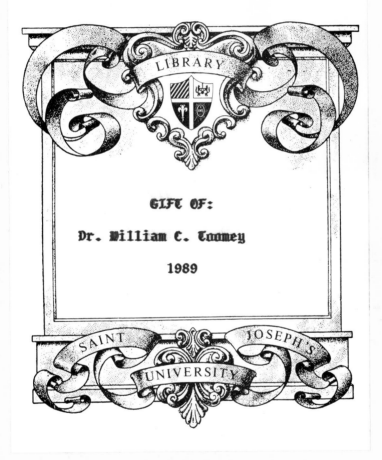

Criminal Behavior and Social Systems

Criminal Behavior and Social Systems

Contributions of American Sociology
Second Edition

Anthony L. Guenther
College of William and Mary

Rand McNally
College Publishing
Company

Chicago

RAND McNALLY SOCIOLOGY SERIES

Copyright © 1976, 1970
  by Rand McNally College Publishing Company
All rights reserved
Printed in U.S.A.
Library of Congress Catalog Card Number 75-20667

76 77 78 10 9 8 7 6 5 4 3 2 1

CONTRIBUTORS

HOWARD S. BECKER
Department of Sociology
Northwestern University

DAVID J. BORDUA
Department of Sociology
University of Illinois

JAMES H. BRYAN
Department of Psychology
Northwestern University

WILLIAM J. CHAMBLISS
Department of Sociology
University of California, Santa Barbara

MARSHALL B. CLINARD
Department of Sociology
University of Wisconsin

DONALD R. CRESSEY
Department of Sociology
University of California, Santa Barbara

NORMAN K. DENZIN
Department of Sociology
University of Illinois

EMILE DURKHEIM
Late of the University of Paris

KAI T. ERIKSON
Department of Sociology
Yale University

DON C. GIBBONS
Department of Sociology
Portland State University

ANTHONY L. GUENTHER
Department of Sociology
College of William and Mary

MARY QUINN GUENTHER
Virginia Social Service Bureau
York County

MARTIN R. HASKELL
Department of Sociology
California State University, Long Beach

GORDON J. HAWKINS
Faculty of Law
University of Sydney, Australia

FRANCIS A. J. IANNI
Department of Educational
    Administration
Teachers College of Columbia University

JENNIE MCINTYRE
Department of Sociology
University of Maryland

PETER K. MANNING
Departments of Sociology and Psychiatry
Michigan State University

HANS W. MATTICK
Center for Research in Criminal Justice
University of Illinois, Chicago Circle

SHELDON MESSINGER
Department of Criminology
University of California, Berkeley

DONALD J. NEWMAN
School of Criminal Justice
State University of New York, Albany

RICHARD QUINNEY
Department of Sociology
Brown University

ALBERT J. REISS, JR.
Department of Sociology
Yale University

JONATHAN RUBINSTEIN
Brooklyn, New York

ROBERT J. SEIDMAN
Law School
University of Wisconsin

THORSTEN SELLIN
Department of Sociology (Emeritus)
University of Pennsylvania

NEAL SHOVER
Department of Sociology
University of Tennessee

WESLEY G. SKOGAN
Department of Political Science
Northwestern University

GRESHAM M. SYKES
Department of Sociology
University of Virginia

ELIZABETH W. VORENBERG
Cambridge, Massachusetts

JAMES VORENBERG
Law School
Harvard University

JAMES Q. WILSON
Department of Government
Harvard University

LEWIS YABLONSKY
Department of Sociology
California State University, Northridge

FRANKLIN E. ZIMRING
Center for Studies in Criminal Justice
University of Chicago

CONTENTS

PREFACE

The second edition of a work provides the author or editor with an opportunity to reflect upon changes that may have occurred both in his own thinking and in his subject matter. Since the late 1960s, when the first edition of this book was prepared, changes in the social order have swept aside many of the notions I held about the proper focus of criminology. The *field* changed too as "young Turks," articulate, impatient with conventional wisdom, and prolific, struck a new course of inquiry.

Ten years ago the vast majority of criminologists were trained as sociologists or were located in sociology departments. Interest in the study of criminal behavior has expanded well beyond traditional boundaries (the FBI Academy at Quantico, Virginia now offers a course in "Advanced Criminology") and I have broadened the emphasis of this new edition in response. However, for criminologists to be found among numerous disciplines in no way diminishes my conviction that we have rigorous expectations of their scholarship.

The support of research, development, and educational programs in criminal justice has, of course, benefited academic criminologists as well. Despite a reputation for controversy and frequent charges of misguidance, the Law Enforcement Assistance Administration (LEAA) and its research arm, the National Institute of Law Enforcement and Criminal Justice, have funded innovative and/or comprehensive programs on a scale unimaginable before LEAA's creation by the Omnibus Crime Control and Safe Streets Act of 1968. All indications point to its continued development as an agency supportive of research and evaluation.

The essays included in this edition are selected from a broad spectrum of the discipline. Some are classics that have stimulated major response, a few are position papers that represent dominant styles of description or analysis, and others are imaginative writings on current problems in American criminology. Two-thirds of the selections are new to this revision of the book. Additionally, the introduction for each section has been completely rewritten and each bibliography has been updated. In an Appendix, those not already familiar with the literature of criminology will find brief guidelines and a listing of thirty journals selected for their persistent use as reference material.

Most of what I learned about crime over the last several years came from a more intimate knowledge of the people—on both sides of the law—who spend more or less of their lives in the crime-control business. I have been the fortunate recipient of counsel from self-acknowledged thieves, homicide detectives, penitentiary inmates, dope dealers, prison correctional officers, police sergeants, transvestites, and a handful of wardens. No one could ask for a more sophisticated set of tutors.

For sheer gratification I will follow the convention of acknowledging others' forbearance during the preparation of this volume. Linda R. Caviness taught my classes at William and Mary over several semesters while I shambled off to write and to observe detectives; her infectious enthusiasm for things criminological is emulable. Good friends in Williamsburg somehow forgave the usual dalliance (my work pace is best captured by the nautical term, "dead slow"), but I sorely missed their camaraderie. Finally, and as all who know her are aware, my wife Mary Quinn is in every sense the coeditor of this volume. Her critical overview of the first edition, suggestions for its improvement, and close attention to all details of the new manuscript—correspondence, substantive editing, typescript preparation—amounted to unusual deprivation. I am reminded anew of the profound influence she has upon my enjoyment of scholarship.

Anthony L. Guenther

August 1975
Criminal Investigations Division
Metropolitan Police Department
Washington, D.C.

PART I

Criminology in Historical and Legal Perspective

The field of criminology had its origins among physicians and anthropologists of the late nineteenth century and then prospered for three-quarters of a century among sociologists. In the past decade, however, criminal behavior has also stimulated interest among proponents of such diverse disciplines as economics, forensic science, law, geography, history, English, political science, psychology, and, of course, criminal justice. These newcomers have changed the dimensions and complexion of criminology, making it both more sophisticated in its methodology and more modest in its claims of predictive power. As the enormous outpouring of research monographs, journal articles, books, and conference proceedings accelerates each year, it becomes more evident that almost nothing studied about crime —its origins, disposition and impact—can be considered definitive.

The vitality of this field is evident from the numerous controversies it embraces. Among these are:

- Police practices and the assurance of defendant's rights
- The deterrent effects of capital punishment
- Gun control legislation and its consequences
- Victimless crimes and the decriminalization of certain behaviors
- The functions and dysfunctions of imprisonment
- Career criminals and the commission of serious crimes
- Drug law enforcement and its public support
- The insidiousness of organized crime
- Pretrial detention or bail provisions for defendants

Although these issues all stimulate strong emotion and are frequently debated in the media, little systematic information exists upon which public policy may be based. Therein lies one rationale for the scientific study of crime.

Modern criminology proceeds by asking how public sentiment regarding obnoxious, harmful, or immoral conduct is transformed into law. This, in fact, is a basic task of legal sociologists, who ask: (1) What activities lead to the perception that specific forms of conduct are unacceptable to the community; and (2) How is community opinion about behavior deserving moral condemnation collectively translated into legal regulation? An important distinction, then, is made by sociologists of law between the evolution of law—which is a function of political institutions —and the enforcement of law—which falls to the police, prosecutors, courts, and correctional agencies.

The research styles of criminologists are differentiated roughly in terms of these two dimensions. Sociologists of law and legal historians often find themselves studying comparative legal structure or anthropological jurisprudence. The majority of American criminologists, however, focus their inquiry upon major components of the criminal justice system.

The present quest for knowledge appears more pragmatic than ever before. On the one hand, this is a function of the sentiments among funding agencies, who increasingly ask: How can a proposed study contribute to more intelligent decision-making among practitioners in the criminal justice field? A disturbing feature of this trend, however, is that many studies may ultimately reflect the priorities of sponsoring or funding agencies, a condition tantamount to the most crass form of "contract" research. On the other hand, recent advances in gathering and analyzing data on crime and the reaction to it of official agencies have changed criminologists' perspectives along more extensive and comparative lines. Thus, a study of sentencing disparity is now likely to be conducted in multiple jurisdictions, selected on the basis of demographic variables or differences in court structure. Similarly, a feasibility project examining the use of ex-offenders as paraprofessionals in probation and parole settings will probably be more extensively implemented now than at an earlier time.

Recent trends in criminology, moreover, reflect an emphasis on longitudinal research. Study directors seem more willing to gather evidence from a given research setting or a selected group of clients over a lengthy time period. Correlated with this trend is the consideration of social-organizational factors which may, indirectly but significantly, affect the study's objective, e.g., shifts in community power structure and demographic changes. Longitudinal analysis of social behavior was once considered prohibitively expensive; the scientific community has since learned that it can afford the luxury of deferred findings.

Finally, a trend noted among the agencies forming a system of criminal justice is to employ members of the legal profession in operational as well as advisory capacities. Criminologists are actively studying: (1) the effects of legal assistance given to indigent defendants; (2) lawyers' representation of groups advocating a public interest at quasi-judicial proceedings conducted by governmental agencies—referred to as "public interest law"; and (3) the impact of counsel given to offenders who seek relief or redress of grievances while imprisoned. Just as the general society has become litigation-conscious, those who find themselves caught up in criminal proceedings now expect legal intervention on their behalf, and the consequences of this movement are being closely monitored by criminologists.

The first selection by Thorsten Sellin traces the historical origins of criminology and shows how competing explanations of criminal conduct emerged from the work of physicians, social philosophers, and early sociologists. Although no adequate history of criminology is yet available, Sellin's essay could well serve as its outline.

Martin R. Haskell and Lewis Yablonsky's essay, taken from a longer treatment of crime and the criminal law, examines these concepts with regard to their essential components. Following this, the authors develop a discussion of norms and types of laws.

"The Rise of Critical Criminology," by Gresham M. Sykes, is an analysis of the skepticism shown by criminologists who question the fundamental theories, methodologies, and substantive interests of the field. Sykes traces the emergence of "critical criminology" (known in some circles as "radical criminology") in the last ten or fifteen years.

For further reading in areas suggested by this brief overview, the following are among the better sources of information.

1. *Criminology: Its History and Changing Focus*
Chambliss, William J., "The State, the Law, and the Definition of Behavior as Criminal or Delinquent," in *Handbook of Criminology*, ed. Daniel Glaser (Chicago: Rand McNally, 1974), pp. 7–43.
Fink, Arthur E., *Causes of Crime: Biological Theories in the United States, 1800–1915* (Philadelphia: University of Pennsylvania Press, 1938).
Grupp, Stanley E., ed., *The Positive School of Criminology* (Pittsburgh: University of Pittsburgh Press, 1968).
Hood, Roger, and Sparks, Richard, *Key Issues in Criminology* (New York: McGraw-Hill, 1970).
Mannheim, Hermann, *Comparative Criminology* (Boston: Houghton Mifflin, 1965).
———, ed., *Pioneers in Criminology*, second edition, enlarged (Montclair, N.J.: Patterson Smith, 1972).
Mills, C. Wright, "The Professional Ideology of Social Pathologists," *American Journal of Sociology* 49 (1942): 165–80.

National Advisory Commission on Criminal Justice Standards and Goals, *Community Crime Prevention* (Washington, D.C.: U.S. Government Printing Office, 1973).

————, *Corrections* (Washington, D.C.: U.S. Government Printing Office, 1973).

————, *Courts* (Washington, D.C.: U.S. Government Printing Office, 1973).

————, *Criminal Justice System* (Washington, D.C.: U.S. Government Printing Office, 1973).

————, *A National Strategy to Reduce Crime* (Washington, D.C.: U.S. Government Printing Office, 1973).

————, *Police* (Washington, D.C.: U.S. Government Printing Office, 1973).

Reasons, Charles E., "The Politicizing of Crime, the Criminal and the Criminologist," *Journal of Criminal Law and Criminology* 64 (1973): 471–77.

Taylor, Ian; Walton, Paul; and Young, Jock, *The New Criminology: For a Social Theory of Deviance* (London: Routledge & Kegan Paul, 1973).

Wilkins, Leslie T., "Crime and Criminal Justice at the Turn of the Century," *The Annals of the American Academy of Political and Social Science* 408 (1973): 13–29.

Wilson, James Q., "Crime and the Criminologists," *Commentary* 58 (1974): 47–53.

2. *Essays on the Sociology of Law*

Evan, William M., ed., *Law and Sociology* (New York: Free Press, Macmillan, 1962).

Gibbs, Jack P., "The Sociology of Law and Normative Phenomena," *American Sociological Review* 31 (1966): 315–25.

Pound, Roscoe, "Sociology of Law," in *Twentieth Century Sociology*, ed. Georges Gurvitch and Wilbert E. Moore (New York: Philosophical Library, 1945), pp. 297–341.

Schur, Edwin M., *Law and Society: A Sociological View* (New York: Random House, 1968).

Schwartz, Richard D., and Skolnick, Jerome H., eds., *Society and the Legal Order* (New York: Basic Books, 1970).

Selznick, Philip, "Sociology of Law," in *International Encyclopedia of the Social Sciences,* vol. 9, ed. David L. Sills (New York: Free Press, Macmillan, 1968), pp. 50–57.

————, "The Sociology of Law," in *Sociology Today: Problems and Prospects,* ed. Robert K. Merton, Leonard Broom, and Leonard S. Cottrell, Jr. (New York: Basic Books, 1959), pp. 115–27.

Turk, Austin T., *Legal Sanctioning and Social Control* (Rockville, Md.: National Institute of Mental Health, 1972).

Quinney, Richard, "Introduction: Toward a Sociology of Criminal Law," in *Crime and Justice in Society* (Boston: Little, Brown, 1969), pp. 1–30.

Zeisel, Hans, "The Law," in *The Uses of Sociology,* ed. Paul F. Lazarsfeld, William H. Sewell, and Harold L. Wilensky (New York: Basic Books, 1967), pp. 81–99.

1

Criminology

Thorsten Sellin

It is proper to use the term *criminology* to designate either (*a*) a body of scientific knowledge about crime, including its causes and prevention, the handling of offenders, and the pursuit of such knowledge regardless of where it stems from; or (*b*) a didactic discipline, which assembles, analyzes, and integrates the findings of criminological research in all scientific disciplines and indicates the best way in which they can be applied in practice to secure socially desirable ends.

Since Raffaele Garofalo (1885) invented the term, no agreement has been reached on the definition of criminology. Traditionally, it has concerned itself with the study of violations of the criminal law and of those who commit them, but opinions vary on the nature and scope of such study. Some hold that it should concentrate on the scientific investigation of the causes of crime and form a subclass of a more general catch-all discipline called "criminal science." Criminal science would be composed of many specialized branches of study, some concerned with etiology—criminology, further subdivided into biological, psychological, and sociological criminology—and others with police science, substantive and procedural legal problems, and penology. By contrast, there are those who would regard all these branches as parts of criminology, a view reflected in American textbooks in particular, which consequently employ the term merely as a pedagogical device. This custom is opposed by those who see in criminology an empirical and naturalistic science, but even this more restrictive view raises problems. This is because the scientific study of offenses, offenders, and the

From Thorsten Sellin, "Criminology," in David L. Sills (ed.), *International Encyclopedia of the Social Sciences,* vol. 3 (New York: Free Press, Macmillan, 1968), pp. 505–10, by permission of the author and publisher. Copyright © 1968 by Crowell Collier and Macmillan, Inc.

whole complex of penal and law-enforcing institutions is carried on by researchers in a variety of scientific fields, each having its own theories, hypotheses, and techniques of investigation, which are often poorly understood, misunderstood, or rejected by researchers in other fields— either in principle or because of faulty interdisciplinary communication arising from increasing specialization in research activity. One cannot, therefore, speak of a science of criminology in the narrow sense of a discipline that possesses universally accepted theoretical concepts.

THE SEARCH FOR CAUSES

It is in the search for an understanding of why people commit crime that most research has occurred. The history of such inquiries can be said to have begun with the nineteenth century, which witnessed the development of the psychological and social sciences. Previously, indeed going back to antiquity, the problem of criminal conduct occupied the minds of natural philosophers and protoscientists, and various theories were advanced to explain it. Observers of the social scene also speculated on the causes of criminality long before sophisticated inquirers with more adequate sources of data began their studies. Generally speaking, one might say that the search for the causes of crime has been made either by those who believe that criminal conduct can be explained chiefly by the biological or mental characteristics of offenders, or by those who believe that environmental conditions and circumstances are the chief operative factors. We shall call the former the individualists and the latter the environmentalists.

The Individualists

Attempts to interpret the significance of relationships between body and mind led in ancient times to the development of *physiognomics.* This method of character diagnosis survived well into the Middle Ages, and one of its practitioners, Giambattista della Porta (1536–1615), may have been the first criminologist. He is said to have made anthropometric measurements on criminals in order to establish a typology. These medieval studies are not unlike some that appeared in the last century, and della Porta's drawings comparing human and animal faces have found counterparts in relatively recent studies by responsible scientists working with different underlying hypotheses. However, physiognomics soon fell into disrepute and remained so until Lombroso revived it in a new connection.

A different approach to the explanation of crime was that of Franz Joseph Gall (1758–1828), the greatest brain anatomist of his age, who was influenced by the faculty psychology of the time. His study of the brain and the nervous system caused him to propound a theory of the localization of brain functions, each operating through an organ in a cluster of other organs distributed over the outer layer of the brain. Criminal conduct then occurred if an overdeveloped organ of combativeness or acquisitiveness, for instance, was too stimulated. In vogue for a few decades, Gall's theory was abandoned, but it called attention to the necessity of studying the offender in order to understand his conduct. Following Gall's lead, Lauvergne (1841) studied prisoners at Toulon and described a criminal type that Lombroso later was to call a criminal by nature.

Psychiatrists were also interested in the etiology of crime. Benjamin Rush (1786), a Philadelphia physician, published an essay on the influence of physical causes on the moral faculties, in which he described persons who, although in other respects normal, became criminals because their moral faculty was impaired, a disease he called anomia. This theory, later elaborated by Philippe Pinel and Jean E. D. Esquirol, given the name "moral insanity" by James C. Prichard, and strongly defended by Prosper Despine and Henry Maudsley, took on a new lease of life in the late 1930s when the notion of the constitutional psychopathic inferior aroused a discussion that seems likely to continue.

The political revolutions of the eighteenth century may have proclaimed the equality of man, but scientists of the period were fully aware of the great variations within the human species. The prevalence of physical and mental defects, ill health, poverty, and criminality gave rise to B. A. Morel's theory of "degeneration" (1857), which held that all these phenomena were the results of a progressive pathological process in which heredity played an important role. This process led to the formation of a variety of human types, which he described in a monograph (Morel, 1864) that contained many of the ideas later adopted by the Lombrosians. He also suggested the need for a science of "morbid anthropology." Dugdale's study of the Jukes (1877) shows some affinity with Morel's ideas.

In 1876 a work with the title *L'uomo deliquente* ("The Criminal Man"), by Cesare Lombroso (1835–1909), introduced a new variant among individualistic theories—the most important one, judging from its ultimate influence rather than its intrinsic value. On the basis of clinical and anatomical studies of criminals, Lombroso was convinced that the criminal was a throwback (atavism), a person who has the body and mind of our primitive ancestors, a kind of vestigial survivor from a day when mankind stood on a lower rung of the ladder of evolution, who, acting in a way natural to such a person, breaks the laws of modern society. The theory is a perfect example of the confluence of many contemporary sources of ideas. Jacob Moleschott and Friedrich K. C. L. Büchner supplied the materialistic doctrine, Charles Darwin the framework, Ernst H. Haeckel's biogenetic principle of recapitulation the mechanism that, interfered with, would account for the atavism (Mendel's discovery was still unknown), psychiatrists the concepts of moral insanity and degeneration, Paul Broca the techniques and instruments of anthropometry, the psychophysicists the methods of psychometrics, and Joseph A. de Gobineau the documentary data on the customs of primitive man.

Lombroso's theory aroused both support and opposition among researchers, not to mention the clergy or the laity represented by the legal profession. The first serious attempt to test it was done by C. B. Goring (1913), who found no support for it, and the last by E. A. Hooton, who failed to substantiate the claims he made for it. It no longer survives anywhere in its original formulation, but the orientation it represents, namely the stress on the importance of biological factors, still dominates criminological thought in Italy, the Iberian peninsula, and the Latin American countries.

A parallel avenue has been followed by the constitutionalists, seeking a correlation between somatic body types and criminality. The rediscovery of Mendel's hypothesis and the development of new psychometric devices such as intelligence tests led to numerous researches on the relationship of hereditary or psychological factors in delinquency, best demonstrated in studies of identical twins. It is within this context that we should appraise the psychoanalytic theories advanced in explanation of crime. Biological theories also fall under this head; indeed, it looks as if ancient beliefs in the role of body fluids in shaping temperaments have reappeared in a new guise in physiological studies of endocrine influences on behavior. As each new hypothesis of biological or psychological nature has appeared, or new diagnostic devices have been found (the electroencephalograph or projective psychological tests, for instance), attempts have been made to determine their usefulness in research explaining criminal conduct.

The Environmentalists

The earliest environmentalists were probably the astrologers, who believed that traits ascribed to planets were mysteriously transmitted to humans, and that persons born when certain planets were in ascendancy or conjunction were doomed to crime. In later ages, such primitive conceptions were replaced by beliefs in the effect of climate on behavior (cf. Montesquieu), systematized less than a century ago by

Enrico Ferri (1881a) in his discussion of telluric factors in the etiology of crime. Today, observed seasonal changes in criminality are recognized but explained in social terms. Indeed, the contributions of the environmentalists to an understanding of criminality have been predominantly sociological. Their ideas, at first based on commonplace experience and observation, have undergone many different, if not always basic, changes because of improved sources of data, greater methodological sophistication, and the stimulus of scientific developments of the behavioral sciences in general.

It is said that Galen, noting the malpractice of Roman physicians, claimed that their conduct was made possible only by the anonymity of city life. Had they lived in small towns, where everybody would have known them, they could not have persisted in their conduct. The effect of poverty on crime was seen by Sir John Fortescue in the fifteenth century, and described by Sir Thomas More and Juan Luis Vives in the sixteenth century. The economic and social consequences of the Black Death and the endemic wars of the following three centuries created a criminal class, the existence of which was attributed to social causes. Eighteenth-century writers like Bernard Mandeville, Henry Fielding, and Patrick Colquhoun cited police corruption, the moral contagion of prisons, poor law enforcement, gambling, the saloon, illiteracy and ignorance, etc. as responsible for criminality. Both Fielding and Colquhoun gave graphic descriptions of organized crime, as did Avé-Lallemant in Germany half a century later.

It is during the last three quarters of the nineteenth century that we discern in the social sciences a development paralleling that already described in our discussion of the individualists. In 1825 France set up the first system of judicial criminal statistics. It was to be imitated by most other European countries. These annual series of data inspired the first important statistical studies by Charles J. M. Lucas (1827) on the relation of education to crime, by Adolphe Quetelet in 1831 on the relation of age to criminality, and by André M. Guerry (1833) on economic conditions, education, sex, etc. as related to crime. To facilitate the understanding of their tables, they presented maps of France showing the distribution of some of the phenomena they investigated, a technique much employed by contemporary and later authors and revived in the present century by American social ecologists.

The socioeconomic consequences of the industrial revolution were seen as criminogenic by numerous authors, especially those influenced by the economic theories of Karl Marx. Indeed, two of them, Napoleone Colajanni (1889) and Enrico Ferri (1881b), produced the first treatises on criminal sociology. Ferri's work became particularly influential. His effort to reconcile the divergent views of the social scientists and the criminal anthropologists led to a multiple-factor approach to the study of causation, which took account of anthropological, telluric, and social factors. His earliest studies (Ferri, 1881*a*) were statistical analyses of criminality in France since 1825.

Two French sociologists were to have considerable influence on criminological thought—Gabriel Tarde (1843–1904) and Emile Durkheim (1858–1917). Both presented sociological theories of criminality worthy of comparison with the biological theories of men like Morel and Lombroso, and the dates of their formulation are evidence of the comparatively later maturation of sociological thought. Tarde (1890) held that as a special activity criminality was explained by the laws of imitation. The criminal represented a social class. Forms of crime originated in the upper classes and spread downward by imitation; thus an individual might be born vicious, but societal influences make him a criminal. Durkheim's best contribution was his theory of anomie, a condition that he held to be created by social evolution, as it transforms homogeneous societies into heterogeneous ones by the increasing division of labor, and by the rise of more and more social groups with divergent norms that may be in conflict with legal norms. Both of these authors, and especially Durkheim, have influenced the thinking of American criminologists.

CRIMINOLOGY IN MODERN TIMES

In this brief review, scores of names of scholars and scientists who have engaged in criminological research and who have assisted in enriching it have necessarily been omitted. And it will be noticed that, with one exception, Benjamin Rush, only Europeans have been mentioned. This is because in the United States, until the present century, studies of criminality or criminals only imitated work done abroad. The poverty of criminal statistics, which is still a problem, made the kind of social investigations done in Europe impossible. Psychologists and psychiatrists faced no such problem; the publication of Healy's *The Individual Delinquent* (1915) marked the beginning of a new era for their studies. Sociologists had to find different approaches. Before World War I, no leading American sociologist, except perhaps Charles H. Cooley, Franklin H. Giddings, or E. A. Ross, showed any theoretical interest in criminology. Courses in criminology were offered in many American colleges and universities by 1905, but they were largely concerned with social reform. Only in the last forty years has a scientific orientation grown up in American sociological research on crime, as in other sociological areas of inquiry. Such research has tended to focus on the causation of crime. Psychiatric research in criminology, clinically oriented, has also increasingly come to recognize the significance of social and cultural influences on criminal conduct.

Whereas in the United States criminological research has been done mostly by sociologists, elsewhere clinical criminology, practiced mainly by psychiatrists, dominated research until World War II. In most countries of basically Latin culture, this is still the case. Since then, however, sociological research has been gaining in importance in many countries and has reversed the psychiatric dominance, especially in northern Europe. This process has been largely due to the phenomena of postwar criminality and delinquency and to the growing familiarity with the products of American empirical criminological research, which before World War II seemed to be almost unknown outside the United States.

Sociologists have also become interested in the study of correctional institutions seen as social systems; significant research in that connection has been conducted in the United States, England, and Norway. The effectiveness of various forms of correctional treatment is being studied in many countries. Such research may be expected to have an influence on legislation on crimes, their sanctions, and correctional administration. Attempts are also being made in some countries to develop prognostic instruments useful in spotting future delinquents among young children, in the selection of offenders for placement on probation or parole, and in the assignment of prisoners to different types of treatment programs. In this connection, the central diagnostic clinics established by many state or national correctional departments, of which California, France, and Italy offer good examples, have aided in bringing about closer cooperation among staff representatives of the various disciplines concerned with criminal conduct.

Concurrent with the growth of scientific research activity and with the proliferation, especially in the United States, of state or local programs and agencies for the prevention of crime and delinquency and for the treatment of offenders has been the increase in the demand for criminologically trained research and treatment personnel. Pedagogical institutes of criminology, aiming to broaden the knowledge of the judiciary and of correctional administrators or candidates for such civil service offices, have existed for more than half a century at law schools in many foreign countries. Institutes combining staff research and teaching have appeared more recently. The most active are those at Cambridge, England, and Vaucresson, France. In the United States, a few universities offer programs of graduate study leading to advanced degrees related to criminology. Such courses are, with rare exceptions, designed to train teachers of criminology or correctional administrators rather than researchers; the same holds true for the offerings of the institute recently established in Japan by the United Nations.

BIBLIOGRAPHY

No adequate history of criminology exists, and the textbooks give scanty information. A broader view may be gained from Niceforo, 1941; Kan, 1903; Bonger, 1905; Bernaldo de Quirós, 1898; Antonini, 1900; Montes, 1911; Fink, 1938; Vold, 1958; Mannheim, 1960. The discussion of the scope and nature of criminology continues unabated, as witnessed by such works as Bianchi, 1956; Pelaez, 1960. Two national dictionaries of criminology are worthy of note: Elster and Lingemann, *Handwörterbuch der Kriminologie,* 1933–1936 and the *Dizionario di criminologia,* 1943. Good bibliographical tools are now available; especially useful are the *International Review of Criminal Policy; International Bibliography on Crime and Delinquency; Annales internationales de criminologie; Excerpta criminologica; Current Projects in the Prevention, Control, and Treatment of Crime and Delinquency.* Textbooks are numerous. Among the many current American ones, all written by sociologists, the best known is Sutherland and Cressey, 1924. Of foreign texts, among the leading titles are Agge, 1955; Greeff, 1946; Hurwitz, 1947; Bemmelen, 1942; Pinatel, 1963. Many criminological journals are being published; among them, in the United States, are the *Journal of Criminal Law, Criminology, and Police Science; Archives of Criminal Psychodynamics; Journal of Research in Crime and Delinquency.*

In England, the leading publication is the *British Journal of Criminology.* In Germany, the *Archiv für Kriminologie* and the *Monatsschrift für Kriminologie und Strafrechtsreform* are both well-established journals, as are the Belgian *Revue de droit pénal et de criminologie,* the Dutch *Nederlands tijdschrift voor criminologie,* and the Swiss *Revue internationale de criminologie et de police technique.* France and Italy, both of which have long traditions of criminological research, produce, respectively, the *Revue de science criminelle et de droit pénal comparé* and the *Quaderni di criminologia clinica.* More extensive listings of journals will be found in International Society of Criminology, 1961. The teaching of criminology in different countries, including the United States, is described in International Society of Criminology, 1957. Also worth reading in this connection is Radzinowicz, 1961. National societies for the study and promotion of scientific criminology exist in many countries. International exchange between criminologists has been organized since the late nineteenth century; no fewer than seven international congresses of "criminal anthropology" were held between 1885 and 1911. The International Society of Criminology, organized in 1937, has held such congresses in 1938, 1950, 1955, 1960, and 1965.

Agge, Ivar, et al., 1955. *Kriminologi.* Stockholm; Wahlström & Widstrand.

Annales internationales de criminologie. Published by the Société Internationale de Criminologie. From 1951 to 1961 it was called the *Bulletin* (of the International Society of Criminology.)

Antonini, Giuseppe, 1900. *I precursori di C. Lombroso.* Turin: Bocca.

Archiv für Kriminologie: Unter Besonder Berücksichtigung der naturwissenschaftlichen Kriminalistik. Published since 1898.

Archives of Criminal Psychodynamics. Published since 1955.

Bemmelen, Jacob M. van, 1958 (1942). *Criminologie: Leerbock der misdaadkunde,* 4th ed. Zwolle (Netherlands): Tjeenk Willink.

Bernaldo de Quirós, Constancio, 1911 (1898). *Modern Theories of Criminality.* Boston: Little, Brown. First published as *Las neuvas teorias de la criminalidad.*

Bianchi, Hermanus, 1956. *Position and Subject-Matter of Criminology: Inquiry Concerning Theoretical Criminology.* Amsterdam: North-Holland Publishing.

Bonger, William A., 1916 (1905). *Criminality and Economic Conditions.* Boston: Little, Brown. First published as *Criminalité et conditions économiques.*

Branham, Vernon C., and Kutash, Samuel, B., eds., 1949. *Encyclopedia of Criminology.* New York: Philosophical Library.

British Journal of Criminology. Published since 1960 by the Institute for the Study and Treatment of Delinquency. From 1950 to 1960 published as *British Journal of Delinquency.*

Colajanni, Napoleone, 1889. *La sociologia criminale,* 2 vols. Catania (Italy): Tropea.

Current Projects in the Prevention, Control, and Treatment of Crime and Delinquency. Published from 1962 to 1964 by the National Council on Crime and Delinquency. Now published by the National Clearing House for Mental Health Information, U.S. Department of Health, Education, and Welfare, Public Health Service.

Dizionario di criminologia, 2 vols., ed. E. Florian, A. Niceforo, and N. Pende, 1943. Milan: Vallardi.

Dugdale, Richard L., 1910 (1877). *The Jukes: A Study in Crime, Pauperism, Disease, and Heredity,* 4th ed. New York: Putnam.

Elster, Alexander, and Lingemann, Heinrich, eds., 1933–1936. *Handwörterbuch der Kriminologie und der anderen strafrechtlichen Hilfswissenschaften . . .* Berlin: de Gruyter.

Excerpta criminologica. A journal of abstracts, published since 1961 by the Excerpta Criminologica Foundation, Amsterdam.

Ferri, Enrico, 1881a. *Studi sulla criminalità in Francia dal 1826 al 1878.* Rome: Botta.

Ferri, Enrico, 1917 (1881*b*). *Criminal Sociology.* Boston: Little, Brown. First published as *I nuovi orizzonti del diritto e della procedura penale.* Title later changed to *Sociologia criminale.*

Fink, Arthur E., 1938. *The Causes of Crime: Biological Theories in the United States, 1800–1915.* Philadelphia: University of Pennsylvania Press. A paperback edition was published in 1962 by Barnes & Noble.

Garofalo, Raffaele, 1914 (1885). *Criminology.* Boston: Little, Brown. First published in Italian.

Goring, Charles B., 1913. *The English Convict: A Statistical Study.* London: H. M. Stationery Office.

Greeff, Etienne de, 1947 (1946), *Introduction à la criminologie,* 2d ed. Brussels: Vandenplas.

Guerry, André M., 1833. *Essai sur la statistique morale de la France.* Paris: Crochard.

Healy, William, 1915. *The Individual Delinquent: A Text-book of Diagnosis and Prognosis for All Concerned in Understanding Offenders.* Boston: Little, Brown.

Hurwitz, Stephan, 1952 (1947). *Criminology.* London: Allen & Unwin. First published in Danish.

International Bibliography on Crime and Delinquency. Published since 1963, first by the National Research and Information Center on Crime and Delinquency, National Council on Crime and Delinquency, now by the National Clearing House for Mental Health Information, U.S. Department of Health, Education, and Welfare, Public Health Service.

International Review of Criminal Policy. Published since 1952 by the United Nations, Department of Social Affairs. Contains an extensive international bibliography of criminology.

International Society of Criminology, 1957. *The University Teaching of Social Sciences: Criminology.* Paris: UNESCO.

International Society of Criminology, 1961. *Selected Documentation on Criminology.* Social Science Clearing House, Reports and Papers in the Social Sciences, no. 14. Paris: UNESCO. A selective bibliography for each of 25 countries.

Journal of Criminal Law, Criminology, and Police Science. Published since 1910 under various titles.

Journal of Research in Crime and Delinquency. Published since 1964 by the National Council on Crime and Delinquency and the Center for Youth and Community Studies, Howard University.

Kan, Joseph van, 1903. *Les causes économiques de la criminalité: Étude historique et critique d' étiologie criminelle.* Paris: Storck.

Kinberg, Olof, 1935. *Basic Problems of Criminology.* Copenhagen: Levin & Munksgaard. A French revision was published in 1960 as *Les problèmes fondamentaux de la criminologie.*

Lauvergne, Hubert, 1841. *Les forçats considérés sous le rapport physiologique, moral, et intellectuel.* Paris: Baillière.

Lucas, Charles J. M., 1827. *Du système pénal et du système répressif en général, de la peine de mort en particulier.* Paris: Béchet.

Mannheim, Hermann, ed., 1960 (1954–1960). *Pioneers in Criminology.* London: Stevens. A collection of biographies that first appeared separately in the *Journal of Criminal Law, Criminology, and Police Science.*

Mannheim, Hermann, 1965. *Comparative Criminology: A Text Book,* 2 vols. London: Routledge.

Middendorff, Wolf, 1959. *Soziologie des Verbrechens.* Düsseldorf: Diederich.

Monatsschrift für Kriminologie und Strafrechtsreform. Published since 1904 under various titles.

Montes, Jerónimo, 1911. *Precursores de la ciencia penal en España: Estudios sobre el delincuente y las causas y remedios del delito.* Madrid: Suárez.

Morel, Benedict A., 1857. *Traité des dégénérescences physiques, intellectuelles, et morales de l'espèce humaine et des causes qui produisent ces variétés maladives.* Paris: Baillière.

Morel, Benedict A., 1864. *De la formation du type dans les variétés dégénérées: Ou, nouveaux éléments d'anthropologie morbide pour faire suite à la théorie des dégénérescences dans l'espèce humaine.* Paris: Baillière.

Nederlands tijdschrift voor criminologie. Published since 1959.

Niceforo, Alfredo, 1949 (1941). *Criminologia,* vol. 1: *Vecchie e nuove dottrine.* Milan: Bocca.

Pelaez, Michelangelo, 1960. *Introduzione allo studio della criminologia.* Milan: Giuffré.

Pinatel, Jean, 1963. *Criminologie,* vol. 3 in Pierre Bouzat and Jean Pinatel, *Traité de droit pénal et de criminologie.* Paris: Dalloz.

Quaderni di criminologia clinica. Published since 1959.

Radzinowicz, Leon, 1962 (1961). *In Search of Criminology.* Cambridge: Harvard University Press.

Revue de droit pénal et de criminologie. Published since 1907.

Revue de science criminelle et de droit pénal comparé. Published since 1936 by the Centre Français de Droit Comparé, Université de Paris, Institut de Criminologie.

Revue internationale de criminologie et de police technique. Published since 1947.

Rush, Benjamin, 1839 (1786). *Inquiry into the Influence of Physical Causes upon the Moral Faculty.* Philadelphia: Cist. Speech delivered before the American Philosophical Society, February 27, 1786. First published as *An Oration ... Containing on Enquiry into the Influence of Physical Causes upon the Moral Faculty.*

Sellin, Thorsten, and Savitz, Leonard, 1963 (1935). "A Bibliographical Manual for the Student of Criminology," 3d ed., rev. *International Bibliography on Crime and Delinquency* 1, no. 3.

Sutherland, Edwin H., and Cressey, Donald R., 1960 (1924). *Principles of Criminology*, 6th ed. New York: Lippincott. First published as a textbook under the title of *Criminology*, with E. H. Sutherland as sole author.

Tarde, Garbriel, 1912 (1890). *Penal Philosophy*. Boston: Little, Brown. First published as *La philosophie pénale*.

Tullio, Benigno di, 1945. *Trattato di antropologia criminale*. Rome: Criminalia.

Vold, George B., 1958. *Theoretical Criminology*. New York: Oxford University Press.

2

The Definition of Crime

Martin R. Haskell and Lewis Yablonsky

The word *crime* has been used so frequently and heard so often that it is taken for granted that everyone means the same thing when he uses the term. Yet definitions of crime differ. To the administrators of justice and to lawyers, a crime is an illegal act. Some social scientists tend to equate the term *crime* with all behavior that is injurious to society. Others view as crimes those acts that deviate greatly from the accepted norms of the society. Religious people regard crime as belonging to the same genre as sin. Others whose personal codes emphasize truth as the ultimate value equate falsehood with crime. The most prevalent tendency is to apply the term *crime* to acts that deviate from rules of behavior valued highly by the dominant segment of the society.

The term *crime* is legally defined in the penal code of every state in the United States. The following is typical of code definition:

A crime or public offense is an intentional act committed or omitted in violation of a law forbidding or commanding it, and to which is annexed either of the following punishments:
1. Death
2. Imprisonment
3. Fine
4. Removal from office; or,
5. Disqualification to hold and enjoy any office of honor, trust, or profit in this state.[1]

From Martin R. Haskell & Lewis Yablonsky, *Criminology: Crime and Criminality,* (Chicago: Rand McNally, 1974) pp. 4–11, by permission of the authors and publisher. Copyright © 1974 by Rand McNally College Publishing Company.

1. *West's California Codes* (St. Paul, Minnesota: West Publishing Co., 1957, as modified by supplements through 1968). Penal Code, secs. 15–20.

Most codes also provide that in every crime there must exist a union or joint operation of act and intent, or criminal negligence.

Some sociologists who object to the exclusive use of the legal definition of crime would broaden the definition to encompass other antisocial behavior. Two arguments in favor of this position are that some antisocial behavior more damaging to our social order than many of the traditional crimes is not made punishable by our criminal codes, and that patterns of behavior closely resembling violations of the criminal law are not included in our criminal codes.

Reasons given for accepting the exclusive legal definition of crime include:

1. Crime statistics are derived from violations of law known to the police, offenses cleared by arrest, court records, and data obtained from persons on probation, in prison, or on parole. Nonnormative and antisocial behavior that does not violate the law is not likely to become part of any public record.
2. There is no general agreement on what constitutes antisocial behavior.
3. There is no general agreement on norms the violation of which would constitute nonnormative behavior of a criminal nature (except for the criminal law).
4. The United States Constitution and laws of the states have provided many safeguards to protect the individual from unjust stigmatization. It would be a mistake to give these up in order to make the term *crime* more inclusive.[2]

Despite some inadequacies in the exclusively legal definition of crime, most sociologists and criminologists find the reasons for accepting it compelling. Immoral or unethical behavior, no matter how socially damaging or reprehensible it may be, cannot be meaningfully equated with criminal behavior because the status of *criminal* is not conferred on the perpetrator. This status, in our society, is conferred only upon those found guilty of a violation of a provision of the criminal law.

There are several specific variables pertaining to the legal definition of crime that deserve our close attention. In order for an act to be a crime, all of the following conditions must be present.

2. Paul W. Tappan, *Crime, Justice and Correction* (New York: McGraw-Hill, 1960), pp. 3–22.

1. *There Must Be an Act or Omission.* That one intends to do something forbidden by law or plans to do a wrong in concert with others is not enough. There must be action. Even in the case of a conspiracy, intending and planning do not suffice. For example, if several men plan to rob a bank, with every intention of carrying out the plan, no crime is committed until there is an overt act in furtherance of the conspiracy. Stealing a getaway car, securing a weapon according to plan, or menacing a bank employee with a weapon would constitute an act in support of the plan. Before anything was done to carry the plan into execution, a member of the group who renounced the conspiracy and refused to have anything to do with it would not have committed a crime. The law takes cognizance of the fact that a man may wish someone dead, even plan to kill him, and change his mind without committing a wrong.

What constitutes an omission? There must be a duty or obligation to do something and a failure to perform that duty. In most states there is no obligation to interfere when one man sees another commit a crime. There are times, however, that the law requires one to take action. California statutes, for example, require a father to furnish his minor children with necessary clothing, food, shelter, and medical attention. Failure to do so constitutes an omission that is punishable as a misdemeanor.

2. *The Act or Omission Must Be in Violation of a Law Forbidding or Commanding it.* Somewhere in the statutory law or case law of the state the act or omission in question must be formally defined as a crime.

3. *There Must Be Criminal Intent* (mens rea) *or Criminal Negligence.* The term *mens rea* is used to describe the nature of the intent. It literally means "guilty mind," and it includes criminal negligence. The offense of larceny involves taking the property of another with *intent* permanently to deprive that person of his property. Taking something by mistake would not be a larceny because the requisite intent would be lacking.

Since people do not ordinarily publicize their intention to steal, direct evidence of intent is unusual. In most cases the court infers the intent from the circumstances surrounding the taking of the property. If the owner testifies, for example, that his automobile is missing and that he did not authorize anyone to take it, the apprehension of an accused driving the car might give rise to an inference that he took the automobile and that the taking was with the intent to steal it. The accused could overcome these inferences by other evidence, such as testimony of witnesses who saw the owner lend him the vehicle.

Some crimes are defined by law in such a way as not to require an intent to do wrong or criminal negligence. Sexual relations with a female below the age of consent constitutes the offense of statutory rape, even if consummated with the consent or at the solicitation of the female. Intent is not an element of the crime of statutory rape.

The killing of a person while the accused is engaged in the commission of a felony constitutes murder, even if the accused in no way intended that crime—indeed, even if the victim was shot by a policeman in the course of a gun battle with the accused. The statute establishing the crime of "felony murder" does not provide for intent to kill as an element of the offense.

4. *There Must Be a Union or Joint Operation of Act and Intent, or Criminal Negligence.* The act, to constitute a crime, *must be the act that the accused intended.* If an accused planned to kill someone by shooting him, and en route to commit the murder accidentally struck the victim with his car, the killing would *not* constitute murder. There would not have been a joint operation of act and intent. The accused might have changed his mind about shooting the victim and the murder might never have taken place.

Criminal negligence, as interpreted by the courts, involves the failure of an individual to exercise the degree of care required of a reasonable person under the circumstances. A man driving an automobile on the main street of a city at a speed of 100 miles an hour would be guilty of manslaughter if he killed someone. Under the circumstances indicated, a reasonable man should know that he was endangering the lives of others.

5. *Punishment Must Be Provided by Law.* Punishment was first introduced into the criminal law to substitute collective vengeance for individual and family vengeance. Wrongs done to individuals were redefined as wrongs done to the state. The state then acted to avenge.

In the eighteenth century, the idea of punishment as a deterrent to offenders was popularized by Cesare Beccaria. It was assumed that if a prospective offender knew in advance the amount of punishment he was risking, he would not commit the crime. The assumption that *punishment deters* is still basic to our criminal law and influences the thinking of many of our legislators. When the incidence of a particular offense increases and this increase attracts public attention, there is generally a demand for more severe penalties for offenders.

The fact that the spirit of vengeance is still with us is evident when we read such statements as "We are coddling delinquents"; "The courts are too easy"; "Criminals are getting away with murder." Unless the statute provides for *punishment* for the prohibited act or omission, the statute is not part of the criminal law and the act is not a crime.

In the light of this decision it becomes apparent that an act or omission is a crime because the government, on some level, has promulgated a law making it a crime and providing for punishment of violators. The use of the criminal law is clearly one way in which our society attempts to get people to refrain from behavior considered undesirable by the political authority.

SOCIAL CONTROL AND THE CRIMINAL LAW

Every society exerts pressures on its members intended to procure a high degree of uniformity of attitude and behavior. Individuals living close to each other in a society and interacting with each other require some way of predicting in advance the response of others to their actions. The term *social control* has been applied to the system of measures, including suggestion, persuasion, restraint, and coercion, by which a society gets individual members to conform to approved patterns of behavior.

It is assumed in this context that the behavior of every member of a society may in some way affect other members. Each person depends on others with whom he has relationships to do what they are supposed to do as defined by the culture, the way of life of the people that make up the society. The "right ways" of doing things are defined for us by our society in rules of behavior that sociologists refer to as *norms.*

The principal norms are called *folkways, mores,* and *laws.* The individual who conforms to a norm is generally rewarded and the one who deviates from it is in some way punished. Rewards are referred to as *positive sanctions* and punishments as *negative sanctions.* Rewards vary from words of approval and general acceptance to selection for positions of great prestige. Punishments—negative sanctions—vary from mild verbal disapproval to ostracism or death. They may be *informally* imposed by people who rebuke or snub the violator of the norm, or they may be formally imposed by an organized group or the society as a whole.

Folkways and Mores

The concept of folkways, or the "ways of the folk," was introduced by William Graham Sumner.[3] The folkways and mores are inculcated early in life. Parents reward conformity and punish deviance in small children many times in an average day. As a result, conformity to these norms becomes habitual. They become invaluable guides to our behavior and help us to predict the behavior of others.

---

3. William Graham Sumner, *Folkways* (Boston: Ginn, 1906).

Violations of the folkways are punished by relatively mild sanctions. A violation of the folkways would include eating without using the appropriate utensils, wearing inappropriate clothing, or failing to show appropriate respect. The violator would be punished mildly by being rebuked, by being criticized, and in some instances by being avoided.

Those folkways considered essential to the society are called *mores.* Incest, molestation of children by adults, murder, and rape are examples of behavior in violation of the mores of our society, and indeed of all societies of which we have knowledge, though the definitions of the terms may vary in detail with time and place. The sanctions imposed on violators of the mores are usually more severe and often include some form of ostracism.

In small societies, informal sanctions are generally sufficient to ensure the maintenance of social control. People dare not risk being ostracized by their friends and neighbors. Since virtually everyone in the small society knows everyone else, deviant behavior by a member comes to the attention of all the others and results in the widespread application of sanctions. In large groups and complex societies, more formal control is required. The deviant can escape informal sanctions simply by relocating to an area in which his deviant behavior is not known. The application of formal controls in the form of published rules with specific penalties contributes greatly to the maintenance of social control.

When informal controls do not work, formal controls are often imposed by an organized group simply by publishing rules and enforcing them. In the early 1960s, for example, girls attending a high school in Los Angeles were expected to wear dresses or skirts that extended below the knees. For years informal controls were sufficient to ensure compliance with this norm. When it became fashionable for girls to wear miniskirts, the school authorities announced publicly that girls were *required* to wear skirts and dresses that did not expose the knees. Until eventually the rule was changed, violators were required to paste on paper additions to bring the garments to the required length. Here we have an illustration of the formalization of a folkway by publication and enforcement of a formal rule. As the new fashion itself became a folkway, and all of the girls favored shorter skirts, the authorities were under pressure to change the rule.

A group may enforce the mores by the imposition of informal or formal sanctions, or by both. People who know that a man has committed incest may ostracize him even though no formal sanctions are applied by the state. On the other hand, the excommunication of a priest who marries without special dispensation illustrates enforcement of the mores of a group by formal sanctions. The Roman Catholic church has a formal regulation forbidding the marriage of a priest. When it excommunicates a violator, the church employs its most severe sanction.

The Law

In complex societies many rules regulating behavior (including folkways and mores) are enacted into law. What distinguishes a law from a folkway, a mos (singular of mores), or a formal regulation of a group is that it is *promulgated* and *enforced* by *political authority*.

There are three types of law regulating behavior: *contract law, tort law,* and *criminal law. Contract law* provides standards for formally arriving at agreements, and designates courts, formal dispute-settling agencies of the state, to decide differences of interpretation in accordance with normative principles and to award damages for breaches of agreements. Every transaction involving the rental or sale or mortgaging of real property, the borrowing of money from a bank, or the purchase of insurance involves a written or oral contract and is obviously regulated by contract law. The pervasiveness of the influence of contract law on our lives becomes more apparent when we consider that the same applies to every situation in which one performs work, labor, and services in exchange for money or other services. Furthermore, virtually every purchase of food, clothing, furniture, or any other item of personal property is made pursuant to a contract, written, oral, or implied, with redress provided by contract law.

Tort law provides redress for one suffering an injury at the hands of another. The victim of a rape, an aggravated assault, or an automobile accident caused by the negligence of another may sue the wrongdoer for damages. Tort law specifies the circumstances under which such actions may be taken to court, designates appropriate courts, and outlines procedures to be followed. A person seeking redress in court for a breach of contract or a tort is awarded a sum of money to compensate him for the loss or injury suffered. This disposition of a case is an example of *distributive justice.* The verdict of the court is intended to make the victim "whole"; that is, to restore him as nearly as possible to the financial position he occupied before the breach of contract or the tort occurred.

Criminal laws specifically forbid certain acts and command certain others, providing punishment for violators. Police departments, prosecuting attorneys, courts, correctional institutions, probation departments, and parole agencies are assigned roles in the enforcement of the criminal law. They differ from contract laws and tort laws in that they prohibit or command specified acts and provide for punishment of violators by the state and on behalf of the state. Violation of a criminal law therefore constitutes an offense against the state. A prosecuting attorney, an agent of the state, brings the case before a criminal court *in the name of the state* against one or more persons accused of violating one or more provisions of the criminal law.

The same act sometimes results in both a tort and a violation of the criminal law. Rape, for example, is a tort, a wrong done to a person. The victim may sue in a civil court to recover damages for injury. Rape is also a violation of the criminal law because the political authority has enacted a statute defining this act as a wrong to the state and providing for punishment of violators. In the United States the victim of rape, aggravated assault, or any other tort must resort to civil action to recover damages. Criminal courts can impose punishment only on behalf of the state and levy fines solely for the benefit of the state. A criminal court cannot award damages to a victim. Punishment provided by the sentence of a criminal court is an example of *retributive justice.*

The increased use of formal controls in our complex society does not eliminate the need for informal controls. Ideally, each type of control supplements the other. A form of behavior in violation of the folkways or mores is further deterred by the passage and enforcement of a law prohibiting it. For example, murder is forbidden by the mores. The law making it a crime provides an additional deterrent. By the same token, a law supported by folkways or mores is easier to enforce than a law that does not have such support.

3

The Rise of Critical Criminology

Gresham M. Sykes

I

In the last ten to fifteen years, criminology in the United States has witnessed a transformation of one of its most fundamental paradigms for interpreting criminal behavior. The theory, methods, and applications of criminology have all been exposed to a new scrutiny, and there seems to be little doubt that the field will be involved in an intricate controversy for many years to come. It is the nature of that controversy, its sources and possible consequences with which this paper is concerned.

In the social turbulence of the 1960s, institutions of higher education were at the center of the storm. Students supplied much of the motive force, and the university frequently served as a stage for, as well as a target of, conflict. The university, however, is more than a place or a social organization. It is also a collection of academic disciplines, and these too felt the tremors of the time. Sociology, in particular, was subjected to a barrage of criticism from a variety of sources, and it is within that framework that we need to examine the change that has overtaken criminology.

It was the special claim of sociology—as almost every introductory textbook in the field was quick to point out—that the discipline had largely freed itself from social philosophy. If the status of sociology as a science was not exactly clear, there was no doubt about its dedication to scientific methods and objectivity.[1] Sociology, it was said, was value-free.

From Gresham M. Sykes, "The Rise of Critical Criminology," *Journal of Criminal Law and Criminology* 65 (1974): 206–13, by special permission of the author and publisher. Copyright © 1974 by Northwestern University School of Law.

1. See, e.g. Mazyur, "The Littlest Science," 3 *American Sociologist* 195 (1968).

It was precisely this point, however, that served as the focus of attack for a number of students and teachers.[2] Sociology, they argued, was still contaminated by the bias and subjectivity of particular interest groups in society. The claim to the cool neutrality of science was a sham. This was especially evident in the area of sociological theory. Social structure, it was said, had been interpreted in terms of consensus, but it was really conflict that lay at the heart of social organization. People in positions of power had traditionally been analyzed in terms of bureaucratic roles aimed at the rational accomplishment of organizational objectives. In reality, people in positions of power were motivated largely by their own selfish interests. A great variety of social problems had been viewed by sociology as flowing from individual pathologies. In fact, however, this approach merely disguised the extent to which the existing social system was at fault, and thus helped to buttress the status quo. Sociology had long been wedded to an evolutionary model of social change, whereas the truth of the matter was that real social change came about not through small increments but through far more radical leaps.

This debate, which broke out into the open in the sixties, involved a great many of the intellectual specialties of sociology, but it was particularly evident in the field of criminology. The study of crime, its causes and its cure had long been regarded as a borrower rather than a lender when it came to the intellectual substance of the social sciences. It had seemed a bit marginal to the major concerns of a science of society, from the viewpoint of many sociologists—perhaps because of its connections with the study of social problems, which many sociologists had viewed as being too deeply enmeshed in value judgments. Now, however, the growing argument about the objectivity of sociology suddenly found many of its crucial themes exemplified in how academic criminology had handled the subject of crime.

II

As a special field of knowledge, criminology had its origins in the attempt to reform the criminal law of the eighteenth century. Bentham, Romilly, and Beccaria were all children of the Enlightenment, and they shared the objective of making the law a more just, humane, and rational instrument of the state. With the rise of the Positivist School in the nineteenth century, however, with its optimistic faith in

2. See, e.g., Gouldner, "Anti-Minotaur: The Myth of a Value-Free Sociology," 9 *Social Problems* 199 (1962).

science, criminology began to move away from the domain of legal thinkers—a movement that became particularly marked in the United States after 1900.[3] In some parts of Europe, and in Latin America, criminology maintained its links with jurisprudence, but in the United States we witnessed a peculiar split. Criminal law became a subject matter for lawyers and law schools; criminology, on the other hand, turned up in the liberal arts curriculum of almost every college and university, largely a creature of the social sciences and particularly sociology.

In some ways, this might have seemed to be a reasonable division of labor. A knowledge of the criminal law was, after all, a part of the lawyer's professional training, even if, until fairly recently, it tended to lack the eclat that attached to areas of law that were potentially more financially productive. The lawyer's interest in the criminal law was apt to center on the nature of the legal rules and their interpretation by the courts; and his concern with why people break the rules and what happens to them after they leave the courtroom was likely to be rather fleeting. These were questions, however, that fell naturally into the theoretical and conceptual framework of the sociologist. Often enough, he had neither the training nor the inclination to enter the thoughtways of the legal scholar to pursue the law's meaning of *mens rea*, search and seizure, and conspiracy.[4]

It is possible that this matter of thoughtways was as important as any special taste in subject matter in the mutual neglect exhibited by criminologists and scholars of criminal law. The study of the law, it has been said, is organized for action, while the social sciences are organized for the accumulation of knowledge; and this aphorism points to a fundamental conflict between the intellectual discipline of law and sociology that helped to keep their practitioners apart. As Robert Merton has indicated, sociologists are guided in their work by the scientific ethos, not in terms of an individual ethical choice, but as a matter of institutionalized professional norms. The search for knowledge is to be undertaken in a spirit of neutrality, and the scientist must have the same passion for proving his hypotheses wrong as for proving them right. The validity of ideas is to be established by impersonal standards of proof; and learned authority must stand on an equal footing with the brashest newcomer when it comes to the empirical testings of facts. Scientific knowledge must be shared with one's colleagues, and no information is to be kept secret because it might bring an advantage or

---

3. See H. Mannheim, *Comparative Criminology* (1965).
4. See R. Quinney, *The Problem of Crime* (1970).

because it might be disturbing. Finally, the scientist is supposed to be under the sway of an organized skepticism that accepts no conclusion as final, no fact as forever proven. Every issue can be reopened and reexamined.[5]

These norms may not always be followed by social scientists as they go about their work, but in a rough way they do guide much scientific behavior, including the behavior of sociologists. The settling of legal disputes, however, is cut on a very different pattern. Lawyers are typically involved as partisans with a far from disinterested concern in the outcome of a case. At law, much is made of the weight of authority, and the discrediting of arguments on an *ad hominem* basis is a familiar occurrence. Information may be withheld on the grounds of privileged communication or with the idea that it would distort the reasoning of the triers of fact. There is a strong impulse to settle cases quickly and not to reopen old disputes.

These differences in the intellectual styles of professional work in sociology and in law appear to have greatly increased the difficulty of exchanging ideas between the two fields, and reinforced their separate development. In any event, the fact that criminal law and criminology tended to remain in separate academic compartments over much of the recent past led to a number of unfortunate consequences. First, many aspects of the criminal law's operation, such as arrest procedures, the activities of the grand jury, trials, and the statutory revision of the criminal law, often remained outside the purview of criminologists. Some attention was given to these matters, it is true, but the bulk of the attention of academic criminology was devoted to questions of crime causation and corrections. One need but review textbooks in criminology of ten or twenty years ago to be struck by the short shrift frequently accorded the criminal law and other issues that loom large in the eyes of the legal scholar and that are, in fact, vital to understanding the relationship between crime and society. Second, the concept of crime was apt to remain singularly crude as the social scientist pursued his goal of building an explanatory schema for criminal behavior. A great variety of acts were frequently lumped together under headings such as "norm violation" and "delinquency," and the careful refinements of legal thought were shoved to one side. Many of the distinctions were quite irrelevant, it is true, from the viewpoint of the social sciences, for they were based on the needs of prosecution, an outmoded concept of man as a hedonistic calculator, and arbitrary, inconsistent categories such as felonies and misdemeanors. But the law at least recognized that "crime" was far from a homogeneous form of

---

5. See R. Merton, *Social Theory and Social Structure* (1949).

behavior, while criminology exhibited a disquieting tendency to speak of crime and the criminal in general. A greater interplay between the two fields might have stimulated efforts to build useful typologies.[6] Third, the fact that the two fields had so little to do with one another meant that many of the findings emerging from criminology received a less than sympathetic ear from those more closely tied to the criminal law. Serious doubts about the effectiveness of juvenile services, prisons, probation, and so on were expressed by criminologists, but their voices seldom seemed to carry beyond the groves of academe.

III

In the late fifties and early sixties, a distinct change began to make its appearance. Topics that had long received relatively little attention in criminology (such as the day-to-day operations of the police) began to be examined by increasing numbers of sociologists. The crude classifications of earlier years began to give way to the empirical study of relatively specific types of criminal activity. The criminal law, which had been taken as a fixed parameter for so long by so many criminologists, began to be examined with a much more inquiring turn of mind. In short, the rather narrow viewpoint of criminology in the United States began to be enlarged and much of its proper subject matter— long left to others—began to be addressed at a serious and systematic level. The change, however, was not mainly because the criminal law and criminology had somehow found a way to end their long estrangement, although this played some part. Rather, a major reason for the shift appears to have been rooted in the same social forces that were modifying sociology as an academic discipline. By the beginning of the 1970s, it was evident that a new strain of thought had entered American criminology, challenging many of its basic assumptions.

Some have spoken of a "radical criminology," but the term is misleading since it suggests a particular ideological underpinning that probably does not exist. I think "critical criminology" is a somewhat better term, at least for the purposes of this discussion, keeping in mind that all such summary phrases can obscure as well as illuminate.

The themes involved in this new orientation can be roughly summarized as follows:

First, there is a profound skepticism accorded any individualistic theory of crime causation. It is not merely biological theories and psy-

---

6. Extended efforts to construct typologies of crime are fairly recent. See Clinard and Quinney, *Criminal Behavior Systems: A Typology* (1973).

chological theories of personality maladjustment that have been abandoned. Sociological theories, dependent on notions of the individual's "defects" due to inadequate socialization or peer group pressures, are also viewed with a wary eye. The problem has become not one of identifying the objectively determined characteristics that separate the criminal and noncriminal, but of why some persons and not others are stigmatized with the label of "criminal" in a social process. "If preconceptions are to be avoided," writes Austin Turk, "a criminal is most accurately defined as any individual who is identified as such. . . ."[7] The roots of this idea in labeling theory are clear enough.[8] A number of writers in criminology today, however, have pushed the idea within a hairline of the claim that the only important reality is the act of labeling —and not because labeling ignores who is a criminal and who is not, but because we are all criminals.

Second, what I have called "critical criminology" is marked by a profound shift in the interpretation of motives behind the actions of the agencies that deal with crime. Many writers, of course, had long been pointing out that the "criminal-processing system" was often harsh and unfair, and, more specifically, that the poor and members of minority groups suffered from an acute disadvantage. Few criminologists, however, were willing to go so far as to claim that the system was inherently unjust. Rather, the usual argument was that our legal agencies were frequently defective due to lack of funds, unenlightened policies, and individual stupidity, prejudice and corruption. Now, however, among a large number of writers, the imputation of motives is of a different order: The operation of legal agencies is commonly interpreted as 1) the self-conscious use of the law to maintain the status quo for those who hold the power in society; or 2) activity aimed at maintaining organization self-interests, with "careerism" as both the carrot and the stick. If the system is unjust, then, we are not to look for relatively minor structural defects or random individual faults. Rather, the criminal law and its enforcement are largely instruments deliberately designed for the control of one social class by another.[9]

---

7. A. Turk, *Criminality and the Legal Order* 18 (1969).

8. See E. Schur, *Labeling Deviant Behavior* (1971).

9. See, e.g., J. Douglas, *Crime and Justice in American Society* xviii (J. Douglas ed. 1971):

If there were no groups trying to control the activities of other groups, and capable of exercising sufficient power to try to enforce their wills upon those other groups through the legislative processes, there would be no laws making some activities "crimes" and there could, consequently, be no "criminals". . . .
    [C]riminal laws are specifically enacted by the middle and upper classes to place the poorer classes under the more direct control of the police. . . .

Third, the rightfulness of the criminal law had been questioned infrequently in the work of American criminologists, even if they were willing to admit that its application sometimes left something to be desired. The insanity plea, the definition of juvenile delinquency, the death sentence, the prohibition of gambling—these areas and a few others were open to vigorous critical scrutiny. By and large, however, the great bulk of the criminal law was taken as expressing a widely shared set of values. In any event, the question of "rightfulness" was not a suitable topic for the social sciences. In the last decade or so, however, there was a growing number of criminologists who found that assumption unrealistic. We could no longer accept the idea presented by Michael and Adler some forty years ago, said Richard Quinney, that "most of the people in any community would probably agree that most of the behavior which is proscribed by their criminal law is socially undesirable."[10] According to the emerging "critical criminology," the criminal law should not be viewed as the collective moral judgments of society promulgated by a government that was defined as legitimate by almost all people. Instead, our society was best seen as a *Gebeitsverband*, a territorial group living under a regime imposed by a ruling few in the manner of a conquered province.[11] The argument was not that murder, rape, and robbery had suddenly become respectable, but that popular attitudes toward the sanctity of property, the sanctity of the physical person, and the rather puritanical morality embedded in the law were far less uniform than American criminology had been willing to admit.

Fourth, American criminologists had long been skeptical of the accuracy of official crime statistics which they nonetheless accepted, reluctantly, as a major source of data for their field. The Uniform Crime Reports of the Federal Bureau of Investigation were, after all, "the only game in town," as far as national figures on criminal behavior were concerned. If the use of other official statistics derived from cities, states, and particular legal agencies were almost always coupled with disclaimers, still, they were used.

The problem with these statistics, as criminologists were quick to point out, was that they could lead to either overestimation or an underestimation of the total amount of crime in any given year, but no one could be sure which was the case. Furthermore, the components of the total crime rate might be in error, and some of the components might be too high while others were too low. The data were based on thou-

---

10. R. Quinney, *The Problem of Crime* 29 (1970).
11. See M. Weber, *The Theory of Social and Economic Organization* 337 (T. Parsons ed. 1947).

sands of local police jurisdictions throughout the country, and even the FBI refused to vouch for their accuracy.

It was clear that a part of the difficulty was the fact that the police had a stake in the amount of crime recorded in official records: if the crime rate went down, the police could win public acclaim for their efficiency in dealing with the crime problem; if the crime rate went up, the police could demand greater financial and political support as they fought their battle with the underworld. This issue, however, was apt to be treated in a rather desultory fashion, in terms of developing a theory about the relationship between crime and society, or simply noted as one more difficulty placed in the path of securing precise data for the construction of a theory of crime causation. The essential task was to find ways to get "better" data, either by seeing to it that official statistics became more accurate, or by finding alternative ways to gather information about the true incidence of criminal behavior, such as self-reporting methods or sociological surveys using the reports of victims to uncover the amount of crime. Since the sixties, however, another view of the matter has become increasingly popular in criminological thought. Rather than dismissing the interest of law enforcement agencies in crime statistics as an unfortunate source of error, the collection and dissemination of information about the incidence of crime has become, for many, an important theoretical variable in its own right. The crime rate, writes Peter Manning, is "simply a construction of police activities," and the actual amount of crime is unknown and probably unknowable.[12] Whether there is more or less "actual" criminality, notes Richard Quinney, is not the issue. "The crucial question is why societies and their agencies report, manufacture, or produce the volume of crime that they do."[13]

The legitimacy of the rules embedded in the criminal law could no longer be taken for granted, then, and neither could the credibility of the government that reported on their violation. The most fruitful line of inquiry with regard to the causes of inaccuracy is not chance error or simple bias. Instead, we must look for a systematic distortion that is part of the machinery for social control.[14]

---

12. Manning, "The Police: Mandate, Strategies, and Appearances," in *Crime and Justice in American Society* 169 (J. Douglas ed. 1971).

13. R. Quinney, supra note 4, at 122.

14. See Biderman and Reiss, Jr., "On Exploring the 'Dark Figure' of Crime," 374 *Annals* 15 (1967):

Any set of crime statistics, including those of the survey, involves some evaluative, institutional processing of people's reports. Concepts, definitions, quantitive models, and theories must be adjusted to the fact that the data are not some objectively observable universe of "criminal acts," but rather those events defined, captured, and processed as such by some institutional mechanism.

IV

"Critical criminology" cannot, I think, be viewed as merely a matter of emphasis, with its major themes no more than bits and pieces of the conventional wisdom of the field. The set of ideas do form a coherent whole that is sufficiently different from much of American criminology of the period immediately before and after World War II to warrant the label "new." At the heart of this orientation lies the perspective of a stratified society in which the operation of the criminal law is a means of controlling the poor (and members of minority groups) by those in power who use the legal apparatus to 1) impose their particular morality and standards of good behavior on the entire society; 2) protect their property and physical safety from the depredations of the have-nots, even though the cost may be high in terms of the legal rights of those it perceives as a threat; and 3) extend the definition of illegal or criminal behavior to encompass those who might threaten the status quo. The middle classes or the lower-middle classes are drawn into this pattern of domination either because 1) they are led to believe they too have a stake in maintaining the status quo; or 2) they are made a part of agencies of social control and the rewards of organizational careers provide inducements for keeping the poor in their place.

The coercive aspects of this arrangement are hidden—at least in part—by labeling those who challenge the system as "deviants" or "criminals" when such labels carry connotations of social pathology, psychiatric illness and so on. If these interpretative schemes are insufficient to arouse widespread distaste for the rule-breaker as "bad" or "tainted," official statistics can serve to create a sense of a more direct and personal danger in the form of a crime wave that will convince many people (including many of the people in the lower classes) that draconian measures are justified.

The poor, according to this viewpoint, may or may not break the legal rules more often than others, although they will certainly be arrested more often and treated more harshly in order to prevent more extensive nonconformity. In a sense, they are expendable in the interest of general deterrence. In any event, they are probably driven in the direction of illegal behavior, even if they do not actually engage in it, because 1) the rules imposed on them from above have little relationship to the normative prescriptions of their own subculture; 2) the material frustrations of the lower classes in a consumer society where the fruits of affluence are publicized for all, but available only to some, prove almost unbearable; and 3) there is generated among the lower classes a deep hostility to a social order in which they are not allowed to participate and had little hand in the making.

36   CRIMINOLOGY IN HISTORICAL AND LEGAL PERSPECTIVE

The perspective sketched in above would seem to fit well with a radical view of American society, or at least with an ideological position on the left side of the political spectrum. While this might possibly account for the attention the perspective has received from some writers in the field of criminology (and some students with a very jaundiced view of the capitalist-industrial social order), I would very much doubt that critical criminology can be neatly linked to any special political position.[15]

At the same time, it does not appear that this new viewpoint in criminology simply grew out of the existing ideas in the field in some sort of automatic process where pure logic breeds uncontaminated by the concerns and passions of the times. Nor does it appear that a flood of new data burst upon the field, requiring a new theoretical synthesis. Instead, as I have suggested at the beginning of this article, it seems likely that the emergence of critical criminology is a part of the intellectual ferment taking place in sociology in general, and both have much of their source in the sociohistorical forces at work in the 1960s.

Among the many elements that have been involved, there are at least three sociohistorical changes that appear to have played a major role. First, the impact of the Vietnam War on American society has yet to be thoroughly analyzed and assessed, but it is clear that it has had an influential part in the rise of a widespread cynicism concerning the institutions of government, the motives of those in power, and the credibility of official pronouncements. The authority of the state has been called into question, including the authority of the state made manifest in the law as its instrument. The good intentions—indeed, the good sense—of those running the apparatus of the state have, for many, become suspect. The truth of official statements, whether it be body counts or crime counts, is no longer easily accepted among many segments of the population. The notion of a Social Contract as the basis of government may have been long recognized as a fiction in American life, but it was also widely accepted as a metaphor expressing a belief in government by consent. In the 1960s, there were many people (including many in the social sciences) who felt that the metaphor was coming apart. Government was far more apt to be seen as manipulation

---

15. In the current intellectual climate, there are a great many pressures to identify particular scientific ideas with particular ideological positions. Ideas and ideology, however, still exhibit a peculiar independence despite strident claims that they must go together; and if some criminologists believe that the viewpoint of critical criminology is something that must be considered, there is no iron necessity that ties them to either a liberal or a conservative stance. For an illuminating examination of the issue in another field, see Herrnstein, "On Challenging an Orthodoxy," 55 *Commentary* 52 (1973).

and coercion, and the legal rules could be more easily interpreted, at least by some, as part of a social order imposed by a ruling elite. "Property is theft," said Proudhon in 1840. In the 1960s, his curt saying had taken on a new bite.

Second, the growth of a counterculture in the United States in the last decade admittedly remains within the realm of those ideas that are far from precise. Yet, there seems no question that a shift in values and ideas did take place and that the use of drugs—particularly marijuana—was a major theme. The arguments about drugs have been repeated so often, the facts and theories elaborated upon in such familiar detail, that discussion of the subject has taken on the appearance of a litany. Nonetheless, for present purposes, it is important to point out that millions of people engaged in behavior they regarded as harmless, but that was defined by society as a crime—not a minor or relatively harmless breach of the law, according to the authorities, but a serious, dangerous offense. Whatever may have been the consequences in terms of popular attitudes toward the law and law-enforcement agencies, another reaction was let loose, namely, a long skeptical look at traditional ideas about the nature of the criminal and the causes of criminal behavior.

In addition, as a consumer-oriented middle class wedded to establishment values emerged as a favorite whipping boy in the analysis of what was wrong with American life, evidence of white-collar crime took on a new prominence.[16] Far from being a form of behavior largely confined to those at the bottom of the social heap, crime was everywhere. "If you are a typical American citizen," says Erik Olin Wright, "chances are that in your life you have committed some crime for which you could have been sent to jail or prison."[17] If this were true, and if the people caught up and punished by the system of criminal justice were so largely drawn from the lower classes, then the machinery of the criminal law must be far from fair or impartial. If you were labeled a criminal, something more than criminal behavior must be involved.

Third, the rise of political protest in the 1960s took on a variety of forms, ranging from heated discussions to bloody confrontations in the streets. It became clear that even the most dispassionate of observers would have to agree that in a number of instances the police power of

16. It should be pointed out, to underline the idea that these ideas were not the sole property of a particular ideological position, that attacks on the middle-class style of life often came from the Right as well as the Left, with much discussion of the perils of a lower-middle class moving into affluence.

17. E. Wright, *The Politics of Punishment* 3 (1973).

the state had been used illegally to suppress political dissent. Some accounts, such as those dealing with the deliberate elimination of the Black Panther leadership, might be shown to have been slipshod in their facts; other accounts might be hopelessly confusing when it came to pinning down precisely the illegality of police actions. Enough evidence remained, however, to show that the police had been used in many instances beyond the limits of the law to silence political opposition. In addition, there were a large number of cases (more murky, perhaps, in terms of being able to disentangle the facts) in which it was believed that the law had acted legally to apprehend and punish a law breaker, but in which the law's actions were due to the individual's social and political beliefs rather than to his criminal behavior. The criminal law, in short, was seen by many as becoming more than a device for controlling run-of-the-mill criminality. It was becoming an arm of Leviathan, not as a matter of abstract theory, but as something directly experienced or immediately observed.[18]

It was the intellectual climate produced by these and similar socio-historical events, I would argue, that played a major part in the rise of critical criminology, as much as any forces at work within the field of traditional criminology itself. The new perspective is touched by ideology, but not determined by it; incorporates points made before, but builds something different; and offers a new interpretation or point of view rather than a vast quantity of new data. All of this, of course, leaves untouched the issue of the potential contribution of this perspective to the study of crime and society.

V

Is critical criminology valid? The question is really an unanswerable one, I believe, because what we are confronted with is not so much a body of precise, systematic theoretical propositions as a viewpoint, a perspective, or an orientation—terms that I have deliberately used throughout the discussion. A theory states the relationships among a number of variables that are well defined; a viewpoint, on the other hand, urges us to look in one direction rather than another, points to promising lines of inquiry, singles out one interpretation from a set of possible interpretations dealing with the same set of facts. In this sense, the viewpoint of critical criminology as it stands today probably cannot be said to be true or false. Rather, it is a bet on what empirical research

---

18. See T. Becker, *Political Trials* (1971).

and theoretical development in the field will reveal in the future. In many ways, I think the bet is not a bad one.

However, before examining what some of the contributions of critical criminology might be, let us look briefly at its more obvious defects. In the first place, criminologists writing from this perspective have a tendency to uncover the latent functions of the criminal law and its operation and then convert these latent functions into manifest ones— unfortunately, all too easily.[19] That is to say, the administration of the criminal law frequently works to the disadvantage of the poor, members of minority groups and the uneducated. It is then assumed, often with little concrete evidence, that this, in fact, is the intended and recognized goal of those administering the criminal law. The task of sociological analysis, however, requires a good deal more than this rather superficial imputation of motive which is apt to degenerate into glib cynicism.

In the second place, a number of writers who are exploring the ideas we have presented under the heading of "critical criminology" often use a model of social stratification that is either overly simplified or ambiguous. We are frequently presented with the poor on the one hand and the Establishment or those in power on the other, with a vaguely defined middle class being portrayed sometimes as another victim of injustice and sometimes as a co-opted agent of those on the top of the socioeconomic scale. In reality, however, there is probably a great deal of variation in different socioeconomic groups in attitudes toward the criminal law and its administration (such as lower-class support of the police and upper-class use of drugs); and, if this is true, the idea that the criminal law is predominantly something imposed from above has need to be substantially modified.

In the third place, we may all indeed be criminals, in the sense that most adults have committed an act at one time or another that would be called a crime by the criminal law. This does not mean, however, that we are all murderers, rapists, robbers, burglars, and auto thieves. Persistent criminals or criminals considered serious may be singled out for the law's attention without reducing a criminal conviction to a mere label that has no connection with an objective reality. Labeling theory in sociology has never quite come to grips with the relationship be-

---

19. I am here following the usage provided by Robert Merton, who defines manifest functions as the objective consequences of social action intended and recognized by the actors involved, whereas latent functions are consequences that are neither intended nor recognized. See R. Merton, supra note 5, at ch. 1.

tween the dynamics of the labeling process and the realities of the behavior being categorized; its tendency toward solipsism had been noted by others.[20] If critical criminology is to make a significant contribution to a sociology of crime, it will need to avoid the error of believing that because the legal stigma of crimes does not match the occurrence of crime in general in the population, the stigma is necessarily based on irrelevant factors such as income and race. Certain patterns of criminal behavior may still have much to do with the matter.

While recognizing these strictures, I think it can be argued that "critical criminology" holds out the promise of having a profound impact on our thinking about crime and society. It forces an inquiry into precisely how the normative content of the criminal law is internalized in different segments of society, and how norm-holding is actually related to behavior. It makes us examine how the legal apparatus designed for the control of crime takes on a life of its own, and begins to pursue objectives that may have little to do with modifying the crime rate. It directs needed attention to the relationship between the political order and nonconformity, thus revitalizing one of sociology's most profound themes, the relationship between the individual and the state. And it impels us, once again, to analyze equality before the law as a basic element of a democratic society. As T. H. Marshall has pointed out, much of the history of the last 250 years or so in Western societies can be seen as an attempt to achieve citizenship for all, which he defines as a kind of basic human equality associated with the concept of full membership in a community.[21] The concept of legal equality emerged in the eighteenth century, the concept of political equality in the nineteenth, and the concept of social equality in the twentieth. But none of the gains can be taken for granted, for they can be lost as well as won. In the administration of the criminal law in our society today, there is ample evidence that our ideals of equality before the law are being compromised by the facts of income and race in an industrial, highly bureaucratized social order. If a "critical criminology" can help us solve that issue, while still confronting the need to control crime, it will contribute a great deal.

---

20. See, e.g., E. Schur, supra note 8.
21. T. H. Marshall, *Citizenship and Social Class* (1950).

PART II

Theoretical Perspectives on Criminal Behavior

Theories, sometimes known as models or paradigms, appear in connection with the study of crime because the major challenge has always been the *explanation* of lawless behavior and control agencies' reaction to it. Theory construction in criminology differs little from theory development in economics, psychology, or other behavioral sciences—all seek a framework within which observations can be organized, arranged in a causal sequence, and used to obtain closure upon a dependent, or predicted, variable. Theory construction has been given such close scientific attention in recent years that the criteria of explanatory power and the elimination of rival hypotheses have become very sophisticated.

When criminology first became a recognized discipline in the United States, many scholars felt that the tool bag of concepts and theorems useful for explaining criminal and delinquent (as opposed to normal) behavior would be unique. Other sociologists and social psychologists attempted to locate the origins of criminality within existing theories. Eventually, common approaches using general sets of hypotheses became standard. Today few researchers claim that one discipline or another has a successful monopoly on the explanation of crime or delinquency.

Criminological theory has developed along several lines. In the beginning, biological explanations based on phrenology and human evolution were very popular, for they suggested a rigorous medical model. Later, as psychometric and personality measurements appeared, these were applied to the study of criminal conduct. Sociological perspectives on lawlessness, creatively initiated in the writings of Emile Durkheim, gave focus to the discipline as it matured, grew, and diversified. Durkheim proposed that a society would be adversely affected by increased population size and density. The resulting condition, which he called *anomie,* is tantamount to a decline in social integration, lessened commitment to the group, magnification of differences between segments of society, and heightened normlessness.

It was many years later that Robert K. Merton formulated an anomie theory of deviant behavior. He pointed out the strain generated when persons are encouraged to structure their aspirations around a set of cultural goals (monetary wealth or occupational success, for example), but are denied access to the legitimate, institutionalized means or avenues for goal achievement. The disjuncture between aspirations and opportunities may be resolved in several ways: withdrawing physically or psychologically; scaling down ambitions so that they are compatible with the means at hand; or selecting an illicit (usually illegal) means for goal achievement.

One significant extension of Merton's work became known as "opportunity theory." It was originally fashioned by Richard A. Cloward and Lloyd E. Ohlin, who held that delinquent gangs employ deviant values in resolving the conflicts that exist between socially approved goals (usually monetary success) and conventional means for realizing those goals. Delinquent behavior, then, is an adaptation to the opportunities the gang members perceive for goal gratification. Just as life-chances for achieving societal goals are unevenly distributed in the social order, so are opportunities for engaging in criminal acts differentially distributed. The importance of this supplement to anomie theory becomes apparent upon inspection of arrest statistics: much of the involvement with stolen merchandise, narcotics, robbery, and other illicit activity reflects the values operative in lower-class society, while embezzling, price collusion, and misappropriation of funds are criminal opportunities available to "white collar" occupations. Nonetheless, opportunity theory is controversial because of its questionable adequacy in explaining recruitment of young people to gang activity, and its failure to be validated by delinquency prevention projects aimed at segments of the population susceptible to deviant values.

Other "culture conflict" theories of criminal behavior made their appearance at the same time, including Albert K. Cohen's theory of delinquent subcultures. Very briefly, he contended that lower-class children are poorly equipped to compete in a world —at school, work, or under the law—where success and other forms of self-actualization are measured by middle-class standards. The lower-class child, according to this position, is frustrated in his attempts to be favorably evaluated. He then rejects middle-class standards, thereby achieving a clean break with the source of his discomfort, and seeks gratification from a delinquent subculture committed to the inverse of middle-class values. A competing theory by Walter B. Miller contends that lawless behavior is a normal part of the lower-class subculture, with its focus upon toughness, excitement, living by wits instead of work, and so on. Miller suggests that these form a distinctive pattern of values and goals which are neither derived from nor competitive with those of the middle class. The positions held by Cohen and by Miller have been attacked on several grounds, not the least of which is their limited capacity for interpreting delinquent gang origins and maintenance.

In 1939 Edwin H. Sutherland published a theory which continues to generate frequent and vigorous debate, yet has stimulated more empirical research in criminology than any competing theory. The magnitude of its impact, moreover, is reflected in the variety of ways it has been used to explain non-criminal social behavior.

Sutherland began by expanding upon the proposition that

44 THEORETICAL PERSPECTIVES ON CRIMINAL BEHAVIOR

behavior, including some that qualifies as criminal, is learned through interpersonal relations. While criminologists during the early decades of the twentieth century may have concentrated excessively upon socially "disorganized" areas of the city or upon one's abnormal, pathological associates, it was Sutherland's position that criminality was somehow related to the *quality* of interpersonal patterns. Thus it was not the culturally disorganized urban area as such, or the undesirable companions, but the *symbolic* influence these had upon the careers of persons involved. According to this argument, a disposition to criminality develops through a preponderance of interpersonal relations with persons whose normative standards are in opposition to those of the middle class.

Sutherland's theory strikingly departed from traditional explanations of crime based upon emotional disorder, psychopathology, or some inherent physiological characteristic of the offender. By emphasizing crime as *learned* behavior, he was able to call attention to such parameters as the sources of learned content, the relative effectiveness of various learning mechanisms, and the ideological transformations necessary to sustain a criminal identity. Learning of criminal conduct, then, involves such symbolic content of interpersonal communications as values, rationalizations, norms, and attitudes.

Three decades of test, modification, and assessment, however, have failed to produce a conclusive verification of Sutherland's theory. The most serious reasons for this appear to be the difficulty experienced in operationalizing, i.e., making testable, the propositions comprising the theory. Some problems arise because Sutherland's writings were inexplicit; others follow an attempt to explain variations in the criminality of individuals, as contrasted with explaining aggregate data on crime.

Another theoretical position which has become prominent in criminology is based upon both official and unofficial reactivity to law violation. Because "crime" is a judgment conferred upon an act by legitimate authority, a number of sociologists have raised questions about the process by which such "labeling" takes place, the complex relations between rule-makers and rule-breakers, and some consequences of being labeled deviant. One explicit concern here has been the implementation of criminal law. When an instance of behavior is suspected to be in violation of a law, the authority of a series of reactive agencies is invoked: the police, courts, and corrections. Contrasted with more traditional criminology, which was devoted to crime causation, this view advocates study of the conditions under which criminal definitions are applied by the state against its citizens and the reactive patterns that follow.

In addition to the labeling perspective, often cited as a type of social control theory, considerable interest has lately been shown in the concept of deterrence. An unusually vigorous group of scholars has inquired about the efficacy of legal threats for securing compliance. Dismissing the simplistic question of whether punishment deters crime, they ask instead: Under what *conditions* will the differential effects of certain criminal sanctions be observable, and what costs will be incurred by all parties in applying sanctions? Perhaps no concept in the recent history of criminology has stimulated more theoretical and empirical fervor than deterrence.

Emile Durkheim's "The Normal and the Pathological" is a classic statement arguing that crime is inherent in the nature of social organization, and that it can be functional for strengthening collective sentiments about normality.

Theoretically linked with Durkheim's writing, Kai Erikson's work, "Deviance and Definition," raises some interesting points about the ways deviance may serve to reestablish the boundaries of propriety and to encourage reaffirmation of group bonds by denoting an occasion when social norms have been violated.

Gibbons's paper on crime causation discusses three major directions that the study of criminal etiology has taken in the last two decades. He suggests that students of adult criminality would profit from closer attention to the advances made in delinquency research.

The essay by Zimring and Hawkins, taken from their larger work on deterrence, describes the naive quality of much thinking about the consequences of crime-control policies. In particular, they show how persons with experience in the field of justice administration may draw faulty conclusions about the nature of deterrence.

Further reading in the development and application of theory in criminology may be found in the following sources.

1. *General Works on Criminological Theory*
Chambliss, William J., "Functional and Conflict Theories of Crime," *Module 17* (New York: MSS Module Publications, 1974).
Schafer, Stephen, *Theories in Criminology* (New York: Random House, 1969).
Shah, Saleem A., and Roth, Loren H., "Biological and Psycho-Physiological Factors in Criminality," in *Handbook of Criminology*, ed. Daniel Glaser (Chicago: Rand McNally, 1974), pp. 101–73.
Vold, George B., *Theoretical Criminology* (New York: Oxford University Press, 1958).

2. *Anomie Theory: Early Formulation and Critical Appraisal*
Clinard, Marshall B., ed., *Anomie and Deviant Behavior* (New York: Free Press, Macmillan, 1964).
Cohen, Albert K., "The Sociology of the Deviant Act: Anomie Theory and Beyond," *American Sociological Review* 30 (1965): 5–14.
Marks, Stephen, "Durkheim's Theory of Anomie," *American Journal of Sociology* 80 (1974): 329–63.
Merton, Robert K., "Social Structure and Anomie," *American Sociological Review* 3 (1938): 672–82.

3. *Subculture Theory*
Cloward, Richard A., and Ohlin, Lloyd E., *Delinquency and Opportunity: A Theory of Delinquent Gangs* (New York: Free Press, Macmillan, 1960).
Cohen, Albert K., *Delinquent Boys: The Culture of the Gang* (Glencoe, Ill.: Free Press, 1955).
Kitsuse, John I., and Dietrick, David C., "Delinquent Boys: A Critique," *American Sociological Review* 34 (1959): 208–15.

Miller, Walter B., "Lower Class Culture as a Generating Milieu of Gang Delinquency," *Journal of Social Issues* 14 (1958): 5–19.

4. *Differential Association Theory*
Burgess, Robert L., and Akers, Ronald L., "A Differential Association-Reinforcement Theory of Criminal Behavior," *Social Problems* 14 (1966): 128–47.
Cressey, Donald R., *Delinquency, Crime, and Differential Association* (The Hague: Martinus Nijhoff, 1964).
Glaser, Daniel, "The Differential-Association Theory of Crime," in *Human Behavior and Social Processes*, ed. Arnold M. Rose (Boston: Houghton Mifflin, 1962), pp. 425–42.
Liska, Allen E., "Interpreting the Causal Structure of Differential Association Theory," *Social Problems* 16 (1969): 485–92.
Sutherland, Edwin H., "Development of the Theory," in *The Sutherland Papers*, ed. Albert K. Cohen, Alfred R. Lindesmith, and Karl F. Schuessler (Bloomington: Indiana University Press, 1956), pp. 13–29.

5. *Labeling Theory: Statements by Proponents and Opponents*
Becker, Howard S., *Outsiders: Studies in the Sociology of Deviance* (New York: Free Press, Macmillan, 1963).
Gibbs, Jack P., "Conceptions of Deviant Behavior: The Old and the New," *Pacific Sociological Review* 9 (1966): 9–14.
Goffman, Erving, *Stigma: Notes on the Management of Spoiled Identity* (Englewood Cliffs, N.J.: Prentice-Hall, 1963).
Gouldner, Alvin W., "The Sociologist as Partisan: Sociology and the Welfare State," *The American Sociologist* 3 (1968): 103–16.
Lemert, Edwin M., "Beyond Mead: The Societal Reaction to Deviance," *Social Problems* 21 (1974): 457–68.
———, *Social Pathology* (New York: McGraw-Hill, 1951), chapters 1–4.
Manning, Peter K., "Deviance and Dogma: Some Comments on the Labeling Perspective," *The British Journal Criminology* 15 (1975): 1–20.
Schur, Edwin M., *Labeling Deviant Behavior: Its Sociological Implications* (New York: Harper & Row, 1971).

6. *Deterrence Theory*

Andenaes, Johannes, *Punishment and Deterrence* (Ann Arbor: University of Michigan Press, 1974).

Gibbs, Jack P., "Sanctions," *Social Problems* 14 (1966): 147–59.

Packer, Herbert L., *The Limits of the Criminal Sanction* (Stanford: Stanford University Press, 1968).

Phillips, Llad, and Votey, Harold L., Jr., "An Economic Analysis of the Deterrent Effect of Law Enforcement on Criminal Activity," *Journal of Criminal Law and Criminology* 63 (1972): 330–42.

Schwartz, Richard D., and Orleans, Sonya, "On Legal Sanctions," *The University of Chicago Law Review* 34 (1967): 274–300.

Tittle, Charles R., "Crime Rates and Legal Sanctions," *Social Problems* 16 (1969): 409–23.

Zimring, Franklin E., and Hawkins, Gordon J., *Deterrence: The Legal Threat in Crime Control* (Chicago: University of Chicago Press, 1973).

4

The Normal and the Pathological

Emile Durkheim

If there is any fact whose pathological character appears incontestable, that fact is crime. All criminologists are agreed on this point. Although they explain this pathology differently, they are unanimous in recognizing it. But let us see if this problem does not demand a more extended consideration.

We shall apply the foregoing rules. Crime is present not only in the majority of societies of one particular species but in all societies of all types. There is no society that is not confronted with the problem of criminality. Its form changes; the acts thus characterized are not the same everywhere; but everywhere and always, there have been men who have behaved in such a way as to draw upon themselves penal repression. If, in proportion as societies pass from the lower to the higher types, the rate of criminality, i.e., the relation between the yearly number of crimes and the population, tended to decline, it might be believed that crime, while still normal, is tending to lose this character of normality. But we have no reason to believe that such a regression is substantiated. Many facts would seem rather to indicate a movement in the opposite direction. From the beginning of the [nineteenth] century, statistics enable us to follow the course of criminality. It has everywhere increased. In France the increase is nearly 300 percent. There is, then, no phenomenon that presents more indisputably all the symptoms of normality, since it appears closely connected with the condi-

From Emile Durkheim, "The Normal and the Pathological," trans. Sarah A. Solovay & John H. Mueller, in George E. G. Catlin (ed.), *The Rules of Sociological Method* (Glencoe, Ill.: The Free Press, 1950), pp. 65–75, by permission of Macmillan Publishing Company, Inc. Copyright © 1938 by George E. G. Catlin, renewed 1966 by Sarah A. Solovay, John H. Mueller, and George E. G. Catlin. Footnotes have been renumbered.

tions of all collective life. To make of crime a form of social morbidity would be to admit that morbidity is not something accidental, but, on the contrary, that in certain cases it grows out of the fundamental constitution of the living organism; it would result in wiping out all distinction between the physiological and the pathological. No doubt it is possible that crime itself will have abnormal forms, as, for example, when its rate is unusually high. This excess is, indeed, undoubtedly morbid in nature. What is normal, simply, is the existence of criminality, provided it attains and does not exceed, for each social type, a certain level, which it is perhaps not impossible to fix in conformity with the preceding rules.[1]

Here we are, then, in the presence of a conclusion in appearance quite paradoxical. Let us make no mistake. To classify crime among the phenomena of normal sociology is not to say merely that it is an inevitable, although regrettable, phenomenon, due to the incorrigible wickedness of men; it is to affirm that it is a factor in public health, an integral part of all healthy societies. This result is, at first glance, surprising enough to have puzzled even ourselves for a long time. Once this first surprise has been overcome, however, it is not difficult to find reasons explaining this normality and at the same time confirming it.

In the first place, crime is normal because a society exempt from it is utterly impossible. Crime, we have shown elsewhere, consists of an act that offends certain very strong collective sentiments. In a society in which criminal acts are no longer committed, the sentiments they offend would have to be found without exception in all individual consciousnesses, and they must be found to exist with the same degree as sentiments contrary to them. Assuming that this condition could actually be realized, crime would not thereby disappear; it would only change its form, for the very cause which would thus dry up the courses of criminality would immediately open up new ones.

Indeed, for the collective sentiments which are protected by the penal law of a people at a specified moment of its history to take possession of the public conscience or for them to acquire a stronger hold where they have an insufficient grip, they must acquire an intensity greater than that which they had hitherto had. The community as a whole must experience them more vividly, for it can acquire from no other source the greater force necessary to control these individuals

---

1. From the fact that crime is a phenomenon of normal sociology, it does not follow that the criminal is an individual normally constituted from the biological and psychological points of view. The two questions are independent of each other. This independence will be better understood when we have shown, later on, the difference between psychological and sociological facts.

who formerly were the most refractory. For murders to disappear, the horror of bloodshed must become greater in those social strata from which murderers are recruited; but first it must become greater throughout the entire society. Moreover, the very absence of crime would directly contribute to produce this horror; because any sentiment seems much more respectable when it is always and uniformly respected.

One easily overlooks the consideration that these strong states of the common consciousness cannot be thus reinforced without reinforcing at the same time the more feeble states, whose violation previously gave birth to mere infraction of convention—since the weaker ones are only the prolongation, the attenuated form, of the stronger. Thus robbery and simple bad taste injure the same single altruistic sentiment, the respect for that which is another's. However, this same sentiment is less grievously offended by bad taste than by robbery; and since, in addition, the average consciousness has not sufficient intensity to react keenly to the bad taste, it is treated with greater tolerance. That is why the person guilty of bad taste is merely blamed, whereas the thief is punished. But if this sentiment grows stronger, to the point of silencing in all consciousnesses the inclination which disposes men to steal, he will become more sensitive to the offenses which, until then, touched him but lightly. He will react against them, then, with more energy; they will be the object of greater opprobrium, which will transform certain of them from the simple moral faults that they were and give them the quality of crimes. For example, improper contracts, or contracts improperly executed, which only incur public blame or civil damages, will become offenses in law.

Imagine a society of saints, a perfect cloister of exemplary individuals. Crimes, properly so called, will there be unknown; but faults which appear venial to the layman will create there the same scandal that the ordinary offense does in ordinary consciousnesses. If, then, this society has the power to judge and punish, it will define these acts as criminal and will treat them as such. For the same reason, the perfect and upright man judges his smallest failings with a severity that the majority reserve for acts more truly in the nature of an offense. Formerly, acts of violence against persons were more frequent than they are today, because respect for individual dignity was less strong. As this has increased, these crimes have become more rare; and also, many acts violating this sentiment have been introduced into the penal law which were not included there in primitive times.[2]

---

2. Calumny, insults, slander, fraud, etc.

In order to exhaust all the hypotheses logically possible, it will perhaps be asked why this unanimity does not extend to all collective sentiments without exception. Why should not even the most feeble sentiment gather enough energy to prevent all dissent? The moral consciousness of the society would be present in its entirety in all individuals, with a vitality sufficient to prevent all acts offending it—the purely conventional faults as well as the crimes. But a uniformity so universal and absolute is utterly impossible; for the immediate physical milieu in which each one of us is placed, the hereditary antecedents, and the social influences vary from one individual to the next and consequently diversify consciousnesses. It is impossible for all to be alike, if only because each one has his own organism and that these organisms occupy different areas in space. That is why, even among the lower peoples, where individual originality is very little developed, it nevertheless does exist.

Thus, since there cannot be a society in which the individuals do not differ more or less from the collective type, it is also inevitable that, among these divergencies, there are some with a criminal character. What confers this character upon them is not the intrinsic quality of a given act but that definition which the collective conscience lends them. If the collective conscience is stronger, if it has enough authority practically to suppress these divergences, it will also be more sensitive, more exacting; and, reacting against the slightest deviations with the energy it otherwise displays only against more considerable infractions, it will attribute to them the same gravity as formerly to crimes. In other words, it will designate them as criminal.

Crime is, then, necessary; it is bound up with the fundamental conditions of all social life, and by that very fact it is useful, because these conditions of which it is a part are themselves indispensable to the normal evolution of morality and law.

Indeed, it is no longer possible today to dispute the fact that law and morality vary from one social type to the next, nor that they change within the same type if the conditions of life are modified. But in order that these transformations may be possible, the collective sentiments at the basis of morality must not be hostile to change and consequently must have but moderate energy. If they were too strong, they would no longer be plastic. Every pattern is an obstacle to new patterns to the extent that the first pattern is inflexible. The better a structure is articulated, the more it offers a healthy resistance to all modification; and this is equally true of functional, as of anatomical, organization. If there were no crimes, this condition could not have been fulfilled; for such a hypothesis presupposes that collective sentiments have arrived at a degree of intensity unexampled in history. Nothing is good indefinitely and to an unlimited extent. The authority which the moral conscience enjoys must not be excessive; otherwise no one would dare criticize it, and it would too easily congeal into an immutable form. To make progress, individual originality must be able to express itself. In order that the originality of the idealist whose dreams transcend his century may find expression, it is necessary that the originality of the criminal, who is below the level of his time, shall also be possible. One does not occur without the other.

Nor is this all. Aside from this indirect utility, it happens that crime itself plays a useful role in this evolution. Crime implies not only that the way remains open to necessary changes but that in certain cases it directly prepares these changes. Where crime exists, collective sentiments are sufficiently flexible to take on a new form, and crime sometimes helps to determine the form they will take. How many times, indeed, it is only an anticipation of future morality—a step toward what will be! According to Athenian law, Socrates was a criminal, and his condemnation was no more than just. However, his crime, namely, the independence of his thought, rendered a service not only to humanity but to his country. It served to prepare a new morality and faith which the Athenians needed, since the traditions by which they had lived until then were no longer in harmony with the current conditions of life. Nor is the case of Socrates unique; it is reproduced periodically in history. It would never have been possible to establish the freedom of thought we now enjoy if the regulations prohibiting it had not been violated before being solemnly abrogated. At that time, however, the violation was a crime, since it was an offense against sentiments still very keen in the average conscience. And yet this crime was useful as a prelude to reforms which daily became more necessary. Liberal philosophy had as its precursors the heretics of all kinds who were justly punished by secular authorities during the entire course of the Middle Ages and until the eve of modern times.

From this point of view, the fundamental facts of criminality present themselves to us in an entirely new light. Contrary to current ideas, the criminal no longer seems a totally unsociable being, a sort of parasitic element, a strange and unassimilable body, introduced into the midst of society.[3] On the contrary, he plays a definite role in social life. Crime, for its part, must no longer be conceived as an evil that cannot be too much suppressed. There is no occasion for self-congratu-

---

3. We have ourselves committed the error of speaking thus of the criminal, because of a failure to apply our rule (*Division du travail social*, pp. 395–96).

lation when the crime rate drops noticeably below the average level, for we may be certain that this apparent progress is associated with some social disorder. Thus, the number of assault cases never falls so low as in times of want.[4] With the drop in the crime rate, and as a reaction to it, comes a revision, or the need of a revision, in the theory of punishment. If, indeed, crime is a disease, its punishment is its remedy and cannot be otherwise conceived; thus, all the discussions it arouses bear on the point of determining what the punishment must be in order to fulfill this role of remedy. If crime is not pathological at all, the object of punishment cannot be to cure it, and its true function must be sought elsewhere.

It is far from the truth, then, that the rules previously stated have no other justification than to satisfy an urge for logical formalism of little practical value, since, on the contrary, according as they are or are not applied, the most essential facts are entirely changed in character. If the foregoing example is particularly convincing—and this was our hope in dwelling upon it—there are likewise many others which might have been cited with equal profit. There is no society where the rule does not exist that the punishment must be proportional to the offense; yet, for the Italian school, this principle is but an invention of jurists, without adequate basis.[5]

For these criminologists the entire penal system, as it has functioned until the present day among all known peoples, is a phenomenon contrary to nature. We have already seen that, for M. Garofalo, the criminality peculiar to lower societies is not at all natural. For socialists it is the capitalist system, in spite of its wide diffusion, which constitutes a deviation from the normal state, produced, as it was, by violence and fraud. Spencer, on the contrary, maintains that our administrative centralization and the extension of governmental powers are the radical vices of our societies, although both proceed most regularly and generally as we advance in history. We do not believe that scholars have ever systematically endeavored to distinguish the normal or abnormal char-

---

4. Although crime is a fact of normal sociology, it does not follow that we must not abhor it. Pain itself has nothing desirable about it; the individual dislikes it as society does crime, and yet it is a function of normal physiology. Not only is it necessarily derived from the very constitution of every living organism, but it plays a useful role in life, for which reason it cannot be replaced. It would, then, be a singular distortion of our thought to present it as an apology for crime. We would not even think of protesting against such an interpretation, did we not know to what strange accusations and misunderstandings one exposes oneself when one undertakes to study moral facts objectively and to speak of them in a different language from that of the layman.

5. See Garofalo, *Criminologie*, p. 299.

acter of social phenomena from their degree of generality. It is always with a great array of dialectics that these questions are partly resolved.

Once we have eliminated this criterion, however, we are not only exposed to confusion and partial errors, such as those just pointed out, but science is rendered all but impossible. Its immediate object is the study of the normal type. If, however, the most widely diffused facts can be pathological, it is possible that the normal types never existed in actuality; and if that is the case, why study the facts? Such study can only confirm our prejudices and fix us in our errors. If punishment and the responsibility for crime are only the products of ignorance and barbarism, why strive to know them in order to derive the normal forms from them? By such arguments the mind is diverted from a reality in which we have lost interest, and falls back on itself in order to seek within itself the materials necessary to reconstruct its world. In order that sociology may treat facts as things, the sociologist must feel the necessity of studying them exclusively.

The principal object of all sciences of life, whether individual or social, is to define and explain the normal state and to distinguish it from its opposite. If, however, normality is not given in the things themselves —if it is, on the contrary, a character we may or may not impute to them —this solid footing is lost. The mind is then complacent in the face of a reality which has little to teach it; it is no longer restrained by the matter which it is analyzing, since it is the mind, in some manner or other, that determines the matter.

The various principles we have established up to the present are, then, closely interconnected. In order that sociology may be a true science of things, the generality of phenomena must be taken as the criterion of their normality.

Our method has, moreover, the advantage of regulating action at the same time as thought. If the social values are not subjects of observation but can and must be determined by a sort of mental calculus, no limit, so to speak, can be set for the free inventions of the imagination in search of the best. For how may we assign to perfection a limit? It escapes all limitation, by definition. The goal of humanity recedes into infinity, discouraging some by its very remoteness and arousing others who, in order to draw a little nearer to it, quicken the pace and plunge into revolutions. This practical dilemma may be escaped if the desirable is defined in the same way as is health and normality and if health is something that is defined as inherent in things. For then the object of our efforts is both given and defined at the same time. It is no longer a matter of pursuing desperately an objective that retreats as one advances, but of working with steady perserverance to maintain the normal state, of re-establishing it if it is threatened, and of rediscovering its conditions if they have changed. The duty of the statesman is no longer to push society toward an ideal that seems attractive to him, but his role is that of the physician: he prevents the outbreak of illnesses by good hygiene, and he seeks to cure them when they have appeared.[6]

---

6. From the theory developed in this chapter, the conclusion has at times been reached that, according to us, the increase of criminality in the course of the nineteenth century was a normal phenomenon. Nothing is farther from our thought. Several facts indicated by us apropos of suicide (see *Suicide*, pp. 420 ff.) tend, on the contrary, to make us believe that this development is in general morbid. Nevertheless, it might happen that a certain increase of certain forms of criminality would be normal, for each state of civilization has its own criminality. But on this, one can only formulate hypotheses.

5

Deviance and Definition

Kai T. Erikson

It is common practice in sociology to picture deviant behavior as an alien element in society. Deviance is considered a vagrant form of human activity which has somehow broken away from the more orderly currents of social life and needs to be controlled. And since it is generally understood that this sort of aberration could only occur if something were wrong within the organization of society itself, deviant behavior is described almost as if it were leakage from machinery in poor condition: it is an incidental result of disorder and anomie, a symptom of internal breakdown.

The purpose of the following remarks will be to review this conventional outlook and to argue that it provides too narrow a framework for many kinds of sociological research. Deviation, we will suggest, recalling Durkheim's classic statement on the subject, can often be understood as a normal product of stable institutions, an important resource which is guarded and preserved by forces found in all human organizations.[1]

I

According to current theory, deviant behavior is most likely to occur when the sanctions governing conduct in any given social setting seem

From Kai T. Erikson, "Notes on the Sociology of Deviance," in Howard S. Becker (ed.), *The Other Side: Perspectives on Deviance* (New York: The Free Press, 1964), pp. 9–21, by permission of the author and Macmillan Publishing Company, Inc. Copyright © 1964 by The Free Press of Glencoe, a division of The Macmillan Company. This is a slightly revised version of a paper that appeared in *Social Problems* 9 (1962): 307–14.

1. Emile Durkheim, *The Rules of Sociological Method*, trans. S. A. Solovay and J. H. Mueller (New York: Free Press, Macmillan, 1958).

to be contradictory[2]—as would be the case, for example, if the work rules posted by a company required one course of action from its employees and the longer-range policies of the company required quite another. Any situation marked by this kind of ambiguity, of course, can pose a serious dilemma for the individual: if he is careful to observe one set of demands imposed upon him, he runs the immediate risk of violating some other, and thus may find himself caught in a deviant stance no matter how earnestly he tries to avoid it. In this limited sense, deviance can be viewed as a "normal" social response to "abnormal" social circumstances, and we are therefore invited to assume that every act of deviation results from some imbalance within the social order—a condition of strain, anomie, or alienation.

This approach to the study of deviant behavior has generated a good deal of useful research, but it has at least one serious drawback for investigators who share an interest in what is known as "social problems." The "anomie" theory (if we may use that convenient label for a moment) is designed to account for all behavior which varies in some technical way from the norms of the community, whether or not that behavior is considered a problem by anyone else. For example, the bank teller who becomes a slave to routine and the armed bandit who relieves him of the day's receipts both register as deviants according to the logic of this scheme, since each is deviating in his own way from the ideal standards of the culture. Yet the most important difference between these men is one that the "anomie" theory cannot easily take into account: the bank teller, no matter how desperate his private needs, does not ordinarily create any concern in the rest of the community, while the bandit triggers the whole machinery of social control into vigorous action. In short, the "anomie" theory may help us appreciate the various ways in which people respond to conditions of strain, but it does not help us differentiate between those people who infringe the letter of the norm without attracting any notice and those who excite so much alarm that they earn a deviant reputation in society and are committed to special institutions like prisons and hospitals.

II

From a sociological standpoint, deviance can be defined as conduct which is generally thought to require the attention of social control

---

2. The best known statements of this general position, of course, are by Robert K. Merton and Talcott Parsons: Merton, *Social Theory and Social Structure*, rev. ed. (New York: Free Press, Macmillan, 1957); and Parsons, *The Social System* (New York: Free Press, Macmillan, 1951).

agencies—that is, conduct about which "something should be done."
Deviance is not a property *inherent in* certain forms of behavior; it is
a property *conferred upon* these forms by the audiences which directly
or indirectly witness them. The critical variable in the study of deviance, then, is the social audience rather than the individual actor, since
it is the audience which eventually determines whether or not any
episode of behavior or any class of episodes is labeled deviant.

This definition may seem a little indirect, but it has the advantage
of bringing a neglected sociological issue into proper focus. When a
community acts to control the behavior of one of its members, it is
engaged in a very intricate process of selection. After all, even the worst
miscreant in society conforms most of the time, if only in the sense that
he uses the correct spoon at mealtime, takes good care of his mother,
or in a thousand other ways respects the ordinary conventions of his
group; and if the community elects to bring sanctions against him for
the occasions when he does misbehave, it is responding to a few deviant
details set within a vast array of entirely acceptable conduct. Thus it
happens that a moment of deviation may become the measure of a
person's position in society. He may be jailed or hospitalized, certified
as a full-time deviant, despite the fact that only a fraction of his behavior
was in any way unusual or dangerous. The community has taken note
of a few scattered particles of behavior and has decided that they reflect
what kind of person he "really" is.

The screening device which sifts these telling details out of the
person's overall performance, then, is a very important instrument of
social control. We know very little about the properties of this screen,
but we do know that it takes many factors into account which are not
directly related to the deviant act itself: it is sensitive to the suspect's
social class, his past record as an offender, the amount of remorse he
manages to convey, and many similar concerns which take hold in the
shifting moods of the community. This may not be so obvious when the
screen is dealing with extreme forms of deviance like serious crimes,
but in the day-by-day filtering processes which take place throughout
the community this feature is easily observable. Some men who drink
too much are called alcoholics and others are not, some men who act
oddly are committed to hospitals and others are not, some men who
have no visible means of support are hauled into court and others are
not—and the difference between those who earn a deviant label and
those who go their own way in peace depends almost entirely on the
way in which the community sifts out and codes the many details of
behavior to which it is witness. In this respect, the community screen
may be a more relevant subject for sociological research than the actual
behavior which is filtered through it.

Once the problem is phrased in this way we can ask: How does a community decide what forms of conduct should be singled out for this kind of attention? The conventional answer to this question, of course, is that society sets up the machinery of control in order to protect itself against the "harmful" effects of deviation, in much the same way that an organism mobilizes its resources to combat an invasion of germs. Yet this simple view of the matter has not always proven to be a very productive one. In the first place, as Durkheim and Mead pointed out some years ago, it is by no means clear that all acts considered deviant in a culture are in fact (or even in principle) harmful to group life.[3] In the second place, it is gradually becoming more evident to sociologists engaged in this area of research that deviant behavior can play an important part in keeping the social order intact.

This raises a number of interesting questions for sociology.

III

In recent years, sociological theory has become more and more concerned with the concept "social system"—an organization of society's component parts into a form which sustains internal equilibrium, resists change, and is boundary-maintaining. In its most abstract form, the "system" concept describes a highly complex network of relations, but the scheme is generally used by sociologists to draw attention to those forces in the social order which promote a high level of uniformity among human actors and a high degree of symmetry within human institutions. The main organizational drift of a system, then, is seen as centripetal: it acts to draw the behavior of actors toward those centers in social space where the core values of the group are figuratively located, bringing them within range of basic norms. Any conduct which is neither attracted toward this nerve center by the rewards of conformity nor compelled toward it by other social pressures is considered "out of control," which is to say deviant.

This basic model has provided the theme for most contemporary thinking about deviation, and as a result little attention has been given to the notion that systems operate to maintain boundaries. To say that a system maintains boundaries is to say that it controls the fluctuation of its constituent parts so that the whole retains a defined range of activity, a unique pattern of constancy and stability, within the larger

---

3. Emile Durkheim, *The Division of Labor in Society*, trans. George Simpson (New York: Free Press, Macmillan, 1952); and George Herbert Mead, "The Psychology of Punitive Justice," *American Journal of Sociology*, 23 (1918): 577–602.

environment.[4] Because the range of human behavior is potentially so wide, social groups maintain boundaries in the sense that they try to limit the flow of behavior within their domain so that it circulates within a defined cultural territory. Boundaries, then, are an important point of reference for persons participating in any system. A people may define its boundaries by referring to a geographical location, a set of honored traditions, a particular religious or political viewpoint, an occupational specialty, a common language, or just some local way of doing things; but in any case, members of the group have some idea about the contours of the niche they occupy in social space. They know where the group begins and ends as a special entity; they know what kinds of experience "belong" within these precincts and what kinds do not.

For all its apparent abstractness, a social system is organized around the movements of persons joined together in regular social relations. The only material found in a system for marking boundaries, then, is the behavior of its participants; and the kinds of behavior which best perform this function are often deviant, since they represent the most extreme variety of conduct to be found within the experience of the group. In this sense, transactions taking place between deviant persons on the one side and agencies of control on the other are boundary-maintaining mechanisms. They mark the outside limits of the area within which the norm has jurisdiction, and in this way assert how much diversity and variability can be contained within the system before it begins to lose its distinct structure, its cultural integrity.

A social norm is rarely expressed as a firm rule or official code. It is an abstract synthesis of the many separate times a community has stated its sentiments on a given kind of issue. Thus the norm has a history much like that of an article of common law: it is an accumulation of decisions made by the community over a period of time which gradually gathers enough moral eminence to serve as a precedent for future decisions. And like an article of common law, the norm retains its validity only if it is regularly used as a basis for judgment. Each time the group censures some act of deviation, then, it sharpens the authority of the violated norm and declares again where the boundaries of the group are located.

It is important to notice that these transactions between deviant persons and agents of control have always attracted a good deal of attention in this and other cultures. In our own past, both the trial and punishment of deviant offenders took place in the public market and gave the crowd a chance to participate in a direct, active way. Today

---

4. Cf. Talcott Parsons, *The Social System.*

we no longer parade deviants in the town square or expose them to the carnival atmosphere of Tyburn, but it is interesting to note that the "reform" which brought about this change in penal policy coincided almost precisely with the development of newspapers as media of public information. Perhaps this is no more than an accident of history, but it is nevertheless true that newspapers (and now radio and television) offer their readers the same kind of entertainment once supplied by public hangings or the use of stocks and pillories. An enormous amount of modern "news" is devoted to reports about deviant behavior and its punishment: indeed the largest circulation newspaper in the United States prints very little else. Yet how do we explain what makes these items "newsworthy" or why they command the great attention they do? Perhaps they satisfy a number of psychological perversities among the mass audience, as commentators sometimes point out, but at the same time they constitute our main source of information about the normative contours of society. In a figurative sense, at least, morality and immorality meet at the public scaffold, and it is during this meeting that the community declares where the line between them should be drawn.

People who gather together into communities need to be able to describe and anticipate those areas of experience which lie outside the immediate compass of the group—the unseen dangers which in any culture and in any age seem to threaten its security. Traditional folklore depicting demons, devils, witches, and evil spirits may be one way to give form to these otherwise formless dangers, but the visible deviant is another kind of reminder. As a trespasser against the group norms, he represents those forces which lie outside the group's boundaries: he informs us, as it were, what evil looks like, what shapes the devil can assume. And in doing so, he shows us the difference between the inside of the group and the outside. It may well be that without this ongoing drama at the outer edges of group space, the community would have no inner sense of identity and cohesion, no sense of the contrasts which set it off as a special place in the larger world.

Thus deviance cannot be dismissed simply as behavior which *disrupts* stability in society, but may itself be, in controlled quantities, an important condition for *preserving* stability.

IV

This raises a delicate theoretical issue. If we grant that deviant forms of behavior are often beneficial to society in general, can we then assume that societies are organized in such a way as to promote this resource? Can we assume, in other words, that forces operate within the social order to recruit deviant actors and commit them to deviant forms of activity? Sociology has not yet developed a conceptual language in which this sort of question can be discussed with any ease, but one observation can be made which gives the question an interesting perspective—namely, that deviant activities often seem to derive support from the very agencies designed to suppress them. Indeed, the institutions devised by society for discouraging deviant behavior are often so poorly equipped for that task that we might well ask why this is considered their "real" function at all.

It is by now a thoroughly familiar argument that many of the institutions built to inhibit deviation actually operate in such a way as to perpetuate it. For one thing, prisons, hospitals, and similar agencies of control provide aid and shelter to large numbers of deviant persons, sometimes enhancing their survival chances in the world as a whole. But beyond this, such institutions gather marginal people into tightly segregated groups, give them an opportunity to teach one another the skills and attitudes of a deviant career, and often provoke them into employing these skills by reinforcing their sense of alienation from the rest of society.[5] It should be pointed out, furthermore, that this process is found not only in the institutions which actually confine the deviant, but throughout the general community as well.

The community's decision to bring deviant sanctions against an individual is not a simple act of censure. It is a sharp rite of transition, at once moving him out of his normal position in society and transferring him into a distinct deviant role.[6] The ceremonies which accomplish this change of status ordinarily have three related phases. They provide a formal *confrontation* between the deviant suspect and representatives of his community (as in the criminal trial or psychiatric case conference); they announce some *judgment* about the nature of his deviancy (a verdict or diagnosis, for example); and they perform an act of social *placement*, assigning him to a special role (like that of prisoner or patient) which redefines his position in society. These ceremonies tend to be events of wide public interest and usually take place in a

---

5. For a good description of this process in the modern prison, see Gresham Sykes, *The Society of Captives* (Princeton: Princeton University Press, 1958). For views of two different types of mental hospital settings, see Erving Goffman, "The Characteristics of Total Institutions," *Symposium on Preventive and Social Psychiatry* (Washington, D.C.: Walter Reed Army Institute of Research, 1957); and Kai T. Erikson, "Patient Role and Social Uncertainty: A Dilemma of the Mentally Ill," *Psychiatry*, 20 (1957): 263–74.

6. Parsons, in *The Social System*, has provided the classical description of how this role transfer works in the case of medical patients.

dramatic, ritualized setting.[7] Perhaps the most obvious example of a commitment ceremony is the criminal trial, with its elaborate formality and ritual pageantry, but more modest equivalents can be found everywhere that procedures are set up to judge whether someone is deviant or not.

Now an important feature of these ceremonies in our own culture is that they are almost irreversible. Most provisional roles conferred by society—like those of the student or conscripted soldier, for example—include some kind of terminal ceremony to mark the individual's movement back out of the role once its temporary advantages have been exhausted. But the roles allotted to the deviant seldom make allowance for this type of passage. He is ushered into the deviant position by a decisive and often dramatic ceremony, yet is retired from it with hardly a word of public notice. As a result, the deviant often returns home with no proper license to resume a normal life in the community. Nothing has happened to cancel out the stigmas imposed upon him by earlier commitment ceremonies; from a formal point of view, the original verdict or diagnosis is still in effect. It should not be surprising, then, that the members of the community seem reluctant to accept the returning deviant on an entirely equal footing. In a very real sense, they do not know who he is.

A circularity is thus set into motion which has all the earmarks of a "self-fulfilling prophesy," to use Merton's fine phrase. On the one hand, it seems obvious that the community's reluctance to accept the deviant back helps reduce whatever chance he might otherwise have for a successful readjustment. Yet on the other hand, everyday experience seems to show that this reluctance is entirely reasonable, for it is a well-known and highly publicized fact that large numbers of ex-convicts return to criminal activity and that many discharged mental patients suffer later breakdowns. The common assumption that deviants are not often cured or reformed, then, may be based on a faulty premise, but this assumption is stated so frequently and with such conviction that it often creates the facts which later "prove" it to be correct. If the returning deviant has to face the community's apprehensions often enough, it is understandable that he too may begin to wonder whether he has graduated from the deviant role—and respond to the uncertainty by resuming deviant activity. In some respects, this may be the only way for the individual and his community to agree as

---

7. Cf. Harold Garfinkel, "Successful Degradation Ceremonies," *American Journal of Sociology*, 61 (1956): 420–24.

to what kind of person he really is, for it often happens that the community is only able to perceive his "true colors" when he lapses momentarily into some form of deviant performance.

Moreover, this prophesy is found in the official policies of even the most advanced agencies of control. Police departments could not operate with any real effectiveness if they did not regard ex-convicts as an almost permanent population of offenders, a pool from which to draw suspects; and psychiatric hospitals could not do a responsible job in the community if they were not alert to the fact that ex-patients are highly susceptible to relapse. Thus the prophesy gains currency at many levels within the social order, not only in the poorly informed opinions of the community at large, but in the best informed theories of most control agencies as well.

In one form or another, this problem has been known in Western culture for many hundreds of years, and the single fact that this is so becomes a highly significant one for sociology. If the culture has supported a steady flow of deviant behavior throughout long periods of historical evolution, then the rules which apply to any form of functionalist thinking would suggest that strong forces must be at work to keep this flow intact—and this because it contributes in some important way to the survival of the system as a whole. This may not be reason enough to assert that deviant behavior is "functional," in any of the many senses of that term, but it should make us wary of the assumption that human communities are organized in such a way as to prevent deviance from occurring.[8]

This in turn might suggest that our present models of society, with their emphasis on the harmony and equilibrium of social life, do a one-sided job of representing the situation. Perhaps two different and often competing currents are found in any well-functioning system: those forces which promote a high overall degree of conformity among its members, and those forces which encourage some degree of diversity so that actors can be deployed throughout social space to patrol the system's boundaries. These different gravitational pulls in the social system set up a constant tension of opposites, outlining the area within which human life, with all its contradiction and variety, takes place. Perhaps this is what Aldous Huxley had in mind when he wrote:

---

8. Albert K. Cohen, for example, speaking for sociologists in general, seems to take the question for granted: "It would seem that the control of deviant behavior is, by definition, a culture goal" ("The Study of Social Disorganization and Deviant Behavior," in *Sociology Today*, ed. Robert K. Merton et al. [New York: Basic Books, 1959], p. 465).

Now tidiness is undeniably good—but a good of which it is easily possible to have too much and at too high a price. . . . The good life can only be lived in a society in which tidiness is preached and practised, but not too fanatically, and where efficiency is always haloed, as it were, by a tolerated margin of mess.[9]

V

These brief remarks are no more than a prelude to further thinking and research, and in the remaining paragraphs we will try to indicate some of the directions this line of reasoning might take.

In the first place, this paper has indirectly addressed itself to one of the oldest problems in sociology. It is all very well for an investigator to conclude that something called a "system" has certain "requirements" in respect to its participants, but the major problem for research is to ask how these needs are imposed upon the people who eventually satisfy them. Ordinarily, the fact that deviant behavior is not evenly distributed throughout the social structure is explained by declaring that something called "anomie" or "disorganization" prevails at certain sensitive points. Deviance leaks out through defects in the social structure; it occurs when the system *fails* to impose its needs on human actors. But if we consider the possibility that even the best organized collectivity needs to produce occasional episodes of deviation for the sake of its own stability, we are engaged in quite another order of inquiry. Perhaps the coherence of some social groupings is maintained only when a few juvenile offenders are enlisted to balance the conformity of an adult majority; perhaps communities can retain a sense of their own territorial identity only if they keep up an ongoing dialogue with deviants who mark and publicize the outer limits of group space; perhaps some families can remain intact only if one of its members becomes a visible deviant to serve as a focus for the rest.[10] If these suppositions prove useful, we should try to learn how a social system appoints certain of its members to deviant roles and how it encourages them to spend a period of service testing the group's boundaries. This is not to suggest that a system necessarily creates the crises which impel people into deviant activity but that it deploys these resources in a patterned, organized way.

---

9. Aldous Huxley, *Prisons: The 'Carceri' Etchings by G. B. Piranesi* (London: Trianon Press, 1949).

10. Cf. Robert A. Dentler and Kai T. Erikson, "The Functions of Deviance in Groups," *Social Problems*, 7 (1959): 98–107.

In the second place, it is evident that cultures vary in the way they regulate deviant traffic moving back and forth from their outer boundaries. We might begin with the observation, for example, that many features of the traffic pattern in our own culture seem to have a marked Puritan cast: a defined portion of the population, largely drawn from young adult groups and from the lower economic classes, is stabilized in deviant roles and often expected to remain there indefinitely. The logic which prevails in many of our formal agencies of control and in the public attitudes which sustain them sometimes seems to echo earlier Puritan theories about predestination, reprobation, and the nature of sin. Be this as it may, different traffic patterns are found in other parts of the world which offer an interesting contrast. There are societies in which deviance is considered a natural mode of behavior for the young, a pursuit which they are expected to abandon once they move through defined ceremonies into adulthood. There are societies which give license to large groups of people to engage in deviant behavior during certain seasons or on certain days of the year. And there are societies which form special groups whose stated business is to act in ways contrary to the normal expectations of the culture. Each of these patterns regulates deviant traffic differently, yet each of them provides some institutional means for a person to give up a deviant career without any kind of permanent stigma. In either of these cases, the person's momentary commitment to deviant styles of behavior is easily reversed—when the group promotes him to manhood, declares a period of festival to be over, or permits him to give up the insignia which marked his membership in a band of "contraries." Perhaps the most interesting problem here from the point of view of pure research is to see whether these various patterns are functionally equivalent in any meaningful way. Perhaps the most interesting problem for those of us who lean over into the applied areas of the field, however, is to ask whether we have anything to learn from those cultures which permit re-entry into normal social life for persons who have spent a period of time in the deviant ranks and no longer have any special need to remain there.

6

Observations on the Study of Crime Causation

Don C. Gibbons

INTRODUCTION

A critical examination of criminology would show that relatively little has been learned about the causation of adult criminal behavior in the several decades since the death of Edwin H. Sutherland. On the whole, criminology is at about the same place as far as knowledge of etiology is concerned that it was in 1950. This situation is in marked contrast to the area of juvenile delinquency analysis, where a massive outpouring of theorizing and empirical research has taken place since 1955.[1] Indeed, some of the best work in the entire field of sociology has occurred in the area of juvenile delinquency. As a result, we know considerably more about causal processes in juvenile lawbreaking than we did two decades ago.

One line of development in criminology in recent years has been to eschew causal inquiry entirely, as reflected, for example, in the writings of Jeffery (1956). He avers that attention should focus on crime instead of criminals, so that, in his view, the most appropriate sociological questions are about the social processes through which groups in

From Don C. Gibbons, "Observations on the Study of Crime Causation," *American Journal of Sociology* 77 (1971): 262–78, by permission of the author and The University of Chicago Press. Copyright © 1971 by The University of Chicago. Footnotes have been renumbered. A revised version of a paper read at the annual meeting of the Pacific Sociological Association, April 1970. I am indebted to Peter Garabedian, Joseph F. Jones, and Dennis Brissett for helpful comments on an earlier draft of this paper. In addition, I would like to acknowledge the incisive comments of several anonymous readers who examined this article for the journal. I have endeavored to strengthen the paper in several important ways suggested by these comments.

1. For a review of this material, see Gibbons (1970).

society manage to get some conduct norms converted into legal norms, as well as about the workings of the legal system and correctional organizations which enforce these norms and label persons as "criminals." Parallel views have been offered by Turk (1969). Also related to this development is the rise of a "sociology of criminal law," concerned with the development of laws, the workings of the legal system, and the like. The anthologies by Simon (1968), Chambliss (1969), and Quinney (1969) contain a good number of writings in this general vein.

—— This discussion starts from the view that continued study of crime causation is desirable and is a proper topic for sociologists. While we agree that the "sociology of criminal law" and sociological analyses of correctional organizations ought to be encouraged, we believe that crime causation continues to be an important topic for sociological study.

Three main currents of work in the area of criminal etiology in the last twenty years can be identified. First, Sutherland's theory of differential association has continued to receive much attention. Second, specific and independent studies of certain offender patterns and other facets of criminality have been reported. Third, there has been a good deal of work on offender typologies, directing attention to the varieties of criminal behavior and collating a mass of data within a typological framework.

In the next section, these lines of work regarding etiology will be briefly examined with an eye toward pointing out their limitations and shortcomings. Next, some new emphases which need to be stressed and some new directions which need to be taken if etiological progress is to be made are discussed. In particular, it is argued that some lessons may be learned from the delinquency literature, where motivational formulations of causation have been supplemented by arguments stressing situational elements in etiology.

CURRENT APPROACHES TO CRIME CAUSATION

Differential Association

Sutherland's theory of differential association holds that offenders are motivated to engage in lawbreaking and in that regard differ from nonoffenders. They are seen as having normal personality structures; they engage in deviance because of an excess of internalized conduct definitions favoring violation of law. These conduct norms were acquired through association with carriers of antisocial standards in social situations of differential social organization (Sutherland and Cressey, 1970, pp. 71–112).

The differential association formulation was first put forth by Sutherland in 1939 and revised in 1947. In this lengthy period of time few investigations have been made to subject it to empirical verification, but these have produced indeterminate results. This ambiguity of findings is attributable to the lack of clarity and specificity of several key ingredients in the theory, including the terms "intensity" and "excess of definitions favorable to violation of law." Investigators have not been able to operationalize successfully these critical elements in the theory. (See Short, 1960.)

More recently, attempts have been made to clean up the logical structure of the differential association argument (DeFleur and Quinney, 1966), and to revise it in the light of modern psychological principles of learning (Burgess and Akers, 1966). Although it is too early to evaluate these efforts in behalf of differential association, to date it does not appear that much progress has been made. I predict that insofar as this formulation is rendered testable by these revisions, the ultimate effect will be to demonstrate its inadequacy as a causal argument. Some new ways of looking at criminality are called for, rather than revisions in differential association theory.

Specific Criminological Studies

Certainly researchers have not been totally inactive in the area of crime causation. Instead, various sociology journals along with publications such as the *Journal of Criminal Law, Criminology and Police Science, Crime and Delinquency,* and the *Journal of Research in Crime and Delinquency* have contained many contributions directly or tangentially concerned with criminal etiology.[2] There has been a modest, continued growth apparent in the criminological literature. For example, Einstadter (1969) has investigated a number of armed robbers. He reports that robbers—unlike professional thieves—are not organized into a behavior system. Their robbery skills are not acquired through differential association but are instead parts of conventional culture which are assimilated. Robbers infrequently exhibit backgrounds of involvement in gang delinquency. Many recruits to armed robbery are from the ranks of "night people" and underworld figures such as "pimps" and the like.

One problem with many of the specific studies in criminology in recent decades is that they have been relatively ad hoc in character, unconnected to one another by linkages to a common theoretical framework. Each study has provided useful descriptive data, but they

---

2. A generous sample of this work is contained in Gibbons (1968, 1970).

have not tended to confirm some general theory of causation, nor has any broad etiological formulation grown out of them. These studies have rarely broken new ground or opened up new leads in the manner of Sutherland's investigations of "white collar crime" (1949). While these inquiries have been useful and helpful, they have tended to confirm traditional generalizations to some extent, instead of serving as stimuli to new approaches and discoveries in crime causation. The combined impact of these works has been to alter the structure of criminological thought a modest amount.

Typological Arguments

One prominent contention in criminology in recent years has centered on typologies. It has been maintained that real progress will come about when the markedly diverse population of offenders is separated into more homogeneous patterns or types. Each of these lawbreaker patterns would then be studied separately, so that etiological factors would be identified for the various types. Presumably, the causal ingredients operating in one form of criminality would be different from those in other patterns. The end product of this kind of work would be a set of miniature criminological theories, each dealing with particular patterns of criminal behavior, rather than some overarching formulation, such as differential association, which endeavors to account for "criminal behavior" as a class of phenomena.

One example of this orientation is the work of Clinard and Quinney (1967), where a large body of evidence was drawn together under a series of rubrics designating types of crime, such as violent personal crime, occupational crime, public order crime, and organized crime. Ferdinand (1966) has pulled together a large number of works on delinquent offenders in the form of an extended essay on delinquent types. Also, Roebuck and Cadwallader (1961) purport to have uncovered a number of offender types made up of individuals exhibiting similar constellations of lawbreaking conduct. Finally, this orientation looms large in several of my books, where offender typologies designed to classify a large number of real criminals and delinquents into homogeneous types are advanced (Gibbons, 1965, 1968, 1970).

Surely lawbreaking is comprised of a vast and heterogeneous collection of deviant acts, as all would agree. At the same time, commonsense observations seem to point to homogeneous types within the lawbreaker population. Moreover, it is possible to find cases of specific criminals who appear to be "professional thieves," "naive check forgers," or other types which have been identified in the criminological literature (see Einstadter, 1969), even though many typological models are relatively terse and vague as to the identifying marks. The heuristic value of typologies is clear enough; they direct attention to more specific hypotheses about causation than differential association and the like.

But some words of caution are in order. There is the danger that the typological approach may be pushed beyond heuristic usefulness. These classification schemes might lead to a criminological picture of offender behavior which oversimplifies and distorts the nature of criminality and perceives types as more crystallized and distinct than they are. This might come about as criminologists go about picking and choosing behavioral observations which fit a typological perspective while ignoring discordant data.[3]

A recent study (Hartjen and Gibbons, 1969) is germane to this point. In it, a fairly explicit and detailed criminal typology was subjected to empirical examination in a probation setting. We used quite crude procedures, and only about half of the probationers were found to fall within a particular typology category. If more refined research techniques had been utilized, even more difficulty might have been experienced in trying to assign actual offenders to pigeonholes in the typology. The half of the probation sample that did not initially fall into the typology was subjected to further study. These individuals were sorted into some rough types such as nonsupport cases, property offenders, and so on. However, these "types" were not clear cut; these offenders were not much different from each other in terms of social backgrounds, nor did they appear to be very different from most law-abiding citizens. Hartjen and I pointed out that much of this lawbreaking appeared to be of the "folk crime" variety (Ross, 1961), in which offenders were not involved in a criminal career. For example, one-quarter were nonsupport [offenders] who had failed to comply with a civil court order to provide child support. Such offenders do not get much attention in contemporary versions of typologies, nor are they the subject of most causal arguments currently fashionable in criminology.

---

3. That the real world is populated by diverse kinds of lawbreakers might be suggested from an examination of Mayhew's classificatory efforts in nineteenth century England. He produced a categorization involving 100 different types. Within his general category of "Those Who Plunder by Manual Dexterity, by Stealth, or by Breach of Trust," Mayhew enumerated "Stock Buzzers," "Tail Buzzers," "Prop Nailers," "Thimble Screwers," "Drag Sneaks," "Snoozers," "Sawney Hunters," as well as a number of other types (Tobias, 1967, pp. 62–64). Sawney Hunters were those who go about purloining bacon from cheesemongers' door steps! Clearly, Mayhew encountered some difficulty in generating a parsimonious typology, so that one might wonder what kinds of obstacles twentieth century efforts in this direction might find.

But if they exist in the real world, their existence will ultimately have to be reflected in criminological thinking.

Moore and I (1970) found similar findings in an investigation of federal probationers. Several hundred probationers were sorted into "types," such as mixed property offenders, selective service violators, income-tax offenders, and car thieves. But these types also seemed not much different from each other, nor did they seem to be markedly unusual or antisocial kinds of citizens. Most of them had been involved in transient criminal episodes, but were reestablished as law-abiding citizens while on probation.

The point is that the existence of a broad class of offenders who might be labeled "situational-casual" criminals ought to be entertained.[4] These persons are involved in various forms of short-run criminality without falling into any clear-cut role-career. In turn, they may be the products of situational forms of causation. The judicious application of typological formulations is called for, by applying them only to those individuals who seem to be involved in career criminality rather than trying to force all of the facts of lawbreaking into this typological mold.[5]

---

4. Actually, "situational" offenders have been acknowledged in a number of criminological essays. For example, Corsini (1949, pp. 110–11) has contended that "situational criminals" constitute one type among a number of patterns observed in penal settings. At the same time, he argued that only those persons who have an inadequate comprehension of the situation are driven to criminality, so that adverse circumstances alone are not sufficient to impel an individual toward lawbreaking. Along the same line, Barnes and Teeters (1959, 53–54) have listed the situational criminal as an offender type, but their commentary is quite brief and superficial. In general, those who have spoken of situational offenders have usually dealt with this category as a residual one within which few persons would be placed. Additionally, little systematic analysis of various situational pressures and inducements to criminality has been pursued.

5. Another point which ought to be made about typologies is that two kinds of role careers or offender types may exist. It may be that some "types" are individuals who get caught up in continuing involvement in deviance out of some kind of genetic or historical process such as differential association (e.g., professional thieves, certain kinds of sex offenders, and some other lawbreakers). There may also be persons who become engaged in a long-term career in deviance, in part as a *result* of correctional handling. They may have been unable to extricate themselves from lawbreaking, once having acquired the stigmatizing identity as a "criminal." There is much speculative commentary holding that correctional institutions are "crime schools," that they have reformative effects upon some persons, or that they are essentially benign in impact upon criminal persons. Similarly, speculative claims abound that other correctional experiences have certain effects. But if situational elements loom larger in etiology than has been assumed in the past, there is a critical need for expanded research attention to correctional experiences as career contingencies or situational influences. Speculation must be replaced by hard facts. Some effort to organize the existing evidence bearing on this point can be found in Gibbons (1968, pp. 236–40; 1970, pp. 221–60).

Concluding Remarks

Differential association theory was described above as providing an answer to the query, how does someone become the kind of person who commits a crime or the kind who refrains from lawbreaking? The differential association perspective asserts that offenders learn definitions favoring violation of law from their social association. Noncriminals acquire law-abiding sentiments from a different set of experiences. This question and the answer to it are actor- or person-oriented, so that it is assumed that various learning experiences operate to put some relatively specific kind of criminal motivation or tendencies inside a person. According to this framework, deviation does not occur without motivation to deviate. I have suggested that if differential association theory could be tested, it would probably turn out to be inaccurate for many lawbreakers. Differential association may be an answer to a defective question that assumes that motivation to criminality must be inside the individuals who engage in criminal conduct. Then too, in differential association theory, definitions favorable to criminality are seen as absent or present in attenuated form in law-abiding individuals, so that they hold an excess of definitions unfavorable to violation of law (Sutherland and Cressey, 1970, pp. 75–76). However, my contention is that many offenders may be no more motivated to engage in criminality than nonoffenders. Their lawbreaking behavior may arise out of some combination of situational pressures and circumstances, along with opportunities for criminality, which are totally outside the actor.

Typological formulations concerning criminals have a closely related deficiency. Typological thinking implies that instead of a single learning experience through which criminal conduct definitions are acquired, different, distinguishable learning experiences produce offender types characterized by separate motivational patterns. My argument is that many lawbreakers do not fit into any role-career kind of typology, that they lack clear-cut criminal motivation and do not derive out of a distinct etiological background. Many of them engage in "folk crimes" or other situationally induced forms of deviance.

If this argument has merit, then criminological attention ought to shift somewhat away from person-oriented perspectives toward more concern with criminogenic situations. It may be that many offenders are virtually indistinguishable from other citizens at the point of initial involvement in deviance, so that traditional views of causal relationships may not hold for many contemporary offenders.

In brief, the argument is for a reexamination of Sutherland's distinction between genetic and situational forms of causation. First, however, let us see what can be gained from recent contributions to the delinquency literature, where motivational arguments have been challenged by situational ones. The review of delinquency work will necessarily be terse and incomplete.

NEW DIRECTIONS IN CAUSAL THEORY

Recent Delinquency Theory and Research

The period since 1955 has been one of prominent growth in delinquency theory and research, particularly in regard to working-class, gang, subcultural delinquency.[6] Cohen's *Delinquent Boys* (1955) was the seminal statement which touched off this surge of work. He argued that gang delinquents were motivated by strongly held feelings of *status* discontent, so that offenders were thought to have shared perceptions that others think ill of them. Working-class youths were regarded as particularly susceptible to these anxieties about social status.

Cohen's essay was followed by a good many others, but the most important alternative formulation was that of Cloward and Ohlin (1960), holding that gang delinquents are motivated by *position* discontent rather than status worries. In their view, working-class boys have high aspirations for material success, while they have only modest expectations for achievement. Those unwilling or unable to reduce their aspirations are the most likely recruits to the delinquent subculture.

These formulations eventually were attacked by those who argued that it may not be necessary to posit strongly held motivation to deviance in order to explain delinquency.[7] For example, Matza (1964) offered a portrait of delinquents as "drifters" into misconduct whose usual attachment to social norms is temporarily broken, and whose neutralizing rationalizations allow them to exculpate themselves for behavior they condemn in principle. Briar and Piliavin (1965) made similar claims, contending that motivational formulations overexplain, that they do not account for real delinquents who fail to exhibit the postulated motivation, nor for spontaneous reform or disengagement from delinquency. Briar and Piliavin proposed a picture of delinquency causation stressing lack of commitment to conformity, rather than positive motivation to deviance. The relatively attenuated stake in confor-

---

6. Much of this theory and research on gang delinquency is summarized in Gibbons (1970, pp. 102–41).

7. An excellent review and analysis of "strain" and "cultural transmission" varieties of motivational theory, along with "social control" arguments, is contained in Hirschi (1969, pp. 3–34).

mity shown by delinquents was traced to certain social class factors and class-related family experiences.

The findings of much of the delinquency research of recent years has supported these latter views more than the motivational arguments. On the whole, the contentions of Cohen, Cloward and Ohlin, and other motivational theorists have received little empirical support (see Gibbons, 1970, pp. 102–41). Instead, a picture of delinquents emerges which stresses their lack of social skills, lack of commitment to conformity, and provocative life circumstances which are conducive to juvenile misbehavior.

One major body of research evidence is that of Short and Strodtbeck (1965), derived from a series of investigations in working-class areas in Chicago. The delinquents they studied generally endorsed middle-class values and standards of "proper" behavior, although they were somewhat more tolerant of "bad" behavior than were nongang boys (pp. 47–76). These investigators also report that delinquents showed limited social skills of various kinds, intelligence scores that put them below nonoffenders from similar backgrounds, and anxieties in the area of sexual adequacy (pp. 217–47). Presumably, these youths had fewer personal resources with which to confront their life situation and a reduced commitment to conformity as a consequence. Short and Strodtbeck interpreted much of the aggression and other misbehavior exhibited by these offenders as a response to threats to their fragile sense of status and well-being gained from membership in gangs. Thus, much of their misconduct was designed to preserve their reputations as courageous fighters or members in good standing in a gang, rather than serving as an attack upon the societal order perceived as unjust. Finally, some of the actions of delinquents—such as becoming fathers of illegitimate children—were interpreted as "aleatory" or chance phenomena, arising accidentally out of the frequent sexual involvement of the youths, rather than from deeply felt motivational sources (Short and Strodtbeck, 1965, pp. 27–46).

Several other lines of evidence support the interpretation which links delinquency to lack of commitment, negative life circumstances, and the like, rather than to positive motivation toward deviance. Downes's (1966, p. 257) study in London of working-class delinquents concluded: "Their illegal behavior seemed to be due not to 'alienation' or 'status frustration,' but to a process of dissociation from middle class dominated contexts of school, work and recreation." Finally Hirschi's (1969) recent investigation in Richmond, California, turned up a good deal of support for the social-control portrait of the delinquent as lacking in commitment to conformity, and with attenuated attachments to parents, school, and peers, so that he is psychologically more "available" to engage in sporadic acts of deviance. ⟩.

The major implication of this work for the study of crime causation should be clear: perhaps more attention ought to be given to the possibility that a number of kinds of criminality are the work of individuals who are not characterized by any sort of clear-cut motivation toward lawbreaking, that their behavior is not the outcome of some kind of differential learning. Instead, there may be a number of forms of criminality in which situational elements loom much larger than acknowledged heretofore. Perhaps it is time to reexamine Sutherland's distinctions between situational and genetic explanations, giving more stress to the former than did Sutherland himself.

Situational versus Genetic Causation

Ironically, it was Sutherland who offered a major alternative perspective on etiology, as well as his ideas about differential association. He noted that differential association was a specific case of the *historical* or *genetic* views of causation, which he contrasted to *mechanistic* or *situational* perspectives (Sutherland and Cressey, 1970, pp. 74–75). The genetic approach seeks those factors in the earlier life history of the criminal or delinquent to which his lawbreaking can be linked. The mechanistic-situational-dynamic view, on the other hand, examines processes operating at or near the moment of the crime. In general, a situational perspective assumes that the causal process operating in some instances of criminality is one which grew out of events closely tied to location and time of the deviant act.

The genetic approach has dominated criminological inquiry. Countless studies have attempted to ferret out the earlier life experiences which propelled persons down criminal paths. By contrast, examples of causal investigations of a situational orientation are less common; Cressey's (1953) examination of rationalizations prior to the deviant act of financial trust violation is one such case.

While Sutherland identified situational or mechanistic causation, he gave it scant attention. He declared: "The objective situation is important to criminality largely to the extent that it provides an opportunity for a criminal act" (Sutherland and Cressey, 1970, p. 74). Different persons will define the same objective situation differently. For some, it is viewed as conducive to criminality; for others, it is not. This is another way of arguing that only those motivated to engage in lawbreaking will do so when confronted by particular situations. In Sutherland's view, these definitions of the situation arise out of prior life experiences of the person, so that a historical or genetic explanation is required to account for the ways in which criminals define their current situations. If this is so, the fundamental etiological task remains to account for the long-term development of the person, his attitudes, and his motivational patterns. In all of this, the image of the offender is that of a person who is different, at least in social-psychological terms, from the nonoffender.

The thesis in this paper is that Sutherland overstated the matter by assuming that the earlier life experiences of offenders, extending over a lengthy time period, are always implicated in criminality. Contrary to Sutherland's assumption, a long-term genetic process may not always be found operating conjointly with situational elements to create lawbreaking. Instead, in many cases, criminality may be a response to nothing more temporal than the provocations and attractions bound up in the immediate circumstances. It may be that, in some kinds of lawbreaking, understanding of that behavior may require detailed attention to the concatenation of events immediately preceding it. Little or nothing may be added to this understanding from a close scrutiny of the early development of the person.

The argument here is *not* for an either-or choice between genetic or situational processes in causation. Instead, the problem for criminologists is one of explicating those relationships where genetic factors weigh most heavily, those where situational elements are most crucial, and those where both sets of influences seem to conjoin to produce the offensive behavior. The end product of this kind of work is likely to be an etiological formulation of considerably greater complexity than those now extant. A number of forms of genetic and situational causation, along with various combinations of these processes, may ultimately be identified.

Genetic Processes in Criminality

Some instances of criminality can be observed in which historical or genetic factors seem to be quite powerful and in which situational elements are of minor significance, such as certain types of deviant sexual conduct involving exhibitionism, voyeurism, or sexually aggressive acts of a pronounced character (Gibbons, 1968, pp. 367–405). Concerning these forms of conduct, Gagnon and Simon (1967, p. 9) have asserted: "In these cases, the causal nexus of the behavior appears to exist in the family and personality structure of the individual and is linked to the contingencies of his biography rather than those of social structure." Aggressive lawbreaking of the kind often labeled "psychopathic" appears to be another form of criminality which arises out of genetic factors—in this case, severe and early parental rejection (Gibbons, 1968, pp. 361–65).

In Sutherland's theorizing, genetic processes in causation revolve around some kind of associational history in which offenders have acquired definitions favoring law violation from their peers or other persons with whom they interact. Some criminologists (e.g., Glaser, 1956) have modified the argument by claiming that some criminals learn definitions from persons with whom they identify but with whom they may not be in direct contact. But there is still another form which genetic etiology may take, in which stable careers in law violation emerge from initial flirtations with deviance, in which criminal definitions emerge in the process, and in which the offender may supply his own reinforcement of these emerging sentiments.

Naive check forgers come to mind as one illustration of this possibility. It may be that the check writer's initial discovery that he can "kite" a check and subsequently settle the matter informally with the store that he has victimized may lead him to conceptualize check writing as a harmless problem-solving technique which is at his disposal. Interaction with others who supply such rationalizations as "You can't kill anyone with a fountain pen" is not involved in the unfolding of this career line in deviance.[8]

Situational Elements in Criminality

Other patterns of offender behavior can be isolated in which situational elements have primacy, so that probing about for genetic factors is unwarranted. For example, consider the report in *Tally's Corner,* where it was noted that the incidence of burglary and other property crimes increased markedly during winter, when Negro construction workers are laid off and turn to crime in order to eke out a living (Liebow, 1967, pp. 29–71). There is little in that report to suggest that criminality is a preferred pattern of behavior by these persons, that they are the carriers of an excess of definitions favorable to violation of

---

8. Several other examples of this kind can be offered. Generalized attitudes holding that stealing is "bad" may become attenuated in amateur shoplifters who start off by experimenting with stealing. To the extent that they manage to avoid detection, they may come to "normalize" shoplifting in their own minds. Another illustration might be taken from Humphreys' study (1970) of impersonal homosexual acts in "tearooms." His data suggest that involvement in this behavior becomes recurrent and stabilized among many of those who engage in it. Many of these persons define participation in "blow-jobs" in positive terms, but those sentiments do not arise out of conversations and social interchange among homosexuals. This example was brought to my attention by one of the readers for the journal.

law, or that their lawbreaking is the outgrowth of a lengthy genetic process of differential socialization. Along the same line, attention ought to be paid to Gould's analysis (1969), which relates the upsurge of car theft and bank robberies over the past several decades to the growing abundance of these "victims." Then, too, consider Camp's research (1967) which shows that bank robberies are usually the work of desperate men. These acts are carried out as a last resort to solve some perceived crisis in the life of the robber, rather than the acts of criminal gangs who make a career of carefully planned heists, or whose lawbreaking has causal antecedents located in criminal associations which occurred years earlier.

Other patterns of offender behavior can be isolated in which situational elements loom large, such as drunk driving and manslaughter. Additionally, Cameron's study (1964) shows that "snitches" or amateur shoplifters are "peripheral" criminals rather than "vocational" offenders. Prior to arrest, they do not think of themselves as thieves, and no clear-cut genetic process emerges in their backgrounds. Some other evidence on juvenile and adult shoplifting supports this characterization of persons who engage in flirtations with deviant acts (Gibbons, 1968, pp. 287–94).

Another case of situational factors is Lemert's report (1967) on naive check forgery, which he contends is the outgrowth of a process of "risk taking." He defines the risk-taking process in the following terms: "This concept refers to situations in which persons who are caught in a network of conflicting claims or values choose not deviant alternatives but rather behavioral situations which carry risks of deviation. Deviation then becomes merely one possible outcome of their actions, but it is not inevitable" (Lemert, 1967, p. 11). An example of this process might be the individual who writes a check while drinking, hoping to be able to reach the bank with funds to cover it before it is presented to the bank. Lemert argues that close examination of other kinds of criminality might also show risk-taking elements.[9]

Interaction of Genetic and Situational Factors

So far, I have argued that some forms of criminal behavior involve a heavy component of genetic etiology, while situational elements loom large in others. However, there probably are many instances where

---

9. Naive check forgery has been offered both as an illustration of genetic and situational processes. This case suggests something of the complexity of causal patterns. A plausible case can be made holding that initial acts of check writing occur in a risk-taking way. Subsequently, discovery that this activity is a low-risk form of criminality may trigger a genetic process of the kind sketched earlier.

both genetic factors and situational contingencies are significant. For example, acts of murder appear to be most frequent among those who have grown up in a "subculture of violence," who have been subjected to a number of disorganizing social influences over an extended period of time, and who are disposed to look upon others as potential assailants. (See Gibbons, 1968, pp. 349–56.) At the same time, not all who share such experiences commit acts of homicide. Those who do engage in murder often do so within situations of marital discord or tavern fights, in which a number of provocative moves and countermoves of interactional partners culminate in acts of homicide. (See Wolfgang, 1958, pp. 264–65.) However, it would be incorrect to suppose that many of the participants in these short-lived sets of events intended them to have this criminal outcome, even a minute or so before the killing actually occurred.

This example of homicide can be viewed as a criminological application of the "value-added" framework employed by Smelser (1963) and Lofland and Stark (1965) in the analysis of collective behavior and social movements. As used by Smelser, the "value-added" formulation refers to a series of stages or events in which each must occur according to a particular pattern in order for a certain outcome to be produced. He notes: "Every stage in the value-added process, therefore, is a necessary condition for the appropriate and effective addition of value in the next stage. The sufficient condition for the final production, moreover, is the combination of *every* necessary condition, according to a definite pattern" (Smelser, 1963, pp. 13–14).[10]

A value-added conception of homicide would assert that the experience of growing up in a subcultural setting where violence is a common theme is a precondition for violent acts, but that specific instances of aggression and homicide do not occur until other events transpire, such as a marital dispute while drinking. Another application of value-added ideas can be made to forcible rape. The available research evidence (see Gibbons, 1968, pp. 384–89) indicates that forcible rapists are usually working-class males from a social situation where exploitative and aggressive themes regarding females are commonplace, but only a small number of those males who regard sexual intercourse as something to be done *to* rather than *with* a female, or who express similar attitudes, become involved in forcible rape. One of the most important

---

10. Cressey's (1953) analysis of financial trust violation can be seen as a case of value-added theory. He argues that nonsharable problems are important in trust violation, but only those persons with these problems who experience certain other life events become engaged in trust violation.

factors in the value-added process, increasing the likelihood that forcible rape will occur, may be the situational one of sexually provocative interaction between a male and female during an evening of drinking.

In both of these illustrations, genetic processes leading to acquisition of definitions favorable to violation of law are acknowledged to be important. However, not all who exhibit these sentiments engage in deviant acts, so that other causal events must also be involved in lawbreaking.

A value-added analysis of criminality would produce a considerably different view of the relationship between genetic and situational factors than the one emphasized by Sutherland. As noted above, he argued that proximate influences of a situational kind were unimportant in criminality compared to conduct definitions acquired from genetic processes. I have suggested in the preceding commentary that situational influences may often be the crucial, final element in a value-added process that ends in lawbreaking. Without the presence of the situational correlates, the necessary and sufficient causes of at least some kinds of criminality fail to occur.

In my view, there is much to be said for the exploration of such familiar notions as "criminogenic culture" from a value-added position which looks for links between genetic and situational factors. For example, it may be that definitions favorable to violation of law in the form of tolerant sentiments toward petty theft are widespread in American society and much less common in some other nations, so that persons in this country commonly do learn these attitudes from some kind of genetic socialization experience. If so, these genetically acquired definitions would account in part for cross-cultural variations in crime rates. They would be etiologically significant, even though additional factors would have to be identified in order to uncover the complete causal pattern producing criminally deviant acts by specific individuals.

SUMMARY

This paper has issued a call for more exploration of situational elements in criminality. I have argued that the lack of progress on etiological questions has been the result of inordinate attention to motivational formulations and genetic processes. Although both genetic and situational factors are implicated in criminality, the thesis here is that the latter may well be more important and more frequently encountered than many criminologists have acknowledged to date. The major tasks for criminological investigation center about identification of those cases where one or both of these sets of influences are operating, explication of the relationships between these factors, and determination of the relative weight to be assigned to these factors in particular cases of criminality.

Limited space precludes spelling out a detailed inventory of the forms of criminal etiology. Nor at present can I offer a full-blown explication of this kind. But some sense of the directions which ought to be explored is contained in the above discussion of particular cases of lawbreaking. Implicit in that material is the view that situational elements are probably involved in a good many nontrivial instances of criminality, so that it is not just the speeding motorist who responds in a criminal fashion to the inducements of the moment. Thus the prisons may be filled with a large number of persons who became enmeshed in criminality more out of adverse situations than of differential learning.[11]

The general programmatic recommendation of this essay is for more exploration of other possibilities where situational factors are operative. Thus close examination might be made of a recent account by Jackson (1969) of the life style of a contemporary Texas "character" (criminal argot for a police character, that is, an offender well-known to law enforcement agencies). This thief is a safe-robber from an upper middle-class background who drifted into deviance after becoming detached from familial ties, rather than being inducted into it through some kind of associational learning. Once involved in the thief life, this offender discovered that he enjoyed stealing and the "wine, women, and song" life style which accompanies it.[12] Another instructive case is Geis's (1968, pp. 103–18) analysis of the occupational cross pressures under which participants in the heavy electrical equipment antitrust cases of 1961 found themselves. These situational inducements to law violation appeared to influence this behavior more than any kind of learning of antisocial sentiments through differential association.

Moving to an area of criminality which has yet to be subjected to intensive investigation, we might wonder what kinds of situational fac-

---

11. Consider the extreme case of contemporary federal prisons which contain many persons sentenced for draft evasion. Many of these youths were responding to differential association of a reverse form to that visualized by Sutherland. They were exposed to extensive and prolonged moral socialization stressing the wrongfulness of killing and warfare. Surely they would not be in prison if the current societal conditions were somewhat different, and it would be hard to characterize them as "antisocial" persons. Joseph F. Jones brought this point to my attention.

12. I have discussed Jackson's book with a criminologist and friend of mine who has served a long sentence in a California prison. He avers that a number of the thieves he knows express positive enjoyment of stealing and the thrills accompanying it once they become enmeshed in that activity.

tors might turn up on income-tax evasion. Suppose that income-tax violations were to be studied by some kind of anonymous self-report technique. We might discover, first, that citizens generally regard petty income-tax evasion as acceptable behavior if one can "get away with it." We might also find that cheating on income-tax returns is class-linked and widespread among those who have opportunities to do so. Laborers and semiskilled workers rarely evade income taxes because their taxes are routinely withheld from their salary checks and they take standard deductions, so that they have little opportunity to file false claims. Persons in higher income brackets are able to falsify their itemized deductions or to withhold payment of tax on hidden forms of income not subject to payroll deduction.

Examples illustrating the need for attention to situational elements in lawbreaking could be enumerated at some length. However, systematic attention to etiological theory is required, rather than the multiplication of illustrations. It is hoped that this paper will trigger some movement toward systematic theory building of the kind hinted at above.

REFERENCES

Barnes, Harry Elmer, and Negley K. Teeters. 1959. *New Horizons in Criminology.* 3d ed. Englewood Cliffs, N.J.: Prentice-Hall.

Briar, Scott, and Irving Piliavin. 1965. "Delinquency, Situational Inducements, and Commitment to Conformity." *Social Problems* 13 (Summer): 35–45.

Burgess, Robert L., and Ronald L. Akers. 1966. "A Differential Association-Reinforcement Theory of Criminal Behavior." *Social Problems* 14 (Fall): 128–47.

Cameron, Mary Owen. 1964. *The Booster and the Snitch.* New York: Free Press.

Camp, George M. 1967. "Nothing to Lose: A Study of Bank Robbery in America." Ph.D. dissertation, Yale University.

Chambliss, William J., ed. 1969. *Crime and the Legal Process.* New York: McGraw-Hill.

Clinard, Marshall B., and Richard Quinney, eds. 1967. *Criminal Behavior Systems.* New York: Holt, Rinehart & Winston.

Cloward, Richard A., and Lloyd E. Ohlin. 1960. *Delinquency and Opportunity.* New York: Free Press.

Cohen, Albert K. 1955. *Delinquent Boys.* New York: Free Press.

Corsini, Raymond. 1949. "Criminal Psychology." In *Encyclopedia of Crime,* edited by Vernon C. Branham and Samuel B. Kutash. New York: Philosophical Library.

Cressey, Donald R. 1953. *Other People's Money.* New York: Free Press.

DeFleur, Melvin L., and Richard Quinney. 1966. "A Reformulation of Sutherland's Differential Association Theory and a Strategy for Empirical Verification." *Journal of Research in Crime and Delinquency* 3 (January): 1–22.

Downes, David. 1966. *The Delinquent Solution.* New York: Free Press.

Einstadter, Werner J. 1969. "The Social Organization of Armed Robbery." *Social Problems* 17 (Summer): 64–83.

Ferdinand, Theodore N. 1966. *Typologies of Delinquency.* New York: Random House.

Gagnon, John H., and William Simon, eds. 1967. *Sexual Deviance.* New York: Harper & Row.

Geis, Gilbert. 1968. *White-Collar Criminal.* New York: Atherton.

Gibbons, Don C. 1965. *Changing the Lawbreaker.* Englewood Cliffs, N.J.: Prentice-Hall.

———. 1968. *Society, Crime, and Criminal Careers.* Englewood Cliffs, N.J.: Prentice-Hall.

———. 1970. *Delinquent Behavior.* Englewood Cliffs, N.J.: Prentice-Hall.

Glaser, Daniel. 1956. "Criminality Theories and Behavioral Images." *American Journal of Sociology* 61 (March): 433–44.

Gould, Leroy. 1969. "The Changing Structure of Property Crime in an Affluent Society." *Social Forces* 48 (September): 50–59.

Hartjen, Clayton A., and Don C. Gibbons. 1969. "An Empirical Investigation of a Criminal Typology." *Sociology and Social Research* 54 (October): 56–62.

Hirschi, Travis. 1969. *Causes of Delinquency.* Berkeley: University of California Press.

Humphreys, Laud. 1970. *Tearoom Trade.* Chicago: Aldine.

Jackson, Bruce. 1969. *A Thief's Primer.* New York: Macmillan.

Jeffery, C. R. 1956. "The Structure of American Criminological Thinking." *Journal of Criminal Law, Criminology and Police Science* 46 (January–February): 658–72.

Lemert, Edwin M. 1967. *Human Deviance, Social Problems, and Social Control.* Englewood Cliffs, N.J.: Prentice-Hall.

Liebow, Elliott. 1967. *Tally's Corner.* Boston: Little Brown.

Lofland, John, and Rodney Stark. 1965. "Becoming a World-Saver: A Theory of Conversion to a Deviant Perspective." *American Sociological Review* 30 (December): 862–75.

Matza, David. 1964. *Delinquency and Drift.* New York: Wiley.

Moore, Robin, and Don C. Gibbons. 1970. "Offender Patterns in a Federal Probation Caseload." Mimeographed. Portland, Ore.: Center for Sociological Research, Portland State University.

Quinney, Richard, ed. 1969. *Crime and Justice in Society.* Boston: Little, Brown.

Roebuck, Julian B., and Merwyn L. Cadwallader. 1961. "The Negro Armed Robber as a Criminal Type: The Construction and Application of a Typology." *Pacific Sociological Review* 4 (Spring): 21–26.

Ross, H. Laurence. 1961. "Traffic Law Violation: A Folk Crime." *Social Problems* 9 (Winter): 231–41.

Short, James F., Jr. 1960. "Differential Association as a Hypothesis: Problems of Empirical Testing." *Social Problems* 6 (Summer): 14–25.

Short, James F., Jr., and Fred L. Strodtbeck. 1965. *Group Process and Gang Delinquency.* Chicago: University of Chicago Press.

Simon, Rita James, ed. 1968. *The Sociology of Law.* San Francisco: Chandler.

Smelser, Neil J. 1963. *Theory of Collective Behavior.* New York: Free Press.

Sutherland, Edwin H. 1949. *White Collar Crime.* New York: Dryden.

Sutherland, Edwin H., and Donald R. Cressey. 1970. *Principles of Criminology.* 8th ed. Philadelphia: Lippincott.

Tobias, J. J. 1967. *Crime and Industrial Society in the 19th Century.* London: B. T. Batsford.

Turk, Austin T. 1969. *Criminality and Legal Order.* Chicago: Rand McNally.

Wolfgang, Marvin E. 1958. *Patterns of Criminal Homicide.* Philadelphia: University of Pennsylvania Press.

7

Deterrence: Theoretical Foundations of Official Beliefs

Franklin E. Zimring and Gordon J. Hawkins

INTRODUCTORY NOTE

There is a celebrated passage in Immanuel Kant's *Philosophy of Law* which runs:

> Even if a Civil Society resolved to dissolve itself with the consent of all its members—as might be supposed in the case of a People inhabiting an island resolving to separate and scatter themselves through the whole world—the last Murderer lying in the prison ought to be executed before the resolution was carried out.[1]

There is an equally celebrated passage in Jeremy Bentham's *An Introduction to the Principles of Morals and Legislation* which runs:

> But all punishment is mischief: all punishment in itself is evil.[2]

The passage from Kant has been qualified by numerous exegetists, and Bentham supplied his own qualification in terms of the prevention of crime. But the juxtaposition of these passages reflects an antithesis which is present in popular thought on the subject of punishment.

For there are those who believe simply that criminals deserve punishment and that the institution needs no further justification.

From Franklin E. Zimring & Gordon J. Hawkins, *Deterrence: The Legal Threat in Crime Control* (Chicago: University of Chicago Press, 1973), pp. 16–32, by permission of the authors and publisher. Copyright © 1973 by The University of Chicago.

1. Kant, *Philosophy of Law* (trans. Hastie, 1887) 198.
2. Bentham, "An Introduction to the Principles of Morals and Legislation," 1 *Works* (1843) 83.

Moreover, even among those who feel the need for further justification in terms of social benefit, the necessity for some positive evidence of advantage gained is often given little weight if it is not disregarded altogether.

There is little doubt that the argument advanced by Professor Van den Haag in a recent article "On Deterrence and the Death Penalty" reflects a widely held popular view. Van den Haag argues that "though we have no proof of the positive deterrence of the penalty, we also have no proof of zero, or negative effectiveness." He goes on to say that therefore "our moral obligation is to risk the possible ineffectiveness of executions."[3] On a most charitable interpretation this is a highly attenuated form of utilitarian justification.

At the opposite extreme there are those who believe that punishment is "futile" and that if we were "honest" about it we would admit that the idea of deterrence "is simply a derived rationalization of revenge."[4] On this view the institution of punishment provides for "the popular masses" a vehicle for "a disguised living out of their own aggressive hostile impulses."[5]

Because such views are held and strongly held, and because attitudes to punishment are among the most deep-rooted of all our beliefs or convictions, it might seem that the approach developed in the pages which follow is unrealistic. Our discussion of such matters as the ethics of deterrence or of the evaluation of penal measures could be said to bear little relation to the way in which people actually think, talk, act, and make political decisions in this sphere. It might be argued that we display a naiveté and a simple-minded rationalism characteristic of the academic when he ventures into the world of realpolitik.

We must therefore point out that our model was conceived and can be interpreted on two different levels. First, it may be regarded as a political paradigm, that is, as an example or pattern of the sort of approach which *should* be adopted in dealing with the problems considered. And insofar as it represents an ideal, to object that it does not correspond to reality, although semantically correct, can scarcely be regarded as a very serious criticism.

On the second level our model reflects an approach to crime con-

3. Van den Haag, "On Deterrence and the Death Penalty" (1969) 60 *J. Crim. Law, Crim., and Police Science* 147.

4. Barnes and Teeters, *New Horizons in Criminology* (2d ed. 1951) 337–38.

5. Alexander and Staub, *The Criminal, the Judge, and the Public* (2d ed. 1956) 221.

trol which in its implementation may create its own constituency. The absence of information can itself both give rise to and ensure the continued dominance of irrational modes of thought and action. For the vacuum created by the absence of data is rapidly filled by the inrush of prejudice, surmise, random speculation, and unsupported assumption. And since the only rational policy is that which is selected as the best on the basis of the observed evidence, the lack of the necessary evidence means that irrationality can often be preemptive. But people's attitudes to punishment are neither always nor wholly irrational. For many, it is likely that information about the effectiveness of crime prevention programs would itself be a decisive factor in determining attitudes.

THE FOUNDATIONS OF OFFICIAL BELIEFS

Official Ideologies

"English judges," says Professor R. M. Jackson in *Enforcing the Law*, "have a great belief in the general deterrent effect of sentences."[6] This belief is not confined to English judges. As Norval Morris has pointed out: "Every criminal law system in the world, except one, has deterrence as its primary and essential postulate. It figures most prominently throughout our punishing and sentencing decisions legislative, judicial and administrative."[7]

And although it would be foolish to regard all those with legislative, judicial, and administrative power in our society as being unquestioning adherents of an established faith in deterrence, it is undeniable that some community of attitude exists. Different groups of officials do appear to share attitudes about deterrence to the extent that generalization does not seem unfair. This is not to say that there is an official dogma which has been formally stated or authoritatively proclaimed. Yet there is an official ideology of deterrence which, though not a system of integrated assertions or an organized body of concepts, does have sufficient definable content to make analytical discussion possible.

When confronted with a crime problem, legislators often agree that the best hope of control lies in "getting tough" with criminals by

---

6. Jackson, *Enforcing the Law* (1967) 207.

7. Morris, "Impediments to Penal Reform" (1966) 33 *U. Chi. L. Rev.* 631. In a footnote it is indicated that the exception referred to is the Greenland Criminal Code of 1962.

increasing penalties.[8] Police subscribe to the notion of "getting tough," but are apt to put more emphasis on what is termed "strict law enforcement,"[9] a concept that accords the major role to policing. Even correctional officers who are publicly committed to a rehabilitative ideal will sometimes privately confess allegiance to a more punitive approach with deterrent purposes in mind.[10] There are of course significant exceptions to these patterns. Many legislators, but far from a majority, now doubt the efficacy of the death penalty as a marginal deterrent when compared with the threat of protracted imprisonment. Many police express less than total faith in the ability of "strict law enforcement" alone to make a very positive contribution in such areas as the control of prostitution and illegal gaming.

But the exceptions are relatively few, and people more often seem to think in a straight line about the deterrent effect of sanctions:[11] If penalties have a deterrent effect in one situation, they will have a deterrent effect in all; if some people are deterred by threats, then all will be deterred; if doubling a penalty produces an extra measure of deterrence, then trebling the penalty will do still better. Carried to what may be an unfair extreme, this style of thinking imagines a world in which armed robbery is in the same category as illegal parking, burglars think like district attorneys, and the threat of punishment will result in an orderly process of elimination in which the crime rate will

---

8. *Crime and Penalties in California* (1968), a publication of the California Assembly Office of Research, discusses two episodes of increased-penalty response to rising rates of marijuana use and assaults on police during the 1961 term of the California legislature (at pp. 10–13). Other frequent candidates for "get tough" legislation in the United States include dangerous drug use and sale, gun robbery, and organized criminal activity.

9. The difference in emphasis between "getting tough" and stricter law enforcement appears to be that the former emphasizes the severity of sanctions while the latter emphasizes the risk of apprehension.

10. In this connection see also Morris and Zimring, "Deterrence and Corrections" (1969) 381 *Annals of AAPSS* at 143: ". . . when the correctional officer faces a disciplinary problem within a prison: then special and general deterrent purposes can be heard resoundingly to dominate decisions."

11. A remarkable example of thinking in a straight line about deterrence can be found in James Fitzjames Stephen's article "Capital Punishment" (June 1864) 16 *Frazer's Magazine* at 753–54. Stephen was convinced that "the punishment of death when vigorously inflicted has tremendous deterring force." He goes on to say that if it were shown that capital punishment did not deter "it would prove too much. It would prove that legal punishments do not deter at all." He concludes: "The truth is that if it is denied that the punishment of death deters from crime, the deterrent theory of punishment ought to be altogether given up, and we ought to resort to the doctrine . . . that crime ought to be treated exclusively as a disease."

diminish as the penalty scale increases by degrees from small fines to capital punishment, with each step upward as effective as its predecessor. Other officials, however—frequently those engaged in correctional work, the discouraging end of deterrence—will sometimes take a different but equally unitary view: Since human behavior is unpredictable and crime is determined by a variety of causes, deterrence is a myth.[12]

Commonly, both those who assert the necessary and universal effectiveness of punishment threats and those who deny their relevance to human behavior do not provide more than alternative slogans or catchwords. So it is impossible to determine what evidential bases their views rest on. The truth is (and it is a cheap point) that deterrence is far too complicated a matter to be contained within either of these procrustean views.[13] Such beliefs have no truth value. Nevertheless, it is of considerable importance to examine the bases upon which they rest. The discussion which follows represents an attempt to provide the necessary analysis.

When crime rates rise, law enforcement officials are frequently held—and many hold themselves—in some degree responsible. Some of them, it is true, may feel either that the problem is insoluble or that the solution lies beyond their sphere of influence. But, for the most part, law enforcement officials and society at large find themselves in agree-

12. This approach is exemplified in Barnes and Teeters, supra note 4, at 337–38. They talk of the "futile contention that punishment deters from crime. In this concept of deterrence there is a childlike faith in punishment. . . . The claim for deterrence is belied by both history and logic." See also Ellingston, *Protecting Our Children from Criminal Careers* (1948) 43: "The belief that punishment protects society from crime by deterring would-be law breakers will not stand up before our new understanding of human behavior."

13. Norval Morris, supra note 7, at 631 says: "The deterrence argument is more frequently implicit than expressed: the debate more frequently polarized than the subject of balanced discussion . . . . There is rarely any meeting of minds on the issue central to the discourse." And it is true that the dialogue frequently exemplifies the mathematician Frank Ramsey's point: "I think we realize too little how often our arguments are of the form—
  A: I went to Grantchester this afternoon.
  B: No, I didn't."
Ramsey, *The Foundations of Mathematics* (1931) 289. As a corrective to this kind of polarization one might refer to Wittgenstein's reply to the question, Why do we punish criminals? "There is" he said "the institution of punishing criminals. Different people support this for different reasons, and for different reasons in different cases and at different times. Some people support it out of a desire for revenge, some perhaps out of a desire for justice, some out of a wish to prevent a repetition of the crime, and so on. And so punishments are carried out." Wittgenstein, *Lectures and Conversations on Aesthetics, Psychology, and Religious Belief* (ed. C. Barrett, 1966) 50.

ment that fluctuations in the crime rate are subject to political control and responsive to crime-control policy.[14]

The law enforcement official, however, soon finds that he has a limited range of crime control options. He is not in a position—nor will he always feel the need—to introduce millennial measures to end poverty or eradicate social and economic inequity. He can make crime physically more difficult in only a limited number of situations—by urging citizens to lock their cars; fostering the use of automatic locks on bank vaults; raising the height of fire alarm boxes to secure them from the whims of five-year-old children; doubling and trebling the number of police on the street to hamper the mugger, the purse thief, and the random attacker.

Many prevention strategies are expensive, and the administrator is the first to feel the brunt of this type of expense. To double the police force, we must more than double our budget for police. If citizens are required to take expensive precautions, they will object. If precautions are not made mandatory, many will not heed warnings. Beyond this, many of the most serious of crimes—homicide, aggravated assault, rape, indoor robbery, larceny, and crimes against trust—are committed where police cannot prevent them.

Thus, a belief in the efficacy of deterrent measures is attractive, because it offers crime control measures where alternatives appear to be unavailable and does so without great apparent cost. It is not surprising that deterrence through threat and punishment is among the most valued official weapons in the war against crime. Nor is this merely a matter of political expedience. For it is difficult to deny that, as Professor Packer puts it, "People who commit crimes appear to share the prevalent impression that punishment is an unpleasantness that is best avoided."[15] To threaten with punishment is therefore a very promising strategy for influencing behavior. And deterrence is a strategy that shows promise of working in areas of behavior where the official has no other technique for crime reduction at hand.

---

14. There is, to be sure, some official ambivalence about the relationship between law enforcement efforts and crime rates. In discussing the nature of homicide, police authorities are quick to point out that there is little by way of direct intervention that police can do to reduce the rate of violent killings. "Criminal homicide is, to a major extent, a social problem beyond police prevention." *Uniform Crime Reports—1967* at 8. At the same time, police and many other officials have asserted a direct relationship between rising crime rates and constitutional restraints on police procedures imposed by the United States Supreme Court in recent years. And four of the eleven factors listed by the FBI as "conditions which will affect the amount and type of crime that occurs from place to place" concern police, prosecution and court policies. See *Uniform Crime Reports 1967* at vi.

15. Packer, *The Limits of the Criminal Sanction* (1968) 149.

Yet it is one thing to believe that deterrent measures may be a promising strategy in some situations and quite another to espouse a monolithic theory of deterrent efficacy. And it is not immediately apparent why so many people do hold monolithic attitudes about deterrence—whether affirming or denying the effectiveness of legal threats. It seems that they allow themselves to hold only one idea about the nature of deterrence. Once the complex of issues about deterrence is transformed into a yes-or-no question, the results are of course predictable. If the only question at issue is whether deterrence is possible or not, those who believe that it is possible will achieve a substantial majority as a matter of common sense. But when a complex series of different issues is bent into the form of a yes-or-no question, the margin of error obtained from answering that question either way approaches 50 percent.

The tendency to have only one idea about deterrence is not peculiar to officials, nor is it confined to those who deal with the subject of deterrence. The "single idea" phenomenon is a characteristic of prescientific speculation in most areas of human knowledge.[16] One factor is no less basic than human nature; we all would prefer to have simple rather than complicated explanations for the questions that perplex us. Complicated explanations evolve from the pressure that experience exerts on our simple initial constructs by a process of trial and error. Since so little evaluative research has yet been done in the area of deterrence, there is little pressure toward rethinking unitary positions. Thus, there are few inconsistent results to sensitize officials to the differences in situation which may, in turn, condition differences in threat effectiveness. Moreover, the limited amount of data available can be comfortably fitted into the official's initial opinion—it can be either accepted at face value or rejected as inconclusive. The absence of reliable research in deterrence does not mean that officials are without any basis for their opinions. In most cases they will have personal and administrative experience in the light of which to test their views of deterrent effectiveness.

The official's personal experience is in most cases likely to lend support to his belief in deterrence. Having worked hard to achieve the regard of his fellows, he is more sensitive than most to the threat of social stigma. He likes to regard himself as a rational man and will be

---

16. The basic fallacy in this context, as in many others (e.g. the causation of crime), was identified over a century ago by that neglected American genius Alexander Bryan Johnson (1786–1867). "The search after the unit is the delusion," he said. Johnson, *A Treatise on Language* (ed. D. Rynin, 1947) 77.

anxious to give himself credit for responding in the only rational manner to threats. The official is also a law-abiding man and attributes some of his obedience to the threat of sanctions. He remembers slowing down when seeing a police car on the highway, remembers considering the possibility of audit when filling out his income tax return. He is less likely to recall deviations.

It is probable that another source of information is the official's own experience with crime control policies. In his official capacity the legislator "tries out" deterrent threats; the results of these trials are integrated into his attitudes about deterrence. In the absence of controlled research, the apparent results of ongoing crime control policy are the most important data available about deterrence, and these results will inevitably have a profound effect on official attitudes. Unhappily, as we shall see, the unquestioning acceptance of the unanalyzed results of experience with crime control policy is not a satisfactory substitute for careful evaluative research.

The Lessons of Experience

We cannot demonstrate the truth of our assertion that an important source of those shared beliefs about deterrence which influence penal policy is to be found in the experience of our lawmakers and law enforcers. Nor can we show conclusively that their beliefs are derived from their experience in the manner which we suggest. We can only adduce argument in support of our view, mainly by showing that officials rationalize their beliefs by pointing to that experience. Moreover the study of such rationalization is itself important.

We do not claim to be, in T. S. Eliot's phrase, "expert beyond experience."[17] But experience as a teacher has defects other than the commonly observed characteristic that it seems to inspire reminiscential garrulity. The truth is that there are different types of experience from which knowledge may be derived, and it is necessary to distinguish from one another at least two meanings of the word *experience.*

First, by experience, we may mean the experiences which men accumulate as a result of direct participation in events and being engaged in a particular activity without making any special effort to explore, investigate, or test hypotheses. Second, we may refer to the special data of experience which men collect by undertaking methodical research and making systematic observations.

---

17. Eliot, "Whispers of Immortality," in *Poems 1909–1925* (1925) 57.

Our contention is that the experience of lawmakers and law enforcement officials is usually of the first kind and that it is subject to serious limitations as a source of knowledge. It is particularly defective when used as a basis for generalization or inductive inference. In order to emphasize some of the common pitfalls that officials encounter in trying to read the significance of the results of crime control policies, we may start with three examples of common errors made in inferring more from statistics than the statistics will support.

Aunt Jane's Cold Remedy.   One common inferential error, or failure to satisfy the conditions of valid or correct inference, can be illustrated by an example drawn from the field of folk medicine. Aunt Jane's Cold Remedy is a mixture of whiskey, sugar, and hot water. It is widely recommended as a treatment for the common cold which can be guaranteed to be effective as a cure within ten days. In a great many cases, moreover, it does appear to be effective. The great majority of those who take the remedy are likely to be quite satisfied with it because every time they take it their cold disappears within the nominated period.

However, apart from some possible temporary, symptomatic relief, Aunt Jane's Remedy has no known effect on the common cold. The cold goes away within ten days because most colds run a course of from three to ten days whether treated or not—that is the nature of the malady. Yet if the adherents of Aunt Jane's Remedy are faithful, they will have no way of knowing that the remedy did not effect a cure. And if, as is quite possible, they have some kind of emotional investment in believing in the cure,[18] they may staunchly resist the suggestion that the remedy is useless, even when their colds go away without being treated with it. Such untreated colds, when recovered from, can be explained away as milder infections.

Legislators and law enforcement officials treat crime, not colds, but they are prone to adopt similar modes of inference. When life is proceeding normally, no great pressure is put on the legislator to increase penalties or on the police official to double or triple patrols. Pressure for strong new countermeasures comes when the crime rate suddenly spurts. Often the scenario then follows this course: (1) spurt in crime rate, (2) countermeasure, (3) return of crime rate to more normal historical level.

---

18. It is characteristic of such folk remedies that they are handed down from parents to children, or within intimate family groups, and thus attract a loyalty which is based on extrinsic factors irrelevant to the nature of the remedy but no less potent for that reason.

Did the countermeasure reduce crime? If so by how much? The headlines read, *Police dogs reduce ghetto crime by 65 percent,* or *Computer reduces false alarms by 35 percent,* and enforcement officials are reluctant to avoid credit for the change. But if we remember that an unusual spurt in the crime rate was responsible for the countermeasure, another possible explanation of the reduction exists: The crime rate simply returned to its usual level, which would have been the case whether or not the computer or police dogs or new patrols had been introduced.

At a later stage we shall be considering documented examples of law enforcement techniques being credited with achieving reductions in crime that were partly the result of other factors. In some cases we find that, after account has been taken of regression to normal levels of crime, the preventive effects attributed to a particular program probably had nothing to do with it. In other cases there may be genuine preventive effects which cannot be explained in terms of regression.

It is sometimes impossible to tell what the crime rate would have been if a particular program had not been introduced. So it is not always possible to determine how much of the reduction can be attributed to natural causes and how much can be credited to the program. But in most cases, knowledge that the program was introduced in a peak period should at least make observers sensitive to the possibility that a good part of the decrease might have been unrelated to the new program. Detailed study of historical trends in the crime rate, or comparisons with untreated areas, could show that the decrease was not solely attributable to Aunt Jane.

Still, if officials desire to maintain a unitary faith in deterrent countermeasures, they can easily do so. Because new programs are normally tried during periods when the rate of the particular crime is high, the official can take credit for any decreases in rate that follow the introduction of the new measures. If the crime rate stays high, who can say that it would not have climbed higher were it not for the new program? Indeed, the rise in crime shows conclusively that we need more of the new countermeasures.[19]

Subjecting our crime prevention strategies to evaluative research will prove less comforting but, in the long run, more valuable. In some situations, close analysis will show that the crime rate could have been

---

19. According to the California Assembly Office of Research study, supra note 8, "In the City of Los Angeles, the rate of attacks on police went from 2.5 per 100 in 1952 to 8.4 in 1961, to 15.8 in 1966. . . . In 1961 the first special penalties for attacks on the police were enacted by the Legislature and such penalties were further increased in . . . 1963 and 1965."

expected to decrease even if no new treatment had been administered; in others, a steady rise in crime over a long period of time that can be attributed to factors such as an increase in the population at risk will indicate that, in the absence of a new treatment, the crime rate would probably have continued to increase.[20] Evaluative research may be able to provide rough estimates of how much the rate would have increased or decreased in the absence of treatment and thus give us a baseline for testing the value of new treatments.

Providing a baseline, so that reliable determinations can be made about the degree of crime reduction attributable to particular countermeasures, is an absolute necessity in any but the most wasteful of crime control policies. Without such a baseline, it may be assumed that some strategies reduce crime when in fact they do not. The preventive effects of other programs may be underestimated because we fail to account for expected increases in crime. When countermeasures do have some effect on crime, overestimating that effect by neglecting the possibility of natural decrease may provoke the use of programs that are not worth their cost—and, worse still, postpone the development of new and more effective strategies.

Tiger Prevention. Alexander King prefaces his *May This House Be Safe From Tigers*—the second volume of his memoirs—with an anecdote about a Buddhist prayer which provides him with his title and will provide us with an illustration.[21]

There are many versions of the story King tells, but that which we favor seems more closely analogous to the way in which what we call the tiger prevention fallacy may both vitiate official thinking and set up a formidable barrier to the revision of crime control strategies. In our version a man is running about the streets of mid-Manhattan, snapping his fingers and moaning loudly, when he is intercepted by a police officer. Their conversation follows:

P.O.: What are you doing?
Gtlm.: Keeping tigers away.

---

20. Thus, it is not possible to conclude, as was done in *Crime and Penalties in California,* supra note 8, at 11, that increased penalties for assaults on a police officer were of no deterrent effectiveness merely because the rate of such crimes continued to increase after penalties for that offense increased.

21. King claims to have a Zen Buddhist friend who, when leaving after a visit, invariably stops in the doorway, presses his hands together Hindu fashion, and says: "May this house be safe from tigers." One day King asked him the meaning of the prayer, and the following dialogue ensued: "What's wrong with my prayer?" he said. "How long have I been saying it to you?" "Oh, about three years, on and off." "Three years," he said. "Well —been bothered by any tigers lately?" King, *May This House Be Safe From Tigers* (1959) v.

P.O.: Why, that's crazy. There isn't a wild tiger within five thousand miles of New York City!

Gtlm.: Well then, I must have a pretty effective technique!

Other factors than the Buddhist's benediction are responsible for Alexander King's immunity from tigers, just as other factors account for the absence of tigers in New York City. But as long as those who practice such preventive methods continue to do so, they will not find that out.

In crime control, the tiger prevention problem is subtle and difficult to resolve. Officials who administer very high penalties acquire the firm conviction that only those penalties stand between them and huge increases in the crime rate. Having assumed that the penalty is the only reason for the absence of a crime wave, the official has "proved" that high penalties deter crime more effectively than less severe penalties.

One of the most celebrated examples of the tiger prevention approach to crime control is British Chief Justice Lord Ellenborough's now classic response to a nineteenth-century proposal that, while the death penalty for shoplifting should remain, the value of the goods stolen which incurred that penalty be raised from five to ten shillings. Speaking in the House of Lords, Ellenborough said:

> I trust your lordships will pause before you assent to an experiment pregnant with danger to the security of property. . . . Such will be the consequence of the repeal of this statute that I am certain depredations to an unlimited extent would immediately be committed. . . . Repeal this law and . . . no man can trust himself for an hour out of doors without the most alarming apprehension that on his return, every vestige of his property will be swept off by the hardened robber.[22]

The proof is the same as that offered by the tiger preventers except in one respect: because penalties may well influence crime rates, it cannot be assumed, as in the tiger examples, that the countermeasure bears no relation to the rate of crime. Being unable to assume that there is no relation between penalty level and crime rate, we can only determine whether and how much the two are related by varying the

22. Parliamentary Debates: House of Lords, 30 May 1810. Cited in Calvert, *Capital Punishment in the Twentieth Century* (1927) 7–8, and subsequently by others too numerous to mention. Another example may be found in the celebrated passage in "The Saint Petersburg Dialogues" in which Joseph de Maistre writes of the public executioner: "And yet all grandeur, all power, all subordination rests on the executioner: he is the horror and the bond of human association. Remove this incomprehensible agent from the world, and at that very moment order gives way to chaos, thrones topple, and society disappears." *The Works of Joseph de Maistre* (ed. J. Lively, 1965) 192.

penalty. But since that would involve risk taking, the status quo and the "proof" of deterrence built into it persist. The tiger prevention argument is not refutable when posed as a barrier to experimental decreases in punishment; it is, however, patently absurd to present high penalties combined with low crime rates as proof of deterrence.

Studies of different areas with different penalties, and studies focusing on the same jurisdiction before and after a change in punishment level takes place, show rather clearly that level of punishment is not the major reason why crime rates vary.[23] In regard to particular penalties, such as capital punishment as a marginal deterrent to homicide, the studies go further and suggest no discernible relationship between the presence of the death penalty and homicide rates.[24] Although imperfect, these studies certainly utilize the best methods available of testing whether more severe sanctions have extra deterrent force in particular situations.

But even in comparative and retrospective studies, the tiger prevention fallacy may crop up in a more sophisticated form. Consider a study that shows homicide to be both the most severely punished and the least often committed crime in a particular jurisdiction.[25] Proof of deterrence? Or tiger prevention? It is quite possible that the rate of homicide would remain low even if the penalty for homicide were less severe, because of the strong social feelings against homicide. Indeed, one reason why the penalty for homicide is so high may be that citizens view this crime as so terrible. Both the low rate and the high penalty may be effects of the same cause: strong social feelings against homicide. Thus, showing that crimes which are punished more severely are committed less often may only be one way of showing how accurately a penalty scale reflects general feeling about the seriousness of crimes.

This problem can also arise in connection with some forms of comparative research. Assume we find out that homicide is punished more severely in one state than in another, and that the homicide rate is much lower in the severe penalty state. Does the higher penalty cause the lower rate? It may be that the higher penalty shows that people in that state have stronger social feelings about homicide; and these feelings, rather than the extra penalty, may explain the difference in homicide rate. In order to test the effect of penalties alone, areas that are similar to each other in all respects except penalties should be sought

---

23. See Rusche and Kirchheimer, *Punishment and Social Structure* (1939) 193–205.

24. See the studies collected in Bedau, *The Death Penalty in America* (1964): also U.N. Dept. of Economic and Social Affairs, *Capital Punishment Developments, 1961–65* (1967).

25. Tittle, "Crime Rates and Legal Sanctions" (1969) 16 *Social Problems* 409.

out and compared. This would be a strategy far more cumbersome than assuming that harsh criminal sanctions are keeping the tigers away but, again, far more reliable and rewarding.

The Warden's Survey. A third type of faulty inference is found most frequently among those who work at what we have called "the discouraging end of deterrence." Once again the argument is based on experience, but this time the conclusion drawn is diametrically opposite to that exemplified above.

The earliest example we have come across of the type of argument we have in mind occurs in a 1931 article by Warden George W. Kirchwey of Sing Sing.[26] Writing as one *"that has known the convict"* (our italics), Kirchwey maintains that "it argues a curious ignorance of human psychology to attach much importance to the doctrine of deterrence." He goes on to say that belief in "the deterrent effect of exemplary punishments or in their moralizing effect on the community at large is "a blind faith."[27]

The same sort of inference is drawn much more explicitly in a book by another celebrated Warden of Sing Sing, Lewis E. Lawes, published in 1940.[28] In his *Meet the Murderer* Lawes states that "the threat of capital punishment lacks the deterrent force most people believe it possesses." On the basis of *"many years' acquaintance with all types of murderers"* (our italics again) he avers that "a person who commits murder gives no thought to the chair."[29]

Lastly, more recently (1962), and even more explicitly we find Warden Clinton T. Duffy of San Quentin giving his views on the effectiveness of the death penalty as a deterrent in his *88 Men and 2 Women.*[30] "But the prison man knows this threat is no deterrent," says Duffy, *"for convicts have told him so again and again"* (our italics).[31]

The warden's survey is unpersuasive for two reasons. First, in none of the instances cited is it at all clear that the prisoners would have told the warden even if they *had* been deterred by penalties at some time in their lives. It could hardly be in their interests to do so. But more significantly, in each case the warden's sample of people to ask about deterrence and base his inference upon is hopelessly biased. For he has

---

26. Kirchwey, "The Prison's Place in the Penal System" (1931) 156 *Annals of AAPSS.*
27. Id. at 17–18.
28. Lawes, *Meet the Murderer* (1940).
29. Id. at 177.
30. Duffy, *88 Men and 2 Women* (1962).
31. Id. at 22.

based his conclusion on experience with groups of men who have evidently *not* been deterred or they would not be in prison.

At a later stage we will be considering more rigorous studies in deterrence and will demonstrate that the warden's survey fallacy is one which recurs even on quite sophisticated levels of inquiry, including a study conducted for the President's Commission on Law Enforcement and the Administration of Justice.[32] In studies which involve this particular fallacy, attention is concentrated on groups of deterrence failures and *general* conclusions are drawn on the basis of evidence relating to *particular* groups, which are unrepresentative precisely because they have not responded to the threat of punishment for crime. All of the law's successes, if there were any, would be found outside these groups.

Our tiger preventers and our wardens make contradictory assumptions about the relation between those criminals in jail and the potential crime problem. The tiger prevention advocate assumes that large numbers of law-abiding citizens are held in check by the threat of penalties; indeed, that only severe penalties can perform this job. The warden seems to assume that, when he interviews prisoners, he is talking to the totality of the potential crime problem, or at least to a representative sample. Consequently, because these assumptions are unsupported, both the "proof" and "disproof" of deterrence must fail.

But the fact that these patterns of thinking fail to prove or disprove deterrence does not mean they are unimportant and can be ignored. Officials will continue to act on severe convictions, whether or not these convictions are well founded. Thus, a significant step toward more rigorous research in deterrence, and ultimately toward a more rational crime control policy, would be to make officials more sensitive to new insights and more understanding of the complexities that undermine monolithic attitudes about deterrence. For this reason, the careful study of "cold remedy," "tiger prevention," and "warden's survey" patterns of inference are an important part of a program for progress in crime control.

---

32. Goodman, Miller, and DeForrest, "A Study of the Deterrence Value of Crime Prevention Measures as Perceived by Criminal Offenders" (1966). Unpublished paper submitted by The Bureau of Social Science Research, Inc., to the Institute for Defense Analysis.

PART III

Issues in Criminological Research

Among the more important tasks confronting the criminologist is the acquisition of knowledge about illegal behavior, including its antecedents and its consequences. Since an offense known to the police generates an enormously complex set of possible responses, e.g., investigation, arrest, charging, indictment, trial, conviction, and sentencing, most students of criminal behavior focus their attention upon a selected aspect of this process. A given project may confine its inquiry to the disposal of robbery or burglary proceeds ("fencing"), or it may analyze the increasing evidence of female offenders at all stages of the criminal justice process. Less pragmatic questions might be: What stigmatizing effects are internalized by young people when they are identified and officially processed as law violators? What social policies will gain support in a society whose citizens perceive crime as increasingly threatening to their property and to them personally?

Beyond the criminologist's imperative to reduce his scope of inquiry to manageable proportions, he must also devise an optimal means for acquiring data on his topic. Many methods of data gathering have evolved over decades of behavioral science research, including interviews, questionnaires, experimentation, official documents, and case studies. A very brief review of these will acquaint the reader with some trends and issues in several of the more productive methodological approaches taken by criminologists and with the data sources at their disposal.

The best-known repository of information on criminal occurrences is police statistics. Nearly every law enforcement agency gathers data at frequent and regular intervals that are matters of public record. For research purposes, however, statistics on crime gathered by public agencies for their own uses are severely limited. In past years they have been subject to political influence (a "reform" chief often promised to reduce crime and did so statistically), but their greatest deficiency is that they include only law violations reported to the police or witnessed by them. Therefore they do not include those criminal events that are not reported to the police. They are also highly susceptible to the skill and discretion exercised by police and to the priorities followed by administrators in the deployment of their officers. In short, official records on crime are an *estimate* of true criminal occurrences at a particular time and in a specific jurisdiction.

The most widely known national collection of data on crimes are the *Uniform Crime Reports* published on an annual basis since 1930 by the Federal Bureau of Investigation. About 11,000 city, county, and state law enforcement agencies submit figures on seven "crime index" or serious offenses: murder, forcible rape, robbery, aggravated assault, burglary, larceny-theft, and motor vehicle theft. Criticisms of the FBI data have persisted in many quarters, but the fact remains that these reports have been the major source of public beliefs about crime for many years.

Not surprisingly, an alternative means for gauging criminal events gained acceptance among those who were distraught over the "wretched" state of official statistics and those who sought data about those events that were beyond the scope of police interests. In the mid-1960s, the President's Commission on

Law Enforcement and Administration of Justice supported a number of pilot projects to survey *victims* of crime, thus inaugurating a mode of inquiry which has combined with other interests to form the subfield of *victimology*.

Surveys designed to elicit information from the victims of criminal offenses have their own problems of reliability and validity, and they are not intended to fully supplant *Uniform Crime Reports*. But they are well suited for comparing offense patterns of different jurisdictions, learning victims' attitudes toward or fears of crime, making temporal analyses of crime trends, and learning more about the social and physical circumstances surrounding criminal acts. When undertaken on a large enough scale, as in a national probability sample of households and businesses, the results of victim data can be invaluable for planning and evaluating crime-reduction programs.

Antecedent even to the collection of crime statistics on the national level was the method of survey research. Most fully developed at the University of Chicago in the 1920s and 1930s, the survey employed local data on crime obtained from official agencies or secured through traditional techniques such as interviews and questionnaires. Many of these studies, directed by Robert Park, Ernest Burgess, and Roderick McKenzie, documented "problem" behavior in metropolitan centers, using Chicago as a "natural laboratory." Park and Burgess (the latter published his "concentric zone" model of urban structure and change in 1925) made seminal contributions to ecological theory, as it was called, and their students over the years wrote research papers on a variety of behaviors considered detrimental to the welfare of society. Out of this program grew a heritage of monographs on suicide, taxi-dance halls, prostitution, divorce, urban vice, skid row life, and mental disorder.

An alternative means of data gathering consisted of the case study. Early sociologists and psychologists referred to this as the "life history" or "own story" technique, and one of the earliest examples of its use was W. I. Thomas's study of Polish girls who turned to careers in delinquency, prostitution, or other illegal conduct. Other well known and highly regarded examples of case studies have used *organizations* as the unit of analysis. Thus analyses of male and female prisons have appeared, together with research on organized crime "families," police departments, the public defender's office, bail-bondsmen, and many others. Case studies of acknowledged, cooperative offenders or organizations share at least two common problems: (1) single cases do not permit verification of causal links between antecedent conditions and ensuing (criminal) behavior; and (2) extrapolation of findings based upon a single organization or criminal career to a universe of similar-appearing ones is tenuous at best.

Case studies often involve the use of participant-observational methods. Any time a criminologist assumes the role of observer, he is confronted with a number of issues—some technical, some ethical or even legal. Often he will be given access to information on illegal transactions or he will be told the details of unsolved crimes. As he acquires field knowledge, scholarly dilemmas arise. What should be done when the police researcher discovers that officers who seize quantities of stolen merchandise dispose of most of the "evidence" for personal gain? Similarly, a prison researcher may discover that certain correctional officers are supplementing their incomes by importing drugs for sale among inmates. Is he under legal obligation to report his findings? What prospects for continued rapport with his subjects will follow?

A major consideration in participant observation is the minimization of "reactive" bias, i.e., the distortion resulting from a respondent's realization that he is under study. The evidence that subjects may adjust their answers to questionnaire or interview items or modify their behavior in observational settings is so compelling that two compensatory techniques have been suggested—concealment of the observer's true identity, and the use of unobtrusive measures. With regard to the first, one's identity can often be made sufficiently congruent with the setting one expects to study that problems of access do not arise. In this approach the researcher covertly participates in a role, gathering observations without the knowledge of his associates. Many of the most perceptive and revealing studies, ranging across professional "fences," thieves, confidence men, numbers operators, transvestites, drug addicts, and burglars, have been products of this method. There are substantial risks involved, as social scientists researching homosexuality, drug use, and prostitution have discovered.

Disagreement about concealing one's role as observer is centered around conflicting ethical responsibilities research personnel have to their colleagues, the citizenry at large, and their study population. If the observer does not disguise himself and his true objectives he may contaminate the research scene, and deny himself the valuable insights that may be shared with those persons they trust.

The second form of compensation is a methodological approach which has gained stature in recent years through the use of unobtrusive or nonreactive measures, i.e., those in which the observer's intrusion has no effect upon his object of study. Thus archival records such as logs, files, and memoranda have great value in determining not only the substance and distribution of critical events, but the *recordkeeping activities of archivists* as well.

Limitations upon sample surveys, participant observation, and other methods of data acquisition have led some scholars to make a case for research triangulation. This design calls for the application of several complementary techniques that converge upon a single objective from independent directions. In the usual case, an investigator could gain a "fix" on his topic through the convergence of interviews, official documents, and field observations.

Albert J. Reiss's essay, "Problems in the Documentation of Crime," is an incisive challenge to the current system of gathering and reporting official data on crime. Using several illustrative cases, he shows how reported crime rates distort the reality of true criminal victimization.

"The Victims of Crime: Some National Survey Findings," written especially for this volume by Wesley G. Skogan, reports upon efforts to overcome many of the limitations of official statistics through the introduction of victim surveys. Skogan compares the results of the 1973 National Crime Survey for certain major crimes with official FBI statistics, presents characteristics of the victims and locations of criminal activity, and analyzes the conditions under which victims initiate police intervention.

Reporting on an unusual study, Jennie McIntyre demonstrates that the general public believes crime is increasing, fears that lawbreaking will probably take the form of attack upon the person by a stranger, and hopes that changes in daily habits can optimize safety. She also shows that persons tend to recommend stern treatment of offenders in the aggregate, but are disposed to leniency and a concern for individual rights in concrete cases.

The selection by Kai T. Erikson takes the position that misrepresenting oneself to gain access to otherwise unavailable settings incurs the risk of being unethical and unscientific. Norman K. Denzin's response debates several points related to the charges made by Erikson and proposes that many of the most significant findings of sociological research have required covert observation. Finally, a rebuttal by Erikson reveals the polarized nature of this issue.

Selected references associated with methodological approaches to crime research appear below.

1. *Some Issues in the Use and Abuse of Crime Statistics*
Black, Donald J., "Production of Crime Rates," *American Sociological Review* 35 (1970): 733–48.
Doleschal, Eugene, *Criminal Statistics* (Rockville, Md.: National Institute of Mental Health, 1972).
Federal Bureau of Investigation, United States Department of Justice, *Uniform Crime Reports for the United States, 1974* (Washington, D.C.: U.S. Government Printing Office, 1975).
Graham, Fred P., "Black Crime: The Lawless Image," *Harper's* 241 (1970): 64–65 ff.
Milakovich, Michael E., and Weis, Kurt, "Politics and Measures of Success in the War on Crime," *Crime and Delinquency* 21 (1975): 1–10.
Newman, Donald J., "The Effect of Accommodations in Justice Administration on Criminal Statistics," *Sociology and Social Research* 46 (1962): 144–55.

Seidman, David, and Couzens, Michael, "Getting the Crime Rate Down: Political Pressure and Crime Reporting," *Law and Society Review* 8 (1974): 457–93.
Simon, Rita James, *The Contemporary Woman and Crime* (Rockville, Md.: National Institute of Mental Health, 1975).
Skogan, Wesley G., "Measurement Problems in Official and Survey Crime Rates," *Journal of Criminal Justice* 3 (1975): 17–31.
Sudnow, David, "Normal Crimes: Sociological Features of the Penal Code in a Public Defender Office," *Social Problems* 12 (1965): 255–76.
Waldo, Gordon P., "Myths, Misconceptions, and the Misuse of Statistics in Correctional Research," *Crime and Delinquency* 17 (1971): 57–66.
Weis, Kurt, and Milakovich, Michael E., "Political Misuses of Crime Rates," *Society* 11 (1974): 27–33.
Wilkins, Leslie T., "Crime: Offense Patterns," in *International Encyclopedia of the Social Sciences* vol. 3, ed. David L. Sills (New York: Free Press, Macmillan, 1968), pp. 476–83.
Wolfgang, Marvin E., "Uniform Crime Reports: A Critical Appraisal," *University of Pennsylvania Law Review* 111 (1963): 708–38.

2. Field Methods in Crime Research

Becker, Howard S., "Practitioners of Vice and Crime," in *Pathways to Data: Field Methods for Studying Ongoing Social Organizations,* ed. Robert W. Habenstein (Chicago: Aldine, 1970), pp. 30–49.
Inciardi, James A., "The Sociologist as Historian and Detective ... An Essay on Methods and the Search for Evidence," in *Careers in Crime* (Chicago: Rand McNally, 1975), pp. 140–55.
Irwin, John, "Participant-Observation of Criminals," in *Research on Deviance,* ed. Jack D. Douglas (New York: Random House, 1972), pp. 117–37.
Polsky, Ned, "Research Method, Morality, and Criminology," *Hustlers, Beats and Others* (Chicago: Aldine, 1967), pp. 117–49.

Wax, Rosalie H., *Doing Fieldwork: Warnings and Advice* (Chicago: University of Chicago Press, 1971).

Wheeler, Stanton, ed., *On Record: Files and Dossiers in American Life* (New York: Russell Sage Foundation, 1970).

Yablonsky, Lewis, "Experiences with the Criminal Community," in *Applied Sociology*, ed. Alvin W. Gouldner and S. M. Miller (New York: Free Press, Macmillan, 1965), pp. 55–73.

———, "On Crime, Violence, LSD, and Legal Immunity for Social Scientist" (letters), *American Sociologist* 3 (1968): 148.

3. *Victimology and Victim Surveys*

Biderman, Albert D., and Reiss, Albert J., Jr., "On Exploring the 'Dark Figure' of Crime," *The Annals of the American Academy of Political and Social Science* 374 (1967): 1–15.

Drapkin, Israel, and Viano, Emilio, eds., *Volume I: Theoretical Issues in Victimology* (Lexington, Mass.: D.C. Heath, 1974).

———, *Volume II: Society's Reaction to Victimization* (Lexington, Mass.: D.C. Heath, 1974).

———, *Volume III: Crimes, Victims and Justice* (Lexington, Mass.: D.C. Heath, 1975).

———, *Volume IV: Violence and its Victims* (Lexington, Mass.: D.C. Heath, 1975).

———, *Volume V: Exploiters and Exploited: The Dynamics of Victimology* (Lexington, Mass.: D.C. Heath, 1975).

Ennis, Phillip H., "Crime, Victims, and the Police," *Trans-Action* 4 (1967):36–44.

Glaser, Daniel, "Victim Survey Research: Theoretical Implications," in *Criminal Behavior and Social Systems: Contributions of American Sociology*, ed. Anthony L. Guenther (Chicago: Rand McNally, 1970), pp. 136–48.

Hentig, Hans von, *The Criminal and his Victim* (New Haven: Yale University Press, 1948).

Schafer, Stephen, *The Victim and his Criminal* (New York: Random House, 1968).

8

Problems in the Documentation of Crime

Albert J. Reiss, Jr.

During the past few years Americans have come to believe that they are being engulfed by a crime wave. In opinion polls, they rank crime as the number one problem of the nation. Indeed, some have even begun to doubt that it is a wave, given the length of time it has been rising. They speak gloomily of moral decay, and of disrespect for the rule of law. The Congress has launched a massive program for law and order in a bill ominously titled The Safe Streets and Omnibus Crime Control Bill.

Clearly, Americans and their legislative representatives are convinced about facts. They regard crime as rising very rapidly. They view with alarm their own safety in the streets and other public places. Many are afraid in their homes. Many believe that the police are hampered in their efforts to control crime and that the courts are not tough enough. All of these are questions of fact. But what are the facts? How much crime is there in American society today? Has there been a change in the crime rate over the past 10 years? How safe are our streets?

Our purpose is to raise some doubts about facts documenting the current crime wave. What we propose to do is to tell you about what recent research on the prevalence and incidence of crime in the United States tells us and what it doesn't tell us. We shall then try to provide a perspective for assessing crime and changes in crime rates.

From Albert J. Reiss, Jr., "Assessing the Current Crime Wave," in Barbara N. McLennan (ed.), *Crime in Urban Society* (New York: Dunellen, 1970), pp. 23–42, by permission of the author and publisher.

Let us begin by making what may appear to be an outrageous statement. No matter that the current rate of crime reported in official statistics of crime in the United States by the FBI is believed to be high; in all likelihood it is at least twice as high. In short, we should prepare to accept the idea that the best factual evidence we have today indicates much higher rates of crime in the United States than any official series of statistics report. We propose now to demonstrate that this is the case.

Oddly enough, we shall begin this demonstration by taking the official report of crimes known to the police as they are summarized and reported in Uniform Crime Reports. Most people are unaware of what is meant by these crime rates. Before discussing these FBI rates, however, we will first indicate some problems posed in measuring crime and developing an index of crime.

PROBLEMS IN MEASUREMENT POSED BY AN INDEX OF CRIME

At first glance, it appears that a single index or measure of the amount of crime in the United States is an important item of information. Just as we measure a death rate, so we may measure a crime rate. Such reasoning rests, nonetheless, on some misconceptions about both death and crime rates.

We shall consider first some misconceptions about the interpretation of simple rates, such as death rates, and then turn to crime rates.

Any simple rate for an event consists of but two elements, a population that is exposed to the occurrence of some event (the denominator) and a count of the events (the numerator). Both of these elements are measured for a point or period of time. In calculating a crude death rate, for instance, it is the practice to report the number of deaths for some unit of population, such as every 100 or 1,000 persons, for some unit of time, such as a month or a calendar year. These rates are deliberately termed crude, because we know that within a given period of time not everyone in the population is equally exposed to the risk of death. There are important differences, for example, according to one's age and sex. For that reason, the denominator often is refined into subgroups and a death rate is calculated separately for each subgroup. These are generally termed specific rates; the death rate for a particular race, age, and sex subgroup—say Negro women, aged 20–24—is a race-age-sex specific death rate.

Though such crude and specific rates are useful for some purposes, they are limited both for an analysis of the causes of death and as a basis for public policies about how to reduce the death rate. The main reason for this limitation is that we know people die from many different causes. Death from an automobile accident is quite different from death due to lung cancer. Obviously public policy when one tries to reduce the death rate due to factors connected with driving automobiles will be quite different from when it has some relationship to lung cancer, such as smoking. To go one step further, we have learned a great deal scientifically about causes of death by classifying types of death and searching for their causes. When one has some understanding of death from a particular cause, one may calculate a separate rate for deaths from that cause. Ever since developing evidence of a strong relationship between smoking and disease, we have calculated a death rate for diseases to which smoking is causally related, including cancer of the lung, larynx, and lip, and chronic bronchitis.[1]

The analogy to crime should be clear. We know that crime is not unitary, nor are causes the same for all types of crime. What causes most types of crime is not clear, but that they have single common causes that affect their incidence seems doubtful. Even in the absence of causal knowledge, we know that policies and practices for crime control differ considerably, depending upon the conditions under which types of crime occur. A policy to control auto theft can be very different from one to control aggravated assault. A simple crime rate, therefore, is of little use either for causal analysis or for public policy.

The analogy between death and crime rates should not be overdrawn, lest it lead to further misconceptions. Some of these differences merit attention because they should influence our choice of social indicators for crime.

First, death is an event that occurs for every member of the population; but every member of the population is not a victim of a crime. In addition, some persons can never be a victim of certain types of crime; men cannot be raped or have their purse snatched, for example. Second, death can occur only once for any member of the population, while crime, like illness or accident, can occur repeatedly. For such events both multiple victimization and multiple offenses are possible. There is, third, the fact that crime is a relational phenomenon—between victims and offenders. One therefore can calculate offense, victim, offender, and/or victim-offender rates. Indeed, a crime may involve a single victim, several victims, an organization, or even a diffuse public. Furthermore, the exposed population is not always made up of persons. It

1. National Center for Health Statistics, *Mortality from Diseases Associated with Smoking: United States, 1950–64,* Series 20, No. 4 (Washington, D.C.: U.S. Government Printing Office, 1966), pp. 2–9.

can consist of organizations such as businesses, or even the general public, as in offenses against public order. Fourth, an offender can commit several crimes at the same point in time. An offender may assault the owner of an automobile and steal his car and the possessions that are in it. He can be charged with assault and two counts of larceny. Fifth, the relative absence of completeness in registration of offenses, offenders, and victims makes difficult the interpretation of changes in rates. With present systems for gathering and processing information on crimes, we lack the knowledge that would permit us to separate any actual increase from any registration increase.

Finally, for many classes of crimes, unlike most classes of death, it is important to know where the crime occurred as well as where the victim resides. The failure to separate place of occurrence from place of residence of victim makes for difficulties in interpreting rates based on an exposed population of residents for any given jurisdiction in the United States. This problem arises from the way data are processed in police registration systems.

It should be evident, therefore, that any simple crime rate, unlike a death rate, lacks the specification necessary for reasonable interpretation. The problem therefore becomes one of deciding what kinds of rates it makes sense to calculate, given our current knowledge of the causes of crime, the situations under which crimes occur, our aims in public information, our goals in the formation of public policy to deal with crime, and our goals in the development of organized strategies to reduce crime.

CRITERIA FOR MEASURING CRIME

More rational ways that crime may be measured than those now in use are possible. We propose three such criteria for a crime rate: (1) that the information in the rate count the crime events only for a population that could be exposed to that crime; (2) that the choice of the rate be appropriate to organized means for gathering it; (3) that the information from the rate permit potential victims, whether persons or organizations, to calculate their chances of victimization more rationally. These are commonly called crime victimization rates, though they are rarely calculated.

Even the official reporting of crime today is highly selective. We lack information, for the most part, on many white-collar crimes, such as fraud, and on much organized crime. For many misdemeanors and minor offenses, it is generally agreed that many of these crimes go unreported. We therefore shall limit discussion primarily to what the

FBI defines as major or index crimes—those that it uses to construct its crime index to measure changes in crime in the United States. These include only criminal homicide, forcible rape, robbery, aggravated assault, larceny over $50, and auto theft. On these crimes hinges the public's information about crime in the United States.

Considering only these offenses, there are many problems in their enumeration and in selecting an exposed population as a base for a crime rate. Not all of these problems are dealt with in what follows, but it should be evident from the illustrations that our current information makes it difficult to construct a highly valid and reliable rate.

For those unfamiliar with the Uniform Crime Reporting System, several important features should be understood before considering specific rates based on them. First, each crime or attempted crime is counted in only one crime classification. When several different major, or Part I, offenses are committed by a person or group at the same time, the offense is classified in the highest-ranking offense in the rank order of Part I offenses: criminal homicide, forcible rape, robbery, assault, burglary, larceny-theft, and auto theft. Thus, a crime involving the murder of a rape victim is classified as a criminal homicide, not as both a rape and a homicide. Legally an offender could be charged with both offenses.

Second, the number of offenses counted in any criminal event is classified differently for crimes against persons and crimes against property. For offenses against the person, the number of offenses counted is the number of persons unlawfully killed, raped, maimed, wounded, or assaulted, plus any attempts to do so. For offenses against property, an offense is counted only for each distinct operation or attempt. The criterion "operation" relates to a crime incident; hence, if 20 people are robbed in a tavern, it is counted as one offense, not 20. The distinction between crimes against persons and crimes against property is not a distinction between persons as victims and households or organizations as victims, since persons are victims when their property is taken.

Third, it should be clear that a distinction is made between the complaint or report of an offense and its bona fide status. The number of offenses reported or known to the police differs from the number of actual offenses reported, in that the latter count results when the former is reduced by the number of false or baseless complaints, as determined from department rules for "unfounding" a complaint.

Finally, there are problems in classifying crimes arising from the organized ways police have for knowing when events that are classified as crimes occur. The main ways they have for knowing them are by responses to citizen complaints that such an event is in progress or has occurred or by some police strategy for gathering intelligence on events that potentially might be crimes, such as by routine patrol or detective work.

A little reflection on what comes to the police as complaints or even as observations by police officers readily suggests that the problem of determining whether an event is to be classified as a crime depends upon the nature of the information received. Generally the police must evaluate information initially received from citizens by investigating whether or not the complaint constitutes a crime event. Obviously both officer discretion or judgment and departmental criteria affect the classification of such an event as a crime. But citizen reports do not present a homogeneous set of events where the same criteria can readily be applied to determine whether or not the event has occurred. This is particularly so for the criteria to judge whether or not the event actually occurred.

The problem of knowing whether an event has occurred is especially difficult when the determination depends upon the status of the complainant, of witnesses, or of offenders. Some offenses are known to the police only through an arrest situation where the offender is present. This is particularly true for offenses involving morals or violations of moral codes. Thus, the police do not usually know about crimes of drunkenness except through the arrest of persons who are called drunks. One clearly cannot have an offense of resisting arrest without some person under arrest engaging in resisting behavior. On the other hand, crimes against property can be known to the police even though no offender is known. Events of shoplifting can be determined only by observation; this is much less likely to be the case for burglary, where evidence of entry, etc., makes determination less difficult. Offenses against the public peace and order occur only when there is a complainant present, while burglary can occur without the presence of a complainant. Some offenses have only testimony or behavior as evidence, while for others there is physical evidence.

Given the diversity of sources and types of information on crimes, the procedures one has for determining whether a crime has occurred must vary. It is doubtful, therefore, whether it makes much logical sense to compute an overall measure of crime, if by that is meant a measure of whether events have occurred. Crime in that sense is unlike births or deaths, where the event is more clearly specified. It is much more like illness, where the organized procedures of medicine are the major basis for knowing and classifying illness. Subjective accounts of either illness or crime by complainants pose problems of validity. So do professional determinations where the procedures rest largely on accounts or judgment rather than on observation or means of measurement. Much of the difficulty in crime reporting, like that in illness reporting, arises from our present procedures of "diagnosing" events that come to our attention.

THE CRIME INDEX

The Uniform Crime Reporting Program uses seven crime classifications to measure the trend and distribution of crime in the United States. These crimes are those of murder or criminal homicide, forcible rape, robbery, aggravated assault, burglary, larceny of $50 and over in value, and auto theft. Basically they were selected to make up the index because they are regarded as the major crimes against persons and their property.

When one reads that the crime index has risen, what does this mean? How significant is any crime in contributing to a rise in value in this index? Three crimes (burglary, larceny over $50 in value, and auto theft) normally account for more than 85 percent of all crime that makes up the index. They are the major crimes against property, not persons. In 1968, for example, these three crimes accounted for 87 percent of the crimes in the index. Burglary accounted for 42 percent; larceny over $50 for 28 percent; and auto theft for 17 percent.[2] It can easily be shown that any rise in the crime index from year to year is largely affected, therefore, by changes in the reporting of crimes against property, a matter we shall return to later.

Of the remaining four crimes, only two are of any additional significance in the crime index—aggravated assaults and robbery. In 1968, aggravated assault and robbery each accounted for 6 percent of all crime that makes up the index.[3] Even here it can be seen that a rise in the robbery rate would have a negligible effect on the index, as, say, compared with a comparable rise in the burglary rate. For every robbery reported, there are more than eight burglaries reported. Finally, forcible rape, with 0.7 percent in 1968, and criminal homicide, with 0.3 percent can be seen as contributing little to any change in the index. In short, major crimes against the person are a relatively small part of the crime index. They accounted for but 13 percent of all index crime in 1968.[4]

2. *Crime in the United States: Uniform Crime Reports, 1968* (Washington, D.C.: U.S. Government Printing Office, 1969), Table 1, p. 58.

3. Ibid.

4. Ibid.

Looking at one's chances of being a victim of a crime as a person as compared with being a victim through property loss, the chances are less than one in five that one will be victimized as a person for one of these major crimes. We now propose to show that even such calculations can be quite misleading.

VICTIMIZATION RATES FOR UCR REPORTS

Let us return now to the problem of providing victimization rates for our current crime statistics and a demonstration that victimization rates are much higher than reported crime rates. For the seven major offenses in the Uniform Crime Index, it should be clear that the exposed or potential victim population is not the same for all of these types of crime. Anyone can be killed or assaulted. A person or a business can be robbed. Only women can be raped. Only dwelling units, businesses, or other organizations can be burglarized. Only automobile owners can have an auto stolen. Few children can be victims of larceny of $50. What is more, some types of larceny, should one be interested in them, refer only to some group, such as pocket-picking to men and purse-snatching to women. Yet the Uniform Crime Reporting system calculates crime rates using every man, woman, and child in the United States as a base for the rate.

It is reasonable, then, to propose that a population which risks crime (the population exposed to victimization) be selected according to the type of offense and the status of the victim in the offense for purposes of calculating crime rates. Quite clearly, where the exposed population is the number of organizations, such rates may be quite different in size from those that would be obtained were the general population of persons used as the base for calculating the rate. This will be evident in the examples below.

Forcible Rape.   Forcible rape is one of the major crimes in the UCR Index for which a rate is calculated. The reported rape rate for the United States, or for any city such as Philadelphia, is based on the population of every man, woman, and child resident in the United States. For 1968, the rape rate was 1.6 for every 10,000 inhabitants. (See Table 8–1).

There may be some use in knowing that there were 1.6 forcible rapes or attempts for every 10,000 inhabitants in the United States in 1968, even though by definition only women can be victims of rape. Generally, however, our police are more interested in the question of how many total rapes there were and where they occurred, since that

TABLE 8-1.   Rates of Forcible Rape for Selected Exposed Civilian Resident
Populations, United States: 1965 and 1968

Exposed population	Year	Total number of persons	Rapes known to police	Rate per 10,000	Ratio of rapes to women
Civilian residents	1968	199,861,000	31,060	1.6	1:6,435
	1965	193,818,000	22,467	1.2	1:8,627
All females	1968	102,291,000	31,060	3.0	1:3,293
	1965	98,704,000	22,467	2.3	1:4,394
Females 14 and over	1968	74,932,000	31,060	4.1	1:2,412
	1965	71,052,000	22,467	3.2	1:3,161

SOURCES: U.S. Bureau of the Census, *Population Estimates,* Current Population Reports, Series P-25,
No. 416, Table 2; *Crime in the United States, Uniform Crime Reports: 1965* and *1968*
(Washington, D.C.: U.S. Department of Justice, Federal Bureau of Investigation, 1966 and
1969).

defines their prevention and control problem. As citizens, we are more
interested in the chances of victimization for women.

What was the victimization rape rate for 1968, the last year for
which a report is available from the FBI? Considering only all women
as the population risking rape, the rape rate in 1968 was a little less than
double that reported, a not unexpected result, since women are slightly
in the majority in the United States. One in every 3,293 women in the
United States in 1968 risked rape, assuming no victims of multiple
rape.

But let us go a step further. While there are occasional forcible
rapes of women under 14 years of age, their number is very small—so
small, in fact, as to have only a negligible effect on the overall rape rate.
When one calculates the rape rate for all women 14 years of age and
over, it turns out to be 4.1 per 10,000 women, or one in every 2,412
women 14 years and older risked being the victim of a forcible rape.
(See Table 8–1.) Thus, realistically, women in the United States had
close to a three times greater chance of being raped than that officially
reported for the United States.

These are rates for the United States. Clearly the probability of
victimization varies considerably by place of residence and even within
places such as cities. [As] one illustration of how much difference there
can be by place of residence, we have calculated the rape rate for the
city of Chicago for 1965. The rape rate for women 14 years of age and
over in Chicago in 1965 was 9.1 per 10,000. A woman in Chicago thus
had a chance of one in 1,100 in 1965 of being raped, assuming no
repeated victimization during the year. Need one add that such
chances were much higher than the (officially reported) one for every
3,161 men, women, and children for that year.

What should be obvious is that current practices of reporting rates of forcible rape for all residents grossly understate the probability of victimization by rape. Indeed, even the rates reported here are less refined than they should or could be, were we to make some slight changes in our reporting system. We know that victims of rape are more likely to be young women than older women, for example. Clearly, the chances that a young woman in Chicago will be raped are quite high—much less than one in 1,000 in 1965. In some areas of the city of Chicago, it may be as high as one in 100.

Robbery. Robbery is a form of theft where the offender uses force or violence to obtain property from a victim or obtains property from the victim by use of threats, weapons, or other means. According to UCR for 1968, the robbery rate was 131 per 100,000 population in the United States, or one robbery for every 763 persons.[5]

Robbery is primarily a crime against city dwellers and businesses, however. In 1968, the 56 major metropolitan cities in the United States with 250,000 or more inhabitants accounted for 74 percent of all robberies. For 1968, the officially reported robbery rate per 100,000 was 433 for cities with more than 250,000 inhabitants, 45 for suburban areas, and only 13 for all other sections.[6]

Although a person is in some sense the victim of a robbery in that all robberies involve a person, the loss is not always sustained by a person. The largest proportion, 58 percent, of all 1968 robberies in the 684 cities with 25,000 or more inhabitants occurred on highways or public ways. Many of these involve businesses, since a very substantial proportion of all robberies are against transportation agencies, with bus and cab drivers the immediate victims. In 1968, 29 percent of all robberies were against businesses, in that they occurred within business settings. Assuming that of the 180,722 robberies reported for these 684 cities, 52,553, or 29 percent, were against businesses,[7] the rate is substantially higher than the 131 reported for all inhabitants. For an estimated 3.5 million employing establishments in the United States in 1968, the robbery rate would be 1,501 per 100,000 establishments, or more than 11 times that for inhabitants. Clearly the likelihood of a business being robbed is much greater than that reported.

During 1968 a sample survey of all United States businesses by the Small Business Administration obtained information on all crimes

---

5. Ibid.
6. Ibid., Table 9, p. 96.
7. Ibid., Table 18, p. 107.

against businesses, whether they were reported to the police or not. Using business establishments as the risk population, we found that roughly one in every 20 businesses was robbed during the previous year. But the rate was much greater for businesses located in ghetto areas. More than one in five ghetto businesses (23 per 100) reported a robbery the previous year.[8] Clearly the risk of robbery is much higher for all businesses than that obtained from our official statistics.

Burglary.   When a person unlawfully enters a dwelling unit, commercial establishment, or any other building or structure to steal or commit any felony, it is considered burglary. It should be clear from this definition that while the victims of burglary are one or more persons—the owners—the unit to which burglary attaches is some structure—a public building, a residence, a commercial house, or any structure attached to a property, such as a garage. Generally persons are not present when burglaries occur. From the standpoint of the problems of policing and of citizens, the logical question would appear to be, what is the likelihood that some residence or establishment I own or rent will be burglarized?

In 1968 the burglary rate reported for the United States was 109 per 10,000 inhabitants, or one burglary for every 91 inhabitants. (See Table 8–2.) When we calculate burglary rates separately for dwelling units (residences) and business establishments (see Table 8–2), the risks change considerably. Thus, one in every 60 residences was burglarized in 1968, assuming no multiple burglaries during the year—a not altogether reasonable assumption, since multiple burglaries occur. For business establishments the figures are more startling, however; one in every four business establishments in the United States risked a burglary in 1968, assuming no multiple burglaries. For households there is not much difference by day or night, while for businesses the risk is far greater at night, a not surprising finding, given the presence of persons on business premises during the day. Clearly, when risks are calculated for owners, renters, or occupants, the risk is much greater than that reported in our official statistics.

Auto Theft.   One other example, the case of auto theft, may serve to show how risks are much higher when one changes the exposed population to a more logical base of risk. Each theft or attempted theft of a

---

8. Albert J. Reiss, Jr., *Field Survey of Crime Against Small Business,* A Report of the Small Business Administration Transmitted to the Select Committee on Small Business, U.S. Senate, 91st Cong., 1st sess., Document No. 91–14, April 3, 1969, pp. 76–77.

TABLE 8-2. Burglary Rates by Type of Burglary, United States, 1965 and 1968

Type of burglary	Year	Number of inhabitants, households, or establishments	Number of burglaries	Rate per 10,000	Ratio of burglaries to inhabitants/ households/ establishments
Total index	1968	199,861,000	1,828,900	91	1:109
	1965	193,818,000	1,173,201	60	1:165
Residence	1968	58,845,000	982,119	166	1:60
	1965	57,251,000	580,735	101	1:98
Night	1968		448,080	76	1:131
	1965		297,993	52	1:192
Day	1968		534,039	90	1:110
	1965		282,742	49	1:202
Nonresidence	1968	3,500,000	846,781	2,419	1:4
	1965	3,384,398	592,466	1,750	1:6
Night	1968		738,876	2,111	1:5
	1965		538,499	1,591	1:6
Day	1968		107,905	308	1:32
	1965		53,967	159	1:62

SOURCES: *Crime in the United States, Uniform Crime Reports: 1965* and *1968* (Washington, D.C.: U.S. Department of Justice, Federal Bureau of Investigation, 1966 and 1969). Table 14 in the *Reports* provides a percentage distribution for burglaries in 646 cities 25,000 and over—this distribution is applied to the burglary total in Table 1 of the *Reports* to provide estimates for total U.S. burglaries; U.S. Bureau of the Census, *Population Estimates,* Current Population Reports, Series P-25, Table 2, total resident population, all ages; *Households and Families by Type,* Current Population Reports, Series P-20 (July 1965; 1968); *1965 and 1967 County Business Patterns,* Table 2.

TABLE 8-3. Auto Theft Rates, United States, 1960, 1965, and 1968

Year	Number of auto thefts	Number of inhabitants	Rate per 10,000 population	Number of motor vehicle registrations	Rate per 10,000 registrations	Ratio of cars stolen to auto registrations
1960	318,500	179,992,000	18	73,877,000	43	1:232
1965	486,568	193,818,000	25	90,357,000	54	1:186
1968	777,755	199,861,000	39	101,039,000	76	1:149

SOURCES: *Crime in the United States, Uniform Crime Reports: 1960, 1965,* and *1968* (Washington, D.C.: U.S. Government Printing Office, 1961, 1966, and 1969), Table 1; U.S. Bureau of the Census, *Population Estimates,* Current Population Reports, Series P-25; U.S. Bureau of Public Roads, *Statistical Summary.*

motor vehicle is counted as an offense. The UCR system calculates auto theft rates for every 100,000 inhabitants, though many of these persons are not even of an age to drive, much less own, an automobile. Logically, only owners can be victims of auto theft. For that reason we used motor vehicle registrations rather than people for the risk population for auto theft. (See Table 8–3.) For 1968, the official auto theft rate was 39 for every 10,000 inhabitants, but it is almost double that for every 10,000 automobile registrations: 76. The ratio of cars stolen to registrations was, in fact, one stolen for every 130 automobile registrations in the United States. Again, it is evident that one's risk as an automobile owner is much higher than that shown in our official statistics for inhabitants.

Thus, victim-oriented statistics show much higher rates than do our present official statistics. For major offenses considered, the rates are more than twice those reported. For some classes of risks, such as businesses, they are generally far greater. Our sense of how much crime there is from the victim point of view should be that it is much higher than we officially recognize.

THE DARK FIGURE OF CRIME

Yet we know that much crime goes unreported. Recent sample surveys for the National Crime Commission and the Small Business Administration demonstrate that much major crime goes unreported. Just how much serious crime does go unreported by citizens? The National Opinion Research Center study of a sample of U.S. citizens showed that in 1965 more than half of all crimes and 38 percent of all UCR Index crimes went unreported to the police. Sample surveys in high crime rate areas of Boston, Chicago, and Washington, D.C., generally showed even higher rates of underreporting of major crimes. For the eight precincts combined in these cities, the survey estimates for index offenses was four times that of the rates known to the police in these cities.[9] There was considerable evidence in the surveys that these estimates are actually conservative ones. There is good reason to believe that one's chances of victimization from major crimes are even greater.

What emerges, then, from an examination of both official statistics and from our sample survey studies is the clear picture that we live with far more major crime than that reported in official statistics.

Naturally one wants to raise the question of why so much crime should go unreported. Sample surveys provide some general answers to this question. For crimes against property, one of the major reasons for nonreporting derives from the insurance of property. Insurance leads both to high reporting by some sectors of the population and to low reporting by others. Many persons and businesses without insurance fail to report crimes against property because they see little to be gained personally from such reporting. They cannot make an insurance claim. Correlatively, insured persons or businesses are more likely to report

9. Albert D. Biderman, "Surveys of Population Samples for Estimating Crime Incidence," *Annals of the American Academy of Political and Social Science*, CCCLXXIV (November, 1967), 16–33.

such crimes unless—and this is important—they are reporting for a home or business in a high crime rate area, and most particularly if they have previously made an insurance claim. The reason for this is fairly obvious. They do not wish to take the risk of having their insurance policy canceled or of having their insurance premium rise because their risk is higher. Hence, many do not report crimes against their property because they are afraid they then would not be covered for the really big claim or that their insurance costs will be so high they cannot afford them.

But these are not the only reasons and certainly do not cover underreporting of major crimes against the person. About one in three citizens in the Washington, D.C., studies of victimization by crime said they did not report the crime because they felt nothing could be done about it.[10] Generally, they take a negative, though perhaps not altogether unrealistic, view of the crime-solving process. They know that most such crimes will go unsolved, and for many, as already noted, there is no personal gain from reporting a crime. The second major reason indicated negative attitudes toward the police—they do not want to get involved with the police because they fear or dislike them, or have little confidence in them to do anything about their crime. About 3 percent feared reprisal if they reported the crime. Other reasons relate to unwillingness to get involved with anyone, seemingly, in many cases, because it was seen as a time-consuming process, again with no net gain to the person reporting.

There is little doubt, then, that a substantial proportion of the citizenry anticipates no personal gain in reporting crimes against them or their property. Some of their unwillingness no doubt relates to their images of the police; much of it, perhaps, because they see either no gain or even an actual loss—such as insurance cancellation or reprisal —if they do report the crime to the police. Such underreporting poses major problems of citizen cooperation and new institutional arrangements if we are to derive a more valid statement of the crime problem in the United States.

IS THE CRIME RATE RISING?

What should now be clear is that neither absolute official crime statistics nor the statistics derived from them are easily interpretable to mem-

---

10. *Report on a Pilot Study in the District of Columbia on Victimization and Attitudes Toward Law Enforcement,* Field Surveys, I, A Report of Research Submitted to the President's Commission on Law Enforcement and the Administration of Justice (Washington, D.C.: U.S. Government Printing Office, 1967), pp. 153–154.

bers of the public. How can the public interpret easily whether the absolute number is large or small and the chances of victimization, given present methods of crime reporting? But an even more difficult question is how anyone can decide whether the crime rate is rising or falling. It is to this problem that we now turn.

What has been presented up to now should cause some real concern as to whether we can tell whether the crime rate rises or falls. Only two facts are established from what we presently know about crime: (1) the official police statistics on crime show increasing numbers of crime each year and, relative to total population, the rate is going up; (2) there is much crime, including index crimes, that goes unreported to the police.

A first major reason, then, why we cannot tell whether the crime rate is rising or falling is the fact that so much crime goes unreported to the police. Anything that will increase either police reporting or police intervention to detect more crimes should increase the amount of crime officially known to the police. In short, official statistics can constantly dip into the dark figure of crime.

Are there reasons to believe that more crime is being made known to the police each year? The answer clearly is yes. Let us explore some of those reasons.

First, we have good reason to believe that police departments are better equipped to receive, record, and process crimes. The upgrading of police technology and greater control of the processing of crime information means there is more crime officially known to the police. Several major changes contribute to this. With centralized communication systems, citizen reporting to the police is made easier. At the same time, it is more difficult for local police commanders to "kill" crimes in their district by not reporting them. Furthermore, the increased use of radio dispatching and an attempt to handle all calls for police assistance undoubtedly add to the official figures. My point is very simply that the better police departments become, the more crime will be known to the police without any actual increase in crime because of reduction of the dark figure of crime—that which occurs but is not presently reported or known to them.

Second, there is good reason to believe that citizens are now more likely to mobilize the police than they have been in years past. Perhaps there are many reasons for this, including the likelihood that when citizens perceive that crime is a major problem, they are more likely to report crimes against themselves. But one of the most important reasons perhaps derives from the changing relationship of Negroes to the police.

We know that at least in many large cities Negroes contribute disproportionately to the increase in the crime rate. But this probably is due largely to two things. First, Negroes are increasingly willing to call the police for assistance, since they are more likely to get such assistance as the police department increases its services to them and becomes more ready to treat their calls as crime matters. Closely related to this is a second reason. Blacks today believe it is their right to be treated with equality and appear to be exercising the right in many ways, including an insistence that police pay attention to crimes against them. In short, there is a minor kind of revolution in which ghetto populations are much more likely today than even a few years ago to report crimes against themselves.

A third major reason for the growing crime rate undoubtedly is the growing insurance industry, and most particularly the advent of the homeowner's policy and automobile insurance policies. This could account in large measure for much of the actual increase in reporting crimes against property. Making an insurance claim generally means that the company will insist that the crime have been reported to the police; at least most citizens believe that to be true. Hence, if one anticipates making an insurance claim, one reports the crime. This factor alone could account for much of the increase in crimes against the property of the so-called propertied classes.

There are several other reasons why we have difficulty in knowing whether the crime rate is rising. These deal with problems in the measurement of crime and the statistics used.

First, we know that crimes are more likely to be committed by young people than older people. We know at the same time that our population bulks heaviest in the younger age group. Some of the rise in crime, then, is due simply to the fact that we now have more young people each year in the crime-prone ages. It has been shown that some of the increase in the crime rate is a function of this changing age composition. Overall rates can be expected to increase or decrease as our age structure changes.

For some crimes, the increase may be due solely to changes that are underway in the society. One such change is secular inflation in the cost of goods. This inflation affects particularly the category of larcenies of $50 and over. Each year many items that are stolen the previous year fall into the category of larceny over $50 simply because goods cost more. Consider only one category. Whereas some years ago any bicycle stolen was a larceny of less than $50, today many bicycles cost more than that. To be sure, economies of scale may also reduce the price of some commodities. What is clear is that we now do not know how much of an increase in the larceny rate may be due to such factors related to the cost of goods.

Closely related to changes in the actual value of goods is police practice in determining the value of goods. There are no uniform national practices for determining the value of goods stolen. Many police departments, in fact, depend upon a citizen's estimate. There is some good reason to believe that not only do citizens increasingly overreport such values for insurance purposes but that they are the mechanism for reporting inflationary prices.

But are there changes that might lead to an actual increase in crime, so that we might say there has been some "upsurge" of crime in this country? Such a question is not easily answered without the careful monitoring of both unreported and reported crimes. The question must even be redefined in some way, since any answer to the question of how much crime there is depends upon some organized means of knowing, each of which has genuine problems of validity and reliability.[11]

Apart from any precise answer, is there reason to conclude that the crime rate may be rising? To answer that question, one should have good causal theory about what causes crime and then see whether there have been marked changes in the causal factors that might lead to an increase in crime.

Can we say much about changes in such causes? One thing is clear, given the rapid increase in crime—officially documented by the FBI as an 89 percent rise in index crimes from 1960 to 1967[12] —we would have to look to some very substantial changes to make the crime rate rise that fast in so short a period of time, changes that occurred during this period of time or during some earlier period that the present crime-producing cohorts experienced. Short of that, it would have to rest in some particular relationship among smaller changes that have suddenly produced a sharp increase.

We are then forced to conclude that no current theory of crime would account very well for such a sharp increase. Therefore, much of the increase must be due to factors already mentioned. Briefly, we are a society that has a much higher rate of crime than what is officially known to the police; our crime rate rises and falls according to how citizens and the police treat matters as crimes for official attention.

---

11. See Albert D. Biderman and Albert J. Reiss, Jr., "On Exploring the 'Dark Figure' of Crime," *Annals of the American Academy of Political and Social Science,* CCCLXXIV (November, 1967), 1–15.

12. *Crime in the United States,* p. 2.

Is there no reason, then, to conclude that the crime rate has been rising, given the fact that many citizens and the police have a strong sense that it is rising? Mention has already been made of the fact that some of the increase in crime is due to our changing age structure. What that says is that assuming there were no changes in what causes crime among the young, we still would have more crime because we have more young.

What may have changed, however, are the opportunities to commit crime and the mobility of persons to take advantage of these opportunities. The argument runs something like this: Americans today are more careless about their possessions and property because they have more of them. They leave auto and house doors unlocked, purses lying around, bicycles unlocked, and so on. These practices create more opportunities for crime. At the same time, Americans of all kinds are freer to move about unquestioned and unhampered by either public or police restrictions. They are in a better position to commit crimes, whether by being freer in public places or by moving more freely to private places. Such freedom may also include greater aggression toward one another, since contact is increased and restraint is decreased.

While it is conceivable that these changes in affluence and in mobility of persons may account for an increase in crime, it is doubtful that they are powerful enough to account for the large changes from year to year. Thus, it seems doubtful that such changes could account for the reported 16 percent increase in major crimes between 1966 and 1967.[13]

CHANGES IN OUR SENSE OF CRIME

Yet, we have already said that both the public and the police sense that crime has increased. We know from our studies that many citizens fear crime. In four high crime rate police precincts we surveyed in Boston and Chicago, 20 percent of the citizens wanted to move because of their fear of crime.[14] What is more, many citizens have taken steps to protect themselves from what they see as a rise in crime. Six of every 10 residents in the high crime rate areas of Boston and Chicago took steps to protect themselves from crime: 50 percent of all residents stay off the streets at night, for example.[15] In the national survey for the National

---

13. Ibid.

14. *Studies in Crime and Law Enforcement in Major Metropolitan Areas*, Field Surveys, III, Vol. 1, A Report of Research Submitted to the President's Commission on Law Enforcement and the Administration of Justice (Washington, D.C.: U.S. Government Printing Office, 1967), p. 31.

15. Ibid., pp. 97–98.

Crime Commission 37 percent said they kept firearms in the house for protection.[16] What is more to the point, almost six of every 10 citizens in the high crime rate areas of Boston and Chicago believe there is more violent crime in their city in recent years.[17] Clearly, people's sense of crime is high, and they regard it as rising.

Might there be reasons why people regard crime as rising even though the actual rise is much less than that which appears? Of course. The fact that people are told crime is rising should convince people that it is true.

Some things about crime appear to have changed. For one thing, its occurrence seems less confined in our cities than formerly. There are areas of Chicago, Philadelphia, New York, Boston, Washington, D.C., or any other major U.S. city where one formerly could walk with reasonable safety but where now the level of crime is such that it appears unwise. One factor may be that as more and more citizens flee to the suburbs—and that flight is very rapid from many cities that have had a large influx of Negroes—less and less of the central city becomes a low crime rate area. Indeed, if one thinks of that area as increasing in a constant ratio to the expansion at the periphery, the expansion of the high crime rate area would be considerable over so short a period as 10 years. One senses that in cities like Detroit, Chicago, and Washington, D.C., for example, where the influx of low-income persons has been very high over the past decades, the unsafe area is larger than in cities like Los Angeles or San Francisco.

Put in another way, there is no good reason to assume that as cities grow, the high crime rate area should remain fixed geographically. There is every reason to assume it will not. Hence, the unsafe area of a city must grow if the city continues to grow. Much research needs to be done to document whether such changes have indeed been taking place.

EPILOGUE

We have tried to say several things. First, we have tried to say that we have a false sense of crime in America. We have both a higher rate of crime than any official statistics disclose because of much unreported crime and a higher rate of victimization because of the way we calculate our statistics on crime.

16. President's Commission on Law Enforcement and the Administration of Justice, *The Challenge of Crime in a Free Society* (Washington, D.C.: U.S. Government Printing Office, 1967), p. 20.

17. Ibid.

Second, we have tried to say that much of the reported increase in crime may be solely a product of dipping into the dark figure of unreported crime.

Third, we have tried to say that we have no causal theory that would explain such a rapid rise in crime as officially reported for the past seven years. This makes it even more likely that the increase is overestimated.

Fourth, we have suggested that some changes may account for an actual increase in crime, particularly an increase in the opportunities to commit crimes and the greater mobility of people to commit them.

Finally, recognizing that many Americans perceive crime to be rising, we have suggested that some of this may be due to the media portrayal of crime, and some may be a consequence of the fact that as our cities grow, the areas that are unsafe must also grow, even with no overall change in the rate of crime.

How much crime is there? Much more than most Americans know. Has it increased? We cannot say with any degree of certainty. Much may be, and probably is, due to changes in how we report and measure crime.

9

The Victims of Crime:
Some National Survey Findings

Wesley G. Skogan

Since the mid-1960s, the problem of "crime on the streets" has been a recurrent theme on the American political agenda. In platforms and campaign speeches, candidates for office have espoused wide-ranging solutions to control crime, from restoring the death penalty or augmenting police departments to radical social and economic reform. This political excitement has been translated into a variety of specific crime-reduction programs. At the local level, rape crisis centers and victim-representation programs have been instituted to provide supportive services for the unfortunate targets of crime. Methadone-maintenance programs have been initiated to respond to the perceived needs of drug users. Halfway houses have been created to facilitate the adjustment of prisoners returning to the community. Police communications hardware and equipment have been upgraded to enable them to respond more rapidly to calls for police assistance, on the presumption that such activity will prevent many crimes from occurring in the first place. The federal government has provided billions of dollars for state and local agencies to initiate and evaluate the effectiveness of such programs, and it has fostered the diffusion of workable ideas throughout the crime-control establishment.

This new attention to the performance of the criminal justice system has highlighted an old problem. In spite of the introduction of innovative programs, we still lack many of the most rudimentary measures necessary to decide which programs work and how our society is

Prepared especially for this volume. This essay was written while the author was a Visiting Fellow at the Law Enforcement Assistance Administration, Washington, D.C. That agency bears no responsibility for its contents or conclusions.

progressing toward reducing crime. Since the 1930s, the primary source of information on crime, criminals, and their victims has been the yearly *Uniform Crime Reports* collected from local police departments by the Federal Bureau of Investigation. Participating departments supply the FBI with the number of crimes of various types that have come to their attention, the number "cleared" (attributed to a firm suspect), and some simple information on the victims of homicide and the recovery of stolen property. They also report the social characteristics (age, race, and sex) of persons arrested for those crimes. These data define the limits of our knowledge about national crime patterns; those limits are quite narrow, and the data themselves are often suspect. In 1967 a Task Force of the Crime Commission concluded:

> [T]he United States is today, in the era of the high speed computer, trying to keep track of crime and criminals with a system that was less than adequate in the days of the horse and buggy. . . . In some respects the present system is not as good as that used in some European countries 100 years ago.[1]

The manifold problems of official crime statistics led the Commission to support a series of sample surveys to gauge independently the volume and distribution of crime. In those surveys, interviewers visited randomly selected samples of households and questioned adult "informants" about the individual victimization experiences of household members, and about burglary and other crimes against property perpetrated against the household unit. The resulting data were used to explore the personal characteristics of victims of various types of crime and to generate new measures of the crime rate for the sampled jurisdictions.[2]

This new source of data on crime closes several gaps in official statistics and circumvents important political and organizational processes that lead the police to undercount or undervalue many kinds of crime in their reports to the FBI. Because participation in the uniform crime reporting system is voluntary, coverage of the United States is far from complete for many key statistics. Sample surveys, on the other hand, can be representative of the entire population. Large, carefully drawn samples yield data more reliable than "complete enumerations," which miss many areas and often elicit incomplete, illegible, or inaccu-

1. President's Commission on Law Enforcement and the Administration of Justice, *Task Force Report: Crime and its Impact—An Assessment* (Washington, D.C.: U.S. Government Printing Office, 1967), p. 123.

2. See Philip H. Ennis, *Criminal Victimization in the United States: A Report of a National Survey* (Washington, D.C.: U.S. Government Printing Office, 1967).

rate accounts of local activity. Furthermore, because they deal with relatively small samples, surveyors can afford to focus upon each individual case in greater depth, thereby eliciting much more thorough descriptions of events. Traditionally, police departments have only collected detailed information on victims, offenders, use of weapons, and physical location in the case of homicide.

Survey measures of crime are also more useful than official statistics in making inter-city comparisons of crime rates and characteristics of crime incidents. The voluntary self-reporting system used by the FBI is plagued by two problems that make comparisons questionable. First, the quality of information kept by local departments varies. The second impediment is differences between standard definitions of specific crimes employed by the FBI for national accounting purposes and the definitions imposed by state criminal codes and city or county ordinances. What is classified as a "robbery" will vary from place to place, and it is not clear that local recordkeeping systems can always be adequately translated into standard form when *Uniform Crime Reports* is compiled. Interview questionnaires, on the other hand, may easily be standardized and deployed in similar fashion across jurisdictions.

Another advantage of surveys is their independence from local authorities. Data gathered and analyzed by organizations not affected by the area's political machinations are not sensitive to local variations in law enforcement politics or police administrative practices. It is easy for the police to cheat. Attempted burglary can be catalogued as vandalism, robbery as purse-snatching, and grand larceny as petty larceny.[3] Rape complaints can be discouraged by rough handling, burglary reports can be "lost," and even homicide can be written off as "suicide" or "hit-and-run" when there is no next-of-kin to raise a ruckus. All of these techniques are useful when they serve the political purposes of the police to "reduce crime," and they may be reversed to achieve the opposite effect as well. Cheating can also take place at the grass-roots level. In departments where the performance of district commanders is evaluated by their ability to manage the local crime rate, they will do so. As one Chicago police officer recently testified, "It's impossible under the present system to write factual and honest official reports and stay out of the commander's office very long."[4]

Finally, even honest official figures can be accumulated only for those crimes that come to the attention of the police. This is both a

3. David Seidman and Michael Couzens, "Getting the Crime Rate Down: Political Pressure and Crime Reporting," *Law and Society Review* 8 (1974): 457–93.

4. *Chicago Tribune*, March 30, 1973.

weakness and a strength of police-based crime statistics. Its weakness lies in the massive undercounting of certain kinds of crime. We have long suspected that many crimes are never reported to the police; European sociologists dubbed this officially unrecognized activity the "dark figure" of crime. In their present organization, the police are primarily a reactive force, intervening upon citizen request. Police rarely observe such events as robbery or burglary, but rely upon victims or their confidants to report crimes to them through calls for assistance. When such calls are not made, the police can neither record nor respond to criminal activities. Unlike official statistics, surveys gather information on many of these unreported victimizations. As we shall see below, nonreporting rates may be as high as eighty percent for some crime categories, and here surveys provide us with the only useful data on victims and offenders.

Surveys of the type reviewed here, however, cannot record many other kinds of crime. They cannot, for example, count crimes without victims. In their "proactive" role, the police detect many events which are not reported to them, but which they must seek out: drug use, public drunkenness, traffic offenses, prostitution. They also determine that events were crimes through intensive investigation; this is how we know, for instance, that a fire was the result of arson. Thus police statistics are the only suitable accounting device for some kinds of crime. In addition, there are other classes of events for which neither official nor survey measures are suitable. It is often impossible to classify an event without knowledge of the perpetrator's motives. When a merchant arrives at his store in the morning and finds a broken front window, shall we label it attempted burglary (a serious crime) or vandalism (not so serious)? When another merchant conducts an inventory and discovers shortages, should we attribute them to shoplifting, to employee theft, or were the goods simply "lost" rather than "stolen"? In the absence of knowledge about specific *events*, even detailed information about the magnitude of a loss is not very useful. Crimes are furtive activities. Offenders attempt to control information that may link them with criminal activity, and when they are successful *no* measurement technique will betray them.

Within these limitations, surveys of crime may still reveal detailed information of considerable importance on suitable events. Since 1972 the Law Enforcement Assistance Administration and the Bureau of the Census have been conducting national and city-level studies of this type. Twenty-six large cities have been chosen for analysis, and approximately 33,000 interviews with city residents and 2,000 interviews with business owners and managers have been conducted in each of those communities. A continuing series of interviews is also being conducted with a national panel of 150,000 individuals and 17,50ᴜ business repre-sentatives. They are questioned every six months in rotation in order to produce quarterly estimates of the crime rate for the United States as a whole. These interviews focus upon a selected set of relatively serious crimes: rape, robbery, assault, burglary, and theft. The section of the survey questionnaire which measures victimization was rigor-ously pretested in three cities to establish procedures that would most accurately assess crime. Questions have been designed particularly to encourage respondents to remember past events, to recall exact dates and details, and to overcome any embarrassment they might feel about discussing their experiences with an interviewer. In addition to report-ing specific crime incidents, victims are asked to describe their assail-ants, the extent of their financial loss and physical injury is probed, it is ascertained if they filed (and if they collected) any insurance claims, and they are asked if anyone reported the event to the police. Together, this information gives us a new and more detailed picture of criminal victimization patterns in the United States.

HOW MUCH CRIME IS THERE?

The victimization surveys uncovered considerable disparity between the number of criminal incidents reported to interviewers and official FBI statistics. Extrapolations from the samples indicate that about 37,-500,000 criminal events occurred in the United States during 1973 alone. The vast majority of these were crimes against property and therefore did not involve personal contact between a victim and an offender. Together, burglary of households (6,400,000 incidents) and commercial establishments (1,400,000), the loss of motor vehicles (1,-300,000), and petty thefts from individuals (over 22,000,000) accounted for 85 percent of the total. Only four percent could be classified as "personal thefts" (robberies, purse-snatches, and other predatory offenses involving direct confrontations between victims and crimi-nals). Slightly over four million instances of interpersonal violence (rapes and assaults) were recorded (11 percent of total reported victim-izations). Assaults were far more frequent than rapes, and a surprising number of both (about 70 percent of rapes and 75 percent of assaults) appear to have been unsuccessful, resulting in little or no physical injury.

Undoubtedly this large figure still falls far short of recording *all* crimes that occurred in the United States during 1973. Rape is probably not well measured in a victim survey, although many more incidents were reported to interviewers than surfaced through official reporting channels in 1973. In general, self-reporting procedures for measuring events are biased when they embarrass the respondent, when the events involve relatives or acquaintances who may be compromised, when the respondent/victim may have been partially responsible for precipitating the event, or when the boundaries that socially define the event are uncertain and shifting. These factors all contribute to measurement error for both rape and assault, and undoubtedly lead victim surveys to underestimate the total number of potentially reportable events in the population. On the other hand, the very large numbers reported above may seriously *overestimate* other classes of offenses. Before they report a crime as having occurred, the police routinely investigate the circumstances surrounding an event; in many cases they conclude that a formal complaint is not required (i.e., no crime has been committed). No such screening is used in these victim surveys, although other surveys employing expert judges to determine if a legally actionable offense has occurred have similarly dismissed a number of citizen-recalled incidents.[5]

It is unlikely, however, that the lack of screening could account for the magnitude of differences between official and survey crime rates revealed here. In some serious categories the ratio of crime uncovered in the interviews to incidents officially recorded is over three to one. While it is impossible to compare official and survey crime figures in every case, Table 9–1 presents such comparisons for those crimes where it is reasonable to do so.

As the figures in Table 9–1 indicate, survey estimates of the crime rate overshadow official counts in every category. Survey data revealed about three times as many rapes, assaults, burglaries, and robberies than reported in *Uniform Crime Reports.* The only crime with a significantly smaller gap between the two figures is vehicle theft. It has been argued that police statistics on auto theft, like those for homicide, are relatively accurate reflections of events that take place in the world. It appears that the magnitude of the loss, the importance of the automobile in daily life, and the widespread belief that a police report must be filed for insurance purposes encourage high reporting rates for auto theft. If the other stages in the crime-recording process function smoothly, this should result in more accurate official figures for vehicle losses.

WHO ARE THE VICTIMS OF CRIME?

The picture of victimization that emerges from the 1973 national crime survey is a familiar one: the burden of crime is unequally distributed in

5. See Ennis, op. cit.

TABLE 9-1. Comparison of Official and Survey Crime Totals
for Selected Categories, 1973

Crime	Survey U.S. Estimate	Official U.S. Total	Ratio	Comments
Rape	153,000	51,000	3.0:1	Should be comparable; both count only individuals; much evidence that both undercount.
Assault	1,313,180	416,270	3.2:1	Both count individuals; official definition requires serious injury or use of weapon; survey estimate is for events with comparable characteristics.
Burglary	7,818,026	2,540,000	3.1:1	Official figures have a wider base, and should total more—the survey figure is for households and businesses only, while the official total includes organizations, governments, etc.
Robbery	1,214,884	382,680	3.2:1	Official base is wider, as for burglary.
Motor Vehicle Theft	1,330,470	923,600	1.4:1	Official base is wider—the survey figure is for auto theft from individual owners only, while official totals include thefts from businesses and organizations.

SOURCE: Official figures are from the *Uniform Crime Reports* for 1973; survey totals were calculated from tabulations supplied by the Bureau of the Census for the 1973 Annual National Crime Survey.

American society, falling heavily upon those who already bear the consequences of other forms of social inequality. The victims of crime are disproportionately young, black, and poor. Further, each of these factors appears to contribute independently to the chances that an individual is the victim of a crime. The effects of age, race, and social status accumulate for those at the bottom of the ladder, leading to extremely high victimization rates for selected subgroups in the population. Let us look at these in succession.

Young people are disproportionately the victims of assaultive violence. Table 9–2 reports assault *victimization rates* (the number of victims divided into the number of persons) for different age groups. Assault rates are extremely high for persons in the sixteen to nineteen age cohort, approaching six per hundred. The rate drops off steadily with age, and it is very small for persons over fifty. There are several reasons for this inverse relationship between assault victimization and age. First, youthful victims are often in close proximity to high-risk offenders, who are also disproportionately other youths: they are on the street, in school yards, and in competitive events with their exuberant peers. Second, until about age sixteen, physical differences between persons of differing ages are often pronounced. Therefore, twelve-year old children will be quite vulnerable to harassment by their immediate elders for several more years.

The differential distribution of interpersonal violence across age cohorts is also presented in Table 9–2; the proportion each group represents in the sample population is contrasted to the proportion each represents in the pool of assault victims. The contrasts are striking: young people are about twice as likely to be assault victims as their numbers in the population would lead us to expect. Persons between ages twelve and twenty-four (who make up *30* percent of the sample population) suffer *60* percent of all assaults recalled in the interviews. Any official policy designed to reduce the overall assault rate in the United States must speak to the particular security needs of the younger component of the population. As we shall see, this will be extremely difficult.

The pool of high-risk victims is further defined by sex: the victimization rate for crimes involving assaultive violence is twice as high among males (3.6 per hundred) as among females (1.9 per hundred). The same proportions describe robbery victimizations as well. Females outdistance males only in two crime categories represented in this survey, rape and purse-snatching (some male victims of each were interviewed).

Rapes which were reported for 1973 were twice as common among black women as among whites. Rape rates were much higher among divorced and single women than among the married, and victims were

TABLE 9-2. Age and Victimization, 1973

Age	Assault Rate (per 100)	Percentage of Total Population (Age 12 and over)	Percentage of Assault Victims
12–15	4.81	10.2	18.3
16–19	5.80	9.6	20.7
20–24	5.28	10.7	21.0
25–34	3.01	17.3	19.4
35–49	1.67	20.8	13.0
50–64	.84	18.8	5.9
65 and over	.38	12.5	1.8
		100.0	100.0

SOURCE: Calculated from tabulations prepared by the Bureau of the Census from the 1973 Annual National Crime Survey. Percentages do not total exactly to 100 percent due to rounding.

concentrated in the sixteen to twenty-four age group. Marital status undoubtedly reflects differential *opportunities* for victimization: single women are more likely to be out at night unescorted or in the presence of males with whom their relationship is uncertain, and are the most accessible targets for attack. The assailant is usually a lone offender: about 80 percent of reported rapes were described in this way, while an additional 10 percent involved two offenders. The victims reported that the offender was a stranger about two-and-one-half times as often as they recalled some previous relationship with him. Strangers may be involved in a far smaller proportion of rapes than these surveys indicate. There is some evidence that rapes in which the victim and the offender are acquainted or related are less likely to be recalled in an interview than the same crimes committed by a stranger. Such crimes by known perpetrators are also less likely to come to the attention of the police.[6]

These attributes of rape help explain why its deterrence presents a difficult problem for the criminal justice system. The structural preconditions of such victimizations involve women's roles, which are certainly less constrained than in the past. This may account in part for the rapid rise of official rape figures in recent years. In addition, the lone, unknown offender is the most difficult to identify and apprehend, reducing the potential impact of police rape-deterrence programs.

The relationship between race and criminal victimization is also clearly patterned: blacks are more likely than whites to be the victims of crime. Table 9–3 presents victimization rates by race for the largest categories of serious crime—robbery, assault, and burglary. In each case, rates for blacks exceed those for whites. Table 9–3 further distinguishes rates for robbery and assault with a weapon and burglary involving breaking and entering. In each of these subcategories, blacks

TABLE 9-3. Race and Victimization Rates, 1973 (per 100)

Type of Offense	Blacks	Whites	Ratio
Assault	3.22	2.64	1.2:1
With a Weapon	1.73	.91	1.9:1
Robbery	1.44	.60	2.4:1
With a Weapon	.85	.29	2.9:1
Burglary	13.55	8.77	1.5:1
Breaking and Entering	6.30	2.56	2.5:1

SOURCE: Computed from tabulations prepared by the Bureau of the Census from the 1973 Annual National Crime Survey.

6. "San Jose Methods Test of Known Crime Victims," *Statistics Technical Report No. 1* (Washington, D.C.: Statistics Division, National Institute of Law Enforcement and Criminal Justice, Law Enforcement Assistance Administration, 1972).

are more likely to be victims. In fact, the ratio between black and white victimization rates is higher in these more serious subcategories (i.e., those involving use of a weapon or breaking and entering) than overall rates for the crimes. Further, the evidence indicates that blacks suffer disproportionately from the serious consequences of crime. Figure 9–1 presents an analysis of the medical problems of the victims of assaultive violence. It reveals a familiar pattern: blacks are more likely to be the victims of such crimes, more likely to suffer a serious assault, more likely to be hospitalized overnight, and less likely to be insured. For a great variety of offenses, black Americans disproportionately suffer the burdens of crime.

The high level of victimization endured by blacks is in part a class phenomenon. In general, lower-income people are more likely than others to be the victims of crime, especially interpersonal violence and personal theft. Several types of property theft, on the other hand, most frequently strike upper-income individuals.

There is an inverse relationship between income and personal violence. Violent victimizations drop as income increases; members of families with incomes over $25,000 suffer [at] only about 60 percent of the rate borne by persons earning less than $3,000. In contrast to as-

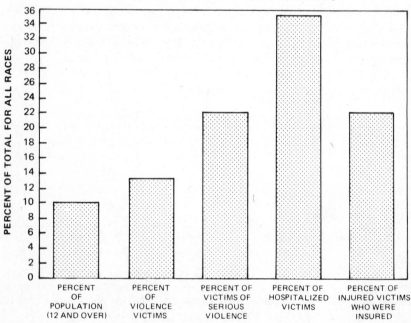

FIGURE 9-1. The Consequences of Victimization for Blacks: The Black Victims
of Personal Violence in the 1973 National Crime Survey

saults, automobile theft and common property theft increase in frequency as we move up the income ladder. These rates seem to reflect the cultural and economic circumstances in which Americans at polar extremes of the income distribution find themselves. Working-class males are more likely to grow up within a cultural milieu which demands that they assert their manhood in a physical manner, and the data indicate that violence within family and acquaintance networks is much more common in lower-income homes. High-income families, on the other hand, are desirable targets for property crime—they have more to steal.

If we simultaneously control for the effects of race and income on victimization rates, the 1973 survey data indicate that each factor is independently important. Both for property offenses and interpersonal violence, rates vary in the fashion described above for blacks and whites *within* income groups, and for high- and low-income people within the *same* racial group. Comparisons of victimization rates within these groupings suggest that income is more important than race in determining the probability of becoming a victim. However, the fact that income is more important should not minimize the effect of race revealed in this survey, for most black families in America do not have very much money. In this national sample, 67 percent of all black households fell into the low-income category (annual income less than $7,500), while 23 percent of all white households and only 8 percent of all black households fell into the high-income category (annual income over $15,000). That white victimization rates for many property crimes are relatively high because whites have more to steal is a two-edged comment on crime in America.

WHERE IS THE ACTION?

Although crime occurs in every corner of the nation, the highest crime rates are concentrated in large cities. Crimes are easy to commit in cities because more strangers are about (making it easier to avoid identification), more goods are available to be stolen, and more people make a point of not knowing their neighbor's business (making it easier to live a "life of crime"). Cities are also places where the rich and poor come into contact daily, increasing opportunities for crime as well as accentuating the differences in their lifestyles.

The relationship between city size and crime is reflected in surveys of the citizenry. Victimization rates are higher among residents of cities than among residents of rural areas; urban rates for interpersonal violence are about one-third higher than those in the country; personal thefts are four times as common in cities; property crime rates in rural places are only about 70 percent of city rates. Rates also increase with city size. Figure 9–2 shows victimization rates for residents of various-sized cities and their suburban rings. (Note that these rates represent the location of victims' residences rather than the location of crimes—the two will differ somewhat, and these data will overestimate suburban crime rates and underestimate central city rates.) As Figure 9–2 indicates, personal theft increases steadily with city size, and the highest rates are achieved by residents of America's urban giants. The relatively high rates of victimization experienced by residents of the rings surrounding these communities reflect the changing character of suburbanization. Many of the suburbs immediately contiguous to our largest cities have acquired a distinctly urban flavor; they tend to be industrial, they contain many apartment units, and they often house lower-income families. These characteristics, in conjunction with the possible displacement of crime to the suburbs as a result of improved central-city policing, may account for high rates of victimization among suburban residents.

WHO CALLS THE POLICE?

Most of the crimes examined here typically are not uncovered by police action, but are brought to their attention by victims or their confidants. Only those that achieve official notice enter police recordkeeping systems. Unreported crimes probably contribute the bulk of those that appeared on the "survey" side of Table 9–1 but that did not appear in "official" totals. Not only are unreported crimes excluded from our social accounts, but they are also unlikely to lead to an arrest. Nonreporting thus limits the deterrent capability of the police.

The determinants of reporting behavior are not well understood. Most research on the problem by criminologists in the past can be summarized as follows: individual reporting rates are shaped by (1) the personal characteristics of individual victims (e.g., race, class, age), (2) the relationship between victims and offenders (webs of kinship or acquaintance), and (3) characteristics of the incidents themselves (e.g., the outrage they engender or their seriousness). Each of these factors is likely to play some role in the reporting decision, and their relative importance may vary from crime to crime. Understanding their influence upon reporting practices is crucial, for such actions shape our knowledge of the dimensions of the crime problem and the potential responsiveness of society to changes in criminal activity.

Analysis of the national crime survey data for 1973 indicates that most of the personal characteristics of individual victims are *unrelated* to reporting. Women are only slightly more likely than men to report

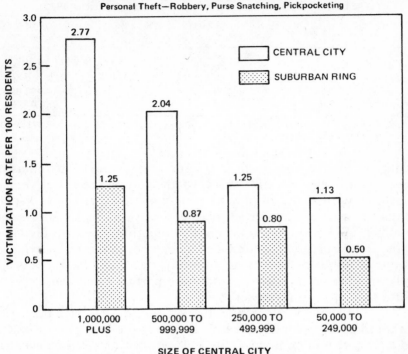

FIGURE 9-2.   Criminal Victimization 1973 by Size of Place
Personal Theft—Robbery, Purse Snatching, Pickpocketing

offenses, and income does not appear to play a significant role in shaping reporting behavior. Surprisingly, neither does race. We would not be astonished if blacks were more unwilling than whites to mobilize the police. Based upon their own experience or accumulated folklore, many black Americans have learned that relationships with the police involve distressing calculations: Will their complaints be taken seriously? Will they face police hostility? Is it wise to become known to the police under any circumstances? For a wide variety of offenses, however, blacks are not noticeably less likely than whites to report their experiences to the police.

The only consistent individual predictor of whether a crime was brought to the attention of the authorities was age. Crimes that affect younger people are not reported as frequently as those that victimize their elders. Table 9-4 divides reporting rates for all crimes against persons (personal theft and interpersonal violence) by age groups. Reporting rates are dramatically lower for those under twenty; in that group, less than one-third of these contact crimes are reported to the police. Table 9-4 also indicates the survey estimate of the *number* of victimizations suffered by each age group. The findings are extremely

TABLE 9-4. Age and Reporting Rates: Crimes Against Persons, 1973

Age	Percentage Reported	Number of Victimizations
12-19	31.5	2,161,940
20-34	49.2	2,304,350
35-49	56.6	747,490
50-64	53.3	494,850
65 and over	53.6	247,300

SOURCE: Computed from tabulations prepared by the Bureau of the Census from the 1973 Annual National Crime Survey.

significant, for the young are also disproportionately the victims of crimes against the person. In 1973, youths between ages twelve and nineteen (mostly males, disproportionately black) experienced 35 percent of all personal-contact victimizations, and very few of these incidents became known to the police. The reporting practices of young people thus exercise an enormous influence over the official violent crime rate in the United States; currently, they keep the rate deceptively low, but an increase in youthful reporting could cause official figures seemingly to skyrocket.

One of the major interests of students of crime has been the *social relationships* between victims and offenders—the bonds of friendship and kinship that unite them. Offenders and their prey often have certain commonalities. They are usually the same race and frequently reside in the same neighborhood. Neither are they always strangers to one another. Close victim-offender relationships are common in murder cases: it is not unusual for 75 percent of the homicides in large cities to involve friends, lovers, relatives, or business partners. It has been assumed that these social bonds frequently inhibit reporting offenses to the police; people do not want their friends or spouses sent to jail, or they define such encounters as "private matters" beyond the scope of the law. National crime survey figures for 1973 indicate that the incidence of crime within personal circles is relatively high. About 40 percent of all assaults, 25 percent of rapes, and 20 percent of violent robberies involved victims and offenders who were *not* strangers. The survey also indicated, however, that such ties between victims and criminals do not appear to inhibit the reporting of most offenses to the police. For example, about 41 percent of the assaults involving strangers were reported, and about 39 percent of the assaults involving relations or acquaintances were reported. The only dramatic difference in reporting rates that appeared in the 1973 figures was for rape. In rape cases, attacks by strangers were reported about 20 percent more often. Again, a methodological caveat is in order: there is some evidence that crimes perpetrated by friends or relatives are underenumerated in the survey, and victims may be more likely to recall in the interview those acquaintanceship crimes that they reported to the police. This would contribute to the pattern of reporting for rape described here. Even if this is the case, it still appears that close victim-offender relationships do not have the dramatic effect on reporting rates that we anticipated.

The strongest and most consistent determinant of citizen reporting to the police is the *seriousness of the offense*. There are at least four major dimensions of seriousness: the value of stolen or damaged property, the extent of personal injury, the use of a weapon which threatens bodily harm, and the extent to which the crime intrudes into the secure lifespace of the victim. Victim surveys reveal that the greater the loss, harm, threat, or insecurity generated by an event, the more likely it is to be reported to the police.

It is not surprising that the value of the loss plays an important role in the reporting decision. Deciding to call the police involves a cost-benefit calculation: the individual weighs the costs of reporting in terms of time, anticipated hostility from the police, and fear of reprisal from the offender or his friends, against the benefits which might accrue from the action (the probability that the offender will be caught and ultimately convicted, or that the property will be recovered). If the amount of the loss is relatively small, reporting costs will most likely outweigh reporting benefits. This is particularly true in the case of property offenses, where the lack of personal contact between victims and offenders makes it virtually impossible to identify suspects. Arrest or clearance rates for such offenses are very low, and the proportion of stolen property recovered is small.

The simple effect of the value of the loss on reporting rates is illustrated in Table 9–5, which compiles reporting rates for all property . thefts in the 1973 survey according to loss values. The reporting rate for successful thefts with small losses (less than ten dollars) was only 8 percent. In the $50–99 range it approached 50 percent, and above $250 it averaged over 80 percent.

The introduction of other elements of seriousness into the equation greatly increases reporting rates, regardless of the value of the loss. Property crime involving an invasion of the home is more readily reported than simple theft away from home. Personal contact crimes that led to serious injury were reported at higher rates than similar offenses that did not result in injuries. Finally, the use of a weapon in a crime appears to have escalated reporting rates in the 1973 data. Table 9–5 also presents survey estimates of the reporting rate for nonviolent rob-

TABLE 9-5. Incident Seriousness and Reporting Rates, 1973

All Household and Personal Property Theft

Value and Loss	Percentage Reported
Less than $10	7.8
$10–49	19.8
$50–99	45.4
$100–249	61.5
$250 and above	82.4

All Robbery Without Personal Assault

Combinations	Percentage Reported
Attempted; no weapon	24.4
Successful; no weapon	39.2
Attempted; weapon	41.0
Successful; weapon	67.8

SOURCE: Computed from tabulations prepared by the Bureau of the Census from the 1973 Annual National Crime Survey.

bery. The figures indicate that the use of a weapon in both successful and unsuccessful robberies increased the reporting rate by 20 to 30 percent. Clearly the threat of harm induced by the display of guns and knives encourages citizens to report incidents to the police.

In sum, the evidence on citizen reporting suggests that the process is highly rational. With the exception of age, reporting rates do not appear to be substantially related to the personal characteristics of individual victims; instead, they are incident-specific. Reporting rates are higher for personal contact crimes, where identifications and arrests are easier to effect. They increase with the value of the loss, when the security of the home is breached, and when the offender threatens serious harm or is considered a menace to the community.

CONCLUSIONS

Until the development of victim surveys, official police records were the only source of information about the distribution of crime and the success or failure of crime-reduction programs. For certain kinds of illegal activity, official statistics remain our only accounting; crimes without victims or crimes that can be uncovered only through police investigations are more difficult to measure by alternative techniques. Valuable new information about other types of crime can be gleaned from interviews with samples of the population. These surveys are unencumbered by many of the well-known limitations of official crime statistics. They make it possible to gather information on incidents that were not reported and therefore could never enter our system of official accounts. They also record the characteristics of events that were ignored or discounted by the police, whether for political or organizational reasons.

Extrapolations from the 1973 national crime survey suggest that the volume of crime in America was about three times larger than recorded in official reports. The total was very large, even though many incidents we would label "criminal" were not covered by the survey. But more important than numbers of incidents are data on the details of those events that are recounted in surveys. One of the chief criticisms of the FBI crime statistics is the paucity of specific information about the distribution of crimes and victims, and the consequences of crime for society. Although they are based upon samples, victim surveys may give us a better picture of these details than more extensive but less accurate enumerations.

Several examples of this detail have been reported here. We have seen the highly skewed inverse relationship between age and distribution of assaultive violence. The victim surveys revealed many more assaults than enter official records, and a considerable proportion affected those under twenty-five. Young people are much less likely than individuals in other age brackets to report any kind of victimization to the police, thereby disguising untold numbers of incidents. Any change in this pattern of nonreporting could cause official crime statistics to fluctuate wildly because of the differential distribution of events. Any concerted societal attack on the problem of assaultive violence would have to deal with this problem, for programs to encourage reporting assaults would have to begin with those under twenty-five. The prompt reporting of events would be necessary to make any crime-reduction policy successful. Other studies of attitudes toward law and the criminal justice system suggest that this would be difficult to achieve. Youths of all races and backgrounds always prove to be the most alienated and suspicious subgroup of the population when we probe their relationships with the police and the courts. Victim surveys would enable us to detect changes in these attitudes, in victim reporting practices, and in the victimization rate for young people. This data would be important because of the tremendous effect such shifts might have on the utility of official crime statistics.

The victim surveys suggest further limitations of crime-reduction policies. Patterns of victimization are far from random, but rather reflect enduring features of the social structure. In the absence of changes in several fundamental social processes, it is unlikely that crime will disappear easily. We have seen, for example, that the probability of victimization is related to the social roles that persons play and the range of victim behaviors those roles demand. Certain roles for women lead them into circumstances under which they are highly vulnerable to rape; commercial establishments with lone operators that are open at night are vulnerable to robbery. Women's roles are related to very fundamental characteristics of the social order, and the directions in which they are evolving are more likely to drive victimization rates up than down. In the absence of a decline in the demand for liquor, groceries, or gasoline (perhaps the latter is likely), opportunities for criminal profit in commercial establishments are not likely to decline either. The distribution of property crime also reflects the social order. Evidence about the frequency of serious theft and the amounts lost in those episodes suggests that target selection is quite rational, and that as long as the distribution of wealth in the society is skewed, the distribution of its victims of property crimes will follow.

Information on these and other topics will continue to flow from the crime surveys, for they are a continuing enterprise. The first results from the 1973 national survey were released in 1974, and in ensuing years a regular cycle of surveys and reports will be established. The national surveys will produce new time-series social indicators, monitoring changes in the victimization rate and patterns of victimization, while more detailed city studies can be used to evaluate the impact of specific governmental programs. In addition, they may be used routinely by local police departments to allocate resources in response to the distribution of crime. We are only beginning to realize the many uses to which this new tool can be put.

10

Public Attitudes Toward Crime and Law Enforcement

Jennie McIntyre

Public concern about crime is neither new nor surprising. An interest which was once manifested in attendance at the public punishment of offenders is now expressed in reaction to the news media's reports of crime and criminals in the local community, the nation, and farther afield.[1] Especially since the growth of the mass news media, there have been, from time to time, surges of public alarm concerning current crime waves. A legal scholar who recently reviewed the literature of the last fifty years noted that in each and every decade, there were prominent articles about the need for strong measures to meet the then-current crisis in crime.[2] From time to time, there were commissions appointed or committees formed to investigate what was seen as intolerable increases in crime. It may be that there has always been a crime crisis.

Sometimes these crime waves have been synthetic, manufactured by journalists. Lincoln Steffens, for example, describes his own creation of a crime wave accomplished by giving headline treatment to the

From Jennie McIntyre, "Public Attitudes Toward Crime and Law Enforcement," *The Annals of the American Academy of Political and Social Science* 374 (1967): 34–46, by permission of the author and publisher. In addition to sources cited herein, the writer has drawn upon the following: unpublished consultant papers prepared by Albert D. Biderman for the National Crime Commission, a search of its archives by the Roper Public Opinion Center, and assistance of Albert H. Cantril in searching recent attitude surveys.

1. For discussions of shifting interpretations of crime as well as the functions of public interest, see Leon Radzinowicz, *Ideology and Crime* (New York: Columbia University Press, 1966); and Kai T. Erikson, "Notes on the Sociology of Deviance," *Social Problems*, 9 (Spring 1962): 307–14.

2. Yale Kamisar, "When the Cops Were Not 'Handcuffed,'" *New York Times Magazine*, November 7, 1965.

ordinary occurrences of the day.[3] The intensity of the current concern regarding crime may be due in part, not to fabrication, but rather to the excellence of news coverage.

An entire nation reads of the fearful mass killing of eight nurses in Chicago and the apparently senseless shooting of thirteen passers-by on a Texas campus by a person not known to them. The unpredictable nature of such violence becomes the more fearful and immediate as citizens across the land view the scene and hear the tales of witnesses on television news programs. The public's perception of the incidence of crime as well as the intensity of its reaction may be influenced by the fact that it receives reports of violent crime drawn from a larger pool of crime-incident reports than ever before.

Nationally oriented communications media tend to draw attention to crime as a national problem. Other conditions, too, encourage the perception of a national crime wave rather than the local phenomenon portrayed by Steffens. The crimes which draw the most attention are urban occurrences. While the primarily rural population of an earlier day could view crime as a characteristic of remote and not quite moral cities, the primarily urban population of today perceives urban crime as more directly threatening. In spite of perennial concern, there is some reason to believe that public concern about crime as a national problem is at an unprecedented level.

An understanding of the attitudes of the public regarding crime, the level of concern, the manner in which this concern affects the lives of people, the beliefs regarding the causes of crime, and the appropriate methods of coping with the problem is for some purposes of as much consequence as an understanding of the nature and extent of crime itself; for the public attitudes on these issues to some extent determine the feasibility of alternative methods of crime prevention and law enforcement. The National Crime Commission in 1966 undertook to assess these attitudes through an analysis of national public opinion polls and surveys conducted for the Commission. . . .

HEIGHTENED CONCERN ABOUT CRIME

The national public opinion polls in recent years provide some evidence of the heightened concern about crime.[4] Until recently, crime was given only peripheral attention by national pollsters. When com-

---

3. Lincoln Steffens, *The Autobiography of Lincoln Steffens* (New York: Harcourt, Brace, 1931), pp. 285–91.

4. Surveys by George Gallup, Director, American Institute of Public Opinion, Princeton, New Jersey, will be referred to as Gallup polls. Those by Louis Harris, public opinion analyst, will be cited as Harris surveys.

pletely open-ended questions were asked by a Gallup poll about the problems facing the nation, international problems invariably topped the lists; until recently, crime was not mentioned by enough persons to appear on the list of top problems. In 1966, when the National Opinion Research Center (NORC) conducted a national survey for the Crime Commission, interviewers asked citizens to pick from a list of six major domestic problems the one to which they had been paying the most attention recently.[5] Crime was the second most frequently selected from this list; only race relations was picked by more persons. (Lower-income nonwhites placed more emphasis on education than crime.)

When local community problems are considered, juvenile delinquency takes on added significance. In 1963 Gallup asked a sample of adults to select the top problem facing their community from a list of thirty-nine. Juvenile delinquency was picked by more persons than almost any other problem; only local real estate taxes were named more frequently. The third most frequently named, the need for more recreational areas, was probably related to the concern with juvenile delinquency.

Whether more concerned about adult or juvenile crime, most people think that the crime situation in their own community is getting worse, and while substantial numbers think the situation is staying about the same, hardly anyone sees improvement. A Gallup survey in April 1965 showed that this pessimistic perception of the problem prevailed among men and women, well-educated and less well-educated, and among all age, regional, income, and city-size groupings. When citizens in Washington, D.C., were interviewed by the Bureau of Social Science Research (BSSR) the next year, 75 percent thought that crime had been getting worse in that city during the past year; 16 percent thought it was about the same.[6]

SOURCES OF ATTITUDES

For the large majority of people, attitudes about crime and crime trends apparently are derived largely from vicarious sources. Whether we judge volume from crimes known to the police or from the far more

5. Phillip Ennis, *Criminal Victimization in the United States: A Report of a National Survey*, President's Commission on Law Enforcement and Administration of Justice Field Survey II (Washington, D.C.: U.S. Government Printing Office, 1967); hereinafter referred to as the NORC study.

6. Albert D. Biderman, Louise A. Johnson, Jennie McIntyre, and Adrianne W. Weir, *Report on a Pilot Study in the District of Columbia on Victimization and Attitudes Toward Law Enforcement*, President's Commission on Law Enforcement and Administration of Justice Field Survey I (Washington, D.C.: U.S. Government Printing Office, 1967); hereinafter referred to as the BSSR study.

generous estimates from public surveys conducted for the Crime Commission, its incidence is not so great as to make personal victimization the major determinant of people's perceptions of the crime problem. This is manifestly true of crimes of violence, which, although relatively rare, are the focus of most people's fears. The experience of being robbed or assaulted might well have a most profound effect on the attitudes and habits of a victim, but such experiences are infrequent.

Even taking into consideration the more common, less serious offenses, most people are not victimized sufficiently often for these experiences to make a major impact on their lives. Neither are those offenses which do occur sufficiently important in people's lives to be remembered vividly for any length of time. These are among the conclusions derived from the intensive methodological work undertaken by the BSSR for the Commission. ... It was necessary to devise and refine special interviewing techniques in order to facilitate recall of incidents of victimization, particularly those that had happened more than a short time prior to the interview. When people were asked about the worst thing that had happened to them that could be called a crime, few remembered anything that had not happened recently.

The seriousness of the incidents recounted to interviewers further suggests that the experiences of victimization are not remembered for any length of time by most people. If persons being interviewed remembered all criminal victimizations, they could be expected to recount numerous trivial incidents, the minor offenses, such as vandalism and bicycle theft, which occur most frequently. Such was not the case, and the seriousness of the incidents reported to interviewers was much the same as that of those reported to the police. It appears that many minor incidents are simply brushed aside and forgotten. Even the more serious offenses, such as burglary, usually involved relatively small monetary loss. Inferentially, then, most incidents of victimization do not appear to constitute very important events in a person's life experience.

If the experience of victimization is not a major event in the lives of most people, it is understandable that this experience does not determine their attitudes regarding crime. The surveys conducted for the commission found little statistical relationship between the experience of victimization and attitudes toward most aspects of the crime problem. The BSSR applied an index of exposure to crime, which included victimization of self, victimization of friends, and having personally witnessed any offense.[7] Scores on this index did not correlate with responses to a variety of questions on attitudes toward crime and to-

---

7. BSSR study, p. 126.

ward law enforcement. Nor was crime exposure related to anxiety about crime. Victims were neither more nor less likely to believe that crime was increasing or to express a sense of uneasiness about their personal safety. The one exception appeared in the case of the Negro male. Negro men who have been the victims of even one criminal incident were more apprehensive about their safety.[8]

The NORC study similarly found little relationship between the experience of victimization and concern about crime.[9] Those who had been victims did worry about the possibility of burglary and robbery somewhat more frequently than did the nonvictims. The difference between men and women was greater than that between victims and nonvictims, however; so that women who had been victimized [worried more often] than men who had. Victims and nonvictims were equally likely to have taken strong household security measures, however: 57 percent of victims and 58 percent of nonvictims had high scores on an index of precautionary behavior which included locking doors during the daytime and keeping a watchdog or weapons for protection.

Anxiety about crime was not a simple function of living in areas where crimes are frequent occurrences. The BSSR study in Washington, D.C., found that the average level of concern with crime in a predominantly Negro precinct that had one of the highest rates of crime in the city, according to police data, was lower than it was in another Negro precinct that had a lower crime rate.[10]

Perhaps the most direct evidence that people form their attitudes about crime on the basis of something other than experience can be found in their own statements. After respondents in Washington were asked for their estimate of an increase or decrease in crime in the city, they were asked where they had obtained their information on this subject. A preponderant majority said that they got their information either from the news media or from what they heard people say.

But if the actual experience of victimization is not a major determinant of attitudes about crime, there is another sense in which vulnerability does influence fear. In the survey in Washington, D.C., the BSSR constructed an index of anxiety about crime.[11] This index reflected a general concern for personal safety as well as the belief that crime is increasing. It found that Negro women had the highest average score, followed by Negro men, white women, and white men. The greater

---

8. Ibid., p. 127.
9. NORC study.
10. BSSR study, p. 125.
11. Ibid., p. 121.

concern of Negroes is consistent with the risks of victimization suggested by police statistics. An analysis of police records in Chicago, for example, indicates that Negroes are far more likely to be the victims of a serious offense against the person than are white persons.[12] The greater anxiety of women than men is not consistent with what is known of the victimization risks, however, and one would have to look for alternative explanations. Anxiety scores were lower at the higher income levels for both Negroes and whites.

CRIME WORSE ELSEWHERE

If most people do not base their attitudes on personal experience, neither do they rely on their understanding of the experiences of others in their immediate environs. While most people questioned thought that the situation is terrible and getting worse all the time, they nevertheless believed that they are relatively safe near their own homes. In the NORC study for the Commission, 60 percent of those questioned compared their own neighborhood favorably to other parts of the community in which they lived, with regard to the likelihood that their home would be broken into, while only 14 percent thought that their area presented a greater hazard.[13] This is true even in areas which are considered crime-ridden by the police—areas which might terrify many suburban dwellers. In the BSSR survey in Washington precincts with average to high crime rates, only one out of five respondents thought that the chances of being beaten were greater in his neighborhood than in other parts of the city.[14] Almost half of the national sample interviewed by NORC said that there was no place in their own city (or suburb or county) where they would not feel safe. Two-thirds of the respondents said that they feel safe walking alone when it is dark if they are in their own neighborhood.[15]

CENTRAL ROLE OF FEAR FOR THE PERSON

When citizens in Washington were asked what steps they had taken to protect themselves from crime, they spontaneously spoke of avoiding

12. Albert J. Reiss, Jr., "Probability of Victimization for Major Crimes Against the Person by Race and Sex Status of Victims and Offenders," in *Studies in Crime and Law Enforcement in Major Metropolitan Areas*, ed. Albert J. Reiss, Jr., President's Commission on Law Enforcement and Administration of Justice Field Survey III (Washington, D.C.: U.S. Government Printing Office, 1967); hereinafter referred to as Reiss studies.

13. NORC study, Table 47, p. 76.

14. BSSR study, p. 121.

15. NORC study.

danger on the streets.[16] They said that they stayed home at night or used taxis, or they avoided talking to strangers. Others spoke of measures to protect themselves and their property at home; they kept firearms or watchdogs or put stronger locks on the doors and windows. In the districts surveyed in Boston and Chicago by the University of Michigan, five out of every eight said that they had changed their habits in one or more of these ways because of the fear of crime.[17] No one mentioned efforts to avoid loss through fraud or overly sharp loan practices or any kind of swindle. It was clear that the crimes which they feared were crimes which might endanger their personal safety, especially attack by a stranger.

The national survey by NORC suggests the same conclusion. While two-thirds of those interviewed feel safe walking in their neighborhoods, one-third do not. Over 80 percent lock their doors at night, and 25 percent lock them during the daytime when family members are at home. Twenty-eight percent said their dogs were primarily watchdogs, and 37 percent that firearms in the home were kept at least partly for protection.[18]

Possibly indicative of the concern of the public is the reaction of citizens to a question posed in the NORC survey: "If you were walking down the street alone around here in the evening and heard footsteps coming from behind, and turned to see a stranger rapidly approaching, what would you do?" A large majority interpreted the situation as dangerous. One-fourth of the respondents said they would "do nothing, just keep right on walking," but the most frequent reply was "Run as fast as I could or call for help."[19] This fear of personal victimization is becoming more intense. In recent years, Harris surveys have found that each year 50 percent of their respondents have said that they are more worried about their personal safety on the streets than they were in the previous year.

Although many persons felt relatively safe in their own neighborhoods, they were not thereby indifferent or unconcerned about personal safety for themselves or their families. Respondents in Washington, D.C., were asked whether they had thought more about the neighborhood or the house when they had selected their current residence. The largest number said that the neighborhood was most important, and nearly as many said that neighborhood and house were

---

16. BSSR study, pp. 128–30.
17. Reiss studies, vol. 1, sec. 2, p. 103.
18. NORC study, Table 44, p. 74.
19. Ibid.

of equal importance.[20] Although some respondents selected a location because of its convenience or aesthetic qualities, 56 percent had placed greatest emphasis on the safety or moral characteristics of the neighborhood. Having selected a location which, within the alternatives available, seemed safe, most felt relatively secure. Nonetheless, 24 percent of the respondents in Washington felt that there was so much trouble in the area that they would like to move. In the areas studied in Boston and Chicago, 20 percent thought that they would like to move because of crime; 30 percent wanted to move out of the higher-crime-rate district in Boston.[21]

SIGNIFICANCE OF THE FEAR OF CRIME

The crimes which the public fears most, crimes of violence, are those which occur least frequently. People are much more tolerant of crimes against property. The average citizen probably suffers the greatest economic loss as a result of crimes against businesses and public institutions which pass on their losses in the form of increased prices and taxes. Nevertheless, most shoplifters are never arrested, and employees suspected of dishonesty are either warned or dismissed.[22]

Furthermore, violence and the threat of violence do not present as great a hazard as do other risks in an industrial society. The number of accidental injuries calling for medical attention or restricted activity of one day or more[23] is far greater than the 1.8 offenses per 1,000 Americans involving violence or threat of violence.[24] Inadequate medical care is another example of risk which does not provoke the same horror as violence. A recent study found the quality, numbers, and distribution of ambulances and other emergency services severely deficient, and estimated that as many as 20,000 persons die each year as a result of inadequate emergency medical care.[25]

Death or injury as a result of violence, however, has a different significance than death by accident or improper care, a significance

---

20. BSSR study, p. 119.

21. Reiss studies, p. 31.

22. Donald J. Black and Albert J. Reiss, Jr., "Problems and Practices for Protection Against Crime Among Businesses and Organizations," in Reiss studies.

23. National Safety Council, *Accident Facts* (Chicago: National Safety Council, 1966), p. 2.

24. U.S. Department of Justice, Federal Bureau of Investigation, *Crime in the United States: Uniform Crime Reports* (Washington, D.C.: U.S. Government Printing Office, 1965), p. 3.

25. Data obtained by interview from American College of Surgeons, Washington, D.C., 1966.

consistent with the repugnance with which Americans view violence. Recent studies have shown that there is a widespread consensus on the relative seriousness of different types of crimes.[26] Offenses involving physical assaults against the person are the most feared, and the greatest concern is expressed about those in which a weapon is used.

The precautions which people take to protect themselves indicate that underlying the fear of crime is a profound fear of strangers. They are afraid that some unknown person will accost them on the street or break into their homes and take their property or attack them personally. Again, the fears are not consistent with the objective risks. Not only are the risks of injury by violence slight relative to the risks of injury or death from other causes, but the risk of serious attack by strangers is about half as great as it is from persons well known to the victim.[27] Injuries in the case of assault are not only more common but more serious when the victim and offender know each other well. This hazard does not even stop at the self, for suicide is twice as common as homicide.

This fear of strangers is impoverishing the lives of many Americans. People stay behind the locked doors of their homes rather than walk in the street at night. Poor people take taxis because they are afraid to walk or use public transportation. Sociable people are afraid to talk to those they do not know. Society is suffering from what the economists would label opportunity costs. When people stay home, they are not enjoying the pleasurable and cultural opportunities in their communities; they are not visiting their friends as frequently as they might. The general level of sociability is diminished. Some are restricting their earning opportunities, as when they ignore job openings in some neighborhoods. Hospital administrators in large cities report difficulty in staffing for night duty. Administrators and officials interviewed by the University of Michigan survey team report that Parent-Teacher Association meetings at night are poorly attended, that library use is decreasing and recreational facilities remain unused, because of stories of robberies and purse-snatching.[28]

As social interaction is reduced and fear of crime becomes fear of the stranger, the social order is further damaged. Not only are there

---

26. Thorsten Sellin and Marvin E. Wolfgang, *The Measurement of Delinquency* (New York: Wiley, 1964), Table 69, p. 289.

27. For a review of findings on the relationship between victim and offender, see President's Commission on Law Enforcement and Administration of Justice, *Task Force Report: Crime and Its Impact—An Assessment* (Washington, D.C.: U.S. Government Printing Office, 1967), pp. 14–15.

28. Stephen Cutler and Albert J. Reiss, Jr., "Crimes Against Public and Quasi-Public Organizations in Boston, Chicago, and Washington, D.C.," in Reiss studies.

fewer persons on the streets and in public places than there might be, but persons who are afraid may show a lack of concern for each other. The logical consequences of this reduced sociability, mutual fear, and distrust can be seen in the reported incidents of bystanders indifferent to cries for help.

RELIANCE ON LAW ENFORCEMENT

The surveys regarding beliefs about the causes of crime indicate a pronounced concern with the morals of the country and the moral training of the country's youth. Few persons blamed social conditions or law enforcement. When Gallup asked the causes of crime, most persons who were interviewed gave answers which could be categorized as poor parental guidance or inadequate home life and supervision of teenagers. "Breakdown of moral standards" was also frequently mentioned. Persons interviewed by Harris blamed disturbed and restless teenagers most frequently. Unemployment, racial problems, broken homes, and low moral standards were next in importance.

When Harris asked why people become criminal rather than for an explanation of the crime rate, then the emphasis on moral training became explicit. Sixty-eight percent of the persons interviewed believed that upbringing or bad environment were the main causes. Many of the other causes named, such as broken homes or wrong companions, could also indicate a concern with the moral training and discipline of youth. Few persons suggested innate defects, and even fewer blamed police failure in any of these polls.

Although a majority saw crime as the consequence of a moral breakdown, most tended to believe that stricter law enforcement was the way to cope with the current crime problem. The BSSR survey in Washington, D.C., asked citizens what they thought was the most important thing that could be done to cut down crime in their city.[29] Responses were classified as to whether a repressive measure, a measure of social amelioration, or one of moral inculcation was being advocated. Sixty percent recommended repressive measures such as more police, police dogs, stiffer sentences, or "cracking down on teenagers." Forty percent believed that the solution lay in social amelioration or moral inculcation. These included such measures as more jobs, recreation and youth programs, better housing, improved police-community relations, better child-training, religious training and revival, community leadership, or simply inculcating discipline. Only 3.5 percent would rely solely on moral measures.

---

29. BSSR study, p. 134.

Another indication that many people believe repressive measures, rather than amelioration of social conditions or moral training of youth, to be the more effective means of cutting down crime lies in attitudes about court actions. The BSSR study in Washington, D.C., asked whether the sentences given by courts in that city were generally too lenient or too harsh. Most respondents, including Negroes, thought that the courts were too lenient. A Gallup survey in 1965 also found that a majority of persons interviewed believed that the courts do not deal harshly enough with criminals; only 2 percent said "too harshly."

Reliance on strict policing and law enforcement is somewhat tempered and not altogether repressive, however. When NORC asked whether the main concern of the police should be with preventing crimes or with catching criminals, over 60 percent placed the emphasis on prevention.[30] Gallup asked respondents how they would deal with a hypothetical youth caught stealing an automobile. The most frequent responses were to give him another chance, be lenient.

When the fate of an actual person is to be decided, the demand for stern treatment of the lawbreaker is further relaxed. The clearest illustration of this in studies undertaken for the Commission can be seen in the survey of employers carried out by the University of Michigan in Boston, Chicago, and Washington, D.C.[31] Only 19 percent of the employers who reported larcenies, fraud, forgery, embezzlement, or misuse of company property by employees said that they had called the police. The most frequent way of handling the offenders was discharge, but in other instances a transfer or demand for restitution sufficed.

More police, more stringent policing, less leniency by the courts— this is how a substantial segment of the population would undertake to reduce crime—except when they are confronted with the necessity of deciding the fate of a particular individual. A smaller proportion of the public believed that social changes could reduce the amount of crime; only a very few suggested improving the moral fiber of the country— although a majority believed that inadequate moral training was responsible for an increase in crime.

CITIZEN RESPONSIBILITY FOR CRIME REDUCTION

Persons who believe that poor upbringing and moral training of youth are a major cause of crime might be willing to assume some responsibility for improved discipline. A Gallup survey which asked adults whether they would be willing to devote one evening a month to

30. NORC study, p. 59.
31. Black and Reiss, op. cit.

working with juvenile delinquents or trying to solve juvenile delinquency problems did, indeed, uncover a considerable potential responsibility. Sixty percent said that they would be willing to spend an evening each month in such activities. On the other hand, citizens in one precinct in Washington were asked whether they had ever "gotten together with other people around here, or has any group or organization you belong to met and discussed the problem of crime or taken some sort of action to combat crime?" Only 12 percent answered affirmatively. Neither did most persons believe that they could do anything about the crime in their own neighborhoods. Just over 17 percent thought that they could do anything.

When administrators and officials of public and quasi-public organizations were asked about the most effective remedies for crime, they suggested the amelioration of social conditions far more frequently than did members of the general public.[32] They also recommended improvement of the moral fiber of the population and better training of youth much more often than the general public. Perhaps because of their broader view of crime reduction, they were also able to see more ways in which they might help to reduce crime. A number thought that they might cooperate with the police in ways calculated to make law enforcement easier. A number thought that they might cooperate in neighborhood and community programs, particularly by donating money for youth and recreation groups. The greatest number of suggestions involved what might be termed an extension of the organization's services. Electric-company executives considered more and brighter street lights; park officials, more recreational activities; and school administrators, more youth programs and adult education. Others believed that they might further community goals through integration of work crews and support of community-relations programs. Although most persons have not become involved in any activity intended to prevent or reduce crime, there does exist the potential for citizen involvement when responsible persons are convinced of its value.

AMBIVALENCE TOWARD LAW ENFORCEMENT

There is a convergence of attitudes and preferences expressed by large numbers of the citizens interviewed which would tend to predispose them to a preference for strong police agencies, unhampered in their efforts to apprehend and convict criminals. A large majority believes that the crime situation is terrible and getting worse. Accounts of crime

---

32. Cutler and Reiss, op. cit.

rates arouse fears of crimes of violence; the quest for safety becomes an important factor in the ordering of personal lives. Their beliefs regarding the causes of crime notwithstanding, a majority would rely on more strict law enforcement and stern treatment of offenders to lower the crime rate. Few seriously considered any personal efforts to reduce crime, even in their own neighborhoods, either by themselves or in concert with other citizens.

It is not surprising, then, to find considerable willingness to permit whatever practices the police consider important. A majority of those interviewed in Washington, D.C. (73 percent) agreed that the police ought to have leeway to act tough when they have to.[33] More than half (56 percent) agreed that there should be more use of police dogs, while fewer than one-third disagreed. Few respondents consistently endorsed either restricting or enlarging police powers, however. Many who take a permissive attitude on one issue refuse to do so on another; more than half of those who oppose the greater use of police dogs are in favor of police freedom to act tough. Neither was there a strong relationship between attitudes toward these issues and more general attitudes toward the police. Respondents were characterized as more or less favorable toward policemen, according to their responses to a six-item scale. Nearly half (47 percent) of those who did not favor police toughness or more police dogs nevertheless indicated strong respect and sympathy for policemen.

A similar ambivalence was observed in the results of the national survey conducted by NORC.[34] Forty-five percent favored civilian review boards (35 percent opposed them; 20 percent were uncertain or indifferent); 52 percent believed that the police should have more power; 42 percent, that police should risk arresting an innocent person rather than risk missing a criminal; and 65 percent favored the ruling that police may not question a suspect without his lawyer being present or the suspect's consent to be questioned without counsel. Most persons were in favor of enlarging police powers on some issues and restricting it on others; only 25 percent were consistently for or against permitting greater powers to the police.

The surveys conducted for the Commission found a strong concern for the civil rights of the individual, including the person who is a suspect or offender, in spite of a wish for strict law enforcement. This is particularly apparent when the issue of rights is explicit. In the districts studied in Boston, Chicago, and Washington, D.C., citizens were

33. BSSR study, p. 146.
34. NORC study.

asked whether they thought that "too much attention is being paid to the rights of people who get into trouble with the police."[35] In each of the three cities, fewer than half (38 percent) agreed. As was true concerning the issue of police practices, this concern for the individual was not derogatory of the police. In Washington, D.C., more than half of those who took a rights position on this question also expressed strong sympathy and respect for the police.

In addition to a tradition of concern for individual rights, a belief that the police discriminate in the way that they treat various groups may account for some of the ambivalence regarding law enforcement. In Washington, D.C., the BSSR study found that 60 percent of the Negro men, 49 percent of the Negro women, and 27 percent of the white citizens thought that Negroes get worse treatment than other people.[36] Among the comments of these respondents were that the police pick on Negroes more, that they are rude to Negroes, use brutality and physical force, or else ignore Negroes more than other people. Others expressed the belief that affluent citizens get better treatment than the poor. In Washington, D.C., half of the persons interviewed agreed that people who have money for lawyers do not have to worry about the police. In Boston and Chicago, there was a tendency for citizens in the predominantly white districts to point out rich and respectable citizens as recipients of more favorable treatment, while citizens in the predominantly nonwhite districts pointed to the less favorable treatment of Negroes by police.[37]

When another issue was posed in economic rather than racial terms, there was again a strong indication of concern with rights of the individual. Almost three-quarters of the persons questioned by the NORC study approved the Supreme Court decision that the state must provide a lawyer to suspects who want one but cannot afford to pay the lawyer's fee.[38] Not only does a strong majority approve the decision, but no income, sex, or racial group opposes it.

NONREPORTING OF CRIMES TO THE POLICE

Americans who believe that crime control is strictly a matter for the police and the courts nevertheless frequently fail to take the one action that they as citizens must take if the police and courts are to intervene

---

35. BSSR study, p. 149, and Reiss studies, p. 82.
36. BSSR study, p. 144.
37. Reiss studies, pp. 43–47.
38. NORC study, Table 40, p. 70.

in any particular situation. Although the surveys undertaken for the Commission represent a more intensive effort to measure the magnitude of nonreported crime than any in the past, students of crime have long recognized the phenomenon of *le chiffre noir* and speculated on the reasons for its existence. In the current studies, persons who were interviewed were asked not only whether they had reported any given incident to the police but also their reasons for not doing so when they had not.[39] The victim's reluctance to get involved was one of the most frequently cited reasons for not calling the police. Sometimes he did not want to take the time to call the police and present evidence, often fearing that this might necessitate spending time in court and away from work.

Some who had witnessed incidents which they thought were crimes denied any responsibility in the matter. An illustration of this sentiment is a comment sometimes made to interviewers: "I am not my brother's keeper." Others said that they did not think that the victim would want the police to be notified or indicated a concern for the offender. The NORC study found that for all classes of offenses except serious crimes against the person, the police were less likely to be notified if the offender were personally known to the victim than if he were a stranger.

The fear of reprisal or other unfortunate consequences sometimes deterred victims or witnesses from notifying the police of an incident. Some feared personal harm might come from the offender or his friends; others, that they themselves would become the subjects of police inquiry or action. Other consequences which the victim might wish to avoid include cancellation of insurance or an increase in rates.

The most frequently cited reason for not calling the police was a resigned belief that any efforts would be useless. The victim simply accepted his losses as irrevocable. This was particularly true in the cases of malicious mischief and vandalism, where it often seemed that there were no clues. The damage could not be undone, nor could the police be expected to apprehend and punish the offender.

Often the victim believed that his evidence was insufficient to convince either the police or the courts that a crime had indeed been committed. This was the reason given by nearly half of the employers who said they had not reported cases of employee dishonesty to the police.[40] Given the belief in the ineffectiveness of a call to police, they preferred the more simple and direct method of discharging or other-

---

39. BSSR study, Tables 3–23 and 3–24, pp. 154–55; NORC study, Table 24, p. 44.
40. Black and Reiss, op. cit.

wise punishing the employee. (Ironically, these same employers often relied on police records for the purpose of screening prospective employees.)

It has been noted that persons interviewed during the national study were far more likely to fail to notify the police if the offender were a relative or person well known to the victim than a stranger. The employer not only knows but is in a special relationship to the employee whom he suspects of dishonesty. In a similar manner, a businessman who cashes a check for a customer has assumed some measure of responsibility for his relationship with this customer. It may be, then, that an undefined sense of responsibility for his own victimization sometimes deters the individual from calling the police. The employers and businessmen who were interviewed had refrained from calling the police more frequently in instances of employee dishonesty and bad checks than shoplifting. Lacking any special relationship with the shoplifter, the businessman could more readily report his offense.

Other persons did not notify the police because of their own uncertainty of what ought to be done. Sometimes they were not sure of what was taking place at the time, or they did not know whether it was a crime or what was the proper procedure for reporting the incident. For these persons, more knowledge of what constitutes reason for calling the police and how to do so would probably increase the rate of reporting. In those cities in which the police department is actively enlisting the aid of the public, dissemination of this information has been effective. Efforts to increase the rate of crime reporting by citizens would have to take into account also the reluctance of most to get involved, to take responsibility for reporting, and to be willing to spend time testifying.

SUMMARY AND CONCLUSIONS

Analysis of the findings of the public opinion polls and the surveys conducted for the Commission indicates a widespread concern about crime, both as a national problem and as a problem in assuring personal safety. Persons who were interviewed expressed a belief that crime is increasing. They tend to equate crime with crimes of violence and to fear most violence at the hands of strangers in unfamiliar surroundings. Crimes against the person are far less common than those against property, and an unknown person is the least likely assailant.

Because of their fear of strangers many people restrict their activities. They forgo opportunities for pleasure or cultural enrichment, and they become less sociable, more suspicious. The level of interaction and mutual trust in the society is reduced; public places may become less safe than they otherwise might be. The crime rate is blamed on a breakdown in morals, and especially on inadequate training and discipline of young people. As a threat to the moral and social order, it becomes fearful even to persons who live in relatively safe circumstances and have no personal experience with crime.

Although attributing an increase in crime to lowered moral standards, most persons would depend on the police and courts for stern treatment of offenders in order to diminish the level of crime. Not as many, but nonetheless a substantial proportion, would recommend increased employment opportunities and other improved social conditions to combat crime. Along with the reliance on law-enforcement officials, there was willingness to permit the police considerable latitude in their efforts to apprehend and convict criminals. This apparent harshness toward offenders was immediately mitigated when the issue of the rights of the individual was posed. Some of this concern is related to the belief that there is discrimination against economic and racial groups. Finally, the recommendation for stern treatment of wrongdoers is further tempered when the fate of an individual offender is considered.

11

Social Settings and Covert Participant Observation

Kai T. Erikson

At the beginning of their excellent paper on the subject, Howard S. Becker and Blanche Geer define participant observation as "that method in which the observer participates in the daily life of the people under study, either openly in the role of researcher or covertly in some disguised role. . . ."[1]

The purpose of this paper is to argue that the research strategy mentioned in the last few words of that description represents a significant ethical problem in the field of sociology. In point of sheer volume, of course, the problem is relatively small, for disguised participant observation is probably one of the rarest research techniques in use among sociologists. But in point of general importance, the problem is far more serious—partly because the use of disguises seems to attract a disproportionate amount of interest both inside and outside the field, and partly because it offers a natural starting point for dealing with other ethical issues in the profession.

In recent years, a handful of studies have been reported in the literature based on the work of observers who deliberately misrepresented their identity in order to enter an otherwise inaccessible social situation. Some of these studies have already provoked a good deal of comment—among them, for instance, the cases of the anthropologist who posed as a mental patient by complaining of symptoms he did not

From Kai T. Erikson, "A Comment on Disguised Observation in Sociology," *Social Problems* 14 (1967): 366–73, by permission of the author and the Society for the Study of Social Problems. This paper was read at the annual meeting of the Society for the Study of Social Problems, Chicago, 1965.

1. Howard S. Becker and Blanche Geer, "Participant Observation and Interviewing: A Comparison," *Human Organization,* 16 (1957): 28–32.

feel,[2] the sociologists who joined a gathering of religious mystics by professing convictions they did not share,[3] the Air Force officer who borrowed a new name, a new birth date, a new personal history, a new set of mannerisms, and even a new physical appearance in order to impersonate an enlisted man,[4] and the group of graduate students who ventured into a meeting of Alcoholics Anonymous wearing the clothes of men from other social classes than their own and the facial expressions of men suffering from an unfortunate disability.[5]

In taking the position that this kind of masquerading is unethical, I am naturally going to say many things that are only matters of personal opinion; and thus the following remarks are apt to have a more editorial flavor than is usual for papers read at professional meetings. But a good deal more is at stake here than the sensitivities of any particular person, and my excuse for dealing with an issue that seems to have so many subjective overtones is that the use of disguise in social research affects the professional climate in which all of us work and raises a number of methodological questions that should be discussed more widely.

I am assuming here that "personal morality" and "professional ethics" are not the same thing. Personal morality has something to do with the way an individual conducts himself across the range of his human contacts; it is not local to a particular set of occupational interests. Professional ethics, on the other hand, refer to the way a group of associates define their special responsibility to one another and to the rest of the social order in which they work. In this sense, professional ethics often deal with issues that are practical in their application and limited in their scope: they are the terms of a covenant among people gathered together into a given occupational group. For instance, it may or may not be ethical for an espionage agent or a journalist to represent himself as someone he is not in the course of gathering information, but it certainly does not follow that the conduct of a sociologist should be judged in the same terms; for the sociologist has a different relationship to the rest of the community, operates under a different warrant, and

2. William C. Caudill et al., "Social Structure and Interaction Processes on a Psychiatric Ward," *American Journal of Orthopsychiatry,* 22 (1952): 314–34.

3. Leon Festinger, Henry W. Riecken, and Stanley Schacter, *When Prophecy Fails* (Minneapolis: University of Minnesota Press, 1956).

4. Mortimer A. Sullivan, Stuart A. Queen, and Ralph C. Patrick, Jr., "Participant Observation as Employed in the Study of a Military Training Program," *American Sociological Review,* 23 (1958): 660–67.

5. John F. Lofland and Robert A. Lejeune, "Initial Interaction of Newcomers in Alcoholics Anonymous: A Field Experiment in Class Symbols and Socialization," *Social Problems,* 8 (1960): 102–11.

has a different set of professional and scientific interests to protect. In this sense, the ethics governing a particular discipline are in many ways local to the transactions that discipline has with the larger world.

The argument to be presented here, then, is that the practice of using masks in social research compromises both the people who wear them and the people for whom they are worn, and in doing so, violates the terms of a contract which the sociologist should be ready to honor in his dealings with others. There are many respects in which this is true, but I will be dealing here in particular with the relationship between the sociologist and (a) the subjects of his research, (b) the colleagues with whom he works, (c) the students he agrees to teach, and (d) the data he takes as his subject matter.

The first of these points has to do with the responsibilities a sociologist should accept toward other institutions and other people in the social order. It may seem a little cranky to insist that disguised observation constitutes an ugly invasion of privacy and is, on that ground alone, objectionable. But it is a matter of cold calculation to point out that this particular research strategy can injure people in ways we can neither anticipate in advance nor compensate for afterward. For one thing, the sheer act of entering a human transaction on the basis of deliberate fraud may be painful to the people who are thereby misled; and even if that were not the case, there are countless ways in which a stranger who pretends to be something else can disturb others by failing to understand the conditions of intimacy that prevail in the group he has tried to invade. Nor does it matter very much how sympathetic the observer is toward the persons whose lives he is studying: the fact of the matter is that he does not *know* which of his actions are apt to hurt other people, and it is highly presumptuous of him to act as if he does —particularly when, as is ordinarily the case, he has elected to wear a disguise exactly because he is entering a social sphere so far from his own experience.

So the sheer act of wearing disguises in someone else's world may cause discomfort, no matter what we later write in our reports; and this possibility raises two questions. The first, of course, is whether we have the right to inflict pain at all when we are aware of these risks and the subjects of the study are not. The second, however, is perhaps more important from the narrow point of view of the profession itself: so long as we suspect that a method we use has at least *some* potential for harming others, we are in the extremely awkward position of having to weigh the scientific and social benefits of that procedure against its possible cost in human discomfort, and this is a difficult business under the best of circumstances. If we happen to harm people who have agreed to act as subjects, we can at least argue that they knew something of the risks involved and were willing to contribute to that vague program called the "advance of knowledge." But when we do so with people who have expressed no readiness to participate in our researches (indeed, people who would presumably have refused if asked directly), we are in very much the same ethical position as a physician who carries out medical experiments on human subjects without their consent. The only conceivable argument in favor of such experimentation is that the knowledge derived from it is worth the discomfort it may cause. And the difficulties here are that we do not know how to measure the value of the work we do or the methods we employ in this way, and, moreover, that we might be doing an extraordinary disservice to the idea of detached scholarship if we tried. Sociologists cannot protect their freedom of inquiry if they owe the rest of the community (not to mention themselves) an accounting for the distress they may have inadvertently imposed on people who have not volunteered to take that risk.

The second problem with disguised observation to be considered here has to do with the sociologist's responsibilities to his colleagues. It probably goes without saying that research of this sort is liable to damage the reputation of sociology in the larger society and close off promising areas of research for future investigators. This is true in the limited sense that a particular agency—say, for example, Alcoholics Anonymous—may decide that its integrity and perhaps even its effectiveness were violated by the appearance of sociologists pretending to be someone else and deny access to other students who propose to use an altogether different approach. And it is also true in the wider sense that any research tactic which attracts unfavorable notice may help diminish the general climate of trust toward sociology in the community as a whole. So long as this remains a serious possibility, the practice of disguised observation becomes a problem for everyone in the profession; and to this extent, it is wholly within the bounds of etiquette for one sociologist to challenge the work of another on this score.

This objection has been raised several times before, and the answer most often given to it is that the people who are studied in this fashion —alcoholics or spiritualists or mental patients, for example—are not likely to read what we say about them anyway. Now this argument has the advantage of being correct a good deal of the time, but this fact does not prevent it from being altogether irrelevant. To begin with, the experience of the past few years should surely have informed us that the press is more than ready to translate our technical reports into news copy, and this means that we can no longer provide shelter for other people behind the walls of our own anonymity. But even if that were not the case, it is a little absurd for us to claim that we derive some measure of protection from the narrowness of our audience when we devote so much time trying to broaden it. The fact is that we are increasingly reaching audiences whose confidence we cannot afford to jeopardize, and we have every right to be afraid that such people may close their doors to sociological research if they learn to become too suspicious of our methods and intentions.

The third objection to be raised here, if only as a note in passing, concerns the responsibilities the profession should accept toward its students. The division of labor in contemporary sociology is such that a considerable proportion of the data·we use in our work is gathered by graduate students or other apprentices, and this proportion is even higher for research procedures that require the amount of energy and time necessary for participant observation. Of the dozen or more observers who took part in the studies I have cited, for example, all but one were graduate students. Now a number of sociologists who have engaged in disguised observation have reported that it is apt to pose serious moral problems and a good deal of personal discomfort, and I think one might well argue that this is a heavy burden to place on any person who is, by our own explicit standards, not yet ready for professional life. I am not suggesting here that students are too immature to make a seasoned choice in the matter. I am suggesting that they should not be asked to make what one defender of the method has called "real and excruciating moral decisions" while they are still students and presumably protected from the various dilemmas and contentions which occupy us in meetings like this—particularly since they are so likely to be academically, economically, and even psychologically dependent upon those elders who ask them to choose.[6]

The fourth objection I would like to raise here about the use of undercover observation is probably the most important—and yet the most remote from what is usually meant by the term "ethics." It seems to me that any attempt to use masquerades in social research betrays an extraordinary disrespect for the complexities of human interaction, and for this reason can only lead to bad science. Perhaps the most important responsibility of any sociologist is to appreciate how little he really knows about his intricate and elusive subject matter. We have at best a poor understanding of the human mind, of the communication

---

6. To keep the record straight, I might add that I first became interested in these matters when I was a graduate student and applied for one of the observer posts mentioned here.

signals that link one mind to another, or the social structures that emerge from those linkages—and it is the most arrant kind of oversimplification for us to think that we can assess the effect which a clever costume or a few studied gestures have on the social setting. The pose might "work" in the sense that the observer is admitted into the situation; but once this passage has been accomplished, how is he to judge his own influence on the lives of the people he is studying? This is a serious problem in every department of science, of course, and a good deal of time has been devoted to its solution. But the only way to cope with the problem in even a preliminary way is to have as clear a picture as possible of the social properties that the observer is introducing into the situation, and this is altogether impossible if we ourselves are not sure who he is. We can *impersonate* other modes of behavior with varying degrees of insight and skill, but we cannot *reproduce* them; and since this is the case, it seems a little irresponsible for a sociologist to assume that he can enter social life in any masquerade that suits his purpose without seriously disrupting the scene he hopes to study.

When people interact, they relate to one another at many different levels at once, and only a fraction of the messages communicated during that interchange are registered in the conscious mind of the participant. It may be possible for someone to mimic the conventional gestures of fear, but it is impossible for him to reproduce the small postural and chemical changes which go with it. It may be possible for a middle-class speaker to imitate the broader accents of lower-class speech, but his vocal equipment is simply not conditioned to do so without arousing at least a subliminal suspicion. It may be possible for a trained person to rearrange the slant of his body and reset his facial muscles to approximate the bearing óf someone else, but his performance will never be anything more than a rough imposture. Now we know that these various physiological, linguistic, and kinetic cues play an important part in the context of human interaction, but we have no idea how to simulate them—and what is probably more to the point, we never will. For one thing, we cannot expect to learn in a matter of hours what others have been practicing throughout a lifetime. For another, to imitate always means to parody, to caricature, to exaggerate certain details of behavior at the expense of others, and to that extent any person who selects a disguise will naturally emphasize those details which *he* assumes are most important to the character he is portraying. In doing so, of course, he is really only portraying a piece of himself. It is interesting to speculate, for example, why the Air Force lieutenant mentioned earlier thought he needed to present himself as a near-delinquent youth with a visible layer of personal problems in order to pose as an enlisted man. Whatever the reasoning behind this particular charade, it would certainly be reasonable for someone to suspect that it tells us more about the investigators' impression of enlisted men than it does about the men themselves—and since we have no way of learning whether this is true or not, we have lost rather than gained an edge of control over the situation we are hoping to understand. What the investigators had introduced into the situation was a creature of their own invention, and it would be hardly surprising if the results of their inquiry corresponded to some image they had in advance of the enlisted man's condition. (It is perhaps worth noting here that impersonation always seems easier for people looking down rather than up the status ladder. We find it reasonable to assume that officers "know how" to portray enlisted men or that sociologists have the technical capacity to pose as drunks or religious mystics, but it is not at all clear that the reverse would be equally true.)

This, then, is the problem. If we provide observers with special masks and coach them in the "ways" of the private world they are hoping to enter, how can we learn what is happening to the people who meet them in this disguise? What information is registered in the unconscious minds of the other people who live in that world? How does the social structure accommodate this peculiar invasion?

It is clear, I think, that something happens—something over which we have no control. Let me relate two incidents drawn from the studies mentioned earlier. The first has to do with the Air Force officer who posed as an enlisted man. In their report of the study, the investigators used several pages of a short paper to describe the elaborate masquerade they had fashioned for the observer and the coaching he had received in the ways of the adolescent subculture. "So successful was the tutoring," reads the brief report, "that when the time for 'enlistment' arrived, the recruiting sergeant . . . suggested that the observer not be accepted by the Air Force because by all appearances he was a juvenile delinquent."[7] And later, during an interview with a service psychologist, the observer was recommended for reclassification on the grounds that he appeared quite anxious over the death of his father. Now these events may indeed suggest that the pose was successful, for the observer *was* trying to look somewhat delinquent and *did* have a story memorized about the death of his father in an auto accident. But who would care to argue that the diagnosis of the sergeant and the psychologist were inaccurate? Surely something was wrong, and if they

---

7. Sullivan, Queen, and Patrick, op. cit., p. 663.

perceived an edge of uneasiness which reminded them of anxiety or detected a note of furtiveness which looked to them like delinquency, they may only have been responding to the presence of a real conflict between the observer and his mask. We may leave it to the psychoanalysts to ask whether vague anxieties about "killing" one's father are an unlikely impression for someone to leave behind when he is parading around with a new name, a new background, a new history, and, of course, a new set of parents. The authors of the article tell us that the observer "did have something of a problem to transform himself from a 27-year-old, college trained commissioned officer into a 19-year-old, near-delinquent high school graduate," and this is certainly easy to believe.[8] What is more difficult to believe is that such a transformation is possible at all—and if it is not, we can have very little confidence in the information gathered by the observer. Since we do not know to what kind of creature the enlisted men were responding, we do not know what sense to make of what they said and did.

The second example comes from the study of the apocalyptic religious group. At one point in the study, two observers arrived at one of the group's meeting places under instructions to tell quite ordinary stories about their experience in spiritualism in order to create as little commotion as possible. A few days afterwards, however, the leader of the group was overheard explaining that the two observers had appeared upset, excited, confused, and unsure of their errand at the time of their original visit, all of which helped confirm her suspicion that they had somehow been "sent" from another planet. In one sense, of course, this incident offered the observers an intriguing view of the belief structure of the cult, but in another sense, the leader's assessment of the situation was very shrewd: after all, the observers *had* been sent from another world, if not another planet, and she may have been quite right to sense that they were a bit confused and unsure of their errand during their early moments in the new job. "In both cases," the report informs us, the visits of the observers "were given as illustrations that 'strange things are happening.' "[9] Indeed, strange things *were* happening; yet we have no idea how strange they really were. It is almost impossible to evaluate the reaction of the group to the appearance of the pair of observers because we do not know whether they were seen as ordinary converts or as extraordinary beings. And it makes a difference, for in the first instance the investigators would be observing a response which fell within the normal range of the group's experience, while in the second

8. Stuart A. Queen, "Comment," *American Sociological Review*, 24 (1959): 399–400.
9. Festinger, Riecken, and Schacter, op. cit., pp. 241–42.

instance they would be observing a response which would never have taken place had the life of the group been allowed to run its own course.

My point in raising these two examples, it should be clear, is not to insist on the accuracy of these or any other interpretations, but to point out that a wide variety of such interpretations is possible so long as one has no control over the effects introduced by the observer. A company of recruits with a disguised officer in its midst is simply a different kind of organization than one without the same ingredient; a group of spiritualists which numbers as many as eight observers among its twenty or so members has a wholly different character than one which does not—and so long as we remain unable to account for such differences, we cannot know the meaning of the information we collect.

In one of the most sensible pieces written on the subject, Julius Roth has reminded us that all social research is disguised in one respect or another and that the range of ethical questions which bear on the issue must be visualized as falling on a continuum.[10] Thus, it is all very well for someone to argue that deliberate disguises are improper for sociologists, but it is quite another matter for him to specify what varieties of research activity fall within the range of that principle. Every ethical statement seems to lose its crisp authority the moment it is carried over into marginal situations where the conditions governing research are not so clearly stipulated. For instance, some of the richest material in the social sciences has been gathered by sociologists who were true participants in the group under study but who did not announce to other members that they were employing this opportunity to collect research data. Sociologists live careers in which they occasionally become patients, occasionally take jobs as steel workers or taxi drivers, and frequently find themselves in social settings where their trained eye begins to look for data even though their presence in the situation was not engineered for that purpose. It would be absurd, then, to insist as a point of ethics that sociologists should always introduce themselves as investigators everywhere they go and should inform every person who figures in their thinking exactly what their research is all about.

But I do think we can find a place to begin. If disguised observation sits somewhere on a continuum and is not easily defined, this only suggests that we will have to seek further for a relevant ethic and recognize that any line we draw on that continuum will be a little artificial. What I propose, then, at least as a beginning, is the following:

---

10. Julius A. Roth, "Comments on 'Secret Observation,' " *Social Problems*, 9 (1962): 283–84.

first, that it is unethical for a sociologist to *deliberately misrepresent* his identity for the purpose of entering a private domain *to which he is not otherwise eligible;* and second, that it is unethical for a sociologist to *deliberately misrepresent* the character of the research in which he is engaged. Now these negative sanctions leave us a good deal of leeway —more, perhaps, than we will eventually want. But they have the effect of establishing a stable point of reference in an otherwise hazy territory, and from such an anchored position as this we can move out into more important questions about invasion of privacy as an ethical issue.

In the meantime, the time has probably come for us to assume a general posture on the question of disguised participant observation even if we are not yet ready to state a specific ethic, and a logical first step in this direction would be to assess how most members of the profession feel about the matter. I am not suggesting that we poll one another on the merits of adopting a formal code, but that we take some kind of unofficial reading to learn what we can about the prevailing climate of opinion in the field. If we discover that a substantial number of sociologists are uncomfortable about the practice, then those who continue to employ it will at least know where they stand in respect to the "collective conscience" of their discipline. And if we discover that only a scattering of sociologists are concerned about the matter, we will at least have the satisfaction of knowing that the profession—as a profession—has accepted the responsibility of knowing its own mind.

12

On the Ethics of Disguised Observation

Norman K. Denzin
and a reply by Kai T. Erikson

Four papers recently published in this journal on the ethics of social research point to an important and as yet unresolved aspect of the sociologist's work.[1] In brief the questions are: "To whom is the sociologist responsible when he makes his observations?" "Does he have the right to observe persons who are unaware of his presence?" And, "What are the ethical consequences of those disguised observations that may disturb, alter, or cause discomfort to those observed?" Ten years ago Shils argued that sociologists have no right to make observations on persons who have not consented to be observed.[2] In several senses the papers to which I make reference follow Shils' dictum; however, it is the paper by Erikson on the ethical consequences of disguised observations that most directly adheres to Shils' position, and it is to this paper that I direct my comments.[3]

Erikson states that observations by the sociologist that either covertly or in some way deliberately disguise the role or intent of the investigator pose significant ethical problems for the sociologist in his relationship to his subjects, his colleagues, his students, and his data. I turn to each of Erikson's arguments and present the counterposition which he submits is either unethical or ethically ambiguous.

From Norman K. Denzin, "On the Ethics of Disguised Observation," and Kai T. Erikson, " A Reply to Denzin," *Social Problems* 15 (1968): 502–6, by permission of the authors and the Society for the Study of Social Problems.

1. *Social Problems*, 14 (Spring 1967). See the papers by Rainwater and Pittman, Erikson, Mills, and Seeley.

2. Edward A. Shils, "Social Inquiry and the Autonomy of the Individual," in Daniel Lerner, ed., *The Human Meaning of the Social Sciences* (Cleveland: Meridian, 1959), pp. 114–57.

3. Kai T. Erikson, "A Comment on Disguised Observation in Sociology," *Social Problems*, 14, no. 4 (Spring 1967):366–73.

First, a comment on my position.[4] I disagree with those who suggest the sociologist has no right to observe those who have not given their consent. I suggest the sociologist has the right to make observations on anyone in any setting to the extent that he does so with scientific intents and purposes in mind. The goal of any science is not willful harm to subjects, but the advancement of knowledge and explanation. Any method that moves us toward the goal, without unnecessary harm to subjects, is justifiable. The only qualification is that the method employed not in any deliberate fashion damage the credibility or reputation of the subject. The sociologist must take pains to maintain the integrity and anonymity of those studied—unless directed otherwise. This may require the deliberate withholding of certain findings from publication entirely, or until those observed have moved into positions where they could be done no harm.[5] My position holds that no areas of observation are in an a priori fashion closed to the sociologist, nor are any research methods in an a priori fashion defined as unethical. This position is clearly at odds with that of Shils and Erikson.

Erikson's first argument against disguised observation is that it represents an invasion of privacy of those studied. Such an interpretation, of course, assumes the sociologist can define beforehand what is a private and what is a public behavior setting. Cavan's recent findings suggest that any given behavior setting may, depending on the time of day and categories of participants present, be defined as either public or private in nature.[6] The implication is that the "privateness" of a behavior setting becomes an empirical question. To categorically define settings as public or private potentially ignores the perspective of those studied and supplants the sociologist's definitions for those studied. Erikson continues his argument by suggesting that when sociologists gain entry into private settings via disguised roles they potentially cause discomfort to those observed. Because the sociologist lacks the means to assess this induced discomfort, he has no right to disguise his intent or role in the research process.

If the research of Goffman is taken seriously, the statement that wearing masks, or disguising one's intents, raises ethical questions and causes discomfort during the research process may be challenged, for

4. See my *The Substance of Sociological Theory and Method: An Interactionist Interpretation* (Chicago: Aldine, tentative title, in process), chap. 14, "The Ethics of Social Research," where this is more fully elaborated.

5. This draws from Howard S. Becker, "Problems in the Publication of Field Studies," in Arthur J. Vidich, Joseph Bensman, and Maurice R. Stein, eds., *Reflections on Community Studies* (New York: Wiley, 1964), pp. 267–84.

6. Sherri Cavan, *Liquor License: An Ethnography of Bar Behavior* (Chicago: Aldine, 1966).

the proper question becomes not whether wearing a mask is unethical (since no mask is any more real than any other), but, rather, "Which mask should be worn?"[7] There is no straightforward answer; for we, as sociologists, assume a variety of masks or selves depending on where we find ourselves (e.g., the classroom, the office, the field, etc.). Who is to say which of these are disguises and which are real? My position is that any mask not deliberately donned to injure the subject is acceptable. To assert that an assumed role during the research process is necessarily unethical and harmful is meaningless in this context.

Second, Erikson argues that the sociologist who assumes a disguised role jeopardizes the broader professional community because in the event of exposure he could simultaneously close doors to future research, while tainting the image of his profession. My position is that any research method poses potential threats to fellow colleagues.[8] The community surveyed twice annually for the past ten years can just as easily develop an unfavorable image of sociology and refuse to be studied as can a local Alcoholics Anonymous club studied by a disguised sociologist. Every time the sociologist ventures into the outside world for purposes of research he places the reputation of the profession on the line, and to argue that disguised observations threaten that reputation more than the survey or the experiment ignores the potential impact these methods can and often do have.

Third, Erikson argues that we, as sociologists, owe it to our students not to place them in situations where they might have to assume a disguised research role. The assumption of such roles, Erikson suggests, places moral and ethical problems on the investigator and students should not have this burden placed on them. My position, based on my own and the experiences related by other colleagues, is that this feeling of uncertainty and ethical ambiguity can just as easily arise from the circumstances surrounding the first interview with an irate housewife in a social survey. Certain persons feel more comfortable in the role of disguised observer than in the role of survey interviewer, known participant observer, or laboratory observer, for example. Therefore the

---

7. Erving Goffman, *The Presentation of Self in Everyday Life* (New York: Doubleday, 1959).

8. Quite obviously, discovery in the disguised role, or the publication of findings from a study in which the research role was not clearly established, can have damaging effects, as the "Springdale" incident indicated. See Arthur J. Vidich and Joseph Bensman, "The Springdale Case: Academic Bureaucrats and Sensitive Townspeople," in Vidich, Bensman, and Stein, op. cit., pp. 313–49, for a review of the circumstances surrounding this incident. This is not the point at issue, however.

belief that encounters with subjects when in the role of disguised observer cause more investigator discomfort may be questioned. I suggest there is nothing inherent in the role that produces ethical or personal problems for the investigator. Instead, it is hypothesized that this represents definitions brought into the role and not definitions inherent in the role itself.

Erikson's fourth argument is that data gathered via the disguised method are faulty because an observer lacks the means to assess his disruptive effects on the setting and those observed. I propose that sociologists sensitive to this problem of disruption employ the method of post-observational inquiry, recently adopted by psychologists, during which the investigator asks the subject what he thought the experiment entailed.[9] After completing observations in the disguised role our presence could be made public and those observed could then be questioned concerning our effect on them. Such a procedure would (1) provide empirical data on our perceived disruptive effect, thereby allowing an assessment of this effect, and (2) allow us to measure empirically the amount of discomfort or harm our disguised presence created. Further, the investigator might make greater use of his day-to-day field notes to measure his own perceived impact.[10] Every time the sociologist asks a question of a subject, he potentially alters behavior and jeopardizes the quality of subsequent data. It seems unreasonable to assume that public research methods (e.g., surveys) do not also disrupt the stream of events under analysis. To argue that disguised roles cause more disruption seems ill-founded and, at the very least, is an empirical question.

Erikson concludes by noting that sociologists never reveal everything when they enter the field. I suggest we not only never reveal everything, but frequently this is not possible because we ourselves are not fully aware of our actual intentions and purposes (e.g., long-term field studies).

Summarizing his position, Erikson offers two ethical dictates: (1) it is unethical to deliberately misrepresent our identity to gain entry into private domains otherwise denied us; and (2) it is unethical to misrepresent the character of our research deliberately.

---

9. See Martin T. Orne, "On The Social Psychology of the Psychological Experiment: With Particular Reference to Demand Characteristics and Their Implications," in Carl W. Backman and Paul F. Secord, eds., *Problems in Social Psychology* (New York: McGraw-Hill, 1966), pp. 14–21.

10. Benjamin D. Paul, "Interview Techniques and Field Relationships," in A. L. Kroeber, ed., *Anthropology Today* (Chicago: University of Chicago Press, (1953), pp. 430–541, presents strategies for this use of field notes.

My reactions are perhaps in the minority among contemporary sociologists, but they indicate what I feel is a necessary uneasiness concerning the argument that sociologists are unethical when they investigate under disguise or without permission. To accept this position has the potential of making sociology a profession that studies only volunteer subjects. I suggest that such an argument misrepresents the very nature of the research process because sociologists have seldom stood above subjects and decided whom they had the right to study and whom they were obligated not to study. Instead, we have always established our domain during the process of research, largely on the basis of our own personal, moral, and ethical standards. In retrospect this can be seen to be so given the fact that such categories of persons as housewives, homosexuals, mental patients, prostitutes, and so on are now viewed as acceptable and legitimate persons for observation.

To conclude, I suggest that, in addition to these ethical questions, sociologists might also concern themselves with the fact that at this point in their scientific career they lack the automatic moral-legal license and mandate to gain entry into any research setting; nor do they have the power to withold information from civil-legal authorities after their data have been obtained.[11] As Project Camelot recently demonstrated, sociology (as a profession and science) has little power in the eyes of the public and broader civil-legal order. To cast ourselves in a position which sanctions research only on what persons give us permission to study continues and makes more manifest an uncomfortable public status. Certainly this need not be the case, as the current examples of psychiatry, medicine, the clergy, and the law indicate.

That my position involves ethical issues of the highest order cannot be denied, for I have placed the burden of ethical decision on the personal-scientific conscience of the individual investigator.[12] My value position should be clear, for I feel sociologists who have assumed those research roles and strategies Erikson calls unethical have contributed more substantive knowledge to such areas as small-group research than have those who have assumed more open roles. But again this is a matter of individual, as well as collective, scientific conscience and standards. The entry into any scientific enterprise potentially threatens someone's values—be it other sociologists or members of some society. We must always ask ourselves, "Whose side are we on?"[13] Unfortu-

11. Ned Polsky also points to this issue in his *Hustlers, Beats, and Others* (Chicago: Aldine, 1967), pp. 117–49.

12. This is also Becker's conclusion. See Becker, op. cit.

13. Howard S. Becker, "Whose Side Are We On?," *Social Problems*, 14 (Winter 1967): 239–48.

nately, I feel Erikson's position removes from the hands of the sociologist the right to make this decision. But perhaps, rather than engaging in polemics and debate, we might as a profession open these matters up to public discussion and empirical inquiry.[14]

NORMAN K. DENZIN

A REPLY TO DENZIN

I have been asked to make my remarks as brief as possible in the interests of preserving space, so I will respond to what I regard the more important of Professor Denzin's arguments in essentially the order that he presented them. Professor Denzin is certainly correct that his position is radically at odds with my own. He contends that any research method is justified so long as it is designed to advance scientific knowledge and does not willfully harm human subjects. This principle, I take, would admit to the roster of legitimate research techniques not only such practices as disguised observation, but the use of wiretapping and eavesdropping devices of one sort or another, and all the rest of the contrivances that come from the new technology of espionage. I suspect that most sociologists—perhaps even Professor Denzin—would prefer to draw a line somewhere short of this. If so, the main point at issue here is not whether sociologists should respect some limits in their search for data, but whether the deliberate use of masks falls inside or outside that line.

My objections to disguised observation are based on a broader set of considerations than are mentioned in Denzin's review. I feel that sociologists should not invade the privacy of other persons, no matter how genial their intentions or how impressive their scientific credentials, because the practice is damaging both to the climate of a free society and to the integrity of the profession that permits it. Now this is largely a personal reflection and I cannot see much point in arguing about it. But even if I agreed with Denzin that the case should rest with the subjects themselves, I would still have serious reservations about disguised observation. This is because I do not think that Denzin or I

---

14. I am currently engaged in a series of studies with Rita James Simon at the University of Illinois which will provide empirical data for a number of issues that to this point can only be taken at face value, or be resolved by personal choice.

An issue not treated in this note is the efficacy and ethicality of unobtrusive measures of observation in sociology. My position would sanction their use but, as I interpret Erikson, he would not. See Eugene J. Webb et al. *Unobtrusive Measures: Nonreactive Research in the Social Sciences* (Chicago: Rand McNally, 1966), where a catalogue of these measures is presented.

or anyone else really *knows* when we are harming other people; and, so long as this continues to be the case, it seems to me that we have no right to let others take the risks for projects that happen to mean something to us without first obtaining their informed consent. I am not at all sure that I know what "informed consent" is, but it is evident that disguised observation does not fit under the heading.

I made four general points in my original article and Professor Denzin has discussed them in order. Regarding the first, I agree that it is sometimes difficult to distinguish between "private" and "public" settings in any objective fashion, but I propose the following rule of thumb: Whenever an investigator goes to all the trouble of disguising his own identity and introducing himself as someone he knows he is not in order to enter a social sphere to which he is not otherwise eligible, then it is fair to infer (*a*) that *he,* at least, defines that sphere as private, and (*b*) that he expects others in that situation to define it similarly. Moreover, I think it is simply not true that "no mask is any more real than any other," and in this assertion I would claim to be a student of Goffman's too. Every man plays many parts, to be sure; but every sane and moral man knows that certain roles in the repertory of his culture are proper for him to play while others are not, and it seems to me that we are completely forgetting what we know about the nature of human personality and the development of social selves if we view the matter as flatly as Denzin suggests. It is one thing for him and me to shift social gears as we move in a reasonably defined orbit from the office to the classroom and out into the field, but it is quite another thing for us to emulate those of our colleagues who join a group of alcoholics dressed in clothes picked out of a garbage can or who impersonate enlisted men while receiving the pay and privileges of officers. The elaborate disguises that most employers of the method have devised in order to "pose" (their word) as someone they are not should be testimony enough to the fact that they are aware of the difference; and, if this is not persuasive, we need only consider what would happen if an unlicensed stranger were to appear in a professional gathering and present himself as an instructor of sociology. We might denounce it as a fraud, diagnose it as a delusion, or pass it off as a prank, but few of us would experience any difficulty determining whether the mask was real or not.

As for the second point, Professor Denzin offers a compelling argument and I will yield. It is of course true that other forms of sociological research have a potential for closing doors to future investigation. I happen to feel that the risks here are considerably greater, but Denzin is correct to suppose that this estimate is based as much on conviction as it is on information.

As for the third point, it may be that Denzin has me there, too. I have no particularly good reasons to insist that students are more compromised while engaged in undercover observation than they are, say, when confronting irate housewives during a door-to-door survey. Granting this, I am left the choice either of arguing that students should be protected from this latter practice as well, or of withdrawing as gracefully as possible. I think a strong case might be made for the first of these options, but instead I will retreat to the second—noting only that my original intention was to point out the incongruities one sees in the arguments of sociologists who discuss the moral ambiguities of disguised observation and then send students out to do the work.

The fourth point is in many ways the critical one, and here I suspect that Professor Denzin has confused the kind of undercover work I was discussing in my paper with other forms of small-group research. He contends that we could measure the effect that disguised observation has on subjects by following up the attempt with such methods as post-observational inquiry and the like. Now I think it is reasonable to assume that researchers wear masks primarily when they cannot show their faces, and I cannot imagine why people who will not respond to a more open kind of investigation in the first instance should submit to a few cheerful rounds of interviewing in the second. People who have seen their trust violated, their privacy invaded, their personal worlds exposed, are not likely to be the most cooperative or reliable informants —unless, of course, Denzin is proposing that a second wave of observers should dress in costumes and follow the first, in which case all the objections I raised earlier are simply doubled. I agree that some empirical evidence would be valuable here: my problem is that no one to date has come up with any and I doubt very much that anyone ever will. The conditions that prompt investigators to wear disguises are almost always conditions that discourage any reasonable hope of measuring the disruptive influence of the observer.

The fact that the position I recommend limits our field of observation to volunteers is, I agree, something of an inconvenience, but any ethical stance is a limitation on one's freedom of movement and I cannot see that this is a reasonable objection. From a purely scientific point of view, after all, it is also an inconvenience that physicians cannot experiment on the persons of patients. The presumption in our society has always been that some things are more important than the needs of researchers.

In this connection, Denzin is concerned that sociologists do not enjoy the license to "gain entry into any research setting" and proposes that this privilege be extended to us. What he fails to appreciate is that none of the professions he lists enjoy this license *when they are engaged in research,* but only when they are serving the interests of clients. If we were to find ourselves dealing only with volunteers, we would certainly be limiting our terrain; but we would then be in exactly the same position as those physicians and lawyers whose status Professor Denzin is so anxious for us to share. The only investigators I can think of who enjoy privileges when engaged in the business of gathering information for their own professional purposes are policemen and espionage agents, and I doubt very much that any of us would like to operate with the general level of trust and respect that they command.

In short, my main disagreement with Professor Denzin is his assumption—stated implicitly, at least—that what is good for sociology is inherently ethical. His "value position," as he informs us near the end of his remarks, is that researchers "who have assumed those research roles and strategies . . . have contributed more substantive knowledge . . . than have those who assumed more open roles." I do not think that this is true by any means, but, even if it were, it would not strike me as the firmest moral ground on which to build a professional ethic. Surely the case should be decided on other merits.

I do not know whether Denzin is in the minority or not, as he seems to feel: but he has stated his case with refreshing candor and I admire his willingness to join the discussion in so straightforward a fashion.

KAI T. ERIKSON

PART IV

Behavior Systems
and Criminal Careers

The framework that we construct to understand social processes in our everyday lives takes form in very subtle ways. Not many of us can recall how and when we first learned to distinguish between categories of persons, the consequences of behaviors, or the tangible products of human endeavor, but we learned quickly that such distinctions were important. Those of us who followed the sciences—behavioral or physical—discovered that precise and inclusive frameworks must be developed to understand, much less predict, our objects of study. The fact that everyday activities in our personal lives require conceptual organization is so obvious that we give little attention to the scientist who seeks to impose order upon reluctant data. Yet scientific explanations cannot proceed systematically without a typology of the phenomena at hand, and nowhere has this task been more arduous than in criminology.

The criminologist is often faced with the need to impose greater precision upon his data than the casual observer or even criminal justice personnel do. Thus, a crime such as "robbery" must further be defined in terms of the presence or absence of a weapon, the proceeds obtained (if any), and the circumstances of the offense. Similarly, "sex offenses" may conceal statutory distinctions based upon the age and sex of the victim and the type of sex act perpetrated. A troublesome generic term is "prisons," which actually forms a typology of precinct lockups, county or municipal jails, reformatories, penitentiaries, halfway houses for prerelease offenders, or correctional field units (work camps or farms). Making such distinctions is one research objective, for in the process of identifying types, much can be learned about their operating dimensions. A second objective is to show how a typology facilitates the explanation of phenomena within its province.

Valuable typologies must meet a number of requirements, including: (1) a precise statement of their intent; (2) explicit defining characteristics on the basis of which classification may be undertaken; and (3) a set of types sharing a common dimension. Although criminal typologies have been developed using the legal definitions of offenses and also using individual characteristics such as sex, personality traits, or biological attributes, most sociologists have built upon the "behavior system" concept, for this perspective appears to have the greatest potential for scientific inquiry. This approach draws attention to the dynamic, patterned features of much criminal behavior: the sources of criminal motivation, the act itself (whether legally or ethically defined), and the victim's role in being exploited. As we have seen earlier in this volume, newly developed interest in the victim has focused upon the social situations in which he routinely operates, the persons with whom he associates, and his styles of interaction with both familiar and unfamiliar persons.

The distinguishing properties of a criminal behavior system are essentially three: (1) each system has common definitions of how offenses are committed, how expertise in criminal matters is attained, and how social relations with others—criminal and noncriminal—should proceed; (2) every system has a distinctive lifestyle or subculture which exists apart from yet governs the behavior of the participants who make it up; and (3) those who partake of a behavior system develop criminalistic conceptions of themselves and identify with others who are similarly disposed. As an illustration, consider the occupation "thief." The subculture of professional thieves includes symbols of expertise and a set of shared perceptions about the police, prisons, plausible targets for criminal exploitation, and "suckers" who work at legitimate jobs for a living. Even the term "thief" itself has a long history of shared denotation among criminals in reference to each other, yet may have little to do with "thieving." Neither is it a term of opprobrium, for it may be complimentary to say, "Oh, yes, I knew him at Leavenworth. He was an old thief out of Kansas City." Similarly a defendant in a criminal case may point to himself with pride as "a stickup man, seven days a week."

Some of the most illuminating work being done by research criminologists concentrates upon the system attributes of check forgery, embezzling, armed robbery, sex offenses, prostitution, homicide, chronic drunkenness, confidence swindling, pool hustling, and organized crime. On the other side of the ledger, interesting system studies have been done on the agencies of response to crime: the police handling skid row residents or the mentally ill, prosecutors systematically "plea bargaining" cases, and bail-bondsmen providing freedom at a price.

An additional attraction of the behavior systems approach is its emphasis upon the *career* features of some offenders. By and large, the preponderance of crime is committed by persons who are not acting out of idiosyncratic and spontaneous motives, but instead have programmed lawlessness into their daily routine. These constitute the recidivist problem shared by most large cities. The concept of career, an important tool for understanding legitimate work roles, also draws attention to common elements of illegitimate occupations as well. Careers of all types involve recruiting new personnel, fostering an identification with the parent organization or their associates, and training recruits in skills pertinent to their role. Since a great deal is known about these elements as they operate in the case of dentists, used-car salesmen, domestic servants, and police officers, the convergence of information on criminal careers with findings on those legitimately employed holds considerable promise.

The first of five selections to follow, by Clinard and Quinney, is drawn from their extensive work on criminal typology. They review some past work in the area, then generate a behavior systems model comprising nine types of criminality.

Howard S. Becker's paper, "Deviant Careers," portrays a sequential paradigm of career transformation, drawing upon a range of deviance from homosexuality to marijuana use. Of particular interest is his contention that reactions of others to the deviant are important determinants of progression through the sequence. Becker's contribution has been the basis for much writing in the area of labeling theory.

The study by James H. Bryan, "Apprenticeships in Prostitution," emphasizes neither the personalities of participants nor the illegal character of their work. Instead Bryan focuses upon their recruitment and initial training period. Data support the view that early call girl socialization is essential to the establishment of an adequate clientele, avoidance of "trouble," and the maintenance of a favorable self-image.

In an excerpt from his book on the Mafia, Francis A. J. Ianni shows how Italian domination of an American way of life has undergone transition. According to his findings, control over organized crime as an avenue of social and economic mobility has diffused to blacks and Hispanics.

The final selection, by Neal Shover, is a study of professional burglary. Analyzing both internal and external dynamics of the role, Shover points out that problems confronting the occupation (e.g., sophisticated security systems and a reduction in negotiable proceeds) may be causing its decline.

Selections from the enormous literature on behavior systems and career criminality are provided below for the interested reader.

1. *Typologies in Criminology: History and Analysis*

Clinard, Marshall B., and Quinney, Richard, *Criminal Behavior Systems: A Typology,* second edition (New York: Holt, Rinehart and Winston, 1973).

Driver, Edwin, D., "A Critique of Typologies in Criminology," *Sociological Quarterly* 9 (1968): 356–73.

Gibbs, Jack P., "Needed: Analytical Typologies in Criminology," *Southwestern Social Science Quarterly* 40 (1960): 321–29.

Glaser, Daniel, "The Classification of Offenses and Offenders," in *Handbook of Criminology,* ed. Daniel Glaser (Chicago: Rand McNally, 1974), pp. 45–83.

Hartjen, Clayton A., and Gibbons, Don C., "An Empirical Investigation of a Criminal Typology," *Sociology and Social Research* 54 (1969): 56–62.

Lindesmith, A. R., and Dunham, H. W., "Some Principles of Criminal Typology," *Social Forces* 19 (1941): 307–14.

Roebuck, Julian B., "Approaches to Criminal Typology," *Criminal Typology* (Springfield, Ill.: Charles C Thomas, 1967), pp. 3–30.

2. *Diverse Research in Criminal Behavior Systems*

Bell, Daniel, "Crime as an American Way of Life," in *The End of Ideology* (New York: Free Press, Macmillan, 1960), pp. 115–36.

Cameron, Mary Owen, *The Booster and the Snitch: Department Store Shoplifting* (New York: Free Press of Glencoe, 1964).

Camp, George M., *Nothing to Lose: A Study of Bank Robbery in America,* unpublished Ph.D. dissertation, Yale University, 1967.

Clinard, Marshall B., *The Black Market: A Study of White Collar Crime* (New York: Rinehart, 1952).

Cressey, Donald R., *Other People's Money* (Glencoe, Ill.: Free Press, 1953).

————, *Theft of the Nation: The Structure and Operations of Organized Crime in America* (New York: Harper & Row, 1969).

Einstadter, Werner J., "The Social Organization of Armed Robbery," *Social Problems* 17 (1969): 64–82.

Geis, Gilbert, "Upperworld Crime," in *Current Perspectives on Criminal Behavior,* ed. Abraham S. Blumberg (New York: Alfred A. Knopf, 1974), pp. 114–37.

Ianni, Francis A. J., *Black Mafia: Ethnic Succession in Organized Crime* (New York: Simon and Schuster, 1974).

Inciardi, James A., "The Adult Firesetter: A Typology," *Criminology* 8 (1970): 145–55.

————, *Careers in Crime* (Chicago: Rand McNally, 1975).

Jackson, Bruce, *A Thief's Primer* (New York: Macmillan, 1969).

Klockars, Carl B., *The Professional Fence* (New York: Free Press, 1974).

Lemert, Edwin M., "The Behavior of the Systematic Check Forger," *Social Problems* 6 (1958): 141–49.

Maurer, David W., *The American Confidence Man* (Springfield, Ill.: Charles C Thomas, 1974).

Roebuck, Julian, "The Negro Numbers Man as a Criminal Type: The Construction and Application of a Typology," *Journal of Criminal Law, Criminology and Police Science* 54 (1963): 48–60.

Shaw, Clifford R., *The Jack-Roller: A Delinquent Boy's Own Story* (Chicago: University of Chicago Press, 1930).

Sutherland, Edwin H., *White Collar Crime* (New York: Dryden Press, 1949).

Wolfgang, Marvin E., *Patterns in Criminal Homicide* (Philadelphia: University of Pennsylvania Press, 1958).

13

The Behavior Systems Approach to Criminal Typology

Marshall B. Clinard and Richard Quinney

TYPOLOGIES IN CRIMINOLOGY

A diverse and wide range of behaviors is included in the category of crime. The one characteristic which all the behaviors have in common is that they have been defined as criminal by recognized political authority. Much of the work in criminology has been concerned with crime in general. Because of the increasing realization, however, that crime refers to a great variety of behaviors, criminologists have in recent years turned their attention to the study of particular types of crime. Thus, criminologists are now giving greater attention to the identification, classification, and description of types of criminal behavior.

Moreover, efforts are being made to delineate categories of crime and criminal behavior which are homogeneous with respect to a specific explanation. In criminology, considering the wide range of phenomena subsumed under the concept of crime, a general theory may be formulated after specific types of crime have been established. [Figure 13–1] illustrates a method of theory construction in criminology.

The interdependence of typology and theory construction is clear. Theoretical assumptions are necessary for the formulation of types, and a typology forces the reformulation of general theory. An adequate explanation of crime will show not only how the explanation applies to all crime but how it is specified to explain the various types of crime.

From Marshall B. Clinard and Richard Quinney, *Criminal Behavior Systems: A Typology*, Second Edition, (New York: Holt, Rinehart and Winston, 1973), pp. 2–21, by permission of the authors and The Dryden Press. Copyright © 1967, 1973 by Holt, Rinehart and Winston, Publishers. Footnotes have been renumbered.

FIGURE 3-1.

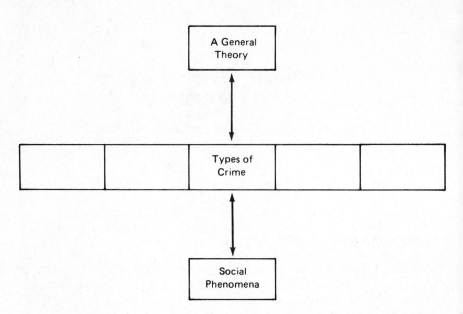

Criminologists in the past have constructed and utilized many different typologies of crime and criminals. The most common typologies have been the legalistic, individualistic, and social.

Legalistic Typologies

The oldest and still the most frequently used forms of classification are based on the legal definition of the offense. A familiar legalistic classification is in terms of the seriousness of the offense as indicated by the kind of punishment provided for the behavior. The most serious offenses are called felonies and are usually punishable by confinement in a state prison or by death. The less serious offenses are called misdemeanors and are usually punishable by fines or by confinement in a local jail. As a classification of crime this is not very useful and is ambiguous because it is difficult to make clear-cut distinctions between the two major types of offenses. For example, many criminal acts classified as felonies in one state are classified as misdemeanors in other states. Also the form of punishment prescribed for a given offense differs from time to time and from place to place.

It is common also to identify the criminal act (or the criminal) in terms of a legal category. Thus, criminals are referred to as murderers, burglars, robbers, embezzlers, and rapists in terms of specific offenses defined in the criminal code. The category of "crimes against the person" includes such illegal acts as murder, assault, and rape; "crimes against property" include burglary, larceny, forgery, and automobile theft; and "crimes against public order" consist of such behavior as prostitution, gambling, drunkenness, disturbing the peace, and the use of narcotics. This method of classifying criminals suffers from a number of disadvantages.[1] For example (1) it tells nothing about the person and the circumstances associated with the offense, nor does it consider the social context of the criminal act, as in the case of rape or the theft of an auto; (2) it creates a false impression of specialization by implying that criminals confine themselves to the kind of crime for which they happen to be caught or convicted; (3) it is a common practice in order to secure easy convictions to allow offenders to receive a reduced sentence by "plea copping" or pleading guilty to a lesser charge that may only slightly resemble the original charge or offense; (4) because the legal definition of a criminal act varies according to time and place, the legal classification of crime presents problems for comparative analysis; and (5) most important of all, the use of legal categories in a classification assumes that offenders with a certain legal label, such as burglars, robbers, auto thieves, and rapists, are all of the same type or are a product of a similar process.

There have been a number of attempts to overcome some of the problems of legalistic classifications, while still utilizing the legal categories. Although the categories of crime defined in the criminal law may not be appropriate for sociological purposes, they may nevertheless be used in various ways in forming types of crime. One possibility is that types may be defined *within* specific legal categories. For example, burglars, depending upon their mode of operation, could be divided into housebreakers, safecrackers, professional burglars, and amateur burglars. Another possibility is that legal categories may be *combined*. Criminologists who favor the strategy of defining types according to legal categories claim that the procedure is desirable because official data concerned with criminal histories exist in terms of legal nomenclature, and because the criminal code contains specific operational definitions of criminal behavior.

Roebuck has constructed a criminal typology based on arrest records of 1,155 prison inmates in the District of Columbia reformatory.[2] On the basis of arrest patterns, Roebuck postulates four main

---

1. See Richard R. Korn and Lloyd W. McCorkle, *Criminology and Penology* (New York: Holt, Rinehart and Winston, 1959), pp. 143–44.

2. Julian B. Roebuck, *Criminal Typology: The Legalistic, Physical-Constitutional-Hereditary, Psychological-Psychiatric and Sociological Approaches* (Springfield, Ill.· Charles C Thomas, Publisher, 1967).

types of careers: the single arrest pattern, the multiple pattern, the mixed pattern, and no pattern. The single pattern refers to those situations in which an individual is arrested three or more times for one type of crime, such as narcotic violations or burglaries. The multiple pattern refers to those situations in which an individual presents two or more patterns. The mixed pattern refers to those situations in which an individual is arrested three or more times but no single pattern emerges. The fourth type, no pattern, refers to those situations in which an individual is arrested fewer than three times. Employing this scheme, thirteen different patterns of crime emerge: single robbery, single narcotics, single numbers game, single burglary, single sex offense, single auto theft, single confidence game, single forgery, double pattern (larceny and burglary), double pattern (assault and drunkenness), triple pattern (larceny, assault, and drunkenness), mixed patterns, and no patterns. His typology includes such offender types as "Negro drinkers and assaulters," "Negro drug addicts," "Negro armed robbers," and "Negro jack-of-all-trades offenders." The types are then described and compared according to the social and personal characteristics of the offenders in each respective type.

Whereas typologies such as this have been useful in pointing out the error of using a single arrest to type an offender and suggesting instead career patterns, they have a number of limitations. One has been the tendency to categorize offenders by race, as a Negro or Caucasian armed robber, which may not be an especially meaningful distinction. Moreover, such inductively derived typologies could mount up indefinitely by this method of using arrests.

Another possibility regarding the use of legal categories is that sociological types may be constructed that *cut across* some of the behaviors included in a number of legal categories. Cressey, for example, included within "criminal violation of financial trust" some of the behaviors officially handled as forgery, confidence game, embezzlement, and larceny by bailee.[3] As practical as these procedures of using various legal classifications appear, they have largely resulted in innumerable unrelated categories of crime lacking a common frame of reference. They have not generated integrated typological schemes.

An important problem remains in the construction of legal typologies of crime. The problem is in respect to the controversy over what behaviors and what persons should be regarded as criminal.[4] This con-

---

3. Donald R. Cressey, *Other People's Money* (New York: The Free Press, 1953).
4. See Paul W. Tappan, "Who Is the Criminal?" *American Sociological Review*, 12 (February 1947), pp. 96–102.

troversy is relevant to the construction of typologies of crime. Posed in question form: At what stage of the criminal defining process should persons and behaviors be regarded as criminal? Is it at the stage of official detection, at the stage of official adjudication, or at the stage of official disposition? Or, to state the extreme, should a typology of crime include persons and behaviors irrespective of official legal action? Even if the criterion of official legal action is dropped in the construction of a typology, there is still the problem of how long a person remains a criminal after he violates the criminal law. Ultimately the selection of the stage of legal action that is going to be used in defining the persons and behavior to be included in a typology of crime depends upon the purpose of the typology and the kinds of research problems that are anticipated.

The use of legal categories of crime is valid when the purpose is to understand the process by which behavior becomes defined as criminal.[5] Since criminality is not inherent in behavior but is a quality conferred upon individuals and acts by others, the study of the formulation and administration of the law is important to the criminologist. The legal definition of crime is the best indication of how the category of crime is created as a form of public policy. Any typology could incorporate the legal aspects of criminal offenses. The legal category itself is a social phenomenon.

Individualistic Typologies

Several Italian criminologists who rejected the legal definitions of crime over seventy-five years ago were instrumental in turning the attention of criminologists to classification and to the use of criteria other than those found in the criminal law.[6] The early criminologists of the Italian or positivist school delimited types of offenders in terms of a heterogeneous collection of personal attributes. Lombroso (1835–1909), for example, identified, to his satisfaction at least, a "born criminal" with a unique, inferior physique. Later, Lombroso recognized other types of criminals, including (1) the insane criminal, (2) the criminal by passion, and (3) the occasional criminal, a type that emphasized the social aspects of the offender as well as individualistic characteristics.

---

5. Richard Quinney, *The Social Reality of Crime* (Boston: Little, Brown & Company, 1970), pp. 3–25; Austin T. Turk, *Criminality and Legal Order* (Chicago: Rand McNally & Company, 1969), pp. 8–18.

6. See Hermann Mannheim, ed., *Pioneers in Criminology* (London: Stevens & Sons, Ltd., 1960), Chaps. 1 and 19; Stephen Schafer, *Theories in Criminology* (New York: Random House, 1969), Chaps. 6 and 7.

Garofalo (1852–1934), an Italian jurist, maintained that criminals are characterized by psychological anomalies. He divided these defectives into four categories: (1) typical criminals, or murderers who kill for enjoyment, (2) violent criminals, (3) criminals deficient in pity and probity, and (4) lascivious criminals. In a not too different fashion, Ferri (1856–1929) distinguished between five types of criminals, namely (1) the insane, (2) the born, (3) the habitual, (4) the occasional, and (5) the passionate.

Clinical psychologists and psychiatrists have subsequently attempted to classify criminal offenders by utilizing either a single personality trait or a syndrome or grouping of traits. Accordingly, criminal offenders have been grouped according to whether they are immature, emotionally insecure, dependent, hostile, antisocial, nonconformists, or aggressive. Sometimes a single trait has been used to apply to a variety of criminal careers differing in both the nature and the seriousness of the activity. Consequently, personality trait syndromes by themselves have little meaning for distinguishing either types of criminal careers or the behavior of criminals from noncriminals who also may have these traits.

In terms of individualistic factors, offenders also have been divided according to their sex, age, rural-urban background, and other personal attributes. Sex is not a meaningful criterion for classification for, with the exception of prostitution, women in the western world now commit as wide a variety of offenses as men, although not as frequently. It is increasingly difficult to distinguish clearly among offenders merely upon the basis of sex. Likewise, age is a somewhat meaningless classification because all types of crime are committed by persons of varying ages. Offenders committing the most overt serious crimes, however, are more frequently under twenty-five years of age, while the so-called white collar crimes of business and professional persons are committed by older persons. Classification of offenders by age has little merit, for the criminal development of an offender may have little relation to his age. An offender may be considered developed criminally if he has unfavorable attitudes toward laws, property, and the police, professional knowledge of techniques to commit crimes and avoid prosecution, and a framework of rationalizations to support his conduct. These qualities can be present in a teen-age offender and be comparatively absent in a middle-aged one.

The individualistic approach to criminal classification employs the questionable assumption that individuals with particular personal characteristics commit certain types of crime. In addition, the individualistic approach implies that persons with these characteristics specialize in particular offenses. Finally, while individualistic classifications may have limited diagnostic possibilities for treatment, they have little utility for the construction of sociological theories of criminal behavior.

Social Typologies

If crime is to be studied as a social phenomenon, it is necessary to delineate types of criminal behavior according to the social context of the criminal offender and the criminal act. A number of such types have been developed. Two European criminologists of the last century, Mayhew and Moreau, proposed criminal types based on the way in which crime is related to the various *activities* of the criminal. Mayhew distinguished between professional criminals, who earn their living through criminal activity, and accidental offenders, who commit criminal acts as a result of unanticipated circumstances. Moreau added one other type of criminal to Mayhew's types. Recognizing that many of the criminals who commit crimes against the person cannot be included in either of Mayhew's types, Moreau designated the *habitual criminal* as one who continues to commit criminal acts for such diverse reasons as a deficiency in intelligence and lack of self-control.

Aware of the Mayhew-Moreau criminal types, Lindesmith and Dunham devised a continuum of criminal behavior ranging from the *individualized criminal* to the *social criminal.*[7] The criminal acts of the individualized criminal are committed for diverse and personal reasons, with the behavior finding little cultural support. The criminal behaviors of the social criminal, on the other hand, are supported and prescribed by group norms. The social criminal through his criminal behavior achieves status and recognition within a group. In addition, although the social criminal uses illegitimate means, the goals he seeks, such as economic gain and security, are valued by the broader culture. The types of criminals found between the extremes share in varying degrees the characteristics of one or the other polar types. In the individualized category is the situational or accidental criminal, for example, a murderer who prior to the crime was a law-abiding person. In the social category is the professional criminal, such as the racketeer or the confidence man. Lindesmith and Dunham also employ a third type, *habitual-situational.* This type is utilized to classify all those criminals who actually are not professional, but are more than situational or accidental offenders. This type of criminal is described as the offender who, while not a professional, is constantly in trouble with the legal

---

7. Alfred R. Lindesmith and H. Warren Dunham, "Some Principles of Criminal Typology," *Social Forces,* 19 (March 1941), pp. 307–314.

authorities, committing in a somewhat fortuitous and free-wheeling manner such crimes as robbery and larceny, intermixed with legitimate economic activities. A slum juvenile delinquent might be described as *habitual-situational.* This trichotomy, while consisting of rather broad categories, does not, however, appear to be exhaustive. For instance, as Lindesmith and Dunham suggest, white collar crime committed by persons in the upper socioeconomic groups does not seem to fit in any of the three categories. It is not a situational or accidental crime, since in many cases the individual criminal may have committed the crime continuously over a lifetime. It is not a professional crime, for in many cases (such as embezzlement) the offender may be a situational criminal. Also, it is not a habitual-situational crime, for Lindesmith and Dunham definitely describe this type as being overt in nature, and white collar crime is characterized by anything but overtness. More important, research subsequent to the development of this typology has indicated considerable group and social factors in such offenses as murder, aggravated assault, and forcible rape which they had tended to regard as of the individual type.

A number of criminologists have stressed vocational aspects of certain forms of crime; that some crimes are committed by persons who pursue criminal behavior as a career. (For example, Reckless has suggested two types of criminal careers: ordinary and professional.[8]) As career crimes, these three types of crime are similar in that they usually involve property offenses for the purpose of gain; the criminals tend to specialize in particular violations; the commission of the offenses requires various degrees of skill and experience; crime is pursued as a way of life; and career criminals continue in crime for a long period of time, possibly for a lifetime. In terms of differences among the career types, ordinary criminals represent the lowest rank of career crime. They engage in conventional crimes, such as robbery, larceny, and burglary, which require limited skill. Ordinary criminals lack the organization to avoid arrest and conviction. Professional criminals, on the other hand, are highly skilled and are thus able to obtain considerable amounts of money without being detected. Because of organization and contact with other professional criminals, these offenders are often able to escape conviction. Professional criminals specialize in offenses that require skill rather than violence, such as confidence games, pickpocketing, shoplifting, sneak thievery, and counterfeiting. Whereas this distinction is important and valid insofar as it goes, it is limited to those who make an occupation or career out of crime.

---

8. Walter C. Reckless, *The Crime Problem,* 4th ed. (New York: Appleton-Century-Crofts, 1967), pp. 279–98.

A more comprehensive typology has been developed by Gibbons. His typology is based primarily on role-careers in which identifiable changes occur in different offender types.

There are some criminal patterns in which role-performance is begun and terminated in a single illegal act, and there are others in which involvement in the deviant role continues over several decades or more, as in the instance of professional criminals. Some delinquent roles lead to adult criminality, whereas other delinquent roles are terminal ones, for they do not normally precede or lead to involvement in adult deviation. In turn, some criminal roles have their genesis in juvenile delinquent behavior, whereas certain other forms of adult criminality develop in adulthood and are not presaged by delinquent careers. Then, too, some role-careers involve more changes in the component episodes of the pattern than do others. Semiprofessional property offenders are one illustration. This pattern begins at the onset of minor delinquent acts in early adolescence. Such a career line frequently leads to more serious forms of delinquency with advancing age: repeated police contacts, commitment to juvenile institutions, "graduation" into adult forms of illegal activity, and more contacts with law enforcement and correctional agencies. Over this lengthy development sequence, the social psychological characteristics of offenders also change. For example, the degree of hostility toward policemen and correctional agents exhibited by the adult semiprofessional criminal is likely to be considerably greater than the antagonism demonstrated by the same person at an early age. The same comment could be made regarding changes in self-image, attitudes, and other matters.[9]

A uniform frame of reference employing the criteria of "definitional dimensions" and "background dimensions" is used by Gibbons. The definitional dimensions consist of: (1) the nature of the offense behavior, (2) the interactional setting with others in which the offense takes place, (3) self-concept of the offender, (4) attitudes toward society and agencies of social control such as the police, and (5) the steps in the role career of the offender. There are four aspects of the "background dimensions" of each type: (1) social class, (2) family background, (3) peer group associations, and (4) contact with defining agencies such as the police, courts, and prisons. On this basis Gibbons set up fifteen adult types and nine juvenile types.

9. Don C. Gibbons, *Changing the Lawbreaker: The Treatment of Delinquents and Criminals,* © 1965, Prentice-Hall, Inc., Englewood Cliffs, N.J., pp. 51–52. Gibbons utilizes his typology in his criminology textbook, *Society, Crime, and Criminal Careers* (Englewood Cliffs, N.J.: Prentice-Hall, 1968), pp. 193–433.

Adult Types	*Juvenile Types*
Professional thief	Predatory gang delinquent
Professional "heavy" criminal	Conflict gang delinquent
Semiprofessional property criminal	Casual gang delinquent
Property offender—"one-time loser"	Casual delinquent,
Automobile thief—"joyrider"	nongang member
Naive check forger	Automobile thief—"joyrider"
White-collar criminal	Drug user—heroin
Professional "fringe" violator	Overly aggressive delinquent
Embezzler	Female delinquent
Personal offender—"one-time	"Behavior problem" delinquent
loser"	
"Psychopathic" assaultist	
Violent sex offender	
Nonviolent sex offender—	
nonviolent "rapo"	
Nonviolent sex offender—	
statutory rape	
Narcotic addict—heroin	

Unfortunately, some of his types are not sharply delineated and tend to overlap or be unclear as to their specific characteristics. Other types depart from an essentially general group and cultural frame of reference and present a largely individualistic psychological orientation which is somewhat contradictory to the overall frame of reference.

A somewhat different typology has been developed by Cavan, which gives principal consideration to the public reaction to crime and the criminal's reaction to the public.[10] In an analysis of the interaction between the public and the criminal, seven types of criminal behavior are constructed: (1) criminal contraculture (professional crime, robbery, burglary), (2) extreme underconformity (for example, occasional drunkenness), (3) minor underconformity (for example, embezzlement), (4) "average" conformity (minor pilfering), (5) minor overconformity (exactness in obeying laws and moral codes), (6) extreme overconformity (attempts to reform society by persuasion and legal means), and (7) ideological contraculture (strenuous efforts to remodel society, possibly through the use of illegal means). Because societal reaction is crucial to the criminal's self-concept and subsequent behavior, it is an important variable to be included in a typology of crime.

---

10. Ruth Shonle Cavan, *Criminology*, 3d ed. (New York: Thomas Y. Crowell Company, 1962), Chap. 3.

An indication of the importance of the typological approach in modern criminology can be seen in the attention devoted to the subject in several contemporary criminology textbooks. Bloch and Geis, for example, give considerable attention to types of criminal behavior systems and to the social and cultural structure in which criminal behavior systems arise.[11] Their types of criminal behavior systems include professional crime, organized crime, homicides and assaults, sex offense, property offenders, white collar crime, and public order offenses.

PRINCIPLES OF CRIMINAL TYPOLOGY

There are several methodological problems in the construction of criminal typologies. These problems serve as the basic principles of criminal typology.

Classification and Typology

While not always followed in practice, a distinction can be made between a classification (composed of classes) and a typology (composed of types). A strict *classification* consists of a set of variables or attributes which are linked to form a number of logically possible classes. A *typology*, in contrast, attempts to specify the ways in which the attributes of observable phenomena are empirically connected in the formation of particular types.

Moreover, in a classification there is the assumption that all cases within a class share the properties of that class to the same extent. The type, however, "acts as a point of reference that determines the extent to which any empirical case conforms to it, the principal consideration therefore being degree of approximation."[12] It is the construction of types rather than classes that interests the criminologist.

Ideal and Empirical Typologies

Another distinction that is commonly drawn is between two kinds of typologies: the ideal and the empirical.[13] Following the lead of Max Weber, an ideal type is an abstraction that does not necessarily describe

11. Herbert A. Bloch and Gilbert Geis, *Man, Crime, and Society*, 2d ed. (New York: Random House, 1970), pp. 101–6, 167–379.

12. John K. Rhoads, "The Type as a Logical Form," *Sociology and Social Research*, 51 (April 1967), p. 348.

13. Edwin D. Driver, "A Critique of Typologies in Criminology," *The Sociological Quarterly*, 9 (Summer 1968), pp. 356–373; Theodore N. Ferdinand, *Typologies of Delinquency: A Critical Analysis* (New York: Random House, 1966), pp. 41–79; Arthur Lewis Wood, "Ideal and Empirical Typologies for Research in Deviance and Control," *Sociology and Social Research*, 53 (January 1969), pp. 227–41.

concrete cases, but represents possible or even extreme cases. An ideal type may be conceived of as a distortion of the concrete. All empirical occurrences can then be viewed in terms of the ideal type.

The empirical typology, on the other hand, is supposedly composed of types that describe exactly the patterns that exist in the real world. While the ideal type is the observer's abstraction, the empirical type is supposed to represent what actually exists.

The distinction between ideal and empirical types is, however, arbitrary. But more than this, the distinction suffers from a faulty epistemology. The problem is related to the age-old controversy between realism and nominalism.

> The question as to whether forms or configurations exist ontologically as the "realist" tradition holds, or whether the form or configuration is merely an abstraction characteristic of the nomenclature as held by the "nominalist" position has persistently been reflected in the argument as to whether types are "real" or merely convenient "fictions." Are types just constructs or are they dictated to observation by some natural arrangement of the phenomena themselves? The literature regarding the "ideal type" has contributed heavily to this controversy. By and large it has been a spurious and fruitless controversy in the social sciences. The question of whether types are real is obviously a metaphysical one and may be of some relevance to philosophers but has little to do with the methodology of the social sciences. The reality of *anything* can be questioned in the same sense that the reality of types is questioned if one wants merely to play the metaphysical game.[14]

Nevertheless, we cannot naively assume that types are "real." But we can dispense with the question of objective reality and the observer's ability to copy it. "There is no reason to believe in the objective reality of anything. Our concern, rather, is with the formulation of constructs that are meaningful for the purposes at hand."[15] Certainly we construct types on the basis of our perceptions and our experiences. Nothing is either totally a priori or completely the result of induction. To conceive of types as developing from either source is to ignore the metaphysical problem of the nature of reality. We construct whatever gives meaning to our lives and to the problems that we pose.

    14. John C. McKinney, "Typification, Typologies, and Sociological Theory," *Social Forces,* 48 (September 1969), p. 5.

    15. Richard Quinney, *The Problem of Crime* (New York: Dodd, Mead & Company, 1970), p. 138.

First and Second Order Constructs

It is obvious that when social scientists develop constructs, such as criminal types, these constructs are removed from the world of the participants in society. Alfred Schutz has noted this most clearly in his discussion of first order and second order constructs: "The constructs of the social sciences are, so to speak, constructs of the second degree, that is, constructs of the constructs made by the actors on the social scene, whose behavior the social scientist has to observe and to explain in accordance with the procedural rules of his science."[16] And following Schutz, types based on first order constructs are what McKinney calls "existential types," or typifications constructed by participants in society; while the types developed by social scientists, based in part on these data, are "constructed types."[17]

The criminologist is thus engaged in the construction of constructions. By means of types, drawing on the commonsensical world of actors, we are able to understand the social world. But as participants ourselves, it is not always clear whether our constructs are entirely first or second order. They are probably both; but to be concerned solely with the problem is again to fall prey to the unanswerable metaphysical problem.

Moreover, our constructions (our types) are not always based on the common sense of the participants. Rather, our constructions may not at times even take into consideration whether or not they are built on the commonsensical world. But no matter. What we always attempt to do is to make the world understandable at least to ourselves and our audience. And that need not—for better or worse—take into consideration what the world means to those we are describing. But it would probably help.

Theoretical Assumptions and Underlying Dimensions

No matter how implicit, some assumptions about crime and society are always present when we construct criminal typologies. In addition, the particular selection of dimensions is guided by the interests of the criminologist. In other words, the purpose at hand determines how the typology is to be constructed. Also, the level of explanation desired by the criminologist will play a part in the particular selection of dimensions in the typology.

---

16. Alfred Schutz, "Concept and Theory Formation in the Social Sciences," Maurice Nathanson, ed., *Philosophy of the Social Sciences* (New York: Random House, 1963), p. 242.

17. McKinney, "Typification, Typologies, and Sociological Theory," pp. 1–3.

General characteristics for the construction of typologies can be developed in the course of criminological research. With the use of such a technique as factor analysis, for example, common characteristics of offenders can be found. These dimensions in turn can be used in the construction of a typological system. Typologies can also be constructed through the use of findings from other research studies of various kinds of crime and delinquency. Once such typologies are constructed, and with the addition of terms, concepts, and postulates, typologies can serve as axiomatic theories whereby further statements regarding types of crime can be deduced.[18]

Related to the selection of characteristics underlying typologies is the problem of the phenomena to be included in the typology. There has been the tendency in criminology, especially in the development of typologies, to avoid distinguishing between the subclasses of phenomena included in the study of crime. The phenomena associated with crime include (1) the formulation and administration of criminal law, (2) the development of persons and behaviors that become defined as criminal, and (3) the social reactions to crime.

The distinction between these three subject areas is crucial in the construction of typologies in criminology. For example, if a typology is based on *criminal law,* attention is focused on the process by which criminal definitions are imposed on human activity by agents of the law. On the other hand, if the objective is a typology based solely on the *criminal and his behavior,* the emphasis is on the process by which persons who are subject to criminal definition acquire their self-conceptions and their values, and how they associate with others in social and cultural contexts. Or a typology could be constructed on the basis of the nature and extent of *social reaction* to crime.

Yet another typology, a *criminal behavior system,* could be constructed that would consider all three areas of phenomena associated with crime. Such a typology would suggest how persons with certain characteristics and behaviors develop patterns that have a certain probability of becoming defined as criminal and receive a particular reaction from society. The development of a multidimensional and integrative typology is our primary concern.

Comprehensiveness and Homogeneity of Types

There is also the question of whether a typology should include the entire range of crime or be limited in scope. A typology that attempts

18. Clarence Schrag, "A Preliminary Criminal Typology," *Pacific Sociological Review,* 4 (Spring 1961), pp. 11–16.

to be comprehensive must necessarily formulate types at a fairly high level of abstraction. When this is done it is unlikely that many cases will remain outside of the typology. Even cases that exhibit a lack of specific patterning could be included in such a type.[19]

Should a typology incorporate both adults and juveniles? Many of the offenses of juveniles are behaviorally the same as those of adults. Therefore, in constructing types, there may be little reason to create separate types of minors and adults. Instead, various forms of juvenile delinquency can be included in a single typology, as we have done. When an offense committed by a juvenile would be a crime if committed by an adult, it is included within our typology. On the other hand, one could construct a typology based on uniquely juvenile offenses, such as truancy, but this is not our intent.

No typology, unless it is on a very low level of abstraction, can contain purely homogeneous types. For every type, several subtypes could be delineated. The level of abstraction of the typology in general and each type in particular determines the extent to which subtyping may be appropriate. It is always the purpose of the analysis combined with the desired level of abstraction that influences the construction of types. Understandably many of our types could eventually be broken down into subtypes, but this will have to wait further criminological research.

Trends in Criminal Typology

Whatever the nature of typological construction, the trend in criminology is clearly toward further study of types of crime. In the development of typologies we cannot, however, expect to achieve a typological system that all criminologists will agree is the most desirable. To be certain, some classifications will at various times be more popular than others. But there are a number of reasons why we cannot look forward to one typology in criminology.

First, as already mentioned, typologies differ according to the purposes they are to serve. Since there will continue to be a multitude of purposes, including levels of analysis and degrees of generality, there will be a number of typologies. Second, there is the fact that crime is relative. That is, the definitions of crime change from time to time and from place to place. Therefore, the behaviors and persons to be included in a typology will vary according to time and place. It may be that future typologies will be developed which will include the crimes

---

19. See Clayton A. Hartjen and Don C. Gibbons, "An Empirical Investigation of a Criminal Typology," *Sociology and Social Research*, 54 (October 1969), pp. 56–62.

of other historical periods. Third, theory within criminology will continue to develop. As this happens, typologies will be altered. Finally, theories, theoretical frameworks, and the related typologies will change as the orientations of criminologists change. Inevitably, as with all intellectual trends, the interests of criminologists will be attuned to the developments in the larger society.

THEORETICAL DIMENSIONS FOR A TYPOLOGY OF CRIMINAL BEHAVIOR

In the typology presented in this book, types of crime are viewed as *systems* of behavior. As heuristic devices, types are necessarily constructed as *systems*. As one writer noted, "The constructed type is a special kind of concept in that it consists of a set of characteristics wherein the relations between the characteristics are held constant for the purpose at hand. Hence, the type is a pragmatically constructed 'system.' "[20] Our *criminal behavior systems* are constructed types that serve as a means by which concrete occurrences can be described and compared within a system of theoretical dimensions that underlie the types.[21]

The theoretical assumptions of our typology are contained in the five dimensions of the typology. The dimensions are:

1. Legal Aspects of Selected Offenses
2. Criminal Career of the Offender
3. Group Support of Criminal Behavior
4. Correspondence between Criminal and Legitimate Behavior
5. Societal Reaction and Legal Processing

Included in these five dimensions are the diverse phenomena associated with crime, that is, the formulation and administration of criminal law, the development of persons and behaviors that may be defined as criminal, and the social reactions to the behaviors. Together the five dimensions with their specific assumptions form the theoretical basis for our typology of criminal behavior systems.

Legal Aspects of Selected Offenses. Crime is a definition of human conduct that is created by authorized agents in a politically organized society.[22] Criminal laws are formulated by those segments of

---

20. John C. McKinney, *Constructive Typology and Social Theory* (New York: Appleton-Century-Crofts, 1966), p. 7.

21. Our typology of criminal behavior systems had its beginnings in Marshall B. Clinard, *Sociology of Deviant Behavior* (New York: Holt, Rinehart and Winston, 1957), pp. 200–209.

22. This theoretical perspective is developed in Quinney, *The Social Reality of Crime*, pp. 15–23.

society that have the power to translate their interests into public policy. Criminal laws thus consist of behaviors that are regarded as threatening to the ruling class. The social history of particular criminal laws is a reflection of changes in the power structure of society.

Criminal Career of the Offender. The behavior of the offender is shaped by the extent to which criminally defined norms and activities have become a part of the individual's career.[23] The career of the offender includes the social roles he plays, his conception of self, his progression in criminal activity, and his identification with crime. Offenders vary in the degree to which criminally defined behavior has become a part of their life organization.

Group Support of Criminal Behavior. The behavior of offenders is supported to varying degrees by the norms of the groups to which they belong. Those who are defined as criminal act according to the normative patterns learned in relative social and cultural settings. Group support of criminal behavior varies according to the associations of the offender with differential norms and the integration of the offender into social groups.

Correspondence between Criminal and Legitimate Behavior. Criminal behavior patterns are structured in society in relation to legitimate and legal behavior patterns. Within this context persons develop and engage in actions that have relative probabilities of being defined as criminal. Criminally defined behaviors thus vary in terms of the extent to which they correspond to legitimate patterns of behavior in society. The behavior of the offender is viewed in relation to the norms of the segments of society that have the power to formulate and administer criminal law.

Societal Reaction and Legal Processing. Criminally defined behaviors vary in the kind and amount of reactions they receive from the public and from the society in general. The social reactions range from the degree of approval or disapproval to the official sanctioning procedures. Different policies of punishment and treatment are established and administered for each type of criminal behavior. Social reactions are also affected by the visibility of the offense and the degree to which the criminal behavior corresponds to the interests of the power structure of society. Finally, the types of criminal behavior vary in the ways that they are processed through the legal system. Patterns of detection, arrest, prosecution, conviction, sentencing, and punishment exist for each type of criminal behavior.

----

23. For the theoretical background of this perspective, see Marshall B. Clinard, *Sociology of Deviant Behavior,* 3d ed. (New York: Holt, Rinehart and Winston, 1968), pp. 251–56.

On the basis of these five theoretical dimensions our typology of criminal behavior systems is constructed.

A TYPOLOGY OF CRIMINAL BEHAVIOR SYSTEMS

Nine types of criminal behavior systems are constructed in relation to the five theoretical dimensions. The types are:

1. Violent Personal Criminal Behavior
2. Occasional Property Criminal Behavior
3. Public Order Criminal Behavior
4. Conventional Criminal Behavior
5. Political Criminal Behavior
6. Occupational Criminal Behavior
7. Corporate Criminal Behavior
8. Organized Criminal Behavior
9. Professional Criminal Behavior

The nine criminal behavior systems [are summarized and diagrammed in Table 13–1.]

Violent Personal Criminal Behavior.   The criminal laws of homicide, assault, and forcible rape are found in most societies, yet the legal categories are qualified and interpreted in their respective social and historical contexts. The offenders do not conceive of themselves as criminals. They are often persons without previous records, but because of certain circumstances commit a personal offense. The offenses are not directly supported by any group, although there may be subcultural definitions favorable to the general use of violence. There is strong reaction to offenses.

Occasional Property Criminal Behavior.   Criminal laws protect the material interests of the propertied classes, specifically prohibiting forgery, shoplifting, vandalism, and auto theft. The offenders do not usually conceive of themselves as criminals and are able to rationalize their criminal behavior. They are usually committed to the general goals of society and find little support for their behavior in group norms. The behaviors violate the value placed on private property. Societal reaction is not severe in those cases where the offender has no previous record. There is leniency in legal processing.

Public Order Criminal Behavior.   Specific criminal laws embody the moral sense of particular segments of the community. Such offenses as prostitution, homosexuality, drunkenness, and drug use may be "victimless," but they are disturbing to some community members. The violators may conceive of themselves as criminals when they are repeatedly defined as criminals by others. There is considerable association with other offenders, and some of the behaviors are supported by rather clearly defined subcultures. There is some correspondence between the illegal behaviors of public order offenders and legitimate patterns. Some of the offenses are desired by part of the legitimate society. There is strong social reaction by some segments of society and weak reaction by others. Only a small portion of the offenses result in arrest.

Conventional Criminal Behavior. The laws that protect private property include such crimes as larceny, burglary, and robbery. Offenders begin their careers early in life, often in gang associations. Offenders vacillate between the values of the larger society and those of a criminal subculture. Some offenders continue primary association with other offenders, while others pursue different careers. The behaviors are consistent with the goal of economic success, but inconsistent with the sanctity of private property. There may be a series of arrests and convictions. Rehabilitation programs preserve the status quo without changing social conditions.

Political Criminal Behavior. Criminal laws are created by governments to protect their own existence. Specific criminal laws, such as conspiracy laws, as well as traditional laws, are made to control amd punish those who threaten the state. However, government or its officials also violate criminal laws. Political offenders, acting out of conscience, do not usually conceive of themselves as criminals. They receive support for their behavior by particular segments of society. The behaviors of citizens against the government are consistent with the ideal of political freedom and basic human rights. Governmental crimes correspond to the belief in political sovereignty. Public acceptance of political crime depends on the extent to which the policies of the government are regarded as being legitimate.

Occupational Criminal Behavior. Legal regulation of occupations has served to protect the interests of occupational groups. The offenders violate the law in the course of their occupational activity. They are able to rationalize their conduct. Some occupations, or groups within occupations, tolerate or even support these offenses. The behavior corresponds to the pursual of business activity. Because such offenses are committed by "respectable" persons, social reaction has traditionally been mild. Official penalties have been lenient, often restricted to the sanctions administered by the professional associations. Public reaction is becoming less tolerant.

Corporate Criminal Behavior. Criminal laws and administrative regulations have been established to regulate the restraint of trade,

TABLE 13-1. Typology of Criminal Behavior Systems

	Violent Personal Criminal Behavior	Occasional Property Criminal Behavior	Public Order Criminal Behavior
Legal Aspects of Selected Offenses	The criminal laws of homicide, assault, and forcible rape are of ancient origin. Yet the legal categories are qualified and interpreted in their respective social and historical contexts. Likewise, the ruling class is able to exclude the forms of violence that enhance its own position.	Criminal laws protect the material interests of the propertied classes. Specific laws prohibit forgery, shoplifting, vandalism, and auto theft.	Specific criminal laws embody the moral sense of particular segments of the community. Such offenses as prostitution, homosexuality, drunkenness, and drug use are disturbing to some community members. Many of the crimes are "victimless" in that only willing participants are involved. Yet it is easier for the power elite to outlaw these behaviors than to either accept them or to change the social arrangements that produced the behaviors.
Criminal Career of the Offender	Crime is not part of the offender's career. He usually does not conceive of self as criminal.	Little or no criminal self-conception. The offender does not identify with crime. He is able to rationalize his behavior.	Most offenders do not regard their behavior as criminal. They do not have a clearly defined criminal career. Ambiguity in self-concept produced in continued contact with legal agents.
Group Support of Criminal Behavior	Little or no group support. Offenses committed for personal reasons. Some support in subcultural norms.	Little group support. Generally individual offenses. Associations tend to be recreational.	Offenses such as prostitution, homosexual behavior, and drug use grow out of, and are supported by, rather clearly defined subcultures. Considerable association with other offenders.
Correspondence between Criminal and Legitimate Behavior	Violations of values on life and personal safety.	Violation of value on private property. Offenders tend to be committed to the general goals of the society.	Some of the offenses are required by legitimate society. Much of the behavior is consistent with legitimate behavior patterns.
Societal Reaction and Legal Processing	Strong social reaction. Harsh punishments. Long imprisonment.	Social reaction is not severe when the offender does not have a previous record. Leniency in legal processing. Probation.	Strong reaction by some segments of society, weak reaction by others. Only a small portion of the offenses result in arrest. Sentences are strong for some offenses, such as the possession of narcotic drugs.

TABLE 13.1. (continued)

Conventional Criminal Behavior	Political Criminal Behavior	Occupational Criminal Behavior
The laws that protect private property include such crimes as larceny, burglary, and robbery. Since the primary interest is in protecting property, general laws regarding property do not need to distinguish the career nature of many property offenders.	Criminal laws are created by governments to protect their own existence. Specific criminal laws, such as conspiracy laws, as well as traditional laws, are made to control and punish those who threaten the state. Yet the government and its officials often violate criminal laws. Political criminal behavior thus includes crimes against government and crimes by government.	Legal regulation of occupations has served to protect the interests of occupational groups, and in some cases to regulate harmful occupational activities. The legal codes that control occupations and professions tend to be made by the occupations and the occupations and the professions themselves, representing their own material interests.
Offenders begin their careers early in life, often in gang associations. Crimes committed for economic gain. Vacillation in self-conception. Partial commitment to a criminal subculture.	Political offenders do not usually conceive of themselves as criminals and do not identify with crime. They are defined as criminal because they are perceived as threatening the status quo (as in crime against government), or they are criminal when they violate the laws that regulate the government itself (crime by government).	Little or no criminal self-conception. Occasional violation of the law, accompanied by appropriate rationalizations. Violation tends to be a part of one's work. Offenders accept the conventional values in the society.
Behavior supported by group norms. Early association with other offenders in slum areas. Status achieved in groups. Some persons continue primary association with other offenders, while others pursue different careers.	Support is received by particular groups or by segments of society. They identify or associate with persons who share similar values. Behavior is reinforced by specific norms.	Some occupations, or groups within occupations, tolerate or even support offenses. The offender is integrated into social groups and societal norms.
Consistent with goals of economic success, but inconsistent with sanctity of private property. Gang delinquency violates norms of proper adolescent behavior.	Crimes against government usually correspond to basic human rights. The actions and beliefs, however, are opposed by those who are threatened by these freedoms. Crimes by government correspond to contrary behavior patterns that promote the sovereignty of government rulers.	Behavior corresponds to the pursual of business activity. "Sharp" practices and "buyer beware" philosophy have guided work and consumption patterns.
A series of arrests and convictions. Institutionalization and rehabilitation of the offender. Agency programs that preserve the status quo without changing social conditions.	Official reactions tend to be severe in the case of crimes against government. Considerable harassment may be experienced and heavy sentences may be imposed. Public acceptance of political offenses depends on the extent to which the policies and actions of the government are accepted. Reactions to governmental crime depends on the consciousness of the public regarding the activities of the government.	Reactions have traditionally been mild and indifferent. Official penalties have been lenient, often restricted to the sanctions administered by the professional association. Public reaction is becomming less tolerant.

TABLE 13.1. (continued)

	Corporate Criminal Behavior	Organized Criminal Behavior	Professional Criminal Behavior
Legal Aspects of Selected Offenses	With the growth of corporations, criminal laws have been created to regulate such activities as restraint of trade, false advertising, fraudulent sales, misuse of trademarks, and manufacture of unsafe foods and drugs. Criminal laws—especially administrative regulations—have been established by the corporations themselves to secure a capitalist economy.	Many traditional laws have been used in the attempt to control organized crime, especially those regarding gambling, prostitution, and drug traffic. The government has more recently enacted special criminal laws in order to infiltrate organized criminal activity in legitimate business and racketeering. But since organized crime is closely tied to the general business economy, these laws tend to invade the privacy of all citizens rather than to control organized crime.	Professional crimes are distinguished by the nature of the criminal behavior rather than by specific criminal laws. Such professional activities as confidence games, pickpocketing, shoplifting, forgery, and counterfeiting are regulated by the traditional laws that protect private property.
Criminal Career of the Offender	The violating corporate official and his corporation have high social status in society. Offenses are an integral part of corporate business operations. Violations are rationalized as being basic to business enterprise.	Crime is pursued as a livelihood. There is a progression in crime and an increasing isolation from the larger society. A criminal self-conception develops.	A highly developed criminal career. Professional offenders engage in specialized offenses, all of which are directed toward economic gain. They enjoy high status in the world of crime. They are committed to other professional criminals.
Group Support of Criminal Behavior	Crime by corporations and corporate officials receives support from similar, even competing, businesses and officials. Lawbreaking is a normative pattern within many corporations. Corporate crime involves a great amount of organization among the participants.	Support for organized criminal behavior is achieved through an organizational structure, a code of conduct, prescribed methods of operation, and a system of protection. The offender is integrated into organized crime.	Professional offenders associate primarily with other offenders. Behavior is prescribed by the norms of professional criminals. The extent of organization among professional criminals varies with the kind of offense.
Correspondence between Criminal and Legitimate Behavior	Corporate crime is consistent with the prevailing ideology that encourages unlimited production and consumption. Only recently has an alternative ethic developed that questions practices that support corporate crime.	While organized crime may be generally condemned, characteristics of American society give support to organized crime. The values underlying organized crime are consistent with those valued in the free enterprise system.	Professional criminal activity corresponds to societal values that stress skill and employment. Some of the offenses depend upon the cooperation of accomplices. The operations of professional crime change with alterations in the larger society.
Societal Reaction and Legal Processing	Strong legal actions have not usually been taken against corporations or their officials. Legal actions have been in the form of warnings and injunctions, rather than in terms of criminal penalties. Public reactions and legal actions, however, are increasing in respect to corporate crime.	Considerable public toleration of organized crime. Offenses are not usually visible to the public. Immunity of offenders, as provided by effective organization, prevents detection and arrest. Convictions are usually for minor offenses.	Considerable public toleration because of the low visibility of professional crime. Offenders are able to escape conviction by "fixing" cases.

false advertising, misuse of trademarks, and the manufacture of unsafe foods and drugs. The laws serve to protect the corporations themselves and to secure a capitalist economy. The criminal behaviors are an integral part of corporate business operations. Violations are rationalized as being basic to business enterprise. Corporate crime involves a great amount of organization among the participants. The offenses are consistent with the prevailing ideology that encourages unlimited production and consumption. Strong legal actions have not usually been taken against corporations and their officials. Public reactions and legal actions are increasing.

Organized Criminal Behavior.   Many of the traditional laws have been used in the attempt to control organized crime. Special laws have been enacted to deal with criminal activity in legitimate business and racketeering. The offenders pursue crime as a livelihood. In the lower echelons they conceive of themselves as criminals, associate primarily with other criminals, and are isolated from the larger society. In the top levels the offenders associate with persons of legitimate society and often reside in the better residential areas. There is considerable correspondence between the criminal activities of organized crime and legitimate society. Illegal services desired by legitimate society are provided by organized crime. The principles of large-scale enterprise are shared by legitimate society. The public tolerates organized crime, partly because of the services it provides and partly because of the problems in dealing with its operation. Conviction is usually for minor offenses.

Professional Criminal Behavior.   Professional crimes are distinguished by the nature of the criminal behavior rather than by specific criminal laws. The laws that protect private property are used to control confidence games, pickpocketing, shoplifting, forgery, and counterfeiting. Professional criminals pursue crime as a livelihood and way of life. They conceive of themselves as criminals, associate with other criminals, and have high status in the world of crime. The extent of organization among professional offenders varies with the kind of offense. There is some correspondence between professional crime and dominant behavior patterns in that professional offenses involve work and skill. The public tolerates many of the offenses because of the low visibility of the behaviors. Many cases of professional criminal behavior are "fixed" in the course of legal processing.

14

Deviant Careers

Howard S. Becker

A useful conception in developing sequential models of various kinds of deviant behavior is that of *career*.[1] Originally developed in studies of occupations, the concept refers to the sequence of movements from one position to another in an occupational system made by any individual who works in that system. Furthermore, it includes the notion of "career contingency," those factors on which mobility from one position to another depends. Career contingencies include both objective facts of social structure and changes in the perspectives, motivations, and desires of the individual. Ordinarily, in the study of occupations, we use the concept to distinguish between those who have a "successful" career (in whatever terms success is defined within the occupation) and those who do not. It can also be used to distinguish several varieties of career outcomes, ignoring the question of "success."

The model can easily be transformed for use in the study of deviant careers. In so transforming it, we should not confine our interest to those who follow a career that leads them into ever increasing deviance, to those who ultimately take on an extremely deviant identity and way of life. We should also consider those who have a more fleeting contact with deviance, whose careers lead them away from it into conventional

From Howard S. Becker, "Kinds of Deviance: A Sequential Model," in *Outsiders: Studies in the Sociology of Deviance* (New York: The Free Press of Glencoe, 1963), pp. 24–39, by permission of the author and Macmillan Publishing Company, Inc. Copyright © 1963 by The Free Press of Glencoe, a Division of The Macmillan Company. Footnotes have been renumbered.

1. See Everett C. Hughes, *Men and Their Work* (New York: Free Press, Macmillan, 1958), pp. 56–67, 102–15, and 157–68; Oswald Hall, "The Stages of the Medical Career," *American Journal of Sociology*, 53 (March 1948): 243–53; and Howard S. Becker and Anselm L. Strauss, "Careers, Personality, and Adult Socialization," *American Journal of Sociology*, 62 (November 1956): 253–63.

ways of life. Thus, for example, studies of delinquents who fail to become adult criminals might teach us even more than studies of delinquents who progress in crime.

The first step in most deviant careers is the commission of a nonconforming act, an act that breaks some particular set of rules. How are we to account for the first step?

People usually think of deviant acts as motivated. They believe that the person who commits a deviant act, even for the first time (and perhaps especially for the first time), does so purposely. His purpose may or may not be entirely conscious, but there is a motive force behind it. We shall turn to the consideration of cases of intentional nonconformity in a moment, but first I must point out that many nonconforming acts are committed by people who have no intention of doing so; these clearly require a different explanation.

Unintended acts of deviance can probably be accounted for relatively simply. They imply an ignorance of the existence of the rule, or of the fact that it was applicable in this case, or to this particular person. But it is necessary to account for the lack of awareness. How does it happen that the person does not know his act is improper? Persons deeply involved in a particular subculture (such as a religious or ethnic subculture) may simply be unaware that everyone does not act "that way" and thereby commit an impropriety. There may, in fact, be structured areas of ignorance of particular rules. Mary Haas has pointed out the interesting case of interlingual word taboos.[2] Words which are perfectly proper in one language have a "dirty" meaning in another. So the person, innocently using a word common in his own language, finds that he has shocked and horrified his listeners who come from a different culture.

In analyzing cases of intended nonconformity, people usually ask about motivation: Why does the person want to do the deviant thing he does? The question assumes that the basic difference between deviants and those who conform lies in the character of their motivation. Many theories have been propounded to explain why some people have deviant motivations and others do not. Psychological theories find the cause of deviant motivations and acts in the individual's early experiences, which produce unconscious needs that must be satisfied if the individual is to maintain his equilibrium. Sociological theories look for socially structured sources of "strain" in the society, social positions which have

2. Mary R. Haas, "Interlingual Word Taboos," *American Anthropologist*, 53 (July–September 1951): 338–44.

conflicting demands placed upon them such that the individual seeks an illegitimate way of solving the problems his position presents him with. (Merton's famous theory of anomie fits into this category.)[3]

But the assumption on which these approaches are based may be entirely false. There is no reason to assume that only those who finally commit a deviant act actually have the impulse to do so. It is much more likely that most people experience deviant impulses frequently. At least in fantasy, people are much more deviant than they appear. Instead of asking why deviants want to do things that are disapproved of, we might better ask why conventional people do not follow through on the deviant impulses they have.

Something of an answer to this question may be found in the process of commitment through which the "normal" person becomes progressively involved in conventional institutions and behavior. In speaking of commitment,[4] I refer to the process through which several kinds of interests become bound up with carrying out certain lines of behavior to which they seem formally extraneous. What happens is that the individual, as a consequence of actions he has taken in the past or the operation of various institutional routines, finds he must adhere to certain lines of behavior, because many other activities than the one he is immediately engaged in will be adversely affected if he does not. The middle-class youth must not quit school, because his occupational future depends on receiving a certain amount of schooling. The conventional person must not indulge his interest in narcotics, for example, because much more than the pursuit of immediate pleasure is involved; his job, his family, and his reputation in his neighborhood may seem to him to depend on his continuing to avoid temptation.

In fact, the normal development of people in our society (and probably in any society) can be seen as a series of progressively increasing commitments to conventional norms and institutions. The "normal" person, when he discovers a deviant impulse in himself, is able to check that impulse by thinking of the manifold consequences acting on it would produce for him. He has staked too much on continuing to be normal to allow himself to be swayed by unconventional impulses.

---

3. Robert K. Merton, *Social Theory and Social Structure* (New York: Free Press, Macmillan, 1957), pp. 131–94.

4. I have dealt with this concept at greater length in "Notes on the Concept of Commitment," *American Journal of Sociology*, 66 (July 1960): 32–40. See also Erving Goffman, *Encounters: Two Studies in the Sociology of Interaction* (Indianapolis: Bobbs-Merrill, 1961), pp. 88–110; and Gregory P. Stone, "Clothing and Social Relations: A Study of Appearance in the Context of Community Life" (unpublished Ph.D. dissertation, Department of Sociology, University of Chicago, 1959).

This suggests that in looking at cases of intended nonconformity we must ask how the person manages to avoid the impact of conventional commitments. He may do so in one of two ways. First of all, in the course of growing up the person may somehow have avoided entangling alliances with conventional society. He may, thus, be free to follow his impulses. The person who does not have a reputation to maintain or a conventional job he must keep may follow his impulses. He has nothing staked on continuing to appear conventional.

However, most people remain sensitive to conventional codes of conduct and must deal with their sensitivities in order to engage in a deviant act for the first time. Sykes and Matza have suggested that delinquents actually feel strong impulses to be law-abiding and deal with them by techniques of neutralization: "justifications for deviance that are seen as valid by the delinquent but not by the legal system or society at large." They distinguish a number of techniques for neutralizing the force of law-abiding values.

In so far as the delinquent can define himself as lacking responsibility for his deviant actions, the disapproval of self or others is sharply reduced in effectiveness as a restraining influence. . . . The delinquent approaches a "billiard ball" conception of himself in which he sees himself as helplessly propelled into new situations. . . . By learning to view himself as more acted upon than acting, the delinquent prepares the way for deviance from the dominant normative system without the necessity of a frontal assault on the norms themselves. . . .

A second major technique of neutralization centers on the injury or harm involved in the delinquent act. . . . For the delinquent . . . wrongfulness may turn on the question of whether or not anyone has clearly been hurt by his deviance, and this matter is open to a variety of interpretations. . . . Auto theft may be viewed as "borrowing," and gang fighting may be seen as a private quarrel, an agreed-upon duel between two willing parties, and thus of no concern to the community at large. . . .

The moral indignation of self and others may be neutralized by an insistence that the injury is not wrong in light of the circumstances. The injury, it may be claimed, is not really an injury; rather, it is a form of rightful retaliation or punishment. . . . Assaults on homosexuals or suspected homosexuals, attacks on members of minority groups who are said to have gotten "out of place," vandalism as revenge on an unfair teacher or school official, thefts from a "crooked" store owner —all may be hurts inflicted on a transgressor, in the eyes of the delinquent. . . .

A fourth technique of neutralization would appear to involve a condemnation of the condemners. . . . His condemners, he may claim, are hypocrites, deviants in disguise, or impelled by personal spite. . . . By attacking others, the wrongfulness of his own behavior is more easily repressed or lost to view. . . .

Internal and external social controls may be neutralized by sacrificing the demands of the larger society for the demands of the smaller social groups to which the delinquent belongs such as the sibling pair, the gang, or the friendship clique. . . . The most important point is that deviation from certain norms may occur not because the norms are rejected but because other norms, held to be more pressing or involving a higher loyalty, are accorded precedence.[5]

In some cases a nonconforming act may appear necessary or expedient to a person otherwise law-abiding. Undertaken in pursuit of legitimate interests, the deviant act becomes, if not quite proper, at least not quite improper. In a novel dealing with a young Italian-American doctor we find a good example.[6] The young man, just out of medical school, would like to have a practice that is not built on the fact of his being Italian. But, being Italian, he finds it difficult to gain acceptance from the Yankee practitioners of his community. One day he is suddenly asked by one of the biggest surgeons to handle a case for him and thinks that he is finally being admitted to the referral system of the better doctors in town. But when the patient arrives at his office, he finds the case is an illegal abortion. Mistakenly seeing the referral as the first step in a regular relationship with the surgeon, he performs the operation. This act, although improper, is thought necessary to building his career.

But we are not so much interested in the person who commits a deviant act once as in the person who sustains a pattern of deviance over a long period of time, who makes of deviance a way of life, who organizes his identity around a pattern of deviant behavior. It is not the casual experimenters with homosexuality (who turned up in such surprisingly large numbers in the Kinsey Report) that we want to find out about, but the man who follows a pattern of homosexual activity throughout his adult life.

One of the mechanisms that lead from casual experimentation to a more sustained pattern of deviant activity is the development of deviant motives and interests. . . . Here it is sufficient to say that many kinds of deviant activity spring from motives which are socially learned. Before engaging in the activity on a more or less regular basis, the person has no notion of the pleasures to be derived from it; he learns

---

5. Gresham M. Sykes and David Matza, "Techniques of Neutralization: A Theory of Delinquency," *American Sociological Review*, 22 (December 1957): 667–69.

6. Guido D'Agostino, *Olives on the Apple Tree* (New York: Doubleday, Doran, 1940). I am grateful to Everett C. Hughes for calling this novel to my attention.

these in the course of interaction with more experienced deviants. He learns to be aware of new kinds of experiences and to think of them as pleasurable. What may well have been a random impulse to try something new becomes a settled taste for something already known and experienced. The vocabularies in which deviant motivations are phrased reveal that their users acquire them in interaction with other deviants. The individual *learns*, in short, to participate in a subculture organized around the particular deviant activity.

Deviant motivations have a social character even when most of the activity is carried on in a private, secret, and solitary fashion. In such cases, various media of communication may take the place of face-to-face interaction in inducting the individual into the culture. . . . Pornographic pictures . . . [are] described to prospective buyers in a stylized language. Ordinary words [are] used in a technical shorthand designed to whet specific tastes. The word "bondage," for instance, [is] used repeatedly to refer to pictures of women restrained in handcuffs or straightjackets. One does not acquire a taste for "bondage photos" without having learned what they are and how they may be enjoyed.

One of the most crucial steps in the process of building a stable pattern of deviant behavior is likely to be the experience of being caught and publicly labeled as a deviant. Whether a person takes this step or not depends not so much on what he does as on what other people do, on whether or not they enforce the rule he has violated. Although I will consider the circumstances under which enforcement takes place in some detail later, two notes are in order here. First of all, even though no one else discovers the nonconformity or enforces the rules against it, the individual who has committed the impropriety may himself act as enforcer. He may brand himself as deviant because of what he has done and punish himself in one way or another for his behavior. This is not always or necessarily the case, but may occur. Second, there may be cases like those described by psychoanalysts in which the individual really wants to get caught and perpetrates his deviant act in such a way that it is almost sure he will be.

In any case, being caught and branded as deviant have important consequences for one's further social participation and self-image. The most important consequence is a drastic change in the individual's public identity. Committing the improper act and being publicly caught at it place him in a new status. He has been revealed as a different kind of person from the kind he was supposed to be. He is labeled a "fairy," "dope fiend," "nut," or "lunatic," and treated accordingly.

In analyzing the consequences of assuming a deviant identity, let us make use of Hughes' distinction between master and auxiliary status traits.[7] Hughes notes that most statuses have one key trait which serves to distinguish those who belong from those who do not. Thus the doctor, whatever else he may be, is a person who has a certificate stating that he has fulfilled certain requirements and is licensed to practice medicine; this is the master trait. As Hughes points out, in our society a doctor is also informally expected to have a number of auxiliary traits: most people expect him to be upper-middle-class, white, male, and Protestant. When he is not, there is a sense that he has in some way failed to fill the bill. Similarly, though skin color is the master status trait determining who is Negro and who is white, Negroes are informally expected to have certain status traits and not to have others; people are surprised and find it anomalous if a Negro turns out to be a doctor or a college professor. People often have the master status trait but lack some of the auxiliary, informally expected characteristics; for example, one may be a doctor but be female or Negro.

Hughes deals with this phenomenon in regard to statuses that are well thought of, desired, and desirable (noting that one may have the formal qualifications for entry into a status but be denied full entry because of lack of the proper auxiliary traits), but the same process occurs in the case of deviant statuses. Possession of one deviant trait may have a generalized symbolic value, so that people automatically assume that its bearer possesses other undesirable traits allegedly associated with it.

To be labeled a criminal one need only commit a single criminal offense, and this is all the term formally refers to. Yet the word carries a number of connotations specifying auxiliary traits characteristic of anyone bearing the label. A man who has been convicted of housebreaking and thereby labeled criminal is presumed to be a person likely to break into other houses; the police, in rounding up known offenders for investigation after a crime has been committed, operate on this premise. Further, he is considered likely to commit other kinds of crimes as well, because he has shown himself to be a person without "respect for the law." Thus, apprehension for one deviant act exposes a person to the likelihood that he will be regarded as deviant or undesirable in other respects.

There is one other element in Hughes' analysis we can borrow with profit: the distinction between master and subordinate statuses.[8] Some

---

7. Everett C. Hughes, "Dilemmas and Contradictions of Status," *American Journal of Sociology*, 50 (March 1945): 353–59.

8. Ibid.

statuses, in our society as in others, override all other statuses and have a certain priority. Race is one of these. Membership in the Negro race, as socially defined, will override most other status considerations in most other situations; the fact that one is a physician or middle-class or female will not protect one from being treated as a Negro first and any of these other things second. The status of deviant (depending on the kind of deviance) is this kind of master status. One receives the status as a result of breaking a rule, and the identification proves to be more important than most others. One will be identified as a deviant first, before other identifications are made. The question is raised: "What kind of person would break such an important rule?" And the answer is given: "One who is different from the rest of us, who cannot or will not act as a moral human being and therefore might break other important rules." The deviant identification becomes the controlling one.

Treating a person as though he were generally rather than specifically deviant produces a self-fulfilling prophecy. It sets in motion several mechanisms which conspire to shape the person in the image people have of him.[9] In the first place, one tends to be cut off, after being identified as deviant, from participation in more conventional groups, even though the specific consequences of the particular deviant activity might never of themselves have caused the isolation had there not also been the public knowledge and reaction to it. For example, being a homosexual may not affect one's ability to do office work, but to be known as a homosexual in an office may make it impossible to continue working there. Similarly, though the effects of opiate drugs may not impair one's working ability, to be known as an addict will probably lead to losing one's job. In such cases, the individual finds it difficult to conform to other rules which he had no intention or desire to break, and perforce finds himself deviant in these areas as well. The homosexual who is deprived of a "respectable" job by the discovery of his deviance may drift into unconventional, marginal occupations where it does not make so much difference. The drug addict finds himself forced into other illegitimate kinds of activity, such as robbery and theft, by the refusal of respectable employers to have him around.

When the deviant is caught, he is treated in accordance with the popular diagnosis of why he is that way, and the treatment itself may likewise produce increasing deviance. The drug addict, popularly considered to be a weak-willed individual who cannot forgo the indecent pleasures afforded him by opiates, is treated repressively. He is forbidden to use drugs. Since he cannot get drugs legally, he must get them

---

9. See Marsh Ray, "The Cycle of Abstinence and Relapse Among Heroin Addicts," *Social Problems*, 9 (Fall 1961): 132–40.

illegally. This forces the market underground and pushes the price of drugs up far beyond the current legitimate market price into a bracket that few can afford on an ordinary salary. Hence the treatment of the addict's deviance places him in a position where it will probably be necessary to resort to deceit and crime in order to support his habit.[10] The behavior is a consequence of the public reaction to the deviance rather than a consequence of the inherent qualities of the deviant act.

Put more generally, the point is that the treatment of deviants denies them the ordinary means of carrying on the routines of everyday life open to most people. Because of this denial, the deviant must of necessity develop illegitimate routines. The influence of public reaction may be direct, as in the instances considered above, or indirect, a consequence of the integrated character of the society in which the deviant lives.

Societies are integrated in the sense that social arrangements in one sphere of activity mesh with other activities in other spheres in particular ways and depend on the existence of these other arrangements. Certain kinds of work lives presuppose a certain kind of family life . . .

Many varieties of deviance create difficulties by failing to mesh with expectations in other areas of life. Homosexuality is a case in point. Homosexuals have difficulty in any area of social activity in which the assumption of normal sexual interests and propensities for marriage is made without question. In stable work organizations such as large business or industrial organizations there are often points at which the man who would be successful should marry; not to do so will make it difficult for him to do the things that are necessary for success in the organization and will thus thwart his ambitions. The necessity of marrying often creates difficult enough problems for the normal male, and places the homosexual in an almost impossible position. Similarly, in some male work groups where heterosexual prowess is required to retain esteem in the group, the homosexual has obvious difficulties. Failure to meet the expectations of others may force the individual to attempt deviant ways of achieving results automatic for the normal person.

Obviously, everyone caught in one deviant act and labeled a deviant does not move inevitably toward greater deviance in the way the preceding remarks might suggest. The prophecies do not always confirm themselves; the mechanisms do not always work. What factors tend

---

10. See *Drug Addiction: Crime or Disease?*, Interim and Final Reports of the Joint Committee of the American Bar Association and the American Medical Association on Narcotic Drugs (Bloomington: Indiana University Press, 1961).

to slow down or halt the movement toward increasing deviance? Under what circumstances do they come into play?

One suggestion as to how the person may be immunized against increasing deviance is found in a recent study of juvenile delinquents who "hustle" homosexuals.[11] These boys act as homosexual prostitutes to confirmed adult homosexuals. Yet they do not themselves become homosexual. Several things account for their failure to continue this kind of sexual deviancy. First, they are protected from police action by the fact that they are minors. If they are apprehended in a homosexual act, they will be treated as exploited children, although in fact they are the exploiters; the law makes the adult guilty. Second, they look on the homosexual acts they engage in simply as a means of making money that is safer and quicker than robbery or similar activities. Third, the standards of their peer group, while permitting homosexual prostitution, allow only one kind of activity, and forbid them to get any special pleasure out of it or to permit any expression of endearment from the adult with whom they have relations. Infractions of these rules, or other deviations from normal heterosexual activity, are severely punished by the boy's fellows.

Apprehension may not lead to increasing deviance if the situation in which the individual is apprehended for the first time occurs at a point where he can still choose between alternate lines of action. Faced, for the first time, with the possible ultimate and drastic consequences of what he is doing, he may decide that he does not want to take the deviant road, and turn back. If he makes the right choice, he will be welcomed back into the conventional community; but if he makes the wrong move, he will be rejected and start a cycle of increasing deviance.

Ray has shown, in the case of drug addicts, how difficult it can be to reverse a deviant cycle.[12] He points out that drug addicts frequently attempt to cure themselves and that the motivation underlying their attempts is an effort to show nonaddicts whose opinions they respect that they are really not as bad as they are thought to be. On breaking their habit successfully, they find, to their dismay, that people still treat them as though they were addicts (on the premise, apparently, of "once a junkie, always a junkie").

A final step in the career of a deviant is movement into an organized deviant group. When a person makes a definite move into an

---

11. Albert J. Reiss, Jr., "The Social Integration of Queers and Peers," *Social Problems,* 9 (Fall 1961): 102–20.

12. Ray, op. cit.

organized group—or when he realizes and accepts the fact that he has already done so—it has a powerful impact on his conception of himself. A drug addict once told me that the moment she felt she was really "hooked" was when she realized she no longer had any friends who were not drug addicts.

Members of organized deviant groups of course have one thing in common: their deviance. It gives them a sense of common fate, of being in the same boat. From a sense of common fate, from having to face the same problems, grows a deviant subculture: a set of perspectives and understandings about what the world is like and how to deal with it, and a set of routine activities based on those perspectives. Membership in such a group solidifies a deviant identity.

Moving into an organized deviant group has several consequences for the career of the deviant. First of all, deviant groups tend, more than deviant individuals, to be pushed into rationalizing their position. At an extreme, they develop a very complicated historical, legal, and psychological justification for their deviant activity. The homosexual community is a good case. Magazines and books by homosexuals and for homosexuals include historical articles about famous homosexuals in history. They contain articles on the biology and physiology of sex, designed to show that homosexuality is a "normal" sexual response. They contain legal articles, pleading for civil liberties for homosexuals.[13] Taken together, this material provides a working philosophy for the active homosexual, explaining to him why he is the way he is, that other people have also been that way, and why it is all right for him to be that way.

Most deviant groups have a self-justifying rationale (or "ideology"), although seldom is it as well worked out as that of the homosexual. While such rationales do operate, as pointed out earlier, to neutralize the conventional attitudes that deviants may still find in themselves toward their own behavior, they also perform another function. They furnish the individual with reasons that appear sound for continuing the line of activity he has begun. A person who quiets his own doubts by adopting the rationale moves into a more principled and consistent kind of deviance than was possible for him before adopting it.

The second thing that happens when one moves into a deviant group is that he learns how to carry on his deviant activity with a minimum of trouble. All the problems he faces in evading enforcement of the rule he is breaking have been faced before by others. Solutions have been worked out. Thus, the young thief meets older thieves who,

---

13. *One* and *The Mattachine Review* are magazines of this type that I have seen.

more experienced than he is, explain to him how to get rid of stolen merchandise without running the risk of being caught. Every deviant group has a great stock of lore on such subjects and the new recruit learns it quickly.

Thus, the deviant who enters an organized and institutionalized deviant group is more likely than ever before to continue in his ways. He has learned, on the one hand, how to avoid trouble and, on the other hand, a rationale for continuing.

One further fact deserves mention. The rationales of deviant groups tend to contain a general repudiation of conventional moral rules, conventional institutions, and the entire conventional world.

15

Apprenticeships in Prostitution

James H. Bryan

While theoretical conceptions of deviant behavior range from role strain to psychoanalytic theory, orientations to the study of the prostitute have shown considerable homogeneity. Twentieth-century theorizing concerning this occupational group has employed, almost exclusively, a Freudian psychiatric model. The prostitute has thus been variously described as masochistic, of infantile mentality, unable to form mature interpersonal relationships, regressed, emotionally dangerous to males, and as normal as the average woman.[1] The call girl, the specific focus of this paper, has been accused of being anxious, possessing a confused self-image, excessively dependent, demonstrating gender-role confusion, aggressive, lacking internal controls, and masochistic.[2]

The exclusive use of psychoanalytic models in attempting to predict behavior, and the consequent neglect of situational and cognitive processes, has been steadily lessening in the field of psychology. Their inadequacy as models for understanding deviancy has been specifically

From James H. Bryan, "Apprenticeships in Prostitution," *Social Problems* 12 (1965): 287–97, by permission of the author and the Society for the Study of Social Problems.

1. H. Benjamin, "Prostitution Reassessed," *International Journal of Sexology*, 26 (1951): 154–60; H. Benjamin and A. Ellis, "An Objective Examination of Prostitution," *International Journal of Sexology*, 29 (1955): 100–105; E. Glover, "The Abnormality of Prostitution," in *Women*, ed. A. M. Krich (New York: Dell, 1953); M. H. Hollander, "Prostitution, the Body, and Human Relatedness," *International Journal of Psychoanalysis*, 42 (1961): 404–13; M. Karpf, "Effects of Prostitution on Marital Sex Adjustment," *International Journal of Sexology*, 29 (1953): 149–54; J. F. Oliven, *Sexual Hygiene and Pathology* (Philadelphia: Lippincott, 1955); W. J. Robinson, *The Oldest Profession in the World* (New York: Eugenics Publishing Co., 1929).

2. H. Greenwald, *The Call Girl* (New York: Ballentine, 1960).

explicated by Becker, and implied by London.[3] The new look in the conceptualization and study of deviant behavior has focused on the interpersonal processes which help define the deviant role, the surroundings in which the role is learned, and limits upon the enactment of the role. As Hooker has indicated regarding the study of homosexuals, one must consider not only the personality structure of the participants, but also the structure of their community and the pathways and routes into the learning and enactment of the behavior.[4] Such "training periods" have been alluded to by Maurer in his study of the con man, and by Sutherland in his report on professional thieves. More recently, Lindesmith and Becker have conceptualized the development of drug use as a series of learning sequences necessary for the development of steady use.[5]

This paper provides some detailed, albeit preliminary, information concerning induction and training in a particular type of deviant career: prostitution, at the call-girl level. It describes the order of events, and their surrounding structure, which future call girls experience in entering their occupation.

The respondents in this study were thirty-three prostitutes, all currently or previously working in the Los Angeles area. They ranged in age from eighteen to thirty-two, most being in their mid-twenties. None of the interviewees were obtained through official law-enforcement agencies, but seven were found within the context of a neuropsychiatric hospital. The remaining respondents were gathered primarily through individual referrals from previous participants in the study. There were no obvious differences between the "psychiatric sample" and the other interviewees on the data to be reported.

All subjects in the sample were call girls. That is, they typically obtained their clients by individual referrals, primarily by telephone, and enacted the sexual contract in their own or their clients' place of

3. H. S. Becker, *Outsiders: Studies in the Sociology of Deviance* (New York: Free Press, Macmillan, 1963). Also see *The Other Side*, ed. H. S. Becker (New York: Free Press, Macmillan, 1964); P. London, *The Modes and Morals of Psychotherapy* (New York: Holt, Rinehart & Winston, 1964). For recent trends in personality theory, see N. Sanford, "Personality: Its Place in Psychology," and D. R. Miller, "The Study of Social Relationships: Situation, Identity, and Social Interaction." Both papers are presented in *Psychology: A Study of a Science*, ed. S. Koch, vol. 5 (New York: McGraw-Hill, 1963).

4. Evelyn Hooker, "The Homosexual Community," *Proceedings of the XIV International Congress of Applied Psychology* (1961), pp. 40–59. See also A. Reiss, "The Social Integration of Queers and Peers," *Social Problems*, 9 (1961): 102–20.

5. D. W. Maurer, *The Big Con* (New York: Signet, 1940); H. S. Becker, *Outsiders;* E. H. Sutherland, *The Professional Thief* (Chicago: University of Chicago Press, 1937); A. R. Lindesmith, *Opiate Addiction* (Bloomington, Ind.: Principia, 1947).

residence or employment. They did not initiate contact with their customers in bars, streets, or houses of prostitution, although they might meet their customers at any number of locations by prearrangement. The minimum fee charged per sexual encounter was $20. As an adjunct to the call-girl interviews, three pimps and two "call boys" were interviewed as well.[6]

Approximately two-thirds of the sample were what are sometimes known as "outlaw broads"; that is, they were not under the supervision of a pimp when interviewed. There is evidence that the majority of pimps who were aware of the study prohibited the girls under their direction from participating in it. It should be noted that many members of the sample belonged to one or another clique; their individually expressed opinions may not be independent.

The interviews strongly suggest that there are marked idiosyncrasies from one geographical area to another in such practices as fee splitting, involvement with peripheral occupations (e.g., cabbies), and so forth. For example, there appears to be little direct involvement of peripheral occupations with call-girl activities in the Los Angeles area, while it has been estimated that up to 10 percent of the population of Las Vegas is directly involved in activities of prostitutes.[7] What may be typical for a call girl in the Los Angeles area is not necessarily typical for a girl in New York, Chicago, Las Vegas, or Miami.

Since the professional literature (e.g., Greenwald, Pomeroy) concerning this occupation and its participants is so limited in quantity, and is not concerned with training per se, the present data may have some utility for the social sciences.[8]

All but two interviews were tape-recorded. All respondents had prior knowledge that the interview would be tape-recorded. The interviewing was, for the most part, done at the girls' place of work and/or residence. Occasional interviews were conducted in the investigator's office, and one in a public park. Interviews were semistructured and employed open-ended questions. One part of the interview concerned the apprenticeship period or "turning out" process.

6. This definition departs somewhat from that offered by Clinard. He defines the call girl as one dependent upon an organization for recruiting patrons and one who typically works in lower-class hotels. The present sample is best described by Clinard's category high-class independent professional prostitute (M. B. Clinard, *Sociology of Deviant Behavior* [New York: Rinehart, 1957]).

7. E. Reid and O. Demaris, *The Green Felt Jungle* (New York: Pocket Books, 1963).

8. H. Greenwald, op. cit.; W. Pomeroy, "Some Aspects of Prostitution" (unpublished paper).

THE ENTRANCE

I had been thinking about it [becoming a call girl] before a lot. . . . Thinking about wanting to do it, but I had no connections. Had I not had a connection, I probably wouldn't have started working. . . . I thought about starting out. . . . Once I tried it [without a contact]. . . . I met this guy at a bar and I tried to make him pay me, but the thing is, you can't do it that way because they are romantically interested in you, and they don't think that it is on that kind of basis. You can't all of a sudden come up and want money for it, you have to be known beforehand. . . . I think that is what holds a lot of girls back who might work. I think I might have started a year sooner had I had a connection. You seem to make one contact or another . . . if it's another girl or a pimp or just someone who will set you up and get you a client. . . . You can't just, say, get an apartment and get a phone in and everything and say, "Well, I'm gonna start business," because you gotta get clients from somewhere. There has to be a contact.

Immediately prior to entrance into the occupation, all but one girl had personal contact with someone professionally involved in call-girl activities (pimps or other call girls). The one exception had contact with a customer of call girls. While various occupational groups (e.g., photographers) seem to be peripherally involved, often unwittingly, with the call girl, there was no report of individuals involved in such occupations being contacts for new recruits. The novice's initial contact is someone at the level at which she will eventually enter the occupation: not a streetwalker, but a call girl; not a pimp who manages girls out of a house of prostitution, but a pimp who manages call girls.

Approximately half of the girls reported that their initial contact for entrance into the profession was another "working girl." The nature of these relationships is quite variable. In some cases, the girls have been long-standing friends. Other initial contacts involved sexual relationships between a Lesbian and the novice. Most, however, had known each other less than a year and did not appear to have a very close relationship, either in the sense of time spent together or of biographical information exchanged. The relationship may begin with the aspiring call girl soliciting the contact. That is, if a professional is known to others as a call girl, she will be sought out and approached by females who are strangers:[9] "I haven't ever gone out and looked for one. All of these have fell right into my hands. . . . They turned themselfs out. . . . They come to me for help."

9. A point also made in the autobiographical account of a retired call girl: Virginia McManus, *Not for Love* (New York: Dell, 1960), p. 160.

Whatever their relationship, whenever the professional agrees to aid the beginner, she also, it appears, implicitly assumes responsibility for training her. This is evidenced by the fact that only one such female contact referred the aspirant to another girl for any type of help. Data are not available as to the reason for this unusual referral.

If the original contact was not another call girl but a pimp, a much different relationship is developed and the career follows a somewhat different course. The relationship between pimp and girl is typically one of lovers, not friends:

> ... because I love him very much. Obviously, I'm doing this mostly for him. ... I'd do anything for him. I'm not just saying I will, I am. ... [After discussing his affair with another woman] I just decided that I knew what he was when I decided to do this for him and I decided I had two choices—either accept it or not, and I accepted it, and I have no excuse.

Occasionally, however, a strictly business relationship will be formed:

> Right now I am buying properties, and as soon as I can afford it, I am buying stocks. ... It is strictly a business deal. This man and I are friends, our relationship ends there. He handles all the money, he is making all the investments and I trust him. We have a legal document drawn up which states that half the investments are mine, half of them his, so I am protected.

Whether the relationship is love or business, the pimp solicits the new girl.[10] It is usually agreed that the male will have an important managerial role in the course of the girl's career, and that both will enjoy the gains from the girl's activities for an indefinite period: "Actually a pimp has to have complete control or else it's like trouble with him. Because if a pimp doesn't, if she is not madly in love with him or something in some way, a pimp won't keep a girl."

Once the girl agrees to function as a call girl, the male, like his female counterpart, undertakes the training of the girl, or refers the girl to another call girl for training. Either course seems equally probable. Referrals, when employed, are typically to friends and, in some cases, wives or ex-wives.

Although the data are limited, it appears that the pimp retains his dominance over the trainee even when the latter is being trained by

---

10. Two of the pimps denied that this was very often so and maintained that the girls will solicit them. The degree to which they are solicited seems to depend upon the nature and extent of their reputations. It is difficult to judge the accuracy of these reports as there appears to be a strong taboo against admitting to such solicitation.

a call girl. The girl trainer remains deferential to the pimp's wishes regarding the novice.

APPRENTICESHIP

Once a contact is acquired and the decision to become a call girl made, the recruit moves to the next stage in the career sequence: the apprenticeship period. The structure of the apprenticeship will be described, followed by a description of the content most frequently communicated during this period.

The apprenticeship is typically served under the direction of another call girl, but may occasionally be supervised by a pimp. Twenty-four girls in the sample initially worked under the supervision of other girls. The classroom is, like the future place of work, an apartment. The apprentice typically serves in the trainer's apartment, either temporarily residing with the trainer or commuting there almost daily. The novice rarely serves her apprenticeship in such places as a house of prostitution, motel, or on the street. It is also infrequent that the girl is transported out of her own city to serve an apprenticeship. Although the data are not extensive, the number of girls being trained simultaneously by a particular trainer has rarely been reported to be greater than three. Girls sometimes report spending up to eight months in training, but the average stay seems to be two or three months. The trainer controls all referrals and appointments, novices seemingly not having much control over the type of sexual contact made or the circumstances surrounding the enactment of the contract.

The structure of training under the direction of a pimp seems similar, though information is more limited. The girls are trained in an apartment in the city in which they intend to work and for a short period of time. There is some evidence that the pimp and the novice often do not share the same apartment, as might the novice and the girl trainer. There appear to be two reasons for the separation of pimp and girl. First, it is not uncommonly thought that cues which suggest the presence of other men displease the girl's customers:

> Well, I would never let them know that I had a lover, which is something that you never let a john know, because this makes them very reticent to give you money, because they think you are going to go and spend it with your lover, which is what usually happens.

(Interestingly, the work of Winick suggests that such prejudices may not actually be held by many customers.)[11] Secondly, the legal

---

11. C. Winick, "Prostitutes' Clients' Perception of the Prostitute and Themselves," *International Journal of Social Psychiatry*, 8 (1961–62): 289–97.

repercussions are much greater, of course, for the pimp who lives with his girl than for two girls rooming together. As one pimp of nineteen years' experience puts it:

> It is because of the law. There is a law that is called the illegal cohabitation that they rarely use unless the man becomes big in stature. If he is a big man in the hustling world, the law then employs any means at their command. . . .

Because of the convenience in separation of housing, it is quite likely that the pimp is less directly involved with the day-to-day training of the girls than the call-girl trainer.

The content of the training period seems to consist of two broad, interrelated dimensions, one philosophical, the other interpersonal. The former refers to the imparting of a value structure, the latter to "do's" and "don'ts" of relating to customers and, secondarily, to other "working girls" and pimps. The latter teaching is perhaps best described by the concept of a short-range perspective. That is, most of the "do's" and "don'ts" pertain to ideas and actions that the call girl uses in problematic situations.[12] Not all girls absorb these teachings, and those who do incorporate them in varying degrees.

Insofar as a value structure is transmitted, it is that of maximizing gains while minimizing effort, even if this requires transgressions of either a legal or moral nature. Frequently, it is postulated that people, particularly men, are corrupt or easily corruptible, that all social relationships are but a reflection of a "con," and that prostitution is simply a more honest or at least no more dishonest act than the everyday behavior of "squares." Furthermore, not only are "johns" basically exploitative, but they are easily exploited; hence they are, in some respects, stupid. As explained by a pimp: "[In the hustling world] the trick or the john is known as a fool. . . . This is not the truth. . . . He [the younger pimp] would teach his woman that a trick was a fool."

Since the male is corrupt, or honest only because he lacks the opportunity to be corrupt, then it is only appropriate that he be exploited as he exploits. "Girls first start making their scores—say one guy keeps them for a while or maybe she gets, you know, three or four grand out of him, say a car or a coat. These are your scores. . . ." The general assumption that man is corrupt is empirically confirmed when the married male betrays his wife, when the moralist, secular or religious, betrays his publicly stated values, or when the "john" "stiffs" (cheats) the

---

12. H. S. Becker, Blanche Geer, E. C. Hughes, and A. L. Strauss, *Boys in White* (Chicago: University of Chicago Press, 1961).

girl. An example of the latter is described by a girl as she reflects upon her disillusionment during her training period.

It is pretty rough when you are starting out. You get stiffed a lot of times. ... Oh, sure. They'll take advantage of you any time they can. And I'm a trusting soul, I really am. I'll believe anybody till they prove different. I've made a lot of mistakes that way. You get to the point, well, Christ, what the heck can I believe in people, they tell me one thing and here's what they do to me.

Values such as fairness with other working girls, or fidelity to a pimp, may occasionally be taught. To quote a pimp:

So when you ask me if I teach a kind of basic philosophy, I would say that you could say that. Because you try to teach them in an amoral way that there is a right and wrong way as pertains to this game ... and then you teach them that when working with other girls to try to treat the other girl fairly because a woman's worst enemy in the street [used in both a literal and figurative sense] is the other woman and only by treating the other women decently can she expect to get along. ... Therefore the basic philosophy, I guess, would consist of a form of honesty, a form of sincerity and complete fidelity to her man [pimp].

It should be noted, however, that behavior based on enlightened self-interest with concomitant exploitation is not limited to customer relationships. Interviewees frequently mentioned a pervasive feeling of distrust between trainer and trainee, and such incidents as thefts or betrayal of confidences are occasionally reported and chronically guarded against.

Even though there may be considerable pressure upon the girl to accept this value structure, many of them (perhaps the majority of the sample) reject it.

People have told me that I wasn't turned out, but turned loose instead. ... Someone who is turned out is turned out to believe in a certain code of behavior, and this involves having a pimp, for one thing. It also involves never experiencing anything but hatred or revulsion for "tricks," for another thing. It involves always getting the money in front [before the sexual act] and a million little things that are very strictly adhered to by those in the "in group," which I am not. ... Never being nice or pleasant to a trick unless you are doing it for the money, getting more money. [How did you learn that?] It was explained to me over a period of about six months. I learned that you were doing it to make money for yourself so that you could have nice things and security. . . . [Who would teach you this?] [The trainer] would teach me this.[13]

It seems reasonable to assume that the value structure serves, in general, to create in-group solidarity and to alienate the girl from "square" society, and that this structure serves the political advantage of the trainer and the economic gains of the trainee more than it allays the personal anxieties of either. In fact, failure to adopt these values at the outset does not appear to be correlated with much personal distress.[14] As one girl describes her education experiences:

> Some moral code. We're taught, as a culture . . . it's there and after awhile you live, breathe, and eat it. Now, what makes you go completely against everything that's inside you, everything that you have been taught, and the whole society, to do things like this?

Good empirical evidence, however, concerning the functions and effectiveness of this value structure with regard to subjective comfort is lacking.

A series of deductions derived from the premises indicated above serve to provide, in part, the "rules" of interpersonal contact with the customer. Each customer is to be seen as a "mark," and "pitches" are to be made.

> [Did you have a standard pitch?] It's sort of amusing. I used to listen to my girl friend [trainer]. She was the greatest at this telephone type of situation. She would call up and cry and say that people had come to her door. . . . She'd cry and she'd complain and she'd say, "I have a bad check at the liquor store, and they sent the police over," and really . . . a girl has a story she tells the man . . . Anything, you know, so he'll help her out. Either it's the rent or she needs a car, or doctor's bills, or any number of things.

Any unnecessary interaction with the customer is typically frowned upon, and the trainee will receive exhortations to be quick about her business. One girl in her fourth week of work explains ["What are some of the other 'don'ts' that you have learned about?"]: "Don't

---

13. The statements made by prostitutes to previous investigators and mental helpers may have been parroting this particular value structure and perhaps have misled previous investigators into making the assumption that "all whores hate men." While space prohibits a complete presentation of the data, neither our questionnaire nor interview data suggest that this is a predominant attitude among call girls.

14. There is, from the present study, little support for the hypothesis of Reckless concerning the association of experienc[ing] trauma and guilt with abruptness of entry into the occupation (W. C. Reckless, *The Crime Problem* [New York: Appleton-Century-Crofts, 1950]).

take so much time. . . . The idea is to get rid of them as quickly as possible." Other content taught concerns specific information about specific customers.

> She would go around the bar and say, now look at that man over there, he's this way and that way, and this is what he would like and these are what his problems are. . . .
> She would teach me what the men wanted and how much to get, what to say when I got there . . . just a line to hand them.

Training may also include proprieties concerning consuming alcohol and drugs, when and how to obtain the fee, how to converse with the customers, and, occasionally, physical and sexual hygiene. As a girl trainer explains:

> First of all, impress cleanliness. Because on the whole, the majority of girls, I would say, I don't believe there are any cleaner women walking the streets, because they've got to be aware of any type of body odor. . . . You teach them to French [fellatio] and how to talk to men.
> [Do they (pimps) teach you during the turning-out period how to make a telephone call?] Oh, usually, yes. They don't teach you, they just tell you how to do it and you do it with your good common sense, but if you have trouble, they tell you more about it.

Interestingly, the specific act of telephoning a client is often distressing to the novice and is of importance in her training. Unfortunately for the girl, it is an act she must perform with regularity, as she does considerable soliciting.[15] One suspects that such behavior is embarrassing for her because it is an unaccustomed role for her to play—she has so recently come from a culture where young women do *not* telephone men for dates. Inappropriate sex-role behavior seems to produce greater personal distress than does appropriate sex-role behavior even when it is morally reprehensible. "Well, it is rather difficult to get on the telephone, when you've never worked before, and talk to a man about a subject like that, and it is very new to you."

What is omitted from the training should be noted as well. There seems to be little instruction concerning sexual techniques as such, even though the previous sexual experience of the trainee may have been quite limited. What instruction there is typically revolves around the practice of fellatio. There seems to be some encouragement not to experience sexual orgasms with the client, though this may be quite variable with the trainer. ". . . and sometimes, I don't know if it's a set rule or maybe it's an unspoken rule, you don't enjoy your dates." "Yes, he did [teach attitudes]. He taught me to be cold."

---

15. The topic of solicitation will be dealt with in a forthcoming paper.

It should be stressed that, if the girls originally accepted such instructions and values, many of them, at least at the time of interviewing, verbalized a rejection of these values and reported behavior which departed considerably from the interpersonal rules stipulated as "correct" by their trainers. Some experience orgasms with the customer, some show considerable affect toward "johns," others remain drunk or "high" throughout the contact.[16] While there seems to be general agreement as to what the rules of interpersonal conduct are, there appears to be considerable variation in the adoption of such rules.

A variety of methods are employed to communicate the content described above. The trainer may arrange to eavesdrop on the interactions of girl and client and then discuss the interaction with her. One trainer, for example, listened through a closed door to the interaction of a new girl with a customer, then immediately after he left discussed, in a rather heated way, methods by which his exit may have been facilitated. A pimp relates:

> The best way to do this [teaching conversation] is, in the beginning, when the phone rings, for instance . . . is to listen to what she says and then check and see how big a trick he is and then correct her from there. . . .
> With every one of them [trainees] I would make it a point to see two guys to see how they [the girls] operate.

In one case a girl reported that her pimp left a written list of rules pertaining to relating to "johns." Direct teaching, however, seems to be uncommon. The bulk of whatever learning takes place seems to take place through observation. "It's hard to tell you, because we learn through observations." "But I watched her and listened to what her bit was on the telephone."

To summarize, the structure of the apprenticeship period seems quite standard. The novice receives her training either from a pimp or from another more experienced call girl, more often the latter. She serves her initial two to eight months of work under the trainer's supervision and often serves this period in the trainer's apartment. The trainer assumes responsibility for arranging contacts and negotiating the type and place of the sexual encounter.

The content of the training pertains both to a general philosophical stance and to some specifics (usually not sexual) of interpersonal behavior with customers and colleagues. The philosophy is one of exploiting

---

16. In the unpublished paper referred to above, Pomeroy has indicated that, of thirty-one call girls interviewed, only 23 percent reported never experiencing orgasms with customers.

the exploiters (customers) by whatever means necessary and defining the colleagues of the call girl as being intelligent, self-interested, and, in certain important respects, basically honest individuals. The interpersonal techniques addressed during the learning period consist primarily of "pitches," telephone conversations, personal and occasionally sexual hygiene, prohibitions against alcohol and dope while with a "john," how and when to obtain the fee, and specifics concerning the sexual habits of particular customers. Specific sexual techniques are very rarely taught. The current sample included a considerable number of girls who, although capable of articulating this value structure, were not particularly inclined to adopt it.

CONTACTS AND CONTRACTS

While the imparting of ideologies and proprieties to the prospective call girl is emphasized during the apprenticeship period, it appears that the primary function of the apprenticeship, at least for the trainee, is building a clientele. Since this latter function limits the degree of occupational socialization, the process of developing the clientele and the arrangements made between trainer and trainee will be discussed.

Lists ("books") with the names and telephone numbers of customers are available for purchase from other call girls or pimps, but such books are often considered unreliable. While it is also true that an occasional pimp will refer customers to girls, this does not appear to be a frequent practice. The most frequent method of obtaining such names seems to be through contacts developed during the apprenticeship. The trainer refers customers to the apprentice and oversees the latter in terms of her responsibility and adequacy in dealing with the customer. For referring the customer, the trainer receives 40 to 50 percent of the total price agreed upon in the contract negotiated by the trainer and customer.[17] The trainer and trainees further agree, most often explicitly, on the apprentice's "right" to obtain and to use, on further occasions, information necessary for arranging another sexual contract with the "john" without the obligation of further "kickback" to the trainer. That is, if she can obtain the name and telephone number

---

17. The fee-splitting arrangement is quite common at all levels of career activity. For example, cooperative activity between two girls is often required for a particular type of sexual contract. In these cases, the girl who has contracted with the customer will contact a colleague, usually a friend, and will obtain 40–50 percent of the latter's earnings. There is suggestive evidence that fee-splitting activities vary according to geographical areas and that Los Angeles is unique for both its fee-splitting patterns and the rigidity of its fee-splitting structure.

of the customer, she can negotiate another contract without fee splitting. During this period, then, the girl not only is introduced to other working colleagues (pimps and girls alike), but also develops a clientele.

There are two obvious advantages for a call girl in assuming the trainer role. First, since there seems to be an abundant demand for new girls, and since certain service requirements demand more than one girl, even the well-established call girl chronically confronts the necessity for making referrals. It is then reasonable to assume that the extra profit derived from the fee-splitting activities, together with the added conveniences of having a girl "on call," allows the trainer to profit considerably from this arrangement. Secondly, contacts with customers are reputedly extremely difficult to maintain if services are not rendered on demand. Thus, the adoption of the trainer role enables the girl to maintain contacts with "fickle" customers under circumstances where she may wish a respite from the sexual encounter without terminating the contacts necessary for reentry into the call-girl role. It is also possible that the financial gains may conceivably be much greater for most trainers than for most call girls, but this is a moot point.

A final aspect of the apprenticeship period that should be noted is the novice's income. It is possible for the novice, under the supervision of a competent and efficient trainer, to earn a great deal of money, or at least to get a favorable glimpse of the great financial possibilities of the occupation and, in effect, be heavily rewarded for her decision to enter it. Even though the novice may be inexperienced in both the sexual and interpersonal techniques of prostitution, her novelty on the market gives her an immediate advantage over her more experienced competitors. It seems quite likely that the new girl, irrespective of her particular physical or mental qualities, has considerable drawing power because she provides new sexual experience to the customer. Early success and financial reward may well provide considerable incentive to continue in the occupation.

A final word is needed regarding the position of the pimp vis-à-vis the call girl during the apprenticeship period. While some pimps assume the responsibility for training the girl personally, as indicated above, as many send the novice to another girl. The most apparent reason for such referral is that it facilitates the development of the "book." Purposes of training appear to be secondary for two reasons: (1) The pimp often lacks direct contact with the customers, so he personally cannot aid directly in the development of the girl's clientele. (2) When the pimp withdraws his girl from the training context, it is rarely because she has obtained adequate knowledge of the profession. This is not to say that all pimps are totally unconcerned with the type of knowledge being imparted to the girl. Rather, the primary concern of the pimp is the girl's developing a clientele, not learning the techniques of sex or conversation.

The apprenticeship period usually ends abruptly, not smoothly. Its termination may be but a reflection of interpersonal difficulties between trainer and trainee, novice and pimp, or between two novices. Occasionally termination of training is brought about through the novice's discovery and subsequent theft of the trainer's "book." Quite frequently, the termination is due to the novice's developing a sufficient trade or other business opportunities. The point is, however, that no respondent has reported that the final disruption of the apprenticeship was the result of the completion of adequate training. While disruptions of this relationship may be due to personal or impersonal events, termination is not directly due to the development of sufficient skills.

DISCUSSION AND SUMMARY

On the basis of interviews with thirty-three call girls in the Los Angeles area, information was obtained about entrance into the call-girl occupation and the initial training period or apprenticeship therein.

The novice call girl is acclimated to her new job primarily by being thoroughly immersed in the call-girl subculture, where she learns the trade through imitation as much as through explicit tutoring. The outstanding concern at this stage is the development of a sizable and lucrative clientele. The specific skills and values which are acquired during this period are rather simple and quickly learned.

In spite of the girls' protests and their extensive folklore, the art of prostitution, at least at this level, seems to be technically a low-level skill. That is, it seems to be an occupation which requires little formal knowledge or practice for its successful pursuit and appears best categorized as an unskilled job. Evidence for this point comes from two separate sources. First, there seems to be little technical training during this period, and the training seems of little importance to the career progress. Length or type of training does not appear correlated with success (i.e., money earned, lack of subjective distress, minimum fee per "trick," etc.). Secondly, the termination of the apprenticeship period is often brought about for reasons unrelated to training. It seems that the need for an apprenticeship period is created more by the secrecy surrounding the rendering or the utilization of the call-girl service than by the complexity of the role. In fact, it is reasonable to assume that the complexity of the job confronting a streetwalker may be considerably greater than that confronting a call girl. The tasks of avoiding the police,

sampling among strangers for potential customers, and arrangements
for the completion of the sexual contract not only require different skills
on the part of the streetwalker, but are performances requiring a higher
degree of professional "know-how" than is generally required of the call
girl.[18]

As a pimp who manages both call girls and "high-class" streetwalk-
ers explains:

> The girl that goes out into the street is the sharper of the two, because
> she is capable of handling herself in the street, getting around the law,
> picking out the trick that is not absolutely psycho . . . and capable of
> getting along in the street. . . . The streetwalker, as you term her, is
> really a prima donna of the prostitutes . . . her field is unlimited, she
> goes to all of the top places so she meets the top people. . . .

The fact that the enactment of the call-girl role requires little
training, and the introduction of the girl to clients and colleagues alike
is rather rapid, gives little time or incentive for adequate occupational
socialization. It is perhaps for this reason, rather than, for example,
reasons related to personality factors, that occupational instability is
great and cultural homogeneity small.

In closing, while it appears that there is a rather well-defined apprenticeship period in the career of the call girl, it seems that it is the
secrecy rather than the complexity of the occupation which generates
such a period. While there is good evidence that initial contacts, primarily with other "working girls," are necessary for entrance into this
career, there seems no reason, at this point, to assume that the primary
intent of the participants in training is anything but the development
of an adequate clientele.

---

18. Needless to say, however, all of the sample of call girls who were asked for status
hierarchies of prostitution felt that the streetwalker had both less status and a less complex
job. It *may* well be that the verbal exchange required of the call girl requires greater
knowledge than that required of a streetwalker, but the nonverbal skills required of the
streetwalker may be considerably greater than those of the call girl.

16

Transitions in Organized Crime: The New Mafia

Francis A. J. Ianni

Organized crime is more than just a criminal way of life; it is an American way of life. It is a viable and persistent institution within American society with its own symbols, its own beliefs, its own logic and its own means of transmitting these systematically from one generation to the next. As an integral part of economic life in the United States it can be viewed as falling on a continuum which has the legitimate business world at one end and what we have come to call organized crime at the other. Viewed in this way, organized crime is a functional part of the American social system and, while successive waves of immigrants and migrants have found it an available means of economic and social mobility, it persists and transcends the involvement of any particular group and even changing definitions of legality and illegality in social behavior.

At present organized crime is in a period of transition. Italian domination has begun to give way to that of a new group: the blacks and Hispanics. During the next decade we will see the presently scattered and loosely organized pattern of their emerging control develop into a new Mafia. This black and Hispanic involvement can be examined as part of the process of ethnic succession. They, like other minorities before them, are inheriting a major instrument to social and economic mobility.

How does this new group differ from its predecessors? What is common and what is different in these groups in comparison to the

From Francis A. J. Ianni, "New Mafia: Black, Hispanic and Italian Styles," *Society* 11 (1974): 26–39, by permission of the author and publisher. Copyright © 1974 by Transaction, Inc.

Italians who preceded them? To answer these questions it is necessary to examine the networks of criminal operation in order to determine the types of relationships which bring people together, foster some kind of criminal partnership, then lead to the formation of organized criminal networks.

To research the nature of crime in America a major study using anthropological field work techniques was undertaken. All of the classifications, descriptions, and anecdotes which follow are drawn from field work. Information was received either from members of networks or from those familiar with criminal networks. Although we focused on the patterns of blacks and Hispanic crime activists, previous research on Italian-American patterns was utilized for comparison.

ORGANIZATION OF CRIME NETWORKS

The first step in determining the pattern or patterns of organization in the networks we observed was to ask the questions: What brings and holds people together in these networks? How are relationships of mutual dependence and responsibility established among people who will engage in organized crime? From our analyses of the networks we found two distinct types of linkages: *causal relationships,* which serve to introduce individuals to each other and into joint criminal ventures; and *criminal relationships,* which are based on a common core of activity in crime. We identified six sets of causal relationships in our networks. All are marked by a sense of mutual trust in the personal characters of those within the relationship.

Childhood. While childhood gangs are an obvious place to look for such friendships, the childhood friendship does not require a gang to establish a potentially criminal relationship. Reggie Martin and Jimmie Brown were childhood friends on 143rd Street, and later, when both were grown and successful in their individual criminal ventures, they joined together to "launder" some of their illicit profits through a joint enterprise in boutiques. The long-term relationship which grows out of childhood friendships is not, of course, restricted to crime circles and is also found in legitimate social relationships. It seems particularly potent in organized crime networks, however. In every case of childhood friendship which grew into an adult criminal partnership, the individuals involved were of the same ethnic or racial grouping and usually of approximately the same age. Obviously, this is not the result of any innate criminality in any of the ethnic groups but rather results from the fact that street society, where kids meet, is based on residential patterns which tend to follow racial and ethnic lines as well as socioeconomic ones. Reggie Martin and Jimmie Brown could just as easily have been meeting in the Grill Room of the Yale Club and discussing the formation of a joint stock venture if their childhood circumstances had been different. But youngsters growing up in the ghetto have a different set of experiences, a different set of role models, and so a different pattern of life chances. One of our interviewees in Central Harlem makes just this point:

> Again I stress the point of making the right kind of friends, from the time you're a little kid, then building up the right kind of respect among your associates, and carrying yourself so that those people who have always known you can continue to depend on you, to think that you are okay. For every friend you have, you have that much more chance to get in on deals, to make it in crime. You are able to be in touch; people will give you their address, their telephone number. Otherwise you are outside looking in—you are nobody. It's a thing in New York that people just don't take you in unless you know somebody. It's a city thing, a poverty thing.

The Recruits.   A second type of linkage develops when an experienced criminal in the neighborhood sees a young boy or gang of young boys with talent and recruits them into organized criminal ventures. This is the most common mode of entry into organized crime and represents the first step in criminal apprenticeship. The War Dragons, a young gang, were recruited in this way following a successful whiskey theft. Recruitment was also the means by which Rolando Solis was brought into the lower echelons of the Cuban Connection (a drug ring) as the first step up the ladder of criminal success. Thus recruitment may involve either individuals, as in the case of Rolando, or groups, as with the War Dragons. Like all social relationships, however, this causal link between younger and older crime activists is two-sided; not only does the older criminal seek out the younger, the youngsters also seek to be recruited and to emulate their elders in crime. It is this role-modeling which gives generational continuity to organized crime and accounts, in part, for its persistence in society.

There were numerous examples throughout the observations and interviews of both blacks and Puerto Ricans which document this apprenticeship system. The process is described by a black from Paterson, New Jersey:

> You can know who is connected and who is involved but you can't go to them and say, 'Hey, man, I want to be one of you!' You can know for certain that Joe Blow is the biggest man in Paterson. He knows me

and I know him but I can't approach that man about it. If I ask him something about that directly he might cuss me out. This is the way it happens. If he has been watching me and he likes what he sees and he wants to give me a little play, he might tell me one day to go see Joe. He won't ever turn around and commit himself to me the first time. You just take this for granted that you don't approach these guys at that level. . . .

Finally, there is the simple, but telling observation by one of our field assistants about the lack of positive influences and legitimate role models for ghetto youngsters:

The ones you see are the ones that interest you. If it had been doctors and lawyers who drove up and parked in front of the bars in their catylacks, I'd be a doctor today. But it wasn't, it was the men who were into things, the pimps, the hustlers and the numbers guys.

Prison Acquaintanceship.   Incarceration can provide very strong and durable links among men who have already been involved in crime and who in the prison atmosphere come to feel themselves segregated from society and find natural linkages among themselves. The chances of these prison links leading to later joint criminal activity and forming the basis for organized crime networks seem to be quite high. Moreover, a multiplier effect is at work here since sometimes being a friend of a friend is enough to establish a link among ex-convicts. The role of prison experience bringing blacks and Puerto Ricans together in crime networks is also an important difference between these groups and the Italians who preceded them. Prison experience, often beginning early in the crime activist's experience, is found very commonly among the blacks and Puerto Ricans in the networks which we have described but seems to have been absent to any sizable degree among Italian-Americans. The strength of kinship and family which binds Italian syndicates together is not found among blacks and is less pronounced among Puerto Ricans than it is among Italians. Thus, the linkages among Italian-Americans are formed early enough so that apprehension and consequent incarceration seem to be less common among Italians than among blacks and Puerto Ricans.

Throughout the networks we found numerous examples of the importance of prison experience in bringing crime activists into contact with each other.

When if I do need him outside [prison], I go to his neighborhood. Everybody is leery of telling me where I can find him or even telling me they know him. But the minute I mention that I did time with him and where, then immediately they come around. They get less scared I may be a cop. When I get to my friend he can take me around so all the people know I'm OK because we did time together.

Prison experience also fosters the strong relationship between a man and "the man who watches my back." The mutual loyalty has been forged during periods of trouble in prison. One inmate protects another. This is one of the strongest links found in black and Puerto Rican crime networks and rivals childhood friendship as a bond.

It sounds strange, but you make your best friends in prison. I could remember a time when something would go down like a strike or something like that. It is like going to a shooting gallery. Someone's waiting to put a shiv in your ribs. But you got friends. The guy in front of me, I'd watch his back; the guy in the back of me watches mine and down the line.

Wives and Lovers. A fourth type of linkage is the infrequent but potent causal type of relationship which seems to exist between individuals in black and, to a lesser extent, Puerto Rican organized crime networks and their wives or lovers. Black and Puerto Rican members of organized crime networks involve women, particularly their lovers, in their criminal activity. Women may be involved in theft rings or in numbers operations. Sometimes they attain fairly high positions within an organization. Here there is a distinctive difference between the emerging black and Puerto Rican organized crime networks and those found traditionally among Italian-Americans. Once again it may represent the strength of family and kinship among Italian-Americans but it may also be a result of the less highly organized and consequently less professionalized relationships among blacks and Puerto Ricans. It is interesting to note that in our field experience we have found that Cubans, who are much more highly organized than either Puerto Ricans or blacks, do not use women in their crime groups. The usual reason given for this by the informants was that the Cubans are "more like the Italians."

Among the blacks there have always been women involved in numbers and dope. You find the same thing in the Puerto Rican race sometimes where they are runners in the numbers; they don't actually "run" numbers from place to place but they do have people come to their house and you leave your number and your money there. Where you don't find any women is with the Cubans. If a Cuban woman gets into drugs or into hustling her ass, she is dead in the Cuban sections, and she better get out as fast as she can.

Kin.   Although family is less important than among the Italian-Americans, kinship ties will sometimes foster a criminal linkage among blacks and Puerto Ricans. Our experience indicates that there is some greater reliance upon kinship among Puerto Ricans than among blacks and that once again, the Cubans seem more like the Italians in that among them, kinship is an important element. One interesting point is that all the kinship ties in our study were between brothers; none were between a father and a son. This could be a function of the limited size of our sample but it could also be a function of the relatively short period of time in which organized crime networks such as those we have described have been in existence in black and Puerto Rican societies. However, the importance of kinship ties, even among blacks, was commented on by a number of informants:

> There is a great deal to the observation that trust is given more easily to a boy if he has a relative—a father, uncle, brother, an aunt—involved in crime. Many times, people want to know who a guy is, that is they want to know his pedigree. A guy is accepted more easily if he has a 'crime-heritage'.

Partners.   The sixth and most common causal type of linkage is the meeting of two men, either through intermediaries or casually, who happen to be in complementary business positions, and consequently form a linkage for common profit. A feeling of mutual trust is established. These kinds of relationships, premised on business, can lead to a great deal of criminal activity. Characteristically, some of the activities are legitimate and some are illegal, but the activity tends to move from one form of organized crime operation to another. Some partnerships are episodic as when a particularly good opportunity arises and two or more individuals along with their associates will join together briefly
for a common venture. In other cases the relationship grows over a period of time as expertise and special skills are required for the continuation of certain types of activities. In either case, the rules of good business practice are as true here as in the world of legitimate business:

> I find that in order for people to put the right kind of opportunities in your path on the streets there must be respect given to the people in positions in crime. They, in turn, must respect your ability as a person or a hustler, or whatever. In this way—through a system of mutual respect—there is the chance that you will be given the opportunity for profit-making in crime. Drug addicts, for instance, are never really successful because they are not respected—they are hooked on dope and cannot be trusted.

CRIMINAL LINKS IN CRIME NETWORKS

In addition to these causal types of linkages in the networks, there are also a number of substantive "criminal relationships," links which develop out of joint criminal operations within a network. Here it is the activity rather than the people which fosters the relationship.

Employer-Employee Relationship.   This is the most common by far, just as it is in the legitimate business world. The employer hires the employee for a salary to do certain things that the employer requires of him. In nearly every one of the networks we find many such relationships. Our study revealed men such as Thomas Irwin who employed a group of thieves, and George the Fence and his employees in the whorehouse, Roberto Mateo and the neighborhood women who worked for him, and Jimmie Mitchell who employed a group of pushers.

Joint Venture.   A second type of substantive criminal relationship is provided in the partnership and joint-venture type of linkage in criminal networks. The partners or associates share equally in the risks, responsibilities and profits. This relationship differs from the employer-employee relationship in that the two individuals involved are in association without a dominant-submissive relationship; there are no fixed leaders or followers. In some cases, however, one partner does seem to have greater authority and perhaps more influence than the others. The childhood gang often operates in this fashion and it appears that older groups do also.

Buyers and Sellers.   A third type of relationship is that which occurs between the buyer and seller of goods. This type of relationship is, of course, very important in the narcotics, boosting, and stolen car trades. However, we have found in most of our networks that this type of relationship exists in a number of the activities of networks. In some cases, it is a well established pattern such as those where illegally acquired goods such as guns or cars are sold either through a middleman or directly as part of the network. In others it tends to be episodic, as when an individual or group learns that someone has some "hot" goods to sell.

Related to the buyer and seller of goods relationship is the buyer and seller of services relationship. In all networks this involves chiefly a specialized criminal skill, such as locksmithing. Other skills such as prostitution or numbers running are less specialized but still important in the networks which include these activities. In the buyer and seller of services relationship, there is usually an established pattern so that the same locksmith, for example, is used repeatedly.

Leaders and Followers.   There is also a complex linkage that exists between a leader of an informal gang and his followers. The most significant examples of this appear in prison life, although it does appear in other networks in some form. This relationship seems to be too informal to maintain a stable operation except in prisons where incarceration keeps inmates in close, continuous association. Here our data are too thin on hierarchical placement, dominance, submission and other organizational features to allow us to do more than speculate that these informal relationships represent first stages in the formalization of leadership in organized crime networks.

Esprit de Corps.   Another type of linkage is that which exists among and between fellow employees, or among and between followers in a gang. Although this type of relationship seldom brings a criminal venture into existence, it is often on this type of relationship that the success of a venture rests. Poor coordination of effort and a lack of cohesion in the group seem to have doomed some of the criminal efforts described in our networks. For example, Luis Santos was a leader of a gang whose downfall was caused by this lack of cohesion. In a traditional legitimate business relationship this would be described as morale, or esprit de corps, within the company.

There are also a few relationships which are somewhat less common than the foregoing but they do emerge with some frequency and seem important to a number of criminal operations. The first of these is that which obtains *between a granter and a grantee of a privilege,* as when, in the Paterson network, Bro Squires inherited his brother's business and his connections and followers as well. In effect this relationship defines property and territorial rights in much the same way as in Italian-American organized crime circles. Another type of relationship which seems to be present in our networks is that which is engendered by bribes and favors; that between *the giver and the recipient of the bribe or favor.* Here the basis of the relationship is the exchange of goods and services based upon mutual needs and the assumption that the exchange is in some fashion mutually beneficial. This is not an uncommon activity even outside of organized crime, but the relationship is an important one for keeping the networks in operation and protected:

> Even to survive with the law you have to be connected. The cops will not take money from just anyone. They are in the business of being a

cop for money and they are interested in pulling in bribes, but they want it in a safe way. The safety comes in knowing the guy from whom they take money. The cop takes the money from a successful man and grants him his protection so that the man can carry out his numbers or dope thing which allows the money to keep flowing to the cop.

Finally, there is a substantive relationship which is not as frequent but should be noted. This is *the relationship engendered by a simple, direct assault.* For example, one of our informants described a policeman in Central Harlem who shakes down addicts to obtain narcotics for resale on the street. We do not have a great deal of data on the use of violence and assault as techniques for compelling behavior in organized crime. Our informants reported repeatedly that violence does occur but is not an important factor since it is the certainty of relationships and the mutual profit among members of the network which keeps it in operation. It is important, however, to remember that criminal business is not always tidy, and consequently violence certainly does occur.

Identification of the causal links which lead to the formation of networks and the criminal links which sustain them helps to clarify the nature of criminal networks and the functional bases on which they are organized. There seem to be two forms of behavioral organization into which all networks can be divided. One type is characterized by the term *associational networks.* These are networks held together by close personal relationships where strong emphasis is placed on mutual trust, and causal links are the usual agents of their formation. We found two forms of associational networks in our field experience.

The first of these is the childhood gang as a beginning criminal partnership. In these associational networks, black or Puerto Rican youngsters growing up in the same neighborhood were involved in criminal activities and then through the process of recruitment became involved in organized crime as a group. The friendships and ties among these youngsters were such that they continued into adulthood. It is important to point out, however, that youthful gangs as such should not be included under organized crime networks because although they might occasionally participate in organized criminal activities, they are not organized entirely for participation in such activities. Rather their importance is as a beginning step and as a source of recruitment into organized crime.

It is this partnership of old neighborhood friends which is most characterized by the sharing of risks and profits, by unclear lines of authority, by expressed concern over many aspects of the personalities of the members, and by the youthfulness of the partnership's members.

This type of network seldom lasts beyond early adulthood, but individual relationships may be maintained long after.

The importance of these childhood relationships in building a "rep" and in forming crime networks is obvious in this excerpt from an interview:

> You've got to be forceful and be willing to do things like putting your life out on the line because somebody just took $10,000 from you. You also have to always be thinking about your business and what you're going to do with it. What happens to it depends on who comes along. Everything works on the basis that you are liked, either because you have qualities that are likeable or because you have qualities that are recognized, such as being a nice guy but still being a regular guy, somebody that is good to be with or a bright kid. These things lead to your being discovered. These are the things that oldtimers look for. It is a tradition.

The second major type of associational network which we found was the prison court, where individuals within prison band together along very strict racial lines and form strong bonds with each other. In addition to racial segregation these prison courts are characterized by strong leadership and a sensitivity to being together under a coercive and authoritarian system. As is true of childhood associations the relationships which are formed tend to be highly personalized and consequently tend to be very lasting. They have the character of partnerships since they do depend on mutual trust and responsibility as well as compatibility of the individuals.

While the chief purposes of the prison court do not include the commission of crime, there is impressive evidence in our data that prison activities are linked to external criminal activities and that base recruitment and basic relationships which serve to structure organized crime networks in the postrelease period are often first formed in prison courts. These prison courts are characterized by (1) a single strong leader and his followers, (2) strict racial segregation, and (3) extreme sensitivity to the closed environment of prison life. It is within these courts that the exchange of favors—the concept of mutual rights and obligations—seems to become well established. The possession or lack of material advantages is an important factor in the adjustment of relations within the prison court. Thus, the individual who is able to provide goods or services is able to achieve a leadership position with the group. The relationships thus established become binding in the sense that there are expectations built up on both sides of each interpersonal relationship.

The second type of behavioral organization is the *entrepreneurial network*. This seems to be a more advanced form among blacks and Puerto Ricans than the associational types. It is the model of the small businessman, the individual entrepreneur, whose illegal activities are carried out through a network of individuals related to him in that activity. In many respects, these crime networks are similar or identical to the kind of network that would coalesce around an individual who establishes his own small legitimate business. The pattern of this type of structure is quite familiar throughout our research and is found in networks ranging from Thomas Irwin's gang of thieves to the gypsy cab industry. Its characteristics seem always the same. One man is basically in charge of the activity by virtue of the fact that he pays the salaries or commissions of the other men. There is not a great deal of hierarchical arrangement among the employees. Most employees seem to have some direct contact with the boss and they identify with him more than they do with other members of the network except in those specific cases where we have seen direct partnerships or long standing relationships among the employee-members. The boss or center of the network is in most cases the only one in the net who has accumulated any risk capital. In fact, if an employee does accumulate risk capital he is likely to try to go off and set up some enterprise of his own. Again it seems that the salaried or commissioned employees, even when they are out on the street, are likely to view their activities as little different from "a job." Similarly, the boss, if the business of the network is successful, is likely to have many of the traits of any good small businessman—economy, prudence, firmness, a sensitivity to when he is being cheated or lied to, and status as a businessman in his neighborhood. It is this relationship between the illegal business set and the community which is most significant as we review the data in the various networks. There are probably no more secrets or confidences within the group of employees in these networks than there would be within any comparable group of employees in legitimate small business. What is different is that despite the illegal nature of the activities, many co-ethnics and neighborhood associates of these networks view them as legitimate.

THE CODE

Like any legitimate organization, criminal networks require a code of rules which regulates relationships between the network and the outside world. It is the code which keeps the network functioning, defines relationships within it, and establishes who is inside and who is outside the net. Control systems of this sort begin with values which define what is "good" and what is "bad." Ultimately, however, human behavior, whether in organized crime or in legitimate enterprises, is guided by specific rules which attempt to operationalize these values and apply them to everyday situations. Thus, while values give us some general sense of what is expected, it is the rule which states what actions will be approved and which forbidden. Rules do not stand alone but are usually grouped into codes or sets of rules which cover specified classes of behavior and the sanctions to be applied when the rule is broken. The rules which govern behavior in organized criminal networks follow just as surely all of these characteristics and direct behavior just as forcefully as do more legitimate codes.

Like so much in the study of organized crime, descriptions of codes for organized criminals have usually been derived by analogy—that is, rather than looking directly at the behavior of criminal syndicate members and extrapolating a code from their words and actions, investigators have tried to apply codes drawn from observations of other groups. One favorite source of analogies for rules of conduct in American criminal syndicates is the "Code of the Mafia," which originated in Sicily. The Task Force on Organized Crime set up in the Johnson Administration, for example, points out that since "there is great similarity between the structure of the Italian-Sicilian Mafia and the structure of the American confederation of criminals, it should not be surprising to find great similarity in the values, norms, and other behavior patterns of the two organizations."

The reason, suggests the report, is that organized crime in America is an offshoot of the Mafia. As the report freely admits, however, the Mafia code itself is also quite similar to those which govern any secret societies such as Mau Mau, or even to those of secret organizations who, like the Irish Republican Army, seek to overthrow the authority in power.

Both Ralph Salerno and Donald Cressey, two leading experts on organized crime in America, further compare these rules of behavior to the Prisoners' Code, an unwritten but widely accepted set of rules which operates among inmates in American prisons. This similarity may be credited to the need of any underground organization for secrecy and control.

Deriving rules of behavior by analogy, however, can only be a valid technique if the values of the organization or group being studied are similar to those of the organization or group from which the analogy is borrowed. There is no certainty that present-day organized crime groups share the values of the Mafia in Sicily in 1900 or, for that matter, of prisoners and thieves. In my recent study of the Lupollo "family," rules were derived from observed behavior rather than by analogy. Our method was to observe and record social action within the Lupollo family and then to seek regularities in behavior which have enough frequency to suggest that the behavior results from the pressures of the shared social system rather than from idiosyncratic behavior. We also asked family members and others about rules, usually by asking why some member of the family behaved in a particular way. Thus, reconstruction of rules of conduct came both from our own observations and from the explanations of observed behavior by the people living under those rules.

In analyzing the data we found three basic rules which organize *(mafia)* behavior in the Lupollo family: (1) primary loyalty is vested in the family rather than in the individual lineages or families which make up the overall organization; (2) each member of the family must act like a man and do nothing which brings disgrace on the family; (3) family business is privileged matter and must not be reported or discussed outside the group. These three rules were the basics for maintaining membership within the group but there were a number of informal rules under each which explain why some members are more successful at playing the game than others.

In studying black and Hispanic organized crime networks, we again tried to extract rules from observed behavior rather than by analogy. A similar but functionally different code of rules exists for each of the two forms of organization we found in our networks.

In associational networks—prison and youthful partnerships—rules seem more likely to speak to intimate personal characteristics:

1. *Don't be a coward.* This rule, which is found in both the prison court and in the youthful networks, enjoins the individual to be a man but has a more physical connotation than we found to be true among the Italian-Americans. Essentially, it indicates that the individual is always willing to fight for his own rights and safety and to a lesser extent for those of his colleagues in the network.

2. *Don't be disloyal.* Here again, the injunction is less positive in terms of its relationship to the group than we found among the Lupollos. What is called for here is a feeling of membership in a group and a basic loyalty rather than the intensely socialized family membership code among the Italian-Americans. Loyalty in this context means acceptance of membership in a group with the consequent requirements that outsiders be rejected.

3. *Don't be a creep.* Here, the rule calls for a normalizing of behavioral relationships among members in the network. What this

rule does is to exclude from membership aberrant individuals—those who are somewhat deficient or who cannot for some reason enjoy full membership—and consequently establishes rules of behavior.

These rules are of course not written and they are usually expressed in terms of punitive or critical actions toward any behavior which violates them. No one says "Be loyal," but when an act by a member of the network is perceived as disloyal by his fellows, he will be subject to verbal and sometimes physical abuse as well. Neither are these rules normally taught in any formal manner; they are learned by experience and taught by example. In effect, these are expected norms of behavior which are socialized into individual network members as a result of their membership in the network in day-to-day experiences.

In prison perhaps more than in the youthful partnerships (and for obvious reasons) shrewdness and the capacity to keep calm seem to be required. Thus, in the prison network we found greater emphasis upon a fourth rule: "Be smart," which enjoins the individual to learn to acquiesce to some regulations which cannot be ignored but at the same time to determine ways to beat the system. This rule, which we found only in the prison networks, is also a rule in what we have earlier called the code of American prisoners. Prisoner-to-prisoner injunctions such as "don't whine ... don't cop out ... be tough ... play it cool and do your own time ... " are responses to the imposed authoritarian environment which is found in prisons but not in the youthful gangs.

In the entrepreneurial networks, rules speak much more to the impersonal requirements of the activities of the network than to the personal qualities we have described in the prison and youthful gang networks. In these business-related networks we found three major rules:

1. *Don't tell the police.* This rule also includes the caution against telling anyone who is likely to tell the police either through malice or weakness. While the rule is strongest within the networks themselves we found that it reaches beyond the networks into the community and that (just as we found among the Italian-Americans) there is a great reluctance on the part of the community to inform on organized crime activities. To some extent this is the result of fear but it also results from an antagonism toward the criminal justice system and a stronger identification on the part of the community members with their co-ethnics in the networks than with the criminal justice system.

2. *Don't cheat your partner or other people in the network.* This rule places a highly "moral" standard on interpersonal behavior within the network but does not carry outside that group. Thus an individual

is expected not to cheat with money inside the network but is not enjoined against doing it externally.

3. _Don't be incompetent in your job._ This rule sets standards of excellence within the network and again it establishes confidence among its members. What this rule suggests is that an individual—thief, numbers runner, prostitute, pimp, locksmith, dealer of stolen goods, narcotics pusher, or hijacker—should do his job well.

These rules seem far less related to personal characteristics than they are to business relationships, because the relationships are more situational or episodic than is true in the prison court or in the youthful gangs. Individuals come together in these entrepreneurial models largely for mutual profit and their dependence upon each other is related entirely to advancing that profit. In the prison court or youthful gang model, however, personal relationships develop out of long-term, intense interaction and are designed to build trust.

While the rules which govern associational networks emphasize personal characteristics and those of entrepreneurial networks emphasize conduct, there is an important relationship between them. The more highly personalized rules take place within networks which might be considered training and testing grounds for the more profitable but also more demanding entrepreneurial networks. Thus recruitment of blacks and Puerto Ricans into sophisticated organized crime networks usually seems to come as a result of prior experience either in a youthful gang or in prison where they are identified as promising individuals. Unfortunately, our data about youth gangs and prison experience among Cubans is quite sparse and we cannot support similar observations there. We do know from our informants that Cubans must go through a preliminary street experience before they are accepted into more important positions. Among blacks and Puerto Ricans, however, enough information is available to codify this process by adding a fifth rule, to be used as a general guide for the entrepreneur type of network which we described earlier: In order to join the "organization" one must have passed through some kind of accredited criminal training course in which it can be assumed that the personal qualities valued in organized crime were duly tested.

Among youthful criminal partnerships, lines of authority seem in general to be poorly drawn—there is little sense of who is obliged to follow whose orders except in particular circumstances. On the other hand, in prison and in the small criminal businesses, certain lines of authority seem to be clearly drawn. In prison, one man in each court is the leader, based on personal qualities and criminal expertise, and all of the others are his followers. In the entrepreneurial network the authority pattern is simple: whoever pays the salaries gives the orders.

Comparing the code of rules for the black and Hispanic network structures with the code of the Lupollo family, there are some obvious similarities and some important differences as well. Both the Italian and the black and Hispanic codes establish who is inside the net and who is an outsider. Those rules demanding loyalty and secrecy serve to establish the boundaries of the network or family and set up behavioral standards as well. It is, of course, not surprising that an organization or network which is engaged in illegal activity should require of its members that they show their loyalty to the group by respecting its confidences and maintaining secrecy. Secret societies of any sort, whether criminal, fraternal, or revolutionary, could not long survive without requiring both loyalty to the organization and some degree of secrecy. Thus the similarity in the two codes results from the generic nature of organized crime as joint clandestine activity. The other similarity between the two codes also derives from the nature of organized criminal activity. These injunctions, which are described in terms such as "be a stand-up guy," "be competent in what you do" or "don't be a coward" are rules which reinforce the feeling of trust among the members of the network or family.

There are also some important differences between the sets of codes. While each of the major rules found among the Lupollos is also found in black and Hispanic networks, these rules do not seem to operate with the same degree of force within the black and Puerto Rican organized crime networks. While the Italian code subordinates the individual and stresses protection of the family—usually a larger organization than a typical black or Puerto Rican network—the latter codes tend to emphasize the individual and secondarily stress loyalty to the network. This may be because of the relatively recent development of networks in comparison to the long history of the Italian crime family.

FUTURE HIERARCHIES

A description of the future of organized crime must be speculative. It is instructive, however, to look at the present pattern of organization, which we found in our study, and the degree of control or power now possessed by the blacks and Hispanics. At present, their networks could not be characterized as big operations, like Italian-American crime families with many layers of authority and countless functionaries and associates, many of whom are not aware of the roles of the others. Black and Hispanic organized crime networks have not yet reached that level of development. We do, however, have enough data on hierarchical arrangements and placement within some of the networks to conclude that while they are growing in complexity, they are still dependent on external sources for supplies and protection. In the Paterson network (the most highly developed of the black networks we examined), the two lowest levels, the street operators who sell drugs, numbers or their bodies as well as their immediate supervisors, the numbers controllers, pimps and small-scale drug suppliers, are all black. It is the next highest, "boss" level which now seems in ethnic transition as Bro Squires, a black, struggles to replace Joe Hajar, a white, as the big man on the hill. Both Squires and Hajar, however, are still dependent on the Italians for police and political protection as well as for drug supplies.

In Harlem in Bedford-Stuyvesant, black networks seem to be free of such dependence on the Italians for protection, but not as yet for drugs except in those cases where they are switching to the Cuban Connection. Internally, these networks do not seem to have developed any new forms of hierarchical arrangement as yet. In the numbers games, the traditional pattern of the carefully articulated runner-controller-banker hierarchy which is still in use by the Italians is also used by both blacks and Puerto Ricans. As we followed the networks upward through the layers of individual black and Puerto Rican entrepreneurs, each with his own little entourage of employees and followers, however, it became obvious that while only in Paterson did we find a direct connection with an Italian syndicate, most of these individual entrepreneurs must relate to Italian families or alternately to the Cuban Connection for drug supplies and for other high-level services such as lay-off banking. Nowhere in our networks did we find blacks or Puerto Ricans who have risen to the point where they are providing major services to other criminals. Neither did we find any systematic pattern of exchange of such services among the various networks. Where we did find any contact among the networks, the individual entrepreneurs seem to be connected to one another either through occasional joint ventures or through straight, one-shot deals for sales or services.

This lack of organizational development in black and Puerto Rican criminal structures coincides with both the newness of blacks and Puerto Ricans in control positions and with the nature of the types of criminal activities which we discovered in these networks. Just as the lack of a sufficient period of time in control positions has hindered any large-scale organizational development, it has also tended to keep the networks in specific types of criminal activities rather than allowing them to achieve hegemony in any one territory. Once again the only exception was in Paterson, where the Italians are still in control. Throughout the networks, however, there is evidence of some embryonic diversification of criminal activity involved in the networks as black control is consolidated. The combinations seem to be fairly stylized: prostitution and drugs, theft and petty gambling, numbers and narcotics are typical patterns. We also found evidence that black crime activists are starting to acquire some legitimate fronts: a boutique, for example, serves to shade some illegal activities, while a gypsy cab is sometimes used for drug transactions and prostitution.

Within this emergent system, mobility is based upon both efficiency needs and power through the accumulation of wealth and territorial control. There is a set of fairly strict rules and norms governing such movement. So it was among the Italians and the evidence suggests that it is becoming so among blacks and Hispanics in organized crime. Successful operations are gaining power increments over time through the scope, extent, and intensity of their dealings. In crime organizations as in more legitimate business enterprises, small operations grow into larger ones and then join with others to maintain territorial control over rich market areas. The market for illegal goods and services is not restricted to the ghetto but at present, with the exception of prostitution, the black or Puerto Rican organized crime networks are excluded from the larger markets which are still dominated by Italians. This same condition prevailed among the Italians in the earlier part of the century until prohibition provided a source for extraghetto profit and power and allowed the Italian mobs to grow into control. But since the present networks among blacks and Hispanics are still relatively small operations, they continue to specialize and have yet to develop into large empires or even interconnected baronies. There are of course a number of indications of connections among networks in the same line of business and some of the activities we observed were on their way to becoming large, but the evidence from our study seems to indicate that the present pattern of loosely structured, largely unrelated networks has now reached its highest stage of development and that what seems to be necessary for these networks to become elaborated into larger combines, like those now present among Italians are: (1) greater control over sectors of organized crime outside as well as inside the ghetto; (2) some organizing principle which will serve as kinship did among the Italians to bring the disparate networks together into larger criminally monopolistic organizations; and (3) better access to political power and the ability to corrupt it.

The first of these conditions, monopolistic control over some sector or sectors of organized crime, can only come about by wresting or inheriting such control from the Italians or, alternately, by developing new forms of illicit goods and services for sale to the public. The current sectors of organized crime—drugs, stolen goods, gambling, prostitution and loan sharking—are presently in a state of transition and their availability to blacks and Hispanics as a source of illicit profit differs. At present, the numbers game is the major organized crime sector coming into obvious and immediate control of blacks and, to a lesser extent, Puerto Ricans. But the short period of control by blacks in this area seems certain to come to an early end. The reasons for its demise are precisely the same as was true in an earlier period when the game's popularity attracted the interest and attention of Jewish and Italian crime syndicates. Now it is the government which seems to be attracted to the immense profits which accrue in this form of gambling. Over the last decade a number of forms of gambling have been legalized, largely as a means of gaining additional revenue for near-bankrupt cities and for state governments as well. In New York, for example, the first step was the establishment of a lottery, ostensibly to defray the costs of education. The success of the lottery, and the lack of a public outcry against it, led to the legalizing of gambling on horse races through the establishment of the Off-Track Betting system. The latter was proposed simply as a means of diverting profits from gambling away from organized crime and directly into the public coffers.

There are now proposals in a number of cities to legalize the numbers as well. Here, however, the conflict between community sentiments and a revenue-hungry government is already beginning to emerge. When Off-Track Betting was established in New York, a number of spokesmen for the black community indicated that now the white middle class had managed to legalize its own preferred form of gambling and even added the convenience of placing the betting parlors throughout the city, doing away with the need to even go to the track. The numbers, however, was a black thing and it remained illegal. Thus, they said it was illegal for blacks to gamble but not for whites. The ghetto dweller's sense of white establishment hypocrisy in legalizing most other forms of gambling while continuing to condemn the numbers is not difficult to understand. On March 6, 1973, the New Jersey edition of the *New York Times* ran a full-column story reporting a police raid on a Puerto Rican numbers operation in East Harlem. The article described the raid by over 40 policemen and detectives, the arrest of 13 people and the confiscation of thousands of dollars worth of equipment. At the bottom of the column, there appeared the black-bordered box which is now present in every issue of the paper:

> The winning New Jersey
> daily lottery number yesterday was:
> 25113

The movement to legalize the numbers seems assured of success within the next few years. The proposals being advanced by a number of blacks are for a system of community control through licensing or franchising arrangements and even the granting of amnesty to present black numbers operators who can run the legal numbers games. The chances for such community control are minimal and even in the unlikely event that it does occur, the important point here is that the numbers, at present the most lucrative form of black organized crime, will certainly disappear through legalization in the near future.

Prostitution, while predominantly organized by black pimps and already operating outside the ghetto, does not actually offer a large enough financial base for further expansion so that among the present forms of organized crime, loan sharking, the theft and sale of goods, and drugs remain as possibilities. Loan sharking and the sale of stolen goods do not seem possible as means of expansion outside the ghetto for black crime activists. It is difficult to imagine that most white Americans would deal with a black salesman pushing stolen goods and even more difficult to envision whites borrowing money from black loan sharks. Thus, while these forms of illicit enterprise may well expand in the ghetto, it is not very probable that blacks can use them as a basis for extending their control over organized crime outside it.

The one sector of organized crime which does seem to present some possibility for black and Hispanic monopolization as a basis for expansion both within and outside the ghetto is drug traffic. First, narcotics and the drug traffic have the same pattern of relationships which surrounded alcohol and bootlegging during the prohibition era. Although there is not as wide a public acceptance of drugs and social opprobrium of hard drug use remains strong, all of the other conditions prevail. Drugs are illegal but in demand. In order for drugs to be produced and wholesaled, some safe haven is necessary for the crime operatives, a place in which they can be assured of at least tacit protection from police by their neighbors. The present movement toward tougher drug laws and stiffer penalties will reduce competition in the drug traffic so that blacks can begin to supply drugs outside the ghetto.

Here, as in prostitution, the willingness of disenfranchized blacks to take risks that other groups need not take to escape poverty will combine with the color blindness of the needs of drug users to break down the racial barriers which impede loan sharking and the sale of stolen goods.

Finally, there is the possibility of corrupting police and other governmental officials without whose protection no form of organized crime could long endure. When the numbers are legalized, the major source of police graft will disappear leaving drugs one of the few remaining sources for the payment of substantial sums to police. All of the conditions for control of distribution within the ghetto are now operative and all that seems necessary is for the blacks and Hispanics to take over the sources of supply and then move into extraghetto distribution. In the East Harlem-Brooklyn Hispanic network, the Cuban Connection is already developing these sources. The importance of cocaine as a street drug has grown tremendously in the last two years and the Cuban Connection has grown apace. Both the police and the underworld, until recently preoccupied with the heroin trade, are now realizing the enormous profits which can be made in cocaine. Its growing popularity among the affluent drug public in penthouses and luxury apartments as well as on the street is equally obvious today. If blacks, either in concert or in competition with Hispanic groups, can take over control of this area then they can develop a national and even international base for operations. Then, as happened among the Italians, they can take their profits and reinvest them in other illicit enterprises. Whether they can also follow the pattern of Italians and use these same monies as a basis for movement into legitimate areas is, however, another question.

The second condition for the elaboration of black organized crime networks into larger combines is the development of some organizing principle which will serve to coalesce black and Hispanic organized crime networks as kinship did for the Italians. Hispanics in organized crime—particularly the Cubans—may well adopt and adapt the existing family model of organization used by the Italians. As we have noted, the bonds of kinship seem stronger in the Hispanic networks we observed than they did among blacks. In fact, there is growing evidence that Hispanics are working in concert with Italian families to a much greater extent than is true of blacks. In September of 1972, for example, Cubans operated the gambling concessions at the San Gennaro festival, New York's annual Italian street fair. Until 1972, of course, the gambling tables and wheels were always operated by Italians. Obviously some arrangement must have been made for the Italians to allow the Cubans to operate, even under franchise, in the heart of Little Italy. While there is a cultural base for a family-type organization among Hispanics, this is not true among blacks.

Instead of family or kinship, however, the blacks may be able to use black militancy as their organizing principle. Previous ethnic groups involved with organized crime—the Irish, the Jews and the Italians—were desperately trying to become white Americans. Now, however, the blacks are beginning to become important in organized crime at a time when being black, being a brother or a sister, serves to create a family-type structure based upon militancy. Even the terminology—brother, sister, mother—expresses a sense of rights and responsibilities to the "family of blacks." More important, blacks and Puerto Ricans involved in organized crime may rightfully feel themselves bound together by the oppressiveness of a system which rejects their attempts at social and political mobility and that during this period when much of black power is negative power—that is demanded and given out of fear—banding together to beat the system by any means may serve as a powerful incentive and organizer.

Patronage, acceptance, and admiration define the attitudes of many of the blacks and Puerto Ricans we spoke with toward blacks and Puerto Ricans in organized crime. The reasons are not difficult to find; the crime activist is making it and he is making it in spite of and in conflict with an oppressive white establishment. Also, the activities he engages in—gambling, boosting and fencing, prostitution and loan sharking—are not considered socially harmful by many ghetto dwellers or indeed by many nonghetto dwellers. Community attitudes toward crime activists change sharply when the drug problem is discussed, but solidarity is even apparent here. The narcotics trafficker is universally detested in the ghetto. Yet the local pusher, even though he is black or Puerto Rican (perhaps because he is black or Puerto Rican) is often not held responsible for the problem of drug addiction. The community's attitude toward the drug pusher is ambiguous. On the one hand, he is a visible symbol of the narcotics traffic and as such becomes an easy target for verbal, sometimes physical, abuse. People living in the community, overwhelmed by the magnitude of the drug problem and not knowing how to deal with it, identify the problem with the pusher. The pusher comes to represent the narcotics problem and the shame and fear community residents feel about drugs. At the same time, community residents assign the responsibility for widespread drug addiction to forces operating on the community from the outside. A conspiracy theory of drugs is widely held in the black and Puerto Rican communities. According to community residents, the widespread use of drugs in the ghetto is the result of a white establishment plot to kill off black and

Puerto Rican youths by allowing or even encouraging drugs in these areas. The role of Italian-American criminal syndicates in narcotics importing and sale is also widely accepted in the ghetto. Community people believe it is Italian-Americans, not blacks and Puerto Ricans, who profit most from the drug trade. Again, this belief mitigates the community's attitude toward the local pusher.

Like most Americans living in our consumer society, ghetto dwellers are hungry for money and for the goods and services it can procure. Ghetto dwellers are cut off from many legitimate ways of obtaining financial security. At the same time they have fewer opportunities than middle-class Americans to achieve the psychological security that can reduce the incidence of crime. When a man is financially secure, happy in his work, has a stable family life, and lives in a stable community, he has little reason to consider criminal activity as a vocational possibility. But blacks and Puerto Ricans, like other ethnics before them, see organized crime as one of the few available routes to success, to financial and thus psychological security. In every society, criminals tend to develop under those social conditions which seem to offer no other way of escaping bondage. Poverty and powerlessness are at the root of both community acceptance of organized crime and recruitment into its networks. Conditions of poverty also nurture community desires for the services organized criminal operations provide. Escapism accounts in part for both widespread drug use and numbers gambling; the resentment that poverty and powerlessness arouse in the subordinated population makes drugs and gambling attractive as mechanisms of rebellion. Organized crime is esteemed for the very reason that society outlaws it.

It is important to note in this context of ethnic succession that none of these characteristics of or attitudes toward organized crime are culture bound: the structures of poverty and powerlessness, rather than the structures of the black and Puerto Rican cultures, seem most responsible. It is of course probable that certain subcultures are more prone to certain kinds of specific behavior as a result of the normative structure of those cultures. As we observed among the Italian-Americans, for example, the cultural model provided by Mafia and other secret criminal organizations in the South of Italy led to a high degree of organizational development in the criminal syndicates operating in the United States. Certainly, if there is a movement toward higher organization within black and Puerto Rican networks, this movement will respond to the culture imperatives of those groups. This, however, is very different from a cultural propensity toward organized crime. Organized crime involves a calculated pattern of offense to one or more of a culture's norms. Its presence is perhaps predictable whenever one culture in a dominating way holds such norms over the head of a lively and energetic dominated subculture. In such a situation, organized crime will probably persist until an adequate degree of assimilation and accommodation takes place. In effect, it can be hypothesized that organized crime results from a conflict of cultures and, further, that organized crime as we know it in the United States requires an underclass of minority-status ethnics in order to be operative.

There seems to be little question that assimilation and accommodation with the larger American society are the chief aims of black and Puerto Rican organized crime activists. This is not to suggest that they are not criminals and that they are not involved in illegal activities but rather that as was true of the Italians, the Jews and the Irish before them, the greater motivation is to achieve social, occupational, and residential mobility. Even while they themselves might never articulate such aims, even when their goals are limited by the scope of their own neighborhood, nevertheless they still exhibit single-minded striving for the material wealth and social security which motivates others in society as well. If some of our informants cannot themselves quite imagine movement toward respectability and security then certainly they want this for their children and their children's children.

Eventually all of these factors could serve to bring together the presently scattered organized crime networks into a classical Mafia. Mafias are first and foremost a form of social protest which can, like the classical Mafia in Sicily and its counterpart among the earlier Italian immigrants to the United States, use crime as a weapon of protest. This protest is expressed in a general attitude toward the law which tends to develop where that law is considered unresponsive or hostile and alien to the culture of the rebellious group. This condition exists in black and Hispanic ghettos today and the coalescence into a new Mafia could prove to be a more effective organizational principle than kinship was among the Italians in organized crime, because its social base is more resistant to social change than kinship bonds are.

The third condition for the elaboration of black and Hispanic crime networks is better access to political power and the ability to corrupt it. The evidence here is more difficult to deal with because it is to some extent contradictory. On the one hand, it is well established in the social history of the city that ethnic groups succeed to power in politics as they do in crime and that the two forms of mobility are often connected. There is evidence that blacks are moving ahead in politics in the large urban areas just as they are in organized crime. What is less evident is that the necessary connections between politics and its corruptibility and black movement in organized crime will coincide. While it is a maxim in the underworld that graft and corruption are color-blind and that police and politicians will take graft regardless of the color of the hand that delivers it, it is difficult to imagine that blacks will be able to insinuate themselves into the kinds of social relationships with white politicians within which deals are made, bribes are offered or sought and protection developed. Again, the black movement in both politics and crime, like so many other processes of social advance among them, comes at a time when much of the power and profit has already been milked from the system by the groups which preceded them. The rampant corruption of our political system reaching up to and now obviously including the White House, could put the costs of corruption to a point where it is prohibitive. This already seems to be the case in New York City, where the revelations of the Knapp Commission on bribe taking by the police seem to have doubled the costs of bribery in just one year's time.

While the growth of a new Mafia is fairly well known or at least perceived in black and Puerto Rican neighborhoods, it would not be unfair to say that, aside from the occasional newspaper headlines, there is little public knowledge that it is going on. To judge from its actions, the greater society seems to consider black and Puerto Rican organized crime as one of the small prices it must pay for the continuance of the many psychological and economic comforts that accrue from the existence of an ethnic underclass. Indeed, when measured against the cost of eliminating such crime, the costs are small. The most visible cost— of the thefts and muggings by narcotic addicts—touch only a few people in the large urban areas. In many respects there is also a continuation of that traditional attitude of the criminal justice system: so long as ghetto dwellers keep their crimes within the ghetto and do not spill outside, leave them to themselves. It is when the muggings and the robberies have reached the nonghetto areas that there is a strong outcry. This attitude, which has traditionally been part of our law enforcement value system, allows organized crime to thrive within the ghetto. Once the organized crime networks find profitable sources of revenue outside the ghetto then the growing economic, political and social impact of organized crime becomes a matter of public interest and social policy. In the meantime, blacks and Hispanics must continue to face the same basic dilemma which confounded earlier generations of Irish, Jews, and Italians: How do you escape poverty through socially approved routes when such routes are closed off from the ghetto? Organized crime resolves the dilemma because it provides a quick if perilous route out.

17

The Social Organization of Burglary

Neal Shover

One of the contributions of American sociologists to the analysis of crime was the early recognition that certain types of criminal pursuits could, like legitimate occupations, be studied as structured and collective activity (Sutherland, 1937; Hollingshead, 1939; Hall, 1952). It was recognized that these structures, or *behavior systems,* commonly consist of distinctive argot, an ideology of defense and legitimation, esoteric knowledge, behavioral norms, and more or less stable relationships between the occupational practitioners and a host of others on whom they are dependent for their successful work performance. Sutherland (1937) applied this sensitizing and organizing concept of the behavior system to theft, insightfully tracing the structure of *professional theft* and the crucial contingencies without which a career as a professional thief could not be realized. This analysis is intended as a continuation in the same tradition. It explicates some of the characteristics of the social relationships which enable one type of burglary offender, the "good burglar," to carry on his activities. The nature of the social relationships between working burglars, and also the relationships between burglars and quasi-legitimate members of the host society, are sketched.

LITERATURE

For Sutherland, the utility of the concept of professional theft as a behavior system stemmed, in part, from the implications this has for

From Neal Shover, "The Social Organization of Burglary," *Social Problems* 20 (1973): 499–514, by permission of the author and the Society for the Study of Social Problems. Tables have been renumbered. The author is grateful to Donald Cressey and Carl Bersani for comments on an earlier version of this paper.

attempts to control professional crime and to understand the activities and careers of thieves (1937, p. 229). However, following Sutherland, others have found that systematic check forgery (Lemert, 1958) and armed robbery (Einstadter, 1969; Camp, 1968) do not appear to conform very closely to this model of professional theft. Unlike the thieves which Sutherland studied, check forgers and armed robbers operate more independently of one another and are not necessarily dependent upon established offenders for tutelage and support. Moreover, they do not maintain ongoing relationships with quasi-legitimate members of the wider society, such as fences and fixers. Thus far, however, burglary and the men who commit it have not been the objects of systematic study.

METHODS

Four different sources of materials were used for this study. First, I read 34 autobiographies of thieves—primarily, though not exclusively, burglars—in their entirety. In addition, 12 novels or journalistic accounts of crime and the activities of criminals were read (e.g., Davis, 1944).[1] Second, a total of 47 interviews were conducted with men incarcerated in the various branches of the Illinois State Penitentiary system. Third, on the basis of these interviews, a lengthy questionnaire was constructed and administered to an additional 88 inmates, in small groups of from three to 12 men at a time. And fourth, interviews were conducted with seven unincarcerated burglars or former burglars, one former fence, and one very peripheral associate of a gang of former bank burglars. All nine of these men were contacted and interviewed without the assistance or cooperation of law enforcement or correctional agencies. Table 17-1 contains limited demographic data on the three different samples. All materials were collected by the author personally.

The collection of data by prison interview and questionnaire proceeded in two steps. First, interviews were conducted with 25 inmates

TABLE 17-1. Demographic Characteristics of the Samples

	Mean (X̄) Age	Race		N
		White	Black	
Prison Interview Sample	23.4	38	9	47
Prison Questionnaire Sample	24.6	71	16	87[a]
Free World Interview Sample	31.6	9	0	9
Total	24.6	118	25	143

[a] Does not include one case for which no records were available.

1. A copy of the list of sources is available upon request from the author.

in various Illinois penal institutions; a topical guide was used to provide minimal structure for these interviews. (The same guide was used to abstract and classify material from the autobiographies.) These interviews each lasted approximately one hour. Following the completion of these initial interviews, the questionnaire was constructed, pretested, and revised. Questionnaire respondents all were new admissions to the Illinois State Penitentiary system for burglary or some related offense (e.g., possession of burglary tools) during the period of the study. Only those men were asked to fill out the questionnaire who were shown by routine testing to be reading at or above a seventh grade level. The questionnaire was usually administered during the first month in the institution, usually in groups of from three to 12 men at a time. Thirteen men declined to complete the questionnaire, in most cases because of suspicion of the author's motives, and in the remaining cases because of feelings of extreme naivete about burglary.

Prison interview respondents were purposively selected, primarily from new admissions to the various institutions. At all times in the selection of interview respondents, I sought to maximize differences in criminal sophistication for comparative purposes. Those respondents who were more criminally sophisticated were all selected by snowballing, after I had made an initial contact with one good burglar. Several of these men were at that time serving sentences for some offense other than burglary; however, each of them had at some time in his life been a skilled burglar. Interviews with 13 men were tape recorded and several of the men were interviewed two or more times. Participation by all respondents was completely voluntary. I repeatedly informed those who participated that "there is no way that you can either be helped or hurt by this."

The use of the questionnaire, autobiographies, and free world interviews were intended to provide a crude triangulation of methods (Denzin, 1970), which was considered especially important in view of the understandable controversy surrounding the use of captive samples (cf. Polsky, 1967; Lemert, 1968). It was recognized, however, that each of the varied methods and research settings contains its own often unique threats to validity. Through the use of a combination of methods and settings, an attempt was made to deal with these validity problems. A more extended discussion of these issues and the methodology can be found in an earlier report (Shover, 1971).

FINDINGS

In the following discussion I present materials on both the *internal* and *external* social organization of burglary. I use the former to refer to the organization of burglary "crews" (i.e., their division of labor) and how they actually operate when "taking off" scores. By the external social organization of burglary, I refer to the relationships between burglars and those outside of their crews with whom they tend to maintain symbiotic social relationships. It is first necessary, however, to discuss the meaning of the concept *good burglar*, since the materials presented here are intended to apply to this type of offender.

The designation "good thief" or "good burglar" is one which is applied selectively by thieves themselves to those who (1) are technically competent, (2) have a reputation for personal integrity, (3) tend to specialize in burglary, and (4) have been at least relatively successful at crime; success in turn is determined by (1) how much money one has made stealing, and (2) how much time, if any, he has done. The good burglar, then, is the man who generally confines his stealing activities to burglary, has been relatively successful, has a reputation as "good people," and is technically competent. At times such a person would be referred to by the more generic designation as a good thief. But in either case the qualitative distinction is most important (cf. Morton, 1950, pp. 18–19).[2]

Of the total number of respondents interviewed for this study, only ten men were considered to be good burglars. These determinations were made on the basis of peer evaluations and material elicited during the interview which indicated past success and sophistication in burglary. All of these men had, at some time, supported themselves solely by criminal activities, the shortest for one year and the longest for approximately 20 years—without incarceration. Of the total questionnaire sample (88), only 20 men were classified as good thieves. This was done on the basis of an arbitrary scoring system applied to (1) the largest sum of money ever received from a single score, and (2) the kind of techniques used to enter places and/or open safes.[3]

Internal Social Organization

Skilled burglary by necessity is a social enterprise. Successful good burglars rarely work alone. The problems simply of managing the act

---

2. An extended discussion of how the social organization of contemporary systematic burglars compares to the behavior system of professional theft as sketched by Sutherland is beyond the scope and space limitations of this paper. I touch upon this issue in the conclusion of this paper.

3. In order to be considered a good burglar a respondent must have (1) received $4,000 or more on his largest score, and either (2) opened a safe at some time by drilling or burning, or (3) entered a place at some time by cutting a hole in the roof or wall. For a more extended discussion of the scoring system used to categorize the sample, see Shover (1971).

requires at least two persons, frequently more. The work is often physically demanding, very time consuming, and must be performed under the apprehension of potential discovery, injury, or arrest. All of these problems must be dealt with, typically by task specialization among members of the burglary crew or "gang." The membership of these crews is in a nearly constant state of flux, as some thieves are arrested, drop out of crime, or are discarded by their crime partners for one reason or another. Although disparate crews may know one another, may hang out in the same joints, and may be linked together to some extent by occasionally overlapping memberships, it is the individual crew which forms the basic unit of social organization among working burglars. These crews are formed from the pool of available manpower which frequents the bars and lounges where thieves hang out, or they may be formed as a result of the assistance of tipsters and fences, who often will introduce burglars to one another.[4]

The key to understanding the social world of the good burglar is found in the recognition that he and his associates form a *category* of individuals, not a society or organization. As Goffman (1963, pp. 23–24) defines it,

> The term category is perfectly abstract and can be applied to any aggregate, in this case, persons with a particular stigma. A good portion of those who fall within a given stigma category may well refer to the total membership by the term "group" or to an equivalent, such as "we" or "our people." Those outside the category may similarly designate those within it in group terms. However, often in such cases the full membership will not be part of a single group, in the strictest sense; they will neither have a capacity for collective action, nor a stable and embracing pattern of mutual interaction. What one does find is that the members of a particular stigma category will have a tendency to come together into small social groups whose members all derive from the category, these groups themselves being subject to overarching organization to varying degrees. And one also finds that when one member of a category happens to come into contact with another, both may be disposed to modify their treatment of each other by virtue of believing that they each belong to the same "group." Further, in being a member of the category, an individual may have an increased probability of coming into contact with any other member, and even forming a relationship with him as a result. A category, then, can function to dispose its members to group-formation and relations, but its total membership does not thereby constitute a group.

---

4. Braly (1967, pp. 233–34) refers to the underworld as a "loosely cohesive and always shifting subworld which include[s] a small manpower pool, fed by a trickle of youngsters outgrowing the teen gangs, and another trickle of men out on parole."

Two men, occasionally three, are usually the largest number of men who will remain together in burglary activities over a relatively long period of time. They tend to confine their burglaries with this same "partner," crew or gang. Whenever the problems expected on some particular score necessitate additional manpower, a not uncommon occurrence, someone who is known to them will be "filled in" for the job. The person who is filled in will be selected on the basis of his trustworthiness, specialized competence, and availability at the time the score is being planned. If he performs well on one job, he may be asked in on other jobs where a person with his qualifications is needed.

As I have indicated, the locus of much of the contact between members of the category of thief or burglar is the hangout, usually a bar, lounge, or restaurant. Gould et al. (1968) have similarly called attention to these hangouts as the places where thieves may recruit partners. In these hangouts thieves spend much of their free time in drinking and socializing. Here they exchange technical information, gossip about one another, talk about "old scores," and plan future ones. The significance of the hangout can be seen in the following remarks, which also tell a great deal about the process by which crews are formed and the loosely knit relationships between working crews.

Q: What are the determinants of whether or not a person gets taken in, or rather taken along, with a good group?

A: Generally you have to know somebody on the crew. Like when I came out of the joint in Iowa I came back to Chicago and I was going out with one guy, a guy I grew up in the neighborhood with. We were going into this joint where the thieves hang out and we made some nice jewelry scores ... And when we went into this joint I got in touch with a couple of fences through the guy that had [owned] this joint ... One particular night this one crew was in there and I got introduced and he more or less told them that I was alright, good people, a good thief and making it. I had a good score that I had looked at so I ran it down to them. So we went over and looked at it and everybody liked it. We all went together and made the score. Owing me something, a couple of weeks later they went out and scored a wholesale house and they called me for a fill in.

For awhile then I didn't work with that crew. But I got filled in with another crew because they needed someone on the radio. One of the guys was in the hospital so I filled in with the crew on a couple of scores. Then I went back to work with the first crew on another score. And [then] this guy that owned the joint, he more or less started working with one guy from this crew and one guy from another crew. They filled me in and we had our own crew.

> And we started operating as a crew—but then we also worked
> intermittently too with other crews (Prison interview, May 1, 1970).

As a consequence of these networks of relationships, even though the
actual span of social organization is extremely limited, working thieves
in even large cities often will know one another, although they may
never have worked together.

> It's like everybody that is stealing—when you have several crews in a
> certain area—they generally know each other ... even though it's no
> big organization thing—20 or 30 burglars and we all have some kind
> of conspiracy—it's just close knit groups and we all know each other.
> If you don't know them all you know two or three here and there, or
> one of your partners knows two or three, or a couple dudes you don't
> know. It's hard to explain. Over the years you get to know everybody
> (Prison interview, May 1, 1970).

Burglary crews, when working, usually function on a partnership
basis (cf. Einstadter, 1969). Such differentiation of authority as does exist
is usually grounded in marked internal differences in age, criminal
experience, or skill. Rarely, however, is there a formally designated
leader (cf. DeBaun, 1950). Tasks during scores are allocated on the basis
of personal strengths and weaknesses, or personal preferences. An easy
informally arrived-at consensus seems to be the rule here. It is not
uncommon for crews to contain at least one man whose mechanical
prowess is quite high as evidenced, among other things, by his ability
to open safes. Nor is it uncommon to find at least one man who seems
to have a particularly good "eye for money" (i.e., who excels at locating
potentially lucrative scores). Although each partner might keep his eyes
open for "something that looked good," one of them would be more
talented along these lines.

Potential scores are located through tips or direct personal selection. The burglar's various "connections" or *occupational contacts* (cf.
Katz, 1958) are the most important source of tips. Burglars themselves
often locate potential scores in a number of different ways. During their
free time, for example, they will often go on automobile trips for hundreds of miles into nearby cities and towns looking over a variety of
places. On "scouting trips" of this nature they will be especially alert
for places similar to those they have made in the past (since chain stores,
for example, will frequently purchase the same type of money safes for
all of their stores).

Having once located a potential score, one or more of the crew will
visit the place to make some preliminary observations. This can range
from driving past a few times in an automobile to possibly walking
around the place or even climbing to inspect the roof during nonbusi-

ness hours. During these early observations the location of the safe is of upmost importance. If it is located near a front window where there is no cover for anyone who would be trying to open it, and if it is also anchored to the floor, it represents a formidable challenge, one which will under most circumstances simply be passed up. On the other hand, if the safe is located in an area of the place which affords cover, the burglars will investigate further. In addition to providing cover from outsiders, the location of the place itself is extremely important. It should, ideally, provide privacy and more than one "out" or avenue of escape. If the place is "bugged," the burglars must determine what type of "bug" it is and the points of vulnerability. If it is a "safe score," they must determine, as precisely as possible, what type of safe it is. If it is a "merchandise score," they will need to know precisely what is to be taken and its location.

To get to and from the score, plans must be made for some kind of transportation. A "work car" is used for this purpose. A stolen car or a used car, commonly purchased for cash under an assumed name, is kept hidden away until needed. A truck might be obtained and used in a similar manner. Occasionally, when the risks and stakes dictate, more than one car or truck will be used during a score; one vehicle might be a legitimate one—valid title and license plates—while one or more others are stolen.

The score itself, as I have emphasized, is planned so that each participant knows exactly what he is expected to do. Three or four men are the most typical size of a crew who take off a score; but here again there is variation, depending upon unique circumstances and conditions. One man is usually left "on point" as a lookout.[5] He can be stationed anywhere that provides good visual coverage of the immediate area, either inside or outside of the place. Depending upon the distance of his station from the building, he might use a walkie-talkie to provide instant warning. Another man will "sit on the calls," listening to police calls on a portable radio, again so that instant warnings of detection can be provided. Another confederate might drive a "pick-up car." Occasionally both the "radio man" and the "point man" will be one and the same person. Most commonly, one or two others will actually make the entry and do the necessary work. This can involve opening a safe and/or preparing merchandise to be hauled away.

Preparations are frequently made in advance for the means and route of escape. The destination is fixed, especially if the burglary in-

---

5. Cf. Einstadter (1969) for an excellent discussion of the social roles involved in heists. Einstadter, it should be noted, was only concerned with the *internal* social organization of armed robbery.

volves merchandise. Generally, in such a case, the first stop will be a "drop" where the fence or one of his agents will inspect the proceeds and arrange for it to be cut up and moved on. If multiple vehicles are used in leaving the score, a legitimate car may be used as a "crash car." The driver of this car will follow the vehicle containing the merchandise and see to it that no one overtakes it from the rear. In the event of failure, and one or more of the participants are arrested, those who escaped are ready and expected immediately to post bail for them.

Members of the crew usually share equally in the proceeds of a score (even "ends"). Any expenses incurred during the planning and carrying out of the score are also shared equally. (And it should be noted that the tools required are sometimes quite expensive.) If there is a "tipster" involved, he will receive an agreed upon percentage of the gross proceeds, frequently a flat ten percent.

External Social Organization

The most important of the social relationships which the good burglar maintains with persons outside his group are closely related to the problems he faces in this work. Collectively these social relationships are known as one's "connections"; the person who is "well connected" has been fortunate in establishing and maintaining a particularly profitable set of such relationships. Systematic burglars face several problems in their work; and their connections are particularly important in helping them to cope with these problems.

First, the good burglar must know before burglarizing a place that it would be worth his while to do so. He wants, above all, to avoid unnecessary exposure to the "bitch of chance" (Braly, 1967, p. 233); so he tries, if possible, to assure himself in advance that a score will be rewarding. Second, if he steals a quantity of merchandise—or anything else that he cannot sell directly—he must have a safe outlet for it; he must be able to sell it without risk to himself of detection. And third, in the event of his arrest, he must be able to so thwart the criminal justice system that he either goes free or else receives an extremely light sentence for his crime(s). The first of these problems, the informational one, is handled by connections with "tipsters"; the second problem, the merchandising problem, is handled by relationships with the "fence"; the third is handled by attorneys, bondsmen, and occasionally, the "fix."[6]

---

6. In many cities gamblers and loan-sharks are also important sources of support for working thieves. Because of their contacts in diverse social circles they are often instrumental in the integration of criminal networks, and in the integration of criminals with quasi-legitimate business and professional men.

The Tipster

A tipster (also known as a "spotter" or "fingerman") is a person who conveys information to a burglar about some premises or its occupants which is intended to aid in burglarizing those premises. Among even moderately successful burglars, tipsters represent an important connection and source of information.

> Your professional burglars depend on information. Any time you read about a darn good burglary, they didn't just happen to be walking along the street and say, Here's a good looking house, let's go in there. They depend upon information from strictly legitimate fellas (Martin, 1953, p. 68).

Tipsters are of several types. Many of them (perhaps the majority) are fences who convey tips to thieves as a way of controlling their inventory. Another type is the ex-thief who holds legitimate employment but still maintains friendships with his old associates. A third type is the active thief who learns about some potentially lucrative score but cannot make it himself because the finger of suspicion would immediately be pointed at him. And finally, another type of tipster is what Hapgood (1903, p. 262) referred to as the "sure thing grafter." This is a person, usually an older thief, who has become extremely selective in his scores. Whenever he hears about a score but does not want to make it himself, he may pass on the tip to some other thief of his acquaintance.

Tipsters of all four types are aware of the value of good information to the burglar; and should they ever receive such information, they are ready to pass it along to someone who can use it. Besides receiving tips from such individuals, the good burglar will, however, occasionally receive information from persons who are not so well informed on burglary and the role of the tipster. This may involve purchasing information from a person who is known to have it; while at other times it may involve the utilization of the knowledge of a personal friend—who may be employed on the premises or may have learned about it some other way.

> In all walks of life you've got people who are morally dishonest. They won't go and steal something themselves. But they'll buy something stolen if they get the right price and they'll give you a little information too. As long as they don't get hurt. Those people are usually legitimate businessmen. They're in a position to give you a lot of information that you couldn't get otherwise. About the protection of different places. About the assets of different places. And the different security measures of different business houses (Martin, 1953, p. 65).

Or the burglar may take a more active part in the search for information.

> This particular place was here in town. I knew a girl that knew a girl that worked there. So I approached this girl and said "Hey I'd like some information about this place. Why don't you ask her and see what she says 'cause I'll pay her for it?" . . . So this girl came back and said, "Yeah, the 15th and 31st there's money there 'cause they cash company payroll checks . . ." Then I sent back for some specific information, what kind of safe it was and how the alarm was tied in . . . We got the place and then I gave this other girl $500 and I never heard anymore about it (Free world interview, March 30, 1971).

Having briefly considered the activities of the tipster, we might now inquire as to just who he is; what kinds of legitimate occupational roles do tipsters occupy? It must be emphasized at the outset that tipsters are not confined to any particular social strata. They are found at all levels of the social structure. As one thief has remarked: "There are some amazing people who come to you with information—people you just wouldn't believe could do such things" (Crookston, 1967, p. 127). The following specific examples of the legitimate occupations of tipsters are mentioned in the autobiographical literature: night watchman (Genet, 1964, p. 58), window cleaner (Page, not dated, pp. 76–77), prostitute (Wilson, 1964, p. 57), attorney (Black, 1926, p. 141; Crookston, 1967, p. 128; Jackson, 1969, pp. 121–22), coal deliveryman (Martin, 1953, p. 65), catering service employee (Malcolm X, 1964, p. 140), jeweler, gambler, detective, and used car dealer (Barnes, 1971, pp. 51–68). In addition, the questionnaire sample was asked if they had "ever received a tip on a place to burglarize." Of the total sample of 88 men, 61 percent replied in the affirmative. These men were then asked to indicate the legitimate occupation of one such person. Responses were given by 26 men, as shown in Table 17-2. The data presented in this table should not be interpreted as a representative picture of the larger population of tipsters. It is presented here only as a means of emphasizing the diversity of backgrounds of tipsters.

TABLE 17-2. Legitimate Occupations Reported for 26 Tipsters

Occupation	N
Tavern Owner or Bartender	7
Owner or Employee of Victimized Place	5
Repairman or Deliveryman	3
Beautician	2
Businessman (unspecified)	2
Other (e.g., police officer, janitor, shipping clerk)	7
Total	26

There is reason to believe that the success of a burglar is directly related to the size of the geographical area over which he maintains connections such as relationships with tipsters (and fences). Some men scarcely know anyone outside of their own city, while others can count on receiving information and assistance from persons in widely separated parts of the United States—or even nearby countries such as Canada and Mexico. The following is a typical account of how these far flung connections are established:

Q: How did you get connected as well as you were?
A: Well, first I was thrown in jail with a man who was pretty well respected throughout the country. I made three or four trips across the country with him, meeting friends of his. And then it just more or less snowballed. It developed that a person in one city [would] say, "If you're going to Miami stop and see so-and-so, tell him I sent you. [There] may be something laying around you can pick up". . . (Free world interview, May 27, 1971).

The value of connections such as these can be appreciated.

Q: You've seen a lot of men, then, who never really amounted to anything stealing. Why was it that they never progressed or became more proficient?
A: Well, one reason is lack of intelligence. [Others are] a lack of connections, a lack of integrity—nobody would trust them—and possibly just no ambition.
Q: You mentioned connections. Do you think they're important?
A: Highly important—well, it depends. Some people are born, raised, steal, and die in the same town. They never get out of the state. They might get out of the city to go to the county jail or penitentiary, then back home. Every policeman in the city knows who they are after they've fallen a couple of times on petty stuff . . . They don't travel far and fast enough.
Q: In what way were connections important to you?
A: They're what I just said in an indirect manner. Because if you're far enough away and fast enough away—through connections—then the local heat don't even bother you. If somebody robbed a safe for $50,000 on westhill today, who would get the blame for it? Where would they start sweeping? All the known safecrackers in this area. Certainly no farther away than Toledo. But suppose someone flew in here from Los Angeles and flew out. He's just about as safe as he can be. Because nobody knows he was here, he don't know anybody in the town except the man who sent for him [tipster]. So he does his little piece of work and goes. The cops are running around picking up everybody in town. But they're not bothering him. You

couldn't do that without connections (Free world interview, June 9, 1971).

The Fence

A fence is a person who buys stolen merchandise, or some other type of commodities (e.g., a coin collection), generally for purposes of resale, which he knows or strongly suspects are stolen. As in the case of tipsters, fences are stratified such that some are better able than others to dispose of a more diversified line of products, a larger quantity of products, and to handle more frequent purchases of products. Additionally, fences can be ordered hierarchically on the basis of how deeply and heavily involved they are in the purchase of stolen goods (cf. Hall, 1952, pp. 155–64; 218–19). The lowest level of fence would be the "square john," who purchases an occasional item from a thief for his own use; the highest level fence would be the person who is able to dispose of nearly any type and quantity of merchandise on the shortest of notices. If it were not for the existence of fences, thieves would have great difficulty disposing of the merchandise they steal. Indeed, systematic theft would be a quite different sort of enterprise without them.

Fences, as already suggested, are one of the most common sources of tips for good burglars. The reason for this is related to the fence's need to exercise some control over the nature and quantity of his inventory. "Giving up scores" (tips) to burglars is one tested and proven technique for doing so. Evidence indicates that this is a very common practice on the part of fences (cf. Malcolm X, 1964, p. 144). In fact, it is this practice which seems to be largely responsible for the fence's having a ready buyer for his products before the thief even "takes off" the score. Giving up scores works, then, to the advantage of both the burglar and the fence. The latter must be seen as occupying a dual role in the behavior system of theft; he purchases stolen goods and simultaneously gathers information about future scores to which the good burglar can be tipped off. By searching out the kinds of merchandise he wants, and then giving the score to burglars, he is able to control his inventory.

But leaving aside the fence's role as a buyer of stolen merchandise, we find that sometimes his relationship with burglars is considerably more complex. Frequently, for example, the fence will be in a position to provide the burglar with several social services (cf. Martin, 1953, pp. 98–99). For example:

> I had . . . this one fence I was doing a lot of business with and he was giving me scores, too. . . . He wasn't a juice man [loan shark] but if you

needed $500 and you did a lot of business with him, if you sold to him regularly, there was no problem. . . . If you had any problem and you needed money quick, say to go out of town to look at something, or if you got sort of short, he could come up with a G-note (Prison interview, March 13, 1970).

Moreover, because of their business contacts, fences occasionally learn about legitimate businessmen or business employees who have gotten themselves into some potentially embarrassing problem. For many of them, this is the kind of problem which could be solved by a contracted "burglary" (cf. Crookston, 1967, pp. 143–44). The fence can put the businessman in touch with a burglar, and the two of them can reach an agreement which works to the benefit of each. Still another service which the fence can provide for the burglar is the introduction of solitary burglars to established crews or gangs, thus helping to link together disparate elements in the thief category.

With few exceptions fences maintain some sort of role in the legitimate business world. Most of them appear, in fact, to be businessmen of one kind or another. According to burglars, there are primarily three reasons for this. First, it is usually only the businessman who has on hand at any given time the ready cash required in dealings with thieves. Second, businessmen can utilize the contacts and knowledge acquired in their legitimate business activities to evaluate and dispose of illicit merchandise (cf. Hall, 1952, pp. 156–57). And third, the fence can use his legitimate business transactions to mask his illicit dealings, thereby making it more difficult for law enforcement officials to build a case against him (cf. Yoder, 1954).

Again, the members of the prison questionnaire sample were asked to indicate the legitimate occupations of "two persons you have personally known who bought stolen merchandise." A total of 61 replies were received and are listed in Table 17–3. There is strong support here for the assertion that most fences are persons who are engaged in some kind of legitimate business. As in the case of Table 17–2, which listed the occupations of tipsters, these data are not presented as representative of the total population of fences, rather they are presented only to give some idea of the types of legitimate occupations found among fences. Actually we would probably be justified in assuming that the data in Table 17–3 are representative of the smaller scale, and less successful, fences.

Bondsmen and Attorneys

Bondsmen and attorneys occupy positions in legitimate society which carry with them the socially sanctioned approval to associate, at least

TABLE 17-3. Legitimate Occupations Reported for 61 Fences

Occupation		N
Tavern owner or Bartender		14
Store owner or Business owner (unspecified)		9
Other business owner		14
service station	4	
restaurant	3	
automobile dealer	3	
pawn shop	2	
barbershop	2	
Policeman		3
Insurance broker		2
Automobile mechanic		2
Television repairman		2
Other (e.g., alderman, jewelry salesman, auctioneer)		15
Total		61

to some extent, with persons who are known to be criminals. That some of them are corrupted in the process is common knowledge (cf. Goldfarb, 1965); of much more fundamental consequence, however, for the stability and perpetuation of the activities of professional criminals— and this includes the good burglar—are the routinized working relationships and understandings which have emerged out of this socially sanctioned link between the underworld and quasi-representatives of the criminal justice system.

For both the attorney and the bondsman there are two extremely important consequences of prolonged contact with members of the underworld. The first of these is a knowledge of the differences in personal integrity which exist among some of the criminal offenders with whom they have contact. The second is a recognition that there are constraints which operate so as to reduce the risks which are run by anyone who, in doing business with thieves, crosses the line of unethical or illegal behavior. Both the attorney and the bondsman learn rather quickly that some members of the underworld are more trustworthy than others. One result of this is recognition that they need not fear the consequences of unethical or illegal transactions so long as they are selective in the types of clients with whom they have potentially embarrassing dealings. Moreover, they learn that members of the underworld usually cannot divulge their guilty knowledge anyway because they themselves would stand to lose much by doing so. They would be sufficiently stigmatized by such disclosures as to make it difficult to acquire competent legal counsel and the services of bondsman on any subsequent criminal charges. This sets the stage for the emergence and flowering of a number of quasi-ethical practices and working relationships.

It must be noted that these practices are further stimulated, and possibly even generated, by certain characteristics of the problems faced by criminal lawyers and bondsmen generally in their work. The former, for example, unlike his corporate counterpart, routinely deals with clients who have little ready cash with which to compensate him for his services.

> Now a criminal lawyer has to give credit, and the main reason for this is that burglars and armed robbers, if they had any money, they wouldn't be out stealing, they'd be partying. It's as simple as that. If they have money, they're partying, and when they're broke, they start to stealing again. If they get caught while they're stealing, they're broke (Jackson, 1969, p. 136).

One result of this is likely to be the attempt by his clients to obtain his services by offering other types of consideration (Carlin, 1966). Among these other kinds of consideration are such things as the sexual favors of wives or girl-friends and property, both real and personal, some of which is almost certainly stolen. The good thief's ability to manipulate the criminal justice system cannot be comprehended unless it is recognized that he differs greatly from the petty thief and first time offender in his knowledge of the workings of the system. Unlike them, he has had a great deal of contact with the various actors which comprise it.

When the good burglar is arrested—as he frequently is—he can count upon receiving the services of both a bondsman and an attorney, even if he has virtually no ready cash. In lieu of a cash down payment the thief will be able to gain his release from confinement, and also preliminary legal representation, on the basis of his reputation and a promise to deliver the needed cash at a later date. He will then search for one or more suitable burglaries (or some other type of crime) which holds out the promise of a quick and substantial reward—so that he can pay his attorney and bondsman. On occasion he will resort to high interest loan sharks ("juice loans") in order to quickly acquire the sums of cash which his attorney and bondsman demand for their services. This period of time when the thief is trying to acquire the cash which he so desperately needs is a particularly stressful one for him. Often he will resort to high risk scores which he would under normal circumstances have passed up. One consequence of this high risk stealing is likely to be another arrest, sometimes in a distant jurisdiction, thus only intensifying his problems.

The principal strategy which the good thief's attorneys use appears to be delay, in the hope that some kind of unforeseen contingency will arise which permits him to gain his client's release or, failing that, to strike a particularly favorable bargain. The fix, which once was relatively common in many American jurisdictions (cf. Byrnes, 1969), has become a much less predictable and available option for the good thief.[7] Admittedly, however, this is an area in which there has never been any thorough research. Nevertheless, if it is true that the fix has become less available for the good thief—as some have contended (cf. Gould et al., 1968)—this could account in part for the alleged decline in the ethical standards of thieves in their dealings with one another (cf. Gould et al., 1968); in a situation in which the probability of serving some time in prison has increased, it would be expected that the willingness of thieves to "cooperate" would similarly increase. And this could lead to a number of working relationships between thieves and the police (cf. Chambliss and Seidman, 1971, pp. 486–88). This also is an area in which more empirical research is needed.

In addition to what has already been noted about the relationships between good burglars and bondsmen and attorneys, other matters should be briefly mentioned. The latter have been known on occasion to provide tips to burglars on places to burglarize. In addition, some of them are alleged occasionally to purchase stolen property from burglars. Finally, in those unusual cases in which the fix can be arranged, attorneys, of course, act as the go-between in working out the details.

CONCLUSION

It should be clear on the basis of what has been said here that an understanding of the activities of the systematic burglar must take into account the social matrix in which he carries on his work, indeed on which he is dependent. To this extent the burglar remains more like the professional thieves which Sutherland sketched, and less like the systematic check forgers studied by Lemert (1958). In some respects, then, the social organization of burglary has continued *relatively* unchanged —at least in comparison with the considerable changes which have occurred in the social organization of check forgery.

Yet even as this is written there is reason to question how much longer it will remain so. For there seems to be near universal consensus that things are changing. In addition to interviews with burglars, the field work for this project included interviews with representatives of two large urban police departments, employees of two safe manufacturers, and a burglary underwriter for a large insurance company. One of

---

7. Space precludes a discussion of the fix as it exists today; however, there is no doubt that the fix is still used in criminal cases. But there is real doubt about how often it is available to the *burglar*. My own views on the contemporary availability of the fix are quite similar to those expressed by Gould et al. (1968) and Jackson (1969).

the points which was made by all of these respondents was their belief that sophisticated burglary is a declining occupation (cf. Gould et al., 1968). Again and again I was told, by thieves as well, that "there's no money in burglary anymore." Two reasons are cited for this change. First, security technology is becoming increasingly sophisticated and represents an ever more formidable challenge to the burglar, which means that many of those offenders who remain in burglary must increasingly confine themselves to easier—and less lucrative—scores. Gone are the days when even a reasonably talented burglar could blow a safe with soap and "oil." Secondly, historical changes in the economy have made cash a declining medium of exchange. There simply is not that much *cash* in safes anymore. Instead, checks and credit cards are used, and it is in the fraudulent manipulation of these that future criminal opportunity will increasingly be found. To the extent that these changes in the economy do in fact produce changes in the attractiveness and social organization of burglary, it will parallel the changes which made check forgery a different kind of offense from what it had been in the very early years of the 20th century (Lemert, 1958).

Another change which many of those interviewed mentioned spontaneously is the gradual erosion of "the Code" among thieves. All seem to agree that the "solid," ethical career criminal seems to be giving way to the "hustler," an alert opportunist who is primarily concerned only with personal—as opposed to collective—security (cf. Irwin, 1970, pp. 8–15; and Gould et al., 1968). Rare is the contemporary autobiography which does not mention and bemoan this trend (cf. MacIsaacs, 1968, pp. 93–94; Crookston, 1967, pp. 140–41). It is always possible that the image of the past is more romance than reality and that this could account in part for the poor showing of our contemporaries (cf. Jackson, 1969, pp. 34–36). We are seriously handicapped here by the absence of any reliable comparative data from earlier periods. Despite this problem, however, it does seem to be true that, compared to the past, when infractions of the code occur today, there is suprisingly little imposed in the way of negative sanctions. This has not, however, altered the strong lip service accorded the code.

Any attempt to explain the apparent changes in burglary and burglary offenders must also take account of improvements in the performance of agents of social control, specifically the police. The existence, for example, of criminal records for police departments who draw upon the services of the FBI has surely done much to eliminate the informational vacuum in which the systematic offender can maneuver in anonymity—and safety. Similarly, the improvement of police technology, which has had the effect of tightening internal controls in police departments (Bordua and Reiss, 1966), has made it more difficult to bargain with isolated individual police officers for their freedom.

Because all of the changes mentioned here are likely to continue, it is reasonable to expect further decline in the ranks of men who approximate the ideal of the good thief.

REFERENCES

Barnes, Robert Earl
1971   *Are You Safe from Burglars?* Garden City, N.Y.: Doubleday.
Black, Jack
1926   *You Can't Win.* New York: A. L. Burt.
Bordua, David J. and A. J. Reiss, Jr.
1966   "Command, control and charisma." *American Journal of Sociology* 72 (July): 68–76.
Braly, Malcolm
1967   *On the Yard.* Boston: Little, Brown.
Byrnes, Thomas
1969   *Professional Criminals of America.* New York: Chelsea House (original published in 1886).
Camp, George M.
1968   "Nothing to lose: A study of bank robbery in America." Unpublished Ph.D. Dissertation. Yale University.
Carlin, Jerome
1966   *Lawyer's Ethics.* New York: Russell Sage Foundation.
Chambliss, William and Robert B. Seidman
1971   *Law, Order, and Power.* Reading, Mass.: Addison-Wesley.
Crookston, Peter
1967   *Villain.* London: Jonathan Cape.
Davis, Clyde B.
1944   *The Rebellion of Leo McGuire.* New York: Farrar and Rinehart.
DeBaun, Everett
1950   "The heist: The theory and practice of armed robbery." *Harpers* (February): 69–77.
Denzin, Norman K.
1970   *The Research Act.* Chicago: Aldine.
Einstadter, Werner J.
1969   "The social organization of armed robbery." *Social Problems* 17 (Summer): 64–82.
Genet, Jean
1964   *The Thief's Journal* (trans. by Bernard Frechtman). New York: Grove Press.

Goffman, Erving
1963   *Stigma*. Englewood Cliffs, N.J.: Prentice-Hall.
Goldfarb, Ronald
1965   *Ransom*. New York: Harper and Row.
Gould, Leroy, Egon Bittner, Sol Chaneles, Sheldon Messinger, Kriss Novak, and Fred Powledge
1968   *Crime As a Profession*. Washington, D.C.: U.S. Department of Justice, Office of Law Enforcement Assistance.
Hall, Jerome
1952   *Theft, Law and Society* (revised edition). Indianapolis: Bobbs-Merrill.
Hapgood, Hutchins
1903   *Autobiography of a Thief.* New York: Fox, Duffield.
Hollingshead, A. B.
1939   "Behavior systems as a field for research." *American Sociological Review* 4(October): 816–822.
Irwin, John
1970   *The Felon*. Englewood Cliffs, N.J.: Prentice-Hall, Inc.
Jackson, Bruce
1969   *A Thief's Primer*. New York: Macmillan.
Katz, Fred E.
1958   "Occupational contact networks." *Social Forces* 37(October): 52–55.
Lemert, Edwin
1958   "The behavior of the systematic check forger." *Social Problems* 6 (Fall): 141–49.
1968   "Book review." *American Journal of Sociology* 73(March): 649–50.
MacIsaacs, John
1968   *Half the Fun Was Getting There*. Englewood Cliffs, N.J.: Prentice-Hall.
Malcolm X (with the assistance of Alex Haley)
1964   *The Autobiography of Malcolm X*. New York: Grove Press.
Martin, John Bartlow
1953   *My Life in Crime*. New York: Signet Books.
Morton, James (Big Jim) (with D. Wittels)
1950   "I was king of the thieves." *Saturday Evening Post* (August 5, 12, and 19): 17–19, 78–81; 28, 92, 94–96; 30, 126, 128, 130–32.
Page, Sir Leo
n.d.   *The Young Lag*. London: Faber and Faber.
Polsky, Ned
1967   *Hustlers, Beats and Others*. Chicago: Aldine.
Shover, Neal
1971   "Burglary as an occupation." Unpublished Ph.D. Dissertation. University of Illinois (Urbana).

Sutherland, Edwin
  1937   *The Professional Thief.* Chicago: University of Chicago Press.
Wilson, Brian
  1964   *Nor Iron Bars a Cage.* London: Wm. Kimber and Co.
Yoder, Robert M.
  1954   "The best friend a thief ever had." *Saturday Evening Post* 227 (December 25): 18–19; 72–73.

PART V

Law Enforcement
and the Criminal

Systematic research on law enforcement agencies was unknown until the early 1960s, when a few scholars began to explore the role of the police in a democratic society. The acceleration of knowledge about the police is attributable to several sources, including: (1) greater willingness on the part of researchers to penetrate traditional barriers surrounding police activities; (2) increased visibility of law enforcement as a means of social control during several years of rapid change in our society; (3) the apparent similarities between functions performed by police organizations and those of other, more widely researched, public bureaucracies; (4) decisions by top police administrators to invite responsible inquiry, hoping that they could thus better cope with complaints of corruption, brutality, selective enforcement of the law, and similar charges made by a disillusioned public; and (5) the need to know what, if any, impact court decisions have made on police operations. In terms of funds expended, research on the police has well exceeded the study of the other components that comprise the criminal justice system.

The enforcement of law by formal agencies of social control is a task relegated to so many diverse organizations that to speak of "the police" is to grossly simplify a complex network of protective services. Distributed among 40,000 autonomous police agencies are about a half million employees, most of whom are sworn officers. Law enforcement personnel consist of the county sheriff and his deputies, metropolitan police, state police, and a variety of federal agencies, including the Federal Bureau of Investigation, the Drug Enforcement Administration, the Secret Service, and the United States Park Police. In the absence of a single federal police in this country, complex jurisdictional arrangements have been made to minimize overlap and duplicity among agencies.

Most local departments are small (about 30,000 have five or less employees), necessitating that personnel be generalists rather than specialists. Large metropolitan departments may be functionally divided into four areas of responsibility: (1) field operations—patrol, criminal investigations, traffic, youth, and special operations divisions; (2) administrative services—community relations, disciplinary review, planning and development, training, and personnel divisions; (3) technical services—communications, property, records, and data processing divisions; and (4) inspectional services—internal affairs, field inspections, and intelligence divisions. Most cities are divided geographically so that districts, boroughs, or precincts centralize and coordinate police services for that area.

Now that published accounts of research are available on many of these organizations and their relationship with the citizenry they serve, certain trends can be noted. First, recent attention has been given to the recruitment, training, and career development of police officers. In part this interest has followed the appearance of women and minority group members at all levels of police activity and the subsequent perception by administrators that their impact needed evaluation. Impetus has also flowed from the belief that better policemen could be provided by more selective recruitment, more sophisticated training, and the provision of career paths that improved upon the usual paramilitary model.

Second, numerous projects have focused upon the roles and functions of the police. At the core of the matter is a conflict among various styles of policing: the maintenance of public order (the "watchman" style); the provision of services to citizens through nonlegal means (the "service" style); and the enforcement of laws regardless of order maintenance (the "legalistic" style). Although a given department or agency may assign greater priority to one of these than to the others at a particular time, as a rule a police officer has enormous discretion. How he exercises that discretion is often a function of his encounters with the public, for just as an officer has culturally induced beliefs about suspects, witnesses, and complainants, they in turn have expectations about the nature and quality of police attention. The discretion police exercise in handling criminal matters is a function of their deployment as *proactive* agents (investigating, stopping, searching, or questioning citizens) or as *reactive* agents (where the initiative for mobilizing them takes the form of citizen complaints or requests for assistance).

Analysis of the police role has led to a number of projects in which traditional police strategies and techniques have been challenged. Among these innovations are designs calling for one-man vs. two-man patrol units in some areas and for neighborhood team policing vs. the usual centralized divisions of patrol/detectives.

A third trend in police research follows a generalized concern over the role of law enforcement in regulating public order and conceptions of morality. Observers have pointed out the ways that police practices are constrained by officers' perceptions of their public. Many scholars have obtained documentation on the differential treatment accorded minority group members, young people, political dissidents, and other "deviants." Other investigators have sought to explain what systems of belief support law enforcement activities directed to different segments of the population. A great deal of attention has been focused upon the involvement of police in certain types of offenses where they have historically acted as "moral entrepreneurs." Most notable among these are gambling, prostitution, abortion, alcohol intoxication, and minor drug cases—often called "victimless" crimes. In many localities one or more of these behaviors now command little notice because they are not considered as serious as other forms of lawlessness, because citizen complaints about them are infrequent, or because changes in the statutes have removed them from police jurisdiction.

A final interest expressed in studies of the police has centered around the organization and control of police forces. In sizeable departments, attempts have been made to measure the efficiency and effectiveness of such aspects of specialization as the centralization of detectives and criminal records, or the use of mobile crime laboratories. Police forces generally have been very sensitive in the last decade to the issue of professionalism. Their original objective was to insulate police work from politics; this eventually led to the expressed need for educational advancements and a restructured police image. More recent projects have analyzed the rapid growth of unions and their ability to influence departmental policy, and have surveyed how well review boards (internal and external) can regulate the integrity of police work.

"Law Enforcement" by David J. Bordua and Albert J. Reiss, Jr. is concerned with the complex transactions between the police as an organization and its environment. The authors begin with a historical account of police systems, show how their accountability to political authority became a major organizational dimension, and how this is related to the nature of encounters between police and citizens.

Peter K. Manning's "Observing the Police" is an essay on the methodology of law enforcement research. In it he discusses the problems of gaining access to the research setting, managing the research role, and dealing with ethical issues that arise in police studies.

Jonathan Rubinstein's "Police Work" is taken from his larger study of the occupational elements in policing. He provides detailed observations on the interpersonal relations between officers, the techniques used to deliver "quality" police work, and the expectations officers develop of working various shifts.

The selection, "The Dilemmas of Police Reform," by James Q. Wilson shows why most police observers feel that a better police force will be an elusive objective. He outlines the disagreements as to what constitutes "better" police and shows what frustrations have been encountered in prior attempts at reform.

The selected bibliography which follows is intended to serve as a partial guide to the literature of law enforcement and the police.

1. *Some General Considerations of Problems and Issues in Law Enforcement*

Alex, Nicholas, *Black in Blue: A Study of the Negro Policeman* (New York: Appleton-Century-Crofts, 1969).

Banton, Michael, *The Policeman in the Community* (New York: Basic Books, 1964).

Bittner, Egon, *The Functions of the Police in Modern Society* (Washington, D.C.: U.S. Government Printing Office, 1970).

Bordua, David J., "Police," in *International Encyclopedia of the Social Sciences,* vol. 12, ed. David L. Sills (New York: Free Press, Macmillan, 1968), pp. 174–81.

_____, ed., *The Police: Six Sociological Essays* (New York: Wiley, 1967).

Buckner, Hubbard T., *The Police: The Culture of a Social Control Agency,* unpublished Ph.D. dissertation, University of California, Berkeley, 1967.

Fox, James C., and Lundman, Richard J., "Problems and Strategies in Gaining Research Access in Police Organizations," *Criminology* 12 (1974): 52–69.

Manning, Peter K., "The Police: Mandate, Strategies, and Appearances," in *Crime and Justice in American Society,* ed. Jack D. Douglas (Indianapolis: Bobbs-Merrill, 1971), pp. 149–93.

_____, *Police Work: Essays in the Social Organization of Policing,* forthcoming.

Niederhoffer, Arthur, *Behind the Shield: The Police in Urban Society* (Garden City, N.Y.: Doubleday, 1967).

The President's Commission on Law Enforcement and Administration of Justice, *Task Force Report: The Police* (Washington, D.C.: U.S. Government Printing Office, 1967).

Reiss, Albert J., Jr., *The Police and the Public* (New Haven: Yale University Press, 1971).

Rubinstein, Jonathan, *City Police* (New York: Farrar, Straus and Giroux, 1973).

Skolnick, Jerome H., *Justice Without Trial: Law Enforcement in a Democratic Society*, second edition (New York: Wiley, 1975).

Wilson, James Q., *Varieties of Police Behavior* (Cambridge: Harvard University Press, 1968).

2. Studies of the Role and Function of the Police

Black, Donald J., "The Social Organization of Arrest," *Stanford Law Review* 23 (1971): 1087–1111.

Clark, John P., and Sykes, Richard E., "Some Determinants of Police Organization and Practice in a Modern Industrial Democracy," in *Handbook of Criminology*, ed. Daniel Glaser (Chicago: Rand McNally, 1974), pp. 455–94.

Cumming, Elaine; Cumming, Ian M.; and Edell, Laura, "Policeman as Philosopher, Guide, and Friend," *Social Problems* 12 (1965): 276–86.

Gardiner, John A., *Traffic and the Police: Variations in Law-Enforcement Policy* (Cambridge: Harvard University Press, 1969).

La Fave, Wayne R., *Arrest: The Decision to Take a Suspect Into Custody* (Boston: Little, Brown, 1965).

Reiss, Albert J., Jr., and Black, Donald J., "Interrogation and the Criminal Process," *The Annals of the American Academy of Political and Social Science* 374 (1967): 47–57.

Sherman, Lawrence W.; Milton, Catherine; and Kelley, Thomas, *Team Policing* (Washington, D.C.: Police Foundation, 1973).

Terris, Bruce J., "The Role of the Police," *The Annals of the American Academy of Political and Social Science* 374 (1967): 58–69.

Tiffany, Lawrence P.; McIntyre, Donald M., Jr.; and Rotenberg, Daniel L., *Detection of Crime* (Boston: Little, Brown, 1967).

Tifft, Larry, "The 'Cop Personality' Reconsidered," *Journal of Police Science and Administration* 2 (1974): 266–78.

Ward, Richard, "The Police Role: A Case of Diversity," *Journal of Criminal Law, Criminology and Police Science* 61 (1970): 580–86.

Weistart, John C., ed., "Police Practices," *Law and Contemporary Problems* 36 (1971).

3. *The Police and Public Order Maintenance*
Bittner, Egon, "Police Discretion in Emergency Apprehension of Mentally Ill Persons," *Social Problems* 14 (1967): 278–92.
_____, "The Police on Skid Row: A Study of Peace Keeping," *American Sociological Review* 32 (1967): 699–715.
McIntyre, Jennie, "Public Attitudes Toward Crime and Law Enforcement," *The Annals of the American Academy of Political and Social Science* 374 (1967): 34–46.
Meyer, John C., Jr., "Patterns of Reporting Noncriminal Incidents to the Police," *Criminology* 12 (1974): 70–83.
Niederhoffer, Arthur, "Criminal Justice by Dossier: Law Enforcement, Labeling, and Liberty," in *Current Perspectives on Criminal Behavior: Original Essays on Criminology*, ed. Abraham S. Blumberg (New York: Alfred A. Knopf, 1974), pp. 47–67.
Reiss, Albert J., Jr., "Discretionary Justice," in *Handbook of Criminology*, ed. Daniel Glaser (Chicago: Rand McNally, 1974), pp. 679–99.
Stinchcombe, Arthur L., "Institutions of Privacy in the Determination of Police Administrative Practice," *American Journal of Sociology* 69 (1963): 150–60.

4. *Popular Accounts of Police Work and its Impediments*
Maas, Peter, *Serpico: The Cop Who Defied the System* (New York: Viking Press, 1973).
McCabe, Bruce, "On the Vice Beat," *The Atlantic* 223 (1969): 122–26.
Wambaugh, Joseph, *The Blue Knight* (Boston: Little, Brown, 1972).
_____, *The New Centurions* (Boston: Little, Brown, 1971).
_____, *The Onion Field* (New York: Delacorte Press, 1973).

5. *The Organization and Control of Police: Trends in Bureaucracy, Malpractice, and Unionization*

LAW ENFORCEMENT AND THE CRIMINAL

Beigel, Herbert, "Investigation and Prosecution of Police Corruption," *Journal of Criminal Law and Criminology* 65 (1974): 135–56.

Bordua, David J., and Reiss, Albert J., Jr., "Command, Control, and Charisma: Reflections on Police Bureaucracy," *American Journal of Sociology* 72 (1966): 68–76.

Chevigny, Paul, *Cops and Rebels: A Study of Provocation* (New York: Random House, Pantheon, 1972).

———, *Police Power: Police Abuses in New York City* (New York: Random House, Pantheon, 1969).

Juris, Hervey, "The Implications of Police Unionism," *Law and Society Review* 6 (1971): 231–45.

Knapp, Whitman et al., *Report of the Commission to Investigate Alleged Police Corruption* (New York: George Braziller, 1972).

Reiss, Albert J., Jr., "How Common is Police Brutality?" *Trans-Action* 5 (1968): 10–20.

Saunders, Charles B., Jr., *Upgrading the American Police* (Washington, D.C.: Brookings Institution, 1970).

Westley, William A., *Violence and the Police* (Cambridge, Mass.: M.I.T. Press, 1971).

18

Law Enforcement

David J. Bordua and Albert J. Reiss, Jr.

Until recently, sociologists paid little attention to police organization and behavior as an object of research. Within the last decade, however, a body of systematic studies has appeared. With what at first sight seems a peculiar perversity, the application of sociology to crime control began at the end of the crime-control process—with corrections—rather than at the beginning—with law enforcement and the police. There are several reasons for this relative neglect. Police until recently have been relatively inaccessible to social science investigation. Sociology itself was identified with the "good government" forces whose purpose was not to study and help the police, but to "expose" them. Moreover, sociologists until recently have been quite uncomfortable in the presence of coercion. They have made their way in the correctional field primarily by providing a "scientific" underpinning to the humanitarian rhetoric that has been so prominent in the correctional reform field.[1]

The professionalization movement in police administration gave sociologists a social base for investigation in much the same way that the high-status prison reform groups did in corrections. The professional administrators by the very fact that they want to professionalize the police emphasize education and the transition from a closed to an open occupation. Moreover, they are increasingly coming to recognize that sociological understanding of organization and behavior is a useful adjunct to the public administration training that most public professionals have gained.

From David J. Bordua & Albert J. Reiss, Jr., "Law Enforcement," in Paul F. Lazarsfeld, William H. Sewell, & Harold L. Wilensky (eds.), *The Uses of Sociology* (New York: Basic Books, 1967), pp. 275–303, by permission of the authors and publisher. Copyright © 1967 by Basic Books, Inc.

1. Joseph P. Eaton, *Stone Walls Not a Prison Make* (Springfield, Ill.: Charles C Thomas, 1962).

The police can be viewed from a variety of sociological perspectives. Those that have informed recent studies of the police have arisen less from the traditional interest in criminology than from more general sociological perspectives. One of these arises from the institutional analysis of the law in the sociology of law. The work of Skolnick, especially, falls in this category. His primary aim was to investigate how value conflicts in a democratic society create conditions that affect the capacity of the police to respond to the rule of law.[2] A second major perspective on the police derives from the study of occupations and social roles. The police are seen as a special occupation group in an occupational organization, the department. The authors of this chapter have emphasized a third perspective, which stresses the transactions between organization and environment.[3] In the case of the police in the United States, both organization and environment are highly complex for any given police organization, and the variations in both are considerable. Moreover, both have been changing over time, so that understanding of current organization requires that attention be given to the historical development of the organization and its transactions with the environment.

Given the generally ahistorical character of American sociology, it is not surprising that sociologists have given little attention to the historical development of law enforcement systems. The writings of Seldon D. Bacon and more recently that of Allan Silver[4] are the major sociological explanations of the emergence of municipal police systems respectively in the United States and England. No attempt has been made to explain their development in the modern period.

EARLY DEVELOPMENTS IN MUNICIPAL POLICE ORGANIZATION

Law enforcement was problematic throughout the history of cities. Yet the modern police department, in the sense of an organization with city-wide jurisdiction, twenty-four-hour responsibility for much of law enforcement, and a regular, salaried, full-time, career police charged with general rather than specific police functions, did not develop until

---

2. Jerome H. Skolnick, *Justice without Trial: Law Enforcement in Democratic Society* (New York: John Wiley & Sons, 1966).

3. Albert J. Reiss, Jr., and David J. Bordua, "Organization and Environment: A Perspective on the Police" in David J. Bordua, ed., *The Police: Six Sociological Essays* (New York: John Wiley & Sons, 1967), pp. 25–55.

4. Allan Silver, "The Demand for Order in Civil Society: A Review of Some Themes in the History of Urban Crime, Police, and Riot in England," in Bordua, ed., op. cit., pp. 1–24.

the nineteenth century. The establishment of the London Metropolitan Police in 1829 and that of New York City in 1844 are the earliest examples of municipal police organization. The underlying social processes that contributed to their establishment were increasing economic specialization, increasing social differentiation, and a growing segregation and density of the urban population.[5]

Increasing economic specialization led to greater citizen dependence on the economic performance of specialists whose performance no longer could be guaranteed by folk control or by market forces. Local governments responded by creating specialized offices of independent inspectors whose duty it was to insure that the populace was not cheated in the market or exploited by their neighbors. As an example, the necessity in New Amsterdam to rely on specialized suppliers of firewood led as early as 1658 to the employment of firewood inspectors. Regulation of butchers, bakers, and hack drivers showed the same consequences of the inability of the citizen to rely on his own resources in a period of increasing specialization. By the time of the emergence of municipal police systems, the list of special regulatory or inspectorial officials had become quite vast.[6] At the time of their formation, some of these inspectors were incorporated into the police department; others were organized in a centralized bureau of inspectors. Although the title of inspector remains in many police departments, most of these inspection services have since been removed to more specialized municipal agencies.

Increasing social differentiation, heterogeneity, and stratification of the population led to lowered consensus on major values and the necessity to develop formal controls if a heterogeneous community was to have at least a minimum of order. Bacon's interpretation covers the ground nicely.

Another method of curbing any overt manifestation of class differences and trying to make compromises or substitute plans of action so that hostility and consequent loss of security will not occur is to set down the acceptable modes of behavior and then place agents at those places and in those times where conflict is likely to arise, to see that the accepted modes of behavior are not infringed upon and to curb at the outset any activity which tends in that direction; this is an expensive adjustment, but not as expensive as the evil it avoids. Like specializa-

---

5. Selden D. Bacon, "The Early Development of American Municipal Police: A Study of the Evolution of Formal Control in a Changing Society," unpublished Ph.D. dissertation, Yale University, New Haven, 1939, Vol. II, Ch. 10.

6. Ibid., p. 767.

tion, class stratification may have its values, but it also has its disadvantages and it is costly to overcome these last and enjoy the benefits.[7]

The "class stratification" to which Bacon refers in the quotation corresponds to differences in "race, nationality, language, major economic function, education, religion, and so forth."[8] Within the rapidly growing American cities, the stage was set for conflict, and conflict there was: struggle over Sunday observance in Boston, near civil war between old inhabitants and immigrants in Philadelphia and between Yankee and Creole in New Orleans, disorders in New York culminating in the Doctors' Riot of 1788, and everywhere problems in the relations between the races. Even slavery under urban conditions became a menace to public order.[9] Matters did not change in the early nineteenth century. The depression years of the 1830's brought riots in three major American cities: a Negro riot in Philadelphia, flour riots in New York City, and riots between firefighting brigades in Boston.

Increasing population density heightened the need to regulate social activity in a variety of ways. It became impossible to continue using the streets as storage facilities, refuse dumps, pastures, or race tracks. Wooden chimneys under congested conditions became a public menace. It became necessary to regulate dogs, kite flying, refuse disposal, handling and storage of explosives, to name but a few. The need for regulation was felt unevenly, and regulation was not always successful. A particularly interesting example of resistance can be found in the swine problem faced by New York City.

> Edict after edict and officer after officer appeared to control this urban problem but their success was limited. The swine were dirty, they dug up the streets, weakened the underpinnings of buildings, attacked small children, were obstructions in the streets and appeared to many people as one of the most obnoxious sights in the city. On the other hand they were a cheap and important supply of food to the poorer people and also acted as a municipal streetcleaning and refuse-disposal department at no cost to the taxpayers.
>
> Various limitations were imposed upon swine: they were ringed; they were forbidden to appear in this or that part of town. Various methods were attempted to enforce the regulations: informers were allowed large fees; the poorhouse officers were allowed to pick up all the hogs they could find and keep the profits for the benefit of their institutions; the constables were ordered to enforce the law; special

---

7. Ibid., pp. 768–69.
8. Ibid., p. 767.
9. Ibid., pp. 769–73.

informers were appointed; any citizen was allowed to claim any swine he might find running loose; hogreeves were appointed.[10]

The problem persisted, however, for 150 years and finally disappeared due to increasing land values and the attendant lack of vacant lots and to the development of street-paving and sanitation services. That the problem persisted whatever the efforts at enforcement illustrated the difficulty of regulation in the face of deep-rooted need and marked division in public opinion. This episode was a preview of enforcement problems in contemporary cities.

City administrations did not respond directly to these underlying processes of specialization, differentiation, and density, however, but rather to the various specific ills which they produced.[11] The rhythms of people, time, and place of city life then as now constituted the basic police reality. Crucial times were nighttimes and holidays; the arrival of many strangers; the advent of war, epidemic, or conflagration. Crucial places were where people of diverse backgrounds and interests were gathered in a limited area—street, marketplace, transport terminal, or theater. Significant objects included animals, weapons, liquor, explosives, and hanging signs. Especially important people were the civic and social "outsiders"—transients (vagabonds), sailors in port, young immigrants, free or slave Negroes.[12]

Situations comprising several of these symptoms were particularly likely to cause trouble. Negroes were dangerous; Negroes with weapons were so dangerous that they were forbidden to have even walking sticks; a drunken Negro with a weapon on a Saturday night at a theater was likely to result in a felony.[13]

The cities studied by Bacon—Boston, New York, Philadelphia, Charleston, and New Orleans—were all important port cities and early in their histories began to display characteristics of many modern American cities, one of the most significant of these being the existence of large populations who were functionally but not normatively integrated into the city. Whole districts became specialized as relatively "lawless," i.e., they housed and catered to the illegal desires of populations especially likely to be disorderly and violent. The "underworld" in early American cities like that in the cities of old consisted of special

---

10. Ibid., pp. 777–78.
11. Ibid., p. 780.
12. Ibid., see Digest, n. p.
13. Ibid., p. 780.

areas of the city where the "lawless" dwelled, not a dispersed minority of criminals organized as a syndicate.

Such "lawless" populations still loom large in the routine problems of policing cities; their ecological concentration helps account for the distribution of police within and among cities. A recent study by Shafter sought to discover why in two small cities of similar populations located sixty miles apart in a Midwestern state there was such a difference in the size of their police departments.[14] "Carbon" with a population of 9,004 in 1960 had five policemen. "Delta" with a population of 9,348 had eighteen policemen. Carbon is a market town that serves a rural hinterland. Delta is a river port and a center for traveling salesmen and seasonal hunters. Moreover, one-third of Delta's population in 1960 was Negro and, except for residence, segregation is complete. Delta could be said to specialize in illegal services and the provision of opportunity for disorder, i.e., in liquor, gambling, prostitution. It is a crime-dependent community, and its economy and social structure require a large police establishment.

EMERGENCE OF A CAREER POLICE

Public response to the problem of order generated by urban change was piecemeal. Not until the establishment of modern police in the middle of the nineteenth century were enforcement officers with general powers and functions to appear. Bacon describes the development of "the night police, the market police, street police, animal police, liquor police, the vagabond and stranger police, vehicle police, fire police, election police, Sunday police and so on."[15] Similarly, we noted that a special inspector office was created each time a new activity had to be regulated. Only slowly did regulation for the public good and the maintenance of order become themselves specializations and the full-time career police develop. The process was, however, extremely slow. In New York it was not until 1741 that a regularly paid night watch was established. These men held full-time jobs in addition and were on duty every third night. It took approximately a century from this point before all the police were organized into a special department of the city.

One of the reasons for the slowness of development was the fiscal problem. Policing is expensive. Financing it on the general tax rolls was politically unpopular. Fiscal difficulties helped account for the wide-

14. Albert J. Shafter, "Numerical Strength of Small Police Departments," *Journal of Criminal Law, Criminology, and Police Science*, LII (1961), 344–46.

15. Bacon, op. cit., p. 781.

spread reliance on informers to be paid out of fines. The financial lure here, of course, was the thought that law enforcement could be partially self-supporting. Also relevant was the idea that paying informers would motivate the citizenry to perform its functions in something like the rural folk pattern.

Paid *Gemeinschaft*, especially on piece rates, had its disadvantages however. Special classes of "professional" informers arose who could use the widespread illegal conduct as a means of livelihood. As would be expected, they themselves tended to be recruited from the less stable and civically integrated segments of the community, and, further, they tended to exploit even weaker and more estranged segments. The very threat to inform became a powerful weapon. Informers were under no organizational discipline whatever.

The most egregious abuse of the informer system in New York was in connection with the control of the behavior of slaves. As early as 1681 the control of slaves "abroad" on the streets became a serious problem. Fees for informers were increased to be paid out of fines levied on the masters who would pay because they disliked seeing their slaves whipped and thereby incapacitated. It was also to the advantage of the city to hold masters responsible for the conduct of slaves. The slave master as a link to the civic outsider seems therefore to have preceded by some years the detached worker in a similar role. Slaves were especially lucrative targets for informers because they as civic nonpersons could not testify in court and challenge the informer's testimony.

The informer system was an attempt to solve several problems that plague policing of cities—how to motivate citizens, how to secure information on crime and evidence for court, how to do so without a politically unsupportable drain on the public purse. The decline of the informer as a paid freelancer still leaves the problem of information and evidence largely unsolved despite the rise of the specialized detective role. Indeed it makes the matter even more complex since the informer was not ordinarily subject to the restrictions on the penetration of private systems which have been increasingly applied to the police in American society.[16]

The motivation of citizen participation in policing was also a live issue. Broadly speaking, in the United States and in England also there has been an evolution from "folk" enforcement based on the solidarities of kin and locality units to an essentially market mechanism based

---

16. Arthur Stinchcombe, "Institutions of Privacy in the Determination of Police Administrative Practice," *American Journal of Sociology*, LXIX (September, 1963), 150–60.

heavily on paid informants (and also piece-rate officers and justices) to a combination of a formally bureaucratized police and the citizen complainant. There is still, however, a widespread use of what are now called informants in police work, especially in offenses where there is no self-defined victim.

The modern informant, however, is "paid" either in foregone prosecutions or in money channeled through police units on a somewhat surreptitious basis. Also of central importance is the fact that informants are not sources of evidence and that indeed testimony of paid informants not only has no special legal standing, but is easily assailed by the defense. Modern informants provide tips, not testimony. Indeed it is possible to describe much modern detective work as the process whereby information satisfactory to the police—tips—is translated into information satisfactory to the courts—evidence.[17]

Formal organization of the police, while a response to the underlying processes and symptoms to which Bacon directs our attention, was also a response to weaknesses and abuses displayed in the informer system. Ideally, formal organization—or bureaucratization—means the interposition between the victim, or complainant, and the offender of a disciplined and disinterested body of men whose decisions are affected by canons of law and formalized bureaucratic discipline rather than by thoughts either of private vengeance or of private gain. Police in a democratic society are to enforce the law and maintain order under the rule of law.

The sequence folk to market to bureaucratic organization may be general in modern societies; it can be seen in the development of armies, of educational systems, and in many other areas where society became too complex for functions to be performed on a folk basis, but where the market mechanism proved unsatisfactory precisely because it made no provision for either reliable execution of collective tasks or for principled conduct and restraint. It is reasonable to suggest that even today the police struggle against the modern versions of these two tendencies—on the one hand for law enforcement to become overwhelmed by private self-help or vigilantism and on the other for protection to be "sold" like a market commodity. Both of these constitute illicit "private" usurpation of "public" functions; they define as central not the relationship of citizen to state, but neighbor to neighbor and buyer to seller. Such "private arrangements" are commonly discussed as a feature of civil law, but of course it is quite appropriate to see them as of much more generic significance.[18]

---

17. See Skolnick, op. cit., Ch. 6, and Reiss and Bordua, op. cit., pp. 41–45.
18. Reiss and Bordua, op. cit., pp. 28–32.

The early form of police bureaucracy was that of paramilitary organization, a form of organization that continues to characterize the police and to render its professionalization not unlike that of the military.[19] The paramilitary form of early police bureaucracy was a response not only, or even primarily, to crime per se, but to the possibility of riotous disorder. Not crime and danger but the "criminal" and "dangerous classes" as part of the urban social structure led to the formation of uniformed and militarily organized police. Such organizations intervened between the propertied elites and the propertyless masses who were regarded as politically dangerous as a class.

In a recent paper, Allan Silver describes the development of the London Metropolitan Police in these terms and points out that a significant difference between England and the United States lies in the tradition of politically articulate riot among the poor in England.[20] The development of the modern police was part of a larger process of expanding normative consensus while solving the political problem by political means, e.g., the eventual reform of the franchise. The "outsiders" of the industrial city were incorporated in the civic body by a combination of legal process and political change.

Police above all link daily life to central authority; moral consensus is extended through the police as an instrument of legitimate coercion. At the same time, the police in performing this function often deflect the hostility of the mass from the class targets to the police themselves. Police in modern societies, therefore, often serve the dubious function of becoming substitute targets of hostility for problems of moral consensus. Much of the difficulty in the relations between Negroes and police in American cities today stems from the fact that the appropriate spheres of legal and political process have been confused. Attempts to provide adequate police protection for the Negro populace while at the same time protecting them from police violation of due process constitute a significant step in the progressive inclusion of this group of civic "outsiders." Nevertheless, no amount of sophistication by police and courts will overcome by itself the effects of housing, employment discrimination, or other problems of urban ghettos. Indeed, it is no exaggeration to say that the police in many American cities are far *ahead* of other segments of civil society in their race relations practices.[21]

---

19. Albert J. Reiss, Jr., "Reflections on Police Bureaucracies in Modern Societies," A Paper for the 6th World Congress of Sociology, Evian, France, September, 1966; also, University of Michigan, Center for Research on Social Organization, Paper No. 20.

20. Silver, op. cit., pp. 1–24.

21. Just as they sometimes are in the problem of relations with adolescents. Trained and specialized juvenile officers probably are better at their jobs than are most school-teachers, especially those teaching in slum schools.

American Negroes will get due process and protection from "whitey's" police long before they get due fellowship from "whitey's" churches.

The problem of civic inclusion of outsiders in Britain was made much simpler by the fact that lines of division were mainly class and not a combination of class, ethnic origin, religion, and race as in the United States. The main "minorities" in the British Isles—the Scots and the Welsh—were integrated into the larger polity party partly by allowing local autonomy in legal administration and in the case of Scotland even a semi-autonomous *corpus juris*.[22]

BUREAUCRATIZATION AND CIVIC ACCOUNTABILITY OF POLICE

Bureaucratization of the police and the attendant control from the top largely solves one crucial problem which confronts societies with organized police—the problem of the political neutrality of the police as a body. Bureaucratization is a device whereby commitment to the occupational organization, to the occupational community, and to its norms of subordination and service takes precedence over extraoccupational commitments. In modern societies the political neutrality and legal reliability of the police is a matter less of the social sources of recruitment than it is a matter of the nature of internal organization, training, and control. Thus the insulation of police from populace which is so often cited as a "problem" in law enforcement is not only a requisite for principled conduct in daily law enforcement, but also a requisite for the removal of police from "high politics" however much they be involved in the "low politics" of patronage and local discretion.

The English solution to the problem of the political reliability of the police was to disarm them and make them directly responsible to the central government. This made it possible for England to have the "best of all possible worlds"—a highly effective police that would not be an internal military threat and therefore not have to be politically balanced by a large standing army. In the nineteenth century the London Metropolitan Police were a local police from the law enforcement standpoint, but a national police from the national political standpoint. In countries centered on a metropolis the way England is centered on London, the high politics of municipal police is of clear significance.[23] Thus, in England the bureaucratic professionalization of the police and

22. Michael Banton, *The Policeman in the Community* (New York: Basic Books, 1964), Ch. 4.

23. David J. Bordua, "The Police," *International Encyclopedia of the Social Sciences* (New York: Crowell Collier, 1967).

the demand that they be able to police the population without firearms were responses not only to the requirements of urban law enforcement, but also to the requirements of high politics.

In the United States, on the other hand, the federal constitution combined with the nonmetropolitan character of most seats of national and state government meant that the problem of political neutrality of the police was never one of "high" politics, but only of "low." Correlatively the demand for rigid internal control of police by administrative elites directly responsible to the executive was less strongly pressed. These conditions when coupled with the general underdevelopment of government services, the successful translation of immigrant votes into municipal patronage, and the restriction of recruitment to local sources meant that, while the purpose of the organized police may have been to suppress the "dangerous classes," the outcome of the development was to staff the police largely with persons drawn from the "dangerous classes" themselves. The mechanisms of staffing the police then were one of the principal devices whereby excluded classes were integrated into the structure of government. "No Irish need apply" definitely did *not* apply to the police.

The inevitable consequence of this situation was police organization of a markedly less "bureaucratic" cast and a strong tendency for immigrant and machine-influenced police to act not as insulated enforcers of abstract law, but rather as intermediaries between the legally and symbolically dominant white Anglo-Saxon Protestant culture and diverse immigrant groups. Through machine politics and ethnic patronage, immigrant groups in the United States were able to some degree to govern the speed of coerced assimilation.[24]

A major organizational dimension of police systems is their accountability to political authority. In modern democratic societies a crucial feature of the accountability of police organizations is the forms of political authority that protect the rights of citizens vis-à-vis the police organization. The mass is in a paradoxical situation in relation to governmental police systems. On the one hand, they are vulnerable to state tyranny enforced through the police organization, i.e., a "police state." On the other hand, they are vulnerable to police tyranny when state authority is unable to directly control the public police organization or hold it accountable.

The organizational form of the accountability system in modern societies bears an important relationship to this paradox. The vulnera-

---

24. The classic source is, of course, William Foote Whyte, *Street Corner Society: The Social Structure of an Italian Slum* (Chicago: University of Chicago Press, 1964).

bility of the citizens to state tyranny has led in some societies to the development of local government police organizational systems that are directly accountable to *local* authority. Local police systems such as in the United States are relatively inaccessible to centralized state control unless their allegiance or compliance can be obtained by other means. These organizational safeguards against state tyranny lead, however, to greater vulnerability of the citizen to local police tyranny, since the state's right and opportunity to intervene generally is limited.

There is an interesting question as to whether the obverse cases obtain: Is the citizen less subject to local police tyranny in centrally organized and controlled police systems? Such systems (at least in the more populated democratic societies) are large-scale bureaucracies. Bureaucratization, of course, is a major way for governments to neutralize civic power. For the police, bureaucratization increases their legal reliability. The neutralization of civic power through bureaucracy makes the citizen less vulnerable to local police tyranny due to local interests, but it opens the way to local bureaucratic tyranny, particularly where the central bureaucracy cannot insure local accountability. To be sure, the central features of bureaucratic "tyranny" apply whether the bureaucracy is local or state controlled, but in a police bureaucracy one need only assure the allegiance of the central commanders to the political elites to insure reasonably effective control of the local organization.

There are a number of important consequences that follow from the organizational form of control and accountability in police systems. In democratic societies, the police bear an important relationship to the resolution of value conflicts in the society, particularly in situations where there is direct civic protest. Some of the important differences in the form and consequences of protest are related to whether the police system is centrally or locally organized and controlled. When there is civic protest involving basic values and the police are centrally organized and controlled, the state is more immediately involved as an organizational actor. The protest is more likely to be defined as an action against the state; if sanctions are applied, they tend to be made across the system. On the other hand, where the police are more locally organized and controlled, such situations are more likely to be defined as protests against local authority; then both sanctions and action taken as a consequence of local protest are defined as local rather than society-wide. Indeed, one might hypothesize that political revolutions and revolutionary situations are more likely to arise in societies with highly centralized bureaucratic police systems. It would follow, then, that where citizens are vulnerable to state tyranny, the state is more vulnerable to revolutionary protest.

One of the major problems in holding the police accountable in all democratic societies is to insure police neutrality in their relations with local elites and interest groups. The criteria governing the legality of police-civil relations in a democratic society are universalistic. A centralized bureaucracy probably is more effective in insuring the legal neutrality of the police from local interests and elites than is a local one.

Yet, this very neutralization of local interests in a centralized system can substantially affect their opportunity to change the police bureaucracy. The problems of civil rights and minority groups in the United States serve as a case in point. The organization of most policing on a local basis has meant that the American Negro minority has had less equity in the legal system, particularly in its southern states. National control of the police undoubtedly would result in a more equitable distribution of justice. At the same time, precisely because of patterns of local control, the Negro minority where effectively organized politically in American cities has changed the quality of police-civil relations and their organizations, changes that have benefited the white majority citizen as well as the Negro minority.

Quite clearly, local organization of the police leads to greater variability among police organizations in the society, both in form and in practice, than does centralized control. Such variability is conductive to innovation as well as to differential application of universalistic norms. It is not surprising, therefore, that police organization in the United States shows both more innovation toward modern police systems and more variability in police-citizen relations than do more centralized systems in other countries.

The organization of police on a local versus a centralized basis also is related to the nature of corruption of the police system when it occurs. In a local system, corruption is highly neutralized because of its linkage to local government and its insulation from the state: The state can neither corrupt nor be corrupted by the police. The situation in a centralized system is quite different. While local bureaucratic corruption occurs, it becomes possible for the police to be corrupted by the state, as well as vice versa.

In the United States, with its local system of policing, one finds again and again instances of "police scandal" involving local government officials and the police or involving local political elites and the police. But it is misleading to conclude that corruption among the police and government officials is widespread in the United States. By the very nature of the local organization of the police, the corruption of both the state political system and of the police is restricted. The recent "Ben Barka" case in France illustrates the contrasting case. With a more centralized police system, the state may corrupt the police or, alternatively, be corrupted by it.

Thus, the problems of crime and public order, of the patterns and varieties of bureaucratization, and of their relationship to the government and organization of cities along with problems of the divergence between formal law and subcultural organization set the stage for the analysis of the police in modern democratic societies.

POLICE PROFESSIONALIZATION AND APPLIED SOCIOLOGY

Sociologists pay little attention to budgets. As Bacon pointed out in his discussion of the development of modern police, however, policing is expensive. We can gain some understanding of the significance of more recent police history and of the professionalization movement in the police by examining briefly the expenditure on police. From 1902 to 1960 annual expenditures for local police in the United States increased from 50 to 1,612 millions of dollars—an increase of 3,124 percent. When account is taken of inflation, population growth, urban concentration, increases in motor vehicles, and increases in the per hour cost of police salaries, the net in funds available to the police is about 20 percent. Although the study from which these data are drawn is still incomplete and considering the extreme difficulty of drawing unequivocal conclusions from trend data, it seems accurate nevertheless to conclude that during the first six decades of the twentieth century, there has been no appreciable real increase in funds available to the local police for crime control use.[25]

Small wonder then that the main thrust of the professionalization movement in the United States has been in the direction of improving operating efficiency, in communications systems and administrative competence, and in the search for ways of conserving and more effectively controlling scarce police manpower. From the beginning of the century to the present we can only conclude that there must have been a dramatic increase in police productivity as a consequence of the technological and managerial rationalization which has accompanied professionalization. Managerial rationalization and increased productivity have not been the only results of the professionalization movement. There can be little doubt that in some cities at least there have been significant gains in the degree to which the police conform to due process. Such conformity is difficult, however, even in the most profes-

---

25. This material on police expenditure is taken from a study currently being made by David J. Bordua and Edward Haurek, University of Illinois.

sionalized departments both because the translation of elite professional perspectives to the rank and file is difficult and because the demands of some enforcement jobs create severe conflict between the requirements for effective enforcement and the demands of due process as enunciated by the courts.[26]

For the first time in American history the emergence of a self-consciously professional police elite coupled with its increasing (though far from complete) success in tightening internal control over department operations provides the organizational conditions whereby not only public demands for efficiency and productivity but also judicial demands for legality can be translated into operations.[27] Developing professionalization of the police also provides the necessary base for the application of sociology to law enforcement concerns. Perhaps even more appropriately put, it provides the base for carrying out the necessary sociological research which in the near future will be translatable into application.

AREAS OF APPLICATION

Applied sociology cannot prosper in the absence of some criteria of effectiveness of personnel and of organization. The police professionalization movement has provided sociologists with a social base and a body of consumers of its material, but it has not provided solid criteria of effectiveness to guide research contributions. Unlike early industrial sociology, which could get along on simple criteria such as increased production or decreased turnover, the problem of criteria in the effectiveness of law enforcement and of policing is extremely complex.

Because of its emphasis on education, the professionalization movement has opened the way for what is probably the most significant "application" of sociology to date. While no definitive data are available, the exposure of police students to sociology in police academies or at the college, junior college, and graduate levels is increasing very rapidly, though in absolute numbers the exposure is probably still small. While the immediate effect on police performance of exposure to academic sociology may be minimal or at best undemonstrable, the proba-

---

26. See Skolnick, op. cit. Also see Wayne R. La Fave, *Arrest: The Decision to Take a Suspect into Custody* (Boston: Little, Brown, 1965); Donald J. Newman, *Conviction: The Determination of Guilt or Innocence without Trial* (Boston: Little, Brown, 1966), esp. Ch. 14.

27. David J. Bordua and Albert J. Reiss, Jr., "Command, Control and Charisma: Reflections on Police Bureaucracy," *American Journal of Sociology*, LXXII (July, 1966), 68–76.

ble long-run effect of helping define policing as an open profession which participates in the general academic dialogue should be of great significance.

Beyond general education of police officers and the explanations of crime and criminality, applications of sociology to law enforcement and police organization can be divided into those touching upon internal organizational structure and process and those dealing with transactions between police organization and the surrounding environment. In both of these broad areas in the immediate future, the application of sociology is more likely to be a matter of providing more sophisticated information and analysis than a matter of operations research.

INTERNAL ORGANIZATION OF POLICE DEPARTMENTS

Changes in internal organization of police departments have resulted in a considerable tightening of internal discipline and centralization of control.[28] At the same time, the police seek to attract more intelligent and better educated personnel. The potential conflict between these objectives of professionalization and centralization of command has been remarked on in the police literature.[29] The sociological analysis of professions and their practice in bureaucratic settings is applicable to the professionalization of the police.

It is common even among sociologists to think of a profession as a special kind of occupation where the job of the professional is technical, the technical knowledge generally having been acquired through long prescribed training, and the knowledge itself being systematic in nature. Furthermore, it is assumed that the professional person follows a set of professional norms that may include a code of ethics that binds the professional to behave ethically toward his clients. Both the training and norms generally fall under legal or professional organizational control, specifying who can practice.

All of these things usually characterize persons who are called professionals. But they miss a central feature that characterizes any profession.[30] At the core of any profession as distinct from a scholarly

28. Ibid.

29. See, for example, Richard A. Myren, "A Crisis in Police Management," *Journal of Criminal Law, Criminology and Police Science*, L (1960), 600–604; Vernon L. Hoy, "A Study of Specialization and Decentralization of Municipal Police Departments with Emphasis on the Specialist in District Stations," unpublished M.S. thesis, University of Southern California, 1958; Ching Pei Tsu, "Police Administration in St. Louis," unpublished M.A. thesis, University of Missouri, 1936.

30. Cf., for example, Harold Wilensky, "The Professionalization of Everyone?" *The American Journal of Sociology*, LXX (September, 1964), 138.

discipline is a relationship with clients. Professions are based on practice, and a major element in all practice is the relationship with clients. What is crucial in defining the professional is the nature of this relationship with clients. We can say that it is technical in nature where the specialized knowledge is utilized in practice, as when the physician calls on his specialized knowledge to diagnose illness. We can say that it is moral or ethical, as when the lawyer treats information from his client as privileged or confidential. Yet a core feature of the relationship with clients is a *decision* about the client—a decision in which the professional person decides something about the client that *relates to his future*. In some professions this decision is given largely in the form of advice. The client presumably is free to ignore or follow the advice. But in other professions and in certain roles within other professions, it is a decision over which the client can exercise little if any choice. We speak of this as a coerced decision, an evaluation, judgment, or a determination. The teacher decides whether the pupil shall pass or fail. The social worker decides whether the applicant is eligible for welfare benefits. The judge decides whether the defendant is guilty and what disposition shall be made for the case. Jurors, by the way, are not professionals, and some of the conflict in the criminal trial procedure today arises over the very question of competence of jurors to decide what have come to be called technical questions. Police are empowered with a decision that involves the fate of their clients—a decision to arrest, a discretionary decision. Police, therefore, are among the few occupations seeking professionalization that share the core feature of a decision that affects the fate of the client.

Studies of the "professionalization" of the police conclude that changes within modernizing police departments have led to professionalization of the department through bureaucratization and centralization of command. These changes work against professionalization of the line officer, particularly the patrol officer where contact is initially made with the public. Three main changes within the organization of police departments militate against professionalization of the line officer.[31]

First, there is the increasing centralization of both command and control in departments—a centralization of decision making. Some police departments have been reorganized so that most of the command and control functions are essentially removed from the precinct level of organization. The precinct functions then primarily to allocate men

---

31. Albert J. Reiss, Jr., "The Role of the Police in a Changing Society," Center for Research on Social Organization, University of Michigan, Paper No. 14, March, 1966, pp. 1–36.

to assignments and supervise them in their work roles. The core of many modern police departments is the centralized communications center where allocative decisions are made under centralized command. The line officer on patrol is commanded from a central headquarters and reports directly to [it] by radio, with reports in some cases being made directly to central headquarters by radio or telephone. Furthermore, the bounds of decision making by the line are officially narrowed so that the officer is left without functions of investigation or, at most, a preliminary report. Although such moves toward a centralized bureaucratic system have not necessarily limited the discretionary decision in practice, they structurally limit professionalization of decision making by the line. A bureaucratic system where decision making is decentralized would be more consistent with professionalization of the line.

Second, most modern police departments centralize the investigative function in a "more technical" elite of the department—the detective bureau. Much overrated in its capacity to investigate and certainly to "solve" most crimes, it nonetheless increasingly bears the "professional" label. Though there is much evidence of increasing bureaucratization of the investigative functions within police departments leading to a large number of special investigation units over and above that of the detective division, there is much less evidence that the requirements of technical knowledge and training are consistent with professionalization of personnel in these units. It is in this sense that we speak of the professionalization of the organizational system, leaving the corollary development of specialization of professional roles relatively untouched.

Finally, there is a growing tendency to make decisions at the staff rather than the operating levels of the department. This is partly due to the fact that increased bureaucratization and introduction of a complex technology necessitate the utilization of other professions within the police system. But such professionals are generally introduced at the staff level or as special consultants inserted for a special reason into operating units. Thus a department employs medical internists and psychiatrists to perform certain applicant or promotion screening functions. The planning or analysis sections may include professional specialists. These professional specialists are generally referred to as "civilians" within the department, separating them not only from the line, but in many cases from the "sworn" staff as well.

The tendency to make decisions at staff rather than operating levels is readily apparent when one examines the staff units of a department. There is considerable evidence that the handling of "human relations" within police departments is largely a staff function. Despite a spate of human relations training for the line, it is the staff units that are regarded as "professional" in human relations work. The training division and the human relations unit of the department are more "professionalized." There is almost no provision for actual implementation of "human relations" in the line except by "central order" and some training of the line in the classroom of the Academy. Without explicit provision for implementation in the line, there is little opportunity for professional treatment of clients. That this characterization of professionalization is not unique to the more recently developed specialized staff functions such as "human relations" cannot be demonstrated here, but a careful examination of almost all new functional units in modernizing police departments serves to bear this out.

A metropolitan police organizational system faces considerable penetration of its organizational environment from organizations and interest groups that lie outside its boundaries. This is so for a number of reasons. Legally charged with responsibility for law enforcement, it nonetheless faces problems of overlapping jurisdiction with county, state, and national enforcement agencies. Law enforcement likewise is intricately linked with a larger organizational system of criminal justice such that its output is an input into the criminal justice system where it is evaluated. Furthermore, it is directly linked to a municipal, county, or state organizational system that controls at least its budget, and it also maintains a host of transactions with other municipal and community organizations in providing "police service." A police system thus engages in transactions not only with its clients who are *citizens* demanding a service and with victims and their violators, but with a multiplicity of organizations where problems of service, its assessment, resource allocation, and jurisdiction are paramount.

How these relationships tend on the whole to militate against the professionalization of the line and how they militate against the professionalization of the staff as well can only be illustrated here. The recent decisions of criminal and appellate courts defining the limits of interrogation, search of the person and property and the seizure of evidence, and of the use of force have been defined by the police and the courts as limits on discretionary decision making. The liberal and minority publics and the appellate courts view the police as exercising too much discretion in their relationships with the public. They generally hold that decision as to method is to be defined on legal professional rather than police professional grounds. In short, one prevailing view is that the police must be controlled by more legitimate authority—authority that is vested in either the law, the public prosecutor, and the courts or in a civil review procedure.

The controversy over the discretionary authority of the police is a classic case of disputes over professional jurisdiction. A group of professionals—in this case largely made up of lawyers and jurists—seeks to restrict the powers of "would-be professionals"—in this case the police. This conflict is not unlike that between medical doctors and nurses or that between prosecutors and judges. In addition to the usual questions of jurisdiction, there is an equally important consideration: professional disputes over jurisdiction generally arise where one group of professionals controls the fate of another group of professionals (or aspirants to professional status) in an intricately balanced organizational system. Much of the conflict between the courts and the police is in this sense inevitable, given the American system of law enforcement and criminal justice. For in that system we have on the one hand institutionalized the introduction of clients into the larger system in the hands of the police, since operationally at least it is the police who exercise the power of arrest. Yet on the other hand we have institutionalized the power of assessing outcome of arrest of the client and assessment of police procedure in the prosecutor and the court. When the ultimate fate of clients rests in another group of clients—and particularly when they are removed from the situation that precipitated the client relationship—conflict is endemic.

Civil review boards pose some barrier to professionalization of the police because they restrict the latitude an occupation or an organization based on an occupation has to "police" itself. That the police have not been altogether ineffective in preventing the creation of civil review boards in the United States is apparent. Much of their success probably is due to the political organization of line officers backed by legitimation of their claims from the police chief. Locally organized, they bring local pressures. Yet lacking effective organization on "professional grounds" across local departments, their long-run influence may be more restricted. Unlike trade unions that increased their bargaining power through extralocal organization, the only extralocal police organization of consequence is the International Association of Chiefs of Police. The line, therefore, is without national power.

The issue for professionalization of the police is whether civic accountability will take the form of an inquiry into an individual's work within an organization, whether it will take the form of accountability of an occupational organization of police, or whether accountability rests with a local police organizational system headed by a chief as the "accountable officer." Traditionally, line organizations of police have "protected" the rights of the officer in charges involving the local organization. Traditionally, the local police organization has been held accountable through control by the mayor, the occasional appointment of "civilian" chiefs, and the sporadic investigations of the department under charges of scandal by "blue-ribbon" committees. Traditionally, the organization of the line has failed to develop standards for control of practice by members of the occupation. The dilemma for the line, then, is that the police occupation exists within a local formally organized police department that controls practice rather than with a professional organization of the police. To shift the balance of review and control to an external review system, however, creates problems both for the operating departmental organization and the occupational association. This is particularly the case when there is external review of an individual's performance within an organization. For this form of accountability interferes with both institutional and organized forms of professional control in the United States. Public school teachers faced the same kind of dilemma. Historically they were under review from both a school organization and a civil review agency—respectively, the school administration and the school board. Increasingly the professional organization of teachers has resisted such review on "professional grounds," thereby coercing the relationship of public school teachers to organizations, employers, and clients more along the lines of traditional professional organizations. It is obvious that police now lack the increasingly effective extralocal organization developed among public school teachers.

Administrative centralization within police departments is partly a consequence of the fact that professionalization often arrives in a department in the form of crisis-produced reform. One area of research and application of great potential benefit to the police involves sociologists in studying the nature and consequences of patterns of supervision and control with a view to the design of systems which maintain the gains of professionalization without the loss of more desirable personnel.

A recent study of police reform indicates that the process of reform-centralization-professionalization heightens the significance of the organization rather than the public as a source of police self-esteem. It implies also that the reform process has increased member attachment—a necessary requisite to any eventual decentralization.[32] Another study of a department in the throes of change indicates that

32. James Q. Wilson, "Police Morale, Reform, and Citizen Respect: The Chicago Case," in Bordua, ed., op. cit., pp. 137–62.

traditional techniques of control coupled with professionalization creates a punishment-centered bureaucracy with high levels of uncertainty among young officers and a consequent emphasis on personal ingratiation with superiors. In this department the formal rules seem more a set of opportunities for punishing officers than a set of bureaucratic imperatives.[33] These results also indicate that reform-based centralization may be necessary to produce sufficient trust and due process within the police department in order that more decentralized decision making may eventually be possible.

Methods of internal control in a police department have great relevance not only to police decision making, but also to problems of recruitment, training, and selection for promotion, as the study by McNamara shows. Beyond the use of written civil service tests, which function more as instruments of equity than of effective selection, there is little sophistication of a social science sort in police selection procedures. Psychiatric screening to spot "bad apples" among potential recruits has appeared in some departments, but there has been little or no contribution by sociologists or sociology. One study in New York City attempts to use a modification of job analysis and the critical incident technique to develop selection instruments at the recruit evaluation level.[34] The study draws on sociological ideas and techniques. It does not, however, display the necessary sensitivity to the organizational position of the policeman which the previously cited study by McNamara indicates to be crucial.[35] Relations between training and role perception and performance are also central to a recently published study of a state police unit.[36]

TRANSACTIONS BETWEEN POLICE AND PUBLIC

Studies of the external performance of the police are even more rare than studies of intra-organizational events. The early work by Westley, and the more recent work by Piliavin and Briar, Bittner, the Cummings, Skolnick, and Black and Reiss are among the few sociological

---

33. John H. McNamara, "Uncertainties in Police Work: The Relevance of Police Recruits' Backgrounds and Training," in Bordua, ed., op. cit., pp. 163–252.

34. Leo R. Eilbert, John H. McNamara, Vernon L. Hanson, *Research on Selection and Training for Police Recruits* (Pittsburgh: American Institute for Research, 1961).

35. Cf. John H. McNamara, op. cit.

36. Jack J. Preiss and Howard J. Ehrlich, *An Examination of Role Theory: The Case of the State Police* (Lincoln: The University of Nebraska Press, 1966).

studies of the external behavior of the police in relation to the police.[37] Apart from the work by Black and Reiss, these studies generally lack criteria of effectiveness of police performance.

Most of these studies focus on the relationship between the demeanor of the citizen and the actions and attitudes of the police. Westley was concerned with the transfer of violence by the police from a legal to a personal resource where violence becomes acceptable to the police as a generalized means. His most significant finding was that at least 37 percent of the police officers he interviewed believed it legitimate to use violence to coerce respect, suggesting that policemen use violence to coerce their audience to respect their occupational status.[38] Piliavin and Briar's studies of police encounters with juveniles likewise emphasize the importance of client demeanor in police behavior. Other than prior record of delinquency, they conclude that the youth's demeanor was the most important factor in apprehension of juveniles by police officers. If the youth was "uncooperative," he was highly unlikely to receive either informal reprimands or admonishment and release; if he cooperated with the officer, they were likely outcomes.[39] Skolnick's study of the processing of traffic violators, narcotics users and peddlers, and prostitutes raises some doubts about personal prejudices and client demeanor in police practice. While he found that the police wanted to implicate the traffic offender more seriously in the criminal process when the violator abused the officer in some way, was a habitual violator who refused to "cop out," or when there were continuing and exacerbated relationships between the officer and the offender, he also found that in police relationships with prostitutes the behavior of the policeman is less likely to involve how he personally feels about the

---

37. Egon Bittner, "Police Discretion in Emergency Apprehension of Mentally Ill Persons," *Social Problems*, XIV (1967), 278–92; Donald J. Black and Albert J. Reiss, Jr., "Coercive Authority and Citizen Rights in Field Patrol Settings"; "Some Aspects of Citizen Behavior in Routine Police Encounters"; "Personal and Property Searches Conducted in Radio-Dispatched Police Work"; "Police-Suspect Transactions in Field Settings According to the Race and Social Class of Suspects"; "Police and Citizen Behavior in Routine Field Encounters: Some Comparisons According to the Race and Social Class Status of Citizens"; "Transactions with Suspects in On-View Police Work," respectively Report Nos. 2, 4, 5, 6, 7, and 8, United States Department of Justice: Office of Law Enforcement Assistance, Grant No. 006, Reports Submitted to the President's Commission on Law Enforcement and the Administration of Criminal Justice, 1966; [Elaine Cumming, Ian M. Cumming, and Laura Edell], "Policeman as Philosopher, Guide and Friend," *Social Problems*, XII (1965); Irving Piliavin and Scott Briar, "Police Encounters with Juveniles," *The American Journal of Sociology*, LXX (1964), 206–14; Skolnick, op. cit.; William A. Westley, "Violence and the Police," *The American Journal of Sociology*, LIX (July, 1953), 34–41.

38. Westley, ibid., p. 39.

39. Piliavin and Briar, op. cit.

suspect. With prostitutes, their relationship to other police goals, such as their informant status, may be more important.[40]

Among the more controversial areas of police behavior in the United States are those pertaining to police conduct in searches, in interrogation, and in confession. Seriously lacking in both public and judicial consideration of these issues has been reliable information about police conduct in these situations. The mass observation studies of Black and Reiss report data on the relative frequency of personal and property searches and interrogations, some of the conditions under which they occur, the response of persons to these practices in settings where they take place, and what the police learn in such situations.[41] They observed that officers very rarely ask for permission to conduct a search or an interrogation; most suspects do not object. The probability that the police will find a dangerous weapon or other evidence in property and personal searches is quite high for the high crime rate areas where the observations took place; about one in five frisks, for example, produced a dangerous weapon while almost one-half of all property searches produced something that the suspect did not wish the police to find. Contrary to expectations, at least a third of all field interrogations involved the interrogation of more than one person concomitantly. In only one in ten situations was there an objection to the interrogation. When objections occurred they were far more likely to be objections to how information was obtained than to the fact that they were questioned. For confessions, it was found that 7 in 10 of the confessions were obtained at the beginning of the police-citizen encounter; in fact, about one-half confessed before any interrogation on the part of the officer. Other than questioning, little or no pressure was applied in 70 percent of the interrogations. Quite clearly, this research shows that much of this police behavior occurs in field settings and outside of the interrogation room or police station where it generally is presumed to occur. Furthermore, given the fact that the research was conducted in the period following the Miranda decision by the United States Supreme Court, compliance with court decisions on informing citizens of their rights was generally quite low, emphasizing again that decision making without organizational implementation generally brings low compliance, if not patterned evasion.

Despite generations of criminological research it is doubtful that sociology can in the near future contribute to the social technology available for apprehending criminals. It has nevertheless contributed to

---

40. Skolnick, op. cit., Ch. 5.
41. Black and Reiss, Jr., op. cit.

police sophistication and success in maintaining order in potentially riotous situations and especially in dealing with potentially dangerous racial tensions.[42] Some recent efforts at crime analysis show the indirect effect of sociological perspectives such as the attempt to develop a typology of sex offenses that would be useful for *modus operandi* files.[43] In general the police have provided more information on crime to sociologists than the reverse. The new computerized information systems provide an opportunity for sociologists to help construct more rationalized information-gathering strategies, as work by Wolfgang demonstrates.[44] Sociologists will have to do much more research on the patterning and determinants of criminal conduct in the field rather than in the prison, and they will have to face up to the hard fact that offenders must be caught before they can be humanely rehabilitated if their research is to be relevant to police organization and policy.

In Western democratic societies the emergence of a police system distinct from the militia and "voluntary service" in a watch system led to the development of a tradition-oriented rather than a rationally efficient bureaucratic system. Primary-group loyalties, often based on a cohort effect of common movement through the ranks, and devotion to duty and honor bound the men in the organization together and brought the commanders close to the men in the line, particularly in those countries that did not recruit a distinct elite corps of staff and command. These traditional loyalties gave way before technical innovation and deliberate organizational strategies in the more rational bureaucratic departments. Their disintegration, however, has created a new set of problems of how the command can insure control—how it could make its orders stick—with less reliance on traditional forms of allegiance to the command.

A related dilemma arises at the staff and command level as well— the dilemma of the "professional managers" vs. the "hero leaders" noted by Janowitz.[45] His characterization for the military profession can be applied to the police. The professional police managers emerge with the highly centralized command based on information technology. A "professional police" must recruit and retrain men for its elite who are

42. Joseph D. Lohman, *The Police and Minority Groups* (Chicago Park District Police, 1947).

43. William W. Hermann, "Acacia: A System for Automating Content and Critical Incident Analysis," Los Angeles: University of Southern California School of Public Administration, 1962.

44. Marvin E. Wolfgang and Harvey A. Smith, "Mathematical Methods in Criminology," *International Social Science Journal*, VIII (1966), 200–223.

45. Morris Janowitz, *The Professional Soldier: A Social and Political Portrait* (Glencoe, Ill.: The Free Press, 1960), esp., pp. 31–36.

skilled in police management. At the same time, a department must recruit officers who can command the allegiance of the men in the line. This problem of leadership is particularly acute in departments that do not recruit solely into the line. While some professional managers command allegiance, many do not.

In rational organizations, symbolic appeals to courage, devotion to duty, and honor often do not ring true. Yet they are essential elements in a police system. The modern trends in police departments make it difficult to perpetuate these elements. The "new" cohorts of officers in the more modern American police department display less enthusiasm for symbolic appeals than their predecessors. Furthermore, an increasing emphasis on civic control of the police in the United States serves further to weaken such appeals—one does a "professional" job, not his duty. How far the police can go in dispensing with symbolism remains an open question. Potentially they should be able to go much further than the military, since, in contrast to the military, their success depends much more on the necessity for and willingness of a population to be policed and on the demand for police service. Because the police are not essentially in a conflict relationship with the public, they need not display the elements of heroic leadership appropriate to combat.

That no bureaucracy conforms to a model of rational organization is well established. While the modern police department places heavy organizational emphasis on modern techniques of personnel selection and training, on technology and technical efficiency, and on rational planning and management, it perhaps cannot altogether dispense with charisma in its leaders and a commitment to duty and honor, particularly in democratic societies, such as the United States, that are fundamentally inhospitable to the police.[46]

A paramilitary organization such as the police displays, and perhaps must continue to display, elements of traditional and rational bureaucracies. In modern democratic societies, however, there are increasing demands that they be human-relations–centered bureaucracies.

Ideally the police should be able to secure compliance with lawful commands while incurring a minimum of citizen hostility. The ability to do so in a heterogeneous society requires formal training in human management rather than merely participation in a common culture. McNamara's study of the training and performance of recruits indicates that neither selection nor training nor postacademy probationary experience provides the necessary sensitivity to differences in values and

---

46. See Bordua and Reiss, "Command, Control and Charisma: Reflections on Police Bureaucracy," op. cit., pp. 73–76.

interpersonal expectations. As a consequence the police tend to become overauthoritative in socially ambiguous situations—securing compliance at the cost of unnecessary levels of hostility.[47] Formal human-relations training is an increasingly common feature of police training and at least some semisociological ideas have been important in the development of training materials.[48]

There is considerable evidence that the American populace, particularly in its larger cities, is no longer content with either the traditional or the rational bureaucratic solutions to police-citizen relations. As noted earlier, the tradition-oriented departments in American society were peculiarly adapted to the accommodation of immigrant interests. More recently, the rational bureaucratic department has moved somewhat to guarantee equity both as to discretionary decisions in application of the law and the legality of means in law enforcement. Yet more is demanded of the officer. He must not only be civil in a rational bureaucratic sense, but he must be "human" or "personal" in his relations with citizens. He must not only be civil in a professional sense, but must also be "client-centered." He must not only be a responsible civil servant, but responsive as well.

Recent studies of the behavior of officers and citizens in police-citizen transactions show that in about three-fourths of police-citizen transactions the officers behaved in a rational bureaucratic manner.[49] Their conduct could be characterized as routinized, impersonal, or businesslike. Only in 16 percent of the encounters could they be characterized as human-relations oriented where humor, interest in the citizen, or similar interpersonal tactics characterized their behavior. For only 6 percent of the encounters did the officers behave in a negative or hostile fashion toward the citizen. Human relations was more characteristic of relations with white than Negro citizens, however. Correlatively, the behavior of citizens toward the police was characterized in three-fourths of the cases as civil with 11 percent behaving deferentially and the remainder with some form of hostility.

The typical encounter between the citizen and a police officer then is one characterized by civility. The officer regards the citizen in a rational bureaucratic framework of civility while the citizen treats the officer with civil conduct. Yet paradoxically, the citizen who is civil toward the officer often regards civility in the officer as a sign of disre-

47. John H. McNamara, op. cit.

48. See, for example, Arthur I. Siegel, Philip J. Federman and Douglas G. Schultz, *Professional Police—Human Relations Training* (Springfield, Ill.: Charles C Thomas, 1963).

49. Black and Reiss, op. cit., Report Nos. 6 and 7.

spect and a failure to regard him in human or personal terms. And the officer perceives civility in the citizen as a failure to command respect. Rational bureaucratic treatment is insufficient for many citizens in their encounters with the police.

Encounters between police and populace with which human-relations training deals have an even broader significance in police work. The populace is, after all, the source of suspects. Moreover, segments of the populace may not only individually but collectively adopt a stance of principled opposition to the police. Where this occurs, police practices of field inquiry, i.e., the systematic search for suspects to match known offenses, may simultaneously result in a challenge to police authority and a further alienation of the suspect group. Nowhere is this problem more apparent than in dealing with slum gangs. In a recent paper Werthman and Piliavin describe encounters between patrol police and Negro gang boys and indicate that the outcome of these encounters may increase hostility, strengthen gang solidarity, threaten police authority, and even help increase social tensions to the point of contributing to violent disorder—all without producing any great payoff to law enforcement.[50] This study also indicates the very real differences in the role of patrol police as compared to that of juvenile officers, who are more a combination of detectives and magistrates.

Yet it remains unclear how much and to what extent the relationship between the police and citizens accounts for the failure of citizens to mobilize the police and to cooperate with them in investigation. Recent studies for the National Crime Commission show that most police officers believe that minority group persons are uncooperative when they attempt to gain information from them.[51] Studies of citizen experiences with crime and the police, however, fail to support the contention that it is police behavior that accounts for citizen failure to mobilize the police or to cooperate with them. Biderman found that of the forty-two respondents who had witnessed a crime and failed to report it to the police, only three of them gave as a reason for their failure to report a negative expectation about dealing with the police.[52] Furthermore, although about four in ten experiences by 104 victims

50. Carl Werthman and Irving Piliavin, "Gang Members and the Police," in Bordua, ed., op. cit., pp. 56–98.

51. Albert J. Reiss, Jr., "Police Officer Attitudes toward Their Work and Job," United States Department of Justice: Office of Law Enforcement Assistance, Grant No. 006, A Report to the President's Commission on Law Enforcement and the Administration of Criminal Justice, 1966.

52. Albert D. Biderman et al., "Salient Findings on Crime and Attitudes toward Law Enforcement in the District of Columbia," Washington, D.C., Bureau of Social Science Research Project 382; United States Department of Justice: Office of Law Enforcement Assistance, May, 1966, Chapter III.

were not reported to the police, citizens rarely gave as their reason for nonreporting a negative expectation about encounters with the police. Rather they emphasized such things as that they saw no useful purpose in doing so as there was nothing that could be done about it or that they wished to avoid the trouble associated with getting involved, such as being a witness later in court. A few feared reprisals from offenders. But two citizens gave a response that they feared the police would give them trouble. Such studies suggest that citizen-police relations are determined more by the general orientation of citizens in American society and the structure of the legal system than by specific experiences with the police or negative images of potential encounters. Clearly further research is necessary to determine how police-citizen encounters influence police-citizen relationships.

One of the few sociological studies that tries to measure the effects of varying techniques among policemen is the attempt by Wattenberg and Bufe to study the effectiveness of juvenile officers.[53] The authors conclude that differences in interpersonal style among officers are related to the probability of later recidivism. If this finding should replicate, it promises to have considerable significance as a guide to juvenile officer training and supervision. Specialized juvenile officers playing quasi-judicial roles are an increasingly significant part of American municipal police systems and a considerable amount of research has been done or is under way on their interactions with juveniles and on the factors involved in police decisions with juveniles.[54]

This review of actual and potential applications of sociology to police and law enforcement can appropriately conclude by pointing out that its central theme—the importance of formal organization—can be applied to the clients of the police as well as to the police themselves. In an increasingly bureaucratized society police decisions may be affected by interorganizational relations. In a recent study Skolnick and Woodworth show that statutory rape complaints may originate in a public welfare agency, and the police morals detail studied was involved not only in the difficult and morale-lowering business of interrogating for statutory rape, but also in a complex interagency information-sharing system.[55] Future developments in centralized in-

---

53. William W. Wattenberg and Noel Bufe, "The Effectiveness of Police Youth Bureau Officers," *Journal of Criminal Law, Criminology and Police Science,* LIV (December, 1963), 470–75.

54. Much of this research is summarized in David J. Bordua, "Recent Trends: Deviant Behavior and Social Control," *The Annals,* CCCLXIX (January, 1967), 149–63.

55. Jerome H. Skolnick and J. Richard Woodworth, "Bureaucracy, Information, and Social Control: A Study of a Morals Detail," in Bordua, op. cit., pp. 99–136.

formation systems and interagency cooperation will raise the whole new issues not only of police expertise, but of the balance between organizational goals and personal liberties.

EPILOGUE: SOME ISSUES OF SOCIOLOGICAL RESEARCH ON LAW ENFORCEMENT

We began by noting that sociological studies of law enforcement and the police were neglected until recently, partly because of the discomfort sociologists experience in the presence of coercion. One might add further that studies of law enforcement and the police create discomfiture because they inevitably raise certain ethical issues, particularly if, as has been the case, much of the data must be gathered by observational techniques.

Skolnick has made a beginning in the discussion of these ethical issues. There are important questions of the invasion of privacy, the effect of an observer's presence on a defendant's fate or constitutional rights, and the deception of his role both for officer and for citizen.[56] Inevitably there are other issues as well, issues that relate to disclosure of information and to an observer's legal obligations as a citizen. Though such issues arise in many social observation studies, they are of particular importance where one is enmeshed in studying the legal system and where legal sanctions on the investigator may be more germane. Quite clearly, continued work on the sociology of law enforcement, to the degree that it partakes of social observation, must cope with the ethical and legal issues generated by the research process.

Sociologists in the field of corrections increasingly have entered prominent roles as administrators and as counsel in the formation of public policy. Within the field of law enforcement, such a role has not as yet clearly emerged. Despite the fact that sociologists were involved in the work of the President's Commission on Law Enforcement and the Administration of Justice, no social scientist was a member of the Commission. The Commission's report itself, while clearly reflecting the research investigations of sociologists, displays less clearly their effectiveness in molding policy recommendations.[57] The entry of sociologists as policy scientists in the field of law enforcement poses problems of relationships not only with the "professionals" in police administration, but with the "professionals" in the law as well.

---

56. Skolnick, op. cit., pp. 37–41.

57. *The Challenge of Crime in a Free Society*, A Report by [the] President's Commission on Law Enforcement and the Administration of Criminal Justice (Washington, D.C.: United States Government Printing Office, February, 1967); also see *Report of the President's Commission on Crime in the District of Columbia* (Washington, D.C.: U.S. Government Printing Office, 1966).

19

Observing the Police

Peter K. Manning

AUTHOR'S INTRODUCTION

The essay partially reprinted here was written in 1969–70. Since that time a number of useful police studies have appeared.[1] Although additional felicitous examples are now available, I would not expect that the argument presented below would require reformulation. On the basis of my recent fieldwork in this country and in England,[2] and seminal critiques of the entire fieldwork enterprise,[3] it is evident that some of the assumptions underlying this research method should be reexamined by those of us interested in the police or any other substantive area. Attention to that task, however, is not our immediate objective.

The ethical and political issues raised in the following essay remain with us. Whether we are pleased with the current status of policing or hope to radically restructure it—either by reduction or by accretion of its coercive power—we are dependent upon the findings of past re-

From Peter K. Manning, "Observing the Police: Deviants, Respectables and the Law," in Jack D. Douglas (ed.), *Research on Deviance* (New York: Random House, 1972), pp. 235–59, 263–68, reprinted by permission of the author and publisher. Copyright © 1972 by Random House, Inc.

1. James C. Fox and Richard J. Lundman, "Problems and Strategies in Gaining Research Access in Police Organizations," *Criminology*, 12 (May 1974), pp. 52–69, note that between the years of 1940 and 1965 articles on the police were published in the two major sociological journals, the *American Sociological Review* and the *American Journal of Sociology*, at a rate of less than one every two years. From 1966 to 1972, this publication rate exceeded three and one-half per year. There is no evidence that this increase in rate has subsided.

2. See Peter K. Manning, *Police Work: Essays in the Social Organization of Policing*, forthcoming.

3. See John M. Johnson, *Fieldwork* (New York: The Free Press, 1975), and Jack D. Douglas, *Investigative Social Research*, forthcoming.

searchers. We must build upon their errors and insights, develop improved techniques to penetrate and illuminate police organizations, and attempt to articulate clearly some criteria for police research. What do we want to know? How can we develop confidence in our findings? How can these findings be made useful for continued research and for policymaking? Some of the past errors are reviewed in my essay below, but much depends upon present and future students, on their research skills, and on their grasp of the dynamics involved.

NEGOTIATING ACCESS TO POLICE ORGANIZATIONS

Police research is alternatively dangerous and boring, frustrating and exciting, sympathy-producing and a source of antagonism, tense and funny, the source of several superior sociological studies and the demise of probably three times that number. It shares some of the problems of social research in general that are entailed by a shift from a "craft model" of social research to an *organizational model.*[4] This shift in the size and organizational complexity of research parallels changes in larger social structures to a more bureaucratically patterned mode of life. The craft model of social research involves the researcher and perhaps an apprentice in the research process from problem definition, research design, data gathering, and analysis through to publication. The typical relationships are dyadic, at both the level of research and training for research. The major research tools are the interview, the questionnaire, and observation. Form characterizes methods texts as "manuals on how the craftsman and his apprentice should gather data on personal or interpersonal behavior." In contrast, considerable recent work (since World War II) has been done by large-scale research bureaus or institutes sharing mutually financed large staffs of service people and facilities. Supporting agencies that provide grants often take an implicit or explicit hand in guiding the nature and type of research done. The organizational model is epitomized by the Institute for Survey Research at the University of Michigan, The National Opinion Research Center at the University of Chicago, and the Bureau of Applied Social Research at Columbia.

Police studies reflect this change in the relationship between research and the researched. The larger research operation encounters more problems regarding *sponsorship* and *legitimation, access* and *role definition.* Parenthetically, it is clear that the model for under-

---

4. William H. Form, "The Sociology of Social Research," in Richard O'Toole (ed.), *The Organization and Management of Research* (Boston: Schenkman, 1970).

standing these problems is the industrial research of the 1930s, but none of the writers mentioned in this article refer to the parallel problems experienced by men seeking access to factories during the period of labor strife and class conflict, which in every way was as tense and potentially explosive as the current era of status-race-age divisions.

The nature of the *sponsorship* obtained by researchers doubtless has an effect on the course of their studies. There are two aspects of sponsorship: the source of *funding,* and the source of *legitimation* within the organization. Most of the studies I have reviewed were connected with large, highly respected universities (M.I.T., University of California at Berkeley, University of Chicago, University of Michigan) and often with research units within them, for example, the Center for the Study of Law and Society at Berkeley, the Center for Research on Social Organization at the University of Michigan. Of the observational studies we are considering here, only two did *not* cite support money from grants: Banton and Buckner. Unfortunately, most of the studies do not provide information on the process of negotiating access to the supporting organization. Those that do imply that the development of the researcher-host organization relationship is almost aleatory.

Skolnick describes the way in which he almost drifted into his research role as a plain-clothes detective in the Westville department:

> The study commenced with observation of the work of the public defender in the fall of 1962. ... Approximately two hundred hours were spent in the office of the public defender.
>
> After several months of such observations, I felt that I had not adequately experienced the law enforcement side of the criminal courts system. It became evident that interactions between the defense attorney and the accused, as individuals, were necessarily more infrequent than those between defense attorney and prosecutor. Thus, an appropriate vision of the system of processing of criminal cases places the prosecutor and the defense attorney at the top as spokesmen and interpreters for the real adversaries who are, on the one hand, the complainant, and on the other, the accused. Given this conception, it seemed necessary to see the system of criminal law processing from the law enforcement side.
>
> By this time, I was fairly well known to several of the deputy district attorneys who had met me while I was looking over the shoulders of men on the public defender's staff. I suggested to the head of the public defender's office that I would like to see how "the other half" lived. Through his recommendation, plus an extended interview with the district attorney, I was permitted to become a participant-observer in that office. After several weeks of observation in the office of the Westville district attorney, it seemed important to know more

about the work of the police. . . . I asked my "contacts" in the prosecutor's office if it would be possible to arrange observation of the police carrying out their duties.

The Chief of Police was willing to entertain the idea. It is again important to emphasize that this police department regarded itself as exemplary. . . .

The Chief assigned his aide, Lieutenant Doyle, to make introductions within the department. The Lieutenant was a genial man who had been on the force for almost twenty years, knew everybody, and was personally liked, as I later learned, throughout the department. We decided that the best place to begin the study was with the patrol division which, in Westville, has one-man vehicles and three ranks: supervising detective, sergeant, and patrolman.

I spent eight nights with these patrolmen, mostly on weekends, on the shift running from 7 P.M. to 3 A.M. All of this time was spent interviewing and observing, talking about the life of the policeman, and the work of the policeman. I understood my job was to gain some insight and understanding of the way the policeman views the world. I found that the most informative method was not to ask predetermined questions, but rather to question actions the policeman had just taken or failed to take, about events or objects just encountered, such as certain categories of people or places of the city. . . .

With the realization that law enforcement is not to be found in its most significant and interesting forms on the streets [italics added], I again consulted with Lieutenant Doyle (who was most helpful and considerate throughout the study). I felt that I ought to begin to study detective work, especially the work of the vice squad, but I also felt that I wanted to learn more about the policeman's use of legal authority in mundane and routine matters. . . .

. . . I decided to attempt to study that portion of it which seemed to me central to an understanding of the police as legal men, and perhaps also the most difficult to study: the working of the vice control squad.[5]

Skolnick apparently presented himself as a single researcher investig‑ ing a problem. His own legal interests probably assisted the ingratiati‑ process, as did his willingness to participate in a wide range of poli‑ activities, for example, shooting on the pistol range, driving vans raids, listening in on phone calls, and signing as a witness to a confessio‑

5. Jerome H. Skolnick, *Justice Without Trial* (New York: Wiley, 1966), pp. 31– [Copyright © 1966 by John Wiley & Sons, Inc. Reprinted by permission of the publishe This is a very important statement of methodological problems written with candor a insight. See also H. Taylor Buckner, "The Police: A Culture of a Social Control Agenc (unpublished Ph.D. dissertation, University of California, Berkeley, 1967), "Appenc Methodology," pp. 465–488.

The impact of Skolnick's observation on the behavior of the policemen he observed, like that of other unknown observers, was probably negligible; at least it is unmentioned in Skolnick's published works.

Large-scale studies, such as the one conducted by Reiss and reported in numerous publications by Black and Reiss, doubtless create more complex problems than did Skolnick's research. The impact of a study as large and systematic as Reiss's presents a threat not only to the patrolmen observed, but to the organization itself. Reiss wrote:

> During the summer of 1966 I conducted a study of crime and law enforcement in major metropolitan areas. Among other things, we investigated police and citizen transactions in eight high crime rate areas of three major metropolitan areas of the United States.
>
> Twelve observers and a supervisor were assigned to each of the cities. Each observer was assigned to an eight-hour watch in a police district six days a week for six to seven weeks. Within each district the watches and beats were sampled and observers rotated across beats. Within this period of time, 92 Negro and 608 white officers were observed at least once. There was a total of 212 eight-hour observation periods of Negro officers and 1,137 observation periods of white officers. The police were mobilized in 5,360 situations; in 3,826 of them they had an encounter with one or more citizens. Some information was gathered on 11,244 citizens who participated in the encounters.
>
> The observers recorded only a minimum of information during the eight-hour period, merely keeping a log of encounters. Following the period of observation, an observation booklet was completed for each encounter of two or more minutes duration. There were four types of booklets depending on whether the mobilization situation was a dispatch, a mobilization by a citizen in a field setting, a police mobilization in a field setting (on-view), or a citizen mobilization in a precinct station. The observer was asked to answer 48 questions about the encounter (if applicable) either by checking a response or writing a descriptive account. They completed 5,360 booklets during the period of the study. In addition, they responded to 23 questions about the observation period itself and the general behavior and attitudes of the officer as they learned it through observation and interviewing during the watch period. There are 1,349 such reports.[6]

This study was sponsored and legitimated by the President's Crime Commission and Office of Law Enforcement Administration. It is un-

6. A. J. Reiss, "Stuff and Nonsense About Social Surveys and Observation," in Howard S. Becker et al. (eds.), *Institutions and the Person* (Chicago: Aldine, 1968), pp. 355–56. Reiss deals with many important similarities between surveys and observation and quite rightly minimizes the *intrinsic* differences between them.

likely that this study could have been accomplished without "high-powered" support and outside political influence.

The importance of the police norm of secrecy can hardly be exaggerated at this point. For even with access, there are often problems in obtaining data. Westley says, "The time consumed in just getting to the data is enormous." He continues:

> The degree of rapport obtained had much to do with whether or not a question was pressed. This was of strategic importance because policemen are under explicit orders not to talk about police work with anyone outside the department; there is much in the nature of a secret society about the police; and past experience has indicated to policemen that to talk is to invite trouble from the press, the public, the administration and their colleagues. The result is that when they got the slightest suspicion that everything was not on an innocuous level they became exceedingly uncooperative and the rest of the men caught on in a hurry. As a matter of fact the principal obstacle in the research was to avoid being defined as a spy. This was more difficult than it seems since it sometimes required that one walk up to a policeman, amidst a hostile group, seeing fear in his eyes, and shake his hand (which he tries not to offer) and at the same time maintain an appearance of joviality and unconcern. The research required a continuous campaign of personal propaganda in order to meet repeated waves of suspicion and consequent lack of cooperation. This meant a constant search for ways to define oneself which would be acceptable. Some of the most successful were that of the man in trouble and the policeman's friend. Each definition seems to wear out in time, however, and a fresh one has to be constructed.[7]

Ironically, the paramilitary structure of the organization can be an asset to data gathering, particularly if it is of the standard questionnaire variety. As soon as administrative permission is granted, orders are issued to report and fill out the materials. The response rates of these studies tend to be very high. Police studies of this sort take on the zero-sum two-person game quality: one is either in possession of an almost complete population of a precinct or post, or one has nothing. The former was the case in a project where a student was able, through his father, a state patrolman, to obtain permission to survey a post and headquarters of a Midwestern state police headquarters.[8]

---

7. William A. Westley, "The Police: A Study of Law, Custom and Morality" (unpublished Ph.D. dissertation, University of Chicago, 1951), pp. 30–31.

8. Robert Trojanowicz was thus able to gather data for "A Comparison of the Behavior Styles of Policemen and Social Workers" (unpublished Ph.D. dissertation, Michigan State University, 1969).

Bordua and Reiss discuss the research implications of the increasing centralization and bureaucratization of police operations:

For the first time in American history the emergence of a self-consciously professional police elite coupled with increasing its (though far from complete) success in tightening internal control over departmental operations provides the organizational conditions whereby not only public demands for efficiency and productivity, but also judicial demands for legality can be translated into operations. Developing professionalization of the police provides the necessary base for the application of sociology of law enforcement concerns. Perhaps even more appropriately put, it provides the base for carrying out the necessary sociological research which in the near future will be translatable into application.[9]

The introduction of professionally oriented, educated, and thoughtful police administrators was a necessary condition for the recent growth of sociological research.[10] The majority of studies we now possess were done in departments that policemen view as "professional": Oakland, San Francisco, Chicago, New York City, and Atlanta.[11]

Police studies demonstrate that police organizations are increasingly ribbed with conflict between blacks and whites, the staff and the line, between the younger and the older policemen, and between those at any level who are professionally oriented and those who are not. The Skolnick Report documents the extent of discontent within the ranks

---

9. David J. Bordua and A. J. Reiss, "Law Enforcement," in P. Lazarsfeld, W. J. Sewell, and H. L. Wilensky (eds.), *The Uses of Sociology* (New York: Basic Books, 1967), p. 287. [Copyright © 1967 by Basic Books, Inc., Publishers, New York.] The implications of professionalization of the police for sociological research are not as clear to me as this statement implies. As the authors point out in detail, the barriers to professionalization are major and not likely to be rapidly dissolved; see especially pp. 289–90.

10. Ibid., p. 275.

11. The exact meaning of "professional" in the context of the police has not satisfactorily been worked out. In my piece, "The Police: Mandate, Strategy and Appearances," in Jack D. Douglas (ed.), *Crime and Justice in American Society* (Indianapolis: Bobbs-Merrill, 1971), I conclude that it is not a useful concept. See James Q. Wilson, *Varieties of Police Behavior: The Management of Law and Order in Eight Communities* (Cambridge, Mass.: Harvard University Press, 1968), and "The Police and Their Problems: A Theory," *Public Policy*, 12 (1963), 189–216; Bordua and Reiss, op. cit.; and David J. Bordua, "Police," *International Encyclopedia of Social Science*, pp. 174–81. *The Challenge of Crime*, Report of the President's Crime Commission (Washington, D.C.: Government Printing Office, 1967), chap. on the police; and *The Police*, Task Force Report (Washington, D.C.: Government Printing Office, 1967) also deal with the issue. The authors of *The Challenge of Crime* are more optimistic than the social scientists cited above, even though there is a considerable overlap between the authors of the report and the writers cited above. The Douglas volume *Crime and Justice* is a criticism of *The Challenge of Crime*.

of the patrolmen. He notes that they see themselves as victims not only of social forces, which they view as a conspiracy, but also of the judiciary, lawyers, and the higher administrators, if they work in large departments.[12]

Research in an organization creates new knowledge of the organization itself, particularly of its various levels, and it soon becomes clear that the researcher (or the person in the organization who controls or deals with him) has potential power over other members of the organization. Secrecy and ignorance play an important part in a punishment-centered bureaucracy, while research raises threats to its power equilibrium. Consequently, the association of research with, and legitimization by, the professional segment of an organization is both an asset and a debit.

The police are involved intimately with many aspects of the criminal justice system, and their actions are, in a sense, publicly reviewed by lawyers and the courts. Bordua and Reiss comment on this fact:

> Law enforcement is likewise intricately linked with a larger organizational system of criminal justice such that its output is an input into the criminal justice system where it is evaluated. Furthermore, it is directly linked to a municipal, county, or state organizational system that controls at least its budget, and also maintains a host of transactions with other municipal and community organizations in providing "police service." A police system thus engages in transactions not only with clients who are *citizens* demanding a service and with victims and their violators, but with a multiplicity of organizations where problems of service, its assessment, resource allocation, and jurisdiction are paramount.[13]

Buckner illustrates the extent to which the police are tied into reciprocal transactions with such community institutions as local businesses (especially restaurants), newspapers, sports arenas, and influential people.[14] As a general proposition, police research is threatening to the police organization in an environment of exchange and negotiation,

---

12. Jerome H. Skolnick (ed.), *The Politics of Protest* (paper ed., New York: Ballantine Books, 1969), pp. 258–268.

13. Bordua and Reiss, op. cit., p. 291.

14. Buckner, op. cit., pp. 117–27. This is not to say that there is a moral consensus as a result; cf. Michael Banton, *The Policeman in the Community* (New York: Basic Books, 1964) and John P. Clark, "The Isolation of the Police: A Comparison of the British and American Situations," in J. Scanzoni (ed.), *Readings in Social Problems* (Boston: Allyn and Bacon, 1967), pp. 384–410. See Arthur Niederhoffer, *Behind the Shield* (Garden City, N.Y.: Anchor Books, 1967), on the cynicism of American policemen.

an organization that provides one of the few points of loyalty and solidarity for the policeman:

> In some cities in the northern parts of the United States the police departments have been demoralized by political control, poor leadership, and low rates of pay. The life of many districts seems competitive and raw; individuals pursue their own ends with little regard for public morality, and the policemen see the ugly underside of outwardly respectable households and businesses. Small wonder, then, that many American policemen are cynics. . . . Couple this experience with the policeman's feeling that in his social life he is a pariah, scorned by the citizens who are more respectable but no more honest, and need it surprise no one that the patrolman's loyalties to his department and his colleagues are often stronger than those to the wider society.[15]

All these aspects of police organizations—secrecy, threat, paramilitary organization, morale problems, internal schisms, and politicalization—have created a police research situation in which the researcher is often best characterized as a "pussyfoot"—that is, he avoids telling the full aims of his research, avoids certain questions and persons, and constantly renegotiates roles.[16]

The more one probes the questions of power and the allocation of resources, issues that threaten the organization as a whole, the greater the problems of negotiating and maintaining access. It is to the credit of sociologists that they have attempted to study very central issues in police action: brutality, response to citizens' calls, budgetary processes, citizens' complaints, and the enforcement of morality.[17]

These questions of access also bear on the role definition the researcher offers at the initiation of his research. It is fundamental to distinguish the initial role definitions, or roles sent and roles received. Roles sent and received by the host organization need not be stable over time and, as a general rule, are not. Some of the more interesting

---

15. Banton, op. cit., pp. 169–70.

16. One police researcher told me he had developed a severe psychosomatic problem in the course of his study of a police department while trying to manage the complex grant monies, the various sponsors, federal and local, and avoiding being thrown out of the department for his research probing. He has since been thrown out. This pattern of avoidance led him to avoid any involvement in one of the major demonstrations in the city, hoping not to be caught in the middle of internal political forces in the department, particularly the scapegoating which followed the events.

17. This is contrary to Form's assertion that sociologists tend to deal with peripheral issues to avoid conflict with the power structure and legitimating members of host organizations. See Form, op. cit.

research chronicles trace the emergence and demise of role relationships of the researcher and the researched.[18]

The placement of the observer within the social system he is observing is an important aspect of role definition vis-à-vis segments of the organization, the data he obtains, and his own view of the world. Buckner felt he began to see the world as a "cop," and apparently this concerned him, although his reasons are not articulated:

> I began to perceive the world from a police point of view, seeing vehicle code violations while driving, watching for accidents and setting out flares when in my private car, knowing certain sections of the city only from their geography of crime and violence, immediately going to a call box when I heard a burglar alarm or saw a traffic hazard while in civilian clothes, noticing suspicious people who seemed out of place, noticing prostitutes and pimps, and thinking of the solution to many problems in police terms.[19]

Westley argues that the secretive nature of police organizations makes the role of outside observer very difficult to play.[20] Buckner, on the other hand, felt constrained by the limited view he was able to gather of the higher levels of the organization.[21] Skolnick thought that "law enforcement is not to be found in its most significant and interesting forms on the streets" and focused his attention on the enforcement of morals in the detective division.[22]

In summary the more "craftlike" the research, the more the focus is on the procedural and the practical (as opposed to the moral and the ethical) aspects of the system operation, the greater the likelihood of gaining access to police organizations. This focus, practically speaking, is to the advantage of the professionalizing segment of the organization and increases the probability of lasting legitimation. These considerations, however, are *not* to be taken as a recipe for the necessary foci of research.

---

18. See articles in Richard N. Adams and Jack Preiss (eds.), *Human Organization Research* (Homewood, Ill.: Dorsey Press, 1960); Phillip E. Hammond (ed.), *Sociologists at Work* (New York: Basic Books, 1964); Gideon Sjoberg (ed.), *Ethics, Politics, and Social Research* (Boston: Schenkman, 1967); and Arthur J. Vidich, Joseph Bensman, and Maurice R. Stein (eds.), *Reflections on Community Studies* (New York: Wiley, 1964). Form, op. cit., suggests several role sets possible: social photographer or ethnographer, public relations expert, social engineer, teacher, scientist, and others. Given the paucity of information on the development and self-definition of police researchers, such a typology would be of little value.

19. Buckner, op. cit., pp. 471–72.

20. William A. Westley, "Violence and the Police," *American Journal of Sociology*, 59 (July 1953), pp. 34–41.

21. Buckner, op. cit., pp. 480–83. Buckner reflects, I think, the feeling of the lower-level patrolman quite accurately.

22. Skolnick, *Justice Without Trial.* op. cit., p. 33.

THE MANAGEMENT OF RESEARCH INSIDE POLICE
ORGANIZATIONS

[R]esearchers who study complex organizations become conscious of their behavior, conscious of their dependency on others, and conscious of how others define them. They must therefore carefully consider what tactics to adopt.[23]

The *tactical aspects of fieldwork* involve interpersonal relationships encountered in the course of the research. A large body of literature on the tactical aspects of managing field roles and interpersonal relationships exists, but, as Form points out, there is relatively little written on matters of politics, interorganizational relationships in which the researcher must move, and large-scale bureaucratic models of social research. Having considered some of the political and power issues above, we turn, in this section, to the interpersonal and interactional "problems" revealed in our studies.

Unfortunately for sociological research, fieldwork (or qualitative analysis) is often taken as synonymous with "soft" or "imprecise" work. In some respects, the "how to do it" aspects of fieldwork are much more carefully developed than the mechanics of large-scale social research—the manipulation of data from large projects, the use of statistical tables to create an argument, and so on.[24] The anthropological tradition provides carefully developed and sensitive orientation to fieldwork, which is otherwise unavailable to students of other modes of research.

There is a tendency for survey techniques and for observational techniques to be defined as polar opposites. It is true that as some researchers use the interview it is insensitive to phenomenological matters, but we have, in fact, little research that systematically compares interview and other sorts of data. However, we have even less on the impact of observers, differences in results and interpretation as a function of role definition, modes of access, sponsorship, and so on. Matters of personal style, class differences, values of observers, simply have not been systematically tested.[25]

A contributing factor to polemics concerning the relative merit of different research techniques is the hesitancy of fieldworkers to develop precise measures and models, as sociologists Becker and Geer have

23. Form, op. cit.
24. See Reiss, in Becker et al., op. cit.
25. Ibid.

attempted to do.[26] This leads to a continued caveat, or warning, prefacing virtually every field study that claims that the study is only exploratory, the conclusions are only tentative and are based on one case, and so forth. These statements are found in the studies at issue, as shown in the following randomly selected apologia.

> In an exploratory study such as this, it is rarely possible to collect precise, numerical data sufficient to permit rigorous analysis. To answer the question of *what is* to be measured, or whether anything *can* be measured, is one reason for doing an exploratory study in the first place. The problem of evidence is not, however, solved by offering such excuses. Much of what is said in this book is asserted, or illustrated, or suggested, but not proved.[27]

Caveats grace the introductory remarks of all but a few of the police studies discussed in this article. Yet, as the bibliography shows, the number and types of these studies are rapidly reaching the state of a "critical mass," where such statements will be indefensible in light of the available information. In short, we have reached a position where more systematic and rigorous studies are needed, and this does not mean more or less quantitative, larger scale, or resembling to a greater degree the natural science–hypothesis-testing type of research. It means research that deals in depth with the social worlds of the participants in their own language and terms. Firsthand immersion in situations that are characteristic of the subjects' lives should result in systematic descriptions that integrate both the categories of social order and the situated management of meanings and are therefore recognizable to the participants. This can be accomplished through a variety of means, but our most fruitful model is that of observer(s), either active or passive, in day-to-day interaction with the empirical world studied. Since the nature of the empirical social world is built up, recognized, modified, constructed, and consistently indicated by people meeting the contingencies of everyday life, I can but suggest the most fruitful general principle of social research articulated by Herbert Blumer:

---

26. See Howard S. Becker, "Inference and Proof in Participant Observation," *American Sociological Review*, 23 (December 1958), pp. 652–60; Howard S. Becker and Blanche Geer, "Participant Observation and Interviewing: A Comparison," *Human Organization*, 16 (Fall 1957), 28–32; and Blanche Geer, "First Days in the Field," in Hammond (ed.), op. cit. These studies are reviewed in Peter K. Manning, "Problems in Interpreting Interview Data," *Sociology and Social Research*, 51 (April 1967), 203–16.

27. Wilson, *Varieties of Police Behavior*, p. 14. This is not an accusation leveled specifically at Wilson—the same statement could have been drawn from any of fifteen studies.

"Respect the nature of the empirical world and organize a methodological stance to reflect that respect"[28] (italics added).

The tactical problems of police studies present us with actual attempts on the part of social researchers to understand the nature of the social reality that the police externalize, objectify, and internalize.[29] The tactical problems of these studies can be organized into three broad areas: *value confrontation,* which results from the interaction of social scientists and policemen; how to deal with the typical problematic scenes characteristic of the occupation to which the researcher must respond by *creating and maintaining a series of viable roles and identities;* and the impact on the researcher of *exposure to the dangerous aspects of police life* and the ideology that surrounds it.

The value system of the police has attracted considerable attention in the mass media. As suggested by the outline of police cultural postulates (above), the themes of life as dangerous and threatening, low self-esteem, men as evil, dishonest, cruel, and unfeeling, and themselves as victims of social conspiracy are very strong among the police and tend to increase with time.[30] The police, having been delegated the task of law enforcement, tend to dwell on those aspects of human life that undermine respect for the law and its enforcers. The police are, however, dependent for their existence on the thing they claim to wish to eliminate: crime and immorality. They come, consequently, to invest a part of themselves in the law. Law-breaking is no longer viewed as the result of random processes or mere ignorance but is taken to represent a thrust at the self of the enforcer. The policeman's respectability and honor are involved in the respect and honor the public confers on the law, and the policeman all too easily finds it operationally difficult to separate the two.

The role seems to attract men who are apparently deeply ambivalent about the law, politically conservative, perhaps reactionary, and persons of lower- or lower-middle-class origins with a high school or less education. The police attributes suggested by the brief listing of the postulates of the police culture—suspiciousness, fear, low self-esteem, and distrust of others—are almost diametrically opposed to the usual conception of the desirable democratic man. The exposure to danger,

---

28. Herbert Blumer, *Symbolic Interactionism* (Englewood Cliffs, N.J.: Prentice-Hall, 1969), p. 60. This book is strongly recommended to students who wish to develop an understanding of the theoretical position that underlies most sociological field studies.

29. These terms are borrowed from Peter Berger, *The Sacred Canopy* (Garden City, N.Y.: Anchor Books, 1969), Chap. 1 and passim.

30. See the Appendix to Neiderhoffer, op. cit., "The Study of Police Cynicism."

the social background of the policeman, the constant exposure to "life as a pornographic movie," low pay, low morale, and vulnerability to a repressive bureaucracy all combine to make the policeman susceptible to the appeals of political groups and to act in accordance with political beliefs in carrying out the wide range of tasks that depend upon discretion.[31] The social scientist, on the other hand, tends to be politically liberal, of middle-class origins, highly educated, and intellectual as contrasted to "action-oriented."

Although sociology has historically been involved in opening up cross-class communication,[32] the kinds of problems encountered by researchers in police studies are only paralleled by problems of studying right-wing groups, end-of-the-world religionists, and so on. That is, the degree of value discrepancy is wide enough to be almost ever-constant, and both parties are aware of it to a considerable degree.

To the police, the social scientist doubtless represents the critical, carping public and the liberal fringe. Many of the recent protest and reform movements are identified with social science and adopt a social science rhetoric ("power structure," "the system," "the elite," "alienation"), which the police see as threatening to their own security and well-being. The tendency for the policeman is to look for extraordinary dress, demeanor, location, or appearance and to interpret them as signs of moral and legal differentiation—in a sense, all minorities are perceived as potential law breakers, and many are ideologically defined as "anticop," such as blacks, peace protesters, hippies, and radicals.[33]

Buckner perceived the extent of his own tension when confronting these differences in personal style, values, and ideology:

> [B]ecoming a participant and going along with whatever is done, as I feel is necessary to truly experience what is going on, will provide the observer with a massive, and extremely difficult to counter, value confrontation. It is very hard to stick to some abstract value conception in the face of firsthand, disconfirming reality. The observer's personal values and the values of the group he is observing are thus in constant tension until some resolution is reached; he finishes his study or he "goes native" accepting and supporting the values he is living and

---

31. This paragraph is taken from Manning, in Douglas (ed.), op. cit.

32. See David Riesman and Mark Benney, "The Sociology of the Interview," in David Riesman (ed.), *Abundance for What?* (Garden City, N.Y.: Anchor Books, 1964), pp. 492–513; and Manning, "Problems . . . ," op. cit.

33. This theme is devloped in Skolnick, *Justice Without Trial*, op. cit.; Irving Piliavin and Scott Briar, "Police Encounters with Juveniles," *American Journal of Sociology*, 70 (September 1964), 206–14; Carl Werthman and Irving Piliavin, in David J. Bordua (ed.), *The Police: Six Sociological Essays* (New York: Wiley, 1967); and Paul Chevigny, *Police Power* (New York: Pantheon, 1969).

working with. Unless an observer is prepared to accept value relativism at an emotional level and to treat his own values as just another set of values "appropriate for some situations," long term participation in a group whose values diverge from his own will be an uncomfortable experience.[34]

Sociologist David Ward claims that it was a difficult experience to have his wife call him "Professor Fuzz" when he came home after observing policemen patrol. The police researcher is often caught between the "liberal" values of his occupational group, his family, and his students—his most significant reference points—and the opinions and attitudes of the policemen he is observing. This situation is a classic example of role conflict, and a variation of cognitive dissonance situations in which two sets of facts are in contradiction and a resolution is demanded.

The resolutions of such role dilemmas take interesting and instructive forms. Reiss, writing of the adaptations his observers took, found a pattern that I have detected in talking with and reading the work of sociologists in the police bag: they tend to become sympathetic to the police problem, almost to the extent of becoming police apologists. One sociologist who has become a popular speaker at police training and educational conventions and at sociological seminars and meetings claims he has two speeches: one, an "antipolice" speech that he delivers to policemen, and the other, a "propolice" speech that he delivers to his sociological colleagues.

This is one resolution of role conflict—the segregation of audiences and messages. In his research, using carefully selected observers from law, police administration, and the social sciences, Reiss found an instructive pattern of adjustment. As we have argued above, observation requires playing not one role, but many roles, and it is simply a truism to state that these performances will in some ways reflect past socialization. Reiss explicates his strategy for selecting observers and training them to take the plain-clothes detective role (without the functions):

> The "fit" between observer role and plainclothesman posed problems both for officers and observers in police and citizen transactions. In our study, it was clear that as observers became sophisticated in the problems of the patrol officer, their potential for "going native" or having officers "thrust" the requirements of the role upon them increased. Indeed, situations occurred all too frequently that served to define and solidify the role of the observer as detective. . . .
>
> As in the study of interviewer effects, we discovered that prior socialization does have an effect on some kinds of data but by no means

---

34. Buckner, op. cit., p. 480.

on all observations. Those with legal background reported more fully and seemingly more accurately on legal matters, social scientists more readily judged the social class position of the citizen, and so on. Generally, these are predictable differences. Yet, in the aggregate, these were not differences in kind but differences in the amount of error introduced into the observation.[35]

Describing one of the only systematic attempts to assess differences in observations and the effects of the observational experience, Reiss continues:

What happened to their original perspectives through the experience of being an observer? They all changed and in the same direction, becoming somewhat more "pro-police." But the change according to original perspective is particularly interesting, since they did not become pro-police in the same way.

The social scientists, among them sociologists, had a beautiful sociological resolution of such role conflict as they experienced in becoming pro-police. Who are the police? They are the "poor men caught in the bad system," human beings like everyone else, some good, some bad, but on the whole really reasonable nice human beings. The job makes them what they are. Why? Well, in part because the environment they deal with makes it hard to be otherwise and more so because police departments make them that way. Now that is an obvious sociological argument that makes sense. It says that roles and organizations make people what they are. Incidentally, and very importantly, their experience made the observers what they were then, and I suspect still are. Participant observation can be socialization with a sociological vengeance.

Because of their association with sociologists as supervisors, some of the observers with training in the law also came to see the problem as poor men caught in a bad organizational system. More importantly, they began to see the law and the legal system not only as malfunctioning, but as lacking in relevance for the problems of police and citizens. They probably never will be students of the law in the same way again. Unlike sociologists who were observers, those from the law responded as would-be-reformers.

The police officers changed least of all in their attitudes toward policing but, with one exception, developed a social science perspective. One of our police officers, from a major eastern city, expressed it clearly by saying that he saw all these things from a new perspective —these questions had never occurred to him. He became more objective and began to see things in broader outlines. The role of investigator had changed him into a man who not only saw, but raised questions.

---

35. Reiss, in Becker et al., op. cit., p. 362.

He also, by the way, became invaluable in getting information that was hard to get. He played an "undercover role" with less conflict. And why not? He had been socialized to do so.

Interestingly, the graduates of police administration programs became more pro-police. They were less likely to take the textbook view of their more liberal professors and of top police administrators of the modern school, whom they now regarded as too far from the line. They no longer were part of the "empty holster" cadre. They knew.[36]

It is imperative, I think, in situations involving major value clashes that are understood by both parties (for example, studies of criminals, policemen, and "deviant groups," where the observer is known) to differentiate your roles from those of the "normal participant." This makes you a "limbo member" of the group. Polsky, in the essay referred to earlier, makes an important point in regard to this value conflict and provides several rules for the study of the deviant that are equally valid for police studies:

If you establish acquaintance with a criminal on some basis of common interest, then, just as soon as possible, let him know of the differences between you if he hasn't guessed them already. [This differentiation of roles and interests may lead to some mutual exchanges of pleas for justification, explanations of "why" things are done, and insights into the meanings of the differences in roles. However, Polsky cautions in an oral interpretation: one should not do favors for criminals; they may expect to be repaid. Repayment may implicate the researcher in immoral, illegal acts, which he would otherwise avoid.]

... It is important to realize that he will be studying you, and let him study you. . . . He has got to define you satisfactorily to himself and his colleagues if you are to get anywhere, and answering his questions frankly helps this process along.

You must draw the line, to yourself and to the criminal. . . . You need to decide beforehand, as much as possible, where you wish to draw the line, because it is wise to make your position on this known to informants rather early in the game. [This is in reference to observing criminal acts, but the police observer has some parallel moral and scientific problems if he wishes to keep his roles straight and if he has strong ethical commitments against assisting the police. This is discussed below.]

Letting criminals know where you draw the line of course depends on knowing this yourself.

---

36. Ibid., pp. 364–65.

Although I have insisted that in studying criminals you mustn't be a "spy," mustn't pretend to be "one of them," it is equally important that you don't stick out like a sore thumb in the criminal's natural environment. . . . In other words, you must walk a tightrope between "openness" on the one hand and "disguise" on the other, whose balancing point is determined anew in each investigation. [This is discussed by Reiss and Skolnick above, and is further discussed in the section on ethics.][37]

The marginality and conflict of policemen and their observers introduces the second theme, that of building viable roles. The observer of any social group, if he is known to take the observer role, and it is most assuredly a role, places himself in the unusual position of being a *stranger.* The scientist in general, of course, plays a stranger-role because he suspends his usual system of personal relevances as well as suspending the personal relevances of those he observes or analyzes. Recall the parallels between the scientist and the cartographer in comparison with the attitudes and actions of the native city dweller. The stranger can be objective. Objective rationality is rare in social life and therefore suspect. This suspicion, which accompanies the stranger-role, means that the usual assumptions that people are "like me" and typical of others in this group are questioned: the observer's loyalty and trustworthiness are at issue.[38]

The problems of "strangeness" are most salient in the early stages of fieldwork, where the oddness of the presence of observers is most unlikely to have been integrated, normalized, and accounted for by the system of everyday assumptions. This suggests that observation is a process of *role-building.* Olesen and Whittaker use a framework derived from this insight in their study of nursing students' socialization. Of particular interest are their three final stages of role-making or building: "proffering and inviting," "selecting and modifying," and "stabilizing and sustaining."[39] (The first stage, "surface encounter," is described in Schutz's essay "The Stranger.") These micro-organizational aspects of social research are an outgrowth of the work of Goffman and others, and are nicely captured by Lofland's notion of role management:

---

37. Ned Polsky, "Research Method, Morality, and Criminology," *Hustlers, Beats and Others* (Chicago: Aldine, 1967), pp. 125–27.

38. Alfred Schutz summarizes this observational problem in his essay, "The Stranger," in Schutz, *Collected Papers, Vol. II: Studies in Social Theory,* ed. Arvid Brodersen (The Hague: Nijhoff, 1964), pp. 91–105.

39. Virginia Olesen and E. Whittaker, "Role-Making in Participant Observation: Processes in the Researcher-Actor Relationship," *Human Organization,* 26 (Winter 1967), pp. 273–81.

Adopting the perspective of someone, some place in particular, behind a role label, the world stretches before him in terms of the immediate present, in terms of the day, and perhaps in terms of weeks and months. First and foremost, reality extends before him in terms of the immediate present and the current day. From behind that label a course of events must be constructed; other persons hiding behind other labels must be dealt with and *managed;* an orderly flow of activity must be negotiated.[40]

The notion of a fragile, processual, social order that is constantly being shaped, defined, and redefined as actors encounter and deal with the intersections of different definitions of social reality lies at the base of such a view of social research. In the stage of proffering and inviting, the system of relevances of the host group, in particular the fit between life roles (age, sex, nonoccupational identities), becomes important. For example, the police culture is essentially a masculine culture with emphasis on virility, toughness, masculinity, and masculine interests such as sexual triumphs, sports, outdoor life, and so forth. (The overlap here with lower-class cultural themes is clear.) The researcher, if known and a male will doubtless be called upon to pass certain "masculinity tests" in the proffering and inviting stage.

David Bordua, in a public address, humorously recounted his own experiences.[41] While doing observation, Bordua normally rode in the back of the patrol car and followed the patrolmen in to investigate a situation. On one occasion, while investigating a complaint, Bordua found himself leading the two policemen with whom he had been riding up a narrow, winding, and dark staircase. Although the order of march in leaving the car had seen the sociologist at the rear (where he definitely preferred to be), the policemen had arranged it so that Bordua was leading.

Similar testing goes on with rookie policemen. Bordua recounted an incident in a black bar in a lower-class area, where a tall, heavy-set black sergeant had arranged for a rookie to precede him on a "premises check" (a walk through a bar to establish that no gambling or illegal activities were going on and, not unimportantly, to establish the presence of the police in the area). As the rookie moved through a narrow aisle, a "drunk" lurched into his path. Every eye attended the scene, awaiting the outcome of this test. The rookie firmly grabbed the man's arm, moved him in front of himself, and sent him on to rest against the

---

40. John Lofland, "Role Management: A Programmatic Statement," Working paper 30, Center for Research in Social Organization (University of Michigan, June 1967), p. 11.

41. David J. Bordua, in an address to the National Institute for Police-Community Relations (Michigan State University, May 20, 1969).

bar. As Bordua describes it, it was an act of skill and grace and established the young man as a potentially "good cop," able to handle himself in a spot without the use of violence or threats. These are risk-taking situations, and most middle-class people prefer to encounter such situations water-skiing or playing cards, where the personal risk is relatively low. They are part of police observation and an intimate part of police life.

This suggests that roles are offered and responded to constantly, and that situations always have definitive properties for members. The question of motives may arise as a result. Why are you doing this anyway? Polsky[42] recounts that criminals assumed he was a "crime buff" or that he had a vicarious interest in crime; other investigators have found that their interest in homosexuality led to imputations by informants that they were "really queer," or "closet queers," unwilling to admit to their true motives. The identity question is always salient in fieldwork (Who am I? Who are they? Why am I here?), and the observed recognize this as well. (I have wondered at my own interest in questions that always seem to involve authority figures and power questions—my research on physicians' political ideology, the police, and deviance in general.) The proffered role may be useful as a fictive device for establishing rapport. Reiss found that his observers were continually being forced into the role of plainclothesman, as did Skolnick, who *became* a detective, for all practical purposes. Skolnick writes:

> I spent six weeks, however, directly observing the vice control squad. In addition, four weeks were spent with the burglary squad and two with robbery and homicide to compare the detective's work where there is typically a citizen complainant. Weeks of intensive observation were spaced over a period of fifteen months, during which time I would drop in at least one or two afternoons a week to keep up acquaintances. I also spent one month in the summer of 1963 studying the La Loma district attorney's office. This is the office to which felony defendants are bound over after a preliminary hearing in Westville. Thus, during three months as participant-observer in the local and county offices of the prosecutor, I frequently came into contact with police.
>
> Under direct observation, detectives were cooperative. They soon gave permission to listen in to telephone calls, allowed me to join in conversations with informants, and to observe interrogations. In addition, they called me at home when an important development in a case was anticipated. Whenever we went out on a raid, I was a detective so far as any outsider could see. Although my appearance does not

42. Polsky, op. cit. Also in paper presented to American Sociological Association, September 1969.

conform to the stereotype of the policeman, this proved to be an advantage since I could sometimes aid the police in carrying out some of their duties. For example, I could walk into a bar looking for a dangerous armed robber who was reportedly there without undergoing much danger myself, since I would not be recognized as a policeman. Similarly, I could drive a disguised truck up to a building, with a couple of policemen hidden in the rear, without the lookout recognizing me.

At the same time, I looked enough like a policeman when among a group of detectives in a raid for suspects to take me for a detective. (It twice happened that policemen from other local departments, who recognized that I was not a member of the Westville force, assumed I was a federal agent.) Even though I posed as a detective, however, I never carried a gun, although I did take pistol training on the police range. As a matter of achieving rapport with the police, I felt that such participation was required. Since I was not interested in getting standard answers to standard questions, I needed to be on the scene to observe their behavior and attitudes expressed on actual assignments.[43]

Skolnick apparently was able to select and modify his roles to fit his interests and those of the observed. This led to stability in the role system. Very little else is written about these interpersonal negotiations in fieldwork on police. It is needed.

The power relationship in fieldwork places the worker in a dependent position vis-à-vis his informants, and he must attempt to exchange valuables to retain interest, sympathy, and cooperation. One of these valuables is simple self-esteem, which flows from being interviewed or observed. The ways in which the observer justified his use and invasion of the lives of his informants tend to take the form of "rhetorics of justification." Science and scientific work are a very useful rhetoric these days, as is the claim to present an objective account of the police problem to the citizens.

It is important to keep in mind that any stability in a role relationship is in a sense "bought" through continual exchange and reciprocity between the observer and the observed.[44] This is speaking both generally and specifically. For example, several investigators have reported that the police asked them to assist in arrests, for example, putting on handcuffs, monitoring a radio message, holding a suspect with a night-

43. Skolnick, *Justice Without Trial*, op. cit., pp. 35–36.

44. This is not an argument for the generality of the exchange notions of social organization. It is relevant where the basis for establishing the role relationship is labeled instrumental by both parties and where the observer is directly asking rights of intrusion.

stick, or verifying a description of field encounters as an "objective observer." (These are further discussed below.) A special class of reciprocity is involved in the observation of police "errors."[45] At times, police observers are placed in a quandary as a result of their observations of violations of departmental regulations or of statutes. One observer in a large Midwestern police department observed such violations (brutality) and was uncertain, since he knew the patrolman knew he had observed the incident, whether to turn the man in and thereby possibly destroy the study or "clam up" and gain the trust of those he observed. Given the possibility that other events might raise questions about his presence, the sociologist also thought that this bit of information might give him leverage later. His decision was not to report the incident to headquarters. On the other hand, a student in this same project who observed policemen harassing blacks in an inner-city area and indignantly reported the event was banned from further observation. (The policemen were temporarily suspended.) These are clearly moral decisions for the observer. This is a salient problem, given the uncertainty of police work and the great discretion allowed the patrolman. According to Buckner, even recording information in the small field diary he carried raised the hackles of his partner:

> The sole feedback of a negative sort which I had was that one officer mentioned that some of the men were worried about me because I was overeducated and wrote down everything in my notebook, unlike many Reserve Officers. I handed him my notebook to let him see that all I wrote down were the details of each incident, which officers are required to do by department policy anyway. I told him to tell anybody who was worried that they could look at anything I wrote at any time they wanted, I had nothing to hide. This was literally true as I kept any private notes at home and did not carry them with me.[46]

A more important question than whether there is a reaction to the presence of the observer (the "reactivity effect") is whether there is an effect on the scene itself—is a "watched cop" the same as one operating only with a partner? Or put another way, what stabilizes a role relationship? None of the observers mention specifically any effect of their

---

45. This is a general problem, as Everett Hughes points out in the chapter, "Mistakes at Work," in *Men and Their Work* (New York: Free Press, 1958). It is made more difficult when the observer is also trained in the same occupation. Dorothy Douglas, an RN-sociologist, faced an extremely difficult moral problem whenever she observed "errors" in an emergency room (personal communication). John MacNamara (personal communication) also comments that the existence of secrets is always a part of the power structure of police organizations. People are likely to "save up" incidents, violations, and errors for strategic use against other parts of the organization or persons.

46. Buckner, op. cit., pp. 477–78. See also, Skolnick, *Justice Without Trial*, op. cit., p. 48.

presence, nor do they speculate about the question—that is, ask what might have been. Skolnick, however, felt his presence was normalized by those he observed, once the observer-observed role relationship had stabilized sufficiently:

One problem that this sort of research approach raises is whether an observer's presence alters the normal behavior of the police. There is no certain control for this problem, but I believe the following assumptions are reasonable. First, the more time the observer spends with subjects, the more used to his presence they become. Second, participant-observation offers the subject less opportunity to dissimulate than he would have in answering a questionnaire, even if he were consciously telling the truth in response to standardized questions. Third, in many situations involving police, they are hardly free to alter behavior, as, for example, when a policeman kicks in a door on a narcotics raid.

Finally, if an observer's presence does alter police behavior, I believe it can be assumed that it does so only in one direction. I can see no reason why police would, for example, behave *more* harshly to a prisoner in the presence of an observer than in his absence. Nor can I imagine why police would attempt to deceive a prisoner in an interrogation to a greater degree than customary. Thus, a conservative interpretation of the materials that follow would hold that these are based upon observations of a top police department behaving at its best. However, I personally believe that while I was not exposed to the "worst," whatever that may mean, most of what I saw was necessarily typical of the ordinary behavior of patrolmen and detectives, necessarily, because over a long period of time, organizational controls are far more pertinent to policemen than the vague presence of an observer whom they have come to know, and who frequently exercises "drop-in" privileges.

If a sociologist rides with police for a day or two he may be given what they call the "whitewash tour." As he becomes part of the scene, however, he comes to be seen less as an agent of control than as an accomplice.[47]

There seems to be some consensus in the work reviewed for this article that the process of role negotiation can lead to a satisfactory research relationship.

Danger is a part of a fair number of occupations, but only in a few does it occupy a significant part of the occupational "line" or public ideology.[48] Being a policeman is one of these occupations. The police possess what might be called a "threat-danger-hero" notion of their

47. Skolnick, *Justice Without Trial,* op. cit., pp. 36–37.
48. On the concept of an occupational "line," or ideology, see Manning, "Problems . . . ," op. cit.; and Oswald Hall, "The Informal Organization of Medical Practice" (unpublished Ph.D. dissertation, University of Chicago, 1944), quoted in Buford Junker (ed.), *Fieldwork* (Chicago: University of Chicago Press, 1960), p. 95.

348   LAW ENFORCEMENT AND THE CRIMINAL

everyday lives.[49] The structure of rewards within police departments is very conducive to this ideology. Violent or dramatic public action— either in solving or preventing a crime, shooting a man, or aggressively patrolling traffic—is a source of promotion to the Detective Bureau, a way to "get out of the bag."[50] In fact, much of police work is boring or involves frustrating, contentious hassles with citizens. The dangerous activities represent considerably less than 10 percent of police patrol time, and less than 1 percent of citizen-initiated complaints concern violent or dramatic crime (rape, murder, assault).[51] This may only be another way of saying that the highly unpredictable, but potentially possible, dangerous scene is always a part of police patrol operations.[52]

---

49. To the policeman, these are considered the "core skills" of the occupation and the "characteristic professional acts." These concepts are found, respectively, in Harvey A. Smith," Contingencies of Professional Differentiation," *American Journal of Sociology,* 63 (January 1958), pp. 410–14; and Rue Bucher and Anselm Strauss, "Professions in Process," *American Journal of Sociology,* 66 (January 1961), pp. 325–334. For an application of these concepts to medicine, especially in regard to associated political attitudes, see Peter K. Manning, "Occupational Types and Organized Medicine: Physicians' Attitudes Toward the American Medical Association" (unpublished Ph.D. dissertation, Duke University, 1966), especially Chap. 3. Although the image of the police and their own self-definition coincide on the danger involved in being a policeman, at least one study found that many other occupations are more dangerous. Policemen kill six times as many people as policemen are killed in the line of duty. In 1955, Gerald D. Robin "Justifiable Homicide by Police Officers," *Journal of Criminal Law, Criminology and Police Science,* 54 (1963), pp. 228–29, found that the rate of police fatalities on duty, including accidents, was 33 per 100,000, less than the rate for mining (94), agriculture (55), construction (76), and transportation (44). Between 1950 and 1960, an average of 240 persons were killed by "criminals." (Summary from Task Force Report, op. cit., p. 189).

50. See John H. MacNamara, "Uncertainties in Police Work: The Relevance of Police Recruits' Backgrounds and Training," in David J. Bordua (ed.), op. cit., pp. 163–252.

51. Donald J. Black, "Police Encounters and Social Organization: An Observational Study" (unpublished Ph.D. dissertation, University of Michigan, 1968). See especially Tables 2 and 18 and discussion thereof. This is a report based on the same project that is discussed by Reiss, in Becker et al., op. cit.

52. The dangerous view of life may have become a self-fulfilling prophecy. Buckner, op. cit., pp. 230–31, lists the astounding weapons he was required to carry:

> The authority of the uniform alone is not sufficient to control many situations which the police encounter, so the police officer is fitted out as a weapons system with a variety of weapons useful in various situations. An officer will routinely carry a .38 caliber revolver and spare ammunition, a 12 to 14 inch truncheon, club or baton, a flashlight, handcuffs and key, call box key and a whistle, a notebook and pen, a citation book, an arrest book, possibly a two-way radio. In addition, he may carry a spare gun, a "come-along" or "bear's claw," brass knuckles, a blackjack, a confiscated switchblade knife, a palm sap, a canister of tear gas or a more potent chemical agent depending on his own preferences and the rule of his department. ... My uniform, which does not include a radio or any additional weapons, weighs almost twenty pounds.

In addition to these weapons which are carried on his person, his patrol car may well contain a shotgun loaded with four rounds of "00" buckshot ([nine .33] caliber pellets per round), additional ammunition, a 26" baton, a riot helmet, a small law library, copies of the department's regulations, forty to fifty types of report forms, flares, blankets, first aid equipment, chalk, measuring tape, a two-way radio, red light and siren, and a "hot sheet" of stolen cars and license plates.

There are, nevertheless, considerations of personal safety for field-workers. Donald Roy, in the preface to an article on union-organizing tactics in the South in a volume dedicated to Everett C. Hughes, makes the ironic observation that fieldwork can be "both fun and safe."

I do not think it too farfetched to claim that Everett Hughes must share responsibility for any inquiry on Southern labor union matters, of which this offering represents a portion. Many years ago, in a course on methods of field research, he taught us that it was fun to sally forth with pencil and notebooks, like newspaper reporters, to observe and to question. I assisted with this course for a time, and learned along with those who took the adventure for credit. We infiltrated an area surrounding the University of Chicago, in team pairs and by task assignments, for reconnoitering, interviewing, and questionnairing. In last-minute reassurance, before his neophytes hit the streets and alleys, our smiling mentor would advise, "My phone number is in the book. If you run into trouble, and need bail, give me a ring—day or night." Thus we learned that field investigation was both fun and safe.

Just the other night, perched on a retaining wall across the street from an entrance to a textile mill, I watched a moving oval of picketing workers and college students attempt to dissuade nonstriking employees from entering the plant grounds to work the graveyard shift. At intervals carloads of incoming millhands would approach the picket line. As they drew up, indicating intent to cross, an otherwise impassive cordon of policemen would quickly form human chains to clear passageway. While a car nosed slowly through the reluctantly yielding mass, the picketers would cry "Scab! Scab! Scab!" in rhythmic unison; and often one of them would manage to advance upon an open car window, before the driver could gun his motor for a fast breakaway, to hiss a parting epithet: "Dirty scab!" "Rotten scab!" or "Dirty, rotten scab!" It was a balmy spring night, with a Carolina moon glowing through the pines to give me enough light to pencil a few lines and to note that police cars and an oversize paddy wagon were parked nearby. Additional police cars and a spare paddy wagon cruised up and down the street to give me a secure, comforted feeling as I jotted down my observations. Field work was fun, indeed, and safe, too, as we had learned from Everett Hughes, so long ago.[53]

Accompanying the police in the role of observer places one on the "right side of the law," minimizing some of the dangers of which Roy speaks, but other risks are involved. Buckner once observed an incredible high-speed chase. It began with a car running a stop sign, which activated the police to give chase. The police pursued the stop sign violator through the city, breaking speed laws, ignoring stop signs, and

---

53. Donald Roy, "The Union-Organizing Campaign as a Problem of Social Distance: Three Crucial Dimensions of Affiliation-Disaffiliation," in Becker et al., op. cit., pp. 49–50.

ending with a crash that totaled the police car in which Buckner was riding. The chase was continued, it was later reported, by other police cars. The chased car was finally run off the road by police cars and smashed against a bridge abutment by one of the police cars. The driver was charged, after a brief fight, with: "Two counts of reckless driving, two counts of assault and battery with an automobile, six counts of running a stop sign, and separate counts of trying to elude police, destroying public property, speeding and drunken driving."[54] A police officer who read Buckner's thesis and made comments added:

> I thoroughly enjoy that kind of challenge. In a way, it is right out of the old West. During such an event you are pressed to your limit. The exhilaration is unmatched. Such events are thoroughly discussed among officers. Exceptional police "hot chase" drivers are known in the department as "wheelmen."[55]

Other sociologists have described similar chases in tones of mixed feelings of fear and excitement.

There are other, perhaps less common, kinds of dangerous situations that are encountered in a day's work: what are euphemistically called "civil disturbances," but that may involve danger from wild shots (most of them from police guns), fights, crowds, and small collective outbursts at rock concerts or high schools. As mundane as it may seem, one of the most dangerous of police activities from the perspective of injury or death is "domestic disputes," or family brawls, for these often involve knives, hand guns, rifles, and other handy missiles.[56]

In summary, then, observing the police involves one in a secrecy-conscious, tightly organized bureaucracy, peopled by men who see the world as dangerous, isolating, and untrustworthy, and who see themselves as the last barrier between the citizen and total social decay. Police research presents some special problems of value conflict, role management, and danger. The structure of the tactics to be used in this type of research is affected by problems of access, research style, sponsorship, location, and perspective on the action.

---

54. Buckner, op. cit., pp. 208–209.

55. Ibid., p. 210. Buckner comments on his admission that he enjoyed the chase and notes that "... every officer within range customarily joins in any high speed chase."

56. Morton Bard, speech delivered at Michigan State University (Spring 1968). This is generally acknowledged among police officers. They view family intervention as "dirty work."

THE ETHICS OF OBSERVATION

A good study, therefore, will make somebody angry.[57]

This section is not a general discussion of the ethical issues in observational research. Several discussions are already available.[58] Rather, it is meant as an overview of certain persistent issues in social observation.

All social research is an enterprise that raises *moral* issues because it involves probing the collective paths along which people organize their lives. Since this probing also involves questions of power and authority, especially within social systems, field research raises *political* issues. Observing the law involves, at times, not observing it. Finally, since one of the obligations of social research is to reveal to other sociologists the ways in which people make their lives accountable to each other, this research raises *scientific* questions.

Intertwined with the initial question of how one constructs a scientific account are questions of *validity*—how accurate is the picture that one reports—and *reliability*—how well does the picture represent what others might find in other times, places, and settings.[59] The validity question has been suggested in the methodological comments of Skolnick and Buckner and is raised by most of the other sociologists whose work is discussed in this article. In any occupation, the problem of dissembling is encountered by the outside observer—that is, how do you know what and whom to believe? Police organizations are *secretive*, and other occupational studies tell us that people stand ready with various "team efforts" to avoid revealing too much of what is private and "backstage"[60] behavior and information.

Front management, dramatization, and concealing and revealing

---

57. Howard S. Becker, "Problems of Publication in Field Studies," in Vidich, Bensman, and Stein (eds.), op. cit., p. 276.

58. See ibid., pp. 267–84, for a general statement and useful bibliography; Lewis Yablonsky, "Experiences with the Criminal Community," A. W. Gouldner and S. M. Miller (eds.), *Applied Sociology* (New York: Free Press, 1965), pp. 55–73; Polsky, op. cit.; and the articles by Lee Rainwater, Theodore Mills, and John Seeley in *Social Problems*, 14 (Spring 1967). See also Norman K. Denzin, "On the Ethics of Disguised Observation," 502–4, and Kai T. Erikson's reply, 505–6, both in *Social Problems*, 15 (Spring 1968); Howard S. Becker, "Practitioners of Vice and Crime," in R. W. Habenstein (ed.), *Pathways to Data* (Chicago: Aldine, 1970); and Lewis Yablonsky, "On Crime, Violence, LSD and Legal Immunity for Social Scientists," *American Sociologist*, 3 (May 1968), 148–49.

59. See Donald W. Ball, "Conventional Data and Unconventional Conduct" (unpublished paper presented to the Pacific Sociological Association, 1967); Becker, "Problems of Publication . . . ," op. cit.; and Polsky, op. cit.

60. These concepts are taken from Erving Goffman, *The Presentation of Self in Everyday Life* (Garden City, N.Y.: Anchor Books, 1959). This is a "field manual" for students embarking on observational research.

roles will occur even if rapport is established at the legitimation stage of the research. Others have asked about the "reactivity effect" (mentioned above), since it bears on validity. There are no simple answers or recipes for solving the validity problem in any situation involving a known observer.[61] Since the observer himself serves as a "measuring instrument," he defines himself situationally largely in terms of the demands of the interpersonal process. In the same way that the policeman has a part of himself lodged in the law, the observer has a considerable portion of himself invested in his data; his data are a part of himself. Writing up a field report is cathartic. It is like viewing a home movie in which one is the principal actor. Separating "data" from "self" becomes a matter of determining analytically the nature of the games in which the researcher and other participants are involved.[62]

Useful formulation of the criteria for establishing validity is suggested by Bittner. His article was based on a year's fieldwork in two large cities, eleven weeks of it in "skid-row work," and approximately a hundred interviews with policemen of all ranks. Bittner proposes a "recognizability" rule "borrowed" from anthropologists.

> The formulations that will be proposed were discussed in these interviews. They were recognized by the respondents as elements of standard practice. The respondents' recognition was often accompanied by remarks indicating that they had never thought about things in this way and that they were not aware of how standardized police work was.[63]

Questions of reliability have seldom reared their threatening heads in police research. The caveat of "exploratory" is raised against such inquiries. It is perhaps weak to claim that there is substantial agreement among sociologists concerning the major points made in this review.

---

61. In many participant-observation studies, this reactivity effect has reached hilarious proportions. Leon Festinger, Henry W. Riecken, and Stanley Schachter's *When Prophecy Fails* (paper ed., New York: Harper Torch Books, 1964) is based on a study of a group of people predicting the world's end. The group was essentially a construction of those who studied it, and during the course of the research, observers probably outnumbered participants at critical points. John F. Lofland, in his study *Doomsday Cult* (Englewood Cliffs, N.J.: Prentice-Hall, 1966), found one of the only converts to the cult that he was doing as a study of conversion. A fascinating fictional treatment that spoofs sociology and sociologists is Alison Lurie's *Imaginary Friends* (New York: Avon, 1968), which insightfully explores the tendency for sociologists to confuse their scientific reality with other people's reality and to confuse both with fantasy. Miss Lurie's books are "sociological" in the best sense of that word; that is, she artistically penetrates the complexity of social experience and reveals the relativity of reality, perspective, feeling, and meaning.

62. See Manning, "Problems . . . ," op. cit.

63. Egon Bittner, "The Police on Skid-Row: A Study in Peace-Keeping," *American Sociological Review*, 32 (October 1967), pp. 699–715. This criterion is suggested by anthropologists; see Ward Goodenough, "Cultural Anthropology and Linguistics," in Dell Hymes (ed.), *Language in Culture and Society* (New York: Harper & Row, 1964).

Given the nature and scope of the studies discussed here—mostly careful ethnographies or descriptions of single types of organizations or problems—the usual reliability questions have little relevance. The information necessary for verification by others is often limited because sociologists conceal the names of the cities, policemen, and citizens involved in their studies. Wilson's *Varieties of Police Behavior* is one of the few studies in which the names of the cities involved are revealed. On the other hand, the cities are generally known by social researchers, and investigators are usually very willing to communicate privately with any other serious researcher about procedures and findings.

Some ethical issues are involved with these questions of scientific procedure. In order to protect their informants, sociologists often have to conceal the information necessary to ascertain usual notions of validity and reliability. A quick scan of other articles in this book will make the problems clear. These problems are most salient for students of criminal behavior, as Polsky and Yablonsky show; witnessing or knowing about a crime is a part of almost any deviant scene, and the sociologist has no legal protection. Some sociologists, Becker, Denzin, and Polsky,[64] have argued for a "philosophic calculus" in which the value of the scientific knowledge gained is weighed against the impact of the information on those studied. Who is benefited by such information? Any information on social life has potential discrediting effects; the functions of ignorance and secrecy in social life are well known.

The issue of overt (or known) versus covert (or unknown) observation further affects the shape of the moral questions. Whose privacy is invaded in what settings when playing what roles? What disruptive effects will the information have if it is gathered under conditions unknown to the observed? What information can ethically be concealed from those studied? For example, when one participates under the guise of science as a legitimating force, is it ever ethical to use the information for political purposes to discredit the organization and people whom you studied?[65] Under what conditions is it ethical?

Yablonsky feels that associations with deviants tend to encourage their deviancy by playing up their deviant roles, roles that, he claims, one should, in fact, be trying to reform.[66] Although I reject any association of reform or therapy with a scientific role in the same research

---

64. Becker, "Problems of Publication . . . ," op. cit.; Denzin, op. cit.; and Polsky, op. cit.

65. One of the police observers cited in this chapter recently wrote an "exposé" of the department he observed in a popular men's magazine. Rumor has it that the department now refuses access to any social researchers. I do not think popular exposés are ethical in light of the usual "scientific research contracts" that legitimate sociologists' access for most of their studies of organizations.

66. Yablonsky, in Gouldner and Miller (eds.), op. cit. Polsky, op. cit., attacks this assertion.

project, Yablonsky's reasoning might have important implications. Does studying the police provide information, a basis for creating more efficient social control? Does improving the practice and theory of police departments serve a metascientific end—providing "the greatest good for the greatest number of people"?

There are at least two levels at which political issues can be explored: the *micro* and the *macro* levels. At the micro level, there are questions of legal liability in witnessing crimes (perhaps being asked to appear in court as an expert witness), and assisting the police in dangerous situations such as those discussed above—holding prisoners, handcuffing them, passing on radio messages, assisting officers in fights where their lives are in danger, and so forth. What guilty knowledge gained as a result of observation should be reported to superiors in the police department, to the public at large in "muckraking articles," or to colleagues only in professional meetings? Police expect help in these kinds of situations. They do not define you in a lasting fashion as an "outsider" (and help in time of stress may be a fairly universal human expectation). You may become friendly with many policemen. Again, the study of deviants supplies a parallel. Does one participate in their activities— drug use, minor theft, abortion, and so forth—in order to legitimate one's own role? There is no simple answer. An a priori decision about where to "draw the line" is urged by many people who are "involved" in dangerous or illegal activities as a result of their research. Not only would this assist the researcher in striking an "honest" research bargain, it would assist him in drawing "identity lines" limning his own social placement, expectations, and obligations.

The political issues at the macro level are almost patently obvious in these days of questioning the establishment and those who enforce the laws of the establishment. Most of the research listed here was sponsored by foundations or by the federal government through the National Institute of Mental Health. However, the Omnibus Crime Control Bill and the legislation issuing from the President's Crime Control Commission's recommendations contain provisions for funding research in such areas as police handling of juveniles, riot control, and police training. Future investigators may consider taking money to study the police equivalent to taking money from the defense department for bolstering the war machine.

If research is undertaken on the police, regardless of sponsorship, political issues still remain. Does the observation, if it occurs, of brutality, harassment, incompetence, or malfeasance *obligate* the researcher to reveal it immediately to the policeman's superiors, or should he overlook them and pussyfoot in the interest of completing the study?

Will a complete study have an even greater cumulative impact on the organization than revelation of instances of wrongdoing?

Radicals have argued, with their usual tendency to dichotomize the world, that any involvement with "the pigs" is prima facie evidence of one's loyalty to the establishment. However, attempts to reorganize police departments in the areas of police-community relations and interpersonal civility, to alter the reward structure and training and recruitment procedures, and to introduce social science knowledge are contributions to a more decent, democratic society.

Two further cautions. First, moral decisions about the focus and scope of research should distinguish between two broad types of research: the first type are those studies that might have an impact in creating more humane, civil police work, that protect the legal rights of the accused, or that assist municipal governments to construct systems of civil accountability for the police; the second type are studies that deal with improving or inventing ineffectual, but perhaps dehumanizing and tyrannizing, systems of scientific surveillance, wire-tapping, or computerized criminal banks or files on "suspects" (which include demonstrators protected by the First Amendment, juveniles who are suspicious, radicals, politically outspoken people, mentally ill people). Second, I see the police problem as more complex than a question of contradictory mandate or of inadequate resources or training. I hold little hope for the "professionalization" rhetoric. Ultimately, it is a political question of *reformulating the law* and bringing police organizations under democratic political control.[67]

---

67. This issue is addressed in Manning, in Douglas (ed.), op. cit.

20

Police Work

Jonathan Rubinstein

The patrolman's conception of his city is different from that of the people he is paid to police. Like all city dwellers he knows the traditional neighborhoods and the nicknames which succeeding generations of people have imposed on their parts of the city in the process of making them their homes. But on his first day at the police academy he is given a city map covered with lines and numbers that do not appear on any street map. His former conception of the city is not erased, but it is gradually embroidered over by these jurisdictional lines of the police districts. As he is gradually introduced to the police craft, these boundaries begin to link up. When he leaves the academy and is initiated into an understanding of what the districts mean in the life of the uniformed police officer, he ceases to see the city as a collection of neighborhoods and begins to see it as a mosaic of linked districts.

There are no painted lines or signs marking the district boundaries, but every policeman (and persons with close connections to the police) knows when he is passing from one district to another. When two officers meet for the first time in a neutral place—at court, the dispensary, a union meeting—they invariably ask two questions of each other before engaging in any conversation: "Where do you work?" and "How much time you got in the business?" The questions are not inspired by simple curiosity but are a policeman's way of placing an unknown colleague. The laconic response "I've been in the Fifty-fifth since I went on the street three years ago" tells the questioner a good deal. He may never have been in the Fifty-fifth district, but he knows where it is, what

From Jonathan Rubinstein, *City Police* (New York: Farrar, Straus & Giroux, 1973), pp. 26–68, by permission of the author, publisher, and International Creative Management. Copyright © 1973 by Jonathan Rubinstein. Footnotes have been renumbered.

kind of people live in it, and what its reputation is, and these are part of the policeman's knowledge of the city. He is also given an opportunity to discuss mutual acquaintances. The familiar language and the acknowledged legitimacy of the questions reflect a common understanding of what they share. But the substance of these questions also indicates an awareness by the men that what they have in common as policemen is tempered by a man's experience and the place he has acquired it. A policeman may feel himself in possession of special rights anywhere in the city, but he knows that it is in his district that he learns his job and is a policeman.

When the graduating rookies are assigned, the news comes in a brief message on the departmental teletype. The captains' clerks scan the sheets to see if their requests for replacements have been granted, while the rookies are being informed whether their prayers or fears are being confirmed. During their three months' training, they learned informally about the districts from their instructors' stories, from friends and relatives in the department, and from other policemen sent to the academy for additional training. Although in Philadelphia they are barred from working the district in which they live[1] and have been warned not to expect the district of their choice, they hopefully fill out the request forms. Most recruits seek to avoid a district which requires a lot of traveling time from their home. Some worry about being assigned to neighborhoods they do not know or privately fear. A few who claim connections in the department confidently predict a good assignment, but most men wait anxiously, happy at the prospect of leaving the academy, which every recruit comes to despise, but worried about where they are going. As graduation day approaches, rumors intensify, fed by instructors who obligingly pass down what they learn from their superiors. After the lengthy wait the disclosure is inevitably anticlimactic. The instructor enters the room with a yellow sheet of teletype and reads off the names as they appear on the paper. No one's request has been satisfied; the class is scattered to districts throughout the city. Those who had boasted connections gamely claim they will get a transfer in a few months, others mutter threats to resign, but most just sit

---

1. The residency regulation is one of many rules designed to curb corruption. It was introduced in a number of cities after World War II, but it is gradually being eliminated as police departments seek ways of bringing their patrolmen into closer contact with neighborhood people. The rule was inspired by the belief that the elimination of prior contacts between the policeman and the people of his area would reduce the likelihood of his refusing to take action for personal reasons, accepting money to protect illegal practices which were locally condoned, and refusing to enforce the law impartially. Its effects have been nil.

silently. The instructor listens for a few moments, smiling, and then calls for order. "Listen, fellas, it ain't as bad as you think. Some of you are going to tough districts, but that's where you are gonna learn to be police officers. Some of you are going to farming districts.[2] Well, the girls are friendly and good-looking and they are good places to study for tests. After a while you can ask for a transfer to an active district. At least you all have someone going with you. It's good to have a couple of familiar faces in the district. I remember when I first went to . . ." but nobody listens any longer. Now the instructor is just another colleague. Everyone is looking at the large map on the front wall, studying the outline of his district, trying to figure out how to get to work and to imagine what the reality of the abstraction before him is like.

THE DISTRICT

The new policeman usually comes to his district knowing little about it except by reputation. He has been ordered to report to the station but not to anyone in particular. Although he is expected, nobody greets him, except possibly another rookie. He stands about awkwardly, adjusting the weight of the unfamiliar equipment which tugs at his belt, fulfilling his first official order by being where he is obliged to be, while his claim to being there crumbles before silence and indifference. Other policemen ignore him or he may wish they did when the grins they cast in his direction are accompanied by comments about his "nice new suit." When the sergeant or corporal finally approaches him and officially recognizes him, he is taken on a tour of the "district," as the men call their station house.

He is assigned a locker, and after leaving the locker room, the only place in a station where policemen have claims on privacy from the public, he is taken through the roll room, a large rectangular hall with a raised platform at one end which is the formal setting for roll calls, magistrate's hearings (police court), community meetings, and holiday parties. He is shown the lockup, where prisoners are held until being transported "downtown" to the central jail, where they are photographed and fingerprinted. He sees the operations room, where the direct communications with the detective divisions and the central police radio are located, the district records maintained, and the paper work produced by the patrolmen during their work tours is processed.

---

2. Until recently the outlying parts of the city were largely uninhabited and some people continued to farm the land. Most of it has now been subdivided and developed, but the population density is low and these places continue to enjoy good reputations among policemen.

If the captain is in his office, the rookie is formally introduced, giving the commander a chance to look over a new prospect for his plainclothes detail. If they have common acquaintances, a few friendly words may be exchanged; otherwise the meeting is brief and perfunctory. He is given a work schedule, told which squad he will work with and when to report. Unless he distinguishes himself or gets into trouble, the new policeman is not likely to speak with his captain again.

The captain is a "line officer" who has risen through the ranks and usually has a distinguished record as a street supervisor. But once he takes command of a district, he rarely has direct contact with his patrolmen. He is an executive who devotes his time to listening to the problems and demands of the residents and merchants of the district; he attends meetings and listens to complaints, checks reports submitted to him by his lieutenants and sergeants, and keeps his inspector, who is rarely seen in the district, informed.

The captain personally selects and commands the plainclothes detail, whose sole responsibility is to enforce the city's gambling, liquor, narcotics, and prostitution laws in the district. These five or six men are the only policemen who are directly under the captain's command. Although he selects his own "captain's men," they must be approved by his inspector and the chief inspector in charge of the patrol divisions. This deprives the captain of the possibility of pursuing an independent vice-enforcement policy. Despite their small number, this detail occupies a considerable part of his time. The plainclothesmen are transferred frequently, requiring the captain to be constantly on the lookout for new men. These transfers are necessary because it is difficult to conceal the men's identities from the "vice characters" against whom they operate and to prevent them from accepting the bribes and payoffs which are offered once they become knowledgeable about the local "action." New policemen are favored for plainclothes because they are less inclined to accept graft, but these men usually cannot make arrests of important vice operators. The department tries to control the possibility of corruption without compromising the quality of arrests made by plainclothesmen by mixing young district policemen with experienced "vice cops" who move often from one district to another.

The captain also recommends and implements changes in the distribution of his manpower and patrol procedures. In every district there are locally important commercial streets that receive the additional protection of a foot patrolman who is regularly assigned to the area during business hours. Businessmen's associations and influential merchants are constantly requesting special treatment and favors. The captain can have a man assigned to a meeting or a social event for a day without seeking the approval of his superiors, but any request for a permanent change in the distribution of his manpower must be decided at the highest levels of the department's command. Once the decision has been made to create a new foot beat, for example, the captain has the privilege of choosing the man for the post.

While the captain may know by name many of the men in his command, he generally deals with them through their sergeants and lieutenants. These men are the street supervisors, as he once was, and he will not interfere with their work unless they fail to provide him with the necessary assurance that they are doing their job properly. But the captain is in an anomalous position. He is an administrator who must enforce the regulations that are funneled to him from headquarters, but at the same time he must also seek to protect and encourage his men, who frequently resent what they consider arbitrary and capricious changes in their operating procedures. He balances his obligations by aligning himself with his men, demonstrating to them in their presence that he is a "good guy," and requiring their adherence to changes only after indicating that he is helpless to do otherwise in the face of superior authority.

One afternoon an order was received by teletype requiring the district to provide two policemen to guard a prisoner in a nearby hospital. When the captain was given the order, he stormed out of his office and denounced it before the fifteen or twenty men who were waiting for their roll call. "That dumb cocksucker who made up this order, he's no street cop. They send men out in one-man cars to break up fights between armed gangs and then expect me to assign two healthy men to guard one half-dead son-of-a-bitch," he shouted. The men were very pleased, although they knew that the order would be complied with.

The relationship between the captain and his subordinates requires them to inform him personally of anything that will open the district's work to scrutiny from outside or above. Any formal statement on a policeman's work—whether it be a recommendation for a commendation for outstanding work or a request to "take someone to the front," that is the laying of formal charges for departmental trial—must be reviewed by the captain before being forwarded up the chain of command. The captain must also sign the annual evaluation that the sergeants must make of each man under their command. If a man seeks a transfer, he must first inform his captain before any formal request can be forwarded to divisional headquarters. Most important of all, the captain must personally approve each application for a search warrant after it has been approved by a sergeant and before it is typed for presentation to a judge. Since warrants are used primarily in vice work, this power combined with his direct command of the district plainclothesmen assures the captain of absolute control over all official vice enforcement by the district police.

The captain assumes that his street supervisors will inform him of any occurrence that has a bearing on the appearance of his command. This is the tacit understanding upon which their relationship rests. In exchange for this, he allows the supervisors almost unrestricted control of the squads.

CO-WORKERS AND COLLEAGUES: THE SQUAD

A patrolman identifies himself to other policemen by his district, but his personal affiliation is with his squad. There are often more than two hundred policemen, organized into four squads, assigned to a district, and only some of the veteran supervisors and "old-timers" know most of them. Although all of these squads work the same ground on different shifts, the men are not encouraged to exchange information and knowledge of their working places with each other. The relations among the squads are formally maintained by direct contacts among the supervisors and through the mediation of their captain. Every man has a chance to meet men from other squads when he works overtime, during emergencies, and on special assignments. At each shift change the men going off are obliged to remain by their cars (frequently they do not) until the relief man takes over, providing a few moments' contact each day. Occasionally a man transfers from one squad to another, bringing with him knowledge of ex-colleagues which he offers to his new colleagues, enriching their knowledge about co-workers who are frequently seen, greeted, chatted with, but rarely known in the personal way as are the fifty policemen, the corporal, two sergeants, and the lieutenants who are in their squad.[3]

Every day each district in Philadelphia is policed by three different squads, while the fourth is off. Each squad works a six-day week, followed by two days off. Every week each squad works a different shift, and over a month's time the men have worked "around the clock" on all three shifts. Each district is policed on "daywork" from 8 A.M. to 4 P.M. by one squad, which is relieved on "nightwork," 4 P.M. to midnight,

---

3. On the differentiation of social and working contacts, see Erving Goffman, "Supportive Interchanges" in his *Relations in Public* (New York, Basic Books, 1971), pp. 69–80, and in his *Stigma* (Englewood Cliffs, N.J.: Prentice-Hall, 1963), Chap. II.

by a second; the last shift of the day is called "last out" and is from midnight to 8 A.M. In the regular rotation a squad works daywork and then returns the following week for last out, which is followed by nightwork.

The district patrolman's working schedule seals him off from other policemen who do not work the same shifts he does and makes it very difficult for him to maintain contacts with people who are not policemen. Not only does he work a different set of hours each week, but he also works a different weekly schedule from the one most people follow. His days off are never the same and he must consult the pocket shift calendar that he always carries with him before he can commit himself to any engagements. He is rarely free on weekends, frequently is working on holidays, and only one week in four does he get home for the evening meal with his family and a chance to go out with his wife.

Throughout the year, on every shift, in all seasons, the patrolman knows he will be working with the same men. It is his squad which helps the rookie learn his job and suffers for his errors. These men exploit his inexperience to lessen their burden as the price for their tolerance, and they decide whether to admit or exclude him from their companionship. None of these things is taught recruits at the police academy, but they are lessons which the policeman remembers throughout his career.

Although his badge has the city's name embossed on it, the patrolman's real employers are his sergeant and lieutenant. They guide him into the nuances of his occupation, teach him his duties, and give him the opportunities to learn his craft. In return for his willingness and commitment to the job, they must protect him from his own mistakes, assume responsibility for his actions if he errs in good faith, and justify his behavior to the captain if the need arises. But if he refuses to do as they desire, they will frequently punish him without permission from above, and if he persists, they will drive him from their midst.

Every squad is divided into two platoons of equal size, about twenty-five men, each directed by a sergeant. The sergeants are of equal rank and are both answerable to their lieutenant, the highest ranking supervisor in the police department, who is in direct contact with the men who actually police the city. Although he is a "white shirt," the squad under his command knows him as a worker who spends his tours of duty riding the street, answering calls when requested by the dispatcher, and intervening at the scene of incidents to control and direct his men. Unlike the captain, he is "there": a crucial distinction in the view of policemen, who see their work as a series of moments and actions that cannot be understood unless directly experienced. Until recently, lieutenants were "house supervisors" who were responsible for commanding the station while the sergeants ruled the street. In an effort to increase the efficiency and reliability of the patrolmen, the department increased the number of supervisors by "streeting" the lieutenant and creating a corporal to assume the management of the station house in the absence of the lieutenant.

When the captain is not in the district (he is almost never there on last out and rarely on nightwork), the lieutenant is the ranking officer responsible for all police functions. Though he is now generally on patrol, he is available to receive complaints or organize liaison with people from other units or other city agencies who have business in the district. He tacitly stresses the executive side of his authority by refraining from directly interfering in his sergeants' handling of their men. If he is involved in a serious conflict with a sergeant over control of the squad, he will occasionally interpose himself, a sure signal to everyone to exercise caution. But when there are only momentary disagreements with his sergeants, he is careful not to reveal these before the men. He tries not to create any barriers between himself and the men in his squad. The men are free to speak with him and ask his advice, and he does not hesitate to give them orders directly. But he will not permit any man to ask favors of him which are the sergeants' to dispense. Anyone who seeks to curry the lieutenant's special favor or to evade his sergeant's authority will be rebuffed.

Each platoon is permanently assigned to one of the two "ends"—east or west, upper or lower—into which the district is informally divided. Although the entire squad works the street at the same time, the two platoons do not really work together. In order to avoid stripping the district of police protection at shift changes, the platoons go on the street a half hour apart. Each platoon has its own roll call and the men from one have gone on patrol before their colleagues have assembled. Since they work at the same time, are always available to come to each other's assistance, and constantly meet in the station when they bring in prisoners and paper work, the men come to know each other quite well. New men frequently work both ends before being permanently assigned to one platoon, and every man occasionally works the "other end" when men are absent. The men who work the other end are not just distant co-workers like policemen in other squads, but they are not as close as the members of a man's own platoon.

The apartness of the platoons is sustained by the two sergeants, who carefully avoid intervening in each other's jurisdiction. Inevitably, one sergeant is the more senior man and he may have closer connections with the lieutenant or the captain than his associate, but he is careful not to diminish the authority of his colleague. When one sergeant is absent, the other generally prefers to allow a senior man from the platoon conduct the roll call, although the sergeant is supposed to assume the responsibility. He must act as their supervisor during the tour, but most sergeants are careful to avoid any actions which impinge on their colleagues' arrangements.

Every squad has its own operations-room crew, which serves as the informal bond between the two platoons. The three or four men who work "inside," under the direction of the corporal, are responsible for maintaining the station, guarding prisoners, and keeping the squad's records. Before the communication system was centralized, the operations crew operated the district call-box system; now these men are mainly responsible for processing mountains of paper work. Each day they must prepare the roll-call report, the assignment sheets, equipment records, and overtime pay lists, and send them all downtown. They compile and code all the tickets, summonses, and reports which are submitted during the tour, record all entries in the official district arrest ledgers, and type up the special reports which patrolmen must submit to other units in the department. They also review the constant stream of messages on the teletype, informing the lieutenant and the sergeants of anything relevant to the squad or the district, and keeping the men informed of official gossip.

The operations room is a sanctuary private citizens are rarely allowed to breach. Squad members use it as a place to take a breather or to have a conversation without being interrupted or overheard by the many people who are constantly coming and going in the station. But the room belongs to the crew; it is the territory of men who are barred from working the street and they do not let their colleagues forget it.

The crew is selected by the squad supervisors, who require the captain's approval only for the turnkey, the man in charge of the lockup. Before the central jail was established, these district cell-blocks were important places. Prisoners were kept there until magistrates set bail or released them. The turnkey had to be a reliable man because of his daily contact with judges, lawyers, bondsmen, and "fixers." People were often kept in the lockups for days, and there were turnkeys who made money by arranging contact with bail bondsmen and selling food, cigarettes, and blankets to people who were entirely at their mercy. Much of this has been eliminated and the turnkey is now mainly a custodian.

Crew members are usually selected from among the older men in the squad, with preference being given to those who volunteer, although men are occasionally obliged to accept an inside job if they wish to remain in the squad and the district. A man whose health makes it difficult or even dangerous to work on the street will be allowed to go inside for a rest or to finish out his career. Occasionally a man with a drinking problem will be ordered off the street to spare everyone trouble. A man who "goes bad," whose work causes numerous complaints, will be moved inside for his own well-being and for the protection of the squad. If a man refuses, he is on his way out of the district. Men who are not working well are frequently moved inside to give them a breather and a hint to try harder. Sometimes a man will be brought inside because he is bored with the street and his bosses hope that the change will revive his interest and keep him from seeking a transfer. While the crew performs the necessary administrative functions required by the department, it informally acts as a kind of safety valve for the squad which is utilized to resolve those personnel issues that are considered internal, private matters.[4]

The rookie takes with him to his district a mixture of admiration for, and fear of, his sergeant which has been fed to him at the academy. "Fellas, don't mess around with your sergeant or you'll have a hard road to travel," the instructor said, holding aloft a copy of the departmental Duty Manual. "If he gives you an order to do something you don't like —do it. If you don't, good luck." His attitudes are reinforced by what he sees of his colleagues' attitudes toward their boss; they are also tempered by a recognition that no successful sergeant is a despot. The men must work as he wishes if they expect to get the recognition, favors, and rewards only he can give, but the sergeant must have men who are happy to be working for him if he expects to show the lieutenant and the captain that he is capable and effective.

The sergeant's power is founded on his control over where each man will work his eight-hour tour. Every sector and foot beat has a distinctive reputation which determines its desirability as a place to work. When there were few patrol cars, any assignment to a car was considered a sign of high regard. Now that most men ride, the favored patrolmen are given the choice sectors. The few remaining foot beats are usually on important commercial streets, and these are given to veteran officers who are excused from shift work and are permanently on daywork. On the other two shifts, these beats are usually assigned to rookies whose capacity is not known or not trusted. Since there is

---

4. A lieutenant said of one man who was eager to return to the street, "He was a hell of a street cop, but he just got too hot [short-tempered]." Another man eager to return to the street was obliged to remain inside because his deteriorating eyesight raised doubts about his reliability on the street at night.

nothing much to do but guard the deserted streets and discourage vandals and window breakers, most men do not relish these assignments. Occasionally a sergeant will assign a veteran officer to a regular beat or one that has been created to deal with an emergency as a warning that he is not performing his job as required. Since everyone understands that these assignments are a form of censure, they provide the sergeant with an informal but direct way of communicating his feelings to his men.

Any assignment to a sector car is considered superior to walking a beat—"In winter the cars are nice and warm and the beats are nice and cold"—but only a rookie regards the chance to work a sector car as a sign of the sergeant's trust. If he interprets the opportunity given to him as an indication of his acceptance as an established member of the platoon, he will be set straight quickly by his colleagues. There are men in every squad—rookies, transfers, "oddballs"—who are used to fill in for men who are absent or on vacation. They "bounce" from one car to another and frequently they are "gypsied" to the other end of the district. Although they are in cars, these men have little standing in their platoon.

The sergeant rewards the men he trusts and likes by giving them a permanent sector assignment. A young patrolman who is given his first permanent assignment does not care whether it is considered a "good" sector because he has been around long enough to know that his sergeant is offering him a secure place in the platoon and informing his colleagues that this is a man he trusts. The patrolman assumes a debt to his sergeant in exchange for this trust, which he must willingly honor if he hopes to retain it. If he does not "produce" as expected, and if his relations with the sergeant deteriorate, he will find himself receiving special assignments or even bouncing about. But he can also increase his claims on the sergeant's affections and place himself in a position to get one of the choice sectors or even an assignment to work a patrol wagon (the "meatwagon" or, most commonly, the "wagon").[5]

The most coveted position in the platoon is a permanent assignment to a patrol wagon. Each platoon has several wagons that are always manned by two men each, and the sergeant reserves these positions for men he trusts completely. Some men decline because they do not like working the "garbage truck" which obliges them regularly to

---

5. A sergeant visited a district at the request of his wife to greet her cousin who had just graduated from the police academy. "I told her I can't do much for the kid, but she insisted. If I knew his lieutenant or sergeant, I could get him off the beat and into a car, if he's not shaky. But that's it."

handle the very ill, the dying, and the dead. The wagons are also used to break in rookies. When a new man comes to the platoon, one of the regular wagon men is temporarily shifted to a patrol car while his partner works with the newcomer, showing him around the district and giving the sergeant an informal appraisal of his character and inclinations. There are men who do not like working with rookies or having partners of any kind and refuse the offer to work in the wagon. This is an assignment which is too important to force on anyone, and if the man is well liked by the sergeant, he will be allowed to choose his own sector. But few patrolmen refuse their sergeant's request.

The wagons are not restricted to patrolling a single sector like a patrol car but have a jurisdiction comprising three or four sectors. Since their primary obligation is to transport the very sick to hospitals and prisoners to the station, the wagon crews are excused from doing a number of jobs that policemen dislike. The police believe that much of their trouble begins immediately after they have made an arrest, and they place great stress on quickly removing prisoners from the scene. (Once a person is arrested, he is a prisoner in the policeman's view.) To assure that wagons are always available for their main work, the wagon crews do not have to perform regular traffic duty or act as schoolcrossing guards, watchmen, or public-relations officers. The wagons must also transport prisoners from the district station to the central jail, a job which gives the crews opportunities to make contacts in other units in the department. The freedom and responsibility of the wagon crews require the sergeant to select men who are dependable and who will do nothing that reflects poorly on him and his superiors.

The sergeant is reluctant to punish a man by shifting him out of his regular assignment because this disrupts the overall efficiency of his men. If he is displeased, there are several warnings he can use to inform the man or the platoon of his attitude, offering them the opportunity to correct their behavior before he acts. There are numerous departmental regulations that even a very conscientious man will occasionally violate. These are normally overlooked, but if the sergeant is unhappy he will make a comment, carefully avoiding any suggestion that he is contemplating official action, but reminding those who may be taking something for granted of the nature of their relationship and the dimensions of his power. If his concern increases, he will comment directly to the men at roll call and threaten them with some kind of action. "You guys have become too lax. There's too much laying down, and if it keeps up the lieutenant is going to be down on my ass. If you keep it up, I will take memos from every man who is late," a sergeant warned his platoon. He had no intention of doing anything with the memos except throwing them away, but policemen regard anything requiring them to commit statements to paper as a threat. If a man is late and is only reprimanded, it is finished, not recorded anywhere, and soon forgotten; but if he must make an official explanation, there is the possibility that it will be filed in his personal record, permanently registered for others to see any time.

If someone is annoying him, the sergeant will withhold the important little rewards which only he has the power to grant. A man who is out of favor will not be allowed to come to work late or leave a few hours early. If he asks the sergeant for a day off, it will not be granted; this privilege is reserved as an incentive to better performance and as a reward for work well done. The police are given compensatory time off for the official holidays when they are obliged to work and they also accumulate sick-leave time. When a patrolman uses holiday time for a day off, he gets paid for the time, but if his sergeant refuses to allow him to use the holiday, the only way he can avoid coming to work without losing the pay is to use some sick time. Any man who calls in sick must be personally visited at home without prior notice by a sergeant from the district where he lives. If his own sergeant does not order the "sick check," the man has a day off with pay. During emergencies and in the summer vacation period, the department cancels the use of holiday time except for genuine family crises, leaving a man no opportunity to get a day off for some private business other than using sick time. A sympathetic sergeant will occasionally let a man off the hook, but any man who does not enjoy a good relationship with his supervisor risks serious punishment for misuse of this regulation.

A man who fails to respond to his sergeant's informal warnings will begin receiving special assignments that take him away from his regular post. The censure can be strengthened by gypsying the man since everyone knows that no sergeant gives away a man he trusts and depends on to do the platoon's work. If trouble persists, the sergeant may try to trade him to another squad or get him transferred from the district. Although the Duty Manual offers almost unlimited opportunities to bring charges against a man ("If you want to get someone, there is no way he can avoid it," a sergeant said), few supervisors like to resort to formal punishment.

About 3 A.M. a patrolman carried a drunken cab driver into the district. The man was bleeding from a head wound inflicted by a robber who had stolen his taxi to make a getaway. The sergeant looked at the man, shook his head, and walked out of the station without saying a word. The corporal said the cab driver was an ex-policeman who had been in the sergeant's platoon. "The sergeant was real good to him," he recalled. "He was real drunk one night and he refused to go home although the sergeant pleaded with him. He wouldn't listen, and when the lieutenant came, he refused again. The lieutenant locked him up for drunk driving. He had been to the front once for AOB (alcohol on his breath), which was a favor to him since the sergeant caught him with a broad in the car. They just fired him. Now he's finished."

Although nobody questions a supervisor's right to punish his men (and every policeman can tell stories of some fabled persecutor), he will exhaust every available alternative before exercising his formal authority. For example, the operations room occasionally fills up with men who come in to drop off their reports and hang around to drink a cup of coffee from the pot the crew keeps constantly fresh. The supervisors, even when they are annoyed, rarely tell the men in a direct fashion to get back on the street. It is common to hear a corporal murmur loudly that the "air in this place is getting awfully warm," or if that does not accomplish his purpose, he will tell them to "hit the bricks," carefully avoiding directing his remarks at anyone. One day a captain from outside the district was about to enter the operations room when he noticed how many policemen were standing inside. He quickly turned away and walked over to the water fountain, where he took a long drink. Their sergeant, who had been urging the men to move just as the captain arrived, said only, "I think he wants to come in here, but he does not want to embarrass anyone so he is waiting for you to leave."

Even when a man is doing something which his superiors dislike and consider dangerous, they will not compel him to change his ways unless it directly affects his work. A young officer, well liked by his supervisors, who considered him an increasingly important member of the platoon, began drinking in a district bar that enjoyed a somewhat lurid reputation. It had been the hangout of a motorcycle gang which often fought with the police, but a new owner had turned them out and welcomed the appearance of the off-duty policemen as protection against their return. When the gang did come back one afternoon and severely beat the bartender and several patrons with chains, the lieutenant was concerned that in the small war that followed his men might be employed as part-time mercenaries, exchanging their presence (and their guns) for a few cheap drinks.

So, after night-shift roll call, he stopped the man and said, "I saw you the other day in that den of iniquity. I didn't say anything because I didn't want to embarrass you and what you do on your own time is your business. But I don't want you to think that I didn't see you. You know it's not up to me, but I think you and your friends should find some other place to drink. There's gonna be more trouble in there and I don't want to see you get hurt. I know the broads aren't as good, but if you feel like it, drop by the Tavern tonight after work." The younger man listened to the lieutenant politely and thanked him for the unusual and generous invitation, but although he said nothing, they both understood that he was not going to do as suggested. He had been warned, and if there was trouble, he could not claim innocence if he pleaded for protection.

The sergeant's and lieutenant's exercise of their authority is tempered by an understanding of their own dependence on the goodwill and cooperation of their men in maintaining the unity of the platoon and the achievement of its goals. They know they can always get rid of a recalcitrant or dangerous man, but they do not want to antagonize their men or encourage them to seek transfer. Every time a man leaves, a new man must be broken in, and there is no guarantee that the replacement will be as good as the man who left. They must also worry about the possibility that an angry man will betray them.

Betrayal, "dropping a dime," is the last resort of the persecuted, the ambitious, the threatened, the fearful, and occasionally the honest. Every supervisor who gives a man a break, lets him off without a sick check, allows someone to go home a few hours early without deducting from his pay, accepts "Christmas money," or goes "on the take" must calculate the possibility of being betrayed by his men. He must not make their lot so distasteful that they will do anything to get away from the district, sacrificing the real advantages which derive from working in a place they know well and taking the risks of being branded as a "gink," a spy.

A sergeant watched as a lieutenant got into his car and drove away. "He's a good man, very good, a first-rate lieutenant, but he's getting a real fucking. The word is that some of the men in his squad were going A.W.O.L. when they were being carried as working. He was on the street where he belonged, but without a corporal inside, he let the men make up the attendance sheets. A couple of them were running a bar downtown, and after signing in, they would go and tend bar for a few hours. It's his fault for trusting them, but it's a shame anyway. A thing like that, you know someone dropped a dime on him. And it's not over yet because they fire guys for stuff like that now."

Since every supervisor violates regulations to produce the conditions and circumstances which enable him to get the required work from his men, each must bear in mind the possibility of betrayal. No matter how rare its occurrence, it is both a barrier against petty tyranny and a brake on the capacity of the supervisors to enforce stringent control over their men. They are as much colleagues as they are executives.

ACTIVITY

The worth of a man to his platoon does not depend on his success in preventing crimes, arresting suspected felons, or even giving service without complaint or injury. A man may be offered a transfer to a choice unit if he makes a spectacular arrest, but catching bank robbers is not the way to develop a sergeant's friendship. That requires something very different.

It is not uncommon to hear a weary man at the end of a busy summer night, scanning his patrol log, in which he records his official work during the tour, say, "Well, we worked tonight but we didn't get any activity[6] for the sergeant." How can a man who has taken fifteen assignments from the radio dispatcher, patiently listened to complaints, and steered his car through clogged and steamy streets say he has had no activity? His shirt is soaked with sweat and filth, his arms ache from wrestling the heavy steering of a car that quickly ages beyond recognition under constant wear and occasional mistreatment. He is tired from no activity?

"Activity" is the internal product of police work. It is the statistical measure which the sergeant uses to judge the productivity of his men, the lieutenant to assure himself that the sergeant is properly directing his men, the captain to assure his superiors that he is capably administering his district, and the department administrators to assure the public that their taxes are not being squandered.

At the end of each tour, the sergeant signs off his men, examines their patrol logs, and enters in his notebook the activity each man has produced during the tour. There are separate categories for "meters" (parking-meter tickets), "parkers" (illegal parking), and "movers" (motor-vehicle-code violations). Each time a patrolman stops a pedestrian or a person driving a car, he is supposed to file a written report giving details of the person and the circumstances. These "car stops" and "ped stops" are separately recorded and used as a measure of a man's aggres-

---

6. See Julius A. Roth, "What is an 'activity'?" *Etc.: A Review of General Semantics*, Vol. XIV (1956), pp. 55–56, for a very useful statement on definitions of activities and nonactivities in a tuberculosis hospital.

siveness and commitment to his patrol duties. Another category is maintained for the citation of juveniles who violate the city's curfew ordinance. There is also an activity category for "damaged car stops," reports filed on cars which have extensive front-end damage indicating possible involvement in hit-and-run accidents.

The sergeant also records all arrests which his men make. During the monthly period used to compute activity, the sergeant separately records arrests for "Part I crimes" (murder, rape, robbery, assault, burglary, larceny, auto theft); "Part II crimes," which are all other offenses excluding violations of the gambling, liquor, prostitution, and drug laws. A man is given personal credit for arresting a drunken driver because this violation of the state penal code is a misdemeanor, a serious offense. If the officer picks a drunk up off the sidewalk, he is granted no personal credit since the man can be charged only with a violation of a city ordinance, which is a summary offense. These minor offenses are individually computed only when the city and the department are making a special effort to demonstrate their effectiveness in a particular area. For example, if there were a public outcry about the number of drunks wandering on the streets, the department would probably institute a separate activity category for this particular work. Arrests for city ordinances generally are computed by the department's statistical division and credited to the total activity of the district and the department. Arrest activity is computed from what the patrolman "puts on the books" and not by the disposition of his cases in court. Since activity is a measure of his work, his sergeant has no interest in what eventually happens to the cases.

Arrests are only one of the many kinds of activity a district man is required to produce, and they do not have particularly high value for him. Platoon members always share arrests so that if two men make a Part I, each of them is credited with one half of an arrest. If a man is well liked by his colleagues and is in need of activity, they willingly "put him in on a pinch," even if he was not there, to help him over a rough spot. There are special crime-prevention units whose only measure of activity is arrests and stops; the men in these units are usually very reluctant to share with needy colleagues.[7]

_____

7. Activity definitions change. Some sergeants record tickets issued for "smokers," automobile air-pollution violations, while others ignore them. This means that they are not yet sufficiently important to warrant sustained attention. When the department demands enforcement of pollution codes, "smokers" will become familiar to all platoons.

The production of activity is not governed by formal quotas, but each squad knows that it is expected to maintain the levels achieved the previous year. Some forms of activity—meters, parkers, movers—are linked directly with the interests and goals of other city agencies which continuously monitor the production of the police and use their influence to assure that there are no lags which will undercut their own performance.[8] When a sergeant tells his men at roll call to "get some meters" or "Come on, fellas, the city paid to have those meters installed and they want their money," he is not nagging them because he has any interest in penalizing people but because he has been told by the captain that the city's collection department or traffic engineers have complained to the commissioner's office. Auto accidents are periodically surveyed by the city engineers, who determine which intersections are particularly hazardous and merit special attention. Any patrolman whose sector contains one of these "selective enforcement" locations knows that he is expected to issue tickets for the specific violations which the engineers say are causing the accidents.

The production of these kinds of activity is so important to the district that the supervisors are willing to violate departmental regulations to assure it. Meters and parkers are written primarily on daywork, which is also the shift on which most vice arrests for gambling are made. Writing tickets is a laborious task requiring continuous attention before a man can get a sizable number of them, but it does not require much skill. In order to keep his best men free for more specialized work, the sergeant, in collusion with his captain and lieutenant, frequently assigns a man to work a tour, or even the whole six-day shift, writing tickets. The man is usually carried on the assignment sheet as working a two-man car while he is actually riding a "silent car," a vehicle which is reported out of service and has no contact with the radio dispatcher. Officially it is not there. Everyone in the platoon knows about this violation of departmental regulations and it cannot be concealed. It is treated as a collusion among colleagues, a violation required to make their work easier and more successful. It also helps to generate internal loyalty and shows the men that their supervisors are almost as dependent on them as they are on the "bosses."

"Working the meter car" is an easy but not necessarily desirable job. Sometimes the sergeant will give it to a man who has been prom-

---

8. On ticketing practices, see John A. Gardiner, *Traffic and the Police* (Cambridge, Mass.: Harvard University Press, 1969).

ised an early dismissal. He will tell him to write a certain number of tickets and allow him to leave when he has finished. With this incentive the man is allowed to determine his own departure time, and the sergeant knows that he will get his tickets. But the assignment is generally given to older men who are no longer interested in doing police work or to rookies the sergeant wants to keep out of the way. Because of its menial character, this job can also be given to an officer as a signal of displeasure, especially if the sergeant knows him to be a man who is interested in trying to make vice arrests.

Individual statistics remain in the districts, and only the totals are forwarded to divisional headquarters. There is no competition among platoons for leadership in activity because of the differences in the territorial character of the areas they police. The number of parking meters varies from area to area, and parking violations are treated differently in business and residential sections. One platoon, working in a largely commercial area, wrote 1,717 movers, 759 parkers, and 994 meters in a year. In the same period the other platoon in the squad wrote only 559 movers and 310 meters, but 785 parkers. They had far fewer meters to check and more disputes over parking because of the residential character of their territory.

The department uses the production of car and ped stops to measure the patrolman's commitment to the prevention and suppression of crime in his sector. Whenever there is an increase in the weekly totals of crimes reported, the men are urged, but not ordered, to be more "aggressive" on patrol and to "increase the number and quality of vehicle and pedestrian stops" they make. This attitude is motivated by the belief that the more actively a man is involved in scanning the people and cars about him, the more likely he is to detect and prevent crime. These car and ped stop reports are also used to provide the department with information about cars and people at specific places and times, facts that may be of aid to other units investigating matters unknown to the patrolman making the report. Whether they are actually of any value has never been demonstrated, but since their introduction (about 1955), they have provided the department with another way of influencing the amount of work each patrolman does.

Individual officers may aggressively seek out opportunities to make felony arrests, but there are no production pressures linked to the arrest rates of squads or patrolmen, except those men who belong to anticrime patrol units. The department is anxious to increase its "clearance rate," the percentage of reported crimes solved by an arrest, and it is believed that aggressive patrol and rapid response to calls are the best ways to accomplish this. In the past, efforts to achieve higher rates of arrest have encouraged patrolmen to make false arrests and to suppress reports of crimes.[9]

A sergeant cannot order his men to go out and make felony arrests without also encouraging them to commit illegal acts. All he can do is tell them to make more stops, although there is no measurable link between the number of stops by a platoon and their success in arresting felons. For example, nobody knows how to evaluate the importance of the 2,626 car stops and 2,575 ped stops made in 1970 by one platoon working a predominantly commercial and industrial area, or the 2,184 car stops and 3,110 ped stops made by the squad's other platoon. There is no way of arguing that these were sufficient, too many, or not enough to assure the "proper" protection of the people and property of the district during the time that squad was working. It is not known how many unrecorded stops these men made, since frequently policemen do not bother to "make paper" if they are not under pressure or if they know the person they stop, but there is no way of evaluating what loss may be incurred by the police and society when any information is allowed to go unrecorded.[10]

Individual patrolmen may produce significantly larger quantities of activity than their colleagues without arousing hostility. Policemen are not piece-rate workers who are paid a bonus for each ticket they write over a minimum number. If one officer meticulously writes up each ped stop he makes, it has no effect on a senior colleague who may write up only a third of the people he interrogates and so give the appearance of doing less work. Even if a squad goes ahead of its previous rate of ticket-writing and creates a higher requirement for the following year, the obligation of each patrolman is not increased by very much and the bulk of the additional work will be carried by the men who work the meter car, those with the lowest status in the group. Patrolmen are much more concerned about efforts by their superiors to increase their work load or to introduce "reforms" into their work. Since the statistical measures used to evaluate their work have no demonstrable effect on the performance of those duties for which they are principally hired— the preservation of order and the protection of life and property—the patrolmen have the means of embarrassing their bosses and exerting significant counterpressure. For example, if the men are ordered to

9. At the turn of the century in London, commanders in high-crime districts were paid a "charge allowance," a bonus for felony arrests which exceeded an informal quota. In order to assure their bonuses, many commanders pressured their men to make false arrests and to add charges. G. Reynolds and A. Judge, *The Night the Police Went on Strike* (London: Weidenfeld–Nicholson, 1969), pp. 25–27.

10. An effort to establish the value of information is made by M. A. P. Willmer, *Crime and Information Theory* (Edinburgh: Edinburgh University Press, 1970).

increase their ticket output, they can exceed their orders by so wide a margin as to assure an outcry from outraged citizens who find their cars ticketed for violations they did not know existed. On the other hand, when ordered to do something which they disapprove, the men can temporarily refuse to do any ticket writing. No police official can say publicly that his men are too zealous and should disregard violations which they discover. Nor can he effectively counter arguments that the men are spending too large a part of their time doing things which fail to increase the security and well-being of the general public. The power of patrolmen to embarrass their superiors without violating their formal obligations enables them to restrict their productivity within the limits they find "normal" and attainable and acts as a brake on those administrators who want to make them more "efficient."[11]

Arrest quotas are rigidly enforced for vice arrests, however, and continuous competition among platoons and individual officers is encouraged by threats and rewards to assure production. Every platoon must exceed its annual total by at least one arrest each year. Regardless of their success in fulfilling other departmental goals, any failure to produce the necessary vice arrests means trouble for the captain, the lieutenants, the sergeants, and all the men in the district who have assignments they want to keep. The kind of vice activity varies from district to district, but the arrests are made principally for numbers,[12] dice games, card playing, horse-betting parlors, prostitution, illegal manufacture and sale of alcohol, the sale of alcohol to minors, or the sale and possession of illegal drugs.

---

11. The restriction of production is a well-known phenomenon in industrial settings where workers are paid piece-rate bonuses. See the very useful studies by Donald Roy, "Quota Restriction and Goldbricking in a Machine Shop," *American Journal of Sociology*, Vol. LVII (1951/52), pp. 427–42; "Work Satisfaction and Social Reward in Quota Achievement: An Analysis of Piecework Incentive," *American Sociological Review*, Vol. XVIII (1953), pp. 507–14; and "Efficiency and 'the Fix': Informal Intergroup Relations in a Piecework Machine Shop," *American Journal of Sociology*, Vol. LX (1954/55), pp. 255–66.

In one New York City precinct a new commander established a quota of fifty tickets a month for his foot patrolmen "to get these people back in the habit of working." His men responded by raising their production from 147 parking tickets on a Friday to 1,154 on Monday and 1,294 on Tuesday. Their efforts produced the desired result: the inspector called off his "reform" effort, *The New York Times* (January 20, 1972). Chicago police recently went on a ticket-writing spree in support of their demand for collective bargaining and other changes. In some districts commanders confiscated ticket books and threatened punishment to halt the flood of tickets, *The New York Times* (October 1, 1972).

12. Numbers is the principal form of urban gambling. It is called policy in New York and has many other names, such as lottery and nigger pool. The best study of numbers is Gustav Carlson, "Numbers Gambling: A Study of a Culture Complex." (Unpublished Ph.D. dissertation, University of Michigan, 1940.)

Vice enforcement, particularly of gambling, has always caused severe problems for all big-city police departments. Often, gambling has been protected by politically powerful people, and the police have been discouraged from pursuing enforcement. This attitude has been aided by the offer of payoffs and bribes to officers. Every department has been touched by scandals and revelations of payoffs for protecting gambling. Many different approaches have been tried to limit the inclinations of some policemen to accept graft from gamblers; in Philadelphia a policy of decentralization is pursued. Instead of concentrating antigambling efforts in one or two specialized units, a competitive situation has been created. It is hoped that this will make men fearful of offering protection to anyone since they cannot know when another unit will intervene and possibly expose them. The district platoons must compete with the captain's men and also with special squads under the direction of the commissioner's office. Each platoon has its own quota, although one successful platoon will frequently "carry" another for several months. Although no distinctions are formally made in the kinds of vice arrests computed, the most important are for gambling. An increase in the number of narcotics arrests, for example, is not an acceptable substitute for the required volume of number pinches.[13]

Everyone in the squad seeks to make a contribution to increasing vice activity. Even the operations crew takes a hand when the opportunity arises, to "create a pinch," as one corporal said. Every arrest must be entered in the district arrest book, and vice arrests are recorded in bright-colored inks, allowing anyone to see at a glance the number of pinches made in a day. When policemen from a special unit bring their prisoners into the district for processing, the operations crew must handle their paper work and record the arrest. If any kind of vice violation is involved, the men are sounded out about the possibility of allowing some of the district men to go on the pinch. This is never done with the captain's men or a downtown squad, since they are in direct competition with the district and they are not supposed to know anything about each other's work. But patrolmen who work in crime-suppression units are often willing to trade a narcotics arrest, for example, with a district man who has made a "gun pinch," or failing anything worthy of trade, they may allow the corporal to add a name along with their own as a way of encouraging good relations with the district personnel. Once there is agreement, the corporal simply writes

---

13. On gambling enforcement see Bruce Smith, Jr., *Police Systems in the United States,* 2d ed. (New York: Harper & Row, 1960), pp. 237–38, 258. In New York City a centralized gambling policy has been followed and the uniformed men have not been responsible for making arrests.

in the name of one or two men from the platoon that works the end where the arrest occurred; they are then formally credited with an arrest and their platoon gets a vice pinch. The men do not appear in court or participate in any way in the legal process initiated by the arrest. The corporal's action is entirely an internal matter, affecting only the norms established by the department to measure the work of its employees. The corporal sees his effort as a harmless but useful act which aids the interests of his closest associates.

There is absolutely no doubt in the mind of the district patrolman about how seriously vice arrests, particularly for gambling, are regarded by his superiors. He may not know what other value they have, since the more experience he acquires in making vice arrests, the clearer it becomes to him that gambling is not deterred by them; he does understand that the department wants a lot of them.

During one nightwork roll call, the sergeant requested two men to come forward to receive letters of commendation from the department for their part in the arrest of some men who were burglarizing a warehouse. He congratulated them warmly, and as they returned to their places in line, he continued, grinning, "Of course, none of this police work counts for much. Only vice pinches count." The men laughed in appreciation and wondered whether they were behind in their obligations.

Each week every district captain is required to submit a report detailing all vice investigations made by his command. These reports are forwarded by the divisional inspectors to headquarters so department administrators can keep abreast of all vice enforcement in the city. Any falling off from the previous year's totals is immediately noticed and pressure is applied directly to the captains. If the lag persists, the inspector will increase the pressure by formally warning all district supervisors that he is personally watching their performance and that he will supersede their captains' power unless there is improvement. One memo from an inspector to a district's squads read in part: "The 89th district is behind eight arrests for illegal lottery and if there is no improvement in the results of the uniformed men, changes will be positively made." Every man was put on notice that his job was in jeopardy unless he produced.

There is a constant demand for vice activity, but when the captain or inspector threatens intervention, the supervisors openly pressure their men by warning of a general reshuffle of assignments. The sergeant speaks to the men individually and warns them collectively at roll call. No opportunity is ignored to remind them that he wants a pinch. When a sergeant calls after a wagon crew heading out the door to begin their tour, "Watch out you don't lose your cushion," they know his smile hides a sincere admonition.

Captains seldom address their men at roll call, but one afternoon following the serious injury of an officer, a captain came to express his solidarity with the injured man's colleagues. When he had finished his little speech, the sergeant stepped forward and said, "While he is here I will mention vice to you. He says that he would like a number pinch, but he will take a bottle, and if not, narcotics. But he wants a vice pinch. He also wants meters. I don't know when you are going to do this, maybe between shootings, but he *will* have a vice pinch." The men smiled silently until the captain laughed, then they burst into a roar.

Rookies and younger officers often impress their sergeants by the activity they generate, but the sergeant knows that eagerness and devotion are of little value in locating a number writer or a speakeasy. This requires skill, knowledge, information, and inclinations which develop only with experience. Even among the veteran members of any platoon, there are only a few who, working closely with their sergeant and lieutenant, produce the flow of information and the arrests which meet their collective requirements. These veterans are rewarded with their choice of sector or a seat in a wagon. They are the men who consistently receive the highest evaluations on their annual performance ratings. As one lieutenant said, "You can be a good guy, a great bullshitter, keep your car clean, make a lot of arrests, but without vice you'll never get an outstanding from me."

A man is capable of producing vice information only after he has been in a district for some time. During the time that he accumulates his experience and knowledge, he also develops contacts and interests in other areas of the department. He knows people, once his colleagues, who have advanced to higher rank and can offer him positions under their command. The men whom sergeants and captains wish most to retain are the ones who are most capable of getting a transfer. Frequently they are content to remain where they are, because their value stems from their unique personal knowledge and connections, which will quickly atrophy when they leave; and their supervisors are willing to go to considerable lengths to keep them happy and encourage them to remain where they are. They are granted freedom in their work and relief from numerous petty obligations, a freedom younger men, who frequently make more arrests and produce the bulk of the platoon's activity, do not have. Activity demands are part of an informal apprenticeship accepted by younger men because they know they cannot make the vice arrests necessary to maintain the platoon's stability and coherence. And without these, they have no assurance that the men who are teaching them how to be policemen will be around to complete the training.

ROLL CALLS

Roll call is a remnant of the decaying military tradition used to discipline the police. When a platoon assembles for roll call, the men are rarely called to order but assemble themselves as their sergeant mounts the platform. There are no claims to a specific place in the rows of eight that line up before the sergeant as the men await the daily attendance call and the issuing of orders and instructions. The policeman does not realize how informal the procedure really is until after he has left the academy, where he was subjected to daily roll calls for twelve weeks, his instructors forcing him to do push-ups and penalty work for not having the proper haircut or the correct shine on his shoes. His recollections of these silly exercises, which contrast so sharply with the reality of his daily life in the district, only deepen his contempt for the training he was given, causing him frequently to disregard many of the more important things he was taught.

"Let's see your tin," the instructor ordered, beginning the final week of training with another mock roll call. The three rows of men stood stiffly in the cold morning air, tugging out their wallets as he shuffled down the front line. Several men had forgotten their badges and another had neglected to cover his with the black band required to honor an officer murdered the week before. The instructor ordered them to submit written explanations of their failure to comply with official orders and canceled their lunch period. "From today you will carry all required equipment and we will have full inspections at all roll calls just like in the districts."

At the afternoon roll call he smiled as the men struggled to hold their gear together without breaking ranks. "Fellas, it's not required but get a heavy rubber band and secure your flashlight, notebook, street guide, and ticket book together or you'll be making a racket at every roll call." He then casually walked through the lines looking at their whistles. "Get a plastic one because those nice shiny ones freeze in winter and will rip up your lips when you go on traffic post." He inspected ball-point pens, wristwatches, clean white handkerchiefs sealed in plastic for emergency first-aid use, change for the telephone (a dime was passed surreptitiously down the line for use by those who did not have one), and a brass key used to open traffic signal control boxes for manual operation. Blue riot helmets lined the ground before the rookies. They shifted awkwardly to show the instructor their handcuffs, slung over belts. They jammed nightsticks into their armpits so their hands would be free to pull out blackjacks from back pockets. Although they had no guns or holsters (these are not issued until graduation day), they were obliged to simulate them on the command of "draw pistols," even jiggling their "gun" to show the instructor that it was loaded.

Equipment checks are rarely held at district roll calls, although policemen know they can be revived at any time as a warning to a faltering platoon or to punish a recalcitrant man. The equipment they carry are the tools of the police trade; it is assumed by most supervisors that the men will come to work with their gear in working condition. After a shooting or an accident, supervisors may conduct gun checks, urging their men to clean their weapons and periodically change the ammunition. Most policemen do not think their colleagues take proper care of their weapons; the department has instituted a program that requires every patrolman to requalify at the pistol range annually. The instructors take this opportunity to inspect and clean the guns, which are, after all, public property.

Formal inspections are held only when there are visitors to the station. Policemen do not like surprises, and there are rarely unannounced visits from higher commanders to a platoon roll call. When an inspector is planning to come to the district to address the men, there is usually ample warning from sympathetic colleagues at divisional headquarters. The captain always informs his lieutenant of any impending visit. "John, the inspector is going to address the men at roll call today. Will you see that they behave themselves accordingly?" The patrolmen know that no one will protect them, regardless of their position in the platoon, if they give cause for embarrassment during these visits. Their response is governed by the visitor's reputation. If he is considered a "ballbuster, the kind that makes you show a dime," they will carefully assemble all the required equipment, borrowing from the operations crew, who do not stand roll call, to replace whatever is missing. If the man is "all right," they will simply take care that their appearance offers no cause for comment.

Only the captain, whose office is near the roll room, attends roll call without prior notice, but when he does, it is usually to comment on some special circumstance and not to check equipment or appearance. It is common to see a captain, obliged to cross the room during a roll call, make certain by the quickness of his movement and an occasional joking remark that nobody will interpret his appearance as ginking or harassment.

The sergeant does not have to resort to discipline and equipment checks to maintain order and attentiveness among his men. He is not a military leader; he is a foreman whose men are scattered over many city blocks. His men rarely work in his direct sight and he needs their goodwill, just as they need his protection and advice to get the job done properly. An understanding of their mutual obligations is sufficient to keep even the most rambunctious in line. Nobody speaks out without permission or interrupts him while he is talking. Any man who is allowed to first-name the sergeant in private is careful to address him formally at roll call. Even someone who disdains his sergeant will refrain from open acts of contempt, except in rare moments of rage or whimsy. But a supervisor who is disliked, especially one whose claims on his men are slight or disintegrating, will be treated contemptuously. Calculated violations of normal conduct, which are insufficient to disrupt the routine and warrant formal punishment, are expressions of opinion rather than rebellion, and they inform the sergeant of his standing. On some occasions these messages can be brutal.

A vacationing sergeant was replaced without warning by a sergeant who had once commanded the squad's other platoon. He had been relieved when the men refused to produce for him. Prior to his departure, several of his men had been transferred to the platoon he was now temporarily commanding. They were displeased and he knew it. "I have a few rules as you know which will be obeyed while I am here. I do not like minutemen. Roll call is on the dot—don't be late. I also have a lot of equipment to carry and I expect you to do the same. Where are your helmets? All of you get them, including the Italian contingent in the back row, and keep them with you at roll call." Silently the men broke ranks, and when they reassembled, one man who had left his helmet visor behind walked from the line to retrieve it while the sergeant was talking. Before returning, he took a long drag from a cigarette he had left burning in an ashtray, staring directly at the sergeant. As he entered the line, the others turned to him and smiled their approval. That was just the beginning.

The next day everyone came prepared for a full-scale inspection. Their equipment was neatly piled up, waiting for the sergeant, who had to content himself with ordering several men to get haircuts. As he passed down the line, each man turned toward him silently, grinning broadly, while the men ahead openly talked to each other. At no time did anyone write down any of his instructions since they had no intention of doing any work for him. On the last day of the shift, at the end of roll call, he ordered a pistol check. Staring directly ahead, the men unholstered their revolvers and, keeping their fingers carefully away from the triggers, pointed them toward the ceiling, while a voice from the back row said quietly, without a hint of menace, "Watch out, Sarge." There were no more inspections.

Roll calls are used by the sergeant to inform his men of their common and mutual obligations as well as to keep them abreast of any departmental news of importance to them. The captain's clerk and the operations crew sift the continual flow of messages from headquarters that are transmitted over the teletype, culling announcements of schedule changes and alterations in administrative procedures to read out at roll call. The sergeant also uses the opportunity to give his men information from official departmental sources and unnamed informers about possible crimes in their end of the district during the tour. If activity is down, he will exhort them all, but only rarely will a sergeant single out an individual for any criticism. Everything that the men are told at roll call is considered general knowledge, intended to help them do their work more efficiently.

The department regularly compiles information regarding criminal activity in the city and the district which is distributed to the men before they go on the street. Every few days a list of stolen auto-license plates, a "hot sheet," is issued for the patrolman's reference to cars that attract his attention on patrol. It is also a source of inspiration for officers who play the numbers. There are lists of serial numbers from reportedly stolen appliances which the man can use, although they rarely have the opportunity, to check against any they find during their tour. The department also prepares information sheets detailing recent trends and techniques in street crime, illustrated descriptions of burglary tools the men may not know, and photographs of people being sought for questioning or arrest.

Each week the men are given a crime bulletin prepared by the divisional staff describing the frequency of reported street crime, burglary, robbery, purse snatching, car theft, assault, noting the sectors which are most active. The rates are compared with the same week in the previous year, and any increases are accompanied by requests to step up car and ped stops. The distribution of these aids is rarely accompanied by any other comment from the sergeant. He knows his men personally, who among them is working hard, who is not; what are their capabilities for the job. Offering them helpful hints will only increase their exasperation with him, not their effectiveness. If he urges or demands that they make arrests, he knows that some of them will ignore the law and the truth to improve their performance. Any hint of complaint from above, which is rare, is angrily rebuffed by the patrolmen, who defend their record by arguing that they are prevented from doing "real police work" (catching criminals) by the heavy load of public services required of them by the men who now criticize their record. When the pressure is strong, the sergeant urges his men to increase their activity, but he does not ask them to make arrests.

Because everyone to whom the patrolman has some obligation is competing for his attention, there is a constant stream of requests, which are read out at roll call. They are not of equal importance and the sergeant has techniques that indicate to the men their relative importance. For example, persons seeking the return of some cherished property, a car or a pet, occasionally offer a monetary reward, prompting him to mention the request rather than simply tacking it on the district bulletin board. More frequently, requests are routed through the captain's office and their announcement is prefaced by saying, "The captain is interested . . ."; this tells the men to pay attention.

If there is a complaint coupled to a request, the sergeant will stress his own concern that the matter be rectified. He does not criticize anyone personally at roll call but simply informs the platoon that they are on notice from him to do their job as he wants it done. "There's been a complaint to the captain that the illegally parked cars on Atlantic Street are not being tagged because the ward committeeman's office is on that street," a sergeant said to his platoon. "That's bullshit. The reason is someone is not doing his job. The captain and I want those cars tagged, and if there is another complaint, I will personally call the sector car and write them myself."

The sergeant may have a personal interest in seeing that a request is fulfilled, and he does not hesitate to let the men know that he considers their careful consideration a courtesy to himself. The wise sergeant does not make a habit of making numerous requests of his men, using up credits which he has accumulated by judicious favors, but his men do not object when he occasionally asks something of them. "There's a woman living on High Street who has been getting threats from her neighbors. Keep an eye on the house when you ride by. She has been helpful to the police in the past," the sergeant said, with a smile. "She was the girl friend of someone who used to be in this squad—so she was helpful." The men smiled as they wrote the address in the notebooks, which they use to record messages and personal information.

Most of the sergeant's remarks are perfunctory warnings designed to keep the men informed of problems in the district that do not require direct action. He mentions playgrounds that have been the scenes of fights and places where special events such as dances or block parties are occurring. This informs them of circumstances that may produce trouble and gives them some idea of what to expect if they receive a call to one of these locations.

Periodically, after complaints from local merchants and residents accumulate, he urges the men to move juveniles off corners where they habitually congregate. These requests are not treated too seriously since most men understand that boys on corners are part of the landscape and driving them off is like the tide washing the shore: it is an endless cycle. But if there has been unusual trouble or if something occurs which is seen as a challenge to the police, the sergeant will make demands that his men treat as a command. "Those deprived children broke every light on Hicks Street last night and made it through an alley before I could catch them. I don't want you to fool with them any longer. I don't want any more ped stops. If they are hanging on the corner tonight, scoop 'em up and bring them in. I mean it, call for a wagon and we'll put 'em on the books and let them have a hearing. Make their parents come after them."

When there is reliable information about a possible problem in the district, the men will be informed, usually without mentioning the source. If, for example, there is a rumor of a holdup, the sergeant will order the sector car and the wagon to check the premises each half hour. If he does not consider the information to be accurate, he will mention it only in passing, covering himself against the possibility that it will turn out to be correct, without giving his men any specific instructions. The man on the sector is then free to treat the information as he sees fit.

The sergeant also uses the roll call to warn his men of any circumstances and conditions in the district which can affect their well-being and his reputation. Since the roll call is the only time when the platoon is assembled as a unit, he uses the occasion to tell them anything which requires general cooperation to avoid embarrassment. These warnings also free him of any obligation to protect anyone who ignores them. "Inspector Blood is riding the district tonight and I expect everyone to answer immediately when radio calls you. If anyone has come to sleep tonight—you know who I mean—you better go off sick right now."

Occasionally, the warnings are graver and consequently more circumspect. The sergeant does not tell the men where his information comes from, nor do they allow themselves to display any curiosity about the warnings. They just listen. "There is a funny wagon with fake door panels parked on the corner of the 1800 block of Vale Street. Don't hang around there, and if you get a job in the area do it right, do it quick, and get out. And don't stare at that wagon when you go by it. Remember, you are strictly on your own out there." Everyone in the platoon understands that the "funny wagon" is a blind for a hidden camera used by the department's internal inspection unit, the ginks, to conduct secret investigations of complaints against policemen. They are what every police officer fears most, even the scrupulously honest. Nobody can know for certain why the wagon is there, but if anyone in the platoon has "something going" in that area he will stay away. Men who are innocent are warned to avoid committing any blunders which might involve them in something they know nothing about. Everyone in the platoon who is doing anything against regulations has been put on notice: the man who intends to slip off for a few drinks, the fellow who is planning to visit the apartment of a woman he knows, the man who is thinking he could use a few dollars. Those who plan to do nothing but the job for which they are paid are made nervous and insecure.

Everyone in the room stares directly ahead while each man tries to figure out who is being investigated. Nobody doubts the truthfulness of the sergeant's warning because his men know that he has no reason to make them fearful. He does not have to resort to subterfuge to make them work; he can simply order them to stay away from any place he does not want them to go. The warning also reminds each man of the limits of collegial intimacy, recalling how little each man knows of what the others are doing on their sectors after they leave the station.

There are things of considerable importance that are never discussed at roll call. The supervisors are constantly getting information about gambling and other vice operations which they do not disclose to the platoons. Although vice arrests are the most consistently demanded work of the platoon, no sergeant seeks to increase the men's effectiveness by encouraging general discussions of vice conditions or exchanges of information about vice characters. Every district is required to maintain a "vice book" containing the photographs and police records of all known characters operating in the area. Departmental regulations require that every man examine the book at least once a year, and the lieutenant is obliged to remind his platoon at roll call and have the men sign a departmental memorandum which acknowledges their compliance with the regulation. "You all know what this is," the lieutenant told the assembled platoon, holding aloft the thick vice book. "You all know where it is and I urge you to go and look at it once in a while." The men laughed. The book is kept in the captain's office, available to any man who requests it. Most men do so rarely. The supervisors distribute their information privately to individual platoon members who enjoy their special trust. The only cooperative aspect of vice enforcement in a platoon is the common understanding of everyone not to ask anyone about what he is doing, where he gets his information, or how it is acquired.

Rookies and new men are told only what is absolutely necessary to maintain the unity of the platoon. Everything the men are told at these daily gatherings is considered public information. Much of the platoon's most important work is never discussed, nor are the men encouraged to discuss among themselves any aspects of the problems they encounter on their sectors. They know that the warnings, the information, and the exhortations given them daily by their sergeant are meant to aid their performance and not to create additional burdens for them. Their attentiveness to his requests and commands strongly affects the chances of each man to advance, to get himself off his feet and into a car, and then into a sector which he can call his own eight hours a day. As he advances, the patrolman learns gradually how much there is to know that is not discussed at roll call. The more of an insider he becomes, the more closely must he adhere to his sergeant, because he is also learning that nothing is permanent. The sergeant affirms this every day by reading out the assignments each man will work. Even men who have worked the same car for years are told anew each day where they will work. This is a little reminder that nobody is in permanent possession of anything, and only their commitment to the unity of the platoon preserves what they already have and keeps open the promise of additional reward and advancement.

GOING TO WORK

At the academy, recruits are introduced to the lore of shift work by instructors who have been relieved, often unwillingly, of the burdens of working around the clock and are now on "steady daywork." There are constant warnings about the dangers to the stomach caused by irregular eating habits, accompanied by opinions of the shifts and how to prepare for them. "Four to twelve is great for working, lots of action, but it's hell on your life. You feel like you're always working or getting ready to go to work. No time for yourself." "Daywork is all bullshit but you get to meet some nice people and make a lot of contacts." "I won't kid you fellas, last out is rough. I tried everything but I could never go to sleep in the morning when I got home. And then maybe you got to go to court. Man, when the sun comes up, it's murder. You just have to drink a lot of coffee and keep shaking your head. But it's part of the job." When he arrives in the district, the rookie knows that each shift has different characteristics; he has only the vaguest appreciation of what they are.

A policeman who understands what he is likely to be doing when he goes to work knows that he has little control over what he may be called on to do. Many claim this unpredictability is a virtue of the trade, an important reason why they prefer police work to other labor. "You never really know what you'll get next in this business, but you can bet it's always something different." However different one "job" may be from the next, he does have some general assumptions about the *kinds* of work he actually must do. He knows, for example, that he must always be ready to give first aid. On any day he may be asked to place himself in danger, consider a suggestion that he discredit his office for personal gain, or perform a solicited service which, while not a requirement of his work, he may consider a fulfillment of his nature. It is a condition of his trade, which all who actively pursue it must acknowledge, that while these may be "part of the job," he cannot know from moment to moment what demand will arise.[14]

While the rookie is learning to adjust his body and his life to the wrenching rhythms of shift work, he is acquiring an understanding of what the department and his sergeant expect of him and an understanding of the people he is paid to police. He is learning about the changing obligations of his work which accompany the progress of the clock and of the seasons, and he is also developing a set of expectations about what he will be doing during his tour that enables him to impose a limit on the uncertainties inherent in his work. As he stands at roll call day after day, listening to his sergeant issue orders, demands, and requests, he begins to formulate concretely his conceptions of the shifts.

Each shift has some compulsory obligations that must be met regardless of other demands. On daywork half the tour is spent directing rush-hour traffic and guarding school crossings. There are other obligations. Shopkeepers and merchants who want protection from robbery and larceny can ask the department for a "store log," which the sector officer must sign, requiring him to visit the place regularly. Logs are also placed inside all banks and subway toll booths. The sector patrolman and the wagon covering the area must sign these every day and the sergeant must sign the bank logs; the subway logs must be signed on all shifts. If the sergeant discovers unsigned logs or receives a complaint, he will order his men to "get your logs," threatening them with the

---

14. The police are not unique in claiming unpredictability as a virtue of their work; cab drivers, salesmen, and newspapermen make similar boasts. These occupations share three things in common: they deal with a public which cannot be screened prior to contact; the work is performed in an open framework, not on an assembly line or in an office where work routines are patterned; and they have low status with the majority of the public.

specter of a headquarters investigation. Daywork is also the primary time for getting meters and parkers, and any pressure on a platoon to improve their production occurs on daywork.

While these obligations consume a large part of each daywork tour, they are subordinate to the continuous pressure for vice arrests. Number writing, the predominant form of urban gambling, is almost exclusively a morning activity. The local "writers" usually finish the day's work by early afternoon; thus most gambling arrests must be made on daywork. Anyone in the platoon who wants to advance himself is trying to obtain some kind of information he can use for a pinch or to give the sergeant as evidence of his effort. In poor neighborhoods, especially in the slums where poor blacks, Puerto Ricans, and Southern white migrants live, speakeasies are common, usually informal affairs operating in someone's parlor. Although they are more numerous on the weekends, Sunday daywork being the most common time for raids, every officer is alert for signs of a "speak" as he patrols and chats with people on his sector.

Because the platoon has so many formal obligations on daywork, the sergeant normally restricts himself to reminding the men of these rather than encouraging them to be alert for other things that commonly occur on daywork. The men know that bank robberies are almost exclusively a daytime event, but if the sergeant urges them to do any more than sign the logs, he will be encouraging them to spend their time on the main business streets when he wants them to be looking for vice and promptly answering the radio calls they are constantly receiving. Similarly, house burglaries are a common daytime occurrence, especially in neighborhoods where a large proportion of the women go out to work, but he rarely mentions this because he knows his men will be alert for housebreakers if they have time to patrol.

The night shift is generally considered the action tour since the men have fewer formal obligations during a time when most people are neither working nor sleeping. Some men will have a traffic post for the homeward rush hour. Others may spend the few hours of the tour before sundown "making statistics" by getting some meters. But the sergeant requests meters only if the platoon is considerably behind, because he believes the night shift is when they "earn their money" and he does not want to burden his men with work that can be done another time. He will urge them to pick up their activity by making car and ped stops; to check for juvenile curfew violators in an effort to cut down car thefts and burglaries, common crimes of night associated by the police with young men. The twilight hours are the likeliest time for street muggings and purse snatches, but he mentions this only if there has been some unusual increase in the district. Holdups too, primarily of bars and liquor stores, are common at night, but special mention will be made of these only if the sergeant has some information. The regular sector men know the places they have to keep an eye on. Also, the night shift brings the heaviest demand for service and the sergeant knows his men will spend a large part of their tour answering radio calls.

The men evaluate the days of the week differentially, profiling them as they do the shifts. Some days are likely to be more active and others have a high probability of being quiet. On daywork, the weekend is most appreciated because many of the formal duties are eliminated, and Sunday, which is considered the quietest tour of all, usually produces only bizarre crimes, the delayed result of weekend celebrations or the eruption of some smoldering kinship connection. The nightwork shift, especially in summer, is viewed as hard work all the time, but in other seasons city policemen believe it is primarily the weekends, which for them begin on Thursday afternoon and end early Sunday morning, that produce most of their action. City police associate much crime with heavy drinking and payday; they believe that the availability of large amounts of cash encourages some people to go drinking and others to rob.

Except for weekend nights, last out is usually a quiet shift. After the bars close, there is little action on the street. Since violations of the closing laws are a vice pinch, some men watch the bars and clubs on their sector closely. The sergeant encourages his men to increase their activity on this shift since the demands on their time are relatively small, and this is the best way he has for combating the professional car thieves and burglars, who prefer to work during these hours. The department also takes advantage of the low demand on the patrolmen's time to order surveys for abandoned cars, potholes in the streets, and defective traffic signals.

Some men enjoy last out because there is relatively less to do and there are few supervisors on the street. Most men feel that "the night is made for loving and sleeping," although there is some disagreement over where these things are best done. Last out produces the highest rate of absenteeism: a man who does not feel like working is most likely to stay put when he has to leave for work at 11 P.M. It is also very difficult to sick-check a man on this shift. His sergeant must have a compelling reason for believing he will not be at home before asking another sergeant to awaken a household after midnight. But a man who makes a habit of not appearing for last out is inviting his sergeant to look into his bag of tricks for informal ways of torturing him.

Unless a sergeant exerts very firm and unrelenting control, there is a considerable likelihood that some men will slip off into holes and others will disappear on private visits. It is not easy even for the conscientious to remain alert throughout the night, and men frequently stop at the station for a cup of coffee and a chat. When the sun begins to rise, the desire to sleep is very strong, and many men pull their cars up and just sit rather than continue to patrol and risk accidents. There are supervisors who allow their men to "go down" and others who continue to employ the tricks and harassments that supervisors have always used to compel their men to toe the mark. A sergeant who suspects someone is sleeping will ask the radio dispatcher to call a man for a meet every hour, day after day, and he will continue to do it until he has convinced the man of his intention to keep him honest. Patrolmen who refuse to sleep often speak contemptuously of their colleagues who do, but every policeman understands the desire to do it, and the obligation to work last out is an important source of the feelings of solidarity that policemen share.[15]

New men often utilize the freedom of last out to explore their district and sector. They nose their cars through back streets, learning which alleys are wide enough for a car and how to travel most directly from one place to another. They are laying the foundations of their territorial knowledge, one of the things which distinguish policemen from most other users of the city streets. They are under no formal pressure to do these things, and many do not, but those who enjoy their work do not need any encouragement to explore.

The policeman's expectations of particular tours and times often fail to materialize, but the belief in the generalizations which are used to characterize them is not shaken. Variations may be ascribed to meteorological or even astrological conditions which are shrugged off as special cases not affecting the validity of the belief. It is sustained by the policeman's need to have firm expectations about his work, although he knows that uncertainty and contingency are two of its fundamental characteristics. He knows that the activity demands made on him have little bearing on his ability to "fight crime," but he also knows that these demands impose clear, defined obligations on him that can be satisfied. These give him a considerable security because he knows that if he produces, he will gain the support and protection of his sergeant. Like any other worker, he seeks the esteem of colleagues and the rewards produced by good work.

---

15. Sleeping on the night shift is common in industry also. See Melville Dalton, *Men Who Manage* (New York: Wiley, 1959), p. 80; and in other branches of public service, Erving Goffman, *Asylums* (New York: Anchor, 1961), p. 204. Nightwork also produces solidarity in other occupational groups, such as musicians and railroad workers who have little in common with policemen. Edward Gross, *Work and Society* (New York: Crowell, 1958), p. 230.

21

The Dilemmas of Police Reform

James Q. Wilson

*There has ... been a traditional political resistance to educating the
police. The root of this resistance lies deeply imbedded in what seems
to me to be a prevailing, but rarely stated, political attitude that if the
police are encouraged to become professional, and thus are made more
effective, they will become a much less controllable arm of the executive branch of government and hence less amenable to the interests of
political influences that almost always lead to partial rather than
impartial enforcement of law.*
—Robert Sheehan, "Police Education and Training," *Law and Disorder,* Tufts University.

Current discussions of the problems of the American police seem
fraught with paradox. While everyone seems to agree about remedies,
criticisms of the police arise out of radically different conceptions of the
police function. Some people see the police as the chief means of ending
or reducing "crime in the streets"; others see them as an agency by
which white society confines and suppresses black ghettos; still others
view them as an organization caught on the grinding edge of a class
conflict among competing standards of order and propriety. Yet despite
these utterly disparate diagnoses, the prescribed treatment tends to be
quite conventional and generally endorsed—higher salaries, better
training, clearer policies, more modern equipment. And a further paradox: despite this apparent agreement on what should be done, little, in
fact, happens. In some places, voters and politicians appear to be universally sympathetic to the needs of the police, but they are unwilling
to appropriate more money to meet those needs. In other places, the

From James Q. Wilson, "What Makes a Better Policeman," *Atlantic* 223 (1969):
129–35, by permission of the author and publisher. Copyright © 1969 by The Atlantic
Monthly Company, Boston, Mass.

extra funds have been spent but the criticisms remain—little, apparently, has changed.

One reason for this confusion or inaction lies, I believe, in the fact that the police perform a number of quite different functions. The controversies in which the police are embroiled reveal this as various disputants emphasize crime prevention, or law enforcement, or the maintenance of order, or political power. Liberty, order, legitimacy—important and fundamental values are in conflict. The adherents of various points of view take refuge in a common (and perhaps peculiarly American) set of proposals: spend money, hire better men, buy more things. I suspect that spending more money and hiring better men *are* essential to police improvement, but I also suspect that one reason so little extra money is spent and so few men are hired is that beneath our agreement on means, we remain in deep disagreement on ends. Spend the money on *what,* and *why?* What *is* a "better" policeman, anyway?

This is not a new issue. The history of the American municipal police is in great part a history of struggles to define their role in our society. What makes the controversy so intense today is only partly that it is linked to the question of race; indeed, in the past the police have repeatedly been in conflict with new urban migrants of whatever color. The reason for the heat generated by the police question is probably the same as the reason for the emotions aroused by the crime issue: we compare present circumstances with an earlier period when we thought we had solved the problem. Police behavior, like crime, was not a major issue in the 1940s and 1950s. When the police did become an issue, it was usually because a department was found to be corrupt, and that discovery produced a standard response—bring in a reform chief, reorganize the force, and get back to work.

CROOK CATCHERS

That work was law enforcement, or so it was thought. The job of the police was to prevent crime and catch crooks. Corruption was a serious problem because it seemed to mean that crime was not being prevented and crooks were not being caught. Organized criminals were buying protection, or petty thieves were putting in a "fix," or the police themselves were stealing on the side. Reforming a department not only meant ending corruption and alliances with criminals; it also meant improving training and developing new methods—more courses on crime detection, tighter departmental discipline to prevent misconduct, better equipment to facilitate getting to the scene of a crime and analyzing clues. When the public was invited to inspect a refurbished

department, it was shown the new patrol cars, the new crime laboratory, the new communications center, and perhaps the new pistol
range. The policeman was portrayed as a "crime fighter," and to an
important degree, of course, he was.

But that was not all or even the most important thing he was. Given
the nature of the crime problem, it was impossible for him to be simply
a crime fighter. Most crime is not prevented and most criminals are not
caught, even in the best-run, best-manned departments. Murder, for
example, is a "private" crime, occurring chiefly off the streets and
among "friends" or relatives. No police methods can prevent it, and
only general domestic disarmament, an unlikely event, might reduce
it. Many, if not most, assaults are similarly immune from police deterrence. Most crimes against property—burglary, auto theft, larceny—are
also crimes of stealth, and though the police might, by various means,
cut the rate somewhat, they cannot cut it greatly because they cannot
be everywhere at once. Street crimes—robberies, muggings, purse
snatches—are more susceptible to police deterrence than any other
kind, though so far few, if any, departments have had the resources or
the community support to carry out a really significant strategy to
prevent street crime.

The result of this state of affairs is that though some police departments are regarded as "backward" and others as "modern" and "professional," neither kind seems able to bring about a substantial,
enduring reduction of the crime rate. If this is true, then the characterization of the police as primarily crime fighters places them in a potentially embarrassing position, that of *being judged by a goal they cannot
attain*. In the 1950s, when crime rates were either stabilized or ignored, this awkward situation and the police response to it were not
apparent.

What most policemen were doing even when they were being
thought of as crime fighters was not so much enforcing the law as
maintaining order. In a recent study, I have tried to show what makes
up the routine workload of patrolmen, the police rank which has the
largest number of men. The vast majority of police actions taken in
response to citizen calls involve either providing a service (getting a cat
out of a tree or taking a person to a hospital) or managing real or alleged
conditions of disorder (quarreling families, public drunks, bothersome
teen-agers, noisy cars, and tavern fights). Only a small fraction of these
calls involve matters of law enforcement, such as checking on a
prowler, catching a burglar in the act, or preventing a street robbery.
The disorders to which the police routinely respond are not large-scale.
Riots and civil commotions are, in any given city, rare occurrences, and

when they happen, the police act en masse, under central leadership. Rather, the maintenance of order involves handling disputes in which only two or three people participate and which arise out of personal misconduct, not racial or class grievances.

The difference between order maintenance and law enforcement is not simply the difference between "little stuff" and "real crime" or between misdemeanors and felonies. The distinction is fundamental to the police role, for the two functions involve quite dissimilar police actions and judgments. Order maintenance arises out of a dispute among citizens who accuse each other of being at fault; law enforcement arises out of the victimization of an innocent party by a person whose guilt must be proved. Handling a disorderly situation requires the officer to make a judgment about what constitutes an appropriate standard of behavior; law enforcement requires him only to compare a person's behavior with a clear legal standard. Murder or theft is defined, unambiguously, by statutes; public peace is not. Order maintenance rarely leads to an arrest; law enforcement (if the suspect can be found) typically does. Citizens quarreling usually want the officer to "do something," but they rarely want him to make an arrest (after all, the disputants are usually known or related to each other). Furthermore, whatever law is broken in a quarrel is usually a misdemeanor, and in most states, an officer cannot make a misdemeanor arrest unless he saw the infraction (which is rare) or unless one party or the other will swear out a formal complaint (which is even rarer).

Because an arrest cannot be made in most disorderly cases, the officer is expected to handle the situation by other means and on the spot, but the law gives him almost no guidance on how he is to do this; indeed, the law often denies him the right to do anything at all *other* than make an arrest. No judge will ever see the case, and thus no judge can decide the case for the officer. Alone, unsupervised, with no policies to guide him and little sympathy from onlookers to support him, the officer must "administer justice" on the curbstone.

EARLY PATTERNS

In the nineteenth century, it was widely recognized that the maintenance of order was the chief function of the police. Roger Lane's informative history, *Policing the City: Boston, 1822–1885* (Cambridge: Harvard University Press, 1967), recounts how that department, the oldest in the United States, was first organized as a night watch to keep the peace in the streets. Beginning in 1834, men drafted from the citizenry were required to take their turns in seeing (as the governing statute required) "that all disturbances and disorders in the night shall be prevented and suppressed." Wild creatures, human and animal alike, were to be kept off the street, and a hue and cry was to be set up should fire or riot threaten.

The job of law enforcement—that is, of apprehending criminals who had robbed or burgled the citizenry—was not among the duties of the watchmen; indeed, it was not even among the duties of the government. A victim was obliged to find the guilty party himself. Once a suspect was found, the citizen could, for a fee, hire a constable who, acting on a warrant, would take the suspect into custody. Even after detectives—that is, men charged with law enforcement rather than the maintenance of order—were added to the force in the nineteenth century, they continued to serve essentially private interests. The chief concern of the victim was restitution, and to that end, the detectives would seek to recover loot in exchange for a percentage of the take. Detectives functioned then as personal-injury lawyers operate today, on a contingency basis, hoping to get a large part, perhaps half, of the proceeds.

Since in those days there was no law against compounding a felony, the detectives were free to employ any methods they wanted to recover stolen property. And with this as their mission, it is not surprising, as Lane notes, that the best detectives were those who by background and experience were most familiar with the haunts and methods of thieves.

The emergence of a municipal police force out of its watchmen antecedents was not so much the result of mounting crime rates as of growing levels of civil disorder. In time, and with the growth of the cities to a size and heterogeneity too great to permit the operation of informal social controls, the problem of order maintenance became too severe to make reliance on part-time or volunteer watchmen feasible. The Boston Police Department was created to deal with riots, as was the Department in Philadelphia. The Boston police first acquired firearms in the aftermath of the Draft Riot of 1863, though they were not fully armed at public expense until 1884.

The Philadelphia case is illustrative of many. Like Boston, that city relied on watchmen rather than organized, quasi-military constabulary. But a series of riots among youthful gangs (The Rats, the Bouncers, the Schuylkill Rangers, and the Blood Tubs, among several) persuaded the city fathers that stronger measures were necessary. To a degree, the riots were under semiofficial auspices, thus magnifying the embarrassment the politicians faced. It seems that volunteer fire companies were organized to handle conflagrations. The young toughs who sat about waiting for fires to happen found this boring and, worse, unrewarding, whereupon some hit upon the idea of starting a fire and racing other companies to the scene to see who could put the blaze out more quickly, and just as important, who could pick up the most loot from the building. Though this competitive zeal may have been a commendable aid to training, it led to frequent collisions between companies speeding to the same fire, with the encounter often leading to a riot. It is only a slight exaggeration to say that the Philadelphia policemen were created in part to control the Philadelphia firemen.

SOMETIMES ON SUNDAY

The growth and formal organization of the police department did not, in themselves, lead to changes in function. The maintenance of order was still the principal objective. What did lead to a change was twofold: the bureaucratization of the detectives (putting them on salary and ending the fee system), and the use of the police to enforce unpopular laws governing the sale and use of liquor. The former change led to the beginning of the popular confusion as to what the police do. The detective became the hero of the dime novel and the cynosure of the public's romantic imagination; he, and not his patrolman colleague, was the "real" police officer doing "real" police work. Enforcing liquor laws caused the police to initiate prosecutions on their own authority rather than on citizen complaint, particularly in cases where the public was deeply divided regarding the wisdom of the law. In Philadelphia, enforcing the Sunday closing laws, especially with regard to saloons, was widely resented, and when the mayor ordered the police to do it, he was, according to a contemporary account, "caricatured, ridiculed, and denounced." In Boston, Mayor Jonathan Chapman was led to remark that police enforcement of temperance laws had created a situation in which "the passions of men are aroused and the community is kept in a constant state of ferment."

What kept the police from being utterly destroyed by the liquor controversy was their determination to do no more than was absolutely necessary, given whatever regime was in power. Edward Savage, the able chief of the Boston force in the 1870s and 1880s, was a man of modest but much exercised literary talents, and in one of his better-known essays, entitled "Advice to a Young Policeman," he set forth the essential rule of good police work: "In ordinary cases, if you find yourself in a position of not knowing exactly what to do, better to do too little than too much; it is easier to excuse a moderate course than an overt act."

In addition, the police provided on a large scale a number of services to citizens, especially to those who, because of drink, indolence, or circumstance, were likely to become sources of public disorder. Roger Lane calculates that in 1856 the Boston police provided "lodgings" to over nine thousand persons, not including those who had been arrested for drunkenness. By 1860 the total exceeded seventeen thousand. Perhaps because the police were the principal city agency to witness the lot of the poor, perhaps because one of the original collateral duties of the police chief was superintendent of public health, the officers provided a wide range of services in addition to lodgings—coal for needy families, soup kitchens for the hungry, and jobs as domestics for girls they thought could be lured away from a life of prostitution.

In time, this service policy, which probably did much to mitigate the hostility between police and public occasioned by the enforcement of liquor laws, was curtailed on the complaint of the leaders of the organized charities who objected, apparently, to unfair competition. The advocates of "scientific charity," it seems, did not believe the police were competent to distinguish between the deserving and the undeserving poor.

The relations between police and public even during the period of free soup were not consistently amicable. One issue was the appointment of Irish police officers. For political purposes, the Boston Whigs demanded that, as we would say today, "representatives of indigenous and culturally-deprived groups" be added to the force. Then as now, the "culturally deprived" were responsible for a disproportionate share of those arrested for crimes. Then as now, the police objected to the appointment of an Irishman on the grounds that the man selected by the politicians was not qualified and had himself been arrested for a crime a few years earlier—it seems he had participated in a riot. The police, of course, denied that they were prejudiced but claimed that appointing a person on grounds of ethnicity would be destructive of morale on the force. The mayor insisted that the appointment take place. On November 3, 1851, the new man reported for work, announcing himself loudly and proudly as "Barney McGinniskin, fresh from the bogs of Ireland!"

THE CHIEF EVIL

By the end of the nineteenth century, the groundwork had been laid for the modern municipal police force, and for the modern problems of the police. The bureaucratization of the detectives and the police enforcement of liquor laws had not as yet overshadowed the order-maintenance function of the police, but two events of the twentieth century ensured that they would—Prohibition and the Depression. The former required the police everywhere to choose between being corrupted and making a nuisance of themselves; the latter focused public attention on the escapades of bank robbers and other desperadoes such as John Dillinger, Baby Face Nelson, and Bonnie and Clyde. Police venality and rising crime rates coincided in the public mind, though in fact they had somewhat different causes. The watchman function of the police was lost sight of; their law enforcement function, and their apparent failure to exercise it, were emphasized.

President Herbert Hoover did what most Presidents do when faced with a major political issue for which the solution is neither obvious nor popular—he appointed a commission. In 1931 the National Commission on Law Observance and Law Enforcement—generally known, after its chairman, as the Wickersham Commission—made its report in a series of volumes prepared by some of the ablest academic and police experts of the day. Though many subjects were covered (especially the question of whether immigrants were more criminal than native-born Americans), the volume on the police was of special importance. On page one, the first paragraph stated a twentieth-century conception of the police function and a new standard by which policemen were to be judged:

> The general failure of the police to detect and arrest criminals guilty of the many murders, spectacular bank, payroll, and other hold-ups, and sensational robberies with guns, frequently resulting in the death of the robbed victim, has caused a loss of public confidence in the police of our country. For a condition so general there must be some universal underlying causes to account for it.

Now, of course there may have been some "universal underlying causes," but the ones that come readily to mind—Prohibition, postwar readjustment, and the economic cycle—were not ones about which a presidential commission could at that time speak very candidly. Besides, it was far from clear what could be done about at least the second and third of these causes. What was necessary was to find a "universal cause" about which something could be done. Needless to say, two groups on whom we have long felt free to cast blame for everything from slums to hoof-and-mouth disease—the police and the politicians— seemed appropriate targets. Accordingly, the Commission wrote:

> The chief evil, in our opinion, lies in the insecure, short term of service of the chief or executive head of the police force and in his being subject while in office to the control of politicians in the discharge of his duties.

SOME PROPOSALS

Following on this analysis, the Commission detailed a number of specific proposals—putting the police on civil service, buying modern equipment ("the wireless"), and of course, hiring better men and giving them better training. In truth, there probably was a need for some police reforms; many departments had become dumping grounds for the fat relatives of second-rate politicians, and modern bank robbers were in many cases more mobile and efficient than the police chasing them. But the "professional" view of the police went further than merely proposing changes in equipment and manpower; it argued in addition that since the police *can* prevent crime, if the crime rate gets out of hand, it is in good measure because the police are incompetent as a result of political influence.

Now, some members of the Commission were no doubt perfectly aware that the police do not cause crime, but, like many commissions anxious to make a strong public impression and generate support for desirable changes, they inevitably overstated the case in their report. A report that said that many improvements in police practice were necessary but that these improvements, if adopted, would have only a slight effect on the crime rate would not generate many headlines. (Thirty-seven years later, the Kerner Commission had not forgotten this lesson; what made the newspapers was not its proposals for action but its charge of "white racism.")

The consequences of assigning to the police a law-enforcement, crime-prevention function to the exclusion of anything else were profound. If the job of the police is to catch crooks, then the police have a technical, ministerial responsibility in which discretion plays little part. Since no one is likely to disagree on the value of the objective, then there is little reason to expose the police to the decision-making processes of city government. *Ergo,* take the police "out of politics." So powerful (or so useful) did this slogan become that within a few decades whenever a big-city mayor tried to pick his own police chief or take charge of his department for the purpose of giving it a new direction, *the police themselves* objected on the grounds that this was an effort to exercise "political influence" over the force.

Furthermore, if the technical objective of law enforcement was primary, then non-law-enforcement duties should be taken away from the police: no more soup kitchens; no more giving lodging to drunks; no more ambulance driving. These things are not "real police work." Let the police see the public only in their role as law enforcers. Let the public, alas, see the police only as adversaries. Of course, these changes were more in the public's mind than in everyday reality. If politics was taken out of the police, the police were not taken out of politics. They continued—in fact, with the decline of party machines, they increased —their involvement in electoral politics, city hall intrigue, and legislative lobbying. And whatever professional police leadership may have said, the patrolman on the beat knew that his job was not primarily law enforcement—he was still handling as many family fights and rowdy teen-agers as ever. But lacking support in the performance of these duties, he came also to believe that his job "wasn't real police work," and accordingly that it was peripheral, if not demeaning.

But perhaps the most important consequence was the police response to the public expectation that they could prevent crime. Their response was perfectly rational and to be encountered in any organization that is judged by a standard it cannot meet—they lied. If police activity (given the level of resources and public support available) could not produce a significant decline in crime rates, police record-keeping would be "adjusted" to keep the rates in line. Departments judged by professional standards but not controlled by professional leaders were at pains to show progress by either understating the number of crimes or overstating the number of crimes "cleared" by arrest. Often this was not the policy of the chief, but the result of judging officers by crime and arrest records.

In the public's eye, the "hero cop" was the man who made the "good pinch." For a while (until the mass media abandoned the standards of the middle-aged and the conservative in favor of the standards of the young and the radical), the ideal cop was the "G Man." FBI agents, of course, are different from municipal police forces precisely because their task *is* law enforcement, and often enforcing important laws against quite serious criminals. Few special agents need to wade into a skid-row brawl. But within city departments, the emphasis on the "good pinch" grew. This was only partly because the newspapers, and thus the public, rewarded such accomplishments; it was also because the departments rewarded it. The patrolman could look forward, in the typical case, to remaining a patrolman all his life *unless* he could get promoted or be made a detective. Promotion increasingly came to require the passing of a written examination in which college men would usually do better than less articulate but perhaps more competent "street men." Appointment as a detective, however, was in many departments available to men with a good arrest record (or a strategically placed friend in headquarters). If you want to get away from drunks, kids, and shrews, then make a pinch that will put you in line for becoming a dick. Though there is in principle nothing wrong with rewarding men for having a good arrest record, one frequent result of this system has been to take the best patrolmen off the street and put them into a headquarters unit.

POLICE REFORM: THE CHOICES AHEAD

Today, the conception of the police role underlying the foregoing arrangements is being questioned. Perhaps the landmark event was the 1967 report of the President's Commission on Law Enforcement and Administration of Justice, the executive director of which was James Vorenberg of the Harvard Law School. Unlike the Wickersham or Kerner Commission reports, this document made relatively few headlines, and the reason, I think, was that it did not provide the reporters with a catchy slogan. The nine volumes of the Vorenberg report insisted that the problems of crime and police work are complicated matters for which few, if any, easy solutions are available. There were no dramatic scandals to uncover; the police "third degree" (on which the Wickersham Commission, in the report drafted by Zechariah Chafee, lavished much attention) had declined in occurrence and significance. Most police departments had been taken out of the control of party machines (in some cases, it would appear, only to be placed under the influence of organized crime). Instead, the Commission devoted considerable attention to the order-maintenance function of the police:

> A great majority of the situations in which policemen intervene are not, or are not interpreted by the police to be, criminal situations in the sense that they call for arrest. . . . A common kind of situation . . . is the matrimonial dispute, which police experts estimate consumes as much time as any other single kind of situation.

The riots in Watts and elsewhere had, by the time the report appeared, already called the attention of the public to the importance (and fragility) of public order. The rise of demands for "community control" of various public services, including the police and the schools, has placed the problem of order on the political agenda. Whether the problems of managing disorder can best be handled by turning city government over to neighborhood groups is a complicated question. (Provisionally, I would argue that war becomes more, not less, likely when a political system is balkanized.) In any case, we have come full circle in our thinking about the function of the police.

Or almost full circle. The current anxiety about crime in the streets continues to lead some to define the police task as wholly or chiefly one of crime deterrence, and thus any discussion of redefining the police role or reorganizing police departments to facilitate performing their other functions tends to get lost in the din of charges and counter-charges about whether or not the police have been "handcuffed." This is unfortunate, not because crime in the streets is a false issue (the rates of street crime, I am convinced, *are* increasing in an alarming manner), but because handling this problem cannot be left solely or even primar-ily to the police; acting as if it could raises false hopes among the citizens and places unfair and distorting demands on the police. At least as much attention to the courts and correctional systems will be necessary if much progress is to be shown in reducing street crime.

The simultaneous emergence of a popular concern for both crime and order does put in focus the choices that will have to be made in the next generation of police reforms. In effect, municipal police depart-ments are two organizations in one serving two related but not identical functions. The strategy appropriate for strengthening their ability to serve one role tends to weaken their ability to serve the other. Crime deterrence and law enforcement require, or are facilitated by, special-ization, strong hierarchical authority, improved mobility and communi-cations, clarity in legal codes and arrest procedures, close surveillance of the community, high standards of integrity, and the avoidance of entangling alliances with politicians. The maintenance of order, on the other hand, is aided by departmental procedures that include decen-tralization, neighborhood involvement, foot patrol, wide discretion, the provision of services, an absence of arrest quotas, and some tolerance for minor forms of favoritism and even corruption.

There is no magic formula—no prepackaged "reform"—that can tell a community or a police chief how to organize a force to serve, with appropriate balance, these competing objectives. Just as slogans de-manding "taking the police out of politics" or "putting the police in cars" have proved inadequate guides to action in the past, so also slo-gans demanding "foot patrolmen" or "community control" are likely to prove inadequate in the future. One would like to think that since both points of view now have ardent advocates, the debate has at last been joined. But I suspect that the two sides are talking at, or past, each other, and not *to* each other, and thus the issue, from being joined, is still lost in rhetoric.

A BASIC READING LIST

The books listed below will be of special interest to general readers who want to know more about the history, training, origins, and special problems of policemen in American life.

The Policeman and the Community, by Michael Banton. New York: Basic Books, 1965.

The Police, ed. by David J. Bordua. New York: John Wiley & Sons, 1967.

Police Power: Police Abuses in New York City, by Paul Chevigny. New York: Pantheon Books, 1969.

Arrest, by Wayne R. LaFave. Boston: Little, Brown and Company, 1965.

Behind the Shield: The Police in Urban Society, by Arthur Niederhoffer. New York: Doubleday & Company, 1967.

The Challenge of Crime in a Free Society, A report by the President's Commission on Law Enforcement and Administration of Justice. Washington: U.S. Government Printing Office, 1967.

Task Force Report: The Police, by the President's Commission on Law Enforcement and Administration of Justice. Washington: U.S. Government Printing Office, 1967.

Justice Without Trial, by Jerome H. Skolnick. New York: John Wiley & Sons, 1966.

Rights in Conflict, by Daniel Walker as submitted to the National Commission on the Causes and Prevention of Violence. New York: E. P. Dutton & Co., 1968.

Varieties of Police Behavior, by James Q. Wilson. Cambridge: Harvard University Press, 1968.

Police Administration, by Orlando W. Wilson. 2nd ed. New York: McGraw-Hill Book Company, 1963.

PART VI

Criminal Conduct
and the Courts

Although social scientists have examined nearly every aspect of the process that has come to be called criminal justice, they have shown an inexplicable tendency to simply assume the operation of the criminal court. The possible exception to this avoidance is an early research series on jury proceedings conducted by social psychologists, a number of studies on judicial decision-making done by political scientists, and recent inquiry by legal scholars into constitutional issues associated with arrest, pretrial custody, and prosecution. Scholars generally have shown lively interest in the deterrent effects of sentencing, but court systems themselves are given altogether too little research attention.

The system of law in this country is complicated by its hierarchical nature and by the recent influence of quasi-legal organizations, especially those of the federal government. Regulatory levels are composed of the United States Constitution, the Bill of Rights, state constitutions, Congress, and state legislatures, followed by the courts and the system of law enforcement designed to serve them. Combined with these are administrative agencies that set guidelines in areas such as environmental protection, employment, civil rights, health, welfare, education, and housing. When these organizations promulgate a set of regulations, they in effect control policy over the quality of life. Such functions were formerly assumed by legislative bodies, but it is readily apparent that future responsibilities in handling these "social problems" will fall to governmental organizations.

Conventional crimes—the traditional interest of criminologists—are brought before trial courts which theoretically conduct adversary proceedings. In practice, however, negotiations at every stage of a citizen's involvement with the law are characteristic. Minor offenses such as misdemeanant and traffic cases are handled by the lesser courts, and major cases such as felonies are heard and adjudicated by courts of wider jurisdiction. The primary objective of these courts is to decide upon issues of fact. In addition, there are appellate courts whose function is not to sit in judgment of fact but to decide issues of law. Appellate courts, of course, review cases on appeal following trial in a lower court, but it is important to note that grounds for appeal are not necessarily related to a convicted defendant's claim of innocence. Instead a case has merit if the original trial was improperly conducted, if prior to trial the defendant's rights were violated, if significantly new and compelling evidence becomes available, or if the law under which conviction was obtained is subsequently ruled unconstitutional. The fact that appellate courts select relatively few cases for review should not obscure their ability to significantly affect human conduct. Consider, for instance, the cases of *Brown* v. *Board of Education* (which required the desegregation of school facilities, 1954), *Miranda* v. *Arizona* (which restricted the latitude of police interrogation upon arrest, 1966), and *In re Gault* (which established certain rules of procedure for juvenile courts, 1967). Appellate courts, then, make decisions that have far greater consequences for the structure of the law than is ordinarily assumed.

The impression most readily gained from studies of justice administration in this country is that no part of the system is immune to criticism or is uncontroversial. Larger metropolitan centers are particularly vulnerable to attack if only because the volume of litigation through their courts is staggering. The largest of cities—New York, Chicago, Los Angeles, Philadelphia—are regularly charged with corruption within their public bureaucracies, and more often than not the accusations focus upon the police or the courts. Perhaps because of their formal, inviolable character, the courts have become a popular scapegoat. Upon them falls the blame for all the constraints suffered by other criminal justice agencies: the police complain bitterly about court decisions related to probable cause, search and seizure, and evidentiary requirements; corrections finds many of its own policies for handling inmates subject to court intervention.

To process defendants so that the courts are not fully inundated, defense attorneys, prosecutors, the judiciary, and other court personnel engage, sometimes unwittingly, in a charade of assembly line justice. Assuming that the accused is duly but not necessarily validly arrested, the first question raised upon arraignment is whether he is likely to reappear for trial. Whether he qualifies for release on personal recognizance, makes bond, or is retained in custody, however, may be more a function of case volume than of personal reliability. At the proceedings that follow, up to and including trial, the defendant can enter a guilty plea. Estimates of the proportion of defendants electing to "cop a [guilty] plea" vary from eighty to ninety percent, which qualifies the guilty plea as the foremost contribution to judicial efficiency. Despite extensive research on guilty pleas, the plea bargaining that may lead to them, and their consequences for the convicted offender, much work in this area is still anticipated.

Finally, findings of judicial research on sentencing practices suggest that critically important discrepancies exist both between and within jurisdictions. Given the discretionary authority of the court, it is hardly surprising that judges inconsistently sentence defendants whose criminal histories, immediate offenses, and other considerations invite comparable legal sanctions. Sentencing disparities arise because plea bargaining may have occurred, or because the applicable statutes may vary considerably between jurisdictions. Suspicion lingers in many quarters, of course, that type and severity of sentence may be a function of less justifiable influences, such as the notoriety of the case, its use as a deterrent to subsequent offenses, or the challenge given law enforcement officers or the prosecutor in bringing the case to trial. As we have seen at other points in the criminal justice system, injustices can readily be identified; their alleviation through litigation has also been demonstrated, even if unsystematically.

Donald J. Newman's "Role and Process in the Criminal Court" is a concise treatment of court structure and functioning. He reviews the personnel and organization of a court setting, traces the process through which cases proceed, and indicates problem areas deserving research.

The essay on "Poverty and the Criminal Process" by William J. Chambliss and Robert J. Seidman is taken from their larger work on a theory of the law in action. Their contention that the legal order is a self-serving system to maintain power and privilege receives full consideration as they examine differential treatment of the poor in the American legal system.

"Early Diversion from the Criminal Justice System" by Elizabeth W. Vorenberg and James Vorenberg is excerpted from a more extensive discussion of alternatives to current treatment of offenders. They show how this important trend gained support and what benefits accrue to the criminal justice system from diversionary programs.

Further readings in the area of the courts and justice administration can be found below.

1. *General Works on the Court and Justice Administration*
Blumberg, Abraham S., *Criminal Justice* (Chicago: Quadrangle Books, 1967).
Cicourel, Aaron V., *The Social Organization of Juvenile Justice* (New York: Wiley, 1968).
Dibble, Vernon K. with Berton Pekowsky, "What is and What Ought to Be: A Comparison of Certain Characteristics of the Ideological and Legal Styles of Thought," *American Journal of Sociology* 79 (1973): 511–49.
Galanter, Marc, "Why the 'Haves' Come Out Ahead: Speculation on the Limits of Legal Change," *Law and Society Review* 9 (1974): 95–160.

Morris, Norval, and Hawkins, Gordon, *The Honest Politician's Guide to Crime Control* (Chicago: University of Chicago Press, 1970).
Nagel, Stuart, *The Legal Process from a Behavioral Perspective* (Homewood, Ill.: Dorsey Press, 1969).
The President's Commission on Law Enforcement and Administration of Justice, *Task Force Report: The Courts* (Washington, D.C.: U.S. Government Printing Office, 1967).
Schur, Edwin M., *Law and Society: A Sociological View* (New York: Random House, 1968).
Selznick, Philip, "Legal Institutions and Social Control," *Vanderbilt Law Review* 17 (1963): 79–90.
Skolnick, Jerome H., "The Sociology of Law in America: Overview and Trends," *Social Problems* 13 (1965): 15–28.
Tapp, June (ed.), "Symposium on Socialization, the Law, and Society," *Journal of Social Issues* 27(1971).

2. Structure and Process in the Criminal Court

Dawson, Robert O., *Sentencing: The Decision as to Type, Length and Conditions of Sentence* (Boston: Little, Brown, 1969).
Goldfarb, Ronald L., and Singer, Linda R., *After Conviction* (New York: Simon and Schuster, 1973).
Hagan, John, "Extra-Legal Attributes and Criminal Sentencing: An Assessment of a Sociological Viewpoint," *Law and Society Review* 8 (1974): 357–83.
Kalven, Harry, Jr., and Zeisel, Hans, *The American Jury* (Boston: Little, Brown, 1966).
Miller, Frank W., *Prosecution: The Decision to Charge a Suspect with a Crime* (Boston: Little, Brown, 1970).
Murphy, John J., Jr., *Arrest by Police Computer: The Controversy over Bail and Extradition* (Lexington, Mass.: D.C. Heath, 1975).
Newman, Donald J., *Conviction: The Determination of Guilt or Innocence Without Trial* (Boston: Little, Brown, 1966).
Oaks, Dallin H., and Lehman, Warren, *A Criminal Justice System and the Indigent* (Chicago: University of Chicago Press, 1968).

Seidman, Robert B., and Chambliss, William J., "Appeals from Criminal Convictions," in *Handbook of Criminology*, ed. Daniel Glaser (Chicago: Rand McNally, 1974), pp. 651–77.

Walker, Nigel, *Sentencing in a Rational Society* (New York: Basic Books, 1971).

Weistart, John C. (ed.), "Judicial Ethics," *Law and Contemporary Problems* 35 (1970).

Wice, Paul B., *Freedom for Sale: A National Study of Pretrial Release* (Lexington, Mass.: D.C. Heath, 1974).

22

Role and Process
in the Criminal Court

Donald J. Newman

THE CRIMINAL COURT IN CONTEXT

The Concept, Structure, and Functions of the Criminal Court

The trial court occupies a central and critical place in the criminal justice system and yet, more than other agencies and offices of this system, it is neither simply defined nor easily delimited. Sometimes the term *court* is used as a synonym for *judge,* but at other times it is used to refer to the entire collection of offices and procedures for processing defendants through the middle stages of the criminal justice system, from postarrest to preincarceration. The difference between the narrower judicial view of the court and its conception as a processing agency is more than a matter of definition. It is, rather, a dramatic illustration of contra-perspectives, of a dichotomy in ideology, that characterizes our entire law-enforcement and criminal justice effort. For both definitions of trial courts are valid, both the judicial and the agency functions apply simultaneously, yet they are related in uneasy and controversial fashion, highlighting Packer's (1964) distinctions between the "due process" and the "crime control" models of the criminal justice system.

In the judicial perspective, the court is a finder-of-fact, a tester of evidence, a judgment-rendering body, whether in the person of the judge or in the combined roles of judge and jury. The court is most clearly the province of law and lawyers, and in spite of admitted short-comings and occasional fallibility, the place where we as people determine guilt or innocence, truth or falseness, in criminal matters. The court's function is to apply to the fullest the constitutional guarantees of due process and procedural regularity in separating the guilty from the innocent, in resolving "beyond all reasonable doubt" disputed questions of fact, and in assuring fair and public trials of those accused of crimes. Indeed, the trial court does have, and does serve, this function.

From the other perspective, the criminal court is simply another criminal justice agency located between the police and the prisons and acting in concert with them, not so much to seek truth by adversary testing but to process the thousands of persons who flow through the system as their status changes from suspect to defendant to convicted offender to inmate and parolee. In this model matters of evidence and proof are of lesser importance than efficiency in moving cases from the street to correctional programs. And, indeed, the trial court does have, and does serve, this function for the vast majority of defendants, whether accused of felonies or misdemeanors, as they move through adjudication to sentencing without trial (Newman, 1966; Skolnick, 1966; President's Commission, 1967a). In this process the jury is absent and the judge, though a central figure, acts primarily to ratify decisions made by the prosecutorial and probation staffs.

Although from an operational point of view the full scale jury trial of a criminal case is comparatively rare, the idealized adversary process has deeper theoretical and symbolic significance. The formal, circumscribed ceremony of the trial, the attention to due process, the separate though presumed balance of legal advantage, the articulation and testing of evidence standards, and even the architecture of the courtroom and the pomp of the proceedings have cultural meanings that cannot be tested simply by measures of efficiency nor denigrated because of infrequent use. Of all the agencies and processes of criminal justice, the court and the trial, in idealized form at least, come closest to what we mean by "justice" in our society. It has been pointed out that the trial model in criminal justice is the one we think we have, or ought to have, but the administrative system for quickly and quietly processing cases is the one we really desire to maintain (Blumberg, 1967, p. 168).

The two models of justice, the different perspectives of the court, have never really been reconciled. Lawyers, legal scholars, sociologists, and appellate courts have long grappled with differences between "law in action" and "law in the books" at various points in criminal processing, but it is only comparatively recently that the nontrial functions of the courts have received sustained scholarly attention and the merger of the prosecutory, adjudicatory, and sentencing functions of the courts were seen and analyzed as a whole, a decision complex of great importance in its own right, not simply a minor alternative to trial (Ohlin & Remington, 1958).

The relationship between the two concepts of court—as trier of fact and as administrative agency—is a subtle and complex one in operational terms as well as in ideology. Aside from its intrinsic importance as a method of adjudication and apart from its symbolic value, the criminal trial, or at least the potential of a trial, has a good deal of administrative significance. In operational terms, it is both a threat and a promise. It is available to all who feel themselves innocent, or at least nonconvictable, and the threat to demand trial is employed by both sides in the plea negotiation process. In the day-to-day processing of thousands of criminal cases, the *avoidance* of trial is of greatest operational significance, the primary objective of both state and accused in the criminal-court process (Newman, 1966).

Officers and Organization of the Criminal Courts

The court stages of the criminal justice process encompass the major decision points of charging, adjudication, and sentencing. Participants in the process include, in addition to defendants, the judge and trial jury, the prosecutor, and in some cases, the grand jury, defense counsel, probation staff, assorted other personnel, such as clerks, bailiffs, stenographers, court administrators, and occasionally others like psychologists or psychiatrists attached to diagnostic clinics, and court-related personnel like jailers and bondsmen. The number and types of personnel involved in court activity vary, not only from one jurisdiction to another but even in a single court, shifting as calendars change, as cases differ, and as the process ebbs and flows between litigation or cooperation—between trial or guilty plea. The relationship among court participants likewise shifts according to activity but even when stable these relationships are amorphous at best, for though the court may be treated analytically as an agency, it is not a line-staff organization of employers and workers in the usual sense. It is much more complex than this, demonstrating internally the complicated structure and role relationships that characterize the entire criminal justice system.

The array of offices and agencies in criminal justice all operate within a delicate balance of authority emanating partly from legislation, partly from appellate-court decree, and partly from agency rule-making power. The system is actually a federation of bureaucracies and professions, interacting in the processing of cases, but structurally independent. The cement that ties the agencies together, the outline of the complex organization, is the flow of its business—the processing of criminal suspects through various decision points from police intake to correctional output (Remington et al., 1969). In the system as a whole, and in the court process as a part, at least four major dimensions of role selection are relevant to both organization and functions: (1) the extent to which personnel occupying any role are required to be professionally trained and educated for their particular function; (2) the method of selection, whether elective, appointive, or the result of competitive examination; (3) the extent of jurisdiction and the basis used for decision reference (whether local or cosmopolitan, whether oriented to a profession or to an agency); and (4) the extent of outside citizen participation and control in both policy formation and decision-making within the functional ambit of the role. Thus, some offices and agencies of the criminal justice system have professional entrance requirements, such as legal training for prosecutors and judges, while others can be staffed by paraprofessionals or by persons without special training. Likewise, some offices are elective, others appointive, and others based on competitive merit, with incumbents drawn from established career lines. Some criminal justice agencies, like correctional services, have broad statewide or even national orientation, whereas others, sheriffs and prosecutors for example, have local authority and regional loyalty. Some agencies, like prisons, are relatively immune from direct citizen control or participation in decision-making, whereas in others "laymen" have, or can have, direct-decision authority, as in the case of the trial jury.

In contrast to national or state agencies, such as corrections and parole, courts are largely local enclaves though not entirely independent from statewide concern and control. By and large, judges, prosecutors, defense counsel, and even probation staff (as well as other court personnel) are indigenous to the area, nontransferable to other locations, and thus heavily responsive to local expectations and demands. However, courts are tied to the larger jurisdiction in a number of ways: by supervision of courts of appeal, by statewide requirements for office or duties fixed by legislation, by loyalty of participants to their profession and professional organizations, by the administrative skills of state-court administrators, and in some ways, by that portion of the court budget that comes from the state or the federal government.

A number of criminal justice agencies, like the police and the custodial staff of prisons, are structured in classic bureaucratic fashion with clear lines of authority and superordinate and subordinate roles. This is not to say that such agencies, organized in paramilitary fashion, are without conflicts and uncertainties; all multifunctional organizations experience power struggles, shifts in authority, competing ideologies, and less-than-stable relationships, as both police and prisons have discovered in times of crisis. Courts, too, have such problems, but they are even more complicated because basic court structure is far different from common administrative bureaucracy, and certainly is not patterned on the military. While the trial judge is the titular head of court activities and may be the actual employer of bailiffs, clerks, and occasionally of probation officers, he is by no means the "boss" of the prosecutor any more than he is of defense counsel who appears before him. While these participants have functional interdependence with the judge and, in the more formalized trial process especially, have some fairly clearly defined reciprocal roles, the primary allegiance of prosecutors, counsel, and probation officers is to their own offices and professions. Such judicial control as exists is indirect and often informal. In short, the overall role structure of the court is more like an affiliation of semiautonomous professionals, closer in a sense to a medical clinic or a university faculty than to an industrial or military bureaucracy. This is so even *within* offices in the court system. Control by the district attorney of his professional staff is generally limited to formulation of general policies and to his powers of persuasion; judgments in legal matters on the part of his lawyer assistants rest primarily on their own professional competence and ethics. Likewise, in multi-judge jurisdictions, the authority of the chief judge is limited largely to matters of the court calendar. In decisions of substance—within gross limits of propriety—his colleagues are immune from his control. So it is with court administrators, now prominent and important participants in many court organizations. In effect, such administrators are business officers and calendar clerks; they can affect budget and work loads, but not substantial decision-making.

The relationship among courts in any jurisdiction is, likewise, an amorphous one: each court is an island of relative autonomy within its jurisdictional authority, yet related to the whole both by legislation, which sets standards, defines limits, and controls some budget, and by the appellate process, where both substance and procedures of the law are interpreted and honed. All states, and the federal jurisdiction, have lower and intermediate trial courts and higher courts of appeal, eventually including the United States Supreme Court. Yet, variety within and between jurisdictions is the rule, and everywhere the control of lower by higher courts is largely indirect (except in cases of gross malfeasance) and inferential by the slow, case-by-case appellate process.

There is no pattern of criminal-court organization common to all jurisdictions, nor are there uniform standards and procedures for selection of court personnel (President's Commission, 1967a). As a matter of fact, inquiry as to the number of criminal courts cannot be answered without many qualifications, for determining what is a criminal court is a matter of choice among various definitions. In the federal as well as all state jurisdictions, there are courts with authority to try felony matters. These courts are located in most counties in all states (there are some regional courts in rural areas that combine counties into common jurisdictions), but there are often many felony courts or many branches of a felony court in metropolitan areas. Even more widely distributed are the so-called lower courts, with jurisdiction to try misdemeanors, traffic violations, ordinance infractions, and the like. Most of these courts, intermediate and lower alike, are involved only part-time with criminal matters; many have concurrent civil jurisdiction and, in fact, operate most frequently there.

Only in the most congested areas with correspondingly high crime rates are there courts with jurisdiction limited solely to criminal matters. Some states have youth courts to process offender populations who fall somewhere between the upper age of delinquency and the lower age of eligibility for felony trial. In some of the largest cities specialization of courts goes beyond even this to include separate courts for dealing with certain types of offenses and offenders. In some cities there are, for example, vice courts, rackets courts, homicide courts, narcotics courts, and the like. There are multi-judge courts and single-judge courts. There are courts with full-time prosecutors and in some rural areas there are courts with district attorneys who are only part-time. In some counties or jurisdictions there may be a single prosecutor to service one or more courts where in others a prosecutor may have hundreds of lawyer assistants, some specializing in certain types of crimes or dealing with certain types of offenders.

This variability in court organization, coupled with the complex mixture of autonomy and functional interdependence of roles found in any court, accounts in good part for both the problems currently confronting criminal courts, from overcrowding to sentence disparity, and the difficulties experienced by virtually all court-reform programs. There is no way to simply order greater efficiency, to command better effectiveness, to legislate uniformity in decision-making. Budget and facilities are important but peripheral to the central concerns of role and function in the court process.

COURT PERSONNEL

The Criminal-Court Judge

The trial judge is not only a symbol of justice but a trier of facts, the chief officer of an administrative agency, and in his own right, a critical decision-maker in criminal justice with his influence having consequences both for the earlier agencies of criminal justice and for postconviction correctional programs as well. The President's Commission put it this way:

> The trial judge is at the center of the criminal process, and he exerts a powerful influence on the stages of the process which precede and follow his formal participation. Many decisions of police, prosecutors, and defense counsel are determined by the trial judge's rulings, by his sentencing practices, and even by the speed with which he disposes of cases. His decisions on sentencing and probation revocation affect the policies and procedures of correctional agencies. And to a great degree the public's impression of justice is shaped by the trial judge's demeanor and the dignity he imparts to the proceedings in his courtroom (1967*a*, p. 65).

Judges are selected for office in a variety of ways. In most states trial judges are elected and, furthermore, in most of these states they run for office on a partisan basis having been nominated by a political party for the judgeship (President's Commission, 1967*a*). In a number of other states judges stand for popular election as nonpartisans, getting their names on the ballot by circulating petitions to obtain a required number of voter signatures. In nine states judges are appointed by the governor or by local executives, and in the federal system judges are appointed by the president with the consent of the Senate. In five states judges are appointed (or, as in Vermont, elected) by the legislature. In ten states judges are selected by the "Missouri Plan" (it was first adopted in Missouri in 1940) that involves the following procedures: qualified candidates are nominated by a nonpartisan commission, judges are originally appointed by the chief executive (the governor, mayor, or other local authority) and approved at the next election by the voters. After a term of office, the incumbent judge runs for office again, not against another candidate but on the basis of his own record. In effect, he asks a vote of confidence from the voters. Should the vote be negative, the selection process begins over again.

Judicial selection procedures are felt by many to be an important way to strengthen or reform the criminal justice system, and there are many long-standing arguments about the relative value of merit selection (nonpartisan, bar-association approval, Missouri Plan) as against political campaigning. In general those favoring merit selection argue that such screening enables the best-qualified, most honest candidates to obtain office without incurring political debt or obligation. On the other hand, critics of merit selection point out that such procedures are essentially political anyway ("Are there nonpolitical federal judges?") and result in selection of judges who are not representative of a large segment of the community, more particularly that such procedures exclude members of minority groups. In general, the President's Commission on Law Enforcement and Administration of Justice took the position that merit selection is the best alternative (1967a, pp. 67–68).

Judges hold office for various lengths of time. The federal judiciary has life tenure, but in some states the terms of office are as short as four years. More commonly terms range from six to ten years, with a possibility of reelection for life or until a mandatory retirement age defined by statute in some states.

At the felony-court level, there is a universal requirement that the judge be minimally qualified by admission to the bar. This does not necessarily mean that he has received a legal education or has graduated from an accredited law school. Though the apprenticeship system is disappearing by both law and custom, in some states persons can still become members of the bar by passing an examination after fulfilling office-practice training requirements. In lower courts (justice-of-the-peace courts, coroner's courts, and other magistrate's courts) incumbents in some jurisdictions are not mandated to be either a member of the bar or a trained lawyer.

By and large, the American trial judge receives no formal training or even any kind of apprenticeship in the judicial function. For example, while most new trial judges have had some prior experience in the private practice of law, a survey by the Institute of Judicial Administration showed that 25 percent of the judges who responded indicated that their practice included *no* criminal cases. No judge who responded had specialized in criminal law practice (President's Commission, 1967a, p. 68). Except in moot-court competition (a voluntary activity), most law schools provide little educational exposure to trial-court activities. In fact, the typical law graduate is much more familiar with the roles and functions of a Supreme Court justice than those of a trial judge.

There are some attempts today to provide judicial training for new judges in short-course summer institutes, like those conducted by the National College of State Trial Judges (an affiliate of the American Bar Association). But here, as in law-school training, the emphasis is largely on the adjudicatory function, stressing the appropriate conduct and procedures for trial. Until very recently, and still more common than not, that component of legal education devoted to criminal law emphasized substantive law and procedure only up through adjudication, with even this focused largely on the trial and not the guilty plea. Sentencing and all postconviction processes (except appeal of conviction) were, and are, largely foreign to legal education and, for that matter, rarely experienced in the practice of law.

By far the most unfamiliar and most uncomfortable task of the new judge is sentencing. There is currently increasing attention to sentencing and the postconviction processes in law-school curricula, and the federal government and many states are conducting sentencing institutes for judges in an attempt to make the process more rational and to reduce sentence disparity (Remington & Newman, 1962).

The Prosecutor

The prosecutor not only has an intrinsically important role in American criminal justice but the office itself is historically and theoretically important in American jurisprudence. Prosecutors have functioned prominently in both federal and state jurisdictions since colonial times. The origins of both the office and the traditional "prosecutor's discretion" have been traced to both early English and French common law (Baker & DeLong, 1934; Grosman, 1969). Interestingly, the prosecutor as we know him is virtually absent from European criminal justice, which operates largely under systems of private prosecution with public prosecutors acting only in very serious or unusual cases. In the United States, however, public prosecutors (generally called district attorneys) are necessary in all jurisdictions, for private prosecution of crimes is not permissible in our system.

In almost all jurisdictions the prosecutor is a locally elected official. In the federal system prosecutors, like judges, are appointed by the president but, unlike the judiciary, do not have life tenure, serving rather at the pleasure of the incumbent executive. Only four states provide for appointment of prosecutors, but even here political considerations play an important role (Nedrud, 1960; President's Commission, 1967a). The tenure of the prosecutor is normally much shorter than that of the judge, with most counties or districts requiring election every two or four years.

By and large, the office of prosecutor is viewed differently from a judgeship by both candidates and incumbents of both offices. Elevation to the bench tends to cap a career of law practice; the typical district attorney is at the beginning or middle of his career, with higher office or a more lucrative practice hoped for in the future. There are comparatively few career prosecutors (Nedrud, 1960) for this office is commonly a stepping-stone into politics or on to the bench (a comparatively high proportion of trial-court judges were at one time or another employed in prosecutor's offices) or, more subtly, candidacy for office (even if unsuccessful) is a way for local attorneys to become known, for the code of professional ethics forbids a lawyer to advertise. In any event, the office of district attorney is highly political, even more so than judges who have achieved office, because of the necessity for the DA to stand more frequently for election. A two-year term for a new DA often means the first year of learning the job, the second of campaigning for reelection. Yet the office is powerful and relatively independent from both the judiciary and from the other criminal justice agencies, including the police.

Like judges, the minimum requirement for prosecutors is membership in the bar; but unlike the situation with most felony-court judges, a number of prosecutors in small rural districts are only part-time office holders, the remainder of their activity being devoted to the private practice of law. In large cities prosecuting attorneys are usually full-time and may have a legal staff numbering in the hundreds, with job security of these assistants protected by civil-service regulations.

In slightly over half of the states, prosecutors share with grand juries the decision of whether to charge a defendant with a crime and, if so, the specific crime and number of counts to be brought. In secret proceedings the prosecutor brings the case to the grand jury, presenting to them such evidence as, in his estimation, is sufficient to convince them to issue an indictment. In the remaining states, where grand juries are not required or may be waived, prosecution is based on a document called an *information* that, like the indictment, lists in formal language the specific criminal charges on which prosecution is based. The information is drafted by the prosecutor without jury screening but is tested for "probable cause" at a preliminary hearing before a judge, unless such hearing is waived by the defendant with consent of the state (Hall et al., 1969).

The value of the grand jury as "shield and sword" of prosecution has been long debated (Hall et al., 1969, pp. 788, 791) for, as might be expected, grand juries indict in the vast majority of cases when requested to do so by the prosecutor (Morse, 1931). But this is also the case with bind-overs following preliminary hearings; in most instances the judge finds sufficient evidence to hold the defendant for trial. The relative worth of each procedure cannot fairly be assessed by whether the prosecutor "wins" or "loses" on probable cause for there are many other factors to be considered, including some that touch basic values in our criminal justice ideology. For example, the grand-jury system represents a method of citizen participation in the charging process, bringing all the pros and cons of judgment by peers to the pretrial stage. Grand-jury deliberations are closed, which has the advantage of preventing detailed and perhaps damaging pretrial publicity, but since they are closed to defense as well as the press, there is no opportunity for the defendant to learn anything of the state's case against him. In contrast the major defense advantage of the preliminary hearing is discovery (Hall et al, 1969; Miller, 1969), but the corresponding disadvantage is public revelation of the state's accusations without, in most cases, the defense being revealed.

The Trial Jury

The right to trial by jury in criminal matters is guaranteed in the Constitution (Article 3, Section 2) and, as a matter of fact, because of the particular wording "trial of all crimes ... shall be by jury," there was a long-standing controversy whether jury trials could be waived, that is, whether all defendants *must* be tried. By and large, court decisions have allowed waiver of jury trial [*Patton* v. *United States,* 281 U.S. 276 (1930)], although waiver is not allowed in some states in certain serious felony matters, particularly where capital crimes are charged (*Cornell Law Quarterly,* 1966, pp. 339, 342–43).

The idea of judgment by peers is deeply imbedded in our political philosophy where, as in criminal matters, the state is seen as potentially repressive and the system as basically punitive. Yet, in practice such judgment is frequently waived by defendants who opt for bench trials (the judge alone) or who plead guilty. When state intervention is defined as beneficent, as in juvenile-delinquency proceedings, the jury ideology weakens [*McKeiver* v. *Penna.* 403 U.S. 528 (1971); Griffiths, 1970]. Criticism of the jury system in criminal cases generally does not challenge its ideological significance, but relates rather to the administration of juror selection procedures and to strategies employed by attorneys to manipulate decisions on emotional rather than rational grounds (Broeder, 1954; Hall et al., 1969).

Extensive studies of criminal juries and their use have shown that jury trials are used in about 15 percent of prosecutions for major crimes (Kalven & Zeisel, 1966, p. 18) and much less frequently in minor crimes and misdemeanors. Judges and juries agree on the outcome of cases about 75 percent of the time, with the jury *less* lenient than the judge in 3 percent of the cases, and more lenient 19 percent of the time (p. 59). While these data suggest that it is advantageous for a defendant to seek judgment by jury, the authors warn against such generalization since the initial decision to take a case to jury trial rests in good part in the belief that it is the type of case to elicit prodefendant sentiment.

The jury studies were concerned with the relative impact of skilled (or unskilled) defense counsel on jury decision-making. In an elaborate analysis of the lawyer factor (the balance of skills between prosecution and defense), Kalven and Zeisel estimate the impact of counsel on the system to be only about 1 percent, but add:

> The figure should not be misread. In 25 per cent of the cases in which defense counsel is superior, he will have some share in moving the jury toward disagreement. But more important, the lawyer's role is not exhausted by consideration of the disagreement cases alone, since in the vast majority of trials, counsel on both sides are evenly matched. And, indeed, it might be well said that the great role of the defense lawyer, as an institution, is to keep the trial process in balance so that the adversary system can function (1966, p. 372).

Selecting a jury of peers, in the common meaning of the term, could perhaps only be realized, if ever, in colonial America when we were a country of small towns and villages. Even then blacks and women were excluded. Today there is a question of the feasibility of even approximating this ideal jury plan, particularly in metropolitan courts and—for a variety of reasons—even in smaller jurisdictions as well. Part of this concern relates to selection procedures, primarily certain exclusion practices that by law or custom keep those without property or permanent residence, particularly members of ethnic and racial minorities, off jury panels. Because criminal defendants are often poor, transient, and members of minority groups, such exclusions are felt to weaken the spirit, if not the letter, of the law in regard to peer judgment. Another part of the concern is with the grossly inadequate facilities and compensation for jurors (and for witnesses as well) that in most jurisdictions make jury duty an unpleasant and unwelcome task for those who are selected. The President's Commission, in recommending improved treatment of both jurors and witnesses, commented:

> Compensation is generally so low that service as a juror or witness is a serious financial burden. . . . The economic impact bears most harshly on people whose wages are usually paid on an hourly or daily basis. Such experiences can only aggravate the feeling of a major segment of the community that the law does them no good (1967a, p. 90).

The trial jury is best known in its adjudicatory capacity. Yet, in a number of jurisdictions, it also has a sentencing function. It is common in those states sanctioning capital punishment for certain crimes to give the jury the final decision as to the death sentence (Virginia Law Review, 1967, p. 968). This is no longer possible because the death penalty was outlawed by the Supreme Court [*Furman* v. *Georgia,* 408 U.S. 238 (1971)]. Twelve states provide for jury sentencing in noncapital cases.

Seven of these give sentencing authority to juries in *all* serious crimes, four restrict the jury function to certain types of offenses, and one (Texas) allows the defendant to request jury sentencing if he so desires [LaFont, 1960, p. 38; Texas Code Crim. Proc., Art. 37.07 (1966)].

The Defense Attorney

Though the right to a jury trial is as old as the Constitution (with an even longer historical precedent), the right of the accused to be represented by counsel at trial is a recent development. While the affluent could always retain lawyers privately to conduct their defenses, indigent defendants had no constitutional right to counsel, except in capital cases, until the Supreme Court so decided in 1963 (*Gideon* v. *Wainwright*, 372 U.S. 335). Overturning a prior Supreme Court holding, the *Gideon* decision extended the right of representation to all defendants, indigent or otherwise, at trial on any charge that carries the possibility of a "substantial prison sentence." This was held to include all felonies and serious misdemeanors, and it was subsequently interpreted to include trials involving petty misdemeanors as well [*Argersinger* v. *Hamlin*, 407 U.S. 25 (1972)]. Though the factual situation in *Gideon* limited the right to counsel at trial, it was subsequently extended to apply to guilty-plea proceedings as well (Newman, 1966). Coming as late in history as it did, the *Gideon* decision probably surprised many Americans who had assumed a right to representation all along. Only those most familiar with courts and criminal procedure were fully aware of the limitations of the right prior to this holding. While a number of states had statutory provisions for counsel, a number did not; but as a result of *Gideon*, the right now applies as a constitutional matter to all jurisdictions. Though representation may be waived by the defendant, it is more common today—in fact, almost routine in many jurisdictions—for defendants in serious criminal cases to be represented by lawyers whether they go to trial, plead guilty, or have charges dismissed.

Privately retained counsel always played an important part in the criminal-court process and the *Gideon* decision and subsequent developments entrenched the counsel's role as a major one in criminal matters and, of course, added great importance to the functions of public defenders or court-assigned lawyers. The initial impact of *Gideon* was to put a strain on available resources, particularly because a series of other Supreme Court decisions at about the same time expanded the right to counsel at "critical stages" other than trial—from early police stages [*Miranda* v. *Arizona*, 384 U.S. 436 (1966)] to sentencing and appeal [*Douglas* v. *California*, 372 U.S. 353 (1963); *Mempa* v. *Rhay*, 389 U.S. 128 (1967)], so that the distribution of legal services became a major problem in many places. Various methods of providing counsel for indigents were developed or expanded, the two major forms being court assignment of lawyers from bar association lists and the development of public defender and other legal-aid services (Silverstein, 1956). Some experimental programs, such as "Judicare," allowed defendants to select their own attorneys with the fee (80 percent of standard fees) being paid by the government.

Studies of the comparative merits of different methods of providing legal services, whether such analysis is based on cost or performance, are generally inconclusive (Silverstein, 1956, p. 73). One argument for the public-defender system is that the lawyer in this office is a specialist in criminal defense and, therefore, more equal in skill to the prosecutor than a randomly assigned lawyer, not only in knowledge of criminal law and procedure but in terms of informal court practices, such as plea negotiation. Assigned lawyers may have neither sufficient criminal-law knowledge nor defense skill and may not even be aware of hallway-bargaining practices. On the other hand, it is argued that if an assignment system is widely used so that eventually all lawyers in a jurisdiction rotate through criminal cases, the result will be involvement of the "better" lawyers, now largely concerned with more lucrative civil practice, in criminal matters. Furthermore, bar-wide involvement of attorneys will generate an interest and concern about criminal justice issues among lawyers at large and, given their collective influence in politics and governmental administration, in turn will eventually lead to improvements in the entire system.

With the exception of experienced public defenders and a handful of specializing criminal lawyers, few members of the bar are really familiar with criminal law and procedure, nor do they rely to any great extent on income derived from the defense of criminal cases. A major study of the *criminal lawyer* used as a working definition of this term lawyers who specified that 10 percent or more of their practice was in criminal law (Wood, 1967). There are a few courthouse regulars in larger communities whose practice is limited to criminal defense but almost all attorneys who appear in criminal court receive the major share of their income and have their major professional interest in other types of law practice (Blaustein & Porter, 1954; Wood, 1967).

Generally speaking, admission to the bar requires formal education, the passing of an examination, and certification as to moral fitness. Though bar admission by apprenticeship in a law office is still with us, increasingly American lawyers are the products of law schools (Carlin, 1962; Johnstone & Hopson, 1967). A fairly large segment of the bar who practice regularly in the criminal courts come from lower- and middle-class families, particularly in large cities. Older minority ethnicity (Irish, Polish, Italian) is heavily represented in criminal law practice; racial minorities are not. Blacks, for example, account for only approximately 1 percent of all American lawyers (Johnstone & Hopson, 1967).

Probation Officers

The authority of the trial court extends beyond imposition of sentence to encompass continued control over offenders who are placed on probation. In addition to his adjudication and sentencing functions, the judge has final responsibility for probation revocation hearings. In any given year over half of all adult felony offenders are placed on probation, thus remaining within the jurisdiction and control of the trial court while they serve their sentences (President's Commission, 1967b). In juvenile courts it is common for the judge to be the chief administrator of the probation service, but in adult felony courts the judge less often has such direct responsibilities as hiring, firing, and setting standards for the work of probation staff. In most jurisdictions adult probation personnel are employees of a state correctional system or of a separate, statewide probation service and, thereby, do not owe job security to any particular judge. In some thirteen states, however, adult probation services are entirely local operations, staffed, funded, and administered by local courts. The reasons for variations in probation organization are many, probably accidents of history in a number of instances, yet it is of some significance that in larger states, particularly those with extensive metropolitan centers, probation is commonly administered on a city or county rather than a statewide basis. In such cases, judicial control and intervention can be much more direct and influential. Attempts to merge probation services into a state organization, whether integrated with parole and other correctional programs or not, have been resisted on various grounds, among them the great cost and administrative complexity that would result if the state attempted to merge myriad local agencies (President's Commission, 1967b, p. 36). It is likely however, that the basis of resistance to merger is more than economic; efforts in this regard threaten the autonomy, lessen the power, and decrease the functions of trial judges.

Whatever the administrative structure in any jurisdiction, probation agents are officers of the trial court and their clients remain under court jurisdiction. Probation officers service the court in two major ways: first by the collection and preparation of presentencing information for the judge to use in sentence determination, and second by community supervision of those offenders whom the court places on probation. In some places probation officers are also expected to conduct recognizance bail investigations, to collect debts, fines, costs, and damages as ordered by the court, to initiate revocations when circumstances call for it, to return absconders, and generally to perform such other duties as the judge may see as relevant to the court's postconviction function.

Although probation officers are accountable to the judge and in some cases are actual employees of the court, probation services are still relatively autonomous, somewhat comparable to the prosecutor's office but with significant differences. Nowhere are probation officers elected officials and the probation agent is the only major participant in the trial-court process who is not a lawyer. He tends to identify his professional development not with law, or even with courts, but with the field of social work generally or corrections in particular (Miles, 1963).

The probation officer ordinarily has a marked effect on the sentencing process because he controls the kind of information that is presented to the judge. The judge rarely knows much from personal contact about the offender before him for sentencing except from impressions formed if there has been a trial. In most cases, of course, conviction is by plea and there has been no trial. The typical arraignment reveals little of use to sentencing. Though sentencing authority is formally vested only with the judge, it is clear in practice that both the preconviction activities of the prosecutor in charging and the presentence investigation reports of probation officers are significant, if not actually determinant, factors in the sentencing decision (Dawson, 1969).

Other Court Personnel

Besides the major actors of judge, jury, prosecutor, defense counsel, and probation staff, there are a variety of other personnel attached to, involved in, or otherwise affecting the criminal-court process. Clerks, stenographers, bailiffs, bondsmen, and jailers are all daily participants in or near the courtroom. Some courts have diagnostic services, often called "psychopathic clinics," attached directly to them and used to test the competency of defendants or witnesses or for making sentencing recommendations. These clinics are staffed by psychiatrists, psychologists, and social workers who act in part as a diagnostic aid to the probation service, yet are independent from it. In addition, in a number of jurisdictions there are court administrators who supervise the budget and logistics of the court process. Controls on the substantive work of courts, that is, on adjudicatory and sentencing decisions, are accomplished by the appellate process; the court administrator, on the other hand, functions to improve the efficiency of the court calendar, to balance work loads, and to supervise the activities of nonjudicial court personnel. The President's Commission recommended that the office of court administrator also function to conduct research on court processes in order to make recommendations to state judicial conferences for trial-court improvements (President's Commission, 1967*a*, pp. 95-96).

Nonjudicial court personnel, while not directly responsible for major decisions about defendants, nevertheless are important actors in ways both direct and subtle in the operations of the court. Calender clerks, for example, play an important informal role by cooperating with defense counsel in the practice of "judge shopping." This is common in multi-judge metropolitan courts where attorneys seek to plead their clients guilty or have them sentenced by a particular judge believed to be lenient in the type of case at hand. To anyone unfamiliar with the daily operations of a trial court, the whole process, even the aura of the courthouse, is confused and cluttered. Court personnel have the important task of steering lawyers, defendants, complainants, witnesses, and family and friends of the accused through the maze of forms and procedures of the court bureaucracy. All this takes place in a setting that is typically overcrowded, staffed by stern officials, and with both defendants and witnesses reluctant, if not hostile. To the extent that the court symbolizes as well as dispenses justice, the impact of processing on defendants and others is dependent, in good part, on the activities of supporting personnel. Decorum may be of minor operational significance, yet the sordidness and appalling confusion that is characteristic of many metropolitan lower courts often makes the entire process a literal degradation ceremony, far from the ideal of ordered liberty and justice.

STAGES IN THE CRIMINAL-COURT PROCESS

Different individuals processed through the entire criminal justice system from arrest to sentence may have significantly diverse experiences though they are accused, indeed convicted, of common offenses. One person may be summoned to the process, appearing in court on his own initiative at a time specified in a citation or summons. Another, suspected of the same crime, may be forcibly arrested by the police with or without warrant, interrogated, held in custody, and taken under secure conditions to the court. At initial court contact, one suspect may be immediately released on bail—monetary or recognizance—while his counterpart is held in detention awaiting further proceedings. A defendant may request and receive privately retained or court-assigned counsel; another may opt to waive his right to representation and go it alone. One may have a full-scale jury trial, the other stand convicted by his own plea. The first may be in court for days, weeks, even months, whereas the entire judicial contact of the other may total only a few minutes. One offender may be placed on probation, the other incarcerated in jail or prison. In brief, while the processes of the criminal justice system can be neatly sketched and the flow of cases traced in uniform array from intake to sentencing, the experiences of different defendants, though formally following the same system, may be grossly different. One defendant can go through the criminal justice system without being in physical custody except momentarily, whereas his counterpart can be forcibly held from the moment of his arrest until the completion of his prison sentence. Obviously, though the system is the same, the objective and subjective experiences of the two defendants in alternative processes are worlds apart.

Beyond the question of bail or jail awaiting trial, and prison or probation following it, defendants' experiences in the processes of the court itself can be quite distinct. A person who is represented by counsel from his initial bail-setting appearance may demand and receive the entire panoply of procedural due process up through and including sentencing. He may challenge his continued custody, the charges brought against him, the admissibility of state's evidence, the decision to bind him over for trial, the quantum of evidence sufficient to convict him beyond a reasonable doubt, and the reasons and rationale for his sentence. Utilizing all available pretrial motions, using the adversary process to its fullest, and taking advantage of appeal procedures mean that the court stage of the process will likely extend over a period of months, even years. In a fully litigated case, a defendant's "day in court" may be a long day indeed. In contrast, a defendant with or without the advice of counsel who waives most formal procedures, including trial, and does nothing to challenge the contentions of the state, indeed cooperates by confessing and pleading guilty, may move very rapidly through the court stages of the process with his day in court shrunk to a few minutes. There is, in fact, some concern on the part of judges and others with too rapid processing. Instances have been noted where defendants, arrested in the morning, have arrived at prison in the afternoon to begin serving a sentence. These "quick justice" convictions are the reciprocal to the problem of delay and, like delay, are receiving increased attention by appellate courts (Newman, 1966).

Given the extremes in both the time and substance of court contacts, it is not possible to trace a single, uniform, typical trial-court process. Various stages where critical decisions about defendants are made can be extracted for analysis but, with the possibility of waiver and of other differential experiences and with variations in procedures from one jurisdiction to the next, at most, these stages remain as abstractions rather than as descriptions of operational reality.

Initial Appearance and Bail

The first court appearance of a suspect arrested for a crime is at a proceeding commonly called *initial appearance before a magistrate.* This is perhaps the least generally understood step in the process, often confused with a preliminary hearing (which is a later proceeding to determine whether or not the state has sufficient evidence to hold the defendant for trial) or with arraignment (which is the time at which a defendant is required to plead to the charges against him). The confusion here is compounded in some jurisdictions where the initial appearance is called *arraignment on the warrant.*

The primary purpose of initial appearance is to determine whether the individual will be released on bail or retained in custody awaiting further processing. In minor offenses the initial magistrate may have jurisdiction to try the case, to accept a guilty plea, and perhaps to levy a fine. This is common, for example, in cases involving traffic violations and other minor misdemeanors. But in serious cases, particularly those involving felonies, the substance of the charge is not litigated here; the jurisdiction of the magistrate is limited to fixing or denying bail. The initial appearance does not test the validity of the arrest, nor is the defendant required to plead to any allegations against him. Provision for initial appearance is made in the statutes or by court rule, and its purpose is to provide a check on the power of the police to hold and interrogate suspects for extended periods of time. A common pattern of control in the criminal justice system is the submission of operational decisions to a neutral authority—judge or referee—in order to provide defendants with protection from excessive intervention by the state. The initial appearance is one illustration of this pattern; the full scale trial, another. Statutory language in most jurisdictions requires that the initial appearance be conducted at the "first opportunity" (i.e., when the court is next open) or within a "reasonable time" after arrest. A significant decision in the federal jurisdiction [*Mallory* v. *United States,* 354 U.S. 449 (1957)] requires suspects to be brought *immediately* before a magistrate. Among other consequences, the "*Mallory* rule" resulted in availability of around-the-clock magistrates in federal jurisdictions. Requirements in most state jurisdictions are not this stringent; in fact, a practice noted in some places is the "Friday-night arrest," giving the police opportunity for in-custody interrogation until the court opens on Monday (LaFave, 1965).

The historical purpose of bail was to control unfettered discretion of the police power of the state by providing defendants with an opportunity for freedom from incarceration prior to trial. The monetary basis of bail—the bail bond—was to insure the return of the defendant with forfeiture added to the other costs and consequences of flight. While some offenses, mostly capital crimes, are defined by statute in some jurisdictions as nonbailable, access to reasonable bail is granted as a right in all jurisdictions for all but these few crimes. The amount of bail fixed by the magistrate must not be "excessive" in violation of the Eighth Amendment to the Constitution.

The monetary bail system in the United States has long been subject to criticism and attack (Foote, 1965; Hall et al., 1969), not only because of the obvious discrimination against poor defendants, but also because of its alleged use for purposes, mostly punitive, other than assurance of appearance at trial (Freed & Wald, 1964; Hall et al., 1969). Within the past decade bail practices have been systematically studied and modified in many jurisdictions. Sparked by the research and experimentation of the Vera Foundation, major bail reforms are now operative many places throughout the country. The basis of this reform is primarily ROR (release on recognizance), in which an investigation of the defendant is made for the purpose of determining his likelihood of reappearing for trial without the necessity of monetary bonding.

Experience has shown that defendants with strong local ties, such as permanent residence and employment, are as likely to show up for later processing on their own word as on their bond (Freed & Wald, 1964). Release-on-recognizance was undoubtedly one of the major reforms in criminal justice administration during the 1960s. Research demonstrated rather dramatically that whether a person was released or not had important subsequent consequences on his fate, including the type of sentence imposed by the judge; defendants released on recognizance were much more likely to receive probation than those held in custody until arraignment or trial (Freed & Wald, 1964, pp. 61–63).

In 1966 Congress enacted a Bail Reform Act, which incorporates provisions for recognizance release (Hall et al., 1969). Although ROR programs proliferated after the early Manhattan Bail Project, there has also been opposition to pretrial release programs. A number of "preventive detention" proposals (of debated constitutionality) would enable the court to deny pretrial release, not so much because of risk of flight, but to prevent the defendant from committing "new crimes" while awaiting trial (Harvard Law Review, 1966; American Bar Association, 1968*b*).

Determination of the Charge

A suspect may be arrested on complaint or suspicion, with or without warrant, and searched and interrogated as incident to the arrest and prior to an initial appearance before a magistrate. Supreme Court decisions of recent years have placed more stringent controls on these processes [*Mapp* v. *Ohio*, 367 U.S. 643 (1961); *Miranda* v. *Arizona; United States* v. *Wade*, 388 U.S. 218 (1967)] but, in general, as a case proceeds onward from the initial intake of arrest, evidence of guilt or innocence accumulates. At some point, sometimes as early as the issuance of an arrest warrant but more often later as evidence builds, the prosecuting attorney is called upon to make a decision in regard to the formal charge or charges he will seek in an indictment or will present at a preliminary hearing.

The charging process is complex (Miller, 1969). Generally, although it is within the prosecutor's authority, in practice it involves the interaction of the police, the grand jury (where necessary), and even the judge (McIntyre, 1968). The charging decision involves more than questions of evidence, although these are of central concern, because it also rests on the discretionary authority of the prosecutor. District attorneys in our system of justice have a traditional power of *nolle prosequi* (sometimes provided in statute, but originating in common law) by which they can decide *not* to prosecute for reasons unrelated to evidence sufficiency (Miller, 1969, pp. 312–16).

Common practice is for the police, after arresting and booking a suspect (and conducting him through initial appearance), to turn over their files to a district attorney for determination of both the desirability of and necessary "probable cause" for prosecution. In some cases, particularly in major crimes, the prosecutor may be involved earlier in the process, perhaps actually conducting all in-custody interrogation or otherwise participating on-scene in the intake process. In more routine cases, however, the district attorney does not see the defendant this early but receives an up-to-date police file on the case after the defendant is arrested and booked. In reading the file and perhaps questioning the arresting officer or the complainant, he decides whether to initiate a charge at all, and if so, which crime or crimes and how many counts of each will be leveled.

In evaluating the evidence at hand and estimating the likelihood of obtaining further evidence, the prosecutor presumably brings his legal training to bear in applying the evidence standard necessary for charging. This is normally phrased as "probable cause" to believe that a crime was committed and that the person in question was the one who committed it. The words of this test, while identical or similar to the "probable cause" or "reasonable cause" necessary to effect an arrest, have a different reference basis for the district attorney than for the policeman on the street. The interest of the prosecutor is the applicability of the evidence at possible trial. While he can, indeed, charge a defendant on evidence less than the "beyond a reasonable doubt" needed to convict, his orientation must be to this higher test. The policeman needs only to look backward, assuring himself that the evidence is sufficient to prevent his paying damages in a civil suit for false imprisonment (commonly called *false arrest*). But in making the charging determination, the prosecutor must weigh numerous factors of the *quality* of his case, such as credibility of witnesses, any likely or probable defenses, the skill or reputation of defense counsel, and similar tactical variables, all tested against the probability of winning or losing at trial. In short, it is possible for a suspect to be validly arrested on probable cause and yet not be charged with a crime when the evidence is assessed by the prosecutor's operational meaning of the probable cause standard.

Assuming a decision to prosecute, the legal task of the district attorney is to translate the factual basis of the complaint into the technical language of appropriate statutes, making reasonably certain that the evidence is sufficient to prove all required elements of the crime, from the mental state required of the perpetrator to the consequences of his conduct. Arrest for homicide is necessarily translated into some degree of murder, manslaughter, or related offense. In addition to determining the statutory basis of each charge, the prosecutor must also decide the number of different charges to bring or the number of counts of any particular crime, for in many cases the alleged criminal conduct of a defendant violates several different statutes or he has been arrested for not one but a series of crimes. Issues of joinder or severance, both of offenses and of codefendants into single or separate trials, are complex, controlled in part by statutory law and in part by policies of prosecutors (Remington & Joseph, 1961; Hall et al., 1969). The American Bar Association has issued standards covering these matters (1968c).

When decisions on the charge or charges rest solely on questions of evidence and the probability of conviction, they reflect the legal competence, experience, and confidence of the prosecutor. Under these conditions, the decision is more or less a traditional lawyer's task, justifying both the need for law training and for some experience in the prosecutorial role. More complex and controversial than reading and applying statutes, however, is the broader exercise of the prosecutor's discretion. This makes the office much more than a gatekeeper of the courts, for it enables the prosecutor to determine the *desirability* of prosecution in addition to determining the odds of conviction or acquittal.

The exercise of this discretion, as with charge determination, has both qualitative and quantitative aspects. Qualitatively, the question is whether, in the judgment of the district attorney, the accused *ought* to be charged with a crime at all, or if in the interest of equity, individualization of justice, or mitigating circumstances, it would be fairer, more just, or sufficient for the purposes of law and the objectives of his office to refrain from prosecuting at all. The quantitative facet relates to the *vigor* of prosecution once it is determined to be possible and desirable. In some cases the prosecutor may charge a crime as serious as the evidence permits, may multiply charges to their fullest, or may even level "extra-maximum" charges by invoking habitual-criminal statutes or similar provisions. Contrariwise, he may ignore the highest crime and prosecute for a lesser included offense, perhaps reduce a felony charge to a misdemeanor, or otherwise pursue prosecution with less vigor than both his authority and the evidence would permit. In operation, the exercise of this quantitative discretion often rests on the desire of the state to negotiate a guilty plea. But apart from plea bargaining, this discretion is clearly within the prosecutor's authority and is an important facet at the charging stage of the process (Baker, 1933; Breitel, 1960; Packer, 1964; Davis 1969; Hall et al., 1969).

Once the district attorney has decided to initiate prosecution, the formal charge is prepared in one of two ways depending upon provisions in the particular jurisdiction. In those states that use the grand-jury system, the prosecutor presents to the jury such evidence as he feels will result in a "true bill"—a formal indictment listing the specific criminal charge or charges on which the defendant will be tried. Grand juries are selected in similar fashion to trial juries, though in composition they are larger and in functioning they are not bound to render a unanimous decision. Typically, such juries are selected and impaneled to meet for a given period of time—a month or a term of the court—acting as needed to consider matters brought to them by the prosecuting attorney. Grand-jury proceedings are secret with neither the defendant nor his counsel normally in attendance. Only the state's side of the case is presented; only that amount of the evidence sufficient to result in indictment need be revealed to the grand jury.

In jurisdictions where the grand jury is not necessary or where it may be waived, the prosecutor drafts the formal charge in an information, testing its sufficiency for bind-over before a judge at a preliminary hearing. This hearing may be waived by the defendant (with consent of the state, which may demand it for a number of reasons, most frequently to preserve testimony which might "disappear" by the time of trial), but, unlike grand-jury proceedings, it is attended by the defendant and counsel and, for that matter, it is open to the press. As with indictment, the prosecutor need introduce only that amount of evidence sufficient to convince the magistrate of probable cause. The defense, however, can challenge the state's evidence if it wishes by cross-examination of witnesses and similar procedures. The defendant has no need to introduce evidence in his own behalf, nor to reply in any way to the evidence presented by the prosecutor, but, at the same time, he cannot demand full disclosure of all the state's evidence. Yet, he may learn something of value to his defense and this is really why defendants, especially those represented by counsel, often demand preliminary hearings. Few defendants actually expect the hearing to result in anything but bind-over; discovery is the major operational motive for defense participation (Fletcher, 1960; Goldstein, 1960). One defendant disadvantage to demanding a hearing is the possibility of adverse publicity because, while it is open to press coverage, it is not a full trial. Generally, only damaging evidence against the defendant is introduced, and partially at that, while the other side of the story, the defense, will not be revealed until the trial, perhaps months in the future.

Arraignment

The next step in the court process is arraignment on the indictment or information, a procedure held in a court of competent trial jurisdiction during which the defendant is notified of his rights (including the right to representation and to jury trial), the formal charges are read, and he is asked to plead to them. Pleas available are not guilty, guilty, and in some instances and at the discretion of the court, *nolo contendere* ("not contested"), a plea that has the criminal effect of conviction but prevents the fact of conviction from being used in any civil damage suits arising from the criminal conduct of the defendants. In some jurisdictions, special pleas indicative of particular defenses to criminal liability are also available. "Not guilty because insane" is one of these. Some jurisdictions require disclosure of some anticipated defenses—insanity or an alibi, for example—at arraignment, in order to give the state time before trial to examine the defendant's mental condition or to investigate his whereabouts as stated in his alibi. If a defendant stands mute at arraignment, refusing to respond when asked to plead, or otherwise seems confused, hesitant, or incompetent, a not-guilty plea is entered for him.

If the plea is not guilty, the defendant is bound over for trial at a future date. Bail is reconsidered, with court options to continue bail or recognizance, increase or decrease the amount of the bond, or to deny bail altogether.

If the plea is guilty and is accepted by the court, a future date is set for sentencing with the intervening time used to conduct a presentence investigation. Occasionally, defendants are sentenced immediately after pleading guilty, particularly where mandatory sentences are prescribed so that the judge has no discretion and, therefore, no need for a presentence report. This is comparatively rare and even where it occurs, a correctional *admissions investigation,* similar to the presentence investigation, is often ordered. Although a defendant may plead guilty even with advice of counsel, the judge need not accept the plea, instead ordering the defendant held for trial. This is rare, occurring primarily because the judge somehow feels that the defendant is confused, ill advised, or that conviction as charged is somehow inappropriate. Some trial judges even *acquit* certain defendants even though they have indicated a willingness to plead guilty. Reasons for this are mixed and sometimes quite complex although, in general, these situations occur when the judge is convinced, in considering the total circumstances of the case, that a mandatory sentence following conviction is not warranted (Newman, 1966).

Procedures for accepting guilty pleas are generally simple, cursory, and quick, although the simplicity of the arraignment is now undergoing change. Traditionally, the judge was required to warn the defendant of his rights, to ascertain the "voluntary" basis of the plea, and to inform him of the consequences of his plea. This latter requirement is generally interpreted as requiring the judge to inform the defendant of the maximum sentence he *could* receive, not necessarily to inform him of all lesser alternatives or to reveal the actual sentence that will follow. Within the past few years, the federal and various state court systems have modified guilty-plea procedures, requiring much more elaboration than in the past. Until now the major inquiry at arraignment was directed to the consent of the defendant; that is, the judge was required to determine that the plea was freely and understandingly offered. If the plea was voluntary, free from coercion and wrongful inducement, evidence of actual guilt was superfluous. Now, however, court rules or statutes in a number of jurisdictions require the judge to satisfy himself that there is a "factual basis" for the plea. In short, some evidence of guilt is required, though it is not expressed as "beyond a reasonable doubt" as at the trial. Furthermore, there are some proposals under consideration at present to develop procedures for making plea-negotiation agreements part of the arraignment record [*People* v. *West*, 477 P. 2d 409 (1970); Fed. Rules Crim. Proc., Proposed Rev. Rule 11].

Pretrial Motions

Because of Supreme Court decisions in the 1960s restricting certain enforcement practices, pretrial hearings increased on the question of exclusion from trial of certain evidence held by the state. This increase in pretrial motions was sparked by the expansion of right to counsel, given substantial impetus by the decisions extending the exclusionary rule (the inadmissibility of illegally seized evidence) to all jurisdictions, and furthered by the *"Miranda warning"* type of control on the admissibility of confessions. Other decisions placed more stringent controls on evidence obtained from wiretapping, the use of lineup identification, and other police practices; in each instance the major method of control was exclusion of evidence from trial. Motions to exclude evidence after the trial has started are generally too late and too cumbersome, hence pretrial hearings involving these practices are common.

Pretrial-motion hearings are frequent enough today to be considered a distinct step in the judicial process. It should be noted, however, that Supreme Court holdings alone are insufficient to account for the increment in such hearings. Increase in enforcement intensity in cases involving organized crime and narcotics, where both eavesdropping and search are common enforcement techniques, also contributed to bringing these issues more frequently into criminal litigation. In most jurisdictions denial of pretrial motions to exclude evidence forces the defendant to go to trial if he wishes to appeal denial of exclusion; this factor alone may account for a significant number of demands for trial with corresponding delay in the court processes. Only New York allows appeal of denial of pretrial motions following a guilty plea [N. Y. Code Crim. Proc., Sec. 813 (C), 1968 Supp.].

The Trial

Defendants who decide to contest the accusations of the state have the option of a bench trial—conducted before the judge sitting without a jury—or a jury trial. Actual trial proceedings in either case are formal and rigidly circumscribed, elaborate ceremonies when serious felony charges are involved, but more casual, even tawdry, in lower courts hearing lesser charges. The trial process in some well-publicized cases has deviated markedly from the ceremonial ideal, with disruptions, violence, and contemptuous behavior—on both sides of the bench

(Schwartz, 1971)—evidenced in the courtroom. Professional organizations have issued standards for the control of courtroom disruptions (American College of Trial Lawyers, 1970) and for the lessening of possibly prejudicial press and media coverage (American Bar Association, 1968d).

The defendant is presumed innocent at the trial—all other stages of the process, from arrest on, operate on increasing probability of guilt —with the state having the burden of proving his guilt as charged, beyond a reasonable doubt. The defendant need not prove his innocence but only raise sufficient doubts of his guilt to win an acquittal. A verdict of not guilty terminates the case; protection against double jeopardy bars retrial. While in a few jurisdictions, the state may appeal an acquittal, the appeal is limited to matters of law—not to the finding of innocence (Kronenberg, 1959). Should the jury render a verdict of guilty, the judge may, in his discretion, set aside the verdict if, in his opinion, it is not substantiated by the evidence or is otherwise unwarranted. In fact, he may direct the jury to bring in a verdict of not guilty if, in his opinion, the evidence is insufficient to convict, but he cannot reverse a jury's decision to acquit even though he may be convinced personally that the defendant is guilty.

Sentencing

It is common practice in felony cases for the judge to order a presentence investigation of the defendant after he stands convicted by trial or plea. This investigation is usually conducted by the probation staff of the court and, depending upon their orientation, skills, case loads, and the time allowed, the report may pull together a wide variety of information about the offender, partly from official records—police, school, and employment—and partly from interviews with the defendant's family, neighbors, friends, and acquaintances. Depending upon custom, the desire of the judge, and the nature of the case, the report may contain diagnostic evaluation of the offender's personality, predictions of his potential for future criminality, and, perhaps, contain a specific sentence recommendation by the probation officer. Traditionally, the presentence report has been considered a confidential document to be read by the judge alone and not disclosed to the defense (Rubin et al., 1963). Increasingly, however, court decisions, rules, and model sentencing proposals are requiring or recommending at least partial disclosure of the report to the defense to enable them to correct mistakes, inaccuracies, or to otherwise challenge its factual content or conclusions [American Law Institute, 1962; Fed. Rules Crim. Proc., Rule 32 (c), 1962].

The defendant has a right to a sentence hearing and a right to be represented by counsel. At this hearing the trial judge (or in some jurisdictions a council of judges) listens to whatever the defendant has to say, then imposes the sentence he believes to be appropriate within whatever limits are set by statute. Sentencing structures vary considerably from one jurisdiction to another (Columbia Law Review, 1960), with legislation in some instances delegating to the judge wide discretion to choose among types, lengths, and conditions of sentence, but in other jurisdictions limiting alternatives by denying the judge authority to use probation in certain cases or by mandating the imposition of specific minimum or maximum sentences for certain crimes.

A judge can effect a probationary sentence in two ways: he can sentence the offender to a term of imprisonment but suspend *execution* of the sentence and place him on probation, or he can suspend *imposition* of sentence in the first place, putting the offender directly on probation for a specified period of time. Where execution is suspended, should the probation be revoked, the previously imposed sentence is applied. Where imposition of sentence has been suspended, however, the offender must be returned to court, not only for a revocation hearing but to be sentenced on the original charge. In some jurisdictions where suspension of execution was the common practice, offenders whose probation was revoked were sometimes moved directly from field supervision to prison without return to court, with the justification that once sentence was imposed the court had no further jurisdiction, with revocation solely the province of the probation field staff. In 1967, the United States Supreme Court declared a constitutional right to a revocation hearing in a case of "deferred sentencing" at which the defendant had the right of representation by counsel (*Mempa* v. *Rhay*). Subsequently, a number of state and federal appellate courts interpreted the procedural requirements of *Mempa* to apply to all forms of probation revocation, whether the grant technically involved suspended execution or deferred imposition.

THE MERGER OF DECISIONS IN THE CRIMINAL-COURT PROCESS: GUILTY-PLEA PRACTICES

In day-by-day routine operations of criminal courts, a substantial majority of felony convictions and the overwhelming percentage of misdemeanor convictions are recorded by a process far less formal and with fewer distinct steps than the procedural flow of contested cases from arrest to sentencing (Newman, 1966). In the guilty-plea process, including as it does various forms of plea bargaining, a number of steps in process are pro forma, with defendant rights waived, so that, in effect, major decision points of charging, adjudication, and sentencing become merged into a single decision complex (Ohlin & Remington, 1958).

Conviction of defendants by their own pleas of guilty is both the norm and *desideratum* of criminal-court processing much as confession is the bread-and-butter of police investigatory activity. Until recently the guilty plea received little attention in legal literature or sociological research. The plea was assumed to be simply a waiver of trial by the obviously guilty, a quick alternative path from detention in jail to sentence in prison or to probation. Within the past few years, however, both the legal dimensions of pleading guilty and the process by which it is done have come to be seen as much more complex—and much more controversial—than traditionally believed. The guilty-plea process, with all of its variations, is understood today to be more than a simple, fast alternative to trial. Rather, it is *the* major form of criminal adjudication in our criminal system. In operational perspective, the full-scale jury trial, in spite of its ideological significance, is the alternative to a guilty plea rather than the reverse.

This alteration in perception of the importance of the plea came about for a variety of reasons, partly the result of sociological research into the pleading process, partly from appellate-court decisions that have more frequently and more frankly confronted issues in pleading, and partly from total systems analysis such as the President's Commission on Law Enforcement and Administration of Justice and the American Bar Foundation studies. All of these have increased general awareness of the shared nature of decision-making in all of criminal justice, including the consequential link among decisions made at one point to others in the process.

The Guilty Plea

There are a number of reasons why most defendants plead guilty rather than go to trial, the first and foremost being the fact that they are guilty of *some* criminal conduct. The checks and screens in the preadjudication stages are designed to prevent totally innocent persons from being subjected to the cost, inconvenience, and reputational damage of trial. Acquittal at the very end of trial is often a hollow victory for the defense for there are real and sometimes lasting negative effects on persons who are arrested, charged, and tried for a crime although they are eventually acquitted. If a defendant avails himself of all pretrial protections, including his right to legal representation, it is unlikely he will stand convicted by his plea if, in fact, he is totally innocent of the crimes charged. The result is less certain, however, if the screens are waived and the defendant pleads without advice of counsel. Much of the present concern about the plea originated with this possibility.

Most suspects who enter the criminal process—who are stopped and questioned or even arrested by the police—are dropped or diverted from the system at some point prior to trial. In some instances, although suspicion is initially proper, brief interrogation or other investigation shows the suspicion to be inaccurate or otherwise unwarranted. In other cases, though the police may have evidence sufficient to arrest, it does not accumulate to standards sufficient for trial or perhaps it is inadmissible, so the suspects are released. In addition to matters of evidence, all participants—police, prosecutors, and judges—exercise discretion, formally recognized or not, by deciding that some individuals do not deserve or do not need full processing to the point of conviction and sentence though technically, based on available evidence, completion of the process is possible (LaFave, 1965; Newman, 1966; Miller, 1969).

All of these matters—the sufficiency of evidence, the propriety of methods used to gather it, and the exercise of discretion—are applicable to the guilty-plea process as well as to trial. But with the plea they have been muted, they are of low intensity and visibility, submerged in a process of maximum efficiency with such advocacy and contest as exist being informal and sub rosa, occurring in offices and hallways, not before the bench.

As a form of adjudication, the guilty plea has a number of advantages over trial for both the state and the accused. The duality of the advantages accounts for its popularity, for, though it is conceded that most defendants who plead guilty are guilty in fact (though the question of convictability is not the same as guilt), the motivation for pleading guilty, in most cases, is not repentance, but sentencing advantage. Likewise, in accepting pleas, even encouraging them, the state acts less because of the uncertainty of outcome if put to trial, than to achieve the ease and efficiency of the pleading itself. No one is challenged, no proof need be put, and conviction is assured. In order for the guilty-plea system to exist, indeed to prevail, mercy must be exchanged for efficiency and, in general, this is the situation. Sometimes, quite often in fact, there is overt preconviction negotiation for this leniency before the plea is offered and accepted. But most guilty pleas contain the seed of a bargain even without overt negotiation. This "implicit bargain," reflected in differential sentencing leniency shown to those who plead guilty over counterparts convicted only after trial, has been common practice but only recently has it been openly discussed and recognized as operationally significant by judges and others (Remington & Newman, 1962; American Bar Association, 1968a).

The guilty-plea process, and each of its overtly negotiated variations, collapses all of the sequentially distinguishable court decisions
into one. Charging and sentencing considerations merge with arraignment used merely to seal the agreement. In effect the prosecutor sentences, while the defendant uses his bargaining power to determine the
charge to which he is willing to plead. The skills exhibited by both
prosecutor and defense counsel in the pleading process are somewhat
different, though reasonably related to the knowledge and art necessary
for trial. Negotiation, compromise, and out-of-court settlement are, indeed, part of the lawyer's craft though more commonly associated with
civil damage suits and labor negotiations than criminal law. Nevertheless, such settlement of criminal cases is common, even in the norm, in
many court systems, with criminal trials infrequent and in some places
even involving different actors (Polstein, 1962). Some defense lawyers,
prosecutors, and even judges specialize (if at all) in trial work, and they
often are not the same personnel who routinely enter and process
guilty-plea defendants.

The Negotiated Plea

In routine operation the criminal court has come to depend upon a
steady and predictable flow of guilty pleas. Courts are staffed, calendars
determined, and budget allocated in anticipation of guilty-plea convictions in about 90 percent of all cases. While it is possible to achieve some
of this by relying on the implicit-sentencing bargain to encourage
pleading, for many defendants—particularly those who have gone the
route before—rewards must be more explicitly stated before they surrender their right to put the state to proof (Newman, 1966). Prearraign-
ment assurance of a sentencing break is the primary defendant
motivation in plea negotiation, although softening of the conviction
label occasionally has significance beyond or in addition to sentence
mitigation. A record of conviction for rape is more repugnant than the
label attached to a number of felonies—burglary, for example—and
conviction of a misdemeanor is almost always better than a felony
record. (Newman, 1966).

Negotiation for pleas takes a number of forms and has somewhat
different strategic objectives depending in good part on the type of
sentencing structure in a particular jurisdiction. The defendant, of
course, hopes to avoid the most severe sentence provided by law and
to achieve the greatest leniency he can—he wishes to minimize the
maximum and maximize the minimum—and where such sentence limits are fixed in legislation, where there are *mandatory* sentences allowing the judge no discretion to modify them, reduction of the charge is
the only way this can be achieved. In jurisdictions where the sentencing

judge has wide choice among alternative types and lengths of sentences, charge reduction may be to no avail unless accompanied by a preconviction sentence promise.

While the comparative frequency of different types of plea negotiations varies from jurisdiction to jurisdiction depending, in good part, on the type of sentencing structure in each instance, plea negotiation is present in virtually all jurisdictions with major differences only in the sequential location of bargaining and the number of offices and persons involved in actual negotiations.

The major forms of plea negotiation involve one or a combination of: (1) reduction of charges to lesser offenses; (2) promise of a lenient sentence, most often probation, by the prosecutor in exchange for the plea; (3) conviction on only one count of multiple charges with other charges being dropped or prosecution dismissed; and (4) in some cases the dropping of "super" charges, such as habitual criminal actions. Reduction of charges may be solely a prosecutor's function, especially if it is worked out before indictment or before the information is filed. In some jurisdictions, consent by the judge to reduction of charges is required but as a practical matter it is a rubber-stamp process. It is difficult for a judge to force the state to prosecute on maximum charges if the prosecutor is unwilling to do so. Of course, reduction in charge from a felony to a misdemeanor is almost always a major labeling and sentencing break, but if processing remains on the felony level, common negotiations involve sentence promises instead of or in addition to charge reduction. The sentence-promise type of negotiation is interesting, because normally the judge who has the sole authority to sentence is not directly involved in the negotiation proceedings. Instead, the defendant elicits from the prosecutor a promise to "recommend" or "not to oppose" probation (or some other lesser sentence) in exchange for the guilty plea. The contract is technically not absolutely binding for the prosecutor is not a principal; he cannot actually promise a sentence nor does he have direct responsibility or authority for sentencing. However, many judges routinely ask for the prosecutor's recommendation and tend to follow it, whether in frank support and acknowledgment of the negotiation process or not, so that for most defendants, a promise by the prosecutor is tantamount to a binding contract for leniency. Misunderstandings, even claims of dishonesty, about sentence promises have plagued courts of appeal for, until recently, records of such bargains were rarely kept (Newman, 1966).

The advantages to the defendant of the negotiated conviction encompass all those that flow from the guilty plea itself, and in addition, plea negotiation makes possible measures of equity, fairness, and individualization of justice that are not likely if strict adherence to evidence —slot machine justice—were the only consideration. From the state's point of view not only is the guilty-plea system—with all of its advantages of efficiency and avoidance of controversy—maintained by plea bargaining, but this process enables the conscientious prosecutor and judge to exercise broader sentencing discretion than provided by strict adherence to legislative mandate. It has been pointed out:

> By downgrading charges and/or by granting probation, the conscientious prosecutor and judge may act to individualize justice by making sensible distinctions between defendants who, although technically guilty of the same criminal conduct, do not deserve either the same record or the same mandatory sentence. Furthermore, plea negotiation and sentencing leniency act to support other parts of the criminal justice system. Leniency in charging or sentencing may be an effective reward for police informers or for cooperative state's witnesses without whom more serious cases could not be developed. Charge reduction and plea negotiation *may* select for the probation staff those offenders most likely to respond to treatment in the community. In short the avoidance of rigidity and slot machine justice—in addition to matters of efficiency and the avoidance of challenge to enforcement methods and quantum of evidence—constitute at least one side of the state's case in plea negotiation (Newman & NeMoyer, 1970, p. 371).

Until very recently, common practices of plea negotiation with accompanying significant administrative consequences were virtually unknown outside the coterie of prosecutors, defense counsel, trial judges, and experienced offenders who participate in the process. Plea bargaining was virtually undiscussed in legal or sociological literature and was of low visibility even to scholars of the courts. It was rarely the basis of appellate litigation and virtually totally ignored in legislation. All this has recently changed. Plea negotiation is currently a matter of interest to researchers and to legal scholars, has recently assumed new importance in appellate litigation, and has been recognized and reflected in court rules and in the mimimum standards of the American Bar Association (1968a).

From essentially a sub rosa process of esoteric interest, plea bargaining has become a matter of major concern and controversy. Questions of the propriety of plea bargaining are now confronting courts, scholars, and various actors in the system, with mixed results. Granting all the advantages of a negotiated justice system, including its use to mitigate the harshness of an automatic sentencing system, questions of its impact on our ideology, of its propriety within our constitutional framework of criminal justice, of its fairness for offenders (some of whom have opportunity to bargain and some do not), and of its impact on the way the general public views court justice in our society are all emerging as issues of major dimensions, all of them as yet unresolved. Whatever the specific concern of critics or supporters of plea bargaining, it is clear that this system of criminal adjudication is much different from the idealized criminal trial though, indeed, it may be no less adversary in its own right.

Critics of negotiated justice argue that it is usurpation of legislative sentencing power by prosecutors and judges. Indeed, the avoidance of legislative mandate is one of the purposes and one of the results of plea negotiation. Supporters of the process answer that negotiation practices simply extend and expand prosecutor and court discretion, enabling justice to be tailored more equitably to the thousands of offenders who pass through the criminal court on their way to jails, prisons, or other correctional programs. Critics argue that inducement of guilty pleas by promises of leniency is really no different from coercion—the third degree—which is clearly an improper basis for law enforcement or adjudication in our society. Opponents answer that inducement and coercion are not different sides of the same coin, that it is quite different and inherently proper to promise and to exercise leniency rather than to threaten, force, or otherwise treat severely. Critics argue with Judge Rives that "Justice and liberty are not the subjects of bargaining and barter" [*Shelton* v. *United States*, 242 F.2d 101, 246 F.2d 571 (5th Cir., 1957)]; opponents point out that plea negotiation already exists as an administrative necessity and that the thing to do is to recognize and control its practice. Critics also argue that plea negotiation lends a general aura of disrespect for the law, comparable to a "fix," and that it breeds cynicism, not reform, in those persons so processed; opponents argue that the purpose of sentencing discretion is to individualize justice, to fit consequences to circumstances, and to do this when such discretion is otherwise prohibited by mandatory sentences. Critics contend that plea negotiation conflicts with both the therapeutic and rational basis of sentencing, allowing sentences to be made in an informal relationship rather than by the careful diagnosis of presentence investigation; proponents, though recognizing the merging of charging and sentencing, propose the establishment of new skills and knowledge in this process, so that both prosecutor and defense become aware of sentencing alternatives and consequences and can appropriately fit cases to different sentence possibilities.

Much about plea negotiation is still unknown, including the full implications of these practices, and much is unresolved. Recently, there have been proposals to recognize the process as appropriate within our court system and to exert some controls on it by building more elaborate procedures into the arraignment process itself [*People* v. *West* (1970); American Bar Association, 1968*a*]. In a United States Supreme Court case, Chief Justice Burger gave explicit approval to the practice of plea bargaining:

> The disposition of criminal charges by agreement between the prosecutor and the accused, sometimes loosely called "plea bargaining" is an essential component of the administration of justice. Properly administered, it is to be encouraged. If every criminal charge were subjected to a full-scale trial, the States and the Federal Government would need to multiply by many times the number of judges and court facilities.
>
> Disposition of charges after plea discussions is not only an essential part of the process but a highly desirable part for many reasons. It leads to prompt and largely final disposition of most criminal cases; it avoids much of the corrosive impact of enforced idleness during pretrial confinement for those who are denied release pending trial; it protects the public from those accused persons who are prone to continue criminal conduct even while on pretrial release; and by shortening the time between charge and disposition, it enhances whatever may be the rehabilitative prospects of the guilty when they are ultimately imprisoned [*Santobello* v. *New York*, 404 U.S. 257 (1971)].

Researchers, legal scholars, and appellate courts will undoubtedly remain occupied with attempts to better understand, describe, and control the process of plea bargaining for, after all, it is the major form of adjudication in our system, and the chief method of operation of our criminal courts.

REFERENCES

American Bar Association
  1968*a* *Standards Relating to Pleas of Guilty.* American Bar Association Project on Standards for Criminal Justice. Chicago: American Bar Association.
  1968*b* *Standards Relating to Pretrial Release.* American Bar Association Project on Standards for Criminal Justice. Chicago: American Bar Association.
  1968*c* *Standards Relating to Joinder and Severance.* American Bar Association Project on Standards for Criminal Justice. Chicago: American Bar Association.
  1968*d* *Standards Relating to Fair Trial and Free Press.* American Bar Association Project on Standards for Criminal Justice. Chicago: American Bar Association.

American College of Trial Lawyers.
1970   *Disruption of the Judiciary Process.* Chicago: American Bar Association.
American Law Institute.
1962   *Model Penal Code.* Proposed Official Draft. Philadelphia: American Law Institute.
Baker, Newman F.
1933   "The prosecutor—initiation of prosecution." *Journal of Criminal Law and Criminology* 23(January–February):770–796.
Baker, Newman F., and Earl DeLong.
1934   "The prosecuting attorney—powers and duties in criminal prosecution." *Journal of Criminal Law, Criminology and Police Science* 24(March–April):1025–1065.
Blaustein, Albert P., and Charles O. Porter.
1954   *The American Lawyer.* Chicago: University of Chicago Press.
Blumberg, Abraham S.
1967   *Criminal Justice.* Chicago: Quadrangle Books.
Breitel, Charles D.
1960   "Controls in criminal law enforcement." *University of Chicago Law Review* 27(Spring):427–437.
Broeder, Dale.
1954   "The function of the jury—facts or fictions?" *University of Chicago Law Review* 21(Spring):386–394.
Carlin, Jerome E.
1962   *Lawyers on Their Own.* New Brunswick, N.J.: Rutgers University Press.
Columbia Law Review.
1960   "Statutory structures for sentencing felons to prison." 60(December):1134–1172.
Cornell Law Quarterly.
1966   "Constitutional law: criminal procedure: waiver of jury trial: *Singer v. United States,* 380 U.S. 24(1966)." 51:339–346.
Davis, Kenneth.
1969   *Discretionary Justice: A Preliminary Inquiry.* Baton Rouge: Louisiana State University Press.
Dawson, Robert O.
1969   *Sentencing: The Decision as to Type, Length and Conditions of Sentence.* Boston: Little, Brown.
Fletcher, Robert L.
1960   "Pretrial discovery in state criminal cases." *Stanford Law Review* 12:293–302.
Foote, Caleb B.
1965   "The coming constitutional crisis in bail." *University of Pennsylvania Law Review* 113(May):959–999.

Freed, Daniel J., and Patricia M. Wald.

1964   *Bail in the United States: 1964.* Working paper of the National Conference on Bail and Criminal Justice. Washington, D.C.: National Conference on Bail and Criminal Justice.

Goldstein, Abraham S.

1960   "The state and the accused: balance of advantage in criminal procedure." *Yale Law Journal* 69(June):1149–1199.

Griffiths, John.

1970   "Ideology in criminal procedure or a third model of the criminal process." *Yale Law Journal* 79(January):359–417.

Grosman, Brian A.

1969   *The Prosecutor.* Toronto: University of Toronto Press.

Hall, Livingston, Yale Kamisar, Wayne R. LaFave, and Jerold H. Israel.

1969   *Modern Criminal Procedure.* St. Paul, Minn.: West Publishing Co.

Harvard Law Review.

1966   "Preventive detention before trial." 79(May):1489–1510.

Johnstone, Quintin, and Dan Hopson, Jr.

1967   *Lawyers and Their Work.* Indianapolis: Bobbs-Merrill.

Kalven, Harry, Jr., and Hans Zeisel.

1966   *The American Jury.* Boston: Little, Brown.

Kronenberg, Jerry.

1959   "A right of a state to appeal in criminal cases." *Journal of Criminal Law, Criminology and Police Science* 49(January–February):473–486.

LaFave, Wayne R.

1965   *Arrest: The Decision to Take a Suspect into Custody.* Boston: Little, Brown.

LaFont, H. M.

1960   "Assessment of punishment—a judge or jury function?" *Texas Law Review* 38:835–846.

McIntyre, Donald M.

1968   "A study of judicial dominance of the charging process." *Journal of Criminal Law, Criminology and Police Science* 59(December):463–490.

Miles, Arthur P.

1963   *The Self-Image of the Wisconsin Probation and Parole Agent.* Madison: Division of Correction, Wisconsin State Department of Public Welfare.

Miller, Frank W.

1969   *Prosecution: The Decision to Charge a Suspect with a Crime.* Boston: Little, Brown.

Morse, Wayne.

1931   "A survey of the grand jury system." *Oregon Law Review* 10:101–295.

Nedrud, Duane R.
   1960   "The career prosecutor," *Journal of Criminal Law, Criminology and Police Science* 51(September–October):343–355.
Newman, Donald J.
   1956   "Pleading guilty for considerations: a study of bargain justice." *Journal of Criminal Law, Criminology and Police Science* 46(March–April):780–790.
   1966   *Conviction: The Determination of Guilt or Innocence Without Trial.* Boston: Little, Brown.
Newman, Donald J., and Edgar C. NeMoyer.
   1970   "Issues of propriety in negotiated justice." *Denver Law Journal* 47:367–407.
Oaks, Dallin H., and Warren Lehman.
   1968   *A Criminal Justice System and the Indigent.* Chicago: University of Chicago Press.
Ohlin, Lloyd E., and Frank J. Remington.
   1958   "Sentence structure: its effect upon systems for the administration of criminal justice." *Law and Contemporary Problems* 23(Summer):495–507.
Packer, Herbert L.
   1964   "Two models of the criminal process." *University of Pennsylvania Law Review* 113(November):1–68.
Polstein, Robert
   1962   "How to settle a criminal case." *Practical Lawyer* 8(January):35–44.
President's Commission on Law Enforcement and Administration of Justice.
   1967a   *Task Force Report: The Courts.* Washington, D.C.: U.S. Government Printing Office.
   1967b   *Task Force Report: Corrections.* Washington, D.C.: U.S. Government Printing Office.
Remington, Frank J., and Allen Joseph.
   1961   "Charging, convicting and sentencing." *Wisconsin Law Review* 1961 (July):528–565.
Remington, Frank J., and Donald J. Newman.
   1962   "The Highland Park Institute on sentence disparity." *Federal Probation* 26(March):3–9.
Remington, Frank J., Donald J. Newman, Edward L. Kimball, Marygold Melli, and Herman Goldstein.
   1969   *Criminal Justice Administration: Material and Cases.* Indianapolis: Bobbs-Merrill.
Rubin, Sol, Henry Weihofen, George Edwards, and Simon Rosenweig.
   1963   *The Law of Criminal Correction.* St. Paul, Minn.: West Publishing Co.

Schwartz, Herman.
1971   "Judges as tyrants." *Criminal Law Review* 7(March):129–138.
Silverstein, Lee.
1956   *Defense of the Poor in Criminal Cases in American State Courts.*
Chicago: American Bar Association.
Skolnick, Jerome H.
1966   *Justice Without Trial.* New York: Wiley.
Virginia Law Review.
1967   "Jury sentencing in Virginia." 53(May):968–1101.
Wood, Arthur Lewis.
1967   *Criminal Lawyer.* New Haven: Yale College and University Press.

23

Poverty and the Criminal Process

William J. Chambliss and Robert J. Seidman

The shape and character of the legal system in complex societies can be understood as deriving from the conflicts inherent in the structure of these societies which are stratified economically and politically. Generally, the legal system in its normative strictures and organizational operations will exhibit those norms and those practices that maintain and enhance the position of entrenched power-holders. Those broad principles underlying the legal order are ramified in and attenuated by the organizational aims of complex societies. The logical structure and its empirical implications, uncovered in our analysis of law, order, and power, may be set forth as a set of propositions. We begin with propositions about the relationship between a group's norms and the law.

PROPOSITIONS

1. One's "web of life" or the conditions of one's life affect one's values and (internalized) norms.
2. Complex societies are composed of groups with widely different life conditions.
3. Therefore, complex societies are also composed of highly disparate and conflicting sets of norms.
4. The probability of a group's having *its* particular normative system embodied in law is *not* distributed equally among the social groups but, rather, is closely related to the group's political and economic position.

From William J. Chambliss & Robert J. Seidman, *Law, Order, and Power* (Reading, Mass.: Addison-Wesley, 1971), pp. 473–83, by permission of the authors and publisher.

5. The higher a group's political or economic position, the greater is the probability that its views will be reflected in the laws.

According to these first five propositions, then, the law will differentially reflect the perspectives, values, definitions of reality, and morality of the middle and upper classes while being in opposition to the morality and values of the poor and lower classes. Given this twist in the content of the law, we are not surprised that the poor should be criminal more often than the nonpoor. The systematically induced bias in a society against the poor goes considerably farther than simply having values incorporated within the legal system which are antithetical to their ways of life. Since, in complex societies, the decision to enforce the laws against certain persons and not against others will be determined primarily by criteria derived from the bureaucratic nature of the law-enforcement agencies, we have the following propositions which explain what takes place within these agencies and the kinds of decisions they are likely to make:

1. The legal system is organized through bureaucratically structured agencies, some of which are primarily norm-creating agencies and others of which are primarily norm-enforcing agencies.
2. The formal role-expectation for each official position in the bureaucracy is defined by authoritatively decreed rules issuing from officials in other positions who themselves operate under position-defining norms giving them the power to issue such rules.
3. Rules, whether defining norm-creating positions or norm-applying positions, necessarily require discretion in the role-occupant for their application.
4. In addition, the rules are for a variety of reasons frequently vague, ambiguous, contradictory, or weakly or inadequately sanctioned.
5. Therefore, each level of the bureaucracy possesses considerable discretion as to the performance of its duties.
6. The decision to create rules by rule-creating officials or to enforce rules by rule-enforcing officials will be determined primarily by criteria derived from the bureaucratic nature of the legal system.
7. Rule-creation and rule-enforcement will take place when such creation or enforcement increases the rewards for the agencies and their officials, and they will not take place when they are conducive to organizational strain.
8. The creation of the rules which define the roles of law-enforcing agencies has been primarily the task of the appellate courts, for

which the principal rewards are in the form of approval of other judges, lawyers, and higher-status middle-class persons generally.

9. The explicit value-set of judges, lawyers, and higher-status middle-class persons generally is that which is embodied in the aims of legal-rational legitimacy.

10. Therefore, the rules created by appellate courts will tend to conform to the requirements of legal-rational legitimacy and to the specific administrative requirements of the court organization.

11. The enforcement of laws against persons who possess little or no political power will generally be rewarding to the enforcement agencies of the legal system, while the enforcement of laws against persons who possess political power will be conducive to strains for those agencies.

12. In complex societies, political power is closely tied to social position.

13. Therefore, those laws which prohibit certain types of behavior popular among lower-class persons are more likely to be enforced, while laws restricting the behavior of middle- or upper-class persons are not likely to be enforced.

14. Where laws are so stated that people of all classes are equally likely to violate them, the lower the social position of an offender, the greater is the likelihood that sanctions will be imposed on him.

15. When sanctions are imposed, the most severe sanctions will be imposed on persons in the lowest social class.

16. Legal-rational legitimacy requires that laws be stated in general terms equally applicable to all.

17. Therefore, the rules defining the roles of law-enforcement officials will require them to apply the law in an equitable manner.

18. Therefore, to the extent that the rules to be applied are potentially applicable to persons of different social classes, the role-performance of law-enforcement officials may be expected to differ from the role-expectation embodied in the norms defining their positions.

Taken as a unit, these propositions represent the basis of a theory of the legal process in complex societies. It is a theory derived essentially from the facts of the operation of criminal law—facts gathered by a large number of researchers into the criminal-law process at each level of the operation.

POVERTY AND THE LEGAL SYSTEM

The empirical data and the propositions based on them make it abundantly clear that the poor do not receive the same treatment at the hands of the agents of law enforcement as the well-to-do or middle class. This differential treatment is systematic and complete. It includes the practice by the police and prosecuting attorneys of choosing to look for and impose punishments for offenses that are characteristically committed by the poor and ignoring those committed by the more affluent members of the community. Where offenses are equally likely to be committed by persons from different social classes (such as gambling), the police will look for these crimes in the lower-class neighborhoods rather than in middle- or upper-class neighborhoods. For example, in almost every American community, medical doctors, dentists, and practicing attorneys are the groups most actively engaged in placing bets with bookmakers. This is so not because of the inherently corrupt tendencies of people in these professions but rather because these people can hide substantial amounts of their income and thus avoid paying taxes on that income. They can then afford to gamble with this tax-free money and declare it as gains only when they substantially increase their wealth. They cannot simply spend the money they do not declare, since to do so would mean living at a much higher level than could be justified by their acknowledged income which makes good grounds for being prosecuted for income tax evasion. Hence, professional groups are the most important financial backers of many forms of gambling. Yet the police virtually never attempt to discover this practice and punish the professional people who are gambling, nor do they very often curtail the activities of those who take the bets (except, of course, where these operations are part of a criminal organization, which subject we shall take up shortly). By contrast, persons who bet on or sell policy numbers (a typically lower-class form of gambling) are often subject to arrest and prosecution. Similarly, middle- and upper-class suburbanites who play poker in their own homes are never sought out or prosecuted for gambling (though in most states there are statutes prohibiting this game). But lower-class persons who shoot dice in the alley or hallway of their apartment house (the apartment itself is of course too small to permit such activities) are constantly in jeopardy of legal intervention. To reduce the visibility of gambling, the devotees may be willing to pay someone a "cup" or the "pot" in order to use their apartment for a game. To do so, however, makes the entire group vulnerable, since this solution to the problem of finding space in which to gamble simultaneously increases the ability of the police and prosecutor to make the game appear as one run by "professional gamblers," thereby justifying arrest and prosecution. As we shall see, in most communities in the United States there is a substantial amount of highly organized gambling activity which takes place with the complicity of the police and the prosecuting attorney's office. The purveyors of these enterprises are generally immune from prosecution. It is ironically the games between friends and acquaintances in lower-class areas which are likely to be chosen for prosecution; similar games among middle- and upper-class members of the community are ignored, as are games handled by truly professional gamblers.

That the selective enforcement by policing agencies is not merely a function of what is most pressingly needed by the society is clearly indicated by a comparison of civil rights law-enforcement and the enforcement of laws prohibiting the use of "dangerous drugs." On the [one] hand, although riots and general discontent are rampant in the urban areas where black ghettos are concentrated, the laws which prohibit discrimination in employment, unions, and housing, consumer fraud, housing violations, and other protections for the poor are effectively ignored at every level of the government—federal, state, and local. By contrast, despite the preponderance of scientific evidence demonstrating that the smoking of marijuana is a relatively harmless pastime (less harmful, most experts agree, than drinking alcohol), laws prohibiting marijuana smoking are enforced vigorously. With respect to unfair employment, housing, and labor practices, enforcement would involve the enforcement agencies in conflicts with politically powerful groups. The federal government, for example, would be involved in serious conflict with the politically powerful trade unions if the section of the National Labor Relations Act prohibiting discrimination in unions were enforced. And if sanctions were inflicted for discrimination in employment, as it can be under Title VII of the Civil Rights Act of 1964, the federal and state governments would be at loggerheads with many of the nation's leading corporations. It is to avoid such clashes that only fourteen of some eight thousand complaints received by the Department of Justice between 1965 and 1968 complaining of discrimination in employment resulted in litigation.[1]

On the other hand, since marijuana smokers were, until quite recently, concentrated among the poor black and Chicano (Mexican-American) populations in the United States, these laws could be enforced at the will of the enforcement agencies and indeed they were. Recently, the spread of marijuana and other "drugs" to middle- and upper-class youths has increased the population of "criminals" substantially. It has also brought into public view some of the problems of selective enforcement which characterize America's legal process. It is possible that this increased visibility of police activities will bring about changes in policy and law. It is unlikely, however, that these changes

1. William F. Ryan, "Uncle Sam's Betrayal," *The Progressive,* May 1968, pp. 25–28.

will substantially alter the tendency of the legal system to select for enforcement laws dealing with acts of the poor.

Since 1941 there has been a constant stream of executive orders prohibiting discrimination in employment by any company holding government contracts. The latest order, Executive Order 11236 issued in 1965, is one of the most stringent. Despite the increased stringency of these executive orders, and despite the fact that most of the companies holding government contracts are covered by these orders, *there has never been a single contract with the government canceled nor sanctions applied because of job discrimination by the employer*,[2] though there are administrative board findings clearly showing discrimination in employment by companies holding government contracts.

By way of digression, this is an appropriate place to point out that it is because of the very great and real gap between "laws" and "enforcement" that the generally held ideal of a "fair" and "just" system of law can be maintained despite widespread tendencies subverting these goals. For few people would be so cynical as to doubt the sincerity of an executive order decrying discrimination in employment and providing for the cancellation of contracts with companies who engage in such practices. Yet the truth of the matter is that the order is totally meaningless; if the sanctions are never imposed and if the enforcement agencies do not seek out violators, it is apparent that the executive order does nothing—it is a rhetorical ritual, empty of content, whose principal significance is the acknowledgement of the need to placate dissenters. It succeeds indeed only in providing a false sense of the inherent justice of the system.

Perhaps the best way to grasp the all-encompassing nature of the differential treatment of the poor in the American legal system is through case studies. The intensive patrol of the police in slum areas presents a constant threat to everyone in the community, whether they are engaged in illegal activities or not.[3]

Case 1.   Ralph worked the four-to-twelve shift in a factory. After work one night he decided to work on his car before going to sleep. Since he had no garage, the only place to work on the car was in the street. He was working on the engine with the hood up when a policeman stopped and asked him what he was doing. He explained that he was fixing his car. The policeman asked to see his driver's license and registration card. Ralph showed these and the policeman left. Within five

---

2. Ibid., p. 25.
3. Field notes of William J. Chambliss.

minutes another policeman had stopped and essentially the same scene took place. Five minutes after the second policeman left, a third patrol car turned the corner and asked Ralph what he was doing. According to the policeman and Ralph the conversation went like this:

> Officer: Whatcha doing to the car, son?
> Ralph (angrily): I'm stealin' the motherfucker.

Ralph was arrested and taken to the station. Later he was released after questioning by the lieutenant.

If a policeman suspects that someone had done something wrong, then the pattern of discriminatory treatment of the poor continues. The following case, adapted from the President's Crime Commission Report,[4] is illustrative of the kinds of problems encountered by the poor as they make their way from arrest through trial and conviction:

Case 2.   Defendant A is spotted by a foot-patrol officer in the skid-row district of town, weaving along the street. When the officer approaches him, the man begins muttering incoherently and shrugs off the officer's inquiries. When the officer seizes his arm, A breaks the hold violently, curses the officer and the police. The patrolman puts in a call for a squad car, and the man is taken to the precinct station where he is booked on a double charge of drunkenness and disorderly conduct.

In the Stationhouse.   Defendant A's belt is removed to prevent any attempts at suicide; [he] is put in the drunk tank to sober up.

> His cellmate lies slumped and snoring on the cell's single steel bunk, sleeping off an all-day drunk, oblivious to the shouts . . . There are at least two men in each 4 X 8 foot cell and three in some . . . The stench of cheap alcohol, dried blood, urine and excrement covers the cell block. Except for the young man's shouts, it is quiet. Most of the prisoners are so drunk they gaze without seeing, unable to answer when spoken to. There are no lights in the cells, which form a square in the middle of the cell block. But the ring of naked light bulbs on the walls around the cell block throw the light into the cells, each of which is equipped with a steel bunk. There are no mattresses. "Mattresses wouldn't last the night," a policeman explains. "And with prisoners urinating all over them, they wouldn't be any good if they did last."

---

4. President's Commission on Law Enforcement and Administration of Justice, *Task Force Report: The Police,* U.S. Government Printing Office, 1967.

The only sound in the cell block is the constant flowing of water through the toilets in each cell. The toilets do not have tops, which could be torn off and broken.

Every half hour or so a policeman checks to see if the inmates are "still warm."

After sobering up, a drunk or disorderly can usually leave the lockup in four or five hours if he is able to post the collateral ($10–$25). No matter how many times he has been arrested before, he will not have to appear in court if he chooses to forfeit the collateral. The drunk without money stays in jail until court opens the next morning. At 6 a.m., the police vans come to collect the residue in the precinct lockups and take them to the courthouse cell blocks to await a 10 a.m. arraignment.

Preliminary Hearing and Arraignment. Defendant A, charged with drunkenness and disorderly conduct, is brought into the court from the bullpen in a shuffling line of dirty, beat, unshaven counterparts, many still reeking of alcohol. Each spends an average of 90 seconds before the judge, time for the clerk to intone the charge and for the judge to ask if he desires counsel and how he pleads. Rarely does a request for counsel or a "not guilty" break the monotony of muttered "guilty" pleas. Lawyers are not often assigned in police courts, and anyone who can afford his own counsel will already have been released from jail on bond—to prepare for trial at a later date or to negotiate with the city prosecutor to drop the charges.

Occasionally, an unrepresented defendant will ask for trial. If the arresting officer is present, he will be tried on the spot. There are no jury trials for drunkenness. The policeman will testify that the man was "staggering," "his breath smelled of some sort of alcoholic beverage," his speech was "slurred," "his eyes were bloodshot and glassy." The man may protest that he had only a few drinks, but there are no witnesses to support his testimony, no scientific evidence to establish the level of alcohol in his blood at the time of arrest, no lawyers to cross-examine the officer. If the defendant pleads not guilty and hopes he can get counsel (his own or court-assigned), he may have his trial postponed a week or two. Meanwhile, he must make bond or return to jail.

Police-court sentencing is usually done immediately after a plea. A few courts with alcoholic rehabilitation court clinics may screen for likely candidates—those not too far along on the alcoholism trail—in the detention pens. Counsel, when available, can ask for a presentence report, but delay in sentencing means jail or bail in the meantime. On

a short-term offense it is seldom worth it. Other kinds of petty offenders
—disorderlies, vagrants, street-ordinance violators—follow a similar
route in court. Guilty pleas are the rule. Without counsel or witnesses,
it is the defendant's word against that of the police. Even when counsel
is present, defense efforts at impeachment founder on the scanty
records kept by the police in such petty offenses. The only defense may
be the defendant's word, which is suspect if he has a record, or hard-to-
find "character witnesses" without records from his slum neighborhood.

Because the crime is more serious, the poor defendant accused of
a felony fares even worse than one who is accused of a misdemeanor.
Frequently the difference between a misdemeanor and a felony charge
is the result of police work to a greater extent than it is a result of the
defendant's criminal act. The following case from Chambliss' research
is illustrative.

Case 3.   Louie, a black militant active in organizing the black community in a middle-sized western city, had failed to pay two traffic tickets.
One ticket was for running a stop sign (at three miles an hour); another
was for driving without a tail light on his car. A warrant was issued for
his arrest. The police pursued him into the night and confronted him
at 11:00 p.m. with the warrant. He was approaching his car when the
policeman commanded him to place his hands on the top of his car and
allow them to search him. He did so, and as he took the stance with his
legs spread apart, the policeman kicked his legs to make him spread
them apart more widely. After searching him, the policeman handcuffed him and began pushing him across the street to the police car.
The policeman also pushed him as he started into the car, causing Louie
to hit his head against the top of the automobile.

A friend of Louie's, Dan, was in a nearby cafe when someone came
in and told him Louie was being arrested. Dan confronted the officer
and demanded to know what Louie was being arrested for. The policeman informed Dan that if he wanted to accompany them to the police
station to see that Louie was not mistreated he could. Dan entered the
car and went with Louie and the policeman to the station.

Dan and Louie argued vehemently at the police station and accused the police of being "white racists" and of arresting them because
they were black. Louie was shoved down to the floor and taken by force
into the elevator and to the jail. Dan began to leave the station but was
informed that he, too, was under arrest for "obstructing arrest." Dan
tried to leave and was forcefully restrained. The police filed charges as
follows:

Louie: charged with resisting arrest, public intoxication, and disorderly conduct (all misdemeanors).

Dan: charged with public intoxication, disorderly conduct, resisting arrest, and battery against a police officer.

The last charge, battery against a police officer, is a felony in the state and, as such, carried with it a possible prison sentence. The alleged battery came about when Dan "threw a pendulum which he was wearing around his neck at a police officer." The policeman claimed to have had his hand nicked by the pendulum.

Bail for Louie was set at $650. He was immediately released when friends posted bond, by paying a bail bondsman $65, which of course is never returned no matter what the result of the trial. Dan could not be bailed out until the hearing the next day, since a hearing is necessary to set the bail in felony cases. Since the arrest occurred on Friday, Dan had to spend the entire weekend in jail.

Friends contacted a lawyer. Dan and Louie insisted they were innocent. The lawyer agreed to talk to the district attorney. The lawyer they hired was with one of the best-known firms in the city. He arranged a bargain with the prosecuting attorney so that in exchange for a guilty plea to the disorderly conduct charges (and a possible six-months jail sentence or up to $1000 fine) the prosecution would drop the other charges. Louie and Dan said they wanted to plead not guilty. The lawyer then informed them that (a) if they pleaded guilty to the lesser offense, his fee would be $500, but (b) if they chose to plead not guilty and the case went to trial (which it probably would), his fee would be a minimum of $1500. He also told them that if they wished, they could ask for a court-appointed lawyer, and he acknowledged that court-appointed lawyers were sometimes excellent.

Ultimately, the men were able to raise $1500 (by a campaign for funds to defend themselves), and the case went to trial. Within two days of testimony the entire case was dismissed without ever going to the jury on the ground that the prosecution did not have sufficient evidence for bringing the case to court. At the hearing, the judge criticized the prosecution and pointed out the expense that the county had incurred. He failed to make note of the expense it had caused Louie and Dan. The two men, who were accused of crimes which they did not commit and which were escalated by police because the latter's insensitivity and belligerence had elicited harsh words from Louie and Dan, were exonerated. But the whole episode cost them over two thousand dollars (the lawyer's fee turned out to be two thousand instead of fifteen hundred) and several nights in jail.

Case 4.   The previous case contrasts sharply with that of Joe, who was arrested for disorderly conduct and malicious mischief against personal property. Joe was a black man who had been sharing an apartment with two white men. The three of them had an argument, and Joe broke some furniture in the apartment and cussed out his roommates. He moved from the apartment two days later, and one of the former roommates pressed charges. Joe was arrested. He spent the night in jail until he raised $125 to pay the bail bondsman (again, not refundable no matter what the outcome of the trial) so he could be released. The bondsman would *not* have been willing to provide bond except for the fact that Joe's employer signed the bond and put his home up for collateral. Joe asked for and was assigned a court-appointed lawyer. The lawyer encouraged Joe to plead guilty to whatever the prosecutor would offer. Joe refused. The lawyer requested that he be withdrawn from the case because he was "about to go on vacation." A new lawyer was appointed. Joe went to the new lawyer's office, and explained what had happened. He told the lawyer that he had witnesses that the property damages consisted of only a plate and that he had not assaulted anyone. The second lawyer suggested that he see still another lawyer, and the court appointed a third one. Each lawyer encouraged Joe to plead guilty. None of them acknowledged that he was being accused unjustly. Meanwhile, the man who had filed the original charge withdrew it and asked the prosecuting attorney's office to drop the charges.

The prosecuting attorney's office refused to do so and determined to pursue the case. After several weeks of postponement, indecision, and changing lawyers, during which no one would give Joe the satisfaction of telling him that he could perhaps win in a court fight, Joe pleaded guilty because, in his words, "I'm tired of all this fucking around, Chambliss." He was sentenced to three months in the county jail. As a consequence, he lost his job and had to drop out of a remedial reading program in which he was enrolled.

For the indigent, free representation by a lawyer is available in two ways: the court may appoint a lawyer chosen from a list supplied by the local bar association or, in states and communities with a public defender system, an indigent defendant may be assigned a public defender. In both instances, whether or not the defendant is indigent and therefore eligible for a court-appointed lawyer or a public defender is a question that must be decided by the judge. Standards of indigency are in no way prescribed and vary considerably from one judge to another.

Case 5. The defendant was charged with petty larceny. He had allegedly stolen a $19.95 sleeping bag from a Sears department store. He was brought to the courtroom handcuffed after spending a night in jail awaiting his preliminary hearing. The judge asked if he could afford a lawyer.

> *Def:* No sir, I would like to have one appointed by the court.
> *Judge:* It's up to me to decide whether or not you should have one appointed by the court. Do you work?
> *Def:* Yes Sir.
> *Judge:* What do you do?
> *Def:* I make sandals.
> *Judge:* How much do you earn making sandals?
> *Def:* About $40 a month.
> *Judge:* Can you live on $40 a month?
> *Def:* (nods yes)
> *Judge:* Do you own any personal property?
> *Def:* No.
> *Judge:* Any musical instruments?
> *Def:* Yes, a sitar.
> *Judge:* How much does a sitar cost?
> *Def:* I paid $150 for it.
> *Judge:* O.K., you can sell your sitar and hire your own attorney. Hearing is set for tomorrow at 11:00 a.m.
> *Def:* How can I sell it and get a lawyer while I'm in jail?
> *Judge:* You'll have to work that out for yourself.

But even when the indigent is assigned a free lawyer, as the case of Joe illustrates, the court-appointed lawyer will conscientiously pursue the best interests of his client only if he can put professional duty without reward of money or status ahead of other more lucrative employment. Even where the state provides public defenders, as was pointed out earlier, the tendency is for the public defender simply to become a pawn of the prosecuting attorney's office. In any event, it is a simple maxim that the best disposition of a poor defendant from the standpoint of the practicing attorney, public defender, prosecuting attorney, judge, police—indeed, everyone in the legal system—is to convince the defendant in one way or another that he should plead guilty to something and throw himself on the mercy of the court. Given the disadvantageous position of the impoverished when confronted with the legal system, it is not surprising that most defendants are coerced into doing just that. It is unlikely that many of them are met with the mercy they plead for.

24

Early Diversion
from the Criminal Justice System

Elizabeth W. Vorenberg and James Vorenberg

INTRODUCTION

In the years since the President's Crime Commission began its work and reform of the criminal justice system became a major national goal, certain words and phrases have become the shorthand for improvements that all "reformers" in the field are deemed to accept. A few examples are "professionalization" and "community service" as applied to the police; "business management techniques" as applied to the courts; and "community treatment" and "collaborative model" as applied to corrections. In hundreds of the criminal justice plans required of the states by the block-grant formulation of the Law Enforcement Assistance Act and in the individual grant applications submitted pursuant to such plans, these and other slogans appear thousands of times, thereby wrapping a particular proposal in the flag of the Crime Commission and the massive subsequent literature. But no word has had quite the power of "diversion" (or, if real specificity is desired, "early diversion") which offers the promise of the best of all worlds: cost savings, rehabilitation, and more humane treatment.

The purpose of this chapter is to explore what we mean by diversion in the criminal justice system, what we have and have not learned from programs or approaches that can fairly use the label, and what the issues are that must be considered in reacting to the concept of diversion generally and to its application to particular situations.

From Elizabeth W. Vorenberg & James Vorenberg, "Early Diversion from the Criminal Justice System: Practice in Search of a Theory," in Lloyd E. Ohlin (ed.), *Prisoners in America* (Englewood Cliffs, N.J.: Prentice-Hall, 1973), pp. 151–83, by permission of the authors and publisher. Copyright © 1973 by The American Assembly, Columbia University.

"Diversion"—or "early diversion"—has no real meaning in relationship to the criminal justice system in the absence of a context that tells us (1) what the process is by which diversion takes place; (2) what the person is diverted from—i.e., what is diversion instead of? and (3) what he is diverted to. Thus, if we take the Perry Mason image of the criminal process by which every person apprehended in a criminal act is arrested, charged, tried, and, if convicted, sentenced to prison, any disposition short of serving the full prison term could fairly be regarded [as] early diversion. This would include a decision of a policeman to let a traffic violation offender go with a tongue-lashing; a district attorney to drop a shoplifting case against a first offender because the store fails to prosecute; a judge to give a convicted person probation or a suspended sentence; or a parole board to release a prisoner at his first parole hearing. These are all diversions from a more serious burden that would have been imposed but for the action taken.

But these early exits from the system are familiar and of long standing and may fairly be regarded as part of the system itself and will generally be so regarded in this chapter. What is usually meant by current calls for early diversion is, to put it simply, something that is *new*. This may consist of (1) recognition that some categories of offenders such as drunks, addicts, and the mentally ill are special candidates for diversion; (2) new procedures or incentives to raise the number, the percentage, or the seriousness-of-offense level of the offenders who leave the system early; (3) new screening devices to select those who will leave; or (4) new places, programs, or opportunities for those who do leave. Many of the most important new programs are built on well-recognized early exit points in the system. Thus the California probation subsidy program is basically a financial and political device to get judges to put more offenders on probation, and the Manhattan Court Employment Project is an elaborate administrative mechanism to encourage and improve a practice long in use in many places—the suspension of prosecution on condition that the offender show the court he can and will hold down a job.

We will try not to agonize over what does and does not qualify as an early diversion program; the chapter will try to focus on issues raised by relatively recent programs.

Although this chapter is [from] a book on corrections, it necessarily looks at diversion at earlier stages of the system. For one of the principal purposes of diversion is to offer an offender the kind of treatment which under certain correctional programs he would receive only after conviction, but without the delays, the pressure on the offender, or the costs of full processing through the system. Thus, in one sense, diversion is simply a way of starting correctional treatment sooner. More broadly, it has become clear that for many purposes the criminal justice system should be seen not as a line but as a closed loop that has as its closing point and its goal the return of the offender to responsibility for his own life. As discussed below there are strong arguments that for many offenders the trip around the circle is meaningless and damaging and costly—and that therefore we should consider whether and under what circumstances we should and can leave offenders where we find them.

Early diversion may be seen as a means of implementing a number of theories that underlie current efforts at correctional reform. Two of these deserve brief mention. Perhaps the most important for our purposes—and central to the Crime Commission's recommendations in the corrections area—is that every effort should be made to avoid relieving an offender of the responsibility and burdens of making decisions and managing his own life, since the goal is to return him to society better able to cope on his own. One manifestation of this theory is that if he must be institutionalized, the offender should have the privilege/burden of participating in decisions affecting him—thus the proposal for "collaborative institutions" that was at the heart of the commission's recommendations about prisons. Another manifestation was that the absence from society—necessitating under the best of circumstances a break in the sequence of responsibility—should be as slight as possible.

Also underlying early diversion is the so-called "labeling" theory. This theory hypothesizes that society's label may be accepted in part by the individual himself. Therefore, imposing the status and label of a convicted criminal makes recidivism more likely. Closely related is the recognition that the label limits or precludes opportunities an offender may have to be reintegrated into lawful society.

It is beyond the scope of this chapter to consider in depth the relation of early diversion to theories of corrections or crime causation, and therefore we have dealt only briefly with those issues. However, in addition to whatever theories may have contributed to the movement for diversion we have a strong sense that perhaps most important of all is the recognition that the system is hopelessly overloaded with cases; is brutal, corrupt and ineffective; and that therefore every case removed is a gain.

Hundreds of projects have been undertaken around the country which have early diversion as a component. Because of the fragmentation of the criminal justice operations among counties, cities, states, and the federal system, it is impossible to make even a rough quantitative assessment of the extent to which offenders are being diverted out of the system. The nation's sources of information about the operation of the conventional parts of the criminal justice system are limited. And since, as will be discussed below, early diversion takes place in many forms and involves many agencies which we normally do not consider to be part of the criminal justice system, we simply must accept that we do not know, except impressionistically, how much real change the movement toward diversion has made. It may be that notwithstanding all the money and all the writing about diversion, only a relatively few offenders are being treated differently than a decade earlier. (One example of how easy it is to be misled on the extent of actual change was the finding by a study at the Harvard Center for Criminal Justice that more than two years after the Crime Commission had recommended community residential facilities and at a time when much was being written and said about them, less than 2 percent of adult offenders in state custody were in residential facilities outside the walls of traditional prisons.)

Unfortunately, the slipshod handling of evaluation and reporting under the Law Enforcement Assistance Act makes it unlikely that even several years from now we will know what the extent of the shift toward early diversion has been or what impact it has had on crime, criminal justice costs, efficiency, morale, or rehabilitation. Despite the lack of any real quantitative information on the scope of early diversion or probing evaluation of its effects, it may be useful to describe briefly as a basis for discussion and analysis some of the major types of diversion projects—both by the points in the system at which diversion takes place (second part of this chapter) and by the type of offender for whom they are designed (third part). Much of the description of these projects draws on or paraphrases secondary literature. . . .

DIVERSION PROJECTS: EXIT POINTS

There are hundreds of new diversion programs being undertaken in the United States. They result in the offender's leaving the traditional criminal justice system at various points from before arrest until after conviction. The way the offender's case is disposed of depends on where and by whom in the system diversion is considered, and the fact of diversion, in turn, has an impact on the various agencies in the system. To try to illuminate some of these issues, this second part of the chapter will consider examples of diversion projects at different points in the system. It needs emphasis that the projects listed here and in the third part are not necessarily the most important or the best of their kind. They are simply among those about which we have been able to obtain enough information to raise issues for consideration. It is also worth noting that the fact that the Vera Institute of Justice of New York City appears repeatedly in this paper is no accident. Vera has carried the concept of early diversion into practice at various stages of the criminal justice system. Because of its pragmatic approach and its record of success in setting up projects, it has provided an important incentive for the development of such projects nationally.

Diversion by Police

In most jurisdictions, the statutory authority of the police to arrest is mandatory not discretionary. Nonetheless, the police everywhere have always exercised broad discretion to decide whether or not to arrest. Of course, if serious crimes or highly dangerous conduct is involved, the police will arrest and participate in an offender's prosecution. But crime connected with family arguments, [and] such misdemeanors as public drunkenness, loitering and disorderly conduct, mildly destructive behavior by juveniles, and minor crimes generally, will often lead to a decision not to arrest or take into custody. Thus at a prearrest stage of the process large numbers of potential offenders have already been diverted in the sense that they have been dropped from the system.

Even after an offender is brought into the station, police power (if not legal authority) to handle a case informally continues. In some cities substantial numbers of cases are dropped at the station-house in a completely invisible, informal, and nonlegal procedure. A case may be dropped unconditionally or on condition that the offender stay out of trouble or make restitution.

On the other hand, in some cities there are well structured hearing procedures for juveniles which are similar to intake hearings of juvenile courts. There are formal notices to parents and minors setting the time and place for a meeting with a "hearing officer." The police officer in charge of the hearing seeks to make a common-sense judgment on whether the juvenile should be sent to court. He takes into account such factors as the juvenile's prior record and his reputation with the police and the community as a troublemaker, the likelihood that the family will cooperate in keeping the juvenile out of trouble, and the extent to which the police may be criticized for being too lenient if the offense was serious or if there is further trouble. While the participation of the juvenile and his parents is voluntary in the sense they can opt for a court appearance, there is in fact great pressure to cooperate in order to stay out of court. Often the police will use this pressure and the juvenile's desire to avoid a police record to get a confession for their files that will enable them to treat the case as closed and which may have an *in terrorem* effect on the future misconduct of the juvenile.

Police Referral. A much broader role for the police is involved in proposals that the police become a referral agency to effect non-criminal disposition of arrested persons. Vera Institute's Manhattan Bowery project for handling drunks (discussed in third part below) is one example, although the police role is a limited one. The New York City Police Department announced in the fall of 1972 that addicts arrested for offenses or misdemeanors will be offered an opportunity to be sent to a drug treatment program with submission of their cases for prosecution held in abeyance. Addicts who agree to treatment and who are accepted by a treatment center would be paroled, with the court's approval, in the custody of the center. One possible role for the community service officer recommended by the President's Crime Commission would be to screen persons arrested for relatively minor crimes and dismiss or refer to social or health agencies those without a serious criminal record.

There is no way of knowing how many police departments are now engaged in such dismissal-referral programs. What is clear is that to the extent they become visible and acknowledged, such programs have an important bearing on the continuing debate about police participation in a social service role. That debate is usually in terms of how police resources should be allocated. But police responsibility for early diversion raises deeper questions as to whether it is inherently inappropriate for the police to make corrections-type decisions and whether the whole postarrest situation is simply too pressured to ensure that a suspect's decision to accept a particular form of treatment (such as participation in a methadone program) is truly voluntary. At least until more is known of the extent and content of diversion by the police in this country, one should probably be cautious about taking a general position about the appropriateness of police agencies undertaking this responsibility. There are undoubtedly some situations—particularly where the decision is not onerous—in which a police role would be generally acceptable. There are others where, without strong protections for the suspect including providing him with a lawyer, there would be general agreement that the police should not take responsibility for diversion. There is one point on which we believe there should be no disagreement. To the extent the police are making arrangements for the conditional dropping of cases, the practice should be openly acknowledged rather than hidden as it so often is.

British Practice. In considering formalized diversion by the police, the British experience may provide some guidance. Great Britain has proceeded further than the United States in formalizing police diversion practices by establishing in 1968 the Juvenile Bureaux within the Metropolitan Police in London. Up to that time the practice of the London police was to arrest and charge juvenile offenders in much the same way as adults. The changes included amending police procedure so that many young offenders would be brought in on a summons instead of a formal charge. But the heart of the new system is use of the "caution" by police as a substitute for court proceedings.

Police Juvenile Bureaux personnel are responsible for gathering information from the Children's Departments, Probation and Education Services, and other [relevant] agencies about a young person brought to the station for an alleged offense. In most cases an officer will visit the juvenile's home. A background report is prepared which, together with the evidence relating to the offense, is considered by the chief inspector in charge of the Bureau who decides whether or not the young offender should be prosecuted. The cautioning procedure, which in 1970 was used for 39 percent of juveniles who committed offenses, is based on the following criteria:

a. The offender must admit the offense.
b. The parents must agree that the child be cautioned.
c. The person victimized must be willing to leave the matter to the police.

The caution is given under formal circumstances at the police station by a chief inspector in uniform. While a juvenile's record is relevant to whether he will have the benefit of the cautioning procedure, the fact that he has been cautioned previously does not necessarily mean that he will be prosecuted if he commits a subsequent offense.

At the outset, other social agencies responsible for juveniles were concerned that the police would not be adequately trained, that they would tend to pass judgment on the character of the juvenile, and that they might abuse confidential information. Representatives of the London Police say that care has been taken in the choice and training of personnel so as to eliminate grounds for such concern.

Diversion from Pretrial Detention

Programs to reduce the extent of pretrial detention have a dual importance in considering early diversion. It is true, of course, that neither the situation from which diversion takes place nor the alternative—release (with or without supervision)—is generally thought of as a correctional program. Nonetheless, diversion from this traditional stage of the criminal justice system is of great importance, because pretrial detention has an enormous and generally damaging impact on many arrested persons. Furthermore, as exemplified by the Des Moines project referred to below, such programs may facilitate subsequent diversion of the defendant after conviction.

The Vera Institute of Justice in New York City has pioneered in developing a "point" system for release on personal recognizance and subsequently adapted that system to enable the New York City Police Department to issue station-house summonses instead of detaining persons accused of minor crimes. If a desk officer in a station house can verify by telephone that an accused person has a sufficient number of points based on "roots in the community," the police can release him with a summons instead of taking him to arraignment court. The Vera summons is now used statewide in New York and is available for all crimes except felonies, unless the accused is under the influence of alcohol or drugs.

A similar program in California showed that more than 90 percent of those arrested persons whose community ties were investigated and who were released appeared for arraignment. Since 1969 police in California are required to consider station-house release of persons charged with misdemeanors.

Similar bail and summons projects based on the Vera experiments have been duplicated in many other cities and states. The Des Moines, Iowa, Model Neighborhood Corrections Project is an example of how pretrial release can be tied to correctional programs. Indeed, the purpose of the project was to permit an offender to show his reliability during his pretrial release period and thereby improve his chances for probation or some other nonprison sentence following trial. The project dealt with persons who did not qualify for release under the Vera-type criteria. After screening, those selected for release were supervised by staff of the project who linked the releasees with social agencies and other existing community resources. Follow-up studies have shown that those released in the project were as good risks as those released on money bail, and that, compared with a similar group of nonreleased defendants, they were less likely to be convicted if tried, less likely to be imprisoned if convicted, and likely to receive shorter sentences if imprisoned.

Pretrial Diversion: Prosecutorial Discretion

A large percentage of cases [are] disposed of in the prosecutor's office. Many of these dispositions are the result of agreed-upon guilty pleas and generally they lead to further processing within the criminal justice system. Some cases are dropped unconditionally on the basis of the prosecutor's judgment that the case is not strong enough or the offense is not serious. In some cases the decision not to prosecute is based on an agreement between the prosecutor and the accused that the accused will seek some other form of treatment or change his life in other ways, such as seeking psychiatric care, getting a job, participating in an educational program, or making restitution to the victim. Generally there are no stated standards or guidelines as to how the prosecutor will act in different kinds of situations. District Attorney William Cahalan of Wayne County, Michigan, has experimented with formalizing the procedures for pretrial conferences and plea negotiation with the aim of relieving the court of the task of docketing criminal cases. During a two-year span, his office reported that the average delay between arrest and trial was reduced from fourteen months to four. Tentative Draft No. 5 of the American Law Institute Model Code of Pre-Arraignment Procedure includes detailed procedures for a precharge screening conference at which the prosecutor and the accused and his lawyer may consider informal disposition of the case including diversion. Section 320.1 of the draft also provides for regulations regarding the conference which "to the extent the prosecutor believes feasible in the effective administration of justice shall include guidelines concerning action which the prosecutor will consider taking in certain types of cases or factual situations."

One interesting elaboration of the notion of a formalized pretrial conference to consider early diversion is a proposed Philadelphia program known as "Arbitration as an Alternative" which is designed to get the parties in a criminal action together so that disputes between them can be settled, all under the control of the district attorney. Arbitration in the settlement of personal injury suits has for some time been in use in Philadelphia, and the proposed experiment represents an extension of this model to criminal proceedings.

One of the most important types of programs for early diversion envisioned by the American Law Institute proposal is the so-called "court employment" project, again based on a Vera Institute innovation, the Manhattan Court Employment Project. This project, begun in 1968, has served as a model for a large number of similar projects around the country and is one of the most promising types of diversion projects at the prosecution stage. The Manhattan Court Employment Project intervenes in the usual court process just after arrest. Accused persons who meet the eligibility criteria are asked if they wish to participate in the project in order to earn a recommendation to the court after 90 days that charges against them be dismissed. In order to be recommended for a dismissal, participants must not be rearrested nor use narcotics. They must keep all appointments with project staff and prospective employers; they must attend and become involved in counseling sessions; and they must make satisfactory vocational adjustments.

During the 90 days, a participant works closely with two people—his representative, who typically has served time in prison himself and serves as counselor, and a career developer, who advises and refers the defendant to job opportunities. Most participants require more than one job placement. They are also encouraged to attend a group session every week, and they receive other appropriate referrals, such as to schools, drug treatment centers, hospitals, and welfare centers.

During the first year of operation, dismissal of charges was recommended and accepted for 39 percent of the participants; for the second year, 46 percent; and for the third year, 61 percent. For "dismissed" participants (those for whom dismissal of charges was successfully obtained) unemployment fourteen months after dismissal was 16.1 percent for a sample group as compared to 40 percent for terminated participants (those who failed in the project). The rearrest rate for "dismissed" participants was 15.8 percent; for participants terminated from the project, 30.8 percent; and for a comparison group drawn from the general court population, 46.1 percent.

In evaluating these figures, it should be noted that eligibility requirements have varied over the life of the project and that the comparison of those who stayed with the project and those who dropped out is necessarily not on a matched basis.

Postconviction Diversion

The problem of defining "diversion" is presented in its most difficult form in the postconviction stage. Probation and suspended sentences are established parts of criminal justice administration, so here it is particularly important to be clear as to what the new practices or programs are that are being considered. In fact we probably can find elements of most of the new postconviction programs in earlier probation programs. What is new may be a difference of degree: the greater numbers of offenders who have an opportunity to participate in the programs or more intensive supervision or services.

Three aspects of postconviction programs deserve discussion: (1) greater willingness now to return to the community offenders who have traditionally been incarcerated; (2) the need for special incentives to encourage the early return of offenders to the community; and (3) the development of new techniques of support or supervision in the community. Since another chapter deals with community treatment programs, we will only give a few examples of each of these developments in order to provide a basis for some observations and questions that bear on diversion at this stage.

Diversion to Community. The two of the most important examples of diverting to the community offenders who traditionally would have been confined are the Community Treatment Program of the California Youth Authority and the closing down of the juvenile institutions by the Massachusetts Department of Youth Services.

The California Community Treatment Program unquestionably was the most influential single source of encouragement for diversion to the community in the late 1960s and early 1970s. It had completed its first phase at the time the President's Crime Commission was in existence, and the commission's report provided a means for disseminating the message of the program: offenders treated in the community will be less dangerous than those incarcerated. Furthermore, this message had enormous influence on the commission's Corrections Task Force in encouraging a broad advocacy of community treatment —not only for juveniles but for adults as well. Although the program was carried on as a research project, the large numbers of offenders in the project and the long period of time over which it has operated entitle it to be regarded as a majority treatment program.

Male and female Youth Authority wards from Sacramento, Stockton, San Francisco, and Modesto were randomly assigned during the first phase of the program to the intensive community program or to the usual Youth Authority traditional institutional structure. During the first two phases (1961–1969) almost 700 cases were studied with an additional 330 in the control group. The project's reports showed that those treated in the community had dramatically lower failure rates than those sent to the Youth Authority's regular institutions. The figures used in the Crime Commission report were 28 percent failure among the Community Treatment group, compared to 52 percent for the control group. However, some observers have suggested that at least part of the differential may be due to more lenient treatment by parole agents and other decision-making authorities of subsequent misconduct by those in the Community Treatment group. In response, it has been suggested that the very fact the Community Treatment group was seen as special may have resulted in its members being under closer surveillance than other youths and hence more likely to come to the attention of the authorities. This issue has not been resolved and may never be, but at least it appears that in terms of cost savings and personal and social adjustment those sent to the community did better.

The most dramatic example of releasing traditionally confined offenders is the closing down of the juvenile institutions in the state program undertaken by Massachusetts Youth Services Commissioner Jerome Miller. After a frustrating attempt to establish therapeutic communities in the institutions and further frustration in gradual closings, Miller in a matter of a few months simply closed down all but the short-term detention facility. He believed a system without juvenile institutions would have less crime, and, having made that judgment, he undertook to find alternatives in the community for the seven hundred juveniles previously held in his institutions. The Harvard Law School Center for Criminal Justice is making an intensive evaluation of this program, including a cohort study, and should over the next few years be able to document its effects.

Incentives for Diversion.   The second issue referred to above—the need for incentives to encourage diversion—raises puzzling questions. If diversion is generally quicker, cheaper, and more humane and if there is doubt that it endangers public safety, why are so many offenders still going the traditional route? Part of the explanation is the lack of reliable data on the effects of diversion on an offender's dangerousness and on the deterrent message of criminal sanctions generally. In the face of this gap in our knowledge, presumably the slowness of change is explained by a degree of real or assumed punitiveness on the part of the public, the inherent conservatism of criminal justice officials, and the natural vested interest that everyone has to continue to do his job as he always has.

The money available under the Law Enforcement Assistance Administration program was designed to provide incentives for change, but the combination of the "block grant" approach in the legislation and weak administration at the federal and state levels has substantially reduced the federal program's effectiveness as an instrument of change. Thus to date it is hard to measure LEAA's impact on diversion. The most comprehensive attempt to provide an incentive for moving offenders to the community is the California Probation Subsidy. This program aims at encouraging counties to divert offenders from the state correctional institutions by offering a financial incentive proportionate to numbers diverted. The funds made available to the counties also enable them to offer better probation supervision and services. Experience during the first two years indicates that the counties can give improved service to five or six probationers with the subsidy saved on every new uncommitted case held at the county level. So far there are no data that would permit an evaluation of the impact of the subsidy program on crime in California or on the lives of those diverted. What does seem clear, however, is that the subsidy technique is an effective method for diverting many offenders from the prison population in a jurisdiction that has made the policy judgment that it wishes to do so.

Improved Supervision. The third aspect of postconviction projects referred to above—improvement of supervision or services in the community—is relevant to diversion at all stages. However, the further along the system an offender proceeds, the greater the pressure to show that the alternative to which he is diverted has real substance. Every postconviction diversion program seeks to justify its existence in large part by the substance of the services and/or supervision it provides to the offender as an alternative to incarceration. Since there is virtually no persuasive evaluation of the effectiveness of the new alternatives, policy-makers and funding agencies necessarily are forced to proceed on the basis of hunch, faith, or desperation about the traditional alternatives. One generalization that can be made about the alternatives offered is that most tend to combine in varying degrees three principal elements: (1) pressure or encouragement to the offender to take responsibility for his life in the community in which he will be living; (2) supportive services; (3) a relatively noncoercive form of supervision.

An example of an early experiment that appears to combine these features is the misdemeanant probation program in Royal Oak, Michigan, in which citizen volunteer sponsors are used on a one-to-one basis with misdemeanant probationers. Started in 1960 by Judge Keith J. Leenhouts, the program had around five hundred misdemeanants on some form of probation by the end of 1969. Twenty-four different treatment techniques are available in the program, including group therapy and assigned work detail projects whereby an offender can earn dismissal of his case and erasure of his record. The number of sponsors available in 1969 was about 250, with 100 awaiting assignments. This allows for considerable freedom in matching sponsors to probationers. An evaluative study of the program found that the recidivism rate for the program probationers was half that of probationers under a conventional misdemeanant probation system.

The Vera Institute has experimented more recently with diverting convicted misdemeanants to nonprison sentences, also using volunteer efforts. The Bronx Sentencing Project began operations in 1968 as an attempt to provide judges with short-form presentence reports. Using the experience of the Bail and Summons projects in developing reliable, verified information about defendants, the project hoped to change sentencing patterns by providing information on some of the 88 percent of convicted adult misdemeanants who were being sentenced by judges who did not have before them reports on the offenders' backgrounds and social histories.

The effect on the increase of nonprison sentences was slight until the project developed a referral capability. Failure rates had suggested that referral to a community agency rather than traditional probation might be more relevant for these offenders (who were indeed higher risks, having been taken from the defendant pool after the lower-risk candidates for probation had been identified). After experimenting with several community agencies, Vera decided to focus on referrals to one, Volunteer Opportunities, Inc. (VOI). And instead of recommending a sentence of conditional discharge for those cases it wished to refer to VOI, it recommended adjournment of the cases for one to six months, with sentencing to take place after the experience of working with VOI. For participants with satisfactory progress, the reward is avoiding a prison sentence. VOI's services include group and individual counseling; assistance on personal problems such as housing, health, job training, and employment; tutoring; and recreation.

The examples given above are necessarily arbitrarily selected from the hundreds of relatively new postconviction diversion programs. Other chapters describe other programs. No one today can have more than an impressionistic view of the extent to which community alternatives are replacing incarceration, and it will be years before we can know the answer to even this preliminary question which requires only a relatively simple "counting" type of research. And, of course, before judgment can be made about the relative effectiveness of diversion-type programs in reducing recidivism, the results of much deeper and more difficult evaluation must be done. Doubts such as those raised about the California Community Treatment project must be resolved. We must have the results of the few in-depth research projects now underway, and long-term and costly research on many existing projects must be undertaken.

Lest the current fashion in this country for diversion projects suggests that the United States is the leader in this movement, it is worth noting that we have probably been relatively slow to seek alternatives to incarceration. In Sweden, noninstitutional treatment is used much more frequently than in the United States. A report of the Advisory Council on the Penal System on Non-Custodial and Semi-Custodial Penalties in Great Britain includes among its recommendations a suggestion that offenders should perform a specified number of hours of service to the community in their spare time in lieu of incarceration.

In Israel, a judge is able to sentence an offender to work in a police station by day and return home at night. This is an outgrowth of a system that existed when Palestine was a British mandate, when the police themselves, not the judge, made the decision to assign prisoners to police station work. A number of prisoners in Israel are also diverted into the army. Those selected are put initially into a military scout program in the prisons, which is followed by three months of additional training under military supervision, then transfer to regular army units. For most participants prison terms are suspended at this point. To cite these examples is not to endorse them—merely to suggest that other nations have been and are grappling with the same issues as we are.

PART VII

Imprisonment
as a Legal Sanction

Among the forms of criminal sanctions thought to be appropriate in our society, none is more controversial than imprisonment. While sentiment is expressed in some quarters against the conferral of a prison sentence upon any offender, others feel that incarceration should be mandatory for convicted felons. The controversy extends further into the administration of prisons and related programs of halfway houses, work-release, study-release, and furloughs. The dilemmas attendant to imprisonment are not likely to be satisfactorily resolved in future decades, for the issues themselves reflect widely varying human values.

Since 1967, when the last capital execution took place in the United States, confinement in prison has been the most severe form of sanction applied by judicial authority. A number of questions have been asked about the aggregation of offenders in secure institutions: What does imprisonment do to benefit society generally and the victim specifically? Assuming that prisons are run along humanitarian lines, what impact—both planned and unplanned—do they have upon inmates? Under what conditions does the act of confinement have a deterrent effect upon criminally disposed persons in the community? If someone commits a crime, is convicted, and sentenced to prison, what rights should he forfeit as a consequence? Does the American public have the commitment to "prison reform" that can surmount the enormous financial, emotional, political, and legal impediments?

Counting persons retained in pretrial custody, well over one million men and women are confined in jails or prisons on any given day. They, of course, do not constitute a random sample of the population. Custodial settings are disproportionately inhabited by minority groups, the poor, and increasingly by women. Present evidence also suggests that institutions for convicted offenders are selective of the more serious, long-term, criminally sophisticated felons. The management and rehabilitative challenges posed by them are both qualitatively and quantitatively greater than in former years.

The effects of imprisonment are not fully understood by any means, but most informed persons feel that alternatives must be found for the majority of offenders. Historically, the court has used probation as a mechanism for sparing first offenders and other, less serious, cases from incarceration. Then, following experiments by quasi-religious organizations that often focused upon drug-related offenders, halfway houses became fashionable. Initially, these were "halfway out" back to the community. Later, "halfway in" houses, used as an option by the court, were established as residential treatment centers. Thus the alternatives available in a convicted felon's career have been expanded; at the same time new problems of decision-making (e.g., how parole decisions are reached, or how violations of halfway house regulations are administratively handled) have appeared.

Another recent trend in corrections is an apparent increase in professionalization. "Correctional institutions" headed by "Superintendents" are replacing penitentiaries run by wardens; inmates are "residents," and guards are "correctional officers." No doubt these changes in nomenclature reflect a concern among prison administrators that corrections work be humane, dignified, and effective. Inmates have become more "professional" as well, particularly regarding legal rights such as due process in disciplinary proceedings, access to the courts and the media, and the redress of grievances. Prison staff contend that they are "losing control" over the prison because institutions are being "run by the courts." As a consequence, the traditional conflict between prisoners and their keepers is not likely to diminish in the near future.

Several approaches to the study of prison systems have been taken by criminologists. One that has stimulated much criticism is to research a type of criminal behavior, as if incarcerated offenders were representative of their counterparts in the outside community. Opponents of this strategy would hold that a study of car thieves, for example, using an imprisoned sample may tell us little about car theft in the community, since many such offenders are not apprehended. A second approach has focused upon the dimensions of inmate society, variously referred to as "inmate culture," "inmate role structure," or the "inmate social system." More recently, some interest has been shown in "staff culture," or the system of beliefs, values, and goals that develops among prison employees. Third, social ecologists and architects have made significant contributions to our knowledge about correctional environments. For example, they have shown how restrictive cell dimensions, security gates, and unimaginative food service heighten the deprivations suffered by imprisoned persons. Fourth, the topic of prison violence has occupied the attention of some criminologists, who argue that institutional life is inherently conflict-ridden and that violence is a traditional means of conflict resolution. Some of the best research on these and other properties of confinement utilizes a comparative approach, i.e., one which attempts to identify organizational characteristics of prisons that predict institutional functioning.

Correctional objectives, whether formulated by political authorities, the administrators of institutions, or inmate councils, have always been criticized for their inconsistencies. It is argued that traditional goals—reformation, incapacitation, and retribution—are inherently abrasive, and that the most sensitive index of this is an enormous recidivism rate. Public indignation about the "failure" of prisons has been given substantial attention by the media in the past few years, following incidents at Attica, San Quentin, and numerous other large institutions. There is some evidence, however, that satisfactory answers to the questions posed did not emerge and that the dilemmas of imprisonment, though better understood in all quarters, will be available to inquiry for a long time. Those who propose a systematic, intensive study of correctional effectiveness can anticipate that the politics of crime and its control will be a major challenge.

———————

Donald R. Cressey's "The Prison and Organizational Goals," taken from a lengthy chapter on the social-system attributes of correctional settings, emphasizes some issues in the philosophy of punishment. Included is a review of societal attitudes and reactions toward imprisoned offenders.

The selection by Gresham M. Sykes and Sheldon Messinger is considered a minor classic in the corrections literature. It analyzes the inmate value system and the normative expectations reflected in role networks among prisoners. Inmate roles are differentiated in terms of prestige, power, verbal and physical adroitness, and commitment to staff or inmate norms.

The Guenthers focus upon the atmosphere of uncertainty in prisons which has important consequences for the conflict between inmates and staff. Compensations by correctional officers to maintain some control over prison incidents are shown to take several forms.

The essay by Hans W. Mattick explains contemporary prison violence in terms of the shifting power bargain reached between inmates and staff. He shows how today's prisoners, more aware socially and politically and less inclined to bargain than the "old cons" were, tend to be less acquiescent.

For the interested reader, selected publications on correctional system theory and research are referred to below.

1. *Prison Goals, Change, and the Concept of Effectiveness*
Adams, Stuart, *Evaluative Research in Corrections: A Practical Guide* (Washington, D.C.: National Institute of Law Enforcement and Criminal Justice, 1975).
Cressey, Donald R., "Contradictory Directives in Complex Organizations: The Case of the Prison," *Administrative Science Quarterly* 4 (1959): 1–19.

Glaser, Daniel, *The Effectiveness of a Prison and Parole System* (Indianapolis: Bobbs-Merrill, 1964).
Lipton, Douglas; Martinson, Robert; and Wilks, Judith, *The Effectiveness of Correctional Treatment: A Survey of Treatment Evaluation Surveys* (New York: Praeger, 1975).
Martinson, Robert, "What Works?—Questions and Answers About Prison Reform," *The Public Interest* 35 (1974): 22–54.
McCleery, Richard H., "The Governmental Process and Informal Social Control," in *The Prison: Studies in Institutional Organization and Change*, ed. Donald R. Cressey (New York: Holt, Rinehart and Winston, 1961), pp. 149–88.
Morris, Norval, *The Future of Imprisonment* (Chicago: University of Chicago Press, 1974).
Nagel, William G., *The New Red Barn: A Critical Look at the Modern American Prison* (New York: Walker, 1973).
Ohlin, Lloyd E., "Conflicting Interests in Correctional Objectives," in Richard A. Cloward et al., *Theoretical Studies in Social Organization of the Prison* (New York: Social Science Research Council, 1960), pp. 111–29.
———, "Organizational Reform in Correctional Agencies," in *Handbook of Criminology*, ed. Daniel Glaser (Chicago: Rand McNally, 1974), pp. 995–1020.
Rothman, David J., "The Invention of the Penitentiary," *The Discovery of the Asylum: Social Order and Disorder in the New Republic* (Boston: Little, Brown, 1971), pp. 79–108.
Schrag, Clarence, "The Correctional System: Problems and Prospects," *The Annals of the American Academy of Political and Social Science* 381 (1969): 11–20.
Singer, Linda R., "Women and the Correctional Process," *The American Criminal Law Review* 11 (1973): 295–308.
Ward, David A., "Evaluative Research for Corrections," in *Prisoners in America*, ed. Lloyd E. Ohlin (Englewood Cliffs, N.J.: Prentice-Hall, 1973), pp. 184–206.
Wilson, James Q., "Locking 'Em Up and Other Thoughts on Crime," *The New York Times Magazine* (March 9, 1975), pp. 11 ff.

2. *Organizational Features of Prisons*
Berk, Bernard B., "Organizational Goals and Inmate Organization," *American Journal of Sociology* 71 (1966): 522–34.

Cressey, Donald R., "Prison Organizations," in *Handbook of Organizations,* ed. James G. March (Chicago: Rand McNally, 1965), pp. 1023–70.

Garson, G. David, "The Disruption of Prison Administration: An Investigation of Alternative Theories of the Relationship Among Administrators, Reformers, and Involuntary Social Service Clients," *Law and Society Review* 6 (1972): 531–61.

Goffman, Erving, "The Characteristics of Total Institutions," in *Complex Organizations,* ed. Amitai Etzioni (New York: Holt, Rinehart and Winston, 1961), pp. 312–40.

Zald, Mayer N., "Power Balance and Staff Conflict in Correctional Institutions," *Administrative Science Quarterly* 7 (1962): 22–49.

3. *Inmate Social Organization*

Buffum, Peter G., *Homosexuality in Prisons* (Washington, D.C.: National Institute of Law Enforcement and Criminal Justice, 1972).

Clemmer, Donald, *The Prison Community* (1940; reissue New York: Rinehart, 1958), chaps. 4–8.

Cressey, Donald R., "Adult Felons in Prison," in *Prisoners in America,* ed. Lloyd E. Ohlin (Englewood Cliffs, N.J.: Prentice-Hall, 1973), pp. 117–50.

Giallombardo, Rose, "Social Roles in a Prison for Women," *Social Problems* 13 (1966): 268–88.

Goffman, Erving, "On the Characteristics of Total Institutions: The Inmate World," in *The Prison: Studies in Institutional Organization and Change,* ed. Donald R. Cressey (New York: Holt, Rinehart and Winston, 1961), pp. 15–67.

Irwin, John, "Adaptation to Being Corrected: Corrections from the Convict's Perspective," in *Handbook of Criminology,* ed. Daniel Glaser (Chicago: Rand McNally, 1974), pp. 971–93.

————, *The Felon* (Englewood Cliffs, N.J.: Prentice-Hall, 1970).

McCorkle, Lloyd W., and Korn, Richard, "Resocialization Within Walls," *The Annals of the American Academy of Political and Social Science* 293 (1954): 80–98.

Sykes, Gresham M., *The Society of Captives* (Princeton: Princeton University Press, 1958).

Ward, David A., and Kassebaum, Gene G., "Homosexuality: A Mode of Adaptation in a Prison for Women," *Social Problems* 12 (1964): 159–77.

Wheeler, Stanton, "Socialization in Correctional Institutions," in *Handbook of Socialization Theory and Research,* ed. David A. Goslin (Chicago: Rand McNally, 1969), pp. 1005–23.

Zeigler, Herb, "Prison: What's It All About?" *Society* 11 (1974): 67–69.

4. *Staff Social Organization*

Giallombardo, Rose, *Society of Women: A Study of a Women's Prison* (New York: Wiley, 1966), chap. 3, "Characteristics of the Staff," and chap. 4, "Organization of the Staff and Relations with Inmates."

Goffman, Erving, "On the Characteristics of Total Institutions: Staff-Inmate Relations," in *The Prison: Studies in Institutional Organization and Change,* ed. Donald R. Cressey (New York: Holt, Rinehart and Winston, 1961), pp. 68–106.

Guenther, Anthony L., *The Culture of Imprisonment* (Englewood Cliffs, N.J.: Prentice-Hall, 1977), chap. 6, "The World of Custodial Staff," and chap. 7, " 'Screws' Versus 'Thugs'."

Lamott, Kenneth, " 'I Didn't Bring Anyone Here, and I Can't Send Anyone Home'," *Saturday Review* 55 (1972), pp. 8 ff.

Sykes, Gresham M., "The Corruption of Authority and Rehabilitation," *Social Forces* 34 (1956): 257–62.

————, *The Society of Captives* (Princeton: Princeton University Press, 1958), chap. 2, "The Regime of the Custodians."

5. *The Development of Correctional Law*

Kraft, Larry, "Prison Disciplinary Practices and Procedures: Is Due Process Provided?" *North Dakota Law Review* 47 (1970): 54–120.

"Prisoners' Rights," *Buffalo Law Review* 21 (1972).

Rubin, Sol, "The Impact of Court Decisions on the Correctional Process," *Crime and Delinquency* 20 (1974): 129–34.

_____, *The Law of Criminal Correction*, second edition (St. Paul, Minn.: West Publishing Company, 1973).

South Carolina Department of Corrections, *The Emerging Rights of the Confined* (Columbia, S.C.: The Correctional Development Foundation, 1972).

25

The Prison and Organizational Goals

Donald R. Cressey

In recent years, variations in the effectiveness and efficiency of different kinds of organizations and in the conditions under which these organizations arise, persist, and change have been studied in many settings, ranging from broad administrative systems to specific governmental and military hierarchies, factories, and hospitals. Almost all such studies could have been made in prisons, which contain systems of a military type designed to keep inmates within walls, industrial systems to maintain the prison and produce goods, and professional or "service" systems to rehabilitate inmates. Moreover, the prison as a whole is a governmental organization designed to administer the activities of the persons in the various roles in these and other subsidiary systems.

Prisons, however, provide more than a convenient opportunity for verifying observations already made by students of social organizations.[1] In two principal respects, prisons seem to differ significantly from factories and similar organizations. First, the administrative hierarchies of prisons are organized down to the lowest level. In factories, there are separate hierarchies of management personnel and of workers, and research has been concerned with the relations of these roles to each other and to their organizational purpose, production. The lowest-status employee in a prison, in contrast, is both a manager and a worker.

From Donald R. Cressey, "Prison Organizations," in James G. March (ed.), *Handbook of Organizations* (Chicago: Rand McNally, 1965), pp. 1023–30, by permission of the author and publisher. Copyright © 1965 by Rand McNally College Publishing Company. Footnotes have been added.

1. The material in this and the following three paragraphs is taken from Donald R. Cressey, "Limitations on Organization of Treatment in the Modern Prison," in Richard A. Cloward et al., *Theoretical Studies in Social Organization of the Prison* (New York: Social Science Research Council, 1960), pp. 78–110.

He is managed in a system of regulations and controls from above, but he also manages in a presumably concordant system the inmates who are in his charge. He is a low-status worker in interaction with management, but a higher-status foreman, "officer," or treatment agent in interaction with inmates. The guard, who in traditional prisons is at the bottom of a hierarchical system which manages his job of managing men, has no counterpart in the business and industrial world. The closest analogy would be the overseer of a crew of slaves, who would be viewed as "outside" the organization designed to utilize their labor effectively. Even this analogy is fallacious except as guards may serve as foremen of inmate industrial or maintenance crews. Most guards have nothing to do but stand guard: they do not "use" inmates productively any more than they themselves are used productively by prison managers. Guards manage and are managed in organizations where management is an end, not a means.

Second, as prisons have grown in size and as concepts of good penology have changed, new services and roles have been added without regard to those already existing. This process seems different from that accompanying similar growth of other bodies, for the new roles have been organized around purposes that are little related to each other. In all prisons there is a line organization of custodial ranks, ranging from warden to guard, and salary differentials and descriptive titles indicate that a chain of command is expected within this hierarchy. However, although all employees are responsibile to the warden, there is no clear expectation that the institution should consist solely of a hierarchy of custodial ranks in reference to which all positions are integrated. Systems of nonline positions, such as those of professional personnel and industrial foremen and superintendents, are essentially separate and have their own salary differentials and titles. They are part of neither the custodial chain of command nor staff organizations. Noncustodial personnel are not advisers to the custodians in the sense that the experts of various sorts who make up the staff organization of factories are advisers, providing specialized knowledge to assist the line organization with its task of production.[2] The structure of prisons provides for three principal hierarchies devoted, respectively, to keeping, using, and serving inmates, but not for the integration of their divergent purposes. The separate organizations concerned with keeping and with serving inmates, for example, not merely are overlapping, but have entirely different and partly contradictory purposes.

---

2. M. Dalton, "Conflicts Between Staff and Line Managerial Officers," *American Sociological Review*, 15 (1950): 342–51.

The objectives of each hierarchy require that its roles and processes of role integration take definite forms. The model of an organization for giving help and treatment to inmates is an archetypical mental hospital; for using inmates, an industrial organization such as a lumber camp, where employees both work and live together; for keeping them, a prison on the order of the early Pennsylvania institutions, where all inmates were kept in solitary confinement. Each organization includes a specific kind of relationship between employees and inmates; a specific pattern of authority, communication, and decision-making; and a specific system for distributing rewards and punishments. These features vary significantly among the different kinds of organization. . . .

Little is known about the processes of modification and accommodation taking place when the three hierarchies are expected to function as parts of an overall organization. There has been little systematic observation of the resulting consequences for each subsidiary organization. There is need for description and analysis of organizational problems stemming from administrative attempts to transform the total system into an organization consistent with only one or another of the subsidiaries. For example, some prison administrators seem committed to establishing, in the presence of treatment and productive organizations, a total system modeled on the custodial archetype.[3] Other administrators, in the presence of productive and custodial organizations, strain to establish and maintain a total system consistent with the treatment archetype. . . .

THE PRISON AND SOCIETY

The variety of occupational activities and organizational patterns characterizing modern prisons has grown out of changing conceptions, in the society as a whole, of what ought to be done to, with, and for criminals. Later sections of this chapter try to show how both conforming behavior and deviant behavior among prison staff members are related to the social pressures arising out of the organizational conditions within which the behavior takes place. It is necessary, therefore, to review briefly some of the history of prisons in order to show how these organizational conditions came into existence. It is erroneous to believe that the prison administrator is free to organize and develop his

---

3. R. L. Jenkins, "Treatment in an Institution," *American Journal of Orthopsychiatry*, 11 (1941): 85–91; Lloyd E. Ohlin, *Sociology and the Field of Corrections* (New York: Russell Sage Foundation, 1956); H. Powelson and R. Bendix, "Psychiatry in Prison," *Psychiatry*, 14 (1951): 73–86; L. N. Robinson, "Contradictory Purposes in Prisons," *Journal of Criminal Law and Criminology*, 37 (1947): 449–57.

prison in any way he considers efficient. The activities which his staff must perform are sharply and rather specifically determined by groups outside the prison itself.

In contemporary American society, there are at least four distinguishable attitudes toward the control of crime, and each of them incorporates a program of action for correctional agencies and institutions.[4] First, there is a desire for retribution. At least since Hammurabi, it has been generally accepted that the criminal deserves to suffer simply because he is a criminal. Taking individual revenge is now usually illegal and/or immoral, but contemporary America does maintain a powerful legal organization for corporate imposition of suffering on offenders. Most of us view this system of officially punishing criminals as highly desirable. By acting collectively to take revenge on criminals, society is said to reinforce its anticriminal values. From this point of view, the future of the offender is unimportant.

Next, there is a desire that suffering be imposed on criminals as a deterrent to potential criminals. Again, the future effects of punishment on the society, not on the criminal, are viewed as the important consideration. The basic notion is that infliction of pain on offenders serves to arouse in others a fear of perpetrating the offense: swift and certain punishment of crime will arouse in noncriminals a fear of transgression. In a narrow perspective, the desire for punishment as a deterrent is based on the assumption that individuals carefully calculate the future consequences of their contemplated acts and do not commit them if they are likely to stimulate punishment. In a broader perspective, the assumption is that administration of the criminal law's penal sanctions by police, courts, and prisons, among others, has long-run effects upon public morality.[5]

Third, in contemporary America there is an obvious desire for protection against the criminal. Whether he is punished or not, the offender must be physically isolated so that the community is safe from him. The attitude here is directed neither at the criminal's fate nor at the indirect effects which punishment has on society's morality. Rather, the criminal is viewed as dangerous, like a poisonous snake or a tornado, and the conclusion is that he must be controlled.

Finally, there is in our society a desire to reduce crime rates by changing criminals. A high crime rate is the result either of a large

---

4. Edwin H. Sutherland and Donald R. Cressey, *Principles of Criminology*, 6th ed. (Philadelphia: Lippincott, 1960), pp. 460–61.

5. Emile Durkheim, *The Division of Labor in Society* (Glencoe, Ill.: Free Press, 1947), pp. 70–110.

number of people committing one crime each or of a few people committing many crimes. Hence, although punishment of the offender may deter many potential criminals, the offender himself must be reformed or rehabilitated if the crime rate is to be substantially reduced. This attitude, of course, is congruent with the notion that society must be protected from criminals; the desire for reformation is merely an implied variation of the proper action to be taken in order to achieve protection from criminals.

These four attitudes are not new. For about 250 years, prison administrators have been charged with implementing each of them. They continue to be charged with such implementation, and this means that prisons must somehow exact retribution, deter potential criminals, and incapacitate and reform convicted criminals. In other words, contemporary prison programs, like those of two centuries ago, are to make life unpleasant for men who have made others' lives unpleasant, to isolate criminals so they cannot commit crimes during certain periods of time, and to reduce crime rates both by deterring the general public from criminal behavior and by reforming criminals. But the conceptions of the proper *procedures* for implementing these attitudes have changed considerably, even in the twentieth century.

In early prisons, few organizational problems arose in connection with meeting these expectations. According to the dominant notions about correctional procedures at the time, each could be fulfilled by an organization designed to inflict punishments of an intensity now labeled "severe." Within the prison walls which were to protect society from dangerous criminals, a rigorous, monotonous, and unpleasant regime was to fill the social needs for retribution, deterrence, and reformation. Gradually, however, conceptions of the proper means to be used for achieving these goals have shifted. First, serious doubts arose about whether there is a social need for retribution and deterrent punishments more severe than "mere" deprivation of liberty. There has been a trend toward the notion that punishment by deprivation of liberty should be substituted for punishment by infliction of physical pain. Next, serious doubts about the necessary degree of severity of punishment and the necessary degree of control have arisen. There has been a trend toward reducing the severity of punishments. Then, more recently, serious doubts have arisen about whether reformation can be achieved by punishment of any kind, including deprivation of liberty. There has been a trend toward increasing acceptance of the notion that reformation, rehabilitation, or "correction" of criminals can be achieved only through nonpunitive treatment methods.

Psychological versus Physical Punishment

Punishment as an instrument of public justice is pain and suffering purposively inflicted on criminals by the state because of some value, such as deterrence or reformation, it is assumed to have. Significantly, the pain and suffering need not be physical: punishment can be deprivation of anything the members of the society cherish, such as money or liberty. One relevant point to note in this connection is that imprisonment as a system for dealing with criminals was hardly known until the time of the great democratic revolutions in the eighteenth century.[6] Until the last part of that century, the primary use of incarceration was for persons awaiting trial; after trial, pain was inflicted on the guilty by corporal punishment. It was no mere coincidence that imprisonment arose when it did, nor is it merely a coincidence that imprisonment has remained the dominant method of dealing with serious offenders in democratic countries. As democracy developed, so did an appreciation of liberty, and restriction of freedom by imprisonment, rather than imposition of physical pain, has come to be regarded as a proper system of punishing criminals. It was in the early democratic period that the current system of criminal laws, each law calling for a measured amount of loss of freedom and thus a measured amount of pain, was initiated.

However, substitution of this kind of suffering for more direct physical suffering has been slow and incomplete. The history of imprisonment is in part a story of the gradual but as yet unfinished modification of the principle that men are sent to prisons *for* punishment rather than *as* punishment. Invention of the notion that criminals should be punished by "mere" deprivation of their freedom, rather than by imposition of physical pain, was not readily accepted by all the groups having significant interests in prisons, and it is not widely accepted, without qualifications, even today. However, in the early days of democracy, people seemed even less sure of themselves than at present, for administrators were more often expected to inflict pain on prisoners while at the same time depriving them of their freedom. In the extreme, prisoners were required to walk treadmills, turn cranks, carry a cannonball for prescribed periods, and to perform other painful tasks. They also were conscientiously forced to live in unpleasant physical surroundings, often depending upon charity for their maintenance. Few opportunities for diversions such as participation in religious services were provided, presumably on the ground that this would mitigate the

---

6. Cressey, "Rehabilitation Theory and Reality, I: The Pain of Restriction," *California Youth Authority Quarterly*, 10 (1957): 6–9.

conditions of suffering which the criminal was thought both to deserve and to need. In this system, reformation was to be produced by the same physically punitive devices which fulfilled the needs for retribution and deterrent punishments.

Prisons soon abandoned harsh corporal punishments and punitive labor as a regime for supplementing the suffering which mere incarceration was expected to produce. Yet "mere incarceration" has never been consistently defined and has meant many things to many people, as has been true of the concept "liberty." In early institutions, such as the Walnut Street Jail in Philadelphia at the end of the Revolutionary War,[7] it meant mere perimeter control, with freedom to commit crime and engage in debauchery within the prison walls. Even today in some prisons perimeter control is stressed, although inmates are not granted the degree of freedom within the walls that they had in the earlier institutions. Such things as petty rackets, stealing, the manufacture, purchase, and consumption of alcohol, homosexuality, fighting, gambling, and other unsupervised activities are not necessarily condoned in these institutions, but they are not prevented either. When these conditions become known to significant outsiders, strong pressures are placed on the administrators to "clean up" and "tighten up" their institutions, pressures which ordinarily arise from assumptions that such prisons are not sufficiently punitive, and therefore are not sufficiently reformative. Further, because the prisoners for whom only perimeter control is exercised do not themselves necessarily develop and maintain high standards of sanitation and hygiene, humanitarian as well as penological considerations enter into evaluations of such institutions as "bad." Control of actions *within* the prison, then, not mere confinement behind walls, becomes a necessary part of punitive imprisonment.

An early and extreme response to this modified interpretation of the meaning of "mere incarceration" was continuous confinement of all prisoners in isolation. "Perimeter control" was in the Pennsylvania institutions in the early nineteenth century extended to the individual inmate, who was confined to a cell. The "abuses" as well as the relatively nonpunitive and nonreformative conditions of freedom within the walls were corrected by solitary confinement under conditions of physical discomfort. Such ultimate restriction of liberty was clearly within the intent of the principle that criminals were to be both punished and reformed by mere incarceration: confinement in solitary would be unpleasant and feared but, at the same time, would make prisoners peni-

---

7. R. C. Gray, *Prison Discipline in America* (London: Murray, 1848).

tent. This system is used for a small minority of the men in present-day prisons, but it has been abandoned as a general regime principally on the theoretical ground that it is "too restrictive" or punitive, and therefore not reformative.

Another early interpretation of the proper mode of handling men whose freedom is being restricted for punitive and reformative purposes was different from the solitary-confinement interpretation only in degree. Inmates were to be allowed some physical mobility within the walls, but every effort was made to insure that a maximum number of their actions and choices was *directed* by prison employees.

A conception of liberty which makes it possible to take this middle ground between interpretation of deprivation of liberty as only perimeter control and interpretation of it as complete individual control has remained the most popular conception today. Control of inmate actions within the prison, not mere confinement behind walls and not individual isolation, has come to be synonymous with imprisonment. Even here there are variations, however, for there is by no means complete consensus on what "individual freedom" and "liberty" means. One conception of deprivation of liberty has it that regulation of almost all the details of the prisoner's life shall be attempted, while a different conception dictates that a much smaller degree of control shall be used. The different ideological positions involved are the same as those which ask for maximum police powers in a community, as opposed to those which insist that police power is undue interference with individual freedom.

Certainly it cannot be inferred that complete transition to imprisonment *as* punishment, rather than *for* punishment, has been made. Physical punishments in forms such as whipping, punitive labor, securing hands in a position high above the head, and battering with a high-pressure stream of water are still used in some prisons. Moreover, restriction of liberty is almost universally interpreted to mean deprivation of some *physical comforts,* with the result that the suffering imposed is physical as well as psychological. For example, within prisons, solitary confinement as punitive restriction of liberty is always supplemented by physical discomforts in the form of a restricted diet and denial of a bed as comfortable as the beds in the rest of the institution. In some cases, the offender in solitary is handcuffed to the bars so that he cannot sit during working hours. Mere restriction of recalcitrant inmates' liberty is viewed as insufficiently punitive. More generally, the practice of sentencing a man to incarceration *under conditions of physical discomfort,* not just to incarceration, is widely accepted in our society. Even in model minimum-security institutions, cells are not equipped with "luxuries" such as comfortable beds, davenports, bathrooms, and overstuffed chairs. Prisoners "do not deserve" such things. Restriction of liberty continues to mean restriction of some degree of comfort, and hence physical as well as psychological punishment.

Nevertheless, significant interest groups with power to control prison practices are, like the society itself, sharply divided on this issue. Prison administrators are under almost constant harassment from interest groups holding that physical deprivation must supplement deprivation of liberty and maintaining that "sentimentalists" are turning our penal institutions into country clubs. They also are under similar harassment from interest groups holding that there can be no punishment at all beyond that stemming from deprivation of liberty and maintaining that "barbarians" and undemocratic "dictators" deprive prisoners of a level of living comparable to that of the middle class, do not permit them to have sexual relationships with their wives, and so on.

Despite the fact that prisoners continue to be physically deprived, there has been a distinct trend in the United States, and in most of the world, toward decreasing use of corporal punishment and punitive labor to supplement the pain coming from loss of liberty. Many contemporary wardens have in their tenure witnessed tremendous humanitarian changes in their own prisons. There also has been a trend toward reducing the degree of control maintained over prisoners. This means that some of the deprivations stemming from loss of liberty, as well as many physical deprivations, have been eliminated. When pain is inflicted by forcing the criminal to live under authoritarian conditions rather than in conditions of freedom, then reduction in the degree of control is a reduction in punishment.[8]

It is possible, of course, to be restrictive and custodial without being punitive. It was specified above that punishment is pain and suffering that are intentionally imposed. It follows that pain and suffering which are unavoidably imposed are not punishment. Thus, a prisoner who has a painful surgical operation performed on him is not being punished, for the pain is an unavoidable part of the treatment. Similarly, neither a man who is drafted into the army, a child who is compelled to attend school, nor a patient who is compelled to live in a hospital is being punished, despite the fact that each loses some degree of freedom. The principal difference between committing a criminal to prison and a psychotic to a mental hospital is that society officially *wants* the crimi-

---

8. Cressey, "Rehabilitation Theory and Reality, II: Organization and Freedom," *California Youth Authority Quarterly*, 10 (1957): 40–47.

nal, but not the psychotic, to suffer from the loss of liberty. The psychotic might suffer from confinement behind bars, just as prisoners do, but imposition of the suffering is an unavoidable correlate of treating him and protecting society from him. No educated person believes that committing a psychotic to a hospital should be based on the assumption that the suffering resulting from his incarceration will, by itself, have value in rehabilitation or in deterring others from becoming patients. This, as indicated, is precisely the assumption behind committing men to prison.

In addition to becoming places where the level of suffering for inmates has been reduced, prisons have increasingly become places where positive, nonpunitive, and nonrestrictive services are offered to offenders. These nonpunitive services are called "treatment." Prisons have almost always relied upon some positive action, as well as on restrictive punishment, to reform criminals, but the degree of interest in changing prisoners by nonpunitive means has increased over the years, principally because new services have been added to those already existing. Thus, religious instruction was introduced shortly after imprisonment was invented, academic education was added about a century ago, vocational education was added in the early twentieth century, and psychological, psychiatric, and social work services of various kinds have been in evidence for a generation. Although the conception of the prison as a place of nonpunitive treatment, rather than as a place of punishment and restriction, has not permeated all institutions to the same degree, the social welfare movement and the growth in popularity of psychiatric interpretations of criminal behavior have meant that prisons have been increasingly concerned with establishing positive programs for rehabilitating prisoners by altering their values, habits, attitudes, psychic structures, and points of view. Despite the fact that in 1958 less than 5 percent of the 27,000 persons employed in American prisons were directly concerned with the administration of treatment or training,[9] it is correct to say that the *idea* that we should attempt to understand the forces and mechanisms of criminality and develop efficient methods of reformation based on that understanding has gained increasing popularity in the last fifty years, and especially in the years since World War II.

In summary, at present there are three popular sanctioned reactions to crime in contemporary American society. One is hostility, with insistence that the criminal be made to suffer in prison, whether the

---

9. A. C. Schnur, "The New Penology: Fact or Fiction?," *Journal of Criminal Law and Criminology*, 49 (1958):331–34.

suffering is physical or psychological. Another reaction is one of human-itarian concern that the punishments in prisons not be too harsh, severe, cruel, or inhuman. A third is inquiry designed to secure compre-hension of the social and psychological processes in criminal behavior, so that control can be based on knowledge.

26

The Inmate Social System

Gresham M. Sykes and Sheldon L. Messinger

In recent years increased attention has been paid to the custodial institution in terms of general sociological theory rather than in terms of social problems, notably with reference to aspects of prison life commonly identified in the relevant literature as the "inmate culture," the "prisoner community," or the "inmate social system." This system of social relationships—its underlying norms, attitudes, and beliefs—as found in the American prison is examined in this paper. After summarizing the salient features of the society of prisoners as presented in the sociological literature of the last two decades, we comment briefly on the major theoretical approach that has been used in discussing prison life in the past. Then we develop a theory of the structure and functioning of the inmate social system, primarily in terms of inmate values and their related roles, and finally we outline some possibilities for future research.

THE PRISON SOCIETY

Despite the number and diversity of prison populations, observers of such groups have reported one strikingly pervasive value system. This value system of prisoners commonly takes the form of an explicit code, in which brief normative imperatives are held forth as guides for the behavior of the inmate in his relations with fellow prisoners and custodians. The maxims are usually asserted with great vehemence by the

From Gresham M. Sykes & Sheldon L. Messinger, "The Inmate Social System," in Richard A. Cloward et al. (eds.), *Theoretical Studies in Social Organization of the Prison* (New York: Social Science Research Council, 1960), pp. 5–19, by permission of the authors and publisher. Copyright © 1960 by the Social Science Research Council. Footnotes have been renumbered.

inmate population, and violations call forth a diversity of sanctions ranging from ostracism to physical violence.

Examination of many descriptions of prison life suggests that the chief tenets of the inmate code can be classified roughly into five major groups:

1. There are those maxims that caution: *Don't interfere with inmate interests,* which center of course in serving the least possible time and enjoying the greatest possible number of pleasures and privileges while in prison. The most inflexible directive in this category is concerned with betrayal of a fellow captive to the institutional officials: *Never rat on a con.* In general, no qualification or mitigating circumstance is recognized; and no grievance against another inmate—even though it is justified in the eyes of the inmate population —is to be taken to officials for settlement. Other specifics include: *Don't be nosey; don't have a loose lip; keep off a man's back; don't put a guy on the spot.* In brief and positively put: *Be loyal to your class—the cons.* Prisoners must present a unified front against their guards, no matter how much this may cost in terms of personal sacrifice.
2. There are explicit injunctions to refrain from quarrels or arguments with fellow prisoners: *Don't lose your head.* Emphasis is placed on the curtailment of affect; emotional frictions are to be minimized and the irritants of daily life ignored. Maxims often heard include: *Play it cool* and *Do your own time.* As we shall see, there are important distinctions in this category, depending on whether the prisoner has been subjected to legitimate provocation; but in general a definite value is placed on curbing feuds and grudges.
3. Prisoners assert that inmates should not take advantage of one another by means of force, fraud, or chicanery: *Don't exploit inmates.* This sums up several directives: *Don't break your word; don't steal from the cons; don't sell favors; don't be a racketeer; don't welsh on debts.* More positively, it is argued that inmates should share scarce goods in a balanced reciprocity of "gifts" or "favors," rather than sell to the highest bidder or selfishly monopolize any amenities: *Be right.*
4. There are rules that have as their central theme the maintenance of self: *Don't weaken.* Dignity and the ability to withstand frustration or threatening situations without complaining or resorting to subservience are widely acclaimed. The prisoner should be able to "take it" and maintain his integrity in the face of privation. When confronted with wrongfully aggressive behavior, whether of inmates or officials, the prisoner should show courage. Although starting a fight

runs counter to the inmate code, retreating from a fight started by someone else is equally reprehensible. Some of these maxims are: *Don't whine; don't cop out* (cry guilty); *don't suck around.* Prescriptively put: *Be tough; be a man.*

5. Prisoners express a variety of maxims that forbid according prestige or respect to the custodians or the world for which they stand: *Don't be a sucker.* Guards are *hacks* or *screws* and are to be treated with constant suspicion and distrust. In any situation of conflict between officials and prisoners, the former are automatically to be considered in the wrong. Furthermore, inmates should not allow themselves to become committed to the values of hard work and submission to duly constituted authority—values prescribed (if not followed) by *screws*—for thus an inmate would become a *sucker* in a world where the law-abiding are usually hypocrites and the true path to success lies in forming a "connection." The positive maxim is: *Be sharp.*

In the literature on the mores of imprisoned criminals there is no claim that these values are asserted with equal intensity by every member of a prison population; all social systems exhibit disagreements and differing emphases with respect to the values publicly professed by their members. But observers of the prison are largely agreed that the inmate code is outstanding both for the passion with which it is propounded and the almost universal allegiance verbally accorded it.

In the light of this inmate code or system of inmate norms, we can begin to understand the patterns of inmate behavior so frequently reported; for conformity to, or deviation from, the inmate code is the major basis for classifying and describing the social relations of prisoners. As Strong has pointed out, social groups are apt to characterize individuals in terms of crucial "axes of life" (lines of interests, problems, and concerns faced by the groups) and then to attach distinctive names to the resulting roles or types.[1] This process may be discerned in the society of prisoners and its argot for the patterns of behavior or social roles exhibited by inmates; and in these roles the outlines of the prison community as a system of action[2] may be seen.

An inmate who violates the norm proscribing the betrayal of a fellow prisoner is labeled a *rat* or a *squealer* in the vocabulary of the

---

1. Samuel M. Strong, "Social Types in a Minority Group," *American Journal of Sociology,* 48 (March 1943): 563–73; Schrag, in "Social Types in a Prison Community," notes the relevance of Strong's discussion for examination of the inmate social system.

2. See Schrag, "Social Types in a Prison Community," and Sykes, "Men, Merchants, and Toughs," for discussion of this approach to the prison as a system of action.

inmate world, and his deviance elicits universal scorn and hatred.[3] Prisoners who exhibit highly aggressive behavior, who quarrel easily and fight without cause, are often referred to as *toughs*. The individual who uses violence deliberately as a means to gain his ends is called a *gorilla;* a prisoner so designated is one who has established a satrapy based on coercion in clear contravention of the rule against exploitation by force. The term *merchant,* or *peddler,* is applied to the inmate who exploits his fellow captives not by force but by manipulation and trickery, and who typically sells or trades goods that are in short supply. If a prisoner shows himself unable to withstand the general rigors of existence in the custodial institution, he may be referred to as a *weakling* or a *weak sister*. If, more specifically, an inmate is unable to endure prolonged deprivation of heterosexual relationships and consequently enters into a homosexual liaison, he will be labeled a *wolf* or a *fag,* depending on whether his role is an active or a passive one.[4] If he continues to plead his case, he may soon be sarcastically known as a *rapo* (from "bum rap") or *innocent*. And if an inmate makes the mistake on allying himself with officialdom by taking on and expressing the values of conformity, he may be called a *square John* and ridiculed accordingly.

However, the individual who has received perhaps the greatest attention in the literature is one who most nearly fulfills the norms of the society of prisoners, who celebrates the inmate code rather than violates it: the *right guy*, the *real con*, the *real man*—the argot varies, but the role is clear-cut. The *right guy* is the hero of the inmate social system, and his existence gives meaning to the villains, the deviants such as the *rat*, the *tough*, the *gorilla*, and the *merchant*. The *right guy* is the base line, however idealized or infrequent in reality, from which the inmate population takes its bearings. It seems worth while, therefore, to sketch his portrait briefly in the language of the inmates.

A *right guy* is always loyal to his fellow prisoners. He never lets you down no matter how rough things get. He keeps his promises; he's dependable and trustworthy. He isn't nosey about your business and doesn't shoot off his mouth about his own. He doesn't act stuck-up, but he doesn't fall all over himself to make friends either—he has a certain dignity. The *right guy* never interferes with other inmates who are conniving against the officials. He doesn't go around looking for a fight,

---

3. The argot applied to a particular role varies somewhat from one prison to another, but it is not difficult to find the synonyms in the prisoners' lexicon.

4. The inmate population, with a keen sense of distinctions, draws a line between the *fag,* who plays a passive role in a homosexual relationship because he "likes" it or "wants" to, and a *punk,* who is coerced or bribed into a passive role.

but he never runs away from one when he is in the right. Anybody who starts a fight with a *right guy* has to be ready to go all the way. What he's got or can get of the extras in the prison—like cigarettes, food stolen from the mess hall, and so on—he shares with his friends. He doesn't take advantage of those who don't have much. He doesn't strong-arm other inmates into punking or fagging for him; instead, he acts like a man.

In his dealings with the prison officials, the *right guy* is unmistakably against them, but he doesn't act foolishly. When he talks about the officials with other inmates, he's sure to say that even the hacks with the best intentions are stupid, incompetent, and not to be trusted; that the worst thing a con can do is give the hacks information—they'll only use it against you when the chips are down. A *right guy* sticks up for his rights, but he doesn't ask for pity: he can take all the lousy screws can hand out and more. He doesn't suck around the officials, and the privileges that he's got are his because he deserves them. Even if the *right guy* doesn't look for trouble with the officials, he'll go to the limit if they push him too far. He realizes that there are just two kinds of people in the world, those in the know and the suckers or squares. Those who are in the know skim it off the top; suckers work.[5]

In summary, then, from the studies describing the life of men in prison, two major facts emerge: (1) Inmates give strong verbal support to a system of values that has group cohesion or inmate solidarity as its basic theme. Directly or indirectly, prisoners uphold the ideal of a system of social interaction in which individuals are bound together by ties of mutual aid, loyalty, affection, and respect, and are united firmly in their opposition to the enemy out-group. The man who exemplifies this ideal is accorded high prestige. The opposite of a cohesive inmate social system—a state in which each individual seeks his own advantage without reference to the claims of solidarity—is vociferously condemned. (2) The actual behavior of prisoners ranges from full adherence to the norms of the inmate world to deviance of various types. These behavioral patterns, recognized and labeled by prisoners in the pungent argot of the dispossessed, form a collection of social roles which, with their interrelationships, constitute the inmate social system. We turn now to explanation of the inmate social system and its underlying structure of sentiments.

---

5. We have not attempted to discuss all the prison roles that have been identified in the literature, although we have mentioned most of the major types. Two exceptions, not discussed because they are not distinctive of the prison, are the *fish*, a novitiate, and the *ding*, an erratic behaver. The homosexual world of the prison, especially, deserves fuller treatment; various role types within it have not yet been described.

THEORETICAL APPROACH TO THE INMATE SOCIAL SYSTEM

The literature shows that few explicit attempts to develop a theory accounting for the norms and behavior of imprisoned criminals have been made. As in literature on other areas of intense public concern, polemics compete with scientific hypotheses, and descriptive anecdotes outnumber empirical generalizations. It may be of greater importance that when the inmate social system has been approached from a theoretical viewpoint, attention has usually been focused on the induction of the individual into inmate society, i.e., the problem of "prisonization."[6] There has been little concerted effort to account for the structure and functioning of the system into which the individual becomes socialized.[7]

It is not difficult to understand why the transformation of the novitiate into a fully accredited convict has received so much emphasis. Penology in the past has been the province primarily of the moralizer and the social reformer, and the major questions have related to how current patterns of adjustment may affect the offender's *future* readjustment to the free community. Thus, the nature of the inmate social system has tended to remain a "given," something to be accepted without systematic explanation, and its functions for current behavior have tended to remain unproblematic. As suggested in the introduction, however, the prison is important as an object of study in its own right; and even from the viewpoint of interest in criminal reform, study only of the socialization process in prison is insufficient, on both theoretical and practical grounds.

On the theoretical side, study of the socialization process in prison leaves a serious hiatus: it does not illuminate the conditions determining the presence (or absence) of inmate society. Acting on the implicit assumption that an inmate behaves like an inmate because of the presence of other inmates who exhibit a distinctive culture, sociologists concerned with the prison have largely failed to provide a theory explaining the remarkable similarity of the inmate social systems found in one custodial institution after another. This fact presses for theoretical consideration at the present time; and if we are to understand the fact, more attention must be given to the social setting in which the inmate population must live and to the problems generated by this

---

6. Cf. Clemmer, *The Prison Community*, pp. 298ff., on the use of this term.

7. Albert K. Cohen, in *Delinquent Boys* (Glencoe, Ill.: Free Press, 1955), especially pp. 18–19, makes a similar point relative to discussions of "delinquency."

setting. We want to know why inmate society "is there," as well as how inmates sustain it.

On the practical side, the major administrative directive that may be traced to studies of socialization in the prison is to separate the "prisonized" from the "nonprisonized." Aside from the financial and administrative imponderables involved in any attempt to carry out this directive, however, we believe that in the long run it would not resolve the basic problem: the development of inmate society under the conditions of imprisonment, only one of which is the presence of formerly incarcerated inmates. Any satisfactory solution to this problem will depend on the development of an adequate theory of the social structure of the inmate world; and only as such a theory is developed will knowledge of the socialization process gain perspective.

A NEW THEORY

The loss of liberty is but one of the many deprivations or frustrations inflicted on imprisoned criminals, although it is fundamental to all the rest. As Hayner and Ash have pointed out, inmates are deprived of goods and services that are more or less taken for granted even at the lowest socioeconomic levels in the free community.[8] Inmates must live in austerity as a matter of public policy. Barnes and Teeters have discussed the constraints imposed by the mass of institutional regulations under which prisoners are required to live.[9] Clemmer, Fishman, and others have stressed the severe frustrations imposed on prisoners by the denial of heterosexual relationships.[10] Numerous other writers have described the various pains of confinement in conditions of prolonged physical and psychological compression.

Although the inmate population may no longer suffer the brutality and neglect that in the past aroused the anger of John Howard and similar critics of penal institutions, prisoners still must undergo a variety of deprivations and frustrations which flow either by accident or intent from the fact of imprisonment. Furthermore, it is of greatest significance that the rigors imposed on the inmate by the prison officials do not represent relatively minor irritants which he can somehow endure; instead, the conditions of custody involve profound attacks on the pris-

---

8. "The Prisoner Community as a Social Group."

9. Harry E. Barnes and Negley K. Teeters, *New Horizons in Criminology*, 2nd ed. (New York: Prentice-Hall, 1951), pp. 438–39.

10. Clemmer, *The Prison Community*, pp. 249–73; Fishman, *Sex Life in American Prisons*.

oner's self-image or sense of personal worth, and these psychological pains may be far more threatening than physical maltreatment.[11] Brief analysis of the nature of these attacks on the inmate's personality is necessary, for it is as a response to them that we can begin to grasp the rationale of the inmate social system.

The isolation of the prisoner from the free community means that he has been rejected by society. His rejection is underscored in some prisons by his shaven head; in almost all, by his uniform and the degradation of no longer having a name but a number. The prisoner is confronted daily with the fact that he has been stripped of his membership in society at large, and now stands condemned as an outcast, an outlaw, a deviant so dangerous that he must be kept behind closely guarded walls and watched both day and night. He has lost the privilege of being *trusted* and his every act is viewed with suspicion by the guards, the surrogates of the conforming social order. Constantly aware of lawful society's disapproval, his picture of himself challenged by frequent reminders of his moral unworthiness, the inmate must find some way to ward off these attacks and avoid their introjection.[12]

In addition, it should be remembered that the offender has been drawn from a society in which personal possessions and material achievement are closely linked with concepts of personal worth by numerous cultural definitions. In the prison, however, the inmate finds himself reduced to a level of living near bare subsistence, and whatever physical discomforts this deprivation may entail, it apparently has deeper psychological significance as a basic attack on the prisoner's conception of his own personal adequacy.

No less important, perhaps, is the ego threat that is created by the deprivation of heterosexual relationships. In the tense atmosphere of the prison, with its perversions and constant references to the problems of sexual frustration, even those inmates who do not engage in overt homosexuality suffer acute attacks of anxiety about their own masculinity. These anxieties may arise from a prisoner's unconscious fear of latent homosexual tendencies in himself, which might be activated by his prolonged heterosexual deprivation and the importunity of others; or at a more conscious level he may feel that his masculinity is threatened because he can see himself as a man—in the full sense—only in a world that also contains women. In either case the inmate is confronted with the fact that the celibacy imposed on him by society means

11. A. H. Maslow, "Deprivation, Threat, and Frustration," *Psychological Review*, 48 (July 1941):364–66.

12. McCorkle and Korn, "Resocialization Within Walls," p. 88.

more than simple physiological frustration: an essential component of his self-conception, his status as male, is called into question.

Rejected, impoverished, and figuratively castrated, the prisoner must face still further indignity in the extensive social control exercised by the custodians. The many details of the inmate's life, ranging from the hours of sleeping to the route to work and the job itself, are subject to a vast number of regulations made by prison officials. The inmate is stripped of his autonomy; hence, to the other pains of imprisonment we must add the pressure to define himself as weak, helpless, and dependent. Individuals under guard are exposed to the bitter ego threat of losing their identification with the normal adult role.[13]

The remaining significant feature of the inmate's social environment is the presence of other imprisoned criminals. Murderers, rapists, thieves, confidence men, and sexual deviants are the inmate's constant companions, and this enforced intimacy may prove to be disquieting even for the hardened recidivist. As an inmate has said, "The worst thing about prison is you have to live with other prisoners."[14] Crowded into a small area with men who have long records of physical assaults, thievery, and so on (and who may be expected to continue in the path of deviant social behavior in the future), the inmate is deprived of the sense of security that we more or less take for granted in the free community. Although the anxieties created by such a situation do not necessarily involve an attack on the individual's sense of personal worth —as we are using the concept—the problems of self-protection in a society composed exclusively of criminals constitute one of the inadvertent rigors of confinement.

In short, imprisonment "punishes" the offender in a variety of ways extending far beyond the simple fact of incarceration. However just or necessary such punishments may be, their importance for our present analysis lies in the fact that they form a set of harsh social conditions to which the population of prisoners must respond or *adapt itself.* The inmate feels that the deprivations and frustrations of prison life, with their implications for the destruction of his self-esteem, somehow must be alleviated. It is, we suggest, as an answer to this need that the functional significance of the inmate code or system of values exhibited so frequently by men in prison can best be understood.

As we have pointed out, the dominant theme of the inmate code is group cohesion, with a "war of all against all"—in which each man

---

13. Bruno Bettelheim, "Individual and Mass Behavior in Extreme Situations," *Journal of Abnormal and Social Psychology,* 38 (October 1943):417–52.

14. Gresham M. Sykes, *Crime and Society* (New York: Random House, 1956), p. 109.

seeks his own gain without considering the rights or claims of others—
as the theoretical antipode. But if a war of all against all is likely to make
life "solitary, poor, nasty, brutish, and short" for men with freedom, as
Hobbes suggested, it is doubly so for men in custody. Even those who
are most successful in exploiting their fellow prisoners will find it a
dangerous and nerve-wracking game, for they cannot escape the company of their victims. No man can assure the safety of either his person
or his possessions, and eventually the winner is certain to lose to a more
powerful or more skillful exploiter. Furthermore, the victims hold the
trump card, since a word to the officials is frequently all that is required
to ruin the most dominating figure in the inmate population. A large
share of the "extra" goods that enter the inmate social system must do
so as the result of illicit conniving against the officials, which often
requires lengthy and extensive cooperation and trust; in a state of complete conflict the resources of the system will be diminished. Mutual
abhorrence or indifference will feed the emotional frictions arising
from interaction under compression. And as rejection by others is
a fundamental problem, a state of mutual alienation is worse than useless as a solution to the threats created by the inmate's status as an outcast.

As a population of prisoners moves toward a state of mutual antagonism, then, the many problems of prison life become more acute. On
the other hand, *as a population of prisoners moves in the direction of
solidarity, as demanded by the inmate code, the pains of imprisonment
become less severe.* They cannot be eliminated, it is true, but their
consequences at least can be partially neutralized. A cohesive inmate
society provides the prisoner with a meaningful social group with which
he can identify himself and which will support him in his struggles
against his condemners. Thus it permits him to escape at least in part
the fearful isolation of the convicted offender. Inmate solidarity, in the
form of toleration of the many irritants of life in confinement, helps to
solve the problems of personal security posed by the involuntary intimacy of men noteworthy for their seriously antisocial behavior in the
past.

Similarly, group cohesion in the form of a reciprocity of favors
undermines one of the most potent sources of aggression among prisoners, the drive for personal aggrandizement through exploitation by
force and fraud. Furthermore, although goods in scarce supply will
remain scarce even if they are shared rather than monopolized, such
goods will be distributed more equitably in a social system marked by
solidarity, and this may be of profound significance in enabling the
prisoner to endure better the psychological burden of impoverishment.

A cohesive population of prisoners has another advantage in that it supports a system of shared beliefs that explicitly deny the traditional link between merit and achievement. Material success, according to this system, is a matter of "connections" rather than skill or hard work, and thus the imprisoned criminal is partially freed from the necessity of defining his material want as a sign of personal inadequacy.

Finally, a cohesive inmate social system institutionalizes the value of "dignity" and the ability to "take it" in a number of norms and reinforces these norms with informal social controls. In effect, the prisoner is called on to endure manfully what he cannot avoid. At first glance this might seem to be simply the counsel of despair; but if the elevation of fortitude into a primary virtue is the last refuge of the powerless, it also serves to shift the criteria of the individual's worth from conditions that cannot be altered to his ability to maintain some degree of personal integration; and the latter, at least, can be partially controlled. By creating an ideal of endurance in the face of harsh social conditions, then, the society of prisoners opens a path to the restoration of self-respect and a sense of independence that can exist despite prior criminality, present subjugation, and the free community's denial of the offender's moral worthiness. Significantly, this path to virtue is recognized by the prison officials as well as the prisoners.

One further point should be noted with regard to the emphasis placed on the maintenance of self as defined by the value system of prisoners. Dignity, composure, courage, the ability to "take it" and "hand it out" when necessary—these are the traits affirmed by the inmate code. They are also traits that are commonly defined as masculine by the inmate population. As a consequence the prisoner finds himself in a situation where he can recapture his male role, not in terms of its sexual aspects, but in terms of behavior that is accepted as a good indicator of virility.

The effectiveness of the inmate code in mitigating the pains of imprisonment depends of course on the extent to which precepts are translated into action. As we have indicated, the demands of the inmate code for loyalty, generosity, disparagement of officials, and so on are most fully exemplified in the behavior of the *right guy*. On the other hand, much noncohesive behavior occurs on the part of the *rat*, the *tough*, the *gorilla*, the *merchant*, and the *weak sister*. The population of prisoners, then, does not exhibit perfect solidarity in practice, in spite of inmates' vehement assertions of group cohesion as a value; but neither is the population of prisoners a warring aggregate. Rather, the inmate social system typically appears to be balanced in an uneasy compromise somewhere between these two extremes. The problems

confronting prisoners in the form of social rejection, material deprivation, sexual frustration, and the loss of autonomy and personal security
are not completely eliminated. Indeed, even if the norms of the inmate
social system were fully carried out by all, the pains of imprisonment
would only be lessened; they would not disappear. But the pains of
imprisonment are at least relieved by whatever degree of group cohesion is achieved in fact, and this is crucial in understanding the functional significance of the inmate code for inmates.

One further problem remains. Many of the prisoners who deviate
from the maxims of the inmate code are precisely those who are most
vociferous in their verbal allegiance to it. How can this discrepancy
between words and behavior be explained? Much of the answer seems
to lie in the fact that almost all inmates have an interest in maintaining
cohesive behavior on the part of others, *regardless of the role they play
themselves,* and vehement vocal support of the inmate code is a potent
means to this end.

There are, of course, prisoners who "believe" in inmate cohesion
both for themselves and others. These hold the unity of the group as a
high personal value and are ready to demand cohesive behavior from
their fellow prisoners. This collectivistic orientation may be due to a
thorough identification with the criminal world in opposition to the
forces of lawful society, or to a system of values that transcends such
divisions. In any case, for these men the inmate code has much of the
quality of a religious faith and they approach its tenets as true believers.
In a second category are those prisoners who are relatively indifferent
to the cohesion of the inmate population as a personal value, but who
are quick to assert it as a guide to behavior because in its absence they
would be likely to become chronic victims. They are committed to the
ideal of inmate solidarity to the extent that they have little or no desire
to take advantage of their fellow captives, but they do not go so far as
to subscribe to the ideal of self-sacrifice. Their behavior is best described
as passive or neutral; they are believers without passion, demanding
adherence from others, but not prepared to let excessive piety interfere
with more mundane considerations. Third, there are those who loudly
acclaim the inmate code and actively violate its injunctions. These men
suffer if their number increases, since they begin to face the difficulties
of competition; and they are in particular danger if their depredations
are reported to the officials. The prisoners who are thus actively
alienated from other inmates and yet give lip service to inmate
solidarity resemble a manipulative priesthood, savage in their expression of belief but corrupt in practice. In brief, a variety of motivational
patterns underlies allegiance to the inmate code, but few inmates can

avoid the need to insist publicly on its observance, whatever the discrepancies in their actions.

We have drawn a picture of the inmate social system as a set of interlocking roles that are based on conformity to, or deviance from, a collection of dominant values; and we have suggested that these values are firmly rooted in the major problems posed by the conditions of imprisonment. The maxims of the inmate code do not simply reflect the individual values of imprisoned criminals; rather, they represent a system of group norms that are directly related to mitigating the pains of imprisonment under a custodial regime having nearly total power. It is hoped that this view of the prison opens fruitful lines of inquiry, which may lead to better understanding of the structure and functioning not only of prison populations but of social groups in general.

BIBLIOGRAPHY

The following contain relevant material:

David Abrahamson, "Evaluation of the Treatment of Criminals," in *Failures in Psychiatric Treatment,* ed. Paul H. Hoch (New York: Grune & Stratton, 1948), pp. 58–77.

Holley Cantine and Dachine Rainer, eds., *Prison Etiquette* (Bearsville, N.Y.: Retort Press, 1950).

Donald Clemmer, "Leadership Phenomena in a Prison Community," *Journal of Criminal Law and Criminology,* 28 (March–April 1938):861–72; *The Prison Community* (Boston: Christopher Publishing House, 1940); "Observations on Imprisonment as a Source of Criminality," *Journal of Criminal Law and Criminology,* 41 (September–October 1950): 311–19.

R. J. Corsini, "A Study of Certain Attitudes of Prison Inmates," *Journal of Criminal Law and Criminology,* 37 (July–August 1946): 132–40; R. J. Corsini and Kenwood Bartleme, "Attitudes of San Quentin Prisoners," *Journal of Correctional Education,* 4 (October 1952):43–46.

George Devereux and Malcolm C. Moos, "The Social Structure of Prisons, and the Organic Tensions," *Journal of Criminal Psychopathology,* 4 (October 1942): 306–24.

Patrick J. Driscoll, "Factors Related to the Institutional Adjustment of Prison Inmates," *Journal of Abnormal and Social Psychology,* 47 (July 1952): 593–96.

Maurice L. Farber, "Suffering and Time Perspective of the Prisoner," *University of Iowa Studies in Child Welfare,* 20 (1944): 153–227.

Joseph F. Fishman, *Sex Life in American Prisons* (New York: National Library Press, 1934).

Vernon Fox, "The Effect of Counseling on Adjustment in Prison," *Social Forces,* 32 (March 1954): 285–89.

L. M. Hanks, Jr., "Preliminary for a Study of Problems of Discipline in Prisons," *Journal of Criminal Law and Criminology,* 30 (March–April 1940): 879–87.

James Hargan, "The Psychology of Prison Language," *Journal of Abnormal and Social Psychology,* 30 (October–December 1935): 359–65.

Ida Harper, "The Role of the 'Fringer' in a State Prison for Women," *Social Forces,* 31 (October 1952): 53–60.

Frank E. Hartung and Maurice Floch, "A Social-Psychological Analysis of Prison Riots: An Hypothesis," *Journal of Criminal Law, Criminology and Police Science,* 47 (May–June 1956): 51–57.

Norman S. Hayner, "Washington State Correctional Institutions as Communities," *Social Forces,* 21 (March 1943): 316–22; Norman S. Hayner and Ellis Ash, "The Prisoner Community as a Social Group," *American Sociological Review,* 4 (June 1939): 362–69; and "The Prison as a Community," *ibid.,* 5 (August 1940): 577–83.

F. E. Haynes, "The Sociological Study of the Prison Community," *Journal of Criminal Law and Criminology,* 39 (November–December 1948): 432–40.

Hans von Hentig, "The Limits of Penal Treatment," *Journal of Criminal Law and Criminology,* 32 (November–December 1941): 401–10.

Alfred C. Horsch and Robert A. Davis, "Personality Traits and Conduct of Institutionalized Delinquents," *Journal of Criminal Law and Criminology,* 29 (July–August 1938): 241–44.

John James, "The Application of the Small Group Concept to the Study of the Prison Community," *British Journal of Delinquency,* 5 (April 1955):269–80.

Benjamin Karpman, "Sex Life in Prison," *Journal of Criminal Law and Criminology,* 38 (January–February 1948): 475–86.

Robert M. Lindner, *Stone Walls and Men* (New York: Odyssey Press, 1946); "Sex in Prison," *Complex,* 6 (Fall 1951): 5–20.

Walter A. Lunden, "Antagonism and Altruism Among Prisoners," in P. A. Sorokin, *Forms and Techniques of Altruistic and Spiritual Growth* (Boston: Beacon Press, 1954), pp. 447–60.

Richard McCleery, *The Strange Journey: A Demonstration Project in Adult Education in Prison,* University of North Carolina extension bulletin 32 (1953); "Power, Communications and the Social Order: A Study of Prison Government" (unpublished doctoral dissertation, University of North Carolina, 1956).

Lloyd W. McCorkle and Richard Korn, "Resocialization Within Walls," *Annals of the American Academy of Political and Social Science,* 293 (May 1954): 88–98.

Hermann Mannheim, *Group Problems in Crime and Punishment* (London: Routledge & Kegan Paul, 1955).

William R. Morrow, "Criminality and Antidemocratic Trends: A Study of Prison Inmates," in T. W. Adorno et al., *The Authoritarian Personality* (New York: Harper, 1950), pp. 817–90.

Victor F. Nelson, *Prison Days and Nights* (Boston: Little, Brown, 1933).

Paul Nitsche and Karl Wilmanns, *The History of Prison Psychosis,* Nervous and Mental Disease Monograph Series no. 13 (1912).

Norman A. Polansky, "The Prison as an Autocracy," *Journal of Criminal Law and Criminology,* 33 (May–June 1942): 16–22.

Harvey Powelson and Reinhard Bendix, "Psychiatry in Prison," *Psychiatry,* 14 (February 1951): 73–86.

Donald Rasmussen, "Prisoner Opinions about Parole," *American Sociological Review,* 5 (August 1940): 584–95.

Hans Riemer, "Socialization in the Prison Community," *Proceedings of the American Prison Association, 1937,* pp. 151–55.

Clarence Schrag, "Social Types in a Prison Community" (unpublished master's thesis, University of Washington, 1944); "Crimeville: A Sociometric Study of a Prison Community" (unpublished doctoral dissertation, University of Washington, 1950); "Leadership among Prison Inmates," *American Sociological Review,* 19 (February 1954): 37–42.

Lowell S. Selling, "The Pseudo Family," *American Journal of Sociology,* 37 (September 1931): 247–53.

Gresham M. Sykes, "The Corruption of Authority and Rehabilitation," *Social Forces,* 34 (March 1956): 257–62; "Men, Merchants, and Toughs: A Study of Reactions to Imprisonment," *Social Problems,* 4 (October 1956): 130–38.

Donald R. Taft, "The Group and Community Organization Approach to Prison Administration," *Proceedings of the American Prison Association, 1942,* pp. 275–84.

Ruth Sherman Tolman, "Some Differences in Attitudes Between Groups of Repeating Criminals and of First Offenders," *Journal of Criminal Law and Criminology,* 30 (July–August 1939): 196–203.

27

"Screws" vs. "Thugs"

Anthony L. Guenther and Mary Quinn Guenther

Almost everyone agrees that something has to be done about [convicts].
The question concerns what is done, who does it, and the nature of the
mandate given by the rest of us to those who do it. Perhaps we give
them an unconscious mandate to go beyond anything we ourselves
would care to do or even to acknowledge.

Everett C. Hughes

According to Everett Hughes's thesis, once we have dissociated ourselves from the people for whom prisons are designed and have declared them a problem, the next logical step is to let someone else do
the dirty work which we would be unwilling to do ourselves. But even
when the work of confining prisoners is delegated to specialized functionaries, questions have been raised in a variety of quarters about the
effectiveness with which prisons accomplish their objectives. The conventional indictments of prisons attack overcrowding, antiquated facilities, personnel turnover, budgetary limitations and public apathy.
Other observers have noted that penitentiaries fail because they must
contend with all the shortcomings and malfunctions of prior stages in
the criminal justice system. What most critics have overlooked as a
major source of prison failure is the set of obstacles faced by correctional
officers.

While it is true that numerous treatment activities have recently
been introduced within walls, e.g., drug abuse, legal assistance and
correctional counselor programs, the most durable and intensive relationships experienced by prisoners are with line correctional officers, an

From Anthony L. Guenther & Mary Quinn Guenther, "Screws vs. Thugs," *Society*
11 (1974): 42–50, by permission of the authors and publisher. Copyright © 1974 by
Transaction, Inc.

increasingly popular synonym for "guard." The task of creating an atmosphere conducive to prisoner change is, in effect, relegated to these officers, who are ill-equipped and poorly motivated to perform such a duty. The everyday operations of correctional work such as locking grilles, making counts, supervising work crews and delivering mail work against prolonged contact between captors and their captives. The presumption that correctional staff have extensive and potentially therapeutic interaction with prisoners, when in fact they don't, may well be an important source of strain in the officer's role. But the most complex and subtle process which can undermine correctional objectives is created by an institutional atmosphere of uncertainty and precariousness.

To study the role of the correctional officer and his perception of both the objectives and realities of his job, data were obtained by the senior author as part of research on custodial staff made over a half-year period at the U.S. Penitentiary in Atlanta, Georgia. Daily contact with officers on all shifts and job assignments as varied as tower duty, the dining hall, the cellhouses, segregation (solitary confinement) and the control center provided opportunity for hundreds of informal interviews. Moreover, all written documents from "jackets" (dossiers) on inmates, records of "incidents" involving theft, assault, escape, etc., to a running log of occurrences during each shift were made available. Supervisors (lieutenants), who were the actual heads of operations for each shift, participated fully in rating all correctional officers on the criteria of technical competence, stability under stress and effectiveness in dealing with inmates. Additional data were secured through lengthy questionnaires returned by three-fourths of the custodial staff.

Complementary data, volunteered by scores of inmates, gave additional insight into the role of correctional officer. Over a dozen prisoners were known to the investigator from another federal penitentiary in past years, and their provision of contacts with the inmate population was indispensable. In combination, these multiple sources of data provided a dynamic assessment of officer-inmate interaction.

The Atlanta Penitentiary is classed as a maximum-security federal facility, and was built 70 years ago as a sister institution to Leavenworth. Some 2,200 men are incarcerated there within the 28 acres enclosed by a wall ("security perimeter") whose height varies between 32 and 40 feet. About 170 correctional officers, civil-service employees at levels of GS-7 and GS-8, comprise the basic custodial staff. This is supplemented by eleven lieutenants, a captain and an associate warden. A parallel but much smaller "treatment" staff including caseworkers, correctional counselors, medical personnel and clergymen handles non-custodial functions.

For inmates, doing time at Atlanta is roughly similar to serving a sentence at any large, older prison. If anything, federal institutions, including this one, reflect the few advances identifiable in American corrections. For example, legal aid is readily accessible, visitation facilities are open and unmonitored and even subscriptions to *Playboy* are permitted. By inmate reckoning, doing a "bit" under federal auspices is less dehumanizing than almost anywhere else. Nevertheless, prisoners who "pull" time here can expect denigrating conditions of psychological separation, lack of privacy, unchallenging jobs, potential danger and routinization. Being referred to by correctional officers as "thugs," "thieves" or "convicts" reinforces the notion that prisoners, with few exceptions, should expect a full allocation of indignities conferred upon them by conviction and incarceration.

In many ways, correctional officers "pull" time as well, for their occupation lacks many of the socially rewarding sources of job satisfaction. Officers find that there are relatively few ways to distinguish themselves and that many job assignments are sheer tedium. Moreover, their occupational self-images hardly benefit from public conceptions of the kind of person who would work in a prison. Within the walls derisive references to officers by inmates as "screws," "hacks" or "cops" are vivid and explicit forms of contempt. Advancement, many officers feel, does not necessarily occur through merit, and the consequences of an error or misjudgment may disqualify them for promotion. The seriousness of committing error is compounded by the uncertainty inherent in prison work; for, at the operational level, it is impossible to predict the behavior of 2,200 men in captive circumstances. Many of the dilemmas encountered by prison correctional officers originate from these unpredictable conditions whose sources and responses are the foci of this study.

Sources of Uncertainty

Outsiders are often surprised and occasionally alarmed to discover that the penitentiary is continually in a state of change. Public stereotypes of the prison as a closed community or total institution convey the image of regimentation, order and control to the extent that any publicized departures from this image suggest incompetence or political corruption. The incidents at Attica, San Quentin and elsewhere in the last three years, for example, invited questions such as: "Why did the guards let the prisoners take over?" and "Have rehabilitative programs for inmates been the victims of legislative apathy?" Officers themselves are acutely sensitive to changes they see taking place on the corrections scene, few of which, from their perspective, are welcome. They cite new challenges such as the reduction in control, an increase in inmate aggressiveness, the incidence of court-ordered policy changes and the new-style inmate (black, inner-city bred, politically aware, articulate and doing "lots of time") as particularly troublesome.

In addition to these recent threats to traditional correctional work, there have always been so many potential sources of incidents in prison that administrators invest a significant portion of custodial manpower in preventive strategies, the objective of which is to anticipate and forestall crises. A lieutenant stated a popular view when he said, "It's hard to believe that we don't get more trouble than we do around here. When you think about how much time these guys are doing and how little experience custodial [officers] have, it scares you half to death." A January 1971 staff report sent to the Bureau of Prisons was more explicit in describing the conditions at Atlanta which confound smooth functioning:

> Conditions at Atlanta would seem to indicate many problems resistant to solution. These are (1) enormous size of the institution, (2) large inmate population, (3) inmate housing facilities which are antiquated, overcrowded, and present substantial control problems, (4) other physical facilities which are outdated, obsolete, or present unusual supervisory problems, (5) difficulties in providing supervision for many operations because of open-door, freedom-of-movement policies, and (6) a large industry operation which runs at night and on weekends [in addition to the daytime].

A crisis or incident in the penitentiary usually has far greater repercussions than an equivalent episode in the outside community. Broadly defined, "incidents" refer to security breaches, personal endangerment, wide-scale disruption of schedules or destruction of property. Their proportions are magnified by the enforced density of men under physical coercion and by the danger posed by some inmates, if freed, to the staff and the community at large.

Conventional advice passed on to new trainees by experienced officers includes pithy references to incidents forestalled (a fracas in the dining hall that "could have turned into a real 'shit-storm' "), as well as to events which occurred despite the best countermeasures available ("We had information that drugs were coming in but the officers shaking down didn't find them"). From the perspective of both staff and inmates, the atmosphere of antagonism, conflict and compression creates incidents which often defy prediction yet require intervention before getting beyond control.

Data obtained at the Atlanta Penitentiary suggest that only a very small proportion of the 2,200 men imprisoned there may be affected by an incident, yet if the crisis is potentially threatening to strained relationships, it must have prompt attention. If, for example, racial animosities have been running high, an incident involving only one or two blacks and a like number of whites may compel large numbers of inmates to choose sides along racial lines. Uncertainty, then, affects correctional work more than many other occupations, for the artificial role relationships of captives and captors, the aggregate of their physical coexistence and an atmosphere of intensified emotions produce a unique organizational climate. The capacity to reduce uncertainty through accurate predictions is highly desirable in corrections work. Yet there is so much behavioral spontaneity within the prison, often precipitated by outside influences, that only estimates of day-to-day occurrences are possible.

The interaction between custodial staff and inmates is affected, generally speaking, by four sources of unpredictability, all of which require compensatory efforts. These are (1) malfunctions of plant or equipment, (2) problems originating among employees, (3) problems created by inmates and (4) difficulties produced by the free community.

The first source of unpredictable occurrences in the prison is a failure of plant or equipment, whether resulting from sabotage, natural deterioration or poor maintenance. A utility breakdown in large cellblocks or dormitories, for example, may necessitate the relocation of large numbers of inmates. Similarly, a disruption in food preparation or service, as can be seen in the following case, may cause an alteration of feeding schedules for the entire institution:

> *July 3, 1972.* Complaints by a number of inmates on "short line" (a work crew eating lunch before the "main line") about "spoiled chicken" were quickly investigated by the staff. Although they thought the "strange taste" was caused by over-seasoning, and most inmates showed no ill effects, the Warden ordered that the chicken be removed. Food Service personnel had less than a half hour to prepare and serve hot dogs as a substitute meat, rather than risk a dining hall incident.

From a custodial standpoint, serious malfunctions which affect large numbers of inmates demand immediate and decisive remedies, though they may involve curtailment of other activities. Not only are inmates likely to be impatient with departures from institutional routine, but some may seize the chance to implement a personal plan. A power failure, for example, may provide an escape-minded inmate with the long-awaited opportunity to "hit the wall" when guard towers are incapacitated.

There is evidence that malfunctions of equipment and mechanical or electrical services are unusually frequent in older U.S. prisons, and these, like Atlanta, often house the most recalcitrant, long-term offenders. Thus it is not surprising that in a large, complex prison, the most conscientious surveillance cannot prevent tools from disappearing, equipment from being sabotaged and existing utility systems from being disrupted. Experienced officers automatically suspect, first, that the breakdown is intended, and second, that it may be a ploy to divert attention from an escape attempt, assault or other nefarious activity. If, by community standards, correctional officers appear cynical in this respect, it is because their experience in penitentiary work does not suggest that prisoners can be trusted or will act in a conventional manner.

A second set of problems leading to unpredictability in prison work is attributable to the employees themselves. Inmates are made so dependent upon correctional staff for the timing, sequence and direction of events that attrition of personnel on a shift cannot be tolerated. Not only would key positions go unmanned, thus compromising security, but also large numbers of confused prisoners may have no guidance. Thus, there can be such serious consequences of a cellhouse officer disabled by a bleeding ulcer, a tower officer suffering a coronary attack or an employee "flipping out" in reaction to prolonged stress that immediate adjustments are required. The importance of staffing the various shifts in a penitentiary schedule is so critical that tardiness is unacceptable, and there is a permanent position on the custodial roster to cover the jobs of officers who may succumb to illness.

But a unique feature of prison work is its inability to allow the standard indiscretions permitted in most other occupational careers. Correctional officers who overextend themselves financially, have marital difficulties or drink to excess not only raise doubts concerning their commitment to the job; they may also be regarded as undependable. As can be seen in the following memorandum, indiscreet behavior, in turn, often means that an injudicious officer can be compromised by an enterprising inmate. (In this and other memos cited here fictitious identities are given to staff and inmates).

March 6, 1972. We became aware that Mr. Senden, a Correctional Officer Trainee, had introduced contraband into the institution for financial gain. He has given a signed affidavit to the F.B.I., admitting he received a package, believed to have contained marijuana, from Beverly Phillipson, the wife of inmate Phillipson 29623. He delivered this package to inmate Woodruff 62472 inside the institution. [Prosecution resulted in a two-year prison sentence for Mr. Senden, the employee, and a sentence of one year's probation for the inmate's wife.]

Observations made of probationary correctional trainees suggested that the most important judgment experienced personnel make is whether or not a new man is reliable. Training sessions for probationary officers emphasize through analysis of past episodes the ways in which personnel often have to assume absolute dependence upon each other. In contrast to many other occupations which require "team efforts," correctional staff working the yard or cellblock must be positive that they have backing when dealing with an explosive situation. The assumption is tacitly made, then, that a new officer is dependable until he proves otherwise, an arrangement which is not very satisfactory because it may be years before one sees his colleagues under acute stress. Having to make the assumption of reliability is discomforting to some officers, particularly if subjective impressions gleaned from verbal, behavioral or biographical evidence discredit that assumption. As a custodial officer with eight years' experience put it:

> I wouldn't give you a plugged nickel for several officers here. You know who I mean; just look at some of the jobs they have to give 'em so they don't get in trouble. When it really begins to hit the fan around here, they're the ones who'll be hiding out.

This kind of speculative comment, based upon the most tenuous impressions, becomes persuasive when it receives interpersonal validation. Thus one of the functions of assembly-room gossip just before a shift begins is to compare hearsay about peer officers. For an officer to be defined as unreliable by his colleagues is highly discrediting and becomes a virtually ineradicable stigma.

Field observations indicated that a third source of unpredictability is deliberate action or inaction by inmates, by far the most frustrating to custodial staff. A lieutenant close to retirement commented:

> The toughest part of this job is the anticipation that goes with each watch. You're constantly under stress because you don't know what will happen, much less what you can do about it until it breaks. No one can remain alert, month after month, year after year, to all the things that can go wrong in this old place.

An officer reporting for duty in most penitentiaries is unlikely to be briefed about the activities of the previous two shifts, and he may even have recently been sick or have had a period of annual leave. Only in exceptional cases, such as alleged imminence of an escape attempt, escalation of racial tensions or abundance of serious contraband, will a shift supervisor have a special briefing for his staff. Thus an officer may take up his assignment in the dining hall or on the yard unaware that "home-brew" has been consumed, a homosexual triangle has evolved or several inmates have just received parole denials. The capacity for handling any events which may follow is nearly always impaired by the attention which must be given to routine details of a job assignment. Besides, many officers would prefer to avoid discretionary matters.

As in other prisons of its type, the Atlanta staff can anticipate during a "normal" day that a number of inmates will become ill, that others will violate regulations by refusing to work and that the behavior of others will be influenced by personal problems. In each instance, a correctional officer or other employee will be involved with an incident whose origin, location, timing and duration are unpredictable. This type of repetitive uncertainty takes as great a toll in strain and apprehension among staff as the more episodic occasions when notorious inmates become assaultive, get inebriated on home-brew or burn out another prisoner's cell. Incidents that reinforce staff beliefs about the capriciousness of prisoners occur almost daily, and, as can be seen in the following illustrations, no amount of training of surveillance can be preventive:

> *December 9, 1969.* At approximately 11:00 A.M., Rackley 33265 was assaulted with a club by Guilford 32007 and was subsequently treated for head injuries. It appeared that Guilford felt Rackley had "put the voodoo" on him, and that he took this action because Rackley had placed a rag doll in his bed with pins stuck in its head. Rackley stated that he "hardly even knew" Guilford.

> *December 12, 1969.* Inmate Tyberson 27222 became inebriated [on home-brew beer] and went berserk in B cellhouse on the evening shift. He was swinging at any inmate near him until restrained and held down by other prisoners. Then he was taken to the hospital and placed in restraints until he sobered up and calmed down.

An additional feature of the second case should be mentioned. It is not at all unusual to find other inmates taking control for they reason that one or more persons may suffer bodily harm, or that unwanted attention ("heat") will be focused upon their domain unless official notice is averted.

Another type of incident, intended to harass or intimidate officers, takes place just often enough to convince the officers that they are "at war" with prisoners:

January 26, 1970. At approximately 5:15 P.M. the officer on duty in C cellhouse was standing just inside the office door when an iron weight of about five pounds was dropped from an upper range. It landed on the metal screen covering the office. It is believed this was a measure of retaliation against the officer who was performing his job in a manner seen as "overzealous" by inmates. We were unable to identify the person(s) who dropped the weight.

February 8, 1968. An electric motor weighing approximately sixty pounds was dropped from the top tier onto the office of D cellhouse. It crashed through the expanded metal roof of the office and struck the officer's desk, causing considerable damage. The officer, Mr. Billingsley, was barely missed and had the drop hit its intended mark, the officer surely would have been severely injured or killed.

Again, it is clear that a conspiracy to vanquish an officer is exceedingly difficult to forestall and may, in fact, be entirely spontaneous. It makes little difference to staff that only a minority of inmates gets involved with assaults; their preconceptions of custodial work include the notions that most inmates have poor impulse control, little tolerance for stress and inherent hostility toward authority.

The correctional officer's orientation to prisoners is structured basically in terms of the axiom that if he does not know a man personally, there is little he can assume about him. This rule determines much of the content and style of interaction with offenders in the cellhouses, the dining hall, on the yard and elsewhere. During interviews officers often emphasized their interest in establishing and maintaining working relationships with inmates—a task made difficult by quarterly job rotations and high inmate-to-officer ratios—for they felt that their ultimate control over inmates during crises was a close function of these associations. The smallest personal knowledge, such as an inmate's name or the job he has in the institution, can be used by an officer to initiate a verbal exchange suggesting trust and a fair settlement.

In addition to these three sources of uncertainty in correctional work, a fourth category of incidents arises from events in the world outside the walls. The man sentenced to a term in federal court and designated for the Atlanta Penitentiary typically comes from those segments of the general population characterized by job instability, poor health, financial crises, emotional disturbance and lack of opportunity. Imprisonment often exacerbates an already tenuous relationship between the new inmate and elements of the outside community. In fact, employees who handle prison casework tasks devote much of their time to the enormous numbers of documents each day which attest to the disruptive effects of incarceration. It is these problems, communicated to the prisoner through visits or correspondence, which are one source of uncertainty precipitated from outside the wall.

Letters from the outside which refer to financial strife or which convey frustrations or even vengeance can be particularly disturbing to the man whose opportunities for response are severely curtailed. Perhaps greatest impact follows a letter from a son or daughter, often written under the guidance of a disillusioned wife:

Daddy

I hope you never get out of there. When you get out stay 15 miles away from us.

I want a father that can stay out of Jail. You never gave me 22 dollars from working on the truck and I'm going to get it. Like it or not.

I want a father that can teach me how to be a good man and show me the right way to do things.

I think I can do better than you are in staying out of trouble.

Your a lousy father I never like you.

I don't work for nothing you know. I hope you like our letters. HA HA HA. You better answer all the letters.

Nicky
HA HA HA

Officers who have supervisory responsibility over inmates rarely examine prisoners' dossiers or consult their caseworkers although knowledge of inmates' problems might prevent an incident. There is an understandable reluctance among officers to get involved in "amateur counseling"; yet they may confront an inmate who has just been sued for divorce, has learned of a death in the family or has just received notice that a detainer (for legal action following the immediate sentence) has been lodged against him. Few correctional officers at the Atlanta institution felt that inmates could cope with these setbacks in a rational or conventional manner.

A second exogenous source of uncertainty originates in decisions made at high administrative levels, many of which call for modifications in existing local policies. In the minds of many officers, too little thought is given to the consequences of a new policy statement or to the ramifications of a court decision. Within the federal prison system, directives to institutions are formulated in Washington, a procedure prompting one lieutenant to observe:

> It's hard to know what you can or can't do with a prisoner these days. If the Bureau [of Prisons] isn't always changing its mind about how we handle these guys, then the courts make us change things just because some character got tired of bellyaching and threw a writ.

Some changes in institutional policy, then, are a reaction to "jailhouse lawyering," or to court-ordered changes brought about by "writ-writers." The perception that "the goddamned courts are running the prisons these days," widely shared among staff, is reinforced by the following episode:

> *February 7, 1972.* Judge Forbes awarded $3,000.00 to Plaintiff [Carruthers 21793] on his complaint of negligence on the part of U.S. Penitentiary officials in failing to provide adequate protection resulting in his being injured (stabbed by another inmate) in A cellhouse on September 8.
>
> The Judge stated that there was an inadequate number of officers assigned to A cellhouse to provide proper protection and supervision of inmates living there. He also stated that although the perpetrators were known to penitentiary officials as an enforcer and gambler, respectively, they were permitted to remain in the general [prison] population rather than be put in Segregation. The Judge also stated that although Carruthers had reported to prison officials threats made toward him by other inmates, and had requested transfer to another institution, this was unfortunately not done.

Correctional officers predictably have little regard for judicial opinions or operating procedures rendered by "absentee authorities" whose familiarity with local problems may be suspect. In addition, if the courts show favor to suits brought by organizations perceived by officers as radical (the American Civil Liberties Union is everybody's whipping boy), correctional administrators must contend with the feeling among their staff members that the authority for running the prison has been surreptitiously undermined. Thus, influences on institutional life which are generated from outside sources convince correctional workers that their line of work is becoming increasingly precarious.

STAFF RESPONSES TO UNCERTAINTY

The socialization of newly hired officers in the federal penitentiary usually involves a transformation of their occupational ideologies. Initially an officer trainee will have high expectations that he can change the man with whom he comes in contact in a socially acceptable direction. It takes little time, however, for a new employee to become disappointed; he soon learns that numerous features of the correctional officer's role impair his effectiveness as a change agent. Gaining experience, he comes to realize that he doesn't have the "tools" with which to achieve his early objective. Because certain posts, such as the towers and patrol duty, are often used specifically for new trainees, he is likely in addition to have little prolonged contact with inmates during his first year. The recollection of a correctional officer with two years' service dramatizes this shift in outlook:

> You enter the [Federal Prison] Service thinking that you can do a better job than others have in helping inmates. It doesn't take long to find out that you aren't going to change anybody. Officers who've been here ten or fifteen years aren't changing anybody either. Oh, you help out some poor old devil every so often, make him feel a little better. But nothing lasting. On top of it all, you've got almost no incentives to offer a prisoner, so how much can you expect?

The awareness that a transformation of offenders into nonoffenders, ostensibly a goal of corrections, takes place only in spite of confinement at Atlanta was an important contributor to the feeling of precariousness and uncertainty among officers. What, then, are the behavioral consequences of working in an atmosphere of low predictability?

Data from questionnaires completed by correctional officers as well as informal interviews reveal that uncertainty has varied effects upon custodial staff. On the one hand, there are those who are exceedingly threatened by the absence of repetition and pattern. They prefer an orderly watch, one which proceeds without disruption or delay. Occasional references by officers to a "convict guard," or a "stick man," identified this particular type as someone who does not usually care for new policies, rule changes, shifts in the composition of the inmate population or changes in the administrative hierarchy. In an attempt to classify the divergent responses to uncertainty Atlanta officers were asked what advice they would give to new trainees. Those subscribing to the "stick man" ideology—about two-thirds of the custodial staff— supported the view that they should expect the worst from the inmate population and would be well-advised to adopt a style which minimizes uncertainty: "Learn all about the inmates who are "hot'"; "Be nosy: check the unusual *and* the usual"; "Give an order and then enforce it at all costs"; and "Say what you mean; mean what you say."

About a third of the staff, however, thrives upon the nonrepetitive, unsystematic features of correctional work. These officers look forward to quarterly job changes, the introduction of new treatment programs, new regulations affecting inmate conduct and a fluid, upwardly-mobile staff. This is not to suggest that they are foolhardy adventurers; on the contrary, they have as great a distaste for disarming an assaultive inmate, coping with a food strike, in short, unstable or dangerous situations, as the others. Their distinctive preference, though, is for a job in which initiative, challenge and ingenuity are required, and they are likely to tailor decisions about inmates individualistically rather than categorically. According to these officers, staff members should anticipate more change, uniqueness and individuality. To the question concerning advice for new trainees, these men replied: "Listen to an inmate's problem with an open mind"; "Be prepared to change jobs and directions often"; "Treat each inmate as an individual and act accordingly"; "Stay flexible with the type person you are dealing with"; and "Consider the varied personalities [staff and inmate] you are dealing with."

One of the unanticipated field observations made during this research arose while recording the operating styles employed by two and sometimes three officers doing the same job. For example, "Quarters Post Orders" which cover the supervision of an inmate housing unit provide the following work description for these officers:

> The most important function of the unit [cellblock] officer is the maintenance of proper security and control in his quarters. In order to achieve success in this goal, the officer should at all times strive to develop a good working relationship with each inmate. This can only be accomplished by frequent individual personal contacts.

Further, he is directed to "maintain continuous accountability for all inmates," to "conduct daily security inspections," enter information of interest in a log book for officers on other shifts such as "rumors of trouble between inmates, suspicious activities [like] plotting escapes, strong-arm gangs and homo activity." Similarly the quarters officer must "supervise the formation and movement of all inmates to and from the cellhouse," and must "screen carefully all individual inmate requests to leave their assigned area."

It was surprising to discover that this job and many others were performed in markedly dissimilar ways despite the existence of uniform instructions. A closer look at the officers involved made it apparent that these behavioral contrasts were important indicators of the polarized correctional ideologies discussed above. For instance, a "stick man" arranges the priorities of his job so that his role is essentially accusatory: anyone entering or leaving the cellblock does so only with his permission; small groups of inmates conversing over a period of time are reprimanded and dispersed; and departures from the schedule of cellblock routine become sources of grave concern. He maintains considerable social distance between himself and inmates and develops a highly structured cellblock environment. The other type of officer, instead, may feel that keeping himself and fellow cellhouse officers accessible to inmates for counsel and assistance takes precedence over attention to out-of-bounds prisoners, cluttered cells and strict adherence to a schedule. He is more apt to "negotiate" rules and to draw the boundaries around permissible conduct more loosely. Thus an inmate often finds that he must adapt to quite varying custodial expectations, even on a given day, because the officers' conceptions of their roles are markedly different.

MINIMIZING LOSS OF CONTROL

Largely in response to their belief that a prison term can be tailored to effectively manage deprivations, a strategy Erving Goffman calls "working the system," inmates adjust in fairly standardized ways. For some, of course, the constraints of imprisonment are nullified only through physical flight; for others, there is psychological escape through fantasy or drugs. Most inmates in Atlanta, however, know how to do time, and the one predictable feature of their existence is the pervasive goal of making-do by manipulating the environment. Compensating by illicit means becomes a game in which prisoners try to "beat" or "con" the staff, who are ostensibly in control. From the inmate perspective making-do by chicanery is rewarding because it reinforces the belief that correctional officers are fallible, it shifts some of the power theoretically held by the staff to inmates and it allocates spoils to the underdog.

Knowing in advance that the prisoners value activities which will reduce the constraints of imprisonment, correctional personnel employ counterefforts to protect themselves against being defrauded or otherwise victimized. There was consensus among Atlanta officers that certain procedures were necessary to minimize uncertainty and inmate opportunism, yet many felt that the steps taken to ensure custody and security were at best a holding action. Nearly every member of the staff commented upon the futility of maintaining control over such a large inmate population in a mega-institution like Atlanta.

Despite a generalized suspicion among custodial staff that the prison's fate is largely indeterminate, several means have evolved over the years to cope with uncertainty. These almost exclusively concentrate upon problems created by inmates since most other sources of unpredictability are beyond staff intervention. The following strategies, therefore, are employed in the penitentiary to minimize loss of control:

The Shakedown.   A central task of correctional personnel is to locate and confiscate goods which are not officially issued to inmates and thus qualify as contraband. Shakedowns hopefully identify persons responsible for the theft, exchange, fabrication or possession of illicit goods, but in practice the zeal with which those responsible are sought is usually contingent upon the nature of the goods. Shaking down can be routinely conducted or it may appear advantageous to vary both the time and location for a search. Experienced officers contend that however productive a shakedown may appear it uncovers only a fraction of the contraband circulating at any given time. The staff use two advantages, information given by informers and judicious timing, to survive in a contest against inmates who have in their favor an almost unlimited number of stashes, including some that are specially engineered, hired lookouts ("jiggers"), a policy of keeping goods moving and, though rarely, the compliance of an intimidated employee.

Shaking down is calculated to reduce the availability of goods which are considered a nuisance or which may pose more serious threats to the welfare of the institution. But the regular appearance of contraband is an unwelcome reminder to officers that many inmates have almost unlimited ingenuity and that the struggle for control can easily shift in favor of the captives.

Information.   It has long been a practice in prison settings to solicit and use secret testimony from inmates about clandestine activities in the institution. Despite the fact that the informer is held in contempt by other prisoners and is derisively referred to as a "snitch," "rat" or "squealer," information is readily available about nearly all matters. An effective means for locating contraband or for coping with trouble such as potential assaults, escape attempts or work strikes is to develop an information system in which prisoners find it profitable to cooperate. They may hope thereby to preclude bodily harm, receive amnesty for their own indiscretions or retaliate against real or imagined aggressors. Even if a large proportion of the information available inevitably has little or no value, as appears to be the case at Atlanta, supervisory personnel hold that the whole system is worth it if just one crisis is averted.

It was apparent during interviews with the Atlanta staff that they were unconcerned with ethical problems associated with prisoner-volunteered testimony. Most correctional officers and their supervisors contended that inmates are going to snitch anyway, in exchange for the obvious benefits to them, and that the welfare of the total prison community is enhanced if trouble is averted.

The Count.   There are several issues in the management of inmate activity which require that choices be made among alternatives. For example, if a prison administrator were to decide that knowing the whereabouts of prisoners at any given time (accountability) had become unacceptably lax, improvements would almost certainly require redeployment or expansion of manpower and curtailment of some treatment programs. In this instance, supervisory personnel must weigh the benefits of accountability, thus increased predictability, against possible costs incurred by manpower changes and decreased inmate satisfaction. Accountability is such an important concept that an elaborate ceremony, the "count," is performed at regular intervals to ensure that a full complement of prisoners can be located. An enumeration in the prison is so critical that nearly all activities are suspended until the count is "cleared." Among custodial officers, moreover, one of the most visible signs of incompetence or carelessness is to submit an erroneous count, and for an inmate to interfere with the count is an exceedingly serious offense.

Officers in the institution nostalgically recalled the "sundown count" that was made in past years after inmates completed the evening meal and then returned to their quarters or went to the yard. Their comments reflected an uneasiness in presuming full accountability during the critical hours when the work day had ended, few custodial staff were on duty and darkness could conceal indecorous activities.

The Siphon.   Atlanta correctional officers contend that "trouble" is the product of a relatively small proportion of the population, and that if it were possible to eliminate troublesome inmates the custodial task would be materially simplified. In the absence of any known screening device or psychological test for trouble-prone inmates, officers invoke conventional stereotypes of problem cases: offenders who are escape risks, are serving long sentences, have committed violent crimes, are known homosexual aggressors, are assaultive or have demonstrated a proclivity for narcotics or other drugs. In Atlanta it is standard procedure to keep a "Hot Book" (referred to by inmates as the "Hunting

List") of selected records on those inmates whose potential for trouble is felt to merit the special attention of employees. Theoretically, staff members consult this volume from time to time, but in practice most officers find out who is "hot" through hearsay. Officers are expected to make informal counts of hot prisoners particularly after the yard is closed or following an entertainment event.

When trouble occurs or conspiracies are detected, suspected prisoners can be detained in a separate facility ("Administrative Segregation") pending a hearing. Knowing that certain notorious inmates have been removed from the population is a source of encouragement to officers whose effectiveness with large numbers of prisoners is compromised by the presence of a few who are belligerent or manipulative. Also included in Segregation are men who need protective custody, that is, who must be secured from intimidation or exploitation by other inmates. Of these, a sizeable number are locked up in Atlanta's prison-within-a-prison at their own request.

For particularly chronic cases, authorization can be obtained from the Bureau of Prisons for a transfer to another penitentiary. In such "separation cases," often instances of one inmate killing another or testifying against another in court, transfer is most frequently made to Leavenworth (Kansas) or Marion (Illinois) where he can be reintegrated with the general prison population. In turn, hot cases at those maximum-security penitentiaries may be transferred to Atlanta. A few inmates whose reputations for trouble have achieved national proportions are said to be kept "on the circuit" between Atlanta, Leavenworth, Marion and McNeil Island (Washington).

Contingency Planning. Any institution must anticipate the occurrence of breakdowns in essential goods and services. For penitentiaries, extensive preparations are made to cope with the disruptive effects of power, heat or water stoppages, fire, natural disaster or widespread sickness. Advance planning is made at Atlanta for another type of acute uncertainty as well: the crisis of an escape, attempted escape, riot or strike. In these instances officers must not only identify suspected prisoners and take them into custody, but the rest of the inmate population must be secured and provided with essential services. Field observations in Atlanta during two escapes and two attempted escapes verified the importance of continuing the normal schedule. Delaying the evening meal, recalling the population from their jobs for a special count or cancelling an entertainment event because a manhunt was underway met with little understanding and sympathy among the 2,000 uninvolved prisoners.

Officers with long experience in these matters hold that no two riots are alike, although, of course, there are significant patterns in all, nor are reactions to any two escapes alike. As in many other staff perceptions of inmate behavior there is the implicit suggestion among correctional officers that even the most extensive contingency planning cannot anticipate all possible outcomes, for whoever gains control is in part a matter of fate, chance or fortuitous circumstance.

Those persons who argue that prisons have historically failed to achieve the multiple objectives given them can find ample reasons for their failure. The problems seem so numerous, in fact, that former governor Lester Maddox was moved several years ago to propose "a better class of inmate" as the solution.

Public expectations of correctional institutions make custody implicit and treatment explicit, but the realities of prison work support a reversal of these objectives. In spite of the introduction of correctional counselors and legal aid assistance, the most immediate and continuing influence upon prisoners is still the custodial staff. Therefore, it is important to understand the nature and the demands of this role. At present, the reality of prison life makes unpredictability a salient feature. Although theoretical expectations about the goals of prisons may emphasize the rehabilitative aspects, the daily task of containing the prisoner, conforming to the latest directive and continuing daily routine forces the average officer to place emphasis upon the custodial rather than the rehabilitative function of his job. This knowledge is essential to any realistic assessment of our objectives for prisons. The whole matter is probably reducible to what we want done within the walls, for what we presently give lip service to is demonstrably more than we currently are willing to invest.

28

The Prosaic Sources
of Prison Violence

*Hans W. Mattick**

It is, perhaps, gratuitous to assert that those who have been convicted
of breaking the law are most in need of having respect for the law
demonstrated to them. We are, moreover, a generous people who are
fond of the notion that the law includes more than a narrow legalism
—". . . for the letter killeth, but the spirit giveth life." In that view,
which we all share in our more virtuous moments, the law approaches
the Platonic ideal of the good, the true and the beautiful. It is a wonder-
ful vision where the law embodies all that is moral, all that is humane,
all that is decent and all that is civilized. But, in the age of Pendleton,
Attica, San Quentin—and all the tragic rest—it may be instructive to
inquire how some of those who act on our behalf have sometimes
demonstrated respect for the law to those who have been convicted of
breaking the law.

It may also be instructive to try to trace some of the correlates of
prison violence—what are popularly referred to as "the causes" of violence—and to do it in such a way as to transcend the usual banalities.
Neither the simpleminded conspiracy theories involving inside or outside agitators that the old-line penal administrators are so quick to
espouse, nor the standard complaints that inmates put forward during
the course of riots, are in themselves sufficient explanations. These are
important and, perhaps, necessary conditions, but they are secondary
because they are constants in the prison situation. They have been

Reprinted by permission of the author. Originally published as one of a series of
Occasional Papers from the Law School, the University of Chicago, March 15, 1972.

*Professor of Criminal Justice and Director of the Center for Research in Criminal
Justice, University of Illinois at Chicago Circle.

present from the beginning of our experience with incarceration, and they are present today, but prison violence fluctuates sporadically and independently of these constants. Much more fundamental is a contra dictory complex of utilitarian and religious ideas of 18th and 19th Cen tury origin, which have been slowly debased into a melange of 20th Century "high school thought," and now serve as the basis for our penal policy. It is, for the most part, a policy of isolation and punishment accompanied by the rhetoric of rehabilitation, which results in the chronic underfinancing, inadequate staffing, deflected sexuality, and general lack of resources and poverty of imagination that characterizes our prisons and jails. But, these too have been constants for the past 200 years and cannot, of themselves, explain sporadic fluctuations in prison violence. If such conditions were both necessary and sufficient, the Naz concentration camps would have been less one-sided in their violence and in a continuous state of revolt. We know that was not the case. To try to explain prison violence, we must penetrate below the surface and get to more fundamental structures and processes.

The massacre at Attica has captured the public imagination, at least for a little while; but as bloody as it was, it is by no means the most calculated use of deadly force in a prison disturbance in recent years That dubious distinction belongs to Pendleton. One can understand the fear, anger and disorganization at Attica, with the lives of hostages seemingly at stake and no clear chain of command to control the situa tion, without condoning the tragic consequences; but there can be no moral justification for what happened at Pendleton. A short account of "the Pendleton incident" was given in the January–February 1970 issue of the *N.C.C.D. News,* an organ of the National Council on Crime and Delinquency:

According to Bruce Nelson, of the *Los Angeles Times,* on September 26, 1969, "12 white men fired repeated volleys of buckshot through a fence [at the Indiana State Reformatory] at young black men who were lying on their stomachs. They killed one and wounded 46. Very few people around the country seemed to notice." Shortly before the shooting, several hundred inmates had congregated in a fenced-in recreation area. They had several demands, including the right to read black literature and to wear their hair in the "Afro" style. Their most important demand was the release of four black inmates who, for unclear reasons, had been isolated. . . . The guards told inmates in the recreation area to leave the vicinity. Many, including all the white inmates, did so. The black inmates asked to present their grievances to [the Superintendent who] refused to talk to the inmates. On the other side of a chain-link fence were 11 white guards and at least one

vocational teacher, dressed in riot helmets and carrying loaded shot-
guns, according to Nelson. The confrontation continued for about 10
to 15 minutes. No attempt was made to disperse the crowd with tear
gas, smoke bombs or nearby fire equipment. The guards fired warning
shots and then, at the command of the Captain . . . the guards began
firing through the fence. . . . One witness said that some of the men
were trying to rise from the ground, raising their hands in a gesture
of surrender, but were told by the guards, "You've had your chance,"
and were shot down. After the shooting, the men were told to leave
the blood-spattered court, and did so, carrying the wounded. Two men
were left lying on the pavement. One of the two . . . was dead. Of the
46 wounded, estimates of those seriously injured run from eight to
twenty."

It may be added that a second inmate died about five months later and,
although this story was covered in the *Los Angeles Times,* some 3,000
miles away, the Chicago newspapers, only 170 miles away, failed to
mention it. For sheer coldbloodedness, Pendleton far surpasses the
emotion-packed atmosphere of Attica.

Such seemingly one-sided incidents of prison violence, unless they
are directed against the authorities, receive very uneven news coverage and slip easily from the memory if, indeed, they ever entered it. But
that does not mean they are rare occurrences. Perhaps a more recent
"incident," that happened after Pendleton and before Attica, will help
reinforce this point. The following account was given in the April 1971
issue of *Civil Liberties,* an organ of the American Civil Liberties Union:

The mass beatings and shootings of inmates at a Florida prison have
led to a massive A.C.L.U. lawsuit alleging violations of federal civil
rights law and state law. . . . On February 12, about 500 prisoners were
peacefully assembled in the prison yard by order of the prison officials.
Guards and other officers, according to the complaint, fired on them
"at point blank range," with absolutely no warning or provocation. The
guards then fired into the windows of occupied cells. Five days of
beatings and tear gassing of prisoners followed. At one point, officers
opened fire into the windows of the prison hospital.

It might be added that February 12th in 1971 was a Friday, followed by a weekend of Saturday and Sunday, which, combined with an
"emergency," is the best of all reasons to close down an institution and
keep all outsiders out. A great deal can be done to prepare an institution
for public scrutiny in three days.

Again, not a very pretty story and, like the affairs at Pendleton and
Attica, not yet finally resolved in the courts. But, if we waited upon

court determination before such matters received any comment, some of the most significant events of our time would have years of silence before they came to public notice. The Chicago Panther Party raid, the Kent and Jackson State killings and the My Lai incident, are typical examples. However the blame for violence at Pendleton and Attica may ultimately be fixed, prison violence is clearly not a simple one-sided affair, with the inmates always aggressing against their keepers. Moreover, although we had serious prison disturbances in both Ohio and Oregon in 1968, and two earlier cycles in the early 1950s and the late 1920s, the massive use of deadly force against groups of prisoners in the last three or four years seems to be a new development.

One would have thought that we could have taken notice sooner that something was seriously amiss in the prison system of the United States when such clear desperation signals as the following were manifest to many public and private observers over the past forty years: (1) In 1968, the celebrated Davis "Report on Sexual Assaults in the Philadelphia Prison System and Sheriffs' Vans" was published. (2) In 1967, the President's Crime Commission, among other things, again revealed the appalling state of American prisons and jails. (3) Earlier in the 1960s, there was some desultory, but subterranean, discussion at the Congresses of the American Correctional Association of the novel punishment methods being used in Arkansas, Florida and Illinois prisons. In Arkansas, the infamous "Tucker Telephone," a hand-operated electric generator that was attached to the genitals of prisoners for punishment purposes, was in frequent use. In Florida, at Raiford Prison, a new use for salt was discovered. Nude inmates, cuffed hand and foot through their cell bars, were seated in piles of salt for periods of 72 hours without relief. In Illinois' Sheridan Reformatory, the members of the inmate boxing team were being used as an indirect disciplinary method, while "shock-therapy" was being converted into punishment at the Menard Psychiatric Division. (4) In the 1950s, the inmates at Rock Quarry Prison in Georgia were breaking each other's legs with 20 pound sledgehammers to achieve transfers, and at Angola Penitentiary in Louisiana, prisoners were crippling themselves for life by cutting their Achilles' tendons in a vain attempt to call attention to their conditions of imprisonment. (5) In 1931, the Wickersham Commission revealed the appalling state of American prisons and jails. (6) That was the year after 317 inmates of the Ohio State Penitentiary died, locked into their cells, in the course of a fire, said to have been set by rioting inmates, although there is some debate about whether the riot began before or after the fire. But, enough is, perhaps, too much. It is clear that violence is no stranger to the prison environment.

With the potential for violence being such a characteristic feature of prison life, it may be a vain pursuit to seek for developmental patterns and explanations in what appears to be a constant. If there is a "pattern," it is a subtle and emergent process that must be stated in tentative terms. Nevertheless, looking back over the past 40 years, prison violence, like a huge, malignant amoeba, seems to have both shape and direction.

There is, to begin with, a change in the proportionate distribution of violence among the wounders and the wounded. In the earlier period (1930–1960), most of the violence was more securely contained within the walls and consisted, for the most part, of assaults between inmates. Then, in descending order of frequency, there were assaults between keepers and kept, self-mutilations by inmates and a few suicides. Except for a few mass disturbances that came to public notice, with few casualties but some property damage, little systematic information about intramural violence exists for the early period.

In the later period (since 1960), self-mutilations seem to have diminished and both suicides and ambiguous deaths, and the proportion of altercations between inmates and guards, have increased. Rebellious inmates have also made more strenuous and self-conscious attempts to communicate their grievances beyond the walls and have begun to find a constituency there. This is, in part, a natural development of the more general civil rights movement and a reflection on the cumulative number of ex-prisoners in the free community who maintain an interest in prison affairs, e.g., every year about 70,000 prisoners leave the prisons and about 3,000,000 persons pass through local jails; to these must be added the increasing numbers of convicted persons being placed on probation, residents of halfway houses and prerelease centers, persons in community treatment programs, and organized groups of ex-prisoners, like the Fortune Society, which are multiplying rapidly. The guards, too, have begun to seek extramural support for their grievances in the form of incipient unionization, associational alliances with police organizations and attempts to influence civil service regulations.

Population shifts and changes in sentencing procedures have also had an impact on prison violence. Geographically, there seems to have been a slow migration of prison violence in a northerly and westerly direction, as white racism has manifested itself in heretofore less tested regions. The southern prisons, in the earlier period, had a much greater tolerance for violence and a more apathetic public audience for what went on among the nether classes in the prisons, while violence that came to public notice in the north tended to generate more public indignation in passing. Thus, while northern prisons got blacker and blacker, incident to Negro migration, and as the increasing use of probation tended to weed out the less violence-prone and more stable prisoners of both races, an exacerbated level of racial conflict was added to the normal level of violence in the northern prisons while southern prisons were still segregated and able to shield their normal level of violence from adverse public scrutiny. The net effect of these population shifts, changes in sentencing practices, and differences in public attitudes was to increase the actual and perceived amount of violence in northern and western prisons, while the amount of violence, actual and perceived, in southern prisons was largely masked. Moreover, while racial conflict between guards and prisoners has a long contributory history to prison violence, with the inmates getting much the worst of it, as active recruitment of Negro prison staff belatedly gets under way, some interesting and unanticipated cross-alliances become possible. It is too early to try to determine what the relation of these new staffing patterns will be to prison violence; all contingencies are possible, but it will be a period of stress for all concerned.

Thus far, we have taken an external view of prison violence by citing some historical examples, pointing out the changing racial composition of prison inmates, indicating some regional differences and referring to changes in sentencing practices, e.g., non-institutional alternatives, like probation, that also change the character of the residual prison population. Such factors, in themselves, do not "explain" prison violence, but they must be understood as contributory elements. We must now place these factors in context and take an internal view of prisons as unisexual, age-graded, total institutions of social control. They are closed communities where real human beings interact in both formal and informal ways, as keepers and kept go through their daily routines. It is in the real humanity of prisoners and guards, and in their mundane routines, that we will find the sources of prison violence.

In any situation where a relatively small group of men control and direct a much larger group, the controllers depend, in a very real sense, on the passive acquiescence of the controlled. Such passivity is purchased by an effective sharing of power. The maintenance of absolute controls requires such implacable social relations that few men are willing to impose them, and even fewer will abide them, for they convert life into death. Prisons are characterized by caste relations where every member of the dominant caste, regardless of personal qualifications, formally rules every member of the subordinate caste, regardless of personal qualifications. Since such personal qualities as intelligence, sophistication, experience, age, strength and energy are differentially distributed among men, regardless of legal status, the formal rules designed to preserve caste relations tend to be subverted. And yet, unless the smaller ruling caste is willing to live in a Hobbesian "state of nature," where the hand of every man is potentially raised against every other, and this for every minute of the day, they know they must come to terms, and do so, with some of the conditions set by the more numerous subordinate caste. It is somewhat like the "social contract" that early philosophers said was necessary for men to emerge from the "state of nature."

Thus the prisoners and their keepers strike a complex bargain. It is a tacit, implicit and informal bargain, somewhat ambiguous as to its precise limits and level, and somewhat variable as to time, place, circumstance and personalities, but one that is unmistakably present. Like the exercise of police discretion in the free community, or plea-bargaining in the criminal courts, such informal arrangements tend to be unacknowledged in daily practice, and are denied altogether when their legitimacy is brought into question by the formal requirements of the criminal justice system, but their weight is disproportionate in the normal prison community. If the average penal administrator or guard were asked, "Who's running this prison, anyway?" they would reply with some degree of self-righteous assertiveness, "Why, we are, of course." In the last analysis, they are right; but the last analysis could mean every prisoner is locked in his cell, gagged and straitjacketed; and then some would be perverse enough to breathe at a rhythm of their own choosing. Few penal administrators want to run a prison that way, for in that direction lies inhumanity and death. It is a question of where the line is drawn, and the line must not only be drawn but accepted. Most penal administrators know where the line is drawn, some will acknowledge it, but a few entertain the delusion of absolute control.

Different prisons strike this bargain at different levels of tolerance, depending upon such factors as the kinds of work or programs the administration wants the prisoners to participate in; the amount of intramural mobility imposed by prison architecture on the routine tasks of prison life; the intelligence and sophistication of guards and inmates; corruption through sentimentality, stupidity, laziness, or venality; the external political climate, custom, tradition and the like. These are the human factors in prison life that make life minimally tolerable for all concerned. Once the level of this power-sharing bargain has been fairly well established, it is difficult to change its terms and limits because very complex social relations, and mutual expectations and obligations, come to depend upon it. To disrupt these informal relations by sudden or extensive social changes, affecting either staff or inmates, is to disrupt prison life; and such disruptions increase the probability of violence.

In the past, when southern prisons were more strictly segregated, and the northern and western prisons still had a racial balance that favored white inmates, prison violence could usually be accounted for in terms of an inadvertent or unavoidable change in the power-sharing bargain. Political elections were followed by key staff changes; groups of prisoners were transferred without notice; the normal turnover of staff and the receipt and discharge of prisoners; the implementation or discontinuance of work assignments or treatment programs; in short, many of the things that had the appearance of the routine could also have very fateful consequences for the informal set of social relations organized around the existing power-sharing bargain. When such routine changes affected important pressure points in the closed prison community, the expectations and obligations of many persons, most of whom were indirectly related to each other, were suddenly disappointed. This would raise the level of tension in an already tense environment, and a precipitating incident that would ordinarily be more easily contained would be the occasion for a sudden flaring of violence.

How was anyone to know that among the inmates who were discharged a few days ago was, for example, inmate "X," who worked in the officer's dining room and was stealing food which he sold, traded or gave away to others who, in turn, were trading or paying off gambling debts to still others, and so on, *ad infinitum?* Similarly, when Captain "A," a grizzled veteran who knew how to survive the prison environment, finally retired and was replaced by Lieutenant "B," who tried to run the cell-house "by the book," a subterranean chain reaction took place, affecting both guards and prisoners, that required many adjustments. Suddenly a whole host of guards who had been having their civilian clothes cleaned, repaired, and pressed in the tailor shop had to turn to outside cleaning shops. Moreover, the tailor shop inmates who had been rewarded in a variety of ways for their extra-curricular work were denied the capital that enabled them to participate in the internal economy.

Such individual examples are only indicative, and necessarily limited in their ramifications. When group transfers, staff shifts, prison industry contracts, elections that affect the upper echelons of prison administration, or too rapid attempts are made to either "tighten up" or "loosen up" the *status quo,* the results can be very serious. Gambling debts go unpaid, borrowed goods are out of control, lovers are separated, incompetent people lose competent help, political or friendship alliances are broken up, mutual service and communication links are disrupted; in short, the social fabric, real and symbolic, is badly torn.

To an outsider, such events have a pedestrian appearance because he is used to the available alternatives and free choices that a free man can make. If a firm's bookkeeper quits his job, another can be hired; if a grocery store closes, there is another in the next block. Some of the routine disruptions of prison life are somewhat akin to the breakdown of utilities or a transportation strike in the free world. Some persons are affected at once, others experience delayed and indirect effects, but only a few have the resources or alternatives to make long-run substitutions. In the closed prison community, life is driven in on itself; there are fewer alternatives and choices, and people are more directly and intensely related, whether they wish it or not. If the routine changes of prison administration, or external politics, press too frequently or too rapidly on the crucial nerve centers and disrupt the social fabric in such a way that the power-sharing bargain is threatened at too many points for too many people, the potential for violence is escalated. Moreover, the actual eruption of violence is likely to be delayed because the latent effects of routine changes take time to ramify through the prison's social structure. Much of what has been considered random or "irrational" prison violence is traceable to such routine prison processes that are simply allowed to happen instead of being carefully planned for and skillfully managed. Invariably, when the violence was "explained," the administration invoked conspiracies and the inmates voiced the ordinary grievances about food, sentences, parole policies and the like. Both were right to some degree, because both the conspiracies and the grievances were real; but they were just as real six months ago and, more than likely, would be just as real six months hence. Such "explanations" are more in the nature of rationalizations than a reflection of actual proximate "causes."

As we approach the present and consider contemporary prison violence, everything that has been said about the power-sharing bargain still has general applicability, but with some important differences. Perhaps most important is the fact that there is a lesser willingness to bargain, and the bargain that is struck, is struck at a much lower level, with fewer benefits for fewer inmates. As, in process of time, the prison population got blacker and blacker, and more Chicano and Puerto Rican as well, the parties to the traditional bargain became more hostile to each other. Much has been said in recent years about a "new breed" of prisoners, and that they are the source of recent violence. A much better case can be made, however, for the existence of an "old breed" of prison guard and penal administrator who have been sheltered, much more than their prisoners, from social changes taking place in the free community. Prisons are isolated, rural, resistant to change and, for the most part, content to remain so. Prisoners are transients who are always upsetting the *status quo*. Moreover, they are more urban, more influenced by current events, more socially aware and naturally concerned about civil rights and the condition of man; but this too is a part of a much wider social movement concerned with equality and justice. Not even the most secure prison can keep it out. A generation ago, penal administrators were deploring the presence of a "new breed" of spoiled and overindulged youthful offenders who were the offspring of permissive parents and bemoaning the absence of the old, professional safecrackers and con-men who "knew how to do time."

In this perspective, every generation of prisoners has been a "new breed" of prisoners. In addition, in recent years, as an accompaniment to the civil rights movement and dissent over the war in Vietnam, we have responded to social dissent by defining a part of it as criminal. The result has been a new mixture of prisoners, and a new kind of exchange of information among them. Radical ideologists have been thrown together with traditional criminal types, and each has taken something from the other at the margin. Thus, the prisons have been "politicalized," and some of the prisoners convicted of traditional crimes have been furnished with a radical critique of imprisonment and all of society, while some of the more radical social dissidents have been furnished with traditional criminal techniques that may be useful in the furtherance of their objectives. It is a stupid arrangement that the older European countries have learned to handle more astutely by wiser separations among these classes of prisoners. And this new mixture of prisoners is regularly delivered into the hands of a predominantly white, rural, conservative, ruling caste in the prisons; a ruling caste which, for the financial, numerical and philosophical reasons mentioned earlier, is wholly inadequate to the task.

No wonder, then, that there is more intransigence and less willingness to compromise in the informal bargaining processes that make prison life minimally tolerable for all concerned. For a while, the guards and penal administrators were still able to bargain in the traditional way with the decreasing proportion of white prisoners, but that form of power-sharing has come to an end. In the prison situation, where outside race relations are reversed, the white minority feels the mounting pressure of the darker majorities. The choice is getting narrower and the potential for violence is increasing; soon the choices will be only open hostility, repression or compromise. This is one interpretation of what the prisoners at the Tombs, at Attica, and elsewhere, meant when the cry went up: "We want to be treated like human beings." It is also one interpretation of what President Nixon meant when he sent his 13 point directive to Attorney General Mitchell on November 13, 1969, and said, "The American system for correcting and rehabilitating criminals presents a convincing case of failure."

There is today, as there was in 1870, some evidence that we are, at long last, ready to face the prison problem. When such an unlikely group as President Nixon, Chief Justice Burger, Attorney General Mitchell and Senator Hruska, on the one hand, and Senators Kennedy and McGovern and Congressman Mikva and former Attorney General Clark, on the other, can agree on the current necessity for penal reform, there might be some hope. Chief Justice Burger, in his State of the Federal Judiciary message last July said, "If any phase of the administration of justice is more neglected than the courts, it is the correctional systems." Attorney General Mitchell, citing the recommendations of the National Congress on Penitentiary and Reformatory Discipline of 1870, citing the Wickersham Commission of 1931, and referring to the findings of the President's Commission on Law Enforcement and Administration of Justice of 1967, at the National Conference on Corrections held at Williamsburg, Virginia on December 6, 1971, was moved to ask: "What was the result of this century of recommendations?" And he answered: "In state after state, most of the prisons have no programs for correcting prisoners."

So there is recognition in high places that a problem exists. Moreover, recent U.S. Court decisions in Arkansas (*Holt* v. *Sarver*, 2/18/70), Rhode Island (*Morris* v. *Travisino*, 3/11/70), California (*Clutchette* v. *Procunier*, 6/21/71) and Virginia (*Landman* v. *Royster*, 10/30/71), have held long-standing prison practices unconstitutional. Even the Quakers, who had such an enormous influence on the form of American imprisonment, have returned to the drawing board after 200 years. A working party of the American Friends Service Committee recently published a report on crime and punishment in America, entitled *Struggle for Justice* (Hill & Wang, Inc., 1971), in which they said, in effect, "We were wrong and must begin again with a different set of premises."

Santayana has admonished that "Those who cannot remember the past are condemned to repeat it." We have been through such a repetitious cycle once before. In 1870, the National Congress on Penitentiary and Reformatory Discipline was held at Cincinnati, Ohio. It was clear to the best penal minds in the country that we had already reached a serious impasse in our methods of imprisonment. Accordingly, after a thorough review of what was wrong with American penology, this National Congress published the famous Declaration of Principles which was to give rise to a New Penology. We can ascertain some measure of what the participants of that National Congress felt they had accomplished by adverting to the sentiments of Zebulon Brockway, the foremost penal administrator of his day, who was present and active. In 1876 he was appointed Warden of the Elmira Reformatory, the "wonder prison" of the western world. Some seventeen years after the National Congress of 1870, he reflected on its accomplishments and was still able to describe it as "an experience similar to that of the disciples of Our Blessed Lord on the Mount of Transfiguration." Last December, just one hundred years later, we held the National Conference on Corrections at Williamsburg, Virginia. Seventeen years hence, will we, as Santayana admonished, have remembered the past, or will we reflect with Goethe that "There is nothing so frightful as ignorance in action?"

APPENDIX

Introductions to the seven sections comprising this book have concluded with a listing of selected articles and books. Readers who require more detailed treatment of a topic may find assistance there. The literature of criminology is so extensive, however, that some additional guidance is warranted. Navigational assistance to those engaged in scholarship is offered, then, with the usual disclaimer that works in print are not, ipso facto, to be regarded as authoritative.

General reference sources to the literature of sociological criminology include (1) *Sociological Abstracts,* which is extensively indexed and reports the major points of articles in many regular journals; (2) *Psychological Abstracts,* a publication which performs the same function for psychologists; (3) *Crime and Delinquency Literature,* a publication of the National Council on Crime and Delinquency; and (4) *Abstracts on Criminology and Penology* (formerly *Excerpta Criminologica*), which is prepared by the Criminologica Foundation in cooperation with the University of Leiden, the Ministry of Justice, and the National Bureau for Child Protection, The Hague, Netherlands. A companion journal is *Abstracts on Police Science.* Both have international coverage and are printed in English.

Three publications deserve special mention because they are exceptionally rewarding to both undergraduates and their instructors. First, the *International Encyclopedia of the Social Sciences* (edited by David L. Sills; New York: Free Press, Macmillan, Inc.) is a seventeen-volume set of specially commissioned essays published in 1968. The fundamental issues and literature of numerous topics in criminology (e.g., "Sociology of Law";

I would like to acknowledge the assistance of Morton S. Goren, Librarian, Law Enforcement Assistance Administration, Washington, D.C. in the preparation of this Appendix.

"White Collar Crime"; "Penology") are succinctly discussed by authorities in various disciplines. Second, the exhaustive *Criminology Index: Research and Theory in Criminology in the United States, 1945–1972* (by Marvin E. Wolfgang, Robert M. Figlio, and Terence P. Thornberry; New York: Elsevier Scientific Publishing Company, Inc.) appeared in 1975. It is an extraordinarily comprehensive (though difficult to use) reference to significant articles and books written by scholars, researchers, and practitioners in the field.[1] Third, Daniel Glaser's *Handbook of Criminology* (Chicago: Rand McNally, 1974) is a carefully edited anthology of specially commissioned essays on some of the foremost topics in criminology. Writing for a sophisticated audience, the contributors to this lengthy volume review the literature on their subjects and provide excellent documentation for the scholar.

Another source often overlooked is the law reviews published by many universities. The *University of Chicago Law Review*, the *University of Pennsylvania Law Review*, the *Yale Law Journal*, and the *Stanford Law Review*, for example, contain valuable articles for criminologists from time to time. The best guide to these is the *Index to Legal Periodicals.*

Generally speaking, the sources consulted most frequently by researchers in the field of criminology are books and professional journals. It is advisable to begin with the latter, for they will yield concise, recent articles which are usually carefully referenced themselves. Sometimes a journal will devote all or a substantial portion of an issue to a topic in the area of criminal behavior or the administration of justice. Examples of this are:

"A Symposium: Women and the Criminal Law," *The American Criminal Law Review*, Winter, 1973

---

1. Antecedent to this work is an early and very useful bibliographical tool prepared by Thorsten Sellin and Leonard D. Savitz and published by the *International Bibliography on Crime and Delinquency*, Volume 1, No. 3, 1963 (separately reprinted as *A Bibliographical Manual for the Student of Criminology*, National Research and Information Center, National Council on Crime and Delinquency, 1965). One other source is Martin Wright (ed.), *The Use of Criminological Literature* (London: Butterworth & Co., 1974), which contains suggestions for doing library research, and includes chapters on the literature of a dozen specialties within the field of criminology. Titles of books, articles, and journals in both the United Kingdom and the United States are cited.

John P. Conrad (ed.), "The Future of Corrections," *The Annals of the American Academy of Political and Social Science,* January, 1969

"Crime and Punishment," *Society,* July/August, 1974

"The Law Enforcement Assistance Administration: A Symposium on its Operation and Impact," *Columbia Human Rights Law Review,* Spring, 1973

"Symposium on Judicial Administration," *Public Administration Review,* March/April, 1971

"A Symposium on White-Collar Crime," *The American Criminal Law Review,* Summer, 1973

"Police Practices," *Law and Contemporary Problems,* Autumn, 1971

To facilitate location of articles that are pertinent to the criminologist, a listing of selected journals appears below. These vary with respect to focus, quality, and intended audience.

American Journal of Correction
    The official publication of the American Correctional Association

American Journal of Sociology
    The oldest journal in American sociology; edited and published at The University of Chicago

American Sociological Review
    An official publication of the American Sociological Association

British Journal of Criminology
    Formerly the *British Journal of Delinquency;* published on behalf of The Institute for the Study and Treatment of Delinquency, London

Canadian Journal of Criminology and Corrections
    Formerly the *Canadian Journal of Corrections;* the official publication of the Canadian Criminology and Corrections Association

Columbia Journal of Law and Social Problems
    Published by Columbia University School of Law

Corrections Magazine
Published by Correctional Information Service, Inc. and supported by the Commission on Correctional Facilities and Research, American Bar Association

Crime and Delinquency
A publication of the National Council on Crime and Delinquency

Criminal Justice and Behavior
The official publication of the American Association of Correctional Psychologists

Criminology
Formerly *Criminologica;* the official publication of the American Society of Criminology

FBI Law Enforcement Bulletin
Published by the U.S. Department of Justice; for professional law enforcement personnel

Federal Probation
Published by the Administrative Office of the United States Courts, in cooperation with the Bureau of Prisons, U.S. Department of Justice

Issues in Criminology
Published by the University of California, Berkeley

Journal of Abnormal Psychology
Formerly the *Journal of Abnormal and Social Psychology;* a publication of the American Psychological Association

Journal of Criminal Justice
Affiliated with the Academy of Criminal Justice Sciences

Journal of Criminal Law and Criminology
Formerly the *Journal of Criminal Law, Criminology and Police Science;* published by the Northwestern University School of Law

Journal of Police Science and Administration
Formerly a part of the *Journal of Criminal Law, Criminology and Police Science;* sponsored jointly by the International Association of Chiefs of Police and the Northwestern University School of Law

Journal of Research in Crime and Delinquency
A publication of the National Council on Crime and Delinquency

Journal of Forensic Sciences
The official publication of the American Academy of Forensic Sciences

Journal of the Forensic Science Society
Published by the Forensic Science Society, Yorkshire, England; also the official publication of the California Association of Criminalists and of the South Australian Branch of the Forensic Science Society

Law and Contemporary Problems
Published by the School of Law, Duke University

Law and Society Review
The official publication of the Law and Society Association

Police Chief
Published by the International Association of Chiefs of Police

Prison Journal
A publication of the Pennsylvania Prison Society

Social Forces
Associated with the Southern Sociological Society; published by the University of North Carolina Press

Social Problems
The official publication of the Society for the Study of Social Problems

Society
Formerly *Trans-Action;* published at Rutgers University

Sociology and Social Research
Published at the University of Southern California

The Annals of the American Academy of Political and Social Science
Published by the American Academy of Political and Social Science, Philadelphia, Pennsylvania

The Journal of Legal Studies
Published by The University of Chicago Law School

Many libraries will have some sources which have been discontinued, but nonetheless are very useful for the periods when they appeared. Examples are the *International Bibliography on Crime and Delinquency* (1963–66), published by the Public Health Service, U.S. Department of Health, Education and Welfare; its successor, *Crime and Delinquency Abstracts* (1966–72), published by the National Institute of Mental Health, U.S. Department of Health, Education and Welfare; and *Police,* published from 1956 to 1972 by Charles C Thomas, Springfield, Illinois. Completely separate from the latter journal yet currently publishing similar articles is *Law and Order.*

Anthony L. Guenther
College of William and Mary

NAME INDEX

Abrahamson, David, 508
Adams, Richard N., 334n.
Adams, Stuart, 480
Adler, 33
Adorno, T. W., 510
Agge, Ivar, 14, 15
Akers, Ronald L., 47, 70, 84
Alex, Nicholas, 291
Alexander, Franz, 88n.
Andenaes, Johannes, 48
Antonini, Giuseppe, 14, 15
Ash, Ellis, 502, 509

Backman, Carl W., 179n.
Bacon, Seldon D., 296–300, 302, 308
Baker, Newman F., 419, 433, 446
Ball, Donald W., 351n.
Banton, Michael, 291, 304n., 327, 332n., 333n., 404
Bard, Morton, 350n.
Barnes, Harry Elmer, 73n., 84, 88n., 91n., 502
Barnes, Robert Earl, 276, 284
Barrett, C., 91n.
Bartleme, Kenwood, 508
Beccaria, Cesare, 22, 28
Becker, Howard S., 47, 57n., 109, 166, 177n., 180n., 188, 214–25, 227, 232n., 329n., 335–36, 340n., 348n., 349n., 350n., 351n., 353
Becker, T., 38n.
Bedau, Hans, 99n.

Beigel, Herbert, 294
Bell, Daniel, 189
Bemmelen, Jacob M. van, 14, 15
Bendix, Reinhard, 487n., 510
Benjamin, H., 226n.
Benney, Mark, 338n.
Bensman, Joseph, 177n., 178n., 334n., 350n.
Bentham, Jeremy, 28, 87
Berger, Peter, 337n.
Berk, Bernard B., 481
Bernaldo de Quiros, Constancio, 14, 15
Bersani, Carl, 266
Bettelheim, Bruno, 504n.
Bianchi, Hermanus, 14, 15
Biderman, Albert D., 34n., 110, 123n., 127n., 149, 151n., 322–23
Bittner, Egon, 285, 291, 293, 316–17, 352
Black, Donald J., 108, 156n., 159n., 163n., 292, 316–17, 318, 321n., 329, 348n.
Black, Jack, 276, 284
Blaustein, Albert P., 424, 446
Bloch, Herbert A., 201
Blumberg, Abraham S., 292, 408, 412, 446
Blumer, Herbert, 336–37
Bonger, William A., 14, 15
Bordua, David J., 284, 290, 291, 294, 295–324, 331, 332, 338n., 343–44, 348n., 404
Bouzat, Perre, 17
Braly, Malcolm, 270n., 274, 284
Branham, Vernon C., 14, 15
Breitel, Charles D., 433, 446
Briar, Scott, 75, 84, 316–17, 338n.
Brissett, Dennis, 68n.
Broca, Paul, 10

Eliot, T. S., 94
Ellenborough, Chief Justice Lord, 98
Ellingston, 91n.
Ellis, A., 226n.
Elster, Alexander, 14, 15
Ennis, Phillip H., 110, 132n., 136n., 151n.
Erikson, Kai T., 45, 57–67, 108, 149n., 166–84, 351n.
Esquirol, Jean E. D., 9
Etzioni, Amitai, 482
Evan, William M., 5

Farber, Maurice L., 508
Federman, Philip J., 321n.
Ferdinand, Theodore N., 71, 85, 201n.
Ferri, Enrico, 11, 12, 15, 16, 196
Festinger, Leon, 167n., 173n., 352n.
Fielding, Henry, 11
Figlio, Robert M., 541
Fink, Arthur E., 4, 15, 16
Fishman, Joseph F., 502, 508
Fletcher, Robert L., 434, 446
Floch, Maurice, 509
Florian, E., 15
Foote, Caleb B., 430, 446
Form, William H., 326n., 333n., 334n., 335
Fortescue, Sir John, 11
Fox, James C., 291, 325n.
Fox, Vernon, 509
Frechtman, Bernard, 284
Freed, Daniel J., 430, 447
Freud, Sigmund, 226

Gagnon, John H., 78, 85
Galanter, Marc, 408
Galen, 11
Gall, Franz Joseph, 8, 9
Gallup, George, 150n., 151, 158, 159
Garabedian, Peter, 68n.
Gardiner, John A., 292, 373n.
Garfinkel, Harold, 64n.
Garofalo, Raffaele, 7, 16, 54, 196
Garson, G. David, 482
Geer, Blanche, 166, 232n., 335–36
Geis, Gilbert, 83, 85, 189, 201
Genet, Jean, 276, 284
Giallombardo, Rose, 482, 483
Gibbons, Don C., 45, 68–86, 189, 199–200, 205n.
Gibbs, Jack P., 5, 47, 48, 188

Giddings, Franklin H., 12
Glaser, Daniel, 4, 46, 47, 79, 85, 110, 189, 292, 293, 410, 411, 481, 482, 542
Glover, E., 225n.
Gobineau, Joseph A. de, 10
Goethe, J. W. von, 540
Goffman, Erving, 47, 63n., 177–78, 182, 216n., 270, 285, 342, 351n., 361n., 391n., 482, 483, 524
Goldfarb, Ronald L., 280, 285, 409
Goldstein, Abraham S., 434, 447
Goldstein, Herman, 448
Goodenough, Ward, 352n.
Goodman, 101n.
Goren, Morton S., 541n.
Goring, Charles B., 10, 16
Goslin, David A., 483
Gould, Leroy, 80, 85, 271, 282, 283, 285
Gouldner, Alvin W., 28n., 47, 110, 351n., 353n.
Graham, Fred P., 108
Gray, R. C., 491n.
Greefe, Etienne de, 14, 16
Greenwald, Harold, 226n., 228
Griffiths, John, 421, 447
Grosman, Brian A., 419, 447
Gross, Edward, 391n.
Grupp, Stanley E., 4
Guenther, Anthony L., 110, 480, 483, 511–28
Guenther, Mary Quinn, 480, 511–28
Guerry, Andre M., 11, 16
Gurvitch, Georges, 5

Haas, Mary R., 215
Habenstein, Robert W., 109, 351n.
Haeckel, Ernst H., 10
Hagan, John, 409
Haley, Alex, 285
Hall, Jerome, 266, 278, 279, 285
Hall, Livingston, 420, 421, 430, 432, 433, 447
Hall, Oswald, 214n., 347n.
Hammond, Phillip E., 334n., 336n.
Hammurabi, 488
Hanks, L. M., Jr., 509
Hanson, Vernon L., 316n.
Hapgood, Hutchins, 275, 285
Hargin, James, 509
Harper, Ida, 509
Harris, Louis, 150n., 155, 158
Hartjen, Clayton A., 72, 85, 189, 205n.
Hartung, Frank E., 509

Shover, Neal, 188, 266–86
Siegel, Arthur I., 321n.
Sills, David L., 6, 7 109, 291, 541
Silver, Allan, 296, 303
Silverstein, Lee, 424, 449
Simon, Rita James, 69, 86, 109, 181n.
Simon, William, 78, 85
Simpson, George, 60n.
Singer, Linda R., 409, 481
Sjoberg, Gideon, 334n.
Skogan, Wesley G., 107, 109, 131–48
Skolnick, Jerome H., 5, 292, 296, 302n.,
   309n., 316–18, 323, 324, 327–29,
   331–32, 334, 338n., 342, 344–45,
   346n., 347, 351, 404, 409, 412, 449
Smelser, Neil J., 81, 86
Smith, Bruce, Jr., 377n.
Smith, Harvey A., 319n., 348n.
Socrates, 53
Solovay, Sarah A., 49n.
Sorokin, Pitirim A., 509
Sparks, Richard, 4
Stark, Rodney, 81, 85
Staub, Hugo, 88n.
Steffens, Lincoln, 149–50
Stephens, James Fitzjames, 90n.
Stein, Maurice R., 177n., 178n., 334n.,
   350n.
Stinchcombe, Arthur L., 293, 301n.
Stone, Gregory P., 216n.
Strauss, Anselm L., 214n., 232n., 348n.
Strodtbeck, Fred L., 76, 86
Strong, Samuel M., 498
Sudnow, David, 109
Sullivan, Mortimer, 167n., 172n.
Sumner, William Grahan, 23
Sutherland, Edwin H., 14, 18, 43–44, 47,
   68, 69–71, 74, 77–79, 82, 83n., 86,
   190, 227, 266–67, 269n., 282, 285,
   488n.
Sykes, Gresham M., 4, 27–40, 63n., 217–18,
   480, 483, 496–510
Sykes, Richard E., 292

Taft, Donald R., 510
Tapp, June, 409
Tappan, Paul W., 20n., 194n.
Tarde, Gabriel, 12, 18
Taylor, Ian, 5
Teeters, Negley K., 73n., 84, 88n., 91n.,
   502
Terris, Bruce J., 292
Thomas, W. I., 105

Thornberry, Terence P., 541
Tiffany, Lawrence P., 292
Tifft, Larry, 292
Tittle, Charles R., 48, 99n.
Tobias, J. J., 72n., 86
Tolman, Ruth Sherman, 510
Trojanowicz, Robert, 330n.
Tsu, Ching Pei, 310n.
Tullio, Benigno di, 14, 18
Turk, Austin T., 6, 32, 69, 86, 195n.

Van den Haag, Ernest, 88
Viano, Emilio, 110
Vidich, Arthur J., 177n., 178n., 334n.,
   350n.
Vives, Juan Luis, 11
Vold, George B., 14, 18, 46
Vorenberg, Elizabeth W., 408, 462–76
Vorenberg, James, 402, 408, 462–76
Votey, Harold L., Jr., 48

Wald, Patricia M., 430, 447
Waldo, Gordon P., 109
Walker, Daniel, 404
Walker, Nigel, 410
Walton, Paul, 5
Wambaugh, Joseph, 293
Ward, David A., 339, 481, 483
Ward, Richard, 292
Wattenberg, William W., 323
Wax, Rosalie H., 110
Webb, Eugene J., 181n.
Weber, Max, 33n., 201
Weihofen, Henry, 445
Weir, Adrianne W., 151n.
Weis, Kurt, 108, 109
Weisart, John C., 293, 410
Werthman, Carl, 322, 338n.
Westley, William A., 294, 316–17, 330, 334
Wheeler, Stanton, 110, 483
Whittaker, E., 342
Whyte, William Foote, 305n.
Wice, Paul B., 410
Wilensky, Harold L., 6, 295, 310n., 331n.
Wilkins, Leslie T., 5, 109
Wilks, Judith, 481
Willmer, M. A. P., 375n.
Wilmanns, Karl, 510
Wilson, Brian, 276, 285

SUBJECT INDEX